Edexcel AS/A level

Psychology

Elizabeth Barkham | Anna Cave | Susan Harty |
Annabel Jervis | Karren Smith |
with **James Bailey** and **Esther O'Neill |**
Series Editor: **Karren Smith**

ALWAYS LEARNING

Published by Pearson Education Limited, 80 Strand, London, WC2R 0RL.

www.pearsonschoolsandfecolleges.co.uk

Copies of official specifications for all Edexcel qualifications may be found on the website: www.edexcel.com

Text © Pearson Education Limited 2015

Designed by Malena Wilson-Max for Pearson

Typeset and illustrated by Phoenix Photosetting, Chatham, Kent

Original illustrations © Pearson Education Limited 2015

Cover design by Malena Wilson-Max for Pearson

Indexed by Sophia Clapham, Index-Now

The rights of James Bailey, Elizabeth Barkham, Anna Cave, Susan Harty, Annabel Jervis, Esther O'Neill and Karren Smith to be identified as authors of this work have been asserted by them in accordance with the Copyright, Designs and Patents Act 1988.

First published 2015

18 17 16 15

10 9 8 7 6 5 4 3 2 1

British Library Cataloguing in Publication Data
A catalogue record for this book is available from the British Library

ISBN (Student Book bundle) 978 1 447 98246 3
ISBN (ActiveBook) 978 1 447 98242 5
ISBN (Kindle edition) 978 1 447 98244 9

Copyright notice

Printed in Slovakia by Neografia

Acknowledgments
For image and text acknowledgments please see page V.

Websites
Pearson Education Limited is not responsible for the content of any external internet sites. It is essential for tutors to preview each website before using it in class so as to ensure that the URL is still accurate, relevant and appropriate. We suggest that tutors bookmark useful websites and consider enabling students to access them through the school/college intranet.

A note from the publisher
In order to ensure that this resource offers high-quality support for the associated Pearson qualification, it has been through a review process by the awarding body. This process confirms that this resource fully covers the teaching and learning content of the specification or part of a specification at which it is aimed. It also confirms that it demonstrates an appropriate balance between the development of subject skills, knowledge and understanding, in addition to preparation for assessment.

Endorsement does not cover any guidance on assessment activities or processes (e.g. practice questions or advice on how to answer assessment questions), included in the resource nor does it prescribe any particular approach to the teaching or delivery of a related course.

While the publishers have made every attempt to ensure that advice on the qualification and its assessment is accurate, the official specification and associated assessment guidance materials are the only authoritative source of information and should always be referred to for definitive guidance.

Pearson examiners have not contributed to any sections in this resource relevant to examination papers for which they have responsibility.

Examiners will not use endorsed resources as a source of material for any assessment set by Pearson.

Endorsement of a resource does not mean that the resource is required to achieve this Pearson qualification, nor does it mean that it is the only suitable material available to support the qualification, and any resource lists produced by the awarding body shall include this and other appropriate resources.

Contents

How to use this book

About this book

This Student Book contains a wealth of features that will help you to access the course content, prepare for your exams, and take your knowledge and understanding further. The pages below show some of the key features and explain how they will support you in developing the skills needed to succeed in psychology.

Key term

Mnemonic: a system for remembering something such as an association or a pattern of letters.

'Key terms' are highlighted in bold in the text and complex terminology or jargon clearly defined in handy boxes close to the main content.

WIDER ISSUES AND DEBATES

Reductionism

This model has been criticised for being overly simplistic: that it underplays the interconnections between the different memory systems by proposing that the memory has distinctly different stores. Artificially breaking up the memory stores makes it easier to study memory experimentally, but this model can be criticised for being reductionist.

'Wider issues and debates' boxes focus on the Issues and Debates sections of the specification, especially important for students taking the A level exam papers. Although not examined in the AS papers, the information in these features will help all students appreciate the relevance of psychology to many of the issues facing society today.

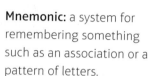

INDIVIDUAL DIFFERENCES

There are several individual differences that can be detected by digit span testing. Dyslexia, which is a problem with learning to recognise words at the level appropriate for age, is associated with a poor digit span (Helland and Asbjørnsen, 2004).

'Individual differences' and 'Developmental psychology' features reflect the importance of recognising these aspects when considering psychological concepts. The examples in the boxes highlight the need to avoid generalisations and will help you to make further links across areas of psychology.

Taking it further

Penfield and Milner's research can be found by searching for the title 'Loss of recent memory after bilateral hippocampal lesions, on the National Center for Biotechnology Information website. Read the summary of the case of HM and other cases of amnesia.

'Taking it further' features provide opportunities for you to explore an aspect of psychology in more detail. The information in these features goes beyond the specification and will help you to deepen your understanding and think like a psychologist.

Exam tip

The aim is an important part of a research investigation because it clearly signposts the topic being investigated. An aim should be as clear and precise as a hypothesis. Once you have read about hypotheses and **operationalisation** later in this topic, it is important that you apply the same detail and accuracy to an aim.

'Exam tips' give practical advice and guidance to ensure you are well prepared for your exams.

Maths tip

It is critical that you show all of your calculations/workings in the exam. Using the formulae, write down step by step how you are calculating the Mann-Whitney as shown above.

'Maths tips' simplify complex calculations and provide practical worked examples to help you apply new methods or formulae to your own work.

Link

For quantitative data analysis including calculating measures of central tendency, frequency tables, measures of dispersion (range and standard deviation) and percentages, please see the Methods section of Topic 1: *Social psychology*.

'Link' boxes show you where related content appears in another topic.

'Thinking bigger' – This feature spread supports A level students with the synoptic content of the specification, which is examined in Paper 3. By analysing an authentic piece of writing and practising your own extended writing, you will develop your ability to combine your knowledge, skills and understanding with the breadth and depth of the subject of psychology.

'Preparing for your exams' – At the end of Topics 4, 8 and 9 you will find detailed exam preparation sections to help consolidate your learning. Exam-style questions, mark schemes and answers, together with useful tips for how to approach the exams, will give you extra confidence in your performance.

Preparing for your exams: A level Paper 2

Advance planning

- You will need to revise the methodology that you have learned about in your first year as this will represent 25 per cent of this paper. The methodology will relate to your chosen application. You will also need to revise all of the statistical tests and mathematical skills. Make sure you include time for this in your revision timetable.
- There are more marks available for Clinical psychology than the application you have learned about. Your revision timetable should reflect this. Spend more time revising the clinical content than your application content.

A level Paper 2 overview

A level Paper 2	Time: 2 hours	
Section A: Clinical psychology (compulsory questions)	A mixture of short answer questions and extended response questions (8–20 marks)	54 marks
Section B: Applications in psychology (Options 1, 2 and 3)	A mixture of short answer questions and extended response questions (8–16 marks)	36 marks
	Total marks =	90 marks

The paper requires the use of a calculator. Statistical tables and formulae are provided at the beginning of the paper.

Section A

Extended response questions will require you to formulate an argument, consider strengths and weaknesses, apply your knowledge, and often come to a reasoned conclusion. It is important to understand the demands of the command words used in this paper and draw up a plan before you commit pen to paper.

You will have learned about schizophrenia and one other mental disorder, either anorexia nervosa, obsessive-compulsive disorder or unipolar depression. In the exam, your option will be referred to as 'one other disorder'.

Section B

This section contains three applications in psychology of which you will have learned about only one. You should ignore the two sections that you have not learned about. Again, you will be asked to draw on your knowledge of research methods and statistics for your chosen application.

Eight-mark questions can ask you to discuss a topic/situation or to evaluate a topic/situation; both require you to describe relevant psychology, explore the issue, consider different viewpoints and judge strengths and weaknesses to form a conclusion. However, if the question asks that you 'make reference to the context', you must instead describe relevant psychology and apply it to the context given. You do not need to evaluate.

Getting the most from your online ActiveBook

This book comes with three years' access to ActiveBook* – an online, digital version of your textbook. Follow the instructions printed on the inside front cover to start using your ActiveBook.

Your ActiveBook is the perfect way to personalise your learning as you progress through your A level Psychology course. You can:

- access your content online, anytime, anywhere

- use the inbuilt highlighting and annotation tools to personalise the content and make it really relevant to you.

Highlight tool

Use this to pick out key terms or topics so you are ready and prepared for revision.

Annotations tool

Use this to add your own notes, for example links to your wider reading, such as websites or other files. Or, make a note to remind yourself about work that you need to do.

*for new purchases only. If this access code has already been revealed, it may no longer be valid. If you have bought this textbook second hand, the code may already have been used by the first owner of the book.

Acknowledgements

The publisher would like to thank the following for their kind permission to reproduce their photographs:

(Key: b-bottom; c-centre; l-left; r-right; t-top)

123RF.com: Adam Radosavljevic 316, alenavlad 97, Andres Rodriques 439, Antonio Guillem 303, Kheng Guan Toh 107; **Alamy Images:** Blickwinkel 105, BSIP SA 311, Detail Nottingham 47, Douglas O'Connor 256, DP RF Alamy 402t, Greatstock Photographic Library 17, Image Source Plus 234, Isobel Flynn 213, Justin Kase z12z 266, MBI 301, 396, OJO Images Ltd 240, P CJones 101, Peter Titmuss 377, Photofusion Picture Library 465, Tommy Trenchard 20, Zuma Press Inc 30; **Blend:** Blend Images 182; **Corbis:** Frederico Gambarini / dpa 402b; **Fotolia.com:** Africa Studio 570 (a), cosma 440, Cromary 236, emirkoo 178b, freie-kreation 231, Highwaystarz 431, Monkey Business 287, roibu 570 (b), Tomsickova 222; **Getty Images:** Ariel Skelley 411, Dan Istitene 374, Image Source 420, Jacqueline Veissid 448, John Moore 72, John Rensten 379, Jonathan Kim 478, Paul J Richards / AFP 218, Peopleimages.com 394, Tom Jenkins 35; **Pearson Education Ltd:** Studio 8 491, MindStudio 469, Jules Selmes 456; **Public Health England:** 95, 518; **Science Photo Library Ltd:** National Institute on Aging 179t, Sam Ogden 523b, Science Source 441tr, Scott Camazine 178tl; **Shutterstock.com:** Edyta Pawlowska 504, Ivica NS 179b, Jordan Tan 166, Kamira 513, Monkey Business Images 259, 334, Sonsedska Yuliia 442, Subbotina Anna 320

All other images © Pearson Education.

The publisher would also like to thank Time to Change and Public Health England for their help with references to their campaigns, the Science Museum for their permission to adapt the illustration, 'Freud's theory of personality', page 168 and the following for their kind permission to reproduce text extracts:

Extract from Diana's Story, page 320, was used with permission from NHS Choices. Article on 'What recycled water reveals about human psychology', page 566, has been reproduced with permission from the Research Digest of the BPS. Original article by guest blogger Sam McNerney.

Every effort has been made to trace the copyright holders and we apologise in advance for any unintentional omissions. We would be pleased to insert the appropriate acknowledgement in any subsequent edition of this publication.

Introduction to Psychology

Psychology is defined as the science of mind and behaviour. But for any new student of psychology it is a different way of thinking about and understanding the world. You will need to learn what is meant by the definition of psychology, and will also have to learn the skills associated with being a psychologist.

This section covers:

- approaches in the study of psychology
- theory, study and methodology
- conventions of report writing and peer review
- what are wider issues and debates?
- common themes
- individual differences and developmental psychology
- understanding how to evaluate.

Approaches in psychology

In psychology many different approaches are taken to understand and study human behaviour. This can be a tricky concept to appreciate as many subjects that you might have studied at GCSE involve learning just one answer, one fact or one perspective about a given topic.

In everyday life there can be many different ways of thinking about the same situation or event. For example, many different people might be interested in a garden: such as a biologist, an artist, a geographer, a gardener and a child. The garden remains the same, but the individuals each have a different perspective on what the garden means to them and will have different interests in it. A biologist would be interested in the ecosystems that exist in the garden borders; the geographer might be interested in the gradient of the landscape; a child would focus on what games can be played in the space; form and colour would be important for the artist, and a gardener would be concerned with the plants and vegetables that are grown there. In the same way, psychologists have different perspectives on what it is important to understand and study about the human mind and behaviour.

Psychologists also differ in the way that they go about studying human behaviour. Using the garden metaphor again, a gardener would use tools, such as a fork and spade, the artist would use an easel and brushes and a biologist would throw a quadrat to measure quantities of species in an area. Psychologists also use different tools to study human mind and behaviour; an experiment can be set up to test mental processing, an observation can be conducted to observe playground behaviour and a case study can be used to study an individual in detail. The research methods used are often contingent on the approach taken to understanding human behaviour.

As you work through the course, you will examine these different approaches and the methods used to investigate humans and animals. It is important to learn the key features of each approach in order to understand their perspectives on psychology, and the tools used to investigate the psychology of mind and behaviour.

Table 1 below shows how each approach views behaviour and the methods of investigation typically used.

Table 1 Approaches in psychology

Approach	Perspective taken	Methods of investigation/methodologies
Social approach/social psychology	Understands human behaviour by examining relationships between individuals, groups, societies and culture. Social psychologists are interested in human behaviours such as prejudice and obedience.	Although they use many methods, such as experiments, observations and correlations, this book draws attention to the self-report methods of the questionnaire and interview.
Cognitive approach/ cognitive psychology	Understands human behaviour as a result of the way we process information. Cognition is our awareness and understanding of the world. Cognition therefore affects the way we respond to an event. Cognitivists are interested in studying topics such as memory, attention, language and intelligence.	Cognitive psychologists typically use experiments to investigate human mental processing. They also use case studies of brain-damaged patients to understand how injury can be linked to **cognitive deficits**.
Biological approach/ biological psychology	Explains human behaviour as resulting from biological mechanisms such as the **nervous and endocrine systems** and ultimately **genetics**. Biological psychologists are interested in many types of normal and abnormal behaviour but this specification focuses on understanding aggression using knowledge of brain mechanisms, hormones and genetics. It links to **evolutionary theory** as human behaviour is a product of psychological adaptations in our evolutionary past.	Biological psychologists often study the behaviours that would be unethical to manipulate or create. They use **correlations** to examine relationships between variables, such as aggression and hormones. They also use scientific methods such as **brain scans** to identify what parts of the brain are responsible for behaviours. **Twin and adoption studies** are used to investigate genetic inheritance.
Learning approach/ learning theories	The learning approach, referred to as behaviourism, explains human behaviour as a product of a learning experience. We acquire behaviour through observation and imitation, association, and the consequences of reward and punishment. Although interested in the acquisition of general behaviour, this specification focuses on learning aggression and phobias.	Learning theorists/behaviourists tend to use animal experiments to understand the building blocks of learning in simple species, although human experiments have been conducted where a new behaviour is deliberately manipulated and studied. This book also focuses on the observation research method used to examine different behaviours.
Psychodynamic approach	The psychodynamic approach is not a main topic in this book but will be touched on when looking at aggression. Sigmund Freud believed that human behaviour could be understood by the expression of different parts of our personality and the nature of the **unconscious mind** as an influence on our behaviour.	The psychodynamic approach typically investigated human behaviour through clinical case studies: in-depth investigations of an individual who presented an abnormal condition that was systematically studied over a long period of time.

The highlighted terms can be found in the glossary.

These approaches vary considerably in their perspectives on the causes of human behaviour, the focus of their interest and the way in which they conduct investigations. But the different perspectives do not necessarily mean that there is only one right answer or explanation. We must consider instead the relative strengths and weaknesses of each perspective and the evidence they use to support their views.

Applications in psychology

In the second year of your course you will be required to apply your knowledge of approaches within specific applications of psychology. Applications are areas of psychology or specialisms, such as child psychology, health psychology, criminological psychology and clinical psychology. Within these applications you will come across the different approaches and methodologies again. In the second year, you will have to use your underpinning knowledge of approaches and apply it to the context of your chosen application and clinical psychology.

Theory, study and methodology

When you study psychology, you will see that there are various components that build up to the bigger picture of understanding human nature. These components can be broadly divided into theory, research study and methodology. We shall examine each in turn.

What is a theory?

Psychology is concerned with explaining human behaviour. It is not possible to explain all human behaviour in totality, so psychologists tend to focus on specific aspects of mind and behaviour that interest them. For example, cognitive psychologists cannot explain all human cognition, as cognition itself involves memory, attention, language, intelligence and problem solving, etc. So a cognitive psychologist may focus their attention on one aspect of cognition, such as memory, and try to explain how memory works. Their explanation is called a **theory**. A theory is an explanation or set of ideas on how something works, or in the case of psychology, how some aspect of mind and behaviour can be explained, and how it can be used to predict future behaviour. In the context of being a science, psychological theories (as with any theory of the natural sciences) cannot be proven or stated as fact, but with supporting evidence they can become 'accepted' theories.

You need to be able to describe, evaluate or use your knowledge of theories. To *describe* a theory involves straightforward recall of the main concepts and ideas that need to be written in logical and coherent prose. To *evaluate* a theory you will need to explain how useful the theory is at helping us to understand the behaviour it claims to explain. To do this you will need to consider the strengths and weaknesses of the theory itself and any research evidence from studies that can be used to support or refute (or contradict) the theory. To *use* the theory requires an application of knowledge to explain a given scenario that is more than simply describing the theory. You will need to consider and select which concepts and ideas within the theory itself are important and can be linked to the scenario you are given and then mould them into an explanation.

What is a study?

A psychologist cannot just claim to have a theory or explanation without the evidence to support it. Psychologists gather this evidence by conducting a research **study** on human or animal participants to demonstrate how their theory might work. Studies are practical investigations that are conducted, analysed, written up and subsequently published in journals to build up a bank of knowledge concerning an aspect of human cognition or behaviour.

Research studies can take many different forms that adopt differing methodologies: clinical trials, experiments, observations, case studies and surveys, among others. They can be conducted over

> ### Key terms
>
> **Theory:** a set of ideas that are used to explain a behaviour.
>
> **Study:** a practical investigation.

a short or long period of time and can differ in the type of data gathered; **quantitative** and/or **qualitative**.

You will need to be able to describe, evaluate and use your knowledge of research studies. To describe a study you will need to show knowledge of the whole study: the name(s) of the researcher(s), the aim of the investigation, the methodology used (including research method, procedure, sample, design, apparatus, controls, variables and ethics), the findings and conclusions drawn. To evaluate the study it is important to have a range of points to ensure that both strengths and weaknesses of the research are included. You may be asked to draw on your knowledge of the study to explain a particular issue, or you can use the research study as evidence to evaluate a particular theory. To use the study as evidence for or against a theory, you only need to refer to the findings and conclusions to explain why it backs up or refutes a theory.

What is methodology?

Broadly speaking, **methodology** refers to a set of principles adopted by an approach or type of procedure used to conduct a research study. Although there are broader definitions of the term within philosophy and other disciplines, in psychology it tends to refer to the type of scientific procedures adopted to study a particular phenomenon. In psychology we classify scientific procedures and label them as research methods. The research method (or methodology) chosen to investigate depends on the nature of what is being investigated and the approach taken by the psychologist. For example, a cognitive psychologist would prefer to use laboratory experiments, case studies of brain-damaged patients, neuroimaging and observations as research methods because they are useful to study aspects of cognition, such as memory. A social psychologist, however, would prefer to use field experiments and observations to study human social interaction or surveys to uncover attitudes about different social groups.

Methodology can also refer to the way in which research was conducted: the procedure used in an investigation.

You will need to be able to describe, evaluate and use your knowledge of methodology throughout the course. Describing the methodology used involves outlining its key features, such as how and when it is likely to be used and the processes involved in the particular method. Evaluation will involve explaining the strengths and weaknesses of the methodology in achieving useful results; this evaluation tends to involve weighing up key elements or features of science (see below) such as control, objectivity, replicability and validity. You can also examine the ethical implications of each research method. Using your knowledge of methodology will involve applying your understanding of methods to a novel situation, perhaps to design an investigation.

You will also have to write about the methodology that you used in your practical investigations.

The nature of scientific investigation

The typical nature of scientific investigation follows a **hypothetico-deductive method** as a way of gathering evidence and generating knowledge. The hypothetico-deductive method means the starting point of science is that a theory is proposed or an observation about human behaviour is made from which a testable hypothesis is generated. A hypothesis is a prediction of what should happen according to the proposed theory. A study is designed to test a hypothesis using a methodology appropriate to the study aim. Once conducted, evidence/data can be collected and the outcome of this research can be used to support or refute the proposed theory.

If a theory is verified by the outcome of the study, the theory can become a supported explanation within a psychological knowledge base. If the theory is refuted by the research, further hypotheses can be proposed or refined and tested again. Therefore, it can be seen that the three elements of theory, study and methodology are equally important for scientific investigation to take place.

Key terms

Quantitative: numerical data (information about quantities, i.e. can be counted).

Qualitative: prose, non-numerical data, such as transcripts of interviews or detailed diary extracts.

Methodology: the way in which we go about conducting research by adopting a research method such as an experiment or case study, for example.

Hypothetico-deductive method: the scientific way of gathering knowledge through testing a proposed theory using evidence gathered by research.

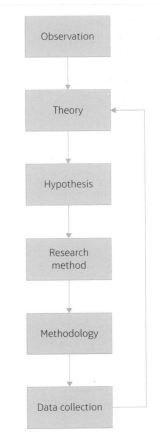

Figure 1 The hypothetico-deductive model

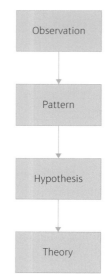

Figure 2 Inductive model

Although the hypothetico-deductive method is widely accepted as a way of generating knowledge in psychology, it is not the only investigative method. The **inductive method** involves firstly making observations and gathering evidence and then generating theories based on observations made. The inductive method can be particularly useful in new areas of research, such as studying the brain, where theories have not yet been established to test. Similarly, case studies often use an inductive method because they involve making observations of an individual or group from which theories can be proposed. Although the inductive research cycle runs in the opposite direction to the hypothetico-deductive cycle, the importance of theory, study and methodology is still obvious. Qualitative research often follows the inductive method because theories often emerge from the qualitative data being analysed.

The conventions of report writing

Academic research, once complete, is written up as a report and often submitted for publication in psychological journals. There is a standard format or convention for report writing that dictates what report structure is followed and how information within the report is presented. Although this varies a little between reports, there is a typical convention used for the subsections of a psychological report:

- Title and author
- Abstract
- Introduction/background research
- Methodology
- Results/findings
- Discussion
- References and appendices

Abstract

The abstract is a short summary of the aims, method, findings and implications of the study which can be found at the very beginning of the report. Its purpose is to provide the reader with a brief account of what was done and found so that they do not have to read the entire article before deciding whether it is relevant for them. Abstracts are also useful when conducting a keyword search online before ordering the entire report at considerable expense.

Introduction/background research

This section provides information about the background theories and previous research on which the current study is based. It provides a rationale for conducting the research and justifies the approach taken and procedure used. The introduction typically begins with an outline of relevant psychological theories and then funnels down into previous research specifically relevant to the current investigation and finally to the aims and hypothesis. This gives the reader a useful introduction to the topic area with narrowed focus and rationale for the aims of the study being described.

Methodology

The methodology section of a report contains information about how the study was conducted. This will include the sampling method and details of the participants' ages, sex, ethnicity and demographics. This information is useful when judging whether the findings of the study are generalisable to the target population or beyond. It also contains details of the variables, apparatus used, procedure, controls and ethical considerations. The methodology can be used to assess the credibility and ethics of research, and also allows replications of the research to be conducted to check for reliability.

Results/findings

This section will present the findings of the study relevant to the aims and hypotheses. Tables and graphs are often used to summarise the data, and statistical conclusions are made with regards to the relevant statistical tests conducted on the data. The findings are simply stated without explanation.

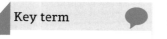

Key term

Inductive method: a way of gathering knowledge through observations generating theory.

Discussion

The discussion section explains the findings in detail, often making reference to theories and research cited in the introduction of the report so that links can be made. This is where the researchers interpret the data and draw conclusions. It is typical for this section to also include a critique of the study with regards to its strengths and limitations, which often makes reference to methodological and ethical issues. This section may also discuss the implications of the research for psychology as a discipline and for the topic area, and applications for use in society. It may also detail how the research could be extended or replicated to further explore the area.

References and appendices

Every report will have a list of references cited in the study to acknowledge the authors mentioned throughout the report. Full references are given in alphabetical order by surname of the main author and typically a referencing format such as the Harvard system is followed. This section can be useful if you want to find out more about a particular theory or study as you can find the citation required to access the full original journal.

An appendix (plural, appendices) is a final section which contains the actual apparatus used or details of the sample or procedure. This can include pictures of the equipment, questionnaires and scales used in the study, standardised instructions, consent forms, etc. Although some researchers do not provide an appendices section, because it can be lengthy, it can be useful to aid replication and judge the validity of the apparatus and procedure.

Peer review

When a researcher has completed a study and written up a psychological report, they will submit this report to relevant publishers of psychological journals. Publishers will use peers who are experts in the relevant field of research to review the report, recommend any changes needed and advise whether the report should be published. This process is known as peer review.

The process of peer review ensures that published psychological knowledge is not invalid, biased or fraudulent. It helps to maintain standards within the discipline and prevent unsubstantiated claims being made by researchers. It also ensures the very best quality contemporary research is published as it is subject to rigorous review of the content, methodology and findings. Researchers whose published work has been successfully reviewed by peers attract a kudos associated with the process and it can also attract funding for the institution with which the research is affiliated.

However, the process of peer review is not without its critics, particularly from those who fail to have their research published. It can involve many amendments being made to the original submission, which can be frustrating for the researcher and costly for the publisher, potentially holding back the progress of research in a psychological area. Some research is never published, and the process is often criticised for failing to publish null findings, leading to a publication bias for positive outcomes that can lead to a distorted view of a subject area. This has the potential to skew the outcomes of a meta-analysis that uses only peer-reviewed research.

Despite seeming an unbiased process, some cynics argue that peer reviewers may use their anonymity to assert their own opinions and settle academic rivalries. Criticisms raised by peer reviewers are based on subjective opinions and can lead to the maintenance of a status quo in published literature; as new and modern techniques in methodology may be misunderstood or rejected as not scientific. This was the case with qualitative research in psychology for many years. Peer reviewers and academics did not initially accept qualitative research which limited its emergence in published journals.

What are issues and debates?

Issues and debates form the synoptic element of assessment and are largely reserved for the GCE assessment, but can be used for the Advanced Subsidiary GCE (AS) too. Issues and debates are considered to be synoptic elements of psychology because they run through the whole course and are used to make broad judgements of theory, methodology and research. Understanding issues and debates gives you a greater understanding of psychology as a whole discipline.

Issues and debates include the following.

Ethical issues

Ethical issues in research (human and animal) refer to the guidelines that serve to protect participants involved in research to ensure their psychological and physical safety and wellbeing. Ethical issues apply directly to research studies that are conducted on humans and animals, so it is important not only to know the ethical guidelines, but also whether or not research has satisfied these guidelines, the reasons for not adhering to the guidelines and the consequences for the participants involved. You will also be conducting your own practical investigations throughout the course to gain the experience of implementing ethical guidelines first hand, and you will need to be aware of the importance of adhering to them.

Reductionism

Reductionism is a debate in psychology that refers to the simplifying of a complex phenomenon. Human mind and behaviour involve undoubtedly complex processes that can be difficult to understand and study without first breaking them down into smaller, simpler components in order to explain them. This is known as reductionism. Reductionism can be desirable as it makes a phenomenon easier to isolate, study and understand, according to the scientific process. However, it can be argued that reductionism inherently oversimplifies, fragments and ultimately limits our understanding of complex human behaviour.

Comparing explanations

It is not uncommon to find two or more theories that could be used to explain the same phenomenon. Comparisons of explanations of behaviour using different themes involves examining opposing theories. Often these themes or theories use different levels of explanation or take a particular approach within their explanation. It is important to understand what approach each theme or theory takes in order to compare the strengths and limitations of each idea.

Psychology as a science

Psychology as a science is a long-standing debate that will be discussed in more depth throughout the course. Psychologists who take a more scientific approach to theory research may argue that psychology is a science but there are aspects of psychology which make it more difficult to meet the criteria of being truly scientific. You may be asked to judge whether a theory, research study or particular methodology is scientific, so it is important to understand what criteria are used.

Science tends to follow the hypothetico-deductive method to ensure that only testable ideas are researched and that evidence can be gathered to support or disconfirm these ideas. Science also follows an empirical tradition. **Empiricism** is a way of thinking and states that only true knowledge can be gathered directly through the senses and should not be simply inferred through logical reasoning (guesswork). Science also involves meeting the criteria of control, objectivity and replication, among others.

Key terms

Reductionism: simplifying or fragmenting a phenomenon.

Empiricism: knowledge can only be gathered through sensory experience. For example, empiricists would argue that you cannot infer that it is raining outside just because you can see people putting up their umbrellas; you can only establish that it is raining by going outside and feeling the rain on your skin.

You will be asked to judge whether an approach or research can be considered to be scientific. Start by making a list of features considered to be scientific (empiricism, **objectivity**, and so on) and then form a judgement about the approach or research by whether or not it matches each criterion. It is also useful to understand that, although being scientific is considered to be a strength, it can be a limitation in psychology. It can prevent certain research from being undertaken because it does not meet the strict criteria of science, so that some research is not conducted in psychology because it may lack credibility. It is also argued that it is not appropriate to study human behaviour as one would study chemicals or plants in strictly controlled conditions, because human behaviour does not exist within an experimental vacuum. Applying science to the study of psychology can be seen as overly mechanistic and highly reductionist. Others argue that it is impossible for psychology, the study of humans, to meet the criteria of science because we can never be truly objective and it ignores the element of consciousness that makes us human.

Culture

Culture is an important issue in psychology because much of the research is conducted in industrialised Western societies so that this view can be over-emphasised within current psychological thinking. This results in culture bias in research which can only therefore be used to explain the behaviour of the culture in which the research has been conducted. When judging the issue of culture bias it can be useful to examine the culture in which the research has taken place, the type of participants involved, the tools used to investigate and the way in which the outcomes of the research are used – do they limit the findings to the culture and sample used, or do they make assumptions about the universality of behaviour?

Ethnocentrism is where we form judgements about other cultures based on culturally biased research, and in some cases assume that other cultures are somehow inferior to the ideals of the developed world. When judging research to be ethnocentric it is important to understand the implications of applying findings to other cultures.

Gender

Gender is an issue in psychology when research either exaggerates differences between men and women (alpha-bias) or minimises them when differences do exist (beta-bias). Alpha-bias is more common and can be found in many areas of psychology. Evolutionary psychology, for example, highlights differences between men and women in terms of physical strength, prowess and dominance. Freud suggested that males were superior to females as women had weaker superego's and suffered 'penis envy' which could only be resolved through procreation. Alpha-bias does tend to support the idea of men being superior to women; however, Bowlby's original theory of attachment (see Topic 7) regarded women as more important in maternal care, so it is not always the case.

It is important to recognise that alpha-bias can often support and perpetuate gender stereotypes that are oversimplified and often exaggerated by a tendency to only publish literature that has found a significant difference rather than no difference at all (null effect).

Beta-bias is when research minimises differences between men and women, which would be a generally fair conclusion based on the fact that there are more psychological similarities than differences between males and females. However, a problem occurs when the research is conducted primarily on male participants but purports to explain the behaviour of both men and women equally. Milgram, for example (see Topic 1), conducted much of his research into obedience on male participants, yet his conclusions were aimed at explaining all human obedience, in men and women alike. This demonstrates an **androcentric** bias in research.

Key terms

Objectivity: impartiality and value-free judgements should be made by the researcher. They should not impose their own opinions on the findings of research.

Androcentric: research representing a male point of view.

When considering gender bias it is useful to know how many males and females were actually tested in the original research and whether the findings of the research suggest a universal human characteristic. It is also important to question statements that seem to categorically suggest that men and women are different in a psychological dimension, as this is rarely the case.

Nature-nurture

This is the debate in psychology about whether psychological characteristics are a product of genetic factors or environmental influence. The former suggests that we inherit genes that determine our biology and psychological characteristics, and as such are predetermined and unavoidable. The latter emphasises the role of environmental influence on the development of psychological characteristics, such as upbringing, education and experiences. Historically the nature-nurture debate saw each standpoint as exclusive, but today we generally accept that we are a product of both nature and nurture in interaction with one another through the course of development both before and after birth. This can simply be represented as a nature-nurture continuum. However, it is important to remember that the debate today is not about how much nature or nurture has an influence, but about how nature and nurture interact to influence the psychological characteristics we possess.

An understanding of how psychological understanding has developed over time

Understanding the historical situation in which an approach, theory or research has been developed or been a dominant way of thinking is important in developing a critical understanding of psychology. This is not simply about learning dates, it involves understanding the time in which knowledge has been developed and the implications of this knowledge at that point in history. For example, psychodynamics is regarded today as the least scientific of the approaches in psychology. It was developed by one of the founding fathers of psychology, Sigmund Freud, at the beginning of the last century. However we can begin to understand that the methods that Freud employed and his explanation of human behaviour were of the time and a result of the techniques that were available.

The use of psychological knowledge within society

Psychological knowledge ultimately has practical use in society. The application of psychological knowledge is far reaching and touches on many aspects of our everyday lives, and in professional and clinical settings. For example, cognitive research has been used to help us revise for exams or tests more effectively, to inform police interview techniques to ensure that witness testimony is reliable, and to help people with dementia who suffer memory loss. Learning theories have been used to reward good behaviour in classrooms, control the behaviour of prisoners and to help people with phobias.

The use of social control in psychology

The issue of social control in psychology concerns how knowledge derived from psychological research can be used to regulate, or control, people's behaviour. Although psychological knowledge can be used to benefit society or an individual, it can have certain social and moral implications as it can involve or imply direct behaviour manipulation. The implications for social control can be obvious in a clinical setting, because psychological therapies such as drug treatments for mental health issues concern altering behaviour so an individual can integrate better into society. However, some psychological knowledge has less obvious social control implications. Behaviourism, for example, is an approach in psychology that assumes that behaviour can be directly manipulated by environmental influences. Operant conditioning is a behavioural theory that describes behaviour as being a product of its consequences; reward or punishment. This may sound innocuous, but ultimately it can be considered a form of social control as it has the potential to directly alter the behaviour of one person by another.

Exam tip
During your study you will come across many applications for psychological knowledge in society. Each time, make a note of how the knowledge is being used, the techniques that have been developed from the knowledge, and whether the application could be considered a form of social control.

Socially sensitive research

Ethical issues are concerns that affect how a participant is treated during the research, but sometimes psychological research has implications beyond the research conditions. Research that has negative implications for the individual or group they represent beyond the confines of a study is considered to be socially sensitive research. This may mean that the research may reflect negatively on people as individuals or may impact negatively on their life, their family, society, profession or the culture to which they belong. Essentially, socially sensitive research puts people at risk. Socially sensitive research often involves taboo topics, such as abuse, immigration, deviance, sexuality, death, etc., which have the potential to distress, harm or threaten the participants or groups in which they are involved.

The problems associated with socially sensitive research are addressed in the British Psychological Society's Code of Human Research Ethics (2014) under the principles of scientific integrity and social responsibility. These principles state that research should be planned, conducted and reviewed in a way that considers how the knowledge gained may have the potential to cause harm, and that the outcomes of research should be used for the 'common good'. In fact, socially sensitive research is an integral theme within the code to ensure that risk of harm is minimised for the individual, and for the groups and communities to which they belong.

With such a broad definition and code to regulate for socially sensitive research, it is likely that most research would be considered to be socially sensitive and therefore not authorised by an ethics committee. It is also of concern that socially sensitive outcomes may not be foreseen by researchers or that the research may only become socially sensitive if the knowledge was misused afterwards. However, avoiding socially sensitive research may mean that important topics of legitimate concern to the discipline of psychology and to society as a whole are overlooked.

Common themes

Throughout the whole course, you will be expected to comment on the credibility, validity, reliability, generalisability, objectivity/subjectivity of theory and research. Therefore it is useful to familiarise yourself with these issues as soon as possible.

Objectivity/subjectivity

A key feature of science is objectivity, that is, research is value free and not contaminated by personal opinion (subjectivity). A researcher should be detached and impartial in the interpretation of information gained during an investigation.

A useful example of subjectivity and objectivity is to consider the length of an object. If you ask people to estimate the length of an object, it is likely to vary between individuals because it is their own personal opinion – this is known as subjectivity. However, if you arm people with a ruler and ask them to measure the length of an object, they are all likely to give the same length because the tool that they have used to measure length is objective. In psychology some methods are more objective than others, but it could be argued that no method can be purely objective because all require an element of interpretation.

The analysis of interview data, observations and other qualitative methods are more subjective because a researcher has to interpret and draw conclusions from data that are more likely to be affected by personal opinion. Similar to using a ruler, objectivity is best achieved by clear **operationalisation** of measurement, that is, defining exactly what is going to be measured and in what way it is to be recorded. In an observation, for example, making clear exactly what behaviours are to be recorded improves objectivity; a researcher looking for how many times a door is opened for someone by another person will be more objective than a researcher looking for polite behaviour, because what constitutes polite behaviour is open to interpretation.

Social control

When considering social control, it is important to recognise the social and moral implications of psychological knowledge as it is used to regulate the behaviour of an individual or society. For example, Bowlby was a developmental psychologist who believed that periods of separation between a child and its mother could have emotional implications on the bond formed and the child's subsequent emotional development. Following the Second World War, this knowledge was used to encourage the female workforce back into domesticity, despite employment being liberating for women across the country. It also ensured that the returning soldiers could regain jobs that had previously been taken by women. Ultimately this psychological knowledge had social implications for the shape of society and for the position of women in it.

Psychological therapies are considered to be a form of social control that has both social and moral implications. Aversion therapy, for example, has social implications because it can be forced on individuals to make them conform to social expectations and values.

 Key term

Operationalisation: defining the variables specifically so that they are directly tested.

Generalisability

Generalisability refers to the extent to which the findings of research can be applied to other people and contexts, other than the ones directly involved in the research itself. Ecological validity is a type of generalisability which questions the extent to which we can generalise from an experimental situation to a natural setting. When we conduct research we cannot investigate everyone, so it is done on a sample of the population. For example, if we conduct research on university students, would these findings also apply to non-university students – the general population?

Reliability

Reliability refers to the consistency of research findings. In order to establish reliability, research needs to be replicated many times to ensure that the outcome was not a one-off. A one-off finding may be because of a methodological issue, subjectivity or that an unstable characteristic is being tested.

Validity

Validity is whether the research is measuring what it intends to measure. For example, if you conduct an IQ test, you want the outcome of the test to accurately reflect the concept of intelligence. Validity is often compromised by poor operationalisation of what is being measured. For example, if you are intending to measure the aggression of children in a playground and you operationalise aggression as pushing, you may find it is not a valid measure of aggression if the children are playing tag, a game where children are supposed to push each other.

Credibility

Credibility is a broad definition given to the trustworthiness of psychological research and the knowledge gained from such research. Credibility is based on a range of factors such as the scientific method, objectivity, reliability and validity of research. The credibility of published psychological research is largely assured by the process of peer review.

Individual differences and developmental psychology

Individual differences

Psychology, as a discipline, has focused on developing laws of human behaviour that can be generalised to everyone. However in modern psychology, there is increasing attention being paid to understanding the differences between individuals as well as the similarities that people share. This new approach has concentrated instead on examining individual differences between people, and the characteristics that vary between us, such as intelligence, personality and abnormality. The assumption that underpins the individual differences approach is that in order to understand the complex nature of human beings, it is important that we recognise the unique differences between us, rather than what we just share in common.

Developmental psychology

Developmental psychology is an area of the discipline which studies the changes that occur as we age through the course of our lifespan; from infancy and childhood, through adolescence, adulthood and old age. Patterns of change occur throughout our development and it is the study of developmental psychology that examines the mechanisms underlying these changes, whether biological or maturational (nature or nurture). We often share these patterns and stages of development cognitively, socially, emotionally and biologically, such as the way in which infants babble before they develop the sounds associated with their native language, but there is also individual variation in development such as the way some of us do not acquire language normally.

Evaluation skills

In psychology you will need to learn how to adopt a critical approach to both psychological theories that have been proposed and psychology research that has been conducted. Being critical involves an awareness of the strengths and weaknesses of an argument or investigation, and an appreciation of the credibility of a theory or study. This critical approach will take some time to develop fully, but there are concepts that can be considered when evaluating psychological research.

Evaluating psychological theories

If you were told that eating five apples a day made you healthy, would you believe it? Most people would. But as a psychologist you need to think critically about the claim, or theory, that eating five apples every day makes you healthy. There are a series of questions you could ask yourself.

- Is there any supporting evidence that eating five apples a day makes you healthy? In psychology you cannot go around making claims unless you have the evidence to back them up. Psychological investigations provide support for theories if they test them and find them to be correct. You should use psychological evidence when evaluating a theory to ensure its credibility. Without evidence, the theory is simply speculation. There is actually no evidence to suggest that eating five pieces of fruit and veg a day actually makes you healthy – how would anyone ever test this theory anyway?

- What kind of evidence is being used to support the theory? If there is evidence to support a claim, what sort of evidence is it? If the evidence comes from anecdotal reports of people claiming to be healthy because they eat five apples a day, you need to question the credibility of these reports. If the support for the claim comes from scientific research then you can be more certain that the evidence is credible.

- Is there any contradicting evidence for apples making you healthy? If unhealthy people eat apples, this may provide some counter-evidence for the claim. Again, the credibility of this evidence should be assessed. If the unhealthy people who eat apples also eat five bags of chips a day, this may discredit the evidence.

- Is the claim that eating apples makes you healthy useful in everyday life? You could certainly claim that it would do no harm, and even introduce healthy snack times to schools or promote free fruit in fast-food restaurants. Therefore it would have useful everyday applications if found to be a true claim.

- Are there any different explanations for being healthy; is it a valid claim? An alternative explanation could be that people who eat apples are more food conscious generally, so have a healthier diet. This would seem a better explanation than apples making you healthy and is probably more grounded in truth.

- Is there anything that the theory fails to explain? Well, the apple claim cannot explain why people who eat five apples a day become unwell. This could not be predicted or explained by the claim, therefore it does not take into account why some people who eat apples are healthy and some people are not.

- It is possible to test the theory that apples cause healthiness? The simple answer is no, this would not be practical or reasonable, you could not restrict a person's diet for an extended period of time (particularly not on apples alone), nor could you control everything else they ate, the amount of exercise, stress at work or school, or indeed any other variable likely to impact on their healthiness.

Exam tip
When evaluating theories and studies, it can be easier to write about the weaknesses rather than the strengths, but both must be considered fully for a balanced evaluation. It is important that you don't just list strengths and weaknesses unless you are asked to. Often a weakness can be countered by a strength or justification.

Learning how to evaluate effectively will help develop your skills without having to remember the precise evaluation for each individual study. However, it is important not to write a generalised evaluation, it needs to be tailored to the study or theory you are evaluating. For example, do not just say that the study was conducted in a laboratory, so was not like real life. Instead detail how the laboratory conditions do not reflect real life for the study, what controls were used that would not be found in an everyday context, and most importantly what are the implications of these being unlike real life.

- Is the theory socially sensitive? That is, does it have a negative effect on the people involved or affected by the claim? Although the apple claim is unlikely to adversely affect anyone really, an extreme view might be that it makes a judgement and implies that unhealthy people are responsible for their own health issues, or that people who cannot afford to buy basket loads of apples feel subordinate to those who can. These are extreme viewpoints, but the issue here is that when a theory is proposed, it can have a negative effect on individuals in some way connected to the theory.

Evaluating psychological research studies

We can use an example of a fictional study on the effect of verbal abuse on performance. Two participants were asked to come to a laboratory and complete a jigsaw puzzle to see if age affected performance. One participant was shouted at by the experimenter and the other was not. Their jigsaw puzzle completion time was recorded and they were told to leave without any explanation.

- Is shouting verbal abuse at someone an ethical thing to do? Not really: it is stressful and the participants were deceived because they thought it was a study about aging, and were not debriefed following the experiment. There is a range of ethical guidelines for research with humans that can be used to evaluate a research study; clearly this example violated many of the ethical guidelines.

- Can you generalise the findings of the study to others? In this example only two participants were used, and only one in each condition of the experiment. The experiment would have to have used a larger sample of participants to be sure that the findings could be generalised to others.

- Is the experiment reliable? To be reliable, it would have to be repeated over and over or on a larger sample of people to be sure the results were consistent. It would also need good controls over factors that might affect the results. In this example, variation between participants, for example resilience or spatial ability, could affect the reliability of the findings.

- Has the research been carried out in a natural environment? This research was conducted in a laboratory, so is artificial and does not reflect real life.

- Is the task ordinary? Perhaps it could be argued that solving a jigsaw puzzle is ordinary, but it depends on the aim of the investigation. If the aim of the study was to find out whether verbal abuse at work affected production, then it could be argued that the simulation does not reflect the aims of the study. In many experiments, participants are required to perform tasks that do not reflect the reality of normal everyday tasks; they lack mundane realism.

- Do the findings have any practical application? If found to be valid research, the findings of this study could have been used to inform the Equality Act (2010) to prevent harassment in the workplace. It could be argued that it has practical application.

- Is the task a useful measure of what was intended to be measured? In this case, is time taken to complete a jigsaw a good measure of performance? It is a restricted measure of performance in that it only measures the ability to recognise patterns and show reasonable spatial awareness. Therefore it is probably not a useful indicator of general performance.

- Are there any other research studies that do not support the findings of this one? Contrasting research may be useful to demonstrate that the research may not be credible.

Methods

You will learn about a range of scientific methods as you progress through your Psychology A level Student Book. You will find that the some methods are repeated in later topics in the specification. This table shows you where you can find information on each method within this book.

Method	Topic 1: Social psychology	Topic 2: Cognitive psychology	Topic 3: Biological psychology	Topic 4: Learning theories	Topic 5: Clinical psychology	Topic 6: Criminological psychology	Topic 7: Child psychology	Topic 8: Health psychology
Experiment		X				X		X
Self-report: questionnaires and interviews	X				X	X	X	
Observation				X			X	
Correlation			X			X		
Biological methods: scanning, twin and adoption studies			X					
Case study		X			X	X		
Cross-cultural research					X		X	X
Longitudinal research					X		X	
Cross-sectional research					X		X	
Meta-analysis					X			
Content analysis				X				
Ethical guidelines	X				X	X	X	X
Animal research and ethics				X				X
Sample selection and techniques	X							
Hypotheses and variables		X						
Descriptive statistics	X							
Inferential statistics		X Mann-Whitney & Wilcoxon test	X Spearman's rho test	X Chi-squared test				
Analysis of correlation data			X					
Scientific status of psychology				X				
Researching mental health					X			
Analysis of qualitative data	X				X			

1 Social psychology

Social psychology is concerned with understanding aspects of human behaviour that involve an individual's relationships to others, groups, society and culture. Social psychologists are interested in topics where people's behaviour can be influenced by others, such as obedience and prejudice. We often observe others in social situations and speculate about their behaviour; social psychology involves a rigorous and scientific investigation of these attitudes and behaviours, using experiments and surveys to establish firm conclusions.

In this topic, you will learn about:

- explanations and research into obedience and prejudice
- factors that affect obedience and prejudice, including individual differences, situation and culture
- the way in which self-report data is gathered and analysed to understand attitudes and behaviour
- a classic and a contemporary study of prejudice and/or obedience
- key issues around the topic of social psychology that are of relevance to society today
- how to carry out a practical research exercise relevant to topics covered in social psychology
- wider issues and debates in social psychology (A level).

1.1 Content
Learning outcomes

In this section, you will learn about:

- theories of obedience, including agency theory and social impact theory
- Milgram's research into obedience
- factors affecting obedience, including individual differences, situation and culture
- theories of and research into prejudice, including social identity theory and realistic conflict theory
- factors affecting prejudice, including individual differences, situation and culture
- developmental psychology in obedience and prejudice research.

An introduction to social psychology

Social psychology developed from a group of people working in Germany in the mid-19th century, called folk psychologists, concerned with understanding the collective or group mind. Notably a French writer, Gustave Le Bon, observed that crowd behaviour was mob-like because individuals within it became part of the collective mob mentality. This notion of the behaviour of an individual can be explained by investigating the context of the group and is central to social psychology today.

The rise of experimental social psychology can be attributed to Floyd Allport (1924). His book outlined a manifesto for social psychology that argued for an experimental approach, giving rise to laboratories to investigate social behaviour. Today, social psychology investigates a range of social behaviours and attitudes such as persuasion and attitude formation, social influence, aggression and group behaviour. This topic focuses on obedience and prejudice.

Obedience

Obedience is a form of **social influence** where the behaviour of an individual is influenced by a real or imagined pressure from another. In terms of obedience, this can be defined as compliance to the real or imagined demands of an authority figure. Yielding to these demands is considered to be obedience, rejecting the demands is known as dissent.

In our everyday lives we obediently follow the instructions of teachers, employers, police officers and the rules of society. Such obedience can prevent accidents and result in social order the majority of the time. However, there are times when obedience has led to horrific consequences. Notably, many atrocities that have been committed against innocent people have been the result of blind obedience. During the Second World War, the Nazi party instructed a mass extermination of millions of Jewish people using inhumane methods. This could only have been achieved through the collective obedience of many German soldiers who carried out these orders.

We are taught to respect authority figures from a young age.

Agency theory of obedience

Stanley Milgram developed a series of classic experiments to investigate obedience under, what he considered to be, conditions that could be used to explain the atrocities committed during the Nazi control of Germany. You may find it useful to read about Milgram's experiments (see page 23) before you read on about agency theory. At the time, historians maintained that the Nazi soldiers had a basic character flaw that rendered them more obedient to orders, so much so that they would be willing to follow instructions to exterminate Jews by an authority figure. Milgram was unconvinced and was influenced by the writings of Hannah Arendt (1963) on the Nazi lieutenant and holocaust organiser Adolf Eichmann. Arendt spoke of Eichmann as an uninspired official with a mild-mannered nature, rather than the monster he was assumed to be and as a result, Milgram set out to investigate whether 'anyone' could be ordered to harm another.

Milgram conducted his obedience experiments on 'normal', healthy participants to investigate whether they would yield to an authority figure and administer electric shocks to an innocent **confederate** of the study. The result of his experiments led Milgram to conclude that we are all capable of complying to the demands of someone in authority, even if this means hurting another person. Using this conclusion as a basis for his agency theory, Milgram believed that we are all capable of extreme obedience, which must serve some evolutionary or societal function.

Key terms

Hierarchical: a system of social organisation that is ranked from top to bottom.

Socialisation: the process by which we learn the rules and norms of society through socialising agents, such as teachers and parents.

Autonomy: acting on one's own free will.

Agency: when one acts as an agent for another.

Moral strain: experiencing anxiety, usually because you are asked to do something that goes against your moral judgement.

Evolution of obedience

Milgram observed that human society was **hierarchical** in nature, with many at the bottom of the hierarchy and a few at the top giving instructions on how they are to behave. He proposed that this hierarchy must have evolved for some survival function, whereby societies that adopted this hierarchy survived and those that did not died out. He also thought that this hierarchical social organisation must have some stabilising function – to create social order and harmony within the group. Obedience within this social organisation is a necessary feature to maintain it. Without obedience there would be challenges to this social order resulting in chaos and societal breakdown.

Just as we are born with the capacity for language, we are innately prepared to be obedient. Exposure to authority figures within the family and education system nurture this preparedness through the process of **socialisation**. Parents are primary socialisers and use a system of rewards and punishments to encourage obedience and discourage dissent in young children. Sanctions and rewards are also institutional within the educational and legal systems, and so perform a large role in ensuring that we develop as subordinates within our society.

Agency and autonomy

Within the hierarchical structure of a social group, there must be a mechanism that ensures obedience. Milgram proposed that humans exist in two different states: **autonomy** and **agency**. In an autonomous state, a human acts according to their own free will. However, when given instruction by an authority figure the human switches to an agentic state of mind, where they see themselves as acting as an agent for the authority figure.

Milgram observed many participants in his obedience study experience **moral strain** when ordered to harm another person. Moral strain occurs when people are asked to do something they would not choose to do themselves, and they feel is immoral or unjust. This moral strain results in an individual feeling very uncomfortable in the situation and, in extreme circumstances, they show anxiety and distress. This anxiety is felt as the individual contemplates dissent and considers behaving in a way that contradicts what they have been socialised to do.

The shift into an agentic state of mind relieves moral strain as the individual displaces the responsibility of the situation onto the authority figure, thereby absolving them of the consequence of their actions. This is not to say that displacement of responsibility is the only way to relieve moral strain. In fact, dissent to authority can also produce relief once an individual has removed themselves from the situation.

WIDER ISSUES AND DEBATES

Nature–nurture

Milgram was attempting to establish that obedience was not a dispositional trait (nature) as historians suggested at the time, but a consequence of the situation in which a person finds themselves (environment). Using the writings of Arendt (1963), he describes obedience as an ingrained behaviour established through the process of socialisation. This behaviour manifests as we are exposed to authority figures under certain environmental conditions conducive to compliance, such as closeness and status of the authority figure.

Evaluation

Milgram's first obedience experiment demonstrated that 65 per cent of participants were willing to obey an authority figure and potentially seriously harm an innocent confederate of the study. This provides evidence for agency theory because the participants showed overt signs of moral strain (anxiety) when given an order. When he debriefed the participants, many reported that their behaviour was the responsibility of the experimenter, and that they had not wanted to do it. This provides evidence for the concept of displacement of responsibility.

Agency theory can also be used to explain verbal reports given after real-life events involving obedience to authority have occurred. During the Vietnam War, a small village called My Lai was approached by American soldiers who were ordered to shoot the occupants who were suspected of being Vietcong soldiers. Lieutenant Calley instructed his division to enter the village and shoot, despite no return of fire. The American soldiers massacred old men, women and children in the village that day after being ordered by Calley. In his court martial following the incident, Calley claimed to be just following orders. This justification has been cited in many real-life cases of atrocities and offers some support for agency theory involving a displacement of responsibility.

Hofling et al. (1966) staged a study in a hospital setting. A stooge doctor telephoned a nurse working on a ward late at night, asking her to administer twice the daily dose of a drug to a patient. Against hospital policy, the stooge doctor informed the nurse that she would sign the prescription later. A total of 21 out of 22 nurses followed the doctor's orders and attempted to give the medication to the patient. Several of the nurses justified their behaviour as being a result of the hierarchy of authority at the hospital. This supports agency theory because the majority of nurses displaced their personal responsibility.

A weakness of agency theory is that it does not explain individual differences – why some people obey and some do not. Disobedience/dissent can occur for many reasons (see page 31), such as personality type, gender and situation. This means that obedience is a more complex process than is being explained by agency theory.

Another weakness with agency theory is that the concepts of autonomy and, in particular, agency are very difficult to define and measure. Agency is a state of mind that, according to Milgram, is switched to when given an order by an authority figure. This concept is an internal mental process that cannot be directly measured, only inferred from the behaviour of an agent. Similarly, there is no direct evidence for the evolutionary basis of obedience. We cannot go back into our evolutionary past and study the development of obedience, nor can we dig up archaeological evidence for this type of behaviour. However, as similar hierarchical systems exist in animal groups, such as primates, with similar sanctions for disobedience, it can be inferred that it has evolved to serve some form of survival function for social groups.

Agency theory does not explain motivational issues behind obedience. French and Raven (1959) identified five bases of power, which are said to motivate and influence behaviour: legitimate power, reward power, referent power, expert power and coercive power. These factors are said to provide a better explanation of obedience, and certainly provide a better explanation for Milgram's findings from his experiments.

Exam tip

You may be asked to apply your knowledge of agency theory to a scenario described in the exam. It is important that you relate your answer directly to the scenario rather than write a generic description of the theory. Practise by relating your knowledge of agency theory to the following scenario.

The Deputy Headmaster of a school, Mr Arrand, was very strict about the wearing of correct school uniform. One of the students wore trainers into school and was sent to Mr Arrand's office. The student was given a detention for a lack of compliance to the school uniform regulations and never wore trainers to school again.

Social impact theory of obedience

Bibb Latané (1981) proposed a theory of social influence that can be used to explain why people are obedient. Latané, consistent with the main social psychological underpinning ideas, proposed that we are greatly influenced by the actions of others; we can be persuaded, inhibited, threatened and supported by other people. These effects are the result of others' actions, and effect changes to how we feel and how we act in response. This is known as social impact because of how others, real or imagined, impact on us.

More specifically, Latané referred to targets and sources of social influence. The target referred to the person being impacted on and the source being the influencer. He developed a formulation of different principles that result in more or less social influence being exerted on the target. Although these principles refer to social influence in general (conformity, bystander behaviour, etc.), they can be used to explain obedience, too.

Principles

Social forces

When a source is affecting the target, the impact of the social influence is a function of the strength, immediacy and number of sources compared to targets. The strength of the source can be determined by status, authority or age. The immediacy is determined by proximity or distance between the source and target and the presence of buffers that could be barriers to the distance. Number refers to how many sources and targets are in the social situation.

In terms of obedience, this suggests that authority figures who are perceived to be legitimate, who are immediate to the individual and who are greater in number, will be more likely to ensure obedience.

The greater the strength, immediacy and number of the source of authority, the greater the impact on the target.

Psychosocial law

It is not simply the case that as strength, immediacy and number of the source increases, so does the social impact they have on the target. The effect is more like that of a lightbulb in a dark room. One lightbulb will have a dramatic effect, a second will improve the lighting conditions, but as more lightbulbs are added, the effect becomes less pronounced.

Berkowitz, Bickman and Milgram (1969) conducted a study at the City University of New York that demonstrates this reduction in social impact. They got between one and 15 confederates to congregate on the street and crane their necks to look up at the sixth floor of the university building. Stanley Milgram was in a sixth floor window video recording the confederates below, and the passers-by who also stopped and craned their necks to look up. The videos were analysed and the number of passers-by who stopped were counted. They found that although increasing the number of confederates craning their neck did increase the number of passers-by imitating their actions, the number of passers-by grew smaller relative to the size of the confederate group. The effect levelled off.

Multiplication versus division of impact

As we have seen, strength, immediacy and number can have a multiplicative effect (up to a point) on the behaviour of a target. But there is also a divisional effect of social impact. Consider a speaker giving a speech to a large audience. The ability of the speaker to persuade the audience is divided among many members of the audience, that is, a divisional effect. Put simply, the number of targets to be influenced affects the impact of the source.

Latané and Darley (1970) demonstrated this divisional effect of social impact in a number of studies on bystander behaviour. They found that a lone person was more likely to help someone in need compared to a group of people; there was a diffusion of responsibility similar to a divisional effect. In terms of obedience, it would suggest that an authority figure would have a diminished capacity to influence someone if that someone had an ally or group of allies.

In a variation study by Milgram, where two peers rebel against the instructions of an authority figure asking them to administer harmful electric shocks to a victim, the presence of peers lowered obedience to 10 per cent. This demonstrates the divisional effect of one source on many targets.

Evaluation

Social impact theory views individuals as passive receivers of others' behaviour towards them, disregarding the active nature of social interaction, and indeed what the target themselves bring to the social situation. Everyone is different, so this theory seems to oversimplify the nature of human interaction and ignore individual differences between each of us. Some of us are more resistant to social impact and some more passive. It is also considered to be a static rather than dynamic theory because it does not take into account how the target and source interact with one another.

The model, therefore, appears to be useful as a general formulation and can predict behaviour under certain conditions. So perhaps it is more descriptive as a theory than explanatory; it does not explain why people are influenced by others, just under what conditions they are more likely to be influenced. However, the theory is quantifiable in that the principles can be observed in everyday behaviour. Research into conformity (Asch, see Taking it further activity) obedience (Milgram) and bystander behaviour (Latané) have all demonstrated the impact of strength, immediacy and number on observable human responses in social situations.

The theory is limited in the type of social situation it is able to explain. It cannot predict what might happen when two equal groups impact on one another. Consider football crowds, where both football team supporting groups are equal in number, strength and immediacy. Who would be the source and who the target? It is not certain whether the principles of the theory would apply in such cases.

Exam tip

In the exam, you may be asked to 'describe' a theory of obedience or prejudice. The term 'describe' is used when you need to give an account of something, in this case a theory. You do not need to justify or explain your response, nor do you need to evaluate the theory or make judgements.

In order to revise the descriptive elements of a theory, it can be useful to devise some prompts to help remember the key elements of a theory. For social impact theory, you might wish to use the following key word prompts:

- strength
- number
- immediacy
- multiplication
- division.

Taking it further

Conduct some independent research on Solomon Asch and his conformity studies. See if you can relate social impact theory to his variations studies.

Exam tip

It is important that you are able to compare explanations for the same behaviour. Drawing up a table of similarities and difference can aid comparison. Use terms such as 'however', 'similarly', 'in contrast to' to ensure that you are making comparisons explicit.

Complete Table 1.1 to compare agency theory and social impact theory. Remember that comparisons can be descriptive or evaluative.

Table 1.1 Agency theory and social impact theory

Agency theory	Term	Social impact theory
Agency theory emphasises the role of evolution and socialisation as a process to ensure obedience.	Whereas	Social impact theory focuses exclusively on the interaction of social forces as situational determinants of obedience.

WIDER ISSUES AND DEBATES

Psychology as a science

To be classed as scientific, a theory must have empirical evidence to support it and be falsifiable. This social impact theory is falsifiable in the sense that a prediction about human behaviour based on the principles of social impact can be observed or not observed. If a prediction based on the theory is not observed, it will falsify the theory.

There has been a large amount of social influence research that supports social impact theory and has gathered empirical evidence for it. Latané, Cappell and Joy (1970) even found evidence for psychosocial law in rats. They housed rats 1, 2, 3, 4 or 6 to a cage and tested them in an open space for social attraction. Isolated rats were more sociable when introduced to others, and the level of sociability increased with the rats housed in more crowded conditions. However, this sociability levelled off and became marginal to the proportion of crowding.

Milgram's research into obedience and three of his variation studies

Aim

Stanley Milgram wanted to investigate whether ordinary people would follow orders and give an innocent person a potentially harmful electric shock. He had criticised earlier research into conformity by Solomon Asch as being unrealistic, and because he was attempting to investigate why ordinary people would commit acts of atrocity in real life, he wanted to make his experiment as close to real 'obedience to commit harm' as possible. He also wanted to establish under what conditions people would display more obedience or dissent. He varied his original experiment to test different factors.

Method

Sample

Milgram placed an advertisement in the local newspaper asking for male participants to take part in a study of memory and learning. The advert asked for all occupations (excluding students) to apply and offered a $4 incentive for their participation. In total, 296 people responded to the advertisement, and Milgram used direct mail invitations to gather more participants and increase his sample. A range of participants with diverse occupations, educational level and ages were recruited. A total of 160 participants were selected and Milgram balanced them out across each of his four initial variation conditions.

Procedure

He contacted specific participants a few days before the experiment to arrange individual appointments. The majority of his experiments were conducted at the Interaction Laboratory at Yale University. A biology teacher was recruited to be a confederate of the study and act as the experimenter, and a middle-aged accountant was recruited to act as the victim.

Individual participants were invited to the laboratory and introduced to another person whom they believed was just another participant of the study but who was actually a confederate. The experimenter briefed both of them about how some people may learn more effectively through punishment, but that this had not been tested on humans of different ages. This brief was a pretext to justify the procedure of the experiment to come, in particular, the use of an electric shock. It also set the scene for the experiment to assign the two roles needed for the study: a teacher and a learner. The experimenter stated that the fairest way of allocating these roles was to draw lots, but unbeknown to the participant, the draw was rigged and both lots had the word teacher written on them. This ensured that the participant was the 'teacher' and the confederate was always the 'learner'.

The teacher and the learner were then taken to another room, and the learner was seated in an electric chair apparatus and his arms strapped down. It was explained to the teacher that this was necessary to avoid excessive movement during the shock procedure. An electrode to administer an electric shock from the shock generator was strapped to the learner's wrist and conductive gel used to avoid blisters from the electric current. The teacher was told at this point that the shocks would be painful but not dangerous. All of this was a ruse to convince the teacher that the learner would be receiving shocks when in fact no shocks would ever be administered.

Key term

Androcentric: focused on men.

Apparatus

The wrist electrode was attached to a shock generator in an adjacent room. The generator was a box with a panel of 30 switches positioned in a horizontal line at the front, increasing in 15-volt increments. Each switch was labelled from 15 to 450 volts and additional labelling above the switches indicated 'Slight Shock', 'Moderate Shock', 'Strong Shock', 'Very Strong Shock', 'Intense Shock', 'Extreme Intensity Shock', 'Danger' and the final two switches were labelled 'XXX'. A light appeared above the switch after it was pressed and a buzzer could be heard. There was also a blue light and a voltage meter dial, which had a hand that oscillated when a lever was pressed. To convince the teacher that the shocks were real, they were given a 45-volt sample shock.

Learning task

Participants were informed that they were to teach the learner a list of word pairs by reading them out, then they were to read out one of the first pair with four possible options. The teacher was to administer a shock from the shock generator if the incorrect pair was given as an answer by the learner. The learner was to respond to the word associate list using a set of four switches that the teacher could see on the top of the shock generator. In fact, the sequence of responses from the learner was also rigged.

Word associate task

The teacher read out a list of word pairs:

- blue box
- nice day
- wild duck
- etc.

The teacher then read out the first word pair and four possible options:

- blue: sky ink box lamp

Instructions

The participant teacher was seated in front of the shock generator and asked to administer successive shocks if the learner gave an incorrect response. Once they reached 450 volts, they were asked to repeat the same shock. The experiment used a series of verbal prods to encourage obedience.

Verbal prods

1. Please continue.
2. The experiment requires that you continue.
3. It is absolutely essential that you continue.
4. You have no other choice, you must go on.

Special prods

In response to particular responses from the teacher, such as whether the procedure was harmful or that the learner refused to go on, the experimenter replied with the special prods:

1. Although the shocks may be painful, there is no permanent tissue damage, so please go on.
2. Whether the learner likes it or not, you must go on until he has learned all word pairs correctly. So please go on.

In a pilot study, Milgram found that participants did not need much encouragement to administer the highest level of shock to the learner. He therefore decided to expose participants to a remote-feedback condition (Experiment 1) where the learner banged on the wall when 300 volts were applied and refused to answer the paired associate task after 315 volts. Of the 40 participants studied, 26 continued to the end of the shock generator.

In Experiment 2, verbal feedback from the learner was heard as the shocks increased in severity. These included verbal protests which began as a grunt at 75 volts, shouting that the shock was painful at 120 volts and painful groans at 135 volts. At 150 volts, the learner cried 'Experimenter get me out of here!', and at 270 volts, agonising screams could be heard. At 300 volts, the learner screamed and refused to continue with the memory experiment, to which the experimenter informed the teacher that a 'no response would be considered an incorrect one' so further shocks should continue. At 330 volts, the learner gave no verbal feedback and no response to the word associate task.

In Experiment 3 (proximity), the learner would be both heard and seen as they were in the same room as the teacher. In Experiment 4 (touch-proximity), the learner was required to place his own hand on a shock plate to receive the shock. At 150 volts the learner refused and the teacher was ordered by the experimenter to force the learners hand onto the plate.

Debrief

Following the end of the experiment, each participant was reconciled with the learner in a friendly manner and informed that the shocks were not real. Both obedient and dissenting participants were reassured that their behaviour was normal and justifiable. Some participants were interviewed at length and all participants were told that they would be sent a report about the investigation and a follow-up questionnaire that would allow participants to express their feelings about the study after greater thought.

Results

Questionnaire

Milgram was interested to see whether people's expectations matched the actual recordings found in his experiment. He invited 39 psychiatrists, 31 college students and 40 middle-class adults to a lecture on obedience and the nature of the experiment and then presented them with a diagram of the shock generator panel. All were asked to predict how far up the shock generator they thought they would go before dissenting. Five of these participants claimed that they would refuse to administer any shocks and most claimed they would break off earlier on in the experiment; none would pass the 300-volt level.

Milgram speculated that perhaps participants responded in a socially desirable way, so then he asked a sample of psychiatrists, students and middle-class adults to plot their predictions for 100 average Americans. The psychiatrists predicted that most of the 100 Americans would not persist beyond the 150-volt shock level, and only 4 per cent would continue to the end.

Experiments 1, 2, 3 and 4

In the remote-feedback condition, all participants gave 300-volt shocks and 26 out of 40 participants (65 per cent) went to the end of the shock generator and continued administering 450 volts for three trials before the experiment was ended. In Experiment 2, the verbal-feedback condition, 25 out of 40 participants (62.5 per cent) went to the 450-volt level. This fell to 40 per cent in the proximity condition (Experiment 3) and 30 per cent on the touch-proximity condition (Experiment 4). During these experiments, participants were observed to protest, twitch nervously and show signs of anxiety.

Conclusion

Milgram concluded that when the learner could not be heard or seen, the participants were more likely to follow orders to cause them harm. When the learner could be seen, the participants empathised more with the learner, which resulted in less obedience.

Variation studies

Milgram repeated his experiment to investigate under what conditions greater or lesser obedience would be found in order to explain why he found such a high level of obedience to authority. The location of his further experiments varied from the original, most being conducted in the basement of Yale University. He also changed the learner voice-feedback to include more verbal protests ('Let me out of here') and the inclusion of comments concerning the learner's heart condition ('My heart is bothering me now').

Telephonic instructions (Experiment 7)

In order to establish whether the proximity of the experimenter had an influence on the level of obedience displayed, Milgram devised a series of three experiments altering the relationship between the teacher and the experimenter. In Experiment 5, the experimenter sat a few feet away from the teacher; in Experiment 6, the nature of the experimenter was altered from hard and technical-looking to soft and unaggressive. In Experiment 7, Milgram wanted to test the effect of physical distance between the experimenter and the teacher. After giving initial instructions to the teacher face to face, the experimenter left the room and continued to give instructions over the telephone.

Milgram found that the number of participants willing to give the maximum 450-volt shock fell from 65 per cent to 22.5 per cent in Experiment 7. He also observed that participants continued to administer lower shocks rather than increase the voltage, and even lied to the experimenter about it, with many assuring that they were increasing the shock level. In a slight modification of this experiment, the experimenter initially gave telephonic instructions until he exhausted his authority, at which point he returned to the laboratory. The participants' initial disobedience soon changed to obedience on his return to the laboratory.

Rundown office block (Experiment 10)

Milgram was aware that the institutional context of Yale University could be encouraging participants to show a higher level of obedience than in less prestigious settings. When follow-up interviews were conducted after the original series of experiments, many participants referred to the integrity of Yale institution having given them the confidence to take part in the study, which they would not have done if the experiments had been done somewhere with less respect.

He relocated his experiment to a rundown commercial office building in a town called Bridgeport, Connecticut. Participants were recruited through mailshot recruitment and paid for their time. Dissociated from Yale University, participants were told that the study was being conducted by Research Associates of Bridgeport, a private company conducting research for commercial industry. The same laboratory procedures were followed as in the basement of Yale University, however, the building was rather sparsely furnished.

Milgram found a slight reduction in obedience of 48 per cent, concluding that the less reputable context reduced the legitimacy of the study. He also reported that participants questioned the credentials of the company on arrival (although these claims were made during debrief).

Ordinary man gives orders (Experiment 13)

In a series of experiments varying the role of the learner and experimenter within the study, Milgram studied the impact of power relations on obedience. Experiments 12–15 altered the power, position and action of the actors during the experiment. In Experiment 13, the role of the experimenter was played by an ordinary man, rather than an experimenter wearing a grey lab coat as portrayed in previous variations. This variation was designed to test the role of authority and status on obedience.

Three people arrived at the laboratory; two of them confederates of the study. A rigged draw was run to determine who would be the teacher, learner and experimenter. The first confederate was given the role of learner, the second confederate was assigned the role of experimenter and given the task of noting times from a clock and was seated at a desk, and the naive participant the role of the teacher. The experimenter followed instructions to strap the learner into the electric shock chair, but did not tell the teacher what levels of shock to give during the study. The experimenter received a phone call to leave the room and departed with a comment to the teacher to continue getting the learner to persist with the word pairs until he had learned them perfectly.

To ensure that some instruction to increase the shock levels was given, the learner said that a good way to conduct the study would be to increase the shock level each time he made a mistake in learning the words. Throughout the experiment, the learner restated this instruction. In this variation, all instructions were given by an ordinary man.

Milgram found that 80 per cent (16 out of 20 participants) broke off before the maximum level of shock, resulting in a 20 per cent obedience level. However, Milgram described this experiment as being strained and the learner had to go to considerable lengths to persuade the teacher to continue administering the shocks in the absence of the experimenter. A further experiment (Experiment 13a, subject as a bystander) was staged to resolve some of this issue. In this adaptation, when the teacher refused to administer shocks at the insistence of the learner, the learner stated that he himself would administer the shocks if the teacher was unwilling to do so. The learner moved in front of the shock generator and instructed the teacher to record the length of shocks administered. In this adaptation, the teacher was to witness self-administration of shocks by a determined learner.

All 16 participants protested to this situation and five physically restrained the learner or tampered with the shock generator to end the experiment. The remaining 11, despite their protests, allowed the learner to self-administer a 450-volt level of shock, resulting in a 68.75 per cent obedience level (or in this case, passivity with some protest).

Evaluation

Milgram's experiments have been discussed on both methodological and ethical grounds. It may be useful to read Topic 2: *Cognitive psychology*, Section 2.2 Methods, and the ethical issues discussed in this section (see page 109) to familiarise yourself with key terms and concepts that will be referred to in this evaluation.

Methodological issues

A strength of Milgram's experiments was that they were highly standardised and controlled. Each participant was briefed in the same way and experienced the same verbal prods, feedback and apparatus in the same way. Behavioural data was gathered about how long participants took to press each switch and for how long the switch was depressed. Both objective qualitative data and qualitative observations were made, making this research highly credible in terms of being scientific.

One criticism levelled at the series of experiments was that the sample of New Haven men and small sample of women are not representative of the general population. One issue is that the participants were recruited by an advertisement and mailshot, resulting in a volunteer (self-selecting sample). This could suggest that the participants were more compliant or more authoritarian in character. When debriefed, Milgram noted that participants took part for a range of reasons, not one single overriding factor that could account for high levels of obedience. Milgram also noted that the participants who gave the greatest level of shock tended to blame the learner for their pain rather than themselves

Taking it further

Milgram's classic series of experiments are widely available on the Internet to watch or listen to audio recordings. Conduct your own search to find original footage.

Derren Brown partially replicated Milgram's experiment more recently in a 2006 program called 'The Heist'. This is also available on the Internet to view.

or the experimenter; a typical trait of an authoritarian character. However, other research into volunteering characters has tended to find them less not more authoritarian.

Another criticism made of Milgram's experiments was that the participants did not really believe that they were administering harmful or serious electric shocks at all, and were just playing along with the game. Milgram dismissed this claim and made two arguments against it. Firstly that the observed anxiety of the teachers throughout the duration of administering shocks was evidence itself that they believed that the shocks were real, and secondly that only two of the 40 participants in Experiment 2 thought that the study was a hoax. Milgram believed that these participants were probably defending their own behaviour so that they were not seen as cruel.

Laboratory research, such as this, is often criticised for being unrealistic and not representative of real behaviour. We can certainly argue that the task lacked mundane realism as it was a unique situation that one would not ordinarily encounter. Milgram maintained that the process of obedience was the same regardless of location or task. Interestingly, the Hofling et al. (1966) field study of the doctor–nurse relationship found far more nurses that were willing to obey the instructions of a doctor than Milgram found in his experiment. Perhaps in real life obedience is greater than Milgram's experiments would predict. Or perhaps the Hofling et al. findings could be explained by the strict hospital hierarchy and the legitimate status of doctors at the time (compared to the grey lab-coat wearing experimenter used by Milgram).

More recently, a virtual reality experiment has been developed by several researchers to test obedience in computer simulation conditions. Slater et al. (2006) used virtual characters as victims and participants were aware, therefore, that the shocks being administered were not real. Consistent with Milgram's experiment, they found that participants who could see the animated victim were less obedient than those who only communicated with the victim via text. This raises the question of whether obedience can be studied under laboratory conditions to good effect and without the ethical implications associated with using live confederates.

Taking it further

Gina Perry conducted an archival analysis of Milgram's reports, video and audio tapes revealing some major issues with Milgram's findings and conclusions.

- She found that Milgram overstated the obedience rate of his research, equating to 65 per cent, which did not represent the high levels of people who dissented throughout his variation studies.
- She claims that many more participants revealed that they knew the study was a hoax and that no real shocks were being administered.
- She claimed that Milgram's procedures were not as standardised as he claimed. Analysis of video and audio recording showed that there was a great deal of improvisation through the experiments by the experimenter, resulting in what she believed to be direct coercion to make the teacher continue with the shocks.

Gina Perry published a book on her findings, *Behind the Shock Machine: The Untold Story of the Notorious Milgram Psychology Experiments* (2012). You can find extracts of her book on the Internet. Use these to find out more about her critique of Milgram's research.

Ethical issues

Diana Baumrind (1964) heavily criticised Milgram's experiments on ethical grounds. She expressed considerable concern for the welfare of the participants and argued that the stress caused was deliberate. Milgram responded by stating that the anxiety induced by the experimental conditions was not deliberate or anticipated. He had discussed the experimental procedures at length with colleagues and none had anticipated the participants' responses. Although it is true that the outcomes of research cannot ever be predicted with reliability, it does not explain the fact that Milgram conducted 18 variations to his study, which involved 636 participants. Although the participants' reactions could not have been foreseen at the beginning, they certainly could have been predicted once the experiments were underway. Milgram justified the anxiety he caused to participants by describing it as 'momentary excitement', which in his view was not the same as harm.

Every experiment that Milgram conducted could also be criticised for involving a considerable amount of deception: participants thought it was a study of memory and learning, not obedience; they were hoaxed into believing the drawing of lots was real when in fact it was rigged; they believed that the confederate learner was a genuine participant; and they thought the shocks administered were real. This deception was a necessary evil for the procedure of the study, but would be ethically problematic by today's ethical standards. Moreover, it could have caused additional stress and embarrassment for the participants when they were debriefed. Milgram, however, went to considerable lengths to ensure that participants did not feel embarrassment. He fully debriefed the obedient participants by explaining that their actions were normal, and the dissenting participants were assured that their decision making was justified. He also ensured a friendly reconciliation between the participant and the learner and followed up with a full written report for all participants and a follow-up questionnaire for them to express their feelings about the experiment after some time. Milgram's post-experimental questionnaire seemed to confirm that participants did not have any negative feeling about their participation, 84 per cent having said that they were glad to have taken part.

Although Milgram clearly offered participants the right to withdraw from the experiment, some argue that their right to leave was violated by the verbal prods used by the experimenter. Milgram briefed participants advising them that they could leave at any time without adverse consequence, and they could even take the money incentive. It is true that Milgram did not tie his participants to their chair. He did, however, enter them into a contract of trust and incentivised their participation with money, and the verbal prods used directly challenged any participant's attempt to leave the situation. In defence of Milgram, the verbal prods were an essential requirement to ensure orders were given that demonstrate obedience, and as 35 per cent (or more) of his participants did end the experiment, it could be argued that the prods merely dissuaded withdrawal.

Milgram vehemently defended his series of experiments, arguing that no one would have been so concerned with the ethical issues associated with the research if they had not found such high levels of obedience from the ordinary man.

Exam tip

If you are asked to 'evaluate' a theory, research study or concept in psychology, you will need to review the strengths and weaknesses of the information, make judgements and form an overall conclusion. For example, if you are asked to evaluate the ethical issues associated with Milgram's research, you will need to consider the weaknesses and strengths of the study in terms of ethics, and consider how the ethical issues could have been justified by the methodology or aims of the study. You will also need to come to a balanced and considered conclusion. It is useful to 'flag up' this conclusion at the end of your answer by stating 'In conclusion,...' This makes it clear to an examiner that you are fulfilling the requirements of the question. You will need to review the main points made in your answer and come to a conclusion based on the material you have presented.

Factors affecting obedience and dissent/resistance to obedience

Situational factors

The series of Milgram's experiments demonstrated that an ordinary person could be capable of harm at the instructions of an authority figure, which dispelled the myth that German soldiers were lacking in a character trait, making them more compliant and obedient. The baseline obedience level of 65 per cent was found (Experiment 1 and 5). The series of experiments also demonstrated that various situational factors increased or decreased levels of obedience and dissent.

- Momentum of compliance: starting with small and trivial requests, the teacher has committed themselves to the experiment. As the request increased, the participants felt duty bound to continue. This is also true of the shock generator as the initial shocks were small but increased slowly in 15-volt increments. The situation created a binding relationship that escalated steadily.

- Proximity: the closer the authority figure, the higher the level of obedience. Distance seemed to act as a buffer to obedience, as found in the telephonic instruction condition. Proximity of the victim also acted as a buffer to obedience. When the learner was in the same room or the teacher had to physically place the hand of the learner onto a shock plate, obedience dropped. This is in contrast to the pilot study where the learner was in a different room and could not be seen or heard throughout, resulting in 100 per cent obedience. Milgram also referred to the shock generator as a physical buffer between the participant and the victim – in the same way that a soldier would be more inclined to drop a bomb than stab an enemy, the generator buffered the distance between them.

- Status of the authority: Milgram stated that obedience could only be established when the authority figure was perceived to be legitimate. This was found to be the case when the experiments were conducted at Yale University, and obedience fell when the experiment was moved to Bridgeport or conducted by an ordinary man.

People are less likely to be obedient when they do not believe the person legitimately has authority over them.

- Personal responsibility: Milgram believed that participants would be more obedient in a situation where personal responsibility is removed and placed onto the shoulders of an authority figure. In a variation study where participants had to sign a contract that stated they were taking part of their own free will and relinquishing any legal responsibility from Yale University, obedience fell to 40 per cent.

Individual differences in obedience and dissent/resistance to obedience

Personality

Milgram conducted a series of follow-up investigations on participants who were involved in the experiments to uncover whether certain individuals would be more likely to obey or dissent. In one study, 118 participants from Experiments 1–4 who were both obedient and disobedient were asked to judge the relative responsibility for giving the shocks out of the experimenter, the teacher and the learner. They indicated who was responsible for the person being given the shocks by moving three hands on a round disc to show proportionate responsibility. He found that dissenting participants gave proportionately more blame to themselves (48 per cent) and then the experimenter (39 per cent), whereas obedient participants were more likely to blame the learner (25 per cent), more so than the dissenters (12 per cent blamed the learner).

Locus of control

It seems that dissenting individuals take more of the blame, whereas obedient people are more likely to displace blame. This can be explained by Rotter's (1966) locus of control personality theory. This theory outlines two different personality types: those with an internal and those with an external locus of control. People with an internal locus of control tend to believe that they are responsible for their own actions and are less influenced by others. People with an external locus of control believe that their behaviour is largely beyond their control but due to external factors such as fate. These people are more influenced by others around them. This seems consistent with Milgram's findings that obedient people have an external locus of control; not only are they more likely to be influenced by an authority figure, but they also believe that they are not responsible for their actions. Dissenters, on the other hand, are more resistant to authority and more likely to take personal responsibility for their actions.

The link between personality and obedience seems a plausible one that can account for individual differences in obedience. However, research in this area is mixed, providing only tentative evidence that individuals with an internal locus of control resist and those with an external locus of control are obedient.

Authoritarian personality

The authoritarian personality will be discussed in more detail when we learn about prejudice (see page 33), but it can also be used here to explain why some individuals are more obedient than others. An authoritarian personality is typically submissive to authority but harsh to those seen as subordinate to themselves. Theodor Adorno et al. (1950) devised the F-Scale (**Fascism** Scale), a questionnaire used to detect the authoritarian personality. Stanley Milgram and Alan Elms (1966) compared the F-Scale scores for 20 obedient and 20 defiant participants involved in his experiments. They found that the obedient participant had a higher F-Scale score, indicating an authoritarian personality type, compared to the dissenters.

Michaël Dambrun and Elise Vatiné (2010) conducted a simulation of Milgram's experiment using a virtual environment/computer simulation and found that authoritarianism was linked to obedience. Those with high authoritarian scores were less likely to withdraw from the study, perhaps because they were submissive to the authority of the experimenter, or showed an inclination to punish the failing learner.

Key term

Fascism: extreme intolerant views based on a right-wing political perspective.

Empathy

It is believed that people who have high levels of empathy would be less likely to harm another person at the instructions of an authority figure. In a recent replication of Milgram's experiment, Jerry Burger (2009) found that although people who score high on empathy were more likely to protest against giving electric shocks, this did not translate into lower levels of obedience. You can read more about this study later in this section.

Gender

Milgram used predominantly male participants in his experiments, although he did conduct one experiment (Experiment 8) that involved 40 female teachers. Previous research had indicated that females were more compliant than males, yet traditionally we think of women as less aggressive. This contradiction would be played out in an experiment that commanded both compliance and aggression. Milgram found that females were virtually identical to males in their level of obedience (65 per cent), 27.5 per cent breaking off at the 300-volt level. Yet their rated level of anxiety was much higher than males for those who were obedient. This was also found in Burger's (2009) replication of the experiment.

Sheridan and King (1972) adapted Milgram's experiment to involve a live puppy as a victim that received genuine shocks from college student participants. They found that all 13 female participants were much more compliant and delivered the maximum levels of shock to the puppy compared to men. However, in a review of 10 obedience experiments, Blass (1999) found that obedience between males and females were consistent across nine of the studies. The study that did not show a similar male/female obedience level was conducted by Kilham and Mann (1974) in a direct replication of Milgram's experiment in Australia. They found females to be far less obedient (16 per cent) than male participants (40 per cent). Although this could have been a result of male teachers being paired with male learners and female teachers with female learners. Perhaps the females joined together against the situation in an alliance to react against the demands of the aggressive male experimenter.

It seems that there is very little, if any, gender differences in obedience, despite traditional beliefs that females would be more compliant to authority.

DEVELOPMENTAL PSYCHOLOGY

According to gender role schema theory (Bem, 1981), individuals develop a sense of masculinity and femininity as they are brought up and socialised. These gender role schema or stereotypes affect how we perceive ourselves and others. They often depict men as strong and aggressive, and females as quiet and compliant. This would predict that females are more obedient, but as we have seen, this may not be an accurate prediction based on experimental evidence.

Table 1.2 Obedience research

Researcher	Country	Percentage of full obedience
Milgram (1962)	US	65%
Edwards et al. (1969)	South Africa	87.5%
Bock (1972)	US	40%
Kilham and Mann (1974)	Australia	28%
Shanab and Yahya (1977)	Jordan	73%
Miranda et al. (1981)	Spain	50%
Schurz (1985)	Austria	80%
Ancona and Pareyson (1968)	Italy	85%
Burley and McGuiness (1977)	UK	50%

Culture

Many behaviours vary across cultures. Culture can be divided broadly into two types: individualistic and collectivistic cultures. Individualistic cultures, such as America and Britain, tend to behave more independently and resist conformity or compliance. Collectivistic cultures, such as China or Israel, tend to behave as a collective group based on interdependence, meaning that cooperation and compliance is important for the stability of the group (Smith and Bond, 1998). We could assume from this that collectivistic cultures are more likely to be obedient.

Thomas Blass (1999) conducted a full review of obedience research (see Table 1.2), analysing research 35 years after Milgram's first series of experiments. His data can be analysed in terms of cultural differences using research employing similar methodology to Milgram.

Although some might argue that obedience levels are not universal, on closer inspection of the methodologies of the research studies, it seems that the variation in percentage of participants who gave the full shock is more a product of the procedure employed than cultural variation.

For example, Ancona and Pareyson's (1968) maximum shock level was 330 volts, compared to Milgram's 450 volts. Milgram found 73 per cent obedience in his proximity studies which is more comparable to the 85 per cent found in Italy, suggesting that 330 volts was perceived to be as less dangerous. In Italy, only student participants were used, which Milgram actively avoided because of their compliant and competitive nature. A similar comparison can be made of Burley and McGuiness (1977), who used only 20 students and a maximum voltage of 225.

Prejudice

Prejudice is one of the greatest problems of humanity, leading to dehumanisation and violence across the world, without cultural or historical boundary. Finding the cause of prejudice is fundamental to understanding how we can prevent it. Prejudice is an attitude and how attitudes are formed, maintained and changed is a key aspect of social psychological research.

Prejudice is an extreme, unfavourable attitude associated with three negative components:

- cognitive: the **stereotypes** we hold.

- affective: feelings of hostility and hatred.

- behavioural: in terms of negative prejudice, this can be displayed as avoidance, assault, joke-making or **discrimination**.

Not all of these components manifest at one time. It can be possible that someone who is prejudiced towards a certain group may have the cognitive and affective component, but would not actively discriminate against them because of prevailing social norms or laws or vice versa.

Causes of prejudice

The Holocaust inspired much of the theoretical work into the roots of prejudice, as much as it spurred on research into obedience. Could the atrocities committed against Jews during the Second World War be explained by group membership? For a long time, social psychology explained atrocities committed during the war as a consequence of dispositional features of the perpetrators. But research into group dynamics was suggesting an alternative explanation. Muzafer Sherif conducted a series of studies at boys' summer camps during the late 1940s and mid-1950s, and using competitions between groups of boys, he observed how competition can cause prejudice.

INDIVIDUAL DIFFERENCES

Following the Second World War, social psychological theories tended to explain prejudice in terms of dispositional factors, such as personality types of individuals, similar to their view about obedience. If prejudice could be explained by individual factors, how can it explain whole cultures and societies being prejudiced? During the War, the majority of the German population was prejudiced against Jews, so surely individual differences cannot account for the attitude of hundreds of thousands of people? Nor can dispositional factors account for the rise and fall of prejudice. For example, in Rwanda the Hutu and Tutsi tribes lived peacefully alongside each other for many years before the conflict led to mass genocide; **anti-Semitism** in Germany grew over a matter of 10 or so years. As a result, we must turn our attention to social factors that can explain how entire populations of people develop prejudiced attitudes towards others over a relatively short period of time. Social identity theory and realistic conflict theory offered an alternative to these dispositional explanations by moving away from individual differences as an explanation and instead focusing on intergroup conflict as a result of social processes.

Exam tip

In the exam, you may be asked 'To what extent...' type questions. For example: To what extent can individual differences explain variation in levels of obedience?

This style of question requires you to review all of the available information and knowledge that you have concerning individual differences in obedience research and theory, and come to a reasoned conclusion that directly answers the question. Similar to an 'evaluate' style of question, it is useful to flag up when you are concluding your review by stating 'In conclusion,...' at the end of your answer.

Key terms

Stereotype: an overgeneralised belief about someone or something typically based on limited information.

Discrimination: the practice of treating one person or group differently from another in an unfair way.

Anti-Semitism: hostility against Jews.

Realistic conflict theory (Sherif, 1966)

Muzafer Sherif (1966) explains prejudice as arising from conflict between groups. This may be caused by a conflict of interest or competition for resources, dominance or land. For example, the Tutsi tribe settled peacefully and intermarried with the Hutu tribe of Rwanda, in Africa, until political rivalry between the groups caused the mass genocide of almost one million Tutsis.

Sherif conducted a series of boys' summer camp experiments, one of which, known as the Robber's Cave Experiment, formed the basis of his realistic conflict theory. He found that if he introduced competition between boys at summer camp, **intergroup conflict** was created. Realistic group conflict is evident in society today. For example, when a new group of immigrants arrive in a country, they can often be met with profound prejudice on the part of the indigenous population because they are viewed as competitors for resources such as jobs, housing and schooling. It results in extreme in-group favouritism and solidarity and a marked hostility towards members of the out-group. However, when groups need to work together for a common aim, there is a reduction in hostility and greater harmony between groups. Sherif believed that intergroup hostility could only be reduced by **superordinate goals,** where all members of each group need to cooperate in order to achieve the intended outcome.

Earlier summer camp experiments involved similar aims to the Robber's Cave, to investigate the development of intergroup hostility in children. The Robber's Cave went on to investigate the reduction of prejudice. All three of these studies show how competition can give rise to intergroup conflict.

Carol and Melvin Ember (1992), social anthropologists, observed that in tribal societies intergroup hostility increases when social or natural conditions mean that competition for these resources are necessary. During periods of famine or natural disasters, warfare was more likely to ensure access to available scarce resources. Similar anthropological studies have suggested that when population is low and land abundant, hostilities between small societies are less likely. However, when populations expand and land becomes in short supply, conflict and violence increase. However, this correlative evidence does not mean that we can confidently establish that competition is responsible for prejudice; there may be other factors involved.

Evaluation

The greatest amount of evidence for realistic conflict theory comes from Sherif's own field studies on intergroup conflict, including the Robber's Cave Experiment which found that competition increased hostility between the groups. These studies, and anthropological studies, are important 'real-life' evidence for prejudice, giving the theory important ecologically valid support.

However, evidence from Sherif's own writings about the experiments indicate that the groups of boys were becoming hostile towards each other even before the introduction of organised competitive events. So, perhaps the mere presence of another group was sufficient to bring about prejudice, as social identity theory suggests.

Aronson et al. (1978) tested realistic conflict theory by introducing cooperation in classrooms where competition was rife. Using the jigsaw technique, where students were divided into small groups that had to succeed in one group task to ensure the success of the overall class project, they found that levels of competition decreased. This demonstrates that the removal of competition decreases prejudice and increases liking between class members. This was similar to the final stage of Sherif's Robber's Cave study, where the boys had to cooperate to fix a water supply or pull the camp bus together. Sherif also found a reduction in intergroup conflict as a result of the removal of competition.

> ### Key terms
>
> **Intergroup conflict:** real conflict experienced between different groups.
>
> **Superordinate goals:** goals that can only be achieved by cooperation of all group members together.

Social identity theory (Tajfel and Turner, 1979)

Henri Tajfel used Sherif's idea of intergroup conflict to investigate prejudice and eventually formulate his social identity theory. Tajfel and John Turner developed a theory of prejudice that proposed the mere presence or perception of the presence of another group can lead to prejudice; that is, this group's formation can lead to prejudice and discrimination. Tajfel and Turner classified groups as either an in-group, to which we have membership, or an out-group, which is another rival group or group to which we do not have membership. They believed that group membership alone, even in the absence of competition, can cause prejudice.

Personal and social identities

Humans continually strive to achieve a positive self-image, so that they look good in the eyes of others and achieve high personal self-esteem. This self-image forms an individual's **personal identity**. Humans also inevitably distinguish themselves by membership to certain social groups; this is known as **social identity**. Because an individual identifies themselves by their membership (social identification), their personal identity is bound up with their social identity. This means that when the social identity is favourable, the personal identity of group members are positive. However, if social identity is not favourable, personal identity will be negative and this lowers the self-esteem of individuals within the group.

Within a group, each individual has a social identity. Unlike personal identity, which is based on personal characteristics unique to the individual, social identity is an image based on the attributes of the group or groups to which we belong. The social identity we have will impact on our personal identity because group memberships are often a source of our self-esteem.

Consider a football team supporter. If their team loses several matches, the lowered social identity of the group will have a negative impact on the individual group member's personal identities.

> ### Key terms
>
> **Personal identity:** our own unique qualities, personality and self-esteem.
>
> **Social identity:** the attributes of the group to which we belong.

The personal identity of a football supporter will be influenced by their social identity as a supporter of their team.

WIDER ISSUES AND DEBATES

Reductionism

Muzafer Sherif was both a professor of psychology and professor of sociology – a sister subject of social psychology more concerned with understanding how society is organised and develops, and how individuals interact with each other and institutions within their social groups and cultures. It is unsurprising, therefore, that Sherif resisted attempts to explain prejudice at a dispositional level, such as the personality theories present at the time of his writing, because he considered them to be too reductionist. Sherif believed that prejudice could not be explained by one strand of thought, but by a range of interconnecting social processes. Drawing on his background in both psychology and sociology, he continually argued for a multidisciplinary approach and believed that psychologists should strive for both laboratory and field research because social problems, such as prejudice, do not occur just in the lab, but in everyday life too.

Taking it further

Social identities and membership are formed through collective activities, emotions and protocols shared by each member of the group. Consider the following groups:

- members of a political party
- a group of teenage girls
- Scouts
- a rugby team
- a group of protesters.

What activities, actions, behaviours do they display that demonstrate social identification between group members?

Key terms

In-group favouritism: seeing our own group and members in a positive light and as unique.

Negative out-group bias: seeing members of a different group as all the same and in a negative light.

Heterogeneous: all different – in-group heterogeneity is the term given to this bias according to social identity theory.

Homogenous: equal or similar – out-group homogeneity is the term given to this bias according to social identity theory.

Social comparison

In order to reconcile a negative social identity, and therefore elevate personal identity, the positive attributes of the in-group need to be raised. This is done by defining the unique characteristics of the in-group and emphasising them, while at the same time comparing and derogating the qualities of the out-group. This is achieved by two processes: **in-group favouritism** and **negative out-group bias**. In-group favouritism is the tendency of group members to see the individuals within their group as unique (**heterogeneous**) and favourable. Negative out-group bias is the tendency to view members of the out-group as 'all the same' (**homogenous**) and in an unfavourable light. This social comparison ensures that the social identity of the group is elevated.

Football supporters are likely to compare their team to another, perhaps make negative comments about the team and supporters, but see their own football team in a favourable light. This ensures that their football team and membership to their group comes out on top.

Research into social identity theory

Tajfel conducted a series of studies called 'Minimal group paradigm experiments' to demonstrate the human tendency for groups to form social identities and produce prejudice.

WIDER ISSUES AND DEBATES

Comparisons between ways of explaining behaviour using different themes
You will have read earlier that Sherif believed that intergroup conflict, and resulting prejudice and discrimination, could be explained by competition between groups. Social identity theory argues that competition is not a necessary condition for conflict, the mere presence of another group is enough to elicit conflict between groups.

This fundamental difference distinguished these theories historically, and accounts for the elaborate 'minimal group paradigm' experiments devised by Tajfel, designed to prevent competition from taking place. The minimal group experiments are designed to ensure that group members are randomly and arbitrarily created, there is no contact between group members, membership is anonymised, and the tokens used as a form of currency to allocate rewards and punishments are of no intrinsic value. These conditions ensured that competition was not driving the behaviour of group members, just the mere presence of another group.

Experiment 1 'accurate or inaccurate estimations'

In the first series of experiments, Tajfel et al. (1971) placed 64 adolescent boys from a comprehensive school in Bristol into a group and tested their discrimination towards another group. The boys were initially asked to estimate how many dots were being flashed up on a screen. In one condition (neutral condition), four groups of eight boys were told that in these types of tasks, some people overestimate how many dots there are and some people underestimate, but that under and over-estimates did not reflect accuracy. In another condition (value condition), a further four groups of eight boys were told that in these types of tasks, some people are more accurate than others. The boys were all then told that the experimenter was interested in different sorts of judgements and that the boys would be studied while they were there.

Following this, the experimenters randomly assigned two of the neutral and value groups to a further procedure. The boys were then told that one group would consist of boys whose estimation of the amount of dots was four, or the highest guesses, and the other group had four of the lowest guesses. The other two neutral and value groups were told that one group would consist of accurate guesses and the other group less accurate guesses.

The boys then had to complete a task where they were required to give monetary rewards or penalties to their own or another group of boys but were not told the identities of the boys in the other group. One by one, each boy was given information about the group that they belonged to and sent off to complete a booklet. Each page of the booklet contained a matrix that had 14 boxes containing sets of two numbers: a top number and a bottom number (see Figure 1.1). For each matrix, the boy was assigning money or penalties to another boy. The top numbers related to rewards and penalties given to their own group member, and the bottom numbers to another group member. The boys had to choose one number set from each of the six matrices shown that would represent the reward given to a member of their own group and a member of another group.

19	18	17	16	15	14	13	12	11	10	9	8	7
5	7	9	11	13	15	17	19	21	23	25	27	29

Figure 1.1 Example of a number box in a matrix

Although the researchers found no difference between the value and neutral condition, they did find a significant amount of in-group favouritism and negative out-group bias by calculating the monetary rewards and penalties given to their own and another group.

Experiment 2 'Klee and Kandinsky'

Tajfel et al. (1971) realised that the social categorisation (neutral and value conditions) were not adequate in the first experiment, so set up a modified Experiment 2. Using 48 boys from the same Bristol comprehensive school, they were arranged into three groups of 16. This time, the boys were categorised into groups according to what they thought was their preference for paintings. The boys were shown various paintings and informed that some of them were from the artist Klee and some from the artist Kandinsky, but they were not told which painting belonged to which artist. They boys were then asked to indicate their preference for each painting.

The boys were randomly assigned to the Klee or Kandinsky condition, regardless of their actual preference, and a similar procedure to Experiment 1 was followed. This time the sets of numbers in each matrix were labelled as rewards for the Klee group (top number in set) or Kandinsky group (bottom number in set). The choice of number set in each matrix would demonstrate whether the boy, in relative terms, rewarded their own or the other group, penalise their own or the other group, or show fairness to both groups.

Tajfel et al. found that the boys consistently rewarded their own group, ignoring the fair alternative, therefore demonstrating in-group favouritism, regardless of the fact that the boys had no idea who was in their own group or indeed in the other group. In fact, the boys failed to maximise their own profit in order to ensure that the other group was sufficiently penalised.

Key term

Demand characteristics: participants behaving in a way they think they should to fit what they perceive to be the aim of the experiment.

Exam tip

Consider the following exam-style question.

To what extent does research into prejudice support social identity theory?

To answer this question, you will need to review the research into social identity theory, evaluate this research in terms of validity, generalisability, credibility, etc., and then come to a conclusion based on the issues that you have discussed.

INDIVIDUAL DIFFERENCES

Social identity theory tends to ignore individual differences between in-group members, in particular that some members may actively choose to discriminate or not based on their personality type. Postmes et al. (2005) argue that it is the individual characteristics that create a social identity, not a social identity that determines individual characteristics.

Evaluation

Tajfel's minimal group paradigm experiments do offer convincing evidence that we have a natural tendency to favour the in-group and discriminate against the out-group, even in the absence of normal intergroup social situations. However, it could be argued that the boys' tendency to ensure rewards for their group could be better explained by competition rather than favouritism. This element of competition giving rise to conflict can be better explained by realistic conflict theory (see page 34). It might also be the case that these laboratory-based experiments encouraged a degree of **demand characteristics**; the boys responded in a way that they believed was expected of them.

There have been many replications of minimal group paradigm experiments, all concluding that the social categorisation of groups inevitably leads to out-group discrimination. Weatherell (1982) suggests that we should not conclude that intergroup conflict is in fact inevitable. In her observations of New Zealand Polynesians, she found them much more likely to favour the out-group than show bias towards their own in-group. Cultures that emphasise collectivism and cooperation are less likely to demonstrate such group prejudice.

Later research by Louise Lemyre and Philip Smith (1985), following the minimal group paradigm procedure, not only replicated the findings of Tajfel, but also indicated that discriminating participants had improved self-esteem following the experiment. This supports the notion that personal identity is bound up in social identity, and that discrimination enhances both aspects.

These early research studies by Tajfel et al. and Lemyre and Smith support social identity theory as an explanation of prejudice, but tend to be restricted to the use of minimal group paradigm experiments, which have their own limitations. More recent research has been applied to understand how mediating social factors influence groups which can explain bullying (Jones et al., 2012) and identification within certain groups, such as heavy drinkers (Livingstone et al., 2011).

In a non-minimal group paradigm study, Cialdini et al. (1976) analysed the results of US university football scores and observed the attending students' clothing after a big football game. They observed that the university students were more likely to wear the football team sweatshirt after a game had been won than lost. They followed this up with a series of interviews on how well they thought their teams had performed during each game. Interestingly, the students referred to the team as 'us' when the team had won the game and 'they' when they had lost. This study demonstrates that an individual's personal identity is affected by their association with a football team (social identity), supporting the social identity theory.

Jane Elliott, a lower school teacher, used a school lesson to teach each class of her third grade pupils about discrimination. This lesson was reported by Aronson and Osherow (1980) and called the 'blue eyes/brown eyes' study. Through the course of a week, Jane Elliott divided her students according to their eye colour. During the first part of the week, the blue eyes were told that they were better, faster and had more desirable traits that the pupils with brown eyes, who were lazy and dishonest. She continued the ruse throughout her lessons, often reinforcing these attributes. Later in the week, she switched their roles. On several measures of performance, the dominant group performed better academically, were more attentive and, importantly, demonstrated discrimination towards the inferior group. This supports social identity theory because it shows how social categorisation, even splitting established friendships, could lead to active prejudice and discrimination.

Taking it further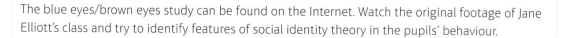

The blue eyes/brown eyes study can be found on the Internet. Watch the original footage of Jane Elliott's class and try to identify features of social identity theory in the pupils' behaviour.

Factors affecting prejudice

Individual differences

Personality

Before social psychology began to focus on group dynamics, dispositional theories of prejudice were common explanations. Theodor Adorno, Else Frenkel-Brunswik, Daniel Levinson and Nevitt Sanford (1950) developed the theory of an authoritarian personality that could explain why some individuals are prejudiced. The authoritarian personality possessed specific characteristics that meant they were more likely to be hostile to people of a different race, social group, age, sexuality or other minority groups. Initially, they interviewed two American college students (Mack and Larry) about their political beliefs, how they were raised and attitudes to minorities. This helped them design a series of questionnaires (scales) that would measure the authoritarian personality; in particular the levels of anti-Semitism, **ethnocentrism** (they preferred to use the term ethnocentrism to prejudice as they felt it better represented the concept) and **conservatism**. They also developed the famous F-Scale (Fascism Scale) to measure **anti-democratic** beliefs. Combined, these scales formed a personality questionnaire designed to measure authoritarianism.

> **Key terms**
>
> **Ethnocentrism:** belief that one's own ethnic group is superior to another.
>
> **Conservativism:** a belief in tradition and social order with a dislike for change.
>
> **Anti-democratic:** views that oppose the fair election of government and majority rule.

The Adorno et al. scales

Here are examples of some of the statements from each scale. Respondents rated their agreement with each statement on a Likert scale.

Anti-Semitism scale

- I can hardly imagine myself marrying a Jew.
- Jews should be more concerned with their personal appearance, and not be so dirty and smelly and unkempt.
- There are a few exceptions, but in general Jews are pretty much alike.

Ethnocentrism scale

- Any group of social movement that contains many foreigners should be watched with suspicion and, where possible, investigated by the FBI.
- One main difficulty with allowing the entire population to participate fully in government affairs (voting, jobs, etc.) is that such a large percentage is innately deficient and incapable.
- A large-scale system of sterilisation would be one good way of breeding out criminals and other undesirable elements in our society and so raise its general standards and living conditions.

Conservativism scale

- The businessman, the manufacturer, the practical man – these are of much greater value to society than the intellectual, the artist, the theorist.
- The best way to solve social problems is to stick close to the middle of the road, to move slowly and to avoid extremes.
- Young people sometimes get rebellious ideas, but as they grow up they ought to get over them and settle down.

The F-Scale items

- Sex crimes, such as rape and attacks on children, deserve more than mere imprisonment; such criminals ought to be publicly whipped.
- No insult to our honour should ever go unpunished.
- Nowadays when so many different kinds of people move around so much and mix together so freely, a person has to be especially careful to protect himself against infection and disease.

You can find an online version of the F-Scale to score your own personality.

Key term

Thematic Apperception Test: where individuals are shown abstract images (inkblots) to interpret in an attempt to uncover motivations and attitudes towards a particular subject.

In addition to the questionnaires, Adorno et al. reported 80 interviews (40 male and 40 female interviewees) covering information about background, beliefs, feelings towards others, and religious and political ideology. This information, the questionnaire data, clinical interviews with Mack and Larry, and **Thematic Apperception Tests** were amassed to produce their theory of prejudice.

They describe the authoritarian personality as hostile to people they see as inferior to themselves, particularly minority groups or people described as out-groups. They are hostile, rigid in thinking and intolerant to change. In fact, they are likely to be very conventional in their attitudes and conform to wider social group norms. On the other hand, they are submissive to authority and obedient to those in positions of power. Often having experienced strict and unaffectionate parenting, they frequently project their anger and aggression onto others. This represents their upbringing because they had to be respectful to their parents, while learning from them that they could be cruel to those who are weak.

DEVELOPMENTAL PSYCHOLOGY

Adorno and his colleagues thought that the authoritarian personality was developed in childhood. Harsh parenting used to ensure obedience leads to a love–hate relationship between a child and its parents. The hate and resentment towards a parent is repressed and displaced onto weaker members of society, such as minorities, while they maintain respect for authority. This theory gives a developmental account of both obedience and prejudice.

While the authoritarian personality seems credible, and certainly explains individual differences such as bullies at school or individuals with extreme political ideas (the National Front), it is unlikely to be a valid explanation for wide-scale prejudice, such as that experienced by the Jews during the Holocaust.

The authoritarian personality theory suggests that certain personality traits that cause prejudice are innate (genetic). A biological basis for prejudice would assume that it is fixed and not changeable, yet through history we see changes to attitudes towards minorities, such as the Rwandan genocide which developed from the harmonious settlement of Tutsis. Such social change cannot be explained by genetics.

Exam tip

You may be asked to assess a theory, study or concept in psychology. The term 'assess' requires that you consider relevant factors and come to a reasoned conclusion. Consider the following example.

Assess whether personality is a viable explanation of prejudice.

You will need to consider evidence that suggests that personality is useful or not as an explanation, and perhaps consider other theories that better-explain prejudice. You must also come to a conclusion based on the evidence and arguments used in your answer.

Culture

Culture can be an influence on prejudice if that culture has existing social norms that legitimise prejudiced practice, has strict religious regimens or laws that endorse prejudice towards targets, or events occur that trigger prejudice towards another group. However, as social norms, laws and events are not static, but are ever changing, it is difficult to establish whether one culture is particularly more prejudiced than another culture. However, the current prejudices held by a culture or society can be explored by investigating national stereotypes.

Katz and Braly conducted a questionnaire on students attending Princeton University in 1933 to investigate the national stereotypes of Americans about other cultures. Giving the students a list of different ethnic groups (Irish, Jewish, etc.), they had to pick 5–6 traits from a list of 84 personality traits (superstitious, lazy, ignorant, etc.) that they thought represented each ethnic group. They found that the majority of American students classified African Americans as superstitious and ignorant, and Jews as shrewd. However, they may have responded in a socially desirable way at the time, and there was no verification that these were actually their personal beliefs. Twenty years later, Karlins et al. (1969) replicated the research and found that while some national stereotypes had changed, others persisted. This suggests that culture does affect prejudice, but as cultures change, so do the prejudices they hold.

Cultures can be generally classified as individualistic or collectivistic based on how the culture views members of its own group. Individualistic cultures tend to emphasise individuals within the group as important, while collectivistic cultures emphasise the importance of the whole group as a collective. This cultural distinction would suggest that individualistic cultures would encourage more interpersonal prejudice and collectivistic cultures more intergroup prejudice (Fujimoto and Härtel, 2004). This is consistent with social identity theory as it would predict that prejudice towards an out-group would be more prominent in collectivistic cultures.

In a cultural comparison of Saudi (collectivist) and American (individualist) people, Al-Zahrani and Kaplowitz (1993) found Saudis to self-report more in-group favouritism and negative out-group bias. Whereas Kleugel (1990) found that collectivism is associated with greater tolerance and lower racism. Comparisons between cultures do not support the idea that one type of culture is more prejudiced than another. However, it should be noted that cross-cultural comparisons of prejudice are extremely hard to measure.

1.2 Methods

Learning outcomes

In this section, you will learn about:

- how to design and conduct a questionnaire and interview
- the issue of researcher effects
- types of survey and questions
- alternative hypotheses
- selecting a sample of participants
- how to analyse and present quantitative data
- the analysis of qualitative data
- the British Psychological Society (BPS) Code of Ethics and Conduct.

Self-report data

A survey is a self-report method, used to gather information about how people feel, their attitudes and opinions, personality types and other traits. Surveys typically are designed to gather a large amount of information, this can be done through a questionnaire or large-scale interview.

Questionnaire

Questionnaires are designed to gather a large amount of data by accessing a large sample. Questionnaires can be administered by post, email, face to face or online, and often consist of questions that require information from participants about their attitudes, opinions, lifestyles and indeed any aspect of a person's life.

Types of question

A questionnaire can gather different types of information or data. **Quantitative data** can be described as information that is or can be converted into numbers, and **qualitative data** can be defined as information that is non-numerical prose. The type of question asked in a questionnaire can yield either quantitative or qualitative data.

Closed questions are questions that have preset fixed answers that a respondent has to select from by circling or ticking the one that is the closest match to their opinion. Closed questions yield quantitative data. These can be yes/no response questions or where a list of options is available.

Although respondents find closed questions easy and quick to answer, and researchers can easily analyse this type of data, they can be frustrating if the possible answers do not match what the participant would like to express. They are also very limited in the amount of information that can be analysed; a researcher cannot know why a respondent has answered in that way, so the level of detail obtained is limited. Attitude scales have been designed to increase the level of detail achieved in a questionnaire.

Attitude scales involve more than a yes/no response, instead offering respondents a range of different options so that their strength of opinion can be gauged. A Likert-type scale involves a respondent selecting from a fixed set of choices to rate agreement to a series of statements. A Likert scale was used in the Adorno et al. survey on authoritarianism (see Section 1.1 Content, *Factors affecting prejudice*).

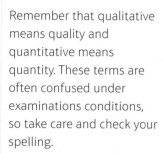

Maths tip

Remember that qualitative means quality and quantitative means quantity. These terms are often confused under examinations conditions, so take care and check your spelling.

Key terms

Quantitative data: numerical data.

Qualitative data: descriptive data.

Fixed-choice questions

Closed questions can be fixed choice, such as yes/no or list of options. Here are some examples:

Are you male or female?

Do you have a pet? Yes/No

Age: 18–40 years/41–60 years/60+ years (please circle)

Which adjective would you use to best describe your personality?
Agreeable Selfish Lonely Happy (please circle)

Likert scale question

Naughty children should be smacked

5	4	3	2	1
Strongly agree	Agree	Neutral	Disagree	Strongly disagree

Ranked scale question

Put the following list of animals in the order in which you fear them; place the most feared in position 1, and so on:

Horse, rat, spider, cat, rabbit, dog, cow

Likert scales involve respondents rating their opinion, and ranked scales involve a respondent ranking their choices relative to other options. To score ranked questions, each preference should be given a weighting. For example, if you ask respondents to rank animals according to how fearful they are of them, the most feared animal would have to be given a higher weighting than the least feared. The animal with the highest score will represent the most feared animal.

Open questions do not involve preset answers, but instead allow respondents to answer freely. This allows them to elaborate on their answers and justify their opinions. However, it does require more time and effort on the part of the respondent and open-ended question responses require a degree of qualitative analysis (see page 54), which can lead to subjective interpretation on the part of the researcher.

Issues with questionnaire design

Social desirability

This occurs when a respondent does not give a genuine answer, but one which depicts them in a more favourable light. That is, they respond to a question in a way that is seen as desirable according to prevailing social norms. For example, very few respondents would say that they agree with segregation or that heterosexuality was the only natural sexuality, because their responses would be contrary to current social norms and they would be seen in a negative light. This can be particularly problematic for research that investigates socially sensitive issues or attitudes that go against social norms. However, many questionnaires have inbuilt lie detectors that can detect socially desirable responses. If too many of these lie-detecting questions are answered in a socially desirable way, the respondents questionnaire can be excluded from further analysis.

Question construction

Designing questions for a questionnaire can be tricky. However, as a researcher is not present when the questionnaire is being completed, it is very important that questions are not too technical, ambiguous or complex. It is also important that questions do not lead or mislead a respondent into giving a particular answer or ask personal questions because this violates the right to privacy.

When designing Likert scale statements, it is important to consider the number of options provided because an odd number of possible answers to a scale means that the middle value may be selected more frequently. Using an even number of answers on a scale forces respondents to make a choice rather than select a 'neutral' or 'neither agree nor disagree' option.

Response bias or response acquiescence can occur when using Likert-style scales. If all the statements in a set of statements are worded favourably or unfavourably, respondents can slip into just agreeing or just disagreeing with all of them. To resolve this, statements should be reversed and mixed up.

Maths tip

Objective means not open to interpretation, while subjective means open to interpretation. For example, if you ask someone to estimate the length of a classroom table, it is likely that their estimation will differ from someone else's. This is a subjective interpretation. However, if you ask someone to use a ruler to measure the length of the classroom table, it is likely that their measurement will be exactly the same as someone else's. This is an objective measure.

Quantitative data is objective because numbers are numbers, and therefore not open to interpretation.

Qualitative data can be subjective because the meanings found in prose can be open to interpretation.

Avoiding response bias

Response bias can be avoided by reversing statements and mixing them up in the questionnaire. Examples of statement reversal:

Marriage helps society to function.	Society does not help marriage to function.
Pets make people happy.	Pets do not make people happy.
Politicians help the economy thrive.	The economy can thrive without politicians.

Questionnaire reliability

Reliability refers to the consistency of a measure or finding. **External reliability** refers to the consistency of a measure or finding over time. **Internal reliability** refers to the consistency of a measure within itself. Some questionnaires and scales lose their external reliability if respondents repeat them on different occasions, so it is important to establish whether this is the case by using the **test-retest method**. This literally means that the same people are given the same questionnaire to complete again on a different occasion. If their responses are the same or very similar, external reliability can be established.

Internal reliability is a problem for questionnaires because often several different questions are used to measure the same trait or attitude. The various scales used by Adorno et al. on conservativism, ethnocentrism, etc., contained many items that collectively measured these concepts. But did they all equally measure the same concept? In order to establish internal reliability, a **split-half method** can be employed. This involves splitting the questions into two halves and comparing the findings from both halves during analysis. If all of the questions are measuring the same concept, both halves should achieve the same score. If they do not, it suggests that some of the questions may be measuring a different concept.

Questionnaire validity

Validity refers to the extent to which something is measuring what it intends to measure. If you design a questionnaire intending to measure attitudes about education, then you need to be sure that you design your questions so that they measure this attitude and nothing else. Sometimes this can be established by simply looking at each question and deciding whether it makes sense in terms of the construct being measured. This is known as **face validity**. This can also be confirmed by asking an expert in the field to review the questions. If a questionnaire is a valid measure of a construct, such as intelligence, then it should have **predictive validity**. This means that it is able to accurately predict the same construct in the future. If an intelligence test has predictive validity, a high intelligence score should correlate with educational success, such as A level or degree grading. Another way of establishing whether the questions in a questionnaire are valid is by comparing it to another test measuring the same construct. This is known as **concurrent validity**.

Interviews

An interview can be used in a survey if it can be administered to a large sample of people relatively easily. This is more likely if it is a structured interview.

Structured interview

Structured interviews are defined by the nature of the questions and the way in which they are asked. Typically, structured interviews are standardised so that all respondents are asked the same questions in the same way, often using closed questions that gather quantitative data. Structured interviews tend to be easy to administer and do not need to establish a rapport between the researcher and respondent. However, the data gathered can be superficial and lack depth, and the respondent may feel stifled and not be able to express their opinions fully, which can be as frustrating as answering closed questions in a questionnaire.

Semi-structured interview

To avoid some of the problems with structured interviews, semi-structured interviews are more conversational and dynamic. A researcher has a set of questions that they aim to be answered, but do not have a standardised format to follow. This means that the conversation can flow a little bit better, while still achieving the research aim and getting relevant information from respondents. This type of interview can gather both quantitative and qualitative data.

Key terms

External reliability: refers to the consistency of a measure.

Internal reliability: refers to the consistency of a measure within itself.

Test-retest method: the same people are given the same questionnaire to complete again on a different occasion.

Split-half method: splitting the questions into two halves and comparing the findings from both halves during analysis to ensure reliability.

Face validity: looking at each question and deciding whether it makes sense in terms of the construct being measured.

Predictive validity: the extent to which results from a test or a study can predict future behaviour.

Concurrent validity: a way of establishing validity that compares evidence from several studies testing the same thing to see if they agree.

Unstructured interview

This type of interview begins with a loose research aim and gathers qualitative information from respondents. Unlike structured interviews, the interviewer needs to be analytical during the interview so that they can probe and seek meaning from respondents. An unstructured interviewer needs to be skilled at achieving a good rapport with respondents and responsive to the information offered; they need good listening skills and should use non-judgemental language.

Ethical issues are important when conducting any type of questionnaire or interview, but critical when using an unstructured interview because the qualitative data gathered can make direct reference to quotes from respondents. It is important that all respondent details are anonymised and personal details disguised. Due to the reflexive nature of an unstructured interview, the interviewer must deal sensitively when asking for personal information to ensure they do not breech the respondent's right to privacy.

Researcher effects

When asking people questions, there are many interviewer characteristics that can influence the respondent; the sex, age, manner and personality of the interviewer can all affect how a person responds, whether they are truthful, and whether they disclose information at all. It is, therefore, important to predict what characteristics might influence respondents and control them. For example, you can predict that a male interviewer will be unlikely to obtain detailed information from a female participant about their view of marriage. This can be controlled by employing a female interviewer.

Alternative hypotheses

In addition to an overall research aim, a study might also make a prediction about what is likely to occur. This prediction is known as an alternative hypothesis. A hypothesis should contain the variables under investigation and be a clear, testable and precise statement at the beginning of a report. This prediction is often guided by previous research in the topic area, but if there is limited previous research or mixed findings, the prediction may have to just state that a difference or relationship might be found between the variables under investigation, but not what direction the difference/relationship may take. You will learn more about hypothesis construction in Topic 2: *Cognitive psychology* (see Section 2.2 Methods).

Sampling techniques

In psychological research it is necessary to recruit participants or respondents to study. The way in which these participants are selected is known as sampling. It is unlikely that a whole population can be studied, so a sample of the population needs to be gathered using a sampling technique. The technique used will depend on the type of research being conducted and the availability of the participants, but the aim of a sampling method is to select a representative sample of participants; that is, a sample that represents the characteristics of the population well. This will ensure that any conclusions drawn from the research can be successfully generalised back to explain the behaviour of the target population as a whole.

Target population

A target population is the population of people being investigated by a study. For example, if you are investigating attitudes about the NHS at a local hospital, the target population will be people at the hospital. A sample will be recruited from this target population using a sampling technique.

Identify the target population in these examples:
- asking teachers at a school about their views on canteen food
- using a gym membership list to recruit participants for a survey about exercise
- stopping people in a street to take part in research
- investigating stress at work in an office building.

If the sample gathered is not representative, because of an over- or underrepresentation of a particular type of participant in the sample use, a sampling bias will occur.

Random sampling

The most likely way to recruit a representative sample is by using a random sampling technique. This should ensure that everyone has an equal chance of being selected. A random sample can be achieved in a number of ways. Computers are capable of producing random sequences of numbers, so every person in a target population can be assigned a number, and the computer-generated numbers can be used to select a sample if the numbers correspond. A simpler way would be to place the names of every member of the target population into a hat, shuffle them and draw at random.

Random sampling should result in a representative sample, although this may not always be the case because you can select an unrepresentative sample at random, too. Even if your random sample is representative of the target population, you still need to obtain consent from each participant selected. If they decide to not take part, you may be left with an unrepresentative sample in the end.

Stratified sampling

If the target population has salient characteristics that need to be proportionately represented in the sample recruited, a stratified sampling technique can be used. For example, if you are researching stress in the workplace in a company, you can find out how many staff occupy different roles within the company, for example office clerks, managers, canteen staff, cleaners, etc. As there may be more clerks than managers, more clerks need to be recruited for the study than managers in order to represent the company staff more fairly. Each subgroup within the company can be randomly sampled by placing the names of all the clerks in a hat, for example, and drawing out a proportionate number.

Opportunity sampling

An opportunity sample makes use of participants who are available. This can involve a researcher going to a student common room and asking people to take part, or investigating passers-by in a high street. Either way, the researcher has limited control over who is recruited and not everyone in a target population has an equal chance of being selected.

Volunteer sampling

Self-selected participants can be recruited by placing an advert in a newspaper or a student common room. Volunteers are self-selecting because they choose to take part; they are not approached and asked by a researcher. The researcher has no control over who volunteers and often a certain type of participant may choose to take part. This can result in a sample bias. However, a researcher may pre-test volunteers before the main study and exclude those with characteristics they feel may not represent the target population.

Sampling bias

Identify the sampling bias in the following examples:

- a researcher recruits student participants in the canteen at lunchtime to find out about attitudes towards A-level reforms

- participants volunteer to take part in a study about eating habits by responding to an advert in a woman's magazine

- a researcher uses the telephone directory to gather a sample of participants for a study on health-related behaviour

- attitudes towards a no-smoking policy are gathered from participants recruited from an outside office smoking area.

Now consider the likely impact of the sampling bias on the conclusions of each study.

Opportunity samples are drawn from a small section from the community so are probably not very representative.

Analysis of quantitative data

Once an investigation has been conducted, the findings of the study need to be analysed. Investigations can produce quantitative data or qualitative data. Quantitative data is numerical data that is gathered. Closed questions and ranked-scale questions produce data that can be easily quantified.

Investigations that gather quantitative data produce numerical results called raw scores. This raw data can be difficult to understand, so it is summarised to make it easier to see the trends being shown and to highlight the differences between groups. Data can be summarised using descriptive statistics; that is, calculations of the measures of central tendency and dispersion.

Data tables

Raw data table

When data has been gathered it is often initially presented in a raw data table. A raw data table is a table of all the individual values measured in the study.

Table 1.3 The individual self-ratings of obedience (out of 10) of males and females

Participant	Males	Females
A	3	7
B	5	9
C	4	6
D	6	8
E	4	7
F	3	6
G	4	9

Using Table 1.3 of raw scores, it is noticeable that females rated themselves as more obedient than males. Not all raw scores show an obvious trend, so other tables can be used to analyse the findings more clearly.

Key terms

Skewed distribution: when the values in a data set do not conform to a normal distribution (many scores around the mean and fewer at the extreme ends).

Interval/ratio data: data where an individual score for each participant is gathered, and the score can be identified using a recognised scale with equal distances between each score, for example time, height.

Ordinal level data: a level of measurement where numbers are rankings rather than scores in themselves, e.g. a rank order for attractiveness on a scale of 1 to 5.

Maths tip

The mean is the most appropriate measure of central tendency for interval level data and should not be used on data with extreme outliers or a data set with a skewed distribution. You will need to look at the raw scores before deciding whether to use the mean.

For example:

Data set: 2, 3, 4, 6, 8, 22 = mean of 7.5. A check of the raw scores reveals that 22 is an outlier that will affect the mean. The mean of 7.5 that has been calculated does not reflect an average score in this data set.

Frequency table

Table 1.4 The frequency of ratings of obedience for males and females

Self-rated obedience	Males	Females
3	2	
4	3	
5	1	
6	1	2
7		2
8		1
9		2

A frequency table shows how many times (the frequency) the scores occurred in a data set. Table 1.4 clearly indicates that females frequently gave a higher obedience rating for themselves than males. Males self-reported lower obedience.

Measures of central tendency

There are a few ways in which data can be summarised, making conclusions easier to draw from the results. Central tendency is a descriptive statistic that calculates the average or most typical value in a data set; that is, the average score recorded. The average score can be calculated in different ways.

The arithmetic mean $\bar{x}$

The arithmetic mean is calculated by adding up all of the values in a data set and dividing the total by the number of scores collected. The formula for calculating the mean is:

$$\bar{x} = \frac{\sum x_i}{n}$$

Where:

$\bar{x}$ = mean

$\sum$ = sum of

n = number of scores

For example:

Data set: 3, 5, 7, 9, 10, 11, 13 $\sum x_i = 58$

Divided by the number of scores = 7

$\bar{x} = 8.3$

The mean is the most sensitive and therefore the most powerful measure of central tendency because all the scores in the data set are used in the calculation, but it can be affected by extreme values or when there is a **skewed distribution** (see page 52). The mean is often used on **interval/ratio level data**.

The median

The median is a measure of central tendency that calculates the middle value when the values in the data set are placed in rank order (from smallest to largest). When the data set has an odd number of scores, it is simply the middle value. However, if there is an even number of scores, the mean of the two middle values needs to be calculated.

For example:

Data set with an odd number of scores: 3, 6, 8, 9, 10 = the median score is 8.

Data set with an even number of scores: 3, 5, 6, 7, 8, 9 = a mean of the middle scores 6 and 7 gives a median score of 6.5.

The median is a simple calculation of the average score and is not affected by extreme scores or a skewed distribution. However, it is less sensitive than the mean and is not useful on data sets that have a small number of values as it may not represent the typically score. The median is typically used on **ordinal data.**

The mode

The mode is a measure of central tendency that calculates the most frequent score in a data set. The mode is the value that occurs most frequently.

Data set: 2, 2, 3, 3, 4, 4, 4, 6, 7, 7, 7, 7, 9 = a mode of 7, the most frequent score.

If there are two most frequent scores, it is referred to as bi-modal and both should be reported. However, if more than two modes are seen the mode becomes a meaningless measure of central tendency. The mode is used on **nominal data** and is very easy to determine. It is not affected by extreme scores. However, it is not a useful measure of central tendency on small data sets with frequently occurring same values.

Measures of dispersion

Dispersion is a descriptive statistic that calculates the spread of scores in the data set. Measures of central tendency can be misleading without knowing the variation between the scores. There are different types of measures of dispersion.

Range

The range is the simplest calculation of dispersion; it is simply the difference between the highest and lowest value. The range is calculated by subtracting the lowest value from the highest value. A high range value indicates that the scores are spread out and a low range value indicates that the scores are closer together.

For example:

Data set: 2, 4, 6, 8, 9, the range is 9 – 2 = 7.

The range is affected by extreme scores, so may not be a useful descriptive statistic if there are outliers in the data set. It also does not tell us if the scores are bunched around the mean score or more equally distributed around the mean.

If a data set has extreme scores, it is often better to calculate the interquartile range. This involves cutting out the lowest quarter and highest quarter of values (the top and bottom 25 per cent) and calculating the range of the remaining middle half of scores.

Standard deviation

A more useful way of looking at the spread of scores is to understand the concept of deviation. Deviation refers to the distance of each value from the arithmetic mean. For example: if the mean average rating for obedience given by the male participants was 7, and one male within in the group was 9, the deviation of the score would be +2. If a different male in the group rated himself as 5 on an obedience scale, the deviation value would be –2.

Clearly each score in a data set would have a deviation value, so to get a single value that represents all deviation scores the standard deviation needs to be calculated. The standard deviation gives a single value that represents how the scores are spread out around the mean. The higher the standard deviation, the greater the spread of scores around the mean value.

The formula for the standard deviation of a sample is

$$SD = \sqrt{\frac{\sum(x - \bar{x})^2}{n - 1}}$$

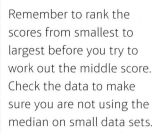

Maths tip

Remember to rank the scores from smallest to largest before you try to work out the middle score. Check the data to make sure you are not using the median on small data sets.

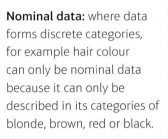

Key term

Nominal data: where data forms discrete categories, for example hair colour can only be nominal data because it can only be described in its categories of blonde, brown, red or black.

Maths tip

In the exam, you are able to use a calculator to work out the mean and the standard deviation. You will need a calculator that can perform statistical calculations or a standard calculator (although this will take a bit longer).

Using a scientific calculator: input each value one at a time, using the 'add' button to do this. Once all scores have been added, press the σ_n−1 symbol button.

Using a standard calculator: calculate the mean of the data set. Subtract each value in the data set from the mean to find the deviation of each score. Square each deviation by multiplying it by itself (for example 20 x 20). Find the sum total of the squared deviations and divide this figure by the number of scores in the data set and minus 1 to find the variance. Find the square root of the variance to find the standard deviation.

Clearly it will be a lot easier to invest in a scientific calculator, but this should only be used to check your workings. In the exam, you will need to show all of your workings.

Key term

Inferential test: a statistical test that is performed on data to establish whether or not the results found were due to chance factors or whether there was indeed a significant relationship or difference found between the data.

To calculate the standard deviation, it is useful to look at an example.

Table 1.5 Example of standard deviation

Score (x)	Mean $\bar{x}$	Deviation $(x - \bar{x})$	Squared deviation $(x - \bar{x})^2$
70	100	−30	900
80	100	−20	400
90	100	−10	100
100	100	0	0
110	100	10	100
120	100	20	400
130	100	30	900
			Sum of deviations squared = 2800

1 In the table above each score has had the mean score subtracted to give the deviation score.

2 Each of these deviation scores need to be squared to give the squared deviations (final column).

3 The sum of the squared deviations should be calculated.

4 Now divide the sum of the squared deviations by the number of scores in the data set minus 1, in this example the sum of squared deviations is 2800 and the number in the sample (7) − 1 = 6. 2800 divided by 6 is 466.6 – this figure is known as the variance.

5 Take the square root of this variance (466.6) = 21.6

Exam tip

If you are asked to calculate a sum in the examination, you must show your workings as well as the figure for the numerical sum achieved.

Summary tables

Summary tables represent measures of central tendency and dispersion clearly.

Table 1.6 A summary table showing the self-rated obedience scores of males and females

	Males	Females
Mean obedience rating ($\bar{x}$)	4.1	7.4
Median obedience rating	4	7
Mode obedience rating	4	6, 7 and 9
Range of obedience ratings	3	3
Standard deviation ($\sigma\bar{x}$)	1	1.2

Using Table 1.6, it is clear that the typical score representing the rating of obedience is higher for females than males. The modal score for females is not useful as three modes have been calculated. The spread of scores, indicated by the range, is the same for both male and female ratings, and the standard deviations are also similar. This suggests a roughly equal spread of scores around the mean for both conditions. It can be concluded that females consistently rate themselves as more obedient than males, and that males consistently rate themselves as less obedient than females.

However, whether the difference in recall is large enough to be a real difference rather than just due to chance can only be established by conducting an **inferential test** on the data. You will learn about inferential tests in Topic 2: *Cognitive psychology*, Section 2.2 Methods.

Graphical representation of data

Graphs can be useful to illustrate summary data or data frequencies. Bar charts are used to present data from a categorical variable, such as the mean, median or mode. The categorical variable is placed on the x-axis, and the height of the bars represents the value of that variable, as shown in Figure 1.2.

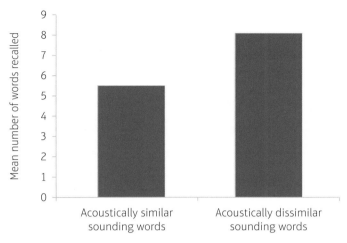

Figure 1.2 A bar graph showing the mean number of words recalled

A histogram is used to present the distribution of scores by illustrating the frequency of values in the data set (see Figure 1.3). Unlike a bar chart, where the bars are separated by a space, the bars on a histogram are joined to represent continuous data rather than categorical (discrete) data. The possible values are presented on the x-axis and the height of each bar represents the frequency of the value.

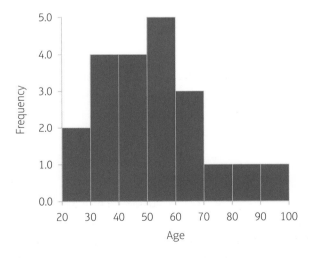

Figure 1.3 A histogram

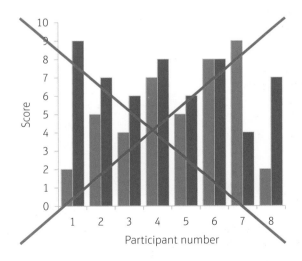

Figure 1.4 Raw scores in a graph – this is bad practice

Normal and skewed distribution

Psychological research can use small samples of participants where only measures of central tendency and dispersion are useful descriptive statistics. When larger samples are gathered, it may be more useful to examine the overall distribution formed by the gathered data. Distribution tells us the overall frequency of the values in a data set. Examining distribution can show trends in the data that cannot be detected using small samples, and we can estimate the distribution of scores in the whole population.

Table 1.7 is an example of the distribution of self-rated obedience scores in a group of individuals gathered using a Likert-style question on a questionnaire.

Table 1.7 The frequency distribution of digit span

Self-reported obedience scores	Frequency	Percentage
1	1	2.04
2	2	4.08
3	3	6.12
4	4	8.16
5	5	10.20
6	6	12.24
7	7	14.29
8	6	12.24
9	5	10.20
10	4	8.16
11	3	6.12
12	2	4.08
13	1	2.04
	Sum total = 49	Cumulative percentage = 100%

> **Raw data for self-reported obedience**
> 1, 2, 2, 3, 3, 3, 4, 4, 4, 4, 5, 5, 5, 5, 5, 6, 6, 6, 6, 6, 6, 7, 7, 7, 7, 7, 7, 7, 8, 8, 8, 8, 8, 8, 9, 9, 9, 9, 9, 10, 10, 10, 10, 11, 11, 11, 12, 12, 13.

Percentage

The percentage score gives an overall indication of the relative proportion of people who achieved a particular obedience score.
To calculate a percentage score, the sum of the values needs to be calculated and each individual value divided by this sum total multiplied by 100.

For example, 5 people achieved an obedience score of 9. This score should be divided by the sum total of 49 and multiplied by 100; that is, 5/49 × 100 = 10.20. This means that 10 per cent of the participants achieved an obedience score of 9.

Normal distribution

When the frequency distribution of a population is calculated, it can be represented on a frequency graph. If the graph illustrates a bell-shaped curve, the data has a normal distribution, as shown in Figure 1.5.

Normal distribution is characterised by its symmetry around the mid-point. The mean, median and mode should be aligned around

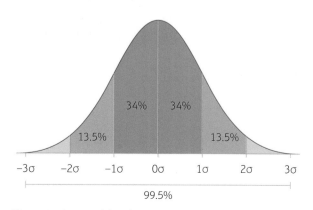

Figure 1.5 A normal distribution curve

the mid-point. The tail ends should not meet the horizontal axis, and we can estimate the percentage of people that fall under the curve at each standard deviation. We know that 68 per cent of the population falls between one standard deviation each side of the mid-point, and that 95 per cent of the population falls between two standard deviations either side of the mid-point. The standard deviation needs to be calculated on the raw scores to understand exactly what value is represented by these intervals.

For example, the standard deviation for obedience scores was 2.8 and the mean, median and mode score was 7. If 7 is placed at the mid-point, +1 standard deviation from the mid-point would be 9.8 and −1 standard deviation from the mid-point would be 4.2. This means that 68 per cent of our sample would achieve an obedience score of between 4.2 and 9.8, and that 95 per cent of our sample would achieve an obedience score 2 standard deviations from the mid-point of between 1.4 and 12.6. The distribution of self-reported obedience would therefore be normal.

Skewed distribution

Some distributions are not normal, but are referred to as skewed because they are not symmetrical (see Figure 1.6). This may be a result of the test administered or the type of sample gathered. If a test is easy or the aptitude of the sample is unusually high, it will mean that most people score highly. This will lead to a negative skew, where many people score above the average or mean score. If the test was particularly difficult or the aptitude of the sample low, it will mean that most people will achieve a low score. This will lead to a positive skew.

> **Maths tip**
>
> It is common to confuse positive and negative skews. Remember that a positive skew has its tail at the positive end of values on the horizontal axis (higher scores) and a negative skew has its tail at the negative end of values on the horizontal axis (lower scores). Another way to remember it is to draw a face on the graph so that it becomes a whale. A whale swimming towards the vertical axis is coming home, so it is positive, and a whale swimming away from the vertical axis is negative because it is leaving home.

Taking it further

Carry out a study of the height of your classmates. Calculate the frequency, mean, median, mode, range, standard deviation of height data gathered and draw a frequency graph to check whether height is equally distributed among the class.

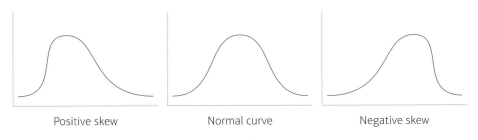

| Positive skew | Normal curve | Negative skew |

Figure 1.6 Examples of distributions

The mean is affected by extreme scores, by the lower scores on a negative skew and by the higher scores on a positive skew. The mean in a negative skew will therefore be lower than the mode, but will be higher than the mode in a positive skew.

Key terms

Thematic analysis: recording themes, patterns or trends within data.

Inductive: using known facts to produce general principles.

Deductive: using the knowledge and information you have in order to understand something.

Analysis of qualitative data using thematic analysis

Qualitative data is non-numerical data gathered often through interviews, questionnaires, case studies and observations. Qualitative data can be converted into quantitative data by counting instances of an event occurring. **Thematic analysis** is a way of analysing data without losing its meaningfulness completely but enables a vast amount of qualitative data to be more manageably reduced into general patterns, trends and themes. Thematic analysis is achieved through reviewing and identifying themes in the qualitative data. This can be done inductively or deductively. Using an **inductive** approach, the researcher would read and reread the qualitative data gathered and themes would emerge from the data without the researcher imposing any of their own ideas or expectations from it. **Deductive** thematic analysis would involve the researcher specifying the themes that they will look for before analysing the data.

Thematic analysis is very flexible, and many researchers use it in different ways. The overall procedure involves carefully reading and considering the qualitative data gathered and identifying the themes present in the data that occur frequently or seem to be a key feature of the data. How frequent or central to the text the theme is depends on the opinion of the researcher and the nature of the material analysed.

The researcher will develop these themes into 'codes', which represent the categories of themes found. The researcher will then use these codes to analyse the data gathered and search for instances where it appears in the data. This is reviewed continually, and changed if necessary, until the themes can be stated, supported and used as a summary of the data.

Analysis of qualitative data, using thematic analysis or other forms of qualitative analysis, is often considered to be unscientific because the themes are highly dependent on the subjective opinions of the researcher, and therefore can lead to researcher bias. For example, if a researcher expected that emergency room service users would be dissatisfied with the waiting times and level of care, they may have preconceived ideas that affect their theme choice and the way interview transcripts are interpreted.

Despite the fact that there is very little control over how a thematic analysis is conducted by individual researchers, qualitative analysis does yield far more detailed and meaningful information than quantitative data.

Ethical guidelines

Psychological research involves working with humans and animals, and certain codes of conduct are used to regulate this. These codes are referred to as ethical guidelines. Research within the UK is regulated by the British Psychological Society (BPS); in America, the American Psychological Association has its own ethical code; and the European Federation of Psychologists' Association regulates Portugal, Spain, France, Italy, Malta and Greece using the Carta Ethica. The BPS Code of Ethics and Conduct (2009) will be discussed here, but most countries are regulated by a similar framework and have similar guidelines.

The purpose of ethical guidelines is to ultimately ensure the safety and well-being of participants within psychological investigations. However, they are also used to ensure that the standards, professionalism and reputation of the subject are upheld.

The BPS ethical code is based around four ethical principles: respect, competence, responsibility and integrity.

Respect

This principle expects psychologists to have a general respect for the dignity of all individuals in terms of their cultural and role differences (ethnicity, age, religion, race, sexual orientation, etc.) and the experience they bring to the research. This respect should maintain the right to **privacy** and **confidentiality** for the safety of the individuals concerned. The principle also maintains that psychologists should seek to gain **informed consent** by disclosing the full nature of the research and avoid **deception** where possible. Participants of research should be offered a **right to withdraw** at any point and without consequence.

Competence

This principle concerns the level of professionalism held by the psychologist conducting research. It maintains that a researcher should be fully aware of the ethical code and if they are uncertain whether their research proposal meets these principles, they are to seek help from experts or supervisors. Psychologists should monitor their own knowledge of the area and recognise their own limits and the limits of their research.

Responsibility

Psychologists not only have a responsibility to their participants, but also to the general public, the profession and to science. They must ensure that their research does not harm others, or result in misuse. They should consider the views of the participants and inform them of any potential for harm and how this harm will be safeguarded. This principle reiterates the participants' right to withdraw and maintains that participation should not be **incentivised**. A **debrief** should always be given at the conclusion of research.

Integrity

Psychologists should be honest and fair in all of their work and avoid situations where they may be seen to exploit others or hold interests which may conflict with the interests of their participants or how the research is likely to be received by the public.

This code of ethical principles forms a framework that regulates research in psychology. However, it cannot address every possible situation that a researcher might face. Such judgements are made by the researcher, and consultation with other professionals in the field is encouraged.

> **Ethical code**
> The main elements of the ethical code can be structured in a brief form, and can be used as a guide for your own practical investigations.
> **Confidentiality**: are the participants anonymised so that they cannot be identified by name or any other personal information about them?
> **Right to withdraw**: are participants aware that they can chose to leave at any point before, during or after the study, and that they can even have their results withdrawn from analysis up to a set period of time?
> **Informed consent**: are participants fully aware of the study aims and nature of their participation? Is any information being withheld?
> **Protection of participants**: participants should not be subject to physical or psychological harm. Researchers should be mindful of how a participant might feel (stressed, embarrassed, fearful) and avoid such situations.
> **Privacy**: participants should not be involved in research that gathers personal or private information that they would not willingly disclose.
> **Deception**: are the participants lied to about the nature of the study?
> **Debrief**: participants will need to be told the nature of their participation when the study has concluded. If deception has been used or information withheld, it must be fully disclosed during a debrief.

Key terms

Privacy: participants should not be asked personal questions that they may find intrusive, and the researcher must not obtain personal data that a participant would not voluntarily disclose.

Confidentiality: participants should not be identified as part of the study. Their names can be anonymised.

Informed consent: participants should be fully aware of the aims, procedure and implications of the research.

Deception: participants should not be lied to or misguided about the nature of the study.

Right to withdraw: participants should be offered the opportunity to leave the study at any point without consequence. This means that they can withdraw their data after the study if they choose (up to a negotiated point in time).

Incentivised: given monetary reward or other form of gift to encourage participation in the study.

Debrief: a statement given to participants on conclusion of a study which discloses fully the nature and implications of the research.

1.3 Studies

Learning outcomes

In this section, you will learn about one classic study:

● Sherif et al. (1954, 1961) Robber's Cave experiment

and three contemporary studies, from which you will need to choose one to learn about:

● Burger (2009) Replicating Milgram: Would people still obey today?

● Reicher and Haslam (2006) Rethinking the psychology of tyranny: The BBC prison study

● Cohrs et al. (2012) Individual differences in ideological attitudes and prejudice: evidence from peer-report data.

Intergroup Conflict and Cooperation: The Robber's Cave Experiment (Sherif et al., 1954, 1961)

Muzafer Sherif, O.J. Harvey, Jack White, William Hood and Carolyn Sherif (1954, 1961) conducted a series of boys' summer camp experiments to investigate intergroup conflict. Each study followed a similar format: 10–12-year-old boys attending a two-week summer camp were divided into groups and made to compete against one another in a series of camp games. The behaviour of the boys was observed and recorded to examine how competition brought about conflict.

Background information

The first in the series of experiments was undertaken on 24 well-adjusted boys who were attending an 18-day summer camp in the isolated Northern Hills of Connecticut in 1949. The boys arrived and spent the first few days together as one group before they were divided into two groups that then participated in competitive camp activities. The groups were housed in separate bunk houses and participated in separate group activities, such as camp outs and hikes. The groups began to evolve separate identities; the groups named themselves Red Devils and Bull Dogs. Within each group, new friendships were formed and a social hierarchy began to develop; they gave themselves nicknames and made up group symbols. Their allegiance and friendships had shifted from the whole group to the separate groups of boys, and conflict between the groups was observed. They even rated individual members of the other group negatively, despite being rated as best friends at the beginning of the camp.

A second study was conducted in upstate New York in the summer of 1953. This time the groups called themselves the Panthers and the Pythons and the research followed a similar format of creating in-group formation and competition. However, this camp was unsuccessful because the boys suspected that the researchers were deliberately trying to create friction between their groups, and the study was stopped. It was also not until the third in the series of experiments that Sherif and his colleagues successfully attempted to reduce prejudice between the groups. It is this third experiment that will be discussed in detail here.

Aim

Sherif and his colleagues wanted to investigate intergroup relations over a period of time when various experimentally induced situations were introduced.

The study was particularly interested in group formation, the effect of competition and the conditions under which conflict could be resolved.

Procedure

The setting for the third experiment was the Robber's Cave camp in Oklahoma, an old hideout for outlaws such as Jesse James.

The study followed three stages:

Stage one: in-groups were created by facilitating tasks that required in-group cooperation.

Stage two: the two groups would be brought together in situations where they would have to compete against one another for goals.

Stage three: superordinate goals were introduced to encourage cooperation between the groups in order to reduce in-group hostility.

Participants

The participants were 22 boys of 11-years-old (one of 12-years-old) similar, 'normally adjusted' and from middle-class Protestant families from schools in Oklahoma City. An initial sample of 200 boys was opportunistically selected from schools in Oklahoma, and 22 were finally selected. The researchers made sure that the boys were not acquainted with each other before the study. A fee of US$25 was paid to parents to incentivise them to not visit the boys throughout the two-week stay at the camp. Unlike the previous two experiments, the boys were not introduced to each other at the start of the study, but divided into equally matched groups using information obtained from parents and teachers about their educational and athletic ability.

Stage one

During the first 5–6 days of the two-week camp, the two groups of boys were kept separate from each other and each group was involved in activities designed to encourage in-group formation. During this initial stage, researchers, who the boys thought were camp staff, observed the verbal and non-verbal communication within each group and the relationships that emerged. **Sociometric data** was gathered on how the boys rated each other in terms of popularity, initiative, etc.

> **Key term**
>
> **Sociometric data:** quantitative data gathered about personal/social relationships.

Stage two

Over the next 4–6 days the boys were brought into contact with each other during competitions as part of a camp tournament. It was necessary for each individual group member to contribute in the competition in order to win points towards the tournament total. Both groups were also subject to orchestrated situations that they would find frustrating and believe were caused by the other group. During this stage, stereotypes between each group were recorded, and behaviours and attitudes towards each group were noted.

Stage three

The final 6–7 days were devoted to bringing about conflict resolution through the introduction of common goals deliberately designed to ensure cooperation between the groups. Three problem situations were set up that could only be resolved if both groups worked cooperatively:

1. Fixing the water tank that provided water to both groups.
2. A joint camp-over where group members had to work together for food and sleeping gear.
3. Starting the broken-down camp bus.

Results

During Stage one, the boys in each group formed their own set of group norms and rules that formed their group identity. They took part in various cooperative activities, and by the end of the stage had defined a name for their group; one called themselves the 'Rattlers' and the other the 'Eagles'. At the end of this stage, the groups were made aware of the other's existence and the formation of an 'us' and 'them' attitude became apparent.

During Stage two, the boys were beginning to show signs of hostility to the other group and persisted in demanding for competitive activities. Leaders to take on the challenges of a tournament emerged in each group and the boys became territorial. When the tournament was announced, the boys began to fight, name call and the Eagles burned the Rattlers' camp flag. There was a strong sense of in-group favouritism and negative out-group bias, resulting in derogatory terms being used (stinkers, braggers, sissies) about the other group and a number of skirmishes and camp raids. When asked to self-report who their friends were out of all of the boys, around 93 per cent selected exclusively from their own in-group.

During the final stage of the study, the researchers attempted to bring the two groups of boys together in various situations. For example, in the dining hall for various mealtimes and watching a movie. However, mere contact alone was not sufficient to reduce hostility between the groups of boys, who persisted in name calling and fighting.

Tasks involving superordinate goals were introduced and the first cooperative task between the Rattlers and the Eagles involved the fixing of the water tank, which had been rigged by the researchers. The boys were divided up and all had a role to play to identify the cause of the camp water shortage. When the water faucet blockage had been identified, the boys were observed to be mingling with each other and no longer name-calling. The harmony, however, did not persist and the boys soon displayed negative out-group bias during supper the same evening, which resulted in derogatory terms being used about the other group and food being thrown.

The boys were informed by staff that they could secure a movie if they collectively paid for it. The boys worked out a strategy for payment and a noticeable reduction in hostility was observed during supper the same evening and turn-taking the following day at breakfast. The boys worked together to pull the camp bus, which was rigged by the researchers to not start.

At the end of the study, the researchers reassessed friendship choices. They found a significant increase in the number of boys whose friendships were now with the out-group compared to those choices made in Stage two.

Conclusions

Sherif and colleagues concluded that strong in-group identities were formed initially, and with the introduction of competition, negative out-group bias quickly emerged. The introduction of superordinate goals had a cumulative effect in reducing negative out-group bias because it removed competition. This research supported the realistic conflict theory that prejudice could be brought about through competition for resources.

Evaluation

The Robber's Cave study had high ecological validity and took place within a natural environment for the boys. Unlike laboratory situations, where group behaviour is heavily manipulated, the behaviour observed between the boys was relatively naturally occurring.

The researchers used a high level of control and careful planning at each stage. The staff were participant observers in the study so that the boys were unaware that their behaviour was being recorded as part of a psychological investigation, and the staff were only permitted to intervene in decision making and conflict between the groups when there was a risk to safety. This control was to ensure the staff did not direct the behaviour of the boys. However, interviews many years later with

---

Tournament activities

A series of researcher-judged and boy-rated activities were created for the tournament. The researcher-judged activities were designed so that the number of points awarded overall could be manipulated. The points were roughly neck and neck throughout the tournament.

Boy-rated activities:

Baseball games

Tug of war

Touch football

Tent pitching

Researcher-judged activities

Cabin inspections

Skits and songs

Treasure hunt

Points would be allocated to winning teams and the prizes were a trophy, medals and a four-bladed knife.

some of the boys who had taken part in the series of studies indicated that the boys were aware of audio equipment in the dining hall and the staff taking notes about their behaviour.

Unpublished researcher notes and interviews with the boys as adults revealed that the researchers may not have been as independent as they were instructed to be. Many of them were reported to be actively encouraging intergroup hostility and creating opportunities for conflict (by breaking down the tents of a rival group and blaming the other group). They were also reported to encourage physical conflict by not intervening, as they should have, in skirmishes between the boys. This invariably fuelled hostility above and beyond what would normally be experienced.

To decrease the influence of individual variables on results once they reached Robber's Cave, Sherif carefully selected the 22 boys based on gender, age, IQ, social class and religion, matching the groups as carefully as possible. This prevented individual differences in character and attributes affecting the behaviour of the boys. However, as only boys were used in the study (two of whom dropped out during the first stage), the sample used may be insufficient and gender biased, meaning the results may not be generalisable. Sherif also selected boys who were reputed to have good athletic ability and were keen on sport. This could explain the degree of conflict between the boys, as they were perhaps naturally competitive.

It was apparent at the end of Stage one that intergroup hostility had already emerged at the mere knowledge of another group, even before competitions formally began. This perhaps offers some support for social identity theory, as competition was not necessary to create prejudice, it merely crystallised later on, in Stage two.

Although the parents had consented to the study, the boys were unaware that they were part of a psychological investigation on intergroup hostility, believing it to be a study about leadership. This means that fully informed consent was not directly obtained from the boys themselves. Many have also questioned the ethical nature of the study as it deliberately induced prejudice and placed the boys in situations where they could have come to harm. This was exacerbated by the fact that Sherif was running out of funding. He had spent considerable funding on the previous two summer camp studies and the Robber's Cave was perhaps the last attempt he could afford to run. This has led to accusations of deliberately inducing high levels of conflict and hostility between the groups to ensure successful study outcomes.

Andrew Tyerman and Christopher Spencer (1983) asserted that it is not a natural condition for strangers to meet and compete against one another, but more likely that in real life the group members will be familiar with one another and have a history of social interaction. Using a Scout troop whose separate patrols normally interacted a couple of times a year, they partially replicated the Sherif et al. summer camp study. Using four patrols that met at a two-week long camp, the patrol leaders assessed the behaviour of the Scouts using a range of different measures: cooperation, atmosphere in camp, solidarity. They found that hostility did not emerge between the groups and competition did not inevitably lead to hostility. As the Scout patrols were familiar with one another, their findings represent a more realistic outcome and therefore, the researchers argue, has greater generalisability than the Robber's Cave. However, the competitions employed by this study did not involve direct contact between the patrols, nor were trophies offered, which may explain the lack of competitive hostility between the groups.

Replicating Milgram: Would people still obey today? (Burger, 2009)

In 2009, Jerry Burger decided to replicate Milgram's (1963) study in contemporary society. He too was interested in whether people would obey an authoritative figure. Some psychologists today believe that people are more aware of the consequences of blindly following orders from an authoritative figure and, as a result, would reconsider their actions when asked to cause potential injury to others. However, Burger believed that despite the large time gap between his study and Milgram's, his study would still produce similar levels of obedience. Burger felt that, although society's culture and values had changed, this would not have a significant effect on obedience.

Burger was also very mindful that Milgram's obedience study had been subject to ethical criticism, and so he needed to adapt his research to adhere more closely to the current ethical guidelines and cause minimal participant distress.

Aim

To investigate obedience by partially replicating Milgram's (1963) study to examine whether situational factors affect obedience to an authoritative figure.

Screening procedures

Individuals responded to advertisements and flyers advertised in a local newspaper and local establishments (library, businesses) as well as online. The advertisements promised US$50 for taking part in two 45-minute sessions. Individuals expressed their interest by phone or by email. Individuals then received a call from a research assistant who began a screening procedure. Participants were asked if they had been to college and if they answered yes, they were also asked if they took psychology lessons. The purpose of such questions was to reject individuals who had two or more psychology classes and to screen out those who may have been familiar with Milgram's original study. The remaining participants were asked about their physical and psychological health and whether they had suffered any traumatic childhood experiences. A further 30 per cent of participants were excluded from further involvement in the study after this.

Participants then continued onto the second screening process led by two clinical psychologists and held at Santa Clara University campus. This screening process required the individuals to complete a number of scales/questionnaires; a demographic sheet asking about age, occupation, education and ethnicity; the Interpersonal Reactivity Index; the Beck Anxiety Inventory; the Desirability of Control Scale; and the Beck Depression Inventory.

Participants were then taken to a room and interviewed by a clinical psychologist to assess participants who might be negatively affected by the study. The interview was structured around the Mini International Neuropsychiatric Interview (MINI) procedure. The MINI interview touches on psychological disorders and allowed the psychologist to identify anyone who should not be part of the study. Each interview lasted approximately 30 minutes. In total, 123 individuals took part in the second screening and 47 (38.2 per cent) were removed from continuing with the study but allowed to gain their money as advertised. Their exclusions and reasons behind their exclusion are unknown due to confidentiality agreements.

A total of 76 individuals were invited back a week later but six dropped out at this point, five of whom expressed awareness of Milgram's research during the second session, leaving a final sample of 29 males and 41 females. They ranged in age from 20–81 years old, with a mean of 42.9 years.

Questionnaires used by the study

- The Interpersonal Reactivity Index, a 28-item scale, is designed to analyse empathy levels.

- The Beck Anxiety Inventory, a 21-item scale, allows individuals to rate their own anxiety levels against 21 different anxiety symptoms.

- The Desirability of Control Scale, a 20-item scale, measures the individual's impressions of themselves in terms of self-control of their lives.

- The Beck Depression Inventory, a 21-item scale, is designed to assess the measure of severity of depression in an individual.

Study procedure

Experiment one – Baseline condition

Participants were split into two groups in an attempt to keep equal ratios of gender in each group. Each participant was introduced to the experimenter and the confederate before starting. Both the experimenter and confederate were selected due to their resemblance to those used in Milgram's study. It was at this point the participant and confederate were both given US$50 and told to keep it even if they chose to withdraw from the study. Burger used a similar script to Milgram's original and explained the procedure of the study to the participant and the use of the electric generator. The role choice was also rigged, similar to Milgram's study, and the confederate always received the role of learner and the participant the teacher. They were both then asked to sign the consent forms.

Exactly like Milgram's study, the learner was put into the adjoining room while the teacher was placed before an electric generator. The teacher was asked to join the experimenter while he prepared the learner for the study. The participant witnessed the experimenter placing an electrode onto the learner's left wrist, sealing it with paste and explaining that it would 'provide a good contact to prevent blisters or burns'.

Burger followed Milgram's procedure and asked the teacher to read out a list of 25 word pairs. The teacher was told that if the learner failed to remember the word pair after being given the first in the pair correctly, an electric shock should be administered using the electric generator in front of them. Each wrong answer would result in a stronger shock being administered. At this point, the confederate revealed a problem with his heart that was detected at a hospital visit.

The learner was shown how to use the electric shock generator and given a 15-volt sample shock. The same four verbal prods from Milgram's study were used in Burger's study and pre-recorded voice feedback grunts from the learner were audible from the 75-volt shock level. At 150 volts, the recording stated 'Ugh. That's all. Get me out of here. I told you I had heart trouble. My heart's starting to bother me now. Get me out of here, please. My heart's starting to bother me. I refuse to go on. Let me out.'

At this point, and after the experimenter used the verbal prods, if the teacher was resistant to continuing, the experiment was ended. The experiment was also forcibly ended at the point where the teacher read out the next instruction following the administering of the 150-volt shock. On finishing the experiment, the experimenter immediately admitted to the teacher that the shocks were not real and the teacher was introduced to the learner to ensure they knew that he was perfectly fine.

Experiment two – Modelled refusal condition

In this variation, all participants followed the same procedure as the baseline condition but with a few minor exceptions. Two confederates were used instead of one. The second confederate posed as a participant, and was the same gender as the real participant. Again, the drawing of roles was rigged and resulted in a learner (confederate), Teacher 1 (a confederate of the study) and Teacher 2, who was a real participant. Teacher 1 took the lead and began the procedure asking the questions and administering shocks while Teacher 2 sat with him/her. At 75 volts, and as scripted, Teacher 1 hesitated after hearing the learner grunt, and at 90 volts Teacher 1 stated 'I don't know about this'. Teacher 1 was prompted by the experimenter, but refused to carry on and pushed his/her chair back from the table. The experimenter would then ask Teacher 2, the real participant, to continue.

Results

Table 1.8 Results from Burger's obedience investigation

Number (%) of participants who stopped	Male	Female	Total
Experiment one – Baseline condition			
Stopped at 150 volts or earlier	6 (33.3)	6 (27.3)	
Went to continue after 150 volts	12 (66.7)	16 (72.7)	28 (70.0)
Experiment two – Modelled refusal condition			
Stopped at 150 volts or earlier	5 (45.5)	6 (31.6)	
Went to continue after 150 volts	6 (54.5)	13 (68.4)	19 (63.3)

In Experiment one, baseline condition, 70 per cent of participants had to be stopped before attempting to continue past 150 volts; a rate that is just lower than Milgram's 82.5 per cent.

In Experiment two, modelled refusal condition, 63.3 per cent went to continue the procedure after 150 volts despite expectations held by Burger and the confederate who withdrew. The results were very similar to the baseline condition.

There was little difference in obedience levels between genders in both experiments. The point at which male and female participants needed the first prod was also similar. Burger then compared the results shown in Table 1.8 with the screening tests of the participants relating to issues of empathy and control. He found little difference between those who stopped and those who continued and their corresponding empathy and control scores. He did find, however, that those who showed reluctance to give the shocks early on in the procedure scored higher on desirability for control in the baseline condition. No difference was found when comparing the modelled refusal condition and base condition to personality scores.

Conclusion

Results found in both experiments are similar to Milgram's research found over 45 years ago. Time and changes in society's culture did not have an effect on obedience levels nor did the refusal of the confederate.

Evaluation

Burger acknowledged the ethical concerns associated with Milgram's original experiments and took several measures to ensure the well-being of the participants in his research. The screening process was rigorous to ensure that participants deemed unsuitable for the study were not used. Participants were informed three times before the experiment that they could leave the study without consequence, to make certain that they understood they had a right to withdraw. Other ethical considerations were also made: participants were only given a 15-volt sample shock rather than the 45 volts given to participants in Milgram's study, and the experimenter in the study was a clinical psychologist instructed to stop the experiment if they detected excessive stress during the procedure. Additionally, the participants were immediately debriefed following the experiment to alleviate any distress or anxiety caused.

Despite these ethical considerations, it still should be considered that the participants involved were deliberately placed in a situation that would cause anxiety, and the verbal prods used by the experimenter effectively removed any previously established right to withdraw, even if only temporarily.

Burger only partially replicated Milgram's study because he did not allow participants to go beyond the 150-volt level due to the ethical concern that they would experience greater amounts of distress beyond this point, as observed in Milgram's study. This is an ethical strength of the study but it can only be assumed that the participants would have continued to obey after 150 volts, as the experiment was stopped at this point. This assumption was based on the fact that the majority of Milgram's participants continued once they had reached this seemingly 'point of no return'. However, we cannot be certain that the participant's involved in Burger's study would have continued to obey.

Compared to Milgram, Burger recruited a more diverse sample of ages and ethnicities, so the findings have greater generalisability. However, similar to Milgram's research, some caution should be maintained when generalising the findings from laboratory research to the real world, particularly the atrocities that have been committed throughout history, which involve many more complex factors than blind obedience to authority. Laboratory research demanding obedience to shock another person based on a word-pair associate task is unlike real-life obedience, which can be a very ordinary experience (complying with the request of a teacher or parent), therefore this research lacks mundane realism.

Rethinking the psychology of tyranny: The BBC prison study (Reicher and Haslam, 2006)

Steve Reicher and Alex Haslam, following a long tradition in social psychology, were interested in explaining the world's history of atrocities, such as the Holocaust and Rwandan genocides. Building on the research of Sherif and Milgram, they sought to replicate another classic experiment conducted by Craig Haney, Curtis Banks, David Jaffe and Philip Zimbardo in 1971 – the Stanford Prison study. In this study, young men were divided into prisoners and guards at a simulated prison in the basement of Stanford University. What emerged from the field study was that the guards conformed to their role and acted brutally towards the prisoners. A two-week experiment was terminated after only six days because of the suffering of the prisoners at the hands of the guards.

The findings of Sherif et al., Milgram, and Haney et al., all suggest that ordinary people are capable of extreme behaviours in particular social situations. However, Reicher and Haslam were quick to point out that this is not always the case and that people are also capable of actively resisting the social influence of others. They pointed out that in the second of the Sherif et al. series of studies on intergroup conflict, the boys refused to compete against one another, and that Milgram found dissent to authority when they had an ally. The prison simulation also showed that prisoners worked together to resist their oppression and resisted the authority of the guards.

Using the understanding that people can be equally compliant and obedient as they are resistant to social influence, the British Broadcasting Company (BBC) *Prison Study* (2006) was set up to partially replicate the Stanford Prison study. The researchers felt that there were several limitations with the original Stanford Prison study, such as a lack of video evidence, and that observational records gathered during the study did not match the conclusions drawn about the participants' psychological states of mind. In particular, Reicher and Haslam maintained that the original study did not clearly show a natural acceptance of the roles adopted by the prisoners and guards, but that these roles were forced by the instructions they were given. In fact, many participants resisted the roles they were assigned.

Aims

In collaboration with the BBC, in 2001, Reicher and Haslam set up their own institution simulation study over a period of eight days. The aim was to simulate an institution that reinforced inequality between groups and to investigate whether inequalities were accepted or resisted. Drawing on the ideas of social identity theory, they wanted to test whether unequal roles were a natural consequence of group formation, or, as the theory suggests, some form of internalisation of the social category to which they are assigned is necessary in order for compliance to occur.

Method

Reicher and Haslam set up an experimental case study to examine the intergroup relations between a dominant and a subordinate group. The institutional setting was created at Elstree Film Studio in London and included prisoner and guard quarters that were separated by a steel mesh fence. The prisoners' quarters had cells that could be locked, showers positioned off a central atrium and an exercise yard, and the guards' quarters had a dormitory, mess room and bathroom.

Participants

The researchers advertised for male participants in national newspapers and leaflets. A total of 332 applicants completed a series of questionnaires used to assess their personality and mental health. In total, 27 men went on to be assessed by a clinical psychologist, following which medical records, police checks and character references for each participant were obtained. A final sample of 15 men were selected for their suitability, representing different ages, social classes and ethnic diversity.

Ethics

Participants recruited for the study were selected after a careful screening process involving clinical, medical and background assessments to ensure that they would not suffer harm or harm other participants. Participants were given information about the study, including that they might experience psychological and physical discomfort and stress, and that they may be locked up and were being watched at all times. The behaviour of the participants was monitored by a clinical psychologist and members of an ethics committee, and security guards were instructed to intervene if any dangerous behaviour was shown. A paramedic was also available at all times. The ethics were approved by the University of Exeter and the BPS.

Procedure

The 15 male participants were randomly assigned to the role of guard or prisoner using a careful matching process. The men were first divided into five groups that matched each other on important dimensions (personality, racism). From each group, one guard was randomly selected and the remaining two participants were assigned the role of prisoner.

The guards were invited to a hotel the evening before the beginning of the study and were given information about the prison timetable, their role to ensure that the prisoner duties were performed, and were asked to draw up a list of prison rules. Although the guards were not given direct instructions on how they should ensure that the prisoners behaved, they were given a list of prisoner rights and told that physical violence would not be tolerated. The guards were escorted to the prison in a van the following morning and briefed about the prison layout, resources and surveillance systems, and given a guard uniform.

Nine prisoners arrived one at a time (the tenth prisoner came to the study later on), had their heads shaved and were given a prisoner uniform with a printed 3-digit number on the T-shirt. The prisoners were informed of the prison rules and their rights.

Manipulations

The guards were informed that their selection was based on their trustworthiness and initiative, but that this was not totally reliable and, in fact, the researchers may have mistakenly assigned one of the prisoners. They asked the guards to be vigilant and look for guard-like characteristics among the prisoners and that correct identification could result in a promotion. This was also announced to the prisoners via loudspeaker. This manipulation was done to encourage the belief that movement between the prisoner and guard roles was possible. Following the promotion of one prisoner to the role of guard, the offer of further promotions was removed. In fact, all prisoners and guards were told that there were no key differences between them and that the groups were now fixed.

Participant 10

The tenth prisoner entered the prison on day five. He was deliberately introduced because he was an experienced trade union representative and the researchers felt that this would bring a different dynamic to the prisoner group, in particular the trade union ideologies of negotiation, equal rights, illegitimacy of the institutional norms that had been established and challenge to authority.

Data collection

The behaviour of the participants was monitored using visual and audio recordings, and their psychological state was assessed using daily questionnaires to measure social identification, right-wing attitudes, rule compliance, citizenship and depression. Levels of cortisol, a stress hormone, were assessed daily through saliva swabs.

Results

Phase one

The prisoners were dissatisfied with their subordinate positions within the institution, and as individuals within the group sought promotion to become a guard, no shared sense of identity was established. When the possibility of promotion was retracted, the prisoners began to develop a sense of shared identity and solidarity against the guards.

The guards' behaviour went against prediction. Instead of forming a group identity based on their superior roles, they were actually reluctant to use their status against the prisoners. This resulted in a lack of role identification and no shared identity was formed.

Using the measures of social identity, the researchers found that the guards identified with each other and their role on the first day, but their social identity scores fell once they had to implement a routine of discipline. In contrast, the social identity scores of the prisoners continually rose, particularly after the promotion was retracted. This also affected the levels of compliance within the groups, the prisoners becoming increasingly reluctant to follow the orders of the guards and becoming increasingly dominant and undermining. The guards' attempt to reassert authority failed and this resulted in decreases in self-efficacy and an increase in depression. On day six, the prisoners broke out of their cells and occupied the guards' quarters; the guards' regime had completely broken down.

Phase two

Following the breakdown of guard rule, the participants initially established a commune environment of equal governance. This led to a reduction in hostility between the groups and a new whole-group identity being formed. However, this was short-lived, and the prisoners who were active in challenging the regime during Phase one became increasingly dissatisfied with the new one. These original dissenters began to break the commune rules and plotted to destroy the new social order. With no rules to cope with such dissent, the new commune system was under threat. Some of the participants formulated a new social order that was harsher than the original prisoner–guard hierarchy, which was met with despondency and minimal resistance by the original founders of the commune. Interestingly during this time, levels of authoritarianism rose in all participants.

With this shift towards right-wing authoritarianism, the researchers decided to stop the study at midday on day eight because any new regime would have probably involved direct force by the new self-appointed guards.

Social identity

The researchers used daily measures of social identity to understand whether the groups were categorising themselves as a group and identifying with group norms. This would establish whether social identity theory (that individual members need to identify with a group) was a better explanation for intergroup hostility compared to mere group formation.

Social identity was measured using a range of questions such as:

- 'I feel strong ties with the prisoners/guards.'
- 'I identify with the prisoners/guards.'
- 'I feel solidarity with the prisoners/guards.'

The participants rated their responses on a 7-point Likert scale (1 – not at all, 7 – extremely).

Conclusions

Reicher and Haslam suggest that people do not inevitably conform to the roles they have been assigned, but a range of factors determine whether or not people identify with their role and the social identity of their group. As such, the mere creation of inequitable groups does not naturally lead to prejudice and intergroup conflict. This does seem to support social identity theory, which suggests that people need to internalise group norms before adopting its social identity.

In addition, when groups fail to form a social identity they are more ready to accept the ideals of a different social group, even one that is more tyrannical, and submit to them. This suggests that oppression can be borne out of conditions of powerlessness and lack of identity. This mirrors the social conditions of Nazi Germany, where extreme right-wing views were adopted by citizens that were confused and disenchanted.

Evaluation

The simulation study can be criticised on many grounds, which the authors acknowledge. Importantly, the participants were fully aware that their behaviour was being recorded and monitored, which could have resulted in artificial behaviour in both the guards and the prisoners. It is not socially desirable to be an oppressor but it is desirable to be a rebel. This could probably account for the reluctance of the guards to exert authority and punish the prisoners, and that the prisoners were quick to dissent. This was probably exacerbated by the knowledge that their behaviour would be shown on national television. It was also the case that the participants' behaviour could have been guided by expectation; they were expected to rebel and form a new social order. Such demand characteristics can seriously affect the validity of the findings. Although the participants could have been 'acting', it would have been harder for them to fake the psychometric measures taken daily during the study. It would also be difficult to understand why they would have suggested a more inequitable social order at the end of the study.

The study can also be criticised as a small sample of men were selected. Some of these men had particularly strong personalities and this may have influenced the dynamics of the group and created dissent among the prisoners initially, and dissent against the commune in Phase two. Although the groups were matched on important personality traits, not all could be controlled or were equally distributed between the prisoner and guard groups. Although the researchers accept that individual differences could have altered the behaviour of the participants, they claim that changes in personality dimensions and attitudes recorded throughout the study could not be explained by the criticism. In particular, individual differences alone cannot explain why rebellion did not occur until after the promotion from prisoner to guard was retracted. If a strong dissenting personality was responsible for rebellion, surely this would have occurred at the start of the study, and not have waited until day four.

Another criticism levelled at the study was that it failed to manufacture any real situations of inequality between the prisoner and guard groups. Despite setting up the environment to favour the guards, with better food and housing conditions, the guards had no real power of authority to exert over the prisoners. The researchers acknowledge this, but insist that the guards did have real power in terms of the rewards and punishments that they could offer, but their failed guard group identity resulted in them not agreeing how to yield such power.

A strength of the study was that there were multiple ways of assessing the behaviour and mental states of the participants that meant they could be sure their experimental manipulations did have an effect on the behaviour of the participants. It was significant that the offer and retraction of the promotion had a direct causal effect on the behaviour and psychological state of individuals and groups in the study.

A further strength was that the diversity of the participants was greater than the sample used by Milgram, therefore the findings have greater generalisability to the ordinary man.

There are significant ethical issues associated with creating groups in a situation where one group can exert power and have the capacity to sanction a subordinate group. Reicher and Haslam did use a range of safeguards to ensure that the experimental procedures were approved by two ethical committees and that the participants were monitored at all times. Their selection process was rigorous and key figures were able to stop the study at any point if they had concerns. The researchers themselves stopped the study before any escalation of threat occurred.

Individual differences in ideological attitudes and prejudice: evidence from peer-report data (Cohrs et al., 2012)

Christopher Cohrs, Nicole Kämpfe-Hargrave and Rainer Riemann (2012) investigated which personality dimensions were good predictors of prejudice. Since the authoritarian personality was suggested to be a personality type associated with prejudice, significant research has gone into identifying which aspects of personality are more closely associated with prejudice. In particular, the five personality dimensions of **neuroticism, extraversion, openness to experience, agreeableness** and **conscientiousness** have been investigated to see whether any of these traits predispose people to develop certain ideological attitudes that result in prejudice. The ideological attitudes of right-wing authoritarianism (RWA) and social dominance orientation (SDO) have been suggested to be associated with certain personalities that can predict prejudice.

However, there have been serious questions raised about how research has made such associations between personality traits, ideological attitudes and prejudice. In particular, the over-reliance of such research on self-report methods. The problem with investigating traits that can be seen as negative, such as prejudice and aggression, is that people do not wish to be seen as having such traits or attitudes because they are not socially desirable. Cohrs and his colleagues set about investigating whether the personality and attitude variables correlated, using both self-reports and peer reports. The use of peer reports was used to cross-check the self-report data as peers' reports tend to be less susceptible to social desirability bias.

Ideological attitudes

Right-wing authoritarianism (RWA): people who are rigid and inflexible in their thinking and behaviour. They dislike change and are not willing to consider the opinions and values of others. They believe that the world is a dangerous place and this results in a desire for stability, security and group cohesion. These people are aggressive to subordinates and submissive to authority figures. They tend to be prejudiced.

Social dominance orientation (SDO): these people are ruthless and tough-minded. They are competitive and work towards their own interests, therefore they desire superiority and dominance associated with an ideology of prejudice.

Previous research suggested that RWA was associated with openness to experience and conscientiousness, and that SDO was associated with agreeableness.

Using a dual-process model of prejudice, Cohrs et al. believed that personality traits and ideological attitudes both mediate prejudice. In particular, they were interested to see if there was a correlation between these factors and prejudice. In addition, they wanted to test the reliability of self-report methods by correlating them with peer reports.

Taking it further

Here are some examples of questions used in the questionnaires.

Prejudice towards foreigners:

1. Germans should not marry foreigners.

2. Foreigners enrich our culture. [−]

Prejudice towards people with disabilities:

1. If I find [he/she finds] out that friends of mine are gay or lesbian, I break [he/she breaks] off the friendship.

2. If somebody tells me [him/her] that he/she is homosexual, I [he/she] can handle this well. [−]

Notice how both question 2s have [−] after them. Although participants could not see this, it was used to reverse the scoring. This means that, on a scale of 1–7, a score of 1 will be converted to a score of 7, or a score of 2 will be converted to a score of 6 for the purpose of analysis.

Consider why reverse-scoring might be a useful strategy in questionnaire construction. How can this be used to evaluate the questionnaire that the researchers used?

Aims

The general aims were to see if the previously established correlations between the five big personality traits, RWA, SDO and prejudice could be found using self-reports, and whether these correlations could be validated by using peer reports.

Method

Study one

Opportunity sampling was used to gather participants from the German population by asking neighbours and acquaintances of the authors to take part. Participants were asked to complete a self-report questionnaire and another questionnaire to give to a peer (acquaintance) to complete about the participant. The questionnaires were fully anonymised.

Study one was focused on measuring prejudice such as negative attitudes to homosexuality, disability and foreigners. The returned questionnaires were screened and those participants indicating that they were homosexual, not of German nationality and lived with disability were excluded from the sample. This left 193 (125 female and 64 male) participants, and their associated peers (97 males and 95 females), who knew the participant they were paired with well.

The participants self-rated their personality and attitudes on modified versions of the personality questionnaire, RWA and SDO scales, and their peers rated the participant. They were also given a questionnaire that measured their prejudice towards gay, disabled and foreign people.

Study two

Half of the sample was gathered from the Jena Twin Registry of multiple births and half from volunteers approached via calling them or approaching them at 'twin clubs'. One twin was given a self-report questionnaire and another questionnaire was given to the other twin and a peer (acquaintance) to complete about the participant. A sample of 424 was achieved, but only 371 of these had both peer reports available and 53 only one peer report available.

The participant and their peers completed further modified versions of the personality, RWA and SDO scales. They also received a questionnaire about gay, disabled and foreign people that was adapted from Study one to include specific references to 'Turks' (largest non-native group in Germany), mental disability and wheelchair users.

Results

Study two

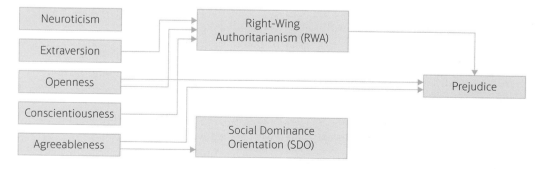

Figure 1.7 Links found between the five big personality traits and right-wing authoritarianism, social dominance orientation and prejudice

They found that associations between personality traits, RWA, SDO and prejudice were similar to those found in previous research. In particular, that the less open to experience (openness), the higher the RWA score; the higher the conscientiousness, the higher the RWA score; the lower the agreeableness, the higher the SDO score; and that RWA correlated positively with prejudice. The peer reports also correlated with the self-reports, although not perfectly, which demonstrated that self-reports were a valid tool for investigating personality, attitudes and prejudice. The two peer reports used in Study two seemed to reduce social desirability bias.

Conclusion

Both self- and peer-reported data suggested openness and conscientiousness attitudes predicted RWA, and RWA predicted prejudice, which was consistent with previous research. It was additionally detected that agreeableness and openness to experience were predictors of prejudice, using both self- and two peer reports, which had been undetected by previous research in this area, perhaps due to social desirability effects. However, SDO did not predict prejudice, but agreeableness did.

The researchers conclude that peer reports are of value when studying personality and prejudice as they can reduce the effects of social desirability.

Evaluation

This research used a very large and diverse sample of participants across both studies, and although they were gathered largely by opportunity, the degree to which they can be generalised to the whole German population is reasonably strong. However, as the data was only gathered from German natives it cannot be generalised to non-native Germans or other cultures around the world.

The purpose of the study was to test whether self-reported personality, attitudes and prejudice were susceptible to social desirability effects. This was controlled by using one or two peers that knew the participant well. This controlled for social desirability as the rate of agreement between participant and peer was assessed when the results were analysed. They also controlled for social desirability effects by asking participants to answer the questions as honestly as possible and return them anonymously.

Because every participant received the same questionnaire in each of the studies, the method was standardised, which makes it possible to replicate to check for reliable findings. They also controlled for specific experiences of prejudice and excluded participants who were non-native, disabled or homosexual. The questions used in the questionnaires were closed, Likert-style questions, which means that the participants' answers are not open to interpretation during qualitative analysis, but it did mean that the participants' answers were restricted to preset responses.

As with any individual difference/dispositional explanation of prejudice, this research can be criticised for ignoring social and cultural explanations of prejudice and instead focusing on personality, which cannot explain widespread prejudices that have occurred throughout history.

WIDER ISSUES AND DEBATES

How psychological knowledge has changed over time

The study of prejudice and theories offered to explain it have changed significantly over the past century. Until the 1920s, race theories were suggested that seemed to legitimise the inequalities that existed between the black and white races. The theories endorsed white supremacy and black inferiority. During the 1920s and 1930s, with the aftermath of the First World War and the rise of the US civil rights movement in the 1950s, a shift in attitude occurred that questioned the legitimacy of racial inequality and instead focused on conceptualising racism as unjust and unfair.

There was a significant shift in social psychology during the 1960s and 1970s to explain behaviour using social and cultural explanations. Research into prejudice became focused on group dynamics. During the 1970s, psychologists began to question whether groups and social conditions could be the whole explanation for prejudice, and suggested that perhaps group processes in interaction with underlying dispositional characteristics could provide a better explanation. With the rise of the cognitive approach, social psychologists became interested in underlying cognitive structures that could be used to explain stereotypes. Today, a more integrative approach is taken.

This section will describe an example of the key issue of how our knowledge of social psychology can be used to explain heroism. However, you can choose your own key issue and relate it to theories, concepts and research used in social psychology.

1.4 Key questions

Learning outcomes

In this section, you will learn about:

- one key issue and its importance to society today
- concepts, theories and research used in social psychology to explain the key issue.

How can social psychology be used to explain heroism?

Heroism is something that is deeply valued across cultures, but how exactly do we define a hero? A heroic act is something that is brave or courageous, a small or large act of kindness, where someone places themselves at risk for another. So far in this topic, we have discussed social influence in a fairly negative manner – destructive obedience to authority, explanations of why we are prejudiced. The same principles, however, can be 'turned on their head' to uncover what situations and characteristics can be used to explain and indeed encourage heroism.

The Heroic Imagination Project, founded by social psychologist Philip Zimbardo, maintains that heroism has four key elements:

- it is voluntary
- it is done to help people or a community in need
- it involves some type of risk – physical, mental and sometimes death
- it is done without the need for compensation of any kind.

Zimbardo founded the Heroic Imagination Project after spending much of his academic career researching the negative aspects of social influence (conformity, obedience and the bystander effect). He has now established a foundation that teaches individuals how to resist the social forces that influence our behaviour in a negative way, and to refocus our behaviour into positive social action. In particular, the programmes teach individuals how to resist conformity and obedience that could result in negative consequence and recognise when and how to act in more prosocial ways. By understanding the tendencies that we all share to being obedient and conformist, we can actively resist such pressures.

As obedience, conformity and prejudice can be explained by situational pressures, rather than dispositional causes, Zimbardo suggests that being a hero is not a unique quality that an individual possesses, but behaviour that anyone can display. He explains that if we teach people to be aware of 'universal human tendencies' that this can lead to individual empowerment. These tendencies are automatic and can be useful, but in situations that are challenging, we over-rely on these human tendencies, which often results in poor decision making. Milgram's research is a good example of an individual being placed in a stressful situation, and the natural default behaviour was to obey the instructions of an authority figure. Understanding this tendency can help an individual to recognise that it can lead to poor decision making and give them the opportunity to consider alternatives.

Universal social tendencies

There are five recognised universal, socially-based tendencies:

1 We have a tendency to react automatically to things that we are not paying attention to. This can lead us to react in dangerous ways and it means that we do not consider other choices that we could make.

2 We have a tendency to rely on labels and categories to make quick judgements of ourselves and others. These judgements may be ill-founded and our quick response to them can be difficult to reverse.

3 We have a tendency to rely on others to help us interpret what is going on around us rather than try to interpret events ourselves. This means that we can over-rely on others and not act ourselves, or misinterpret a situation.

4 We have a tendency to seek acceptance from others and try to avoid rejection. This can mean that we fail to speak out against someone for fear of being ostracised and we go along with the crowd.

5 We have a tendency to believe that we cannot change, which can result in low motivation to change anything.

Links to concepts, research and theory in social psychology

Obedience

Zimbardo draws on Milgram's research into obedience to describe how people can do harmful things at the instructions of an authority figure. This 'natural tendency' to blindly follow orders was demonstrated in Milgram's studies on obedience, when 65 per cent of participants were willing to give a harmful shock to an innocent man. Zimbardo also draws on real-life evidence of obedience and other research that demonstrates how we can be blindly obedient.

Prejudice

Drawing on research using Tajfel's minimal group paradigm (Elliott, in Aronson and Osherow, 1980), Zimbardo describes the natural tendency for humans to become a member of an assigned group, which results in in-group favouritism and negative out-group bias. This division creates a basis for judging others less favourably than our own group and creates prejudice. This was demonstrated in Jane Elliott's blue eyes/brown eyes study, as she divided members of her class into two groups pitted against each other, resulting in prejudice and discrimination.

Bystander behaviour

Zimbardo describes the bystander effect, which is where we tend to avoid personal responsibility to take action when we are in a crowd. In 1964, a young woman called Kitty Genovese was murdered late one night. Despite the assailant returning to attack her on many occasions and her screams, her neighbours only yelled from a window; no one came to her aid. The bystander effect was extensively researched by Bibb Latané following this case, leading to the theory of 'diffusion of responsibility'.

Heroism

Understanding the social influences that serve to prevent us from becoming heroic, Zimbardo developed an educational package to help us become aware of these social forces and be more mindful. The aim is to:

- try to assess a situation rather than be blind to it and give automatic responses

- understand social influence and the dangers of blind obedience, conformity, prejudice and bystander effect.

Taking it further

Visit the Heroic Imagination Project on the Internet and view the video clips that demonstrate real-life obedience and other obedience studies that have been conducted in more natural situations, for example marrying a stranger.

Taking it further

Other social processes and theories can be used to explain why we do not display heroism. For example, social impact theory, social power theory, agency theory and social identity theory can all be used to explain how we may not be heroic. Awareness of these ideas, however, can be used to encourage heroism, too. Read through this section again and develop a heroism project of your own.

Evaluation

Zimbardo's heroism project can be seen as a positive force in society, building awareness and encouraging positive social action. However, there has been little research published that has been able to operationally define heroism and a lack of empirical evidence to suggest that it works. Some critics have suggested that it can involve more harm than good as people may place themselves in situations of danger in order to become heroic.

Zimbardo's project is research based, and an education programme has been undertaken in a school in San Francisco to see whether the heroism strategies effect changes in attitudes, beliefs and behaviour. These findings are yet to be published.

Research into social influence both supports and goes against the principles on which the Heroic Imagination Project is founded. There is plenty of research that suggests our behaviour is guided by social forces, and also research that suggests we have innate characteristics associated with prejudice and obedience. Such personality theories suggest that we cannot just train a person to become a hero, as Zimbardo claims, because it is part of our personality. However, recent research (Walker et al., 2010) investigated the characteristics of people who had received awards for acts of bravery. They found that one-off heroes were no different from ordinary people, which suggests that heroism is not necessarily a personality trait, although the same research found that long-time heroes did possess personality traits that distinguished them from others.

Some types of heroism can be trained while others depend on the unique characteristics of some individuals.

1.5 Practical investigation

Learning outcomes:

In this section, you will learn about:

- designing and conducting a questionnaire to gather both quantitative and qualitative data on a topic in social psychology

- planning and constructing your questionnaire(s), including sampling decisions and ethical considerations

- collecting and presenting your data using appropriate tables, graphs and descriptive statistics

- conducting a thematic analysis on your qualitative data and drawing conclusions

- the strengths and weaknesses of your questionnaire

- reporting conventions to document your procedure, results and discussion.

You have learned about various experiments in social psychology, but as you know, these experiments are ethically not permissible to replicate because they deliberately cause anxiety or embarrassment. Instead, you must conduct a questionnaire that investigates a topic that you have studied to ask for people's opinions and beliefs about their own or others' behaviour. For this example practical investigation, we will be using a questionnaire to gather information about gender and obedience, specifically whether men or women are viewed as more obedient by others. You may wish to conduct your own practical investigation on a different topic in social psychology or adapt this title to investigate how males and females perceive their own obedience.

Before you begin planning your practical investigation, you should review the methodology section in this topic to familiarise yourself with key terms and concepts concerning questionnaires.

Aim

An aim is a general area of interest that the questionnaire is concerned with. In this practical example, the aim of the study is to investigate perceptions of gender differences in obedience. Aims tend to be based on previous research in the area, so this aim is derived from the fact that obedience research tends to predict that there is no difference in actual levels of obedience between men and women, but that females tend to be distressed when they have to comply with orders that they would not voluntarily choose to do.

Before you decide on your study aim, it is important to do a review of the background theory and research into the topic so that your aim is well founded.

Alternative hypotheses

Your practical investigation should have an alternative hypothesis. This is a prediction of what is likely to be found by your investigation based on what has been found in previous studies. Your alternative hypothesis may predict the direction of difference that is likely to be found, in which case it is known as a directional hypothesis. However, if the previous research is mixed or unclear, it may not be possible to predict the direction of difference that you will find, therefore you will need to write a non-directional hypothesis.

Link

The use of directional and non-directional hypotheses can also be found in Topic 2: *Cognitive psychology*. See Section 2.2 Methods.

Directional and non-directional hypotheses examples

In this study, a directional hypotheses will be proposed.

There will be a difference in perceived levels of obedience between men and women.

- This is non-directional because, although experimental research suggests that males are not more or less obedient than females, social norms dictate that females will be either more compliant because they are considered to be less assertive than men or less compliant because they do not want to cause harm to another. This means that perceived levels of obedience could be higher or lower for females compared to males.

- However, if the study was interested in understanding the emotional responses to obedience experienced by males and females, a directional example would be more likely.

Females will be perceived to be more distressed than males if they are ordered to harm another person.

- This hypothesis is directional because both experimental evidence and social norms would predict that females will experience greater distress at harming another at the orders of an authority figure.

Quantitative and qualitative data

For this practical investigation both quantitative and qualitative data collection will be centred around the first hypothesis, which states that there will be a difference in perceived levels of obedience in males and females. The first half of the questionnaire will be designed to consist of a series of closed questions related to perceptions of male and female obedience. Scores will be totalled so that each participant has a rating of perceived obedience for men and women.

Maths tip

It is very important that you consider the type of scoring method that you are going to use and how your data is analysed while constructing your questions and designing the format of your questionnaire. It is often the case that lots of closed questions lead to copious amounts of single raw data figures and bar graphs. This can be unhelpful and time-consuming when it comes to analysis.

Examples of quantitative data gathered through closed questions

1 If a policeman asked a passer-by to pick up litter, who do you think would be more likely to comply with the request?
   man/woman

2 How likely would a man be to agree to make a colleague at work redundant if asked to by his boss?
   very unlikely   unlikely   neutral   likely   very likely

3 A female student is asked by her teacher to photocopy a pile of work, but she does not have the time. How likely is the student to say no to her teacher?
   very unlikely   unlikely   neutral   likely   very likely

Closed questions produce quantitative data, which is relatively easy to analyse. You will need to assign a numerical score for each answer. For example, the answers to the second question can be given a score of 1–5: 1 for very unlikely, 2 for unlikely, 3 for neutral, 4 for likely and 5 for very likely. This means that the higher the score, the greater the perception of obedience. However, you may want to consider response bias, which may occur if your questions are not carefully constructed. You can control this to an extent by question reversal. This means that some of the questions are rephrased to reverse the emphasis. In the examples above, the second question asks about obedience, and the third question asks about dissent. In order to get an overall score for obedience, the score for the third question should be reversed (a score of 1 will be reversed to be 5, 2 will be 4, and so on).

Qualitative data will be gathered by asking participants to complete a story. A story completion method is used to detect underlying attitudes that people may have without directly asking them a question. Typically, a researcher writes the beginning of a story, in this case about obedience, and the participant is asked to finish it. Qualitative analysis can then be done on the themes written about by the participant as they have finished off the story.

Qualitative story completion task

James and Olivia were told to tidy their bedrooms by their mother. Neither James nor Olivia wanted to tidy their rooms but wanted to go out to play instead. Their mother shouted at them and told them that they would not be allowed to go out to play unless their rooms were tidy. Mother put James in his room and Olivia in her room…

Please complete the story, detailing what both James and Olivia do.

You may wish to use a simpler way to gather qualitative data, by using open-ended questions for example.

Examples of open-ended questions

1 In your view, explain whether you think males or females would be more obedient in their workplace.

2 Soldiers often have to comply with the demands of their superior officers, frequently to do things that they would not voluntarily do. Based on this, explain whether you think that soldiers should be male or female.

Sampling decisions

Before you consider which sampling method to choose, you will need to consider the target population that you wish to investigate; this can be the general population or a specific population such as family and friends. Because the aim of this example practical is to investigate perceptions of obedience and gender, it will be important to have a fairly diverse target population with an equal number of males and females. This is because perceptions of gender differences will vary according to sex, age and background. You may choose to try to control for these individual differences by using a random sample from a diverse target population, although this may be difficult and time-consuming. To keep it simple, this practical investigation will use a stratified sampling technique to ensure a proportionate distribution of males and females in a student population.

Stratified sampling technique

The process of gathering a sample using a stratified sampling technique for this practical investigation:

- target population = sixth form college students

- sample required = 50

- gather all the names of students that attend a sixth form college

- calculate the number of males and females in the target population (for example, 55% female, 45% male)

- place all the female names in a hat and pick out 27 (55% of 50 is 27.5 – but we cannot have half a person)

- place all the male names in a hat and pick out 23 (45% of 50 is 22.7 – but we cannot have 0.7 of a person).

You may wish to consider using a simpler sampling technique such as opportunity or volunteer sampling by asking family and friends or placing an advert in a sixth-form common room.

Ethical issues

When designing a questionnaire and considering how and when it will be distributed, a number of specific ethical considerations should be made.

- Has verbal and written consent been obtained by every participant?

- Has the nature of the questionnaire been disclosed? If not, what safeguards do you have in place to protect and debrief participants?

- Are participants aware of their right to withdraw?

- Are the questionnaires anonymous so that confidentiality is assured?

- Do the questions violate participant privacy?

- Are the questions in the questionnaire socially sensitive or offensive?

- Have you put safeguards in place to safely store and destroy the questionnaires after the data has been analysed?

- Will participants have access to their results and the full report once it has been written?

- Have you considered risk management in psychological research?

It is critical that these ethical issues are addressed, particularly the way in which questions are phrased as they may inadvertently cause embarrassment or distress that you may have overlooked. It is sensible to conduct a pilot study of the questionnaire on a small sample of people, family and friends, to ensure that any ethical issues are detected and that the questions are clear and understandable.

Design decisions taken in this experiment

Aim: to investigate perception of gender differences and obedience

Alternative hypothesis (H_1): there will be a difference in perceived levels of obedience between men and women.

Sampling technique: stratified

Procedure: questionnaires to be distributed and completed individually

Ethical issues: consent, privacy, confidentiality, protection from harm

---

Sample brief

Thank you for agreeing to take part in a questionnaire for my psychology investigation. I am interested in how you view obedience in certain situations, so the questions that you will need to answer will be based on incidents involving someone giving orders. For the majority of questions, you will need to decide whether you think a person will obey these orders. You will not be asked any personal questions and you are free to refuse to answer any or all of the questions.

In the second half of the questionnaire, you will be given the beginning of a story that you will be asked to complete.

Please be as honest as possible in answering the questions and please complete the questionnaire on your own so that you are not influenced by others.

It will take you approximately 20 minutes to complete the questionnaire and it will be completely anonymous; you will not have to give your name, only your gender, and you can return the questionnaire to me in the pre-paid postal envelope. Your results and a full write-up of the findings will be available on request. After one week the data will be extracted from your questionnaire response and your questionnaire will be destroyed.

Analysis of quantitative data

Once you have gathered your questionnaires, you will need to begin your qualitative and quantitative analysis. Your closed questions will give you the quantitative data that you can present in tables and graphs, and can be summarised using descriptive statistics.

Table 1.9 An example data table using extract data from Likert-style questions

Participant	Score for perception of male obedience (total)	Score for perception of female obedience (total)
1	25	35
2	20	34
3	14	27
4	22	29
5	19	33
6	17	24
7	21	27
8	21	30
9	18	32

> **Sample size**
>
> A small sample size has been shown for the purpose of this example. It is important to note that the larger the sample size, the more meaningful the analysis will be.

From the data shown in Table 1.9, there is a clear difference in participants' perceptions of male and female obedience, the perception being that females will be more obedient. However, to see this trend more clearly, descriptive statistics should be used.

Descriptive statistics

Table 1.10 An example of descriptive statistics

	Male obedience	Female obedience
Mean perception of obedience ($\bar{x}$)	19.7	30.1
Mode obedience score	21	27
Median obedience score	21	30
Range	11	11
Standard deviation ($\sigma\bar{x}$)	3.16	3.68

The data in Table 1.10 shows a clear difference between participants' perceptions of male and female obedience. Females are believed to be far more obedient than men, and this is consistent in all of the measures of central tendency. The range and standard deviation suggest that the rate of agreement between participants about their perceptions of gender and obedience are relatively similar; that is, there is equivalent variation in perceived obedience scores. With quite a high range, it suggests that there is a reasonably large variation in both perceived male and female obedience scores.

Graphical representation

Any graphical representation of a data set should be meaningful, and take account of the type of data gathered. We can use a bar chart to illustrate the mean score of perceived obedience clearly.

Qualitative data analysis

In this example practical investigation we used a story completion task to gather qualitative data. The first stage of qualitative analysis involves reading the story endings and making a note of any themes that emerge.

Thematic analysis

James and Olivia were told to tidy their bedrooms by their mother. Neither James nor Olivia wanted to tidy their rooms but wanted to go out to play instead. Their mother shouted at them and told them that they would not be allowed to go out to play unless their rooms were tidy. Mother put James in his room and Olivia in her room…

Please complete the story on a separate piece of paper, detailing what both James and Olivia do.

Participant 1

'James was in his room but did not want to tidy up, so he played on his game console instead. Olivia went to her room and tidied away some of her toys, but she was mad, so she did not tidy them all away. James was told off by his mother again and he eventually tidied away some of his toys, however, he stuffed most of them underneath his bed.'

Participant 2

'Olivia went to her room and tidied away all of her toys. She put everything away and then went to help James with his bedroom.'

Participant 3

'James had a tantrum and refused to tidy his bedroom. His sister started tidying her room, but then got bored and decided to shout at her brother. Mum told them both off again, and they both went to their rooms to tidy up.'

Participant 4

'Olivia cried and eventually tidied her room. James shouted and banged his door. Eventually both children tidied their bedrooms, but James was sullen the whole afternoon.'

Key questions to consider

- Is the study ethical?
- Can you generalise the findings to others/ different cultures/ different eras?
- Is the study reliable?
- Is the study carried out in a natural or artificial environment?
- Is the task ordinary?
- Are the findings useful in real life?
- Is the research valid?
- Is there any conflicting evidence from other research?

Not all of these questions will be relevant to your questionnaire, so be selective and pick the strongest comments to make.

Using the story endings, there seem to be themes of resistance, obedience and protest. These themes could be further subdivided into types of resistance, obedience and protest, as shown in Table 1.11.

Table 1.11 Thematic analysis

Themes	Sub themes	Tally/comments
Resistance	Refusal to tidy	I – James had a tantrum
	Not doing a good job	I – Olivia did not tidy them all away I – James stuffed toys under his bed
	Doing something else instead	I – James played games console
Obedience	Tidying room	I – Olivia tidied all her toys (and went to help James) I – Olivia eventually tidied her toys away
Protest	Crying	I – Olivia cried I – James was sullen the whole afternoon
	Shouting	I – Olivia shouted at her brother
	Hitting/banging	I – James banged his door

From the thematic analysis (Table 1.11) it can be seen that there were two instances of clear obedience, both shown by the female (100 per cent), although the amount of protest was equal for both the male and female. Most resistance was put up by the male (75 per cent). Therefore we can conclude from this simple thematic analysis that there is a perception that males are more likely to resist being obedient and both males and females may protest to being given orders, but that females will be more likely to comply.

Evaluation

It is important to consider both the strengths and weaknesses of the practical investigation.

Strengths

By asking participants about other people's levels of obedience, they are less likely to display social desirability in their responses because it is not directly about them. If the questions related directly to the participant's own obedience, they may have answered dishonestly to make themselves appear either compliant, or non-compliant (as this may be seen as a desirable trait in their social group). By using the story completion method, this practical investigation was able to tap into underlying beliefs about male and female obedience without asking participants about it directly; this raises the validity of the questionnaire.

The questionnaire used in this practical example gathered 50 responses, which is quite a large sample to generalise to others from. This is a strength of questionnaires in general, because a high quantity can be distributed and returned. Although, you should be mindful that response rates can be low for questionnaires as people may not have the time to complete them.

Weaknesses

Because each question concerned either male or female obedience, the aim of the study was perhaps quite obvious. This could have resulted in participants answering in a way that they thought the researcher was looking for in the investigation. This may account for the high perceived levels of obedience in females, not males, because social norms would suggest that males are less compliant. Generalisability may also be an issue as only students were used in the sample, therefore the findings may not apply to the whole population as perceptions of obedience may change over time and place.

Suggestions for improvement

Because we were not using an established questionnaire for perceptions of obedience, the questionnaire was not tried and tested for reliability. Many questionnaires, such as those established by Adorno et al. (1950) and Cohrs et al. (2012), discussed earlier in this section, have been tried and tested, so it may be useful to check the reliability of your questionnaire using a test-retest method or split-half technique. A test-retest method would involve asking the same participants to complete the questionnaire again at a later date, although this could be time-consuming. A quicker way to test the reliability of your questionnaire would be to use a split-half procedure. This will involve dividing your questionnaire into two halves and cross checking the scores obtained in the first half and comparing them to the second half. If the scores match, the construct being tested is more likely to be reliable.

Writing up the report

In order to present your practical investigation in a conventional format for psychology, you will need to follow the 'Conventions of report writing'. You can find more information about this in the Introduction.

Conventions of report writing

Abstract: a summary of the background theory/research, aims, hypotheses, method, results and discussion. This is a short paragraph overview of the entire report.

Introduction: an overview of related theories and research in the topic area. The introduction provides a rationale for the current investigation that links prior research to the study aims and hypotheses.

Method: a detailed account of the participants, sampling method, apparatus, procedure, controls and ethical issues.

Results: a detailed account of the data gathered and its analysis using descriptive statistics and graphical representations of the findings.

Discussion: conclusions drawn from the results analysis, reference to prior research, strengths, weaknesses and possible improvements for future research.

1.6 Issues and debates (A level only)

In this section, you will learn about issues and debates relevant to social psychology. You will have already noticed that issues and debates have been mentioned throughout this topic. This section will draw together the main themes and ideas related to the social approach as a whole.

Ethics

During the 1950s and 1960s, social psychologists conducted experiments into prejudice and obedience that would be considered to be ethically and morally reprehensible by today's ethical guidelines. As such, there has been little experimental research conducted, and no direct replications of these studies have been conducted without significant modification to control for ethical issues.

Inherent in obedience research is the risk of causing psychological harm and the removal of a participant's right to withdraw, as participants are gradually ordered to comply with requests to harm another. Similarly, prejudice research also creates the potential for psychological harm as groups are pitted against one another in a host of situations designed to encourage conflict.

We should be aware of the specific ethical issues concerned with research in this area, and also consider the reasons why these issues were necessary to create conditions in which obedience and prejudice could be studied. While researchers may justify the ethical problems with their experiments, often in terms of the results they achieved, it does not excuse the harm that was caused.

Practical issues in the design and implementation of research

There are many issues concerning the design and implementation of obedience research, often creating the ethical problems inherent in such research. One significant practical issue in obedience research is demand characteristics; if participants are aware of the aims of the research, they are unlikely to display natural behaviour. Deception is often used to prevent demand characteristics from occurring, and significant effort has been exerted in disguising research aims. Consider Milgram's obedience research. He deceived his participants by recruiting them under the guise of a memory and learning experiment, used a confederate actor, rigged a lottery for assigning the teacher and learner roles, faked electrocution and the confederate's responses to being shocked, and even gave a sample shock to reinforce the ruse. This elaborate methodology, he felt, ensured that participants believed that they were giving real shocks to a real person.

Prejudice research has its own practical issues, in that people tend to mask their prejudices, particularly in today's social and cultural climate. This results in attempts to measure prejudice being affected by social desirability bias; the tendency for people to respond in a way that society deems more acceptable or which fits better with social norms. Questionnaires that directly ask about prejudiced beliefs can often be criticised for not being able to tap into prejudiced attitudes. Additionally, prejudice today is more ambiguous, less obvious and often too subtle to be detected by questionnaires.

A range of validity and reliability assessments are necessary to ensure that questionnaires accurately tap into prejudice. Test-retest methods are used to ensure that the prejudice being measured is consistent over time, split-half techniques are used to assess the validity of the questionnaire in measuring prejudice and construct validity is validated using other measures, such as peer reports (see Cohrs et al., 2012). Correlations between different measures of prejudice and within the questionnaires themselves often involve complicated analysis, but have resulted in a series of robust questionnaires being created to accurately assess prejudiced attitudes (see Fiske and North, 2014).

Reductionism

Although the endeavours of social psychology are to avoid being reductionist, many theories can be criticised for focusing on specific data drawn from their research to explain complex human social behaviours. In particular, social impact theory (Latané, 1981) can be criticised for developing what can only be described as an equation to calculate how people will behave under certain social conditions. However, the theory does not take account of how the social conditions and individual interact with one another. Ignoring the interrelation between individual and social factors can be considered reductionist.

Dispositional/personality explanations of prejudice and obedience can also be considered to be reductionist as they focus only on the character of the individual and disregard the social conditions in which prejudice and obedience are more likely to occur. Social psychologists such as Sherif rejected personality explanations, arguing that a multifaceted approach to understanding social influence was necessary.

Comparisons between ways of explaining behaviour using different themes

Contrasting explanations of prejudice and obedience can be useful to understand their particular emphasis, which can be subtle. In comparing social identity theory and realistic conflict theory, it can be seen that they both describe the role of groups in the formation of prejudice, using in-group favouritism and negative out-group bias. The key difference between them is that realistic conflict theory describes how competition for resources is a necessary condition for prejudice to occur, whereas social identity theory does not.

Different ways of explaining obedience and prejudice often reflect current social and historical events. Original attempts to explain social attitudes and behaviours have tended to focus on dispositional causes, which reflected attitudes at the time that Germans during the Holocaust were somehow different from the rest of the world. The emphasis shifted to more social explanations and today both dispositional and social theories are dominant as explanations as social psychologists become more aware of their interrelatedness.

Psychology as a science

Social psychology in the early 19th century was concerned with understanding collective thinking and action. It was not until the writings of Floyd Allport (1924) that there was a manifesto for social psychology to focus on experimentation and science. The intention for social psychology from this point was to become more scientific and to focus on experimentation to understand group dynamics and behaviour. Norman Triplett is regarded to have conducted the first social psychology experiment on social facilitation at Indiana University in 1898, testing whether individuals performed better on their own or when faced with competition from others.

This early influence paved the way for many social psychological experiments in the 1950s, 1960s and 1970s, such as the Robber's Cave of Sherif et al. (1961) and Milgram's research into obedience. In these experiments, variables could be controlled and carefully manipulated to ensure cause and effect relationships under laboratory or more naturalistic conditions. Despite an experimental methodology, social psychology can be criticised for studying human social behaviour in a vacuum that cannot be generalised to the real world. Group dynamics rarely exist in a social vacuum, but are affected by social, historical and cultural events which continually change, so any scientific approach taken to study human behaviour through experimentation should acknowledge this.

Comparing agency theory and social impact theory as explanations of obedience
The differences between agency theory and social impact theory as explanations of obedience are more obvious. Social impact theory is strictly focused on the social conditions that encourage social influence, but agency theory takes account of the evolutionary basis of obedience, socialising factors and psychodynamic forces that are at play to reduce the moral strain one experiences and displace responsibility onto another.

Culture and gender

As we have discussed, obedience would be predicted to be greater in females compared to males as gender stereotypes predict that women would be more compliant than male counterparts. However, experimental evidence from Milgram and other social psychologists has not found this to be the case. Social psychological theories of obedience such as agency theory and social impact theory explain obedience as largely a product of social circumstances and forces, which are not mediated by gender. Although research into conformity (Crutchfield, 1955) found women to be more compliant than males, it has been argued to be a result of methodological bias. In particular, male and female participants are exposed to male-orientated persuasion, which may account for greater female compliance, because when exposed to female-orientated persuasion, males are more compliant.

Milgram's obedience experiments have been conducted in many different cultures, most citing over an 80 per cent level of obedience. One study that found very low levels of obedience (Kilham and Mann, 1974) was probably the product of methodological differences rather than any real difference in obedience rates. The distinction between collectivistic and individualistic cultures may be useful in understanding whether social influence is affected by culture. Typically, collectivistic cultures work together cooperatively and interdependently, so it could be predicted that a higher level of obedience and prejudice would be observed. However, cross-cultural obedience research is not methodologically comparable, which may account for the differences in obedience rates found, and prejudice research has produced mixed findings. It is therefore not yet clear whether culture is a mediating factor for either obedience or prejudice, and this is probably because social and cultural conditions are not static. These ever-changing social circumstances affect whether a society is more prone to or resistant to authority, and whether social norms reinforce or dissent against prejudice and discrimination.

Nature–nurture

The greatest distinction in social psychological research is between whether behaviour is affected by dispositional causes (within the person) or situational factors (external to the person). Personality explanations of prejudice focus on the type of character that is more or less likely to be prejudiced and therefore account for the nature side of the debate. Intergroup dynamic theories, such as realistic conflict and social identity theories, focus on the situational conditions that cause conflict, which reflect the nurture side of the debate. This may be an oversimplified distinction, and certainly in the case of personality theories, it is not the case that nurture is ignored completely. In fact, most personality accounts of prejudice explain that such traits arise from the way in which they are brought up. Adorno, for example, explains that the authoritarian character develops from harsh parenting which leads to hostility that is directed at weaker targets.

An understanding of how psychological knowledge has developed over time

Social psychological knowledge has changed over time and is largely influenced by social changes in attitudes and historical events, such as the Holocaust. The classic research by Milgram, Sherif and Zimbardo has been revisited and group processes remain at the forefront of social psychological research. More recent developments in social psychology have attempted to investigate the underlying motivation and mental constructs associated with social influence research, bringing social psychology alongside cognitive psychology.

Issues of social control

As with much of psychology, explanations and research can be used to both good and bad effect. Understanding what makes us obedient can be used to help educate and prevent blind destructive obedience in the future, and helps us understand historical events such as mass genocide at the hands of different groups and even the military. However, it can also be used to manipulate obedience. If we can understand what conditions create the highest levels of obedience, this knowledge can be used to ensure our soldiers obey higher ranking officers, or employees comply with the requests of their employers. This can certainly be seen in everyday life; police officers wear uniforms and have the ability to use punishment to keep our behaviour in line with the law, and majorities work against minorities to encourage conformity to social norms. In the military, positions of authority are clearly identified by the uniform; supervising officers are immediately identifiable to their troops and have the authority to use sanctions to ensure obedience.

The use of psychological knowledge in society

The main application of prejudice research in society has been to reduce prejudice. This has been used in our classrooms (jigsaw technique and other structured learning environments) to reduce racial bias in multi-ethnic schools. Using our knowledge of stereotypes we can educate people to be more mindful of the similarities that exist between different groups rather than focusing on the differences. Langer et al. (1985) found an improvement in how children perceived disability when encouraged to be more mindful; this package reduced stereotypes and increased empathy.

Intergroup hostility is facilitated by a lack of equal status contact. This explains why communities divided by physical barriers or educational and employment integration often experience conflict. This was the case in Northern Ireland, where land was divided into Protestant and Catholic areas and integration was not permitted.

In 1951, Deutsch and Collins took advantage of a desegregation housing project in New York to conduct a social psychological investigation into equal status contact. Using social identity theory as a basis for their research, they predicted that desegregation would reduce negative out-group bias and intergroup conflict between whites and blacks. In accordance with New York State law, two public housing projects were designed to allocate housing regardless of race. They compared these housing projects to two similar projects in New Jersey where whites and blacks were segregated into two different blocks. In the desegregated housing blocks, the housewives mixed regularly when doing their laundry, meeting in the street and at the grocers. Asking a random sample of white housewives, they found that white housewives held black housewives in higher regard and were more in favour of interracial housing compared to the segregated housewives, who held stereotypes of blacks being dangerous and inferior. This proved a lesson in equal status contact that was rolled out in other public housing projects.

In a meta-analysis of over 515 intergroup contact studies, Pettigrew and Tropp (2006) found that contact does reduce prejudice.

Issues related to socially sensitive research

Any research into prejudice and discrimination has the potential to be socially sensitive for the participants involved in the research themselves or the groups which they represent. Very early social research into prejudice can be heavily criticised for exaggerating differences between races and producing biased evidence that whites were superior to blacks. Thankfully this opinion is not held today, but at the time this psychological knowledge legitimised social, educational and economic divisions between races and endorsed discriminatory practices and legislation.

Social control can be positive

Social control can be positive, and research into the social conditions that cause prejudice have led to developments in reducing prejudice. The jigsaw technique (Aronson et al., 1978) is based on the Sherif et al. summer camp studies (1954, 1961) where superordinate goals were used to reduce prejudice. Designing classroom and workplace environments that maximise the jigsaw technique can be used to control levels of intergroup hostility and reduce bullying and negative competition.

Knowledge check

Content

> In the content section you are required to describe, evaluate and apply your knowledge of explanations of obedience and prejudice, and to discuss individual differences and developmental psychology.
>
> To check your evaluation skills, refer to the introduction section of this book and review 'how to evaluate a theory'. Remember that you may be asked to consider issues of validity, reliability, credibility, generalisability, objectivity and subjectivity in your evaluation of theories.

Can you describe agency theory and social impact theory as explanations of obedience?

Are you able to apply the concepts used by agency theory and social impact theory to explain why some people might obey an authority figure?

Can you evaluate agency theory and social impact theory in terms of strengths and weaknesses?

Are you confident that you can describe and apply your knowledge of Milgram's research, including his variations studies, to understand when and why obedience may occur?

Are you able to discuss why there may be individual variation in obedience levels according to gender and personality?

Are you able to discuss why there may be different levels of obedience according to the situation that an individual is in?

Are you able to discuss cultural variations in obedience?

Can you describe social identity theory and realistic conflict theory as explanations of prejudice?

Are you able to apply your knowledge of social identity theory and realistic conflict theory to explain novel cases of prejudice?

Can you describe and evaluate research into prejudice that has investigated social identity theory and realistic conflict theory?

Can you evaluate social identity theory and realistic conflict theory in terms of strengths and weaknesses?

Are you able to discuss individual variation in prejudice in terms of personality differences?

Are you able to discuss why prejudice may differ across different situations?

Are you able to discuss how prejudice may differ according to culture?

Are you able to discuss how prejudice and obedience may develop from our upbringing, according to Adorno?

Methods

Can you describe how questionnaires and interviews are designed and implemented?

Are you able to understand how researcher effects can influence self-reports?

Can you identify and describe different types of self-report (structured, semi-structured and unstructured)?

Can you identify and describe different types of question used in self-reports (open, closed, ranked-scale)?

Can you evaluate questionnaires and interviews as research methods?

Are you able to identify and write alternative hypotheses?

Are you able to identify, describe and evaluate sampling techniques (random, volunteer, stratified and opportunity)?

For quantitative data, can you identify, calculate and understand the analysis and interpretation of measures of central tendency (mean, median and mode), measures of dispersion (range and standard deviation) and percentages?

Can you draw, interpret and select appropriate table and graphical representations of quantitative data (frequency table, bar graph and histogram)?

Are you able to describe and analyse qualitative data using thematic analysis?

Can you evaluate qualitative and quantitative data?

Can you describe, identify and evaluate the BPS Code of Ethics and Conduct (2009) and understand risk management when undertaking psychological research?

Studies

> In the studies section you are required to describe, evaluate and apply your knowledge of one classic and one contemporary study in social psychology.
>
> To check your evaluation skills, refer to the introduction section of this book and review 'how to evaluate a study. Remember that you may be asked to consider issues of validity, reliability, credibility, generalisability, objectivity and subjectivity in your evaluation of studies.

Can you describe the classic study by Sherif et al. (1954/61) Intergroup conflict and cooperation: The Robber's Cave experiment, in terms of its aim, method(s), procedures, results and conclusions?

Are you able to evaluate the Sherif et al. (1954/61) study in terms of strengths and weaknesses?

Are you able to identify and describe the aims, method, procedure, results and conclusions of a contemporary study from the following list and evaluate the study in terms of strengths and weaknesses?

- Burger (2009) Replicating Milgram: Would people still obey today?

- Reicher and Haslam (2006) Rethinking the psychology of tyranny: The BBC prison study

- Cohrs et al. (2012) Individual differences in ideological attitudes and prejudice: evidence from peer-report data.

Key questions

Are you able to identify and describe a key question in social psychology that is relevant to today's society?

Can you explain this key question using concepts, theories and research that you have studied in social psychology?

Practical investigation

Have you designed and conducted a questionnaire(s) to investigate an area of social psychology?

Can you explain how you went about planning and designing your questionnaire(s), justifying your questionnaire construction, sampling decisions and ethical considerations?

Can you describe and analyse (using measures of central tendency and dispersion) the quantitative data that you gathered from your questionnaire and how you presented your data (table and graphical representation)?

Can you describe how you went about conducting a thematic analysis on the qualitative data you have gathered?

Are you able to draw conclusions from the quantitative and qualitative data you gathered and analysed?

> Remember that you may be asked to consider issues of validity, reliability, credibility, generalisability, objectivity and subjectivity in your evaluation of your practical investigation.

Can you explain the strengths and weaknesses of your questionnaire(s) and suggest possible improvements that could have been made?

Are you able to write up the procedure, results and discussion sections in a report style?

Issues and debates (A level only)

> Remember that issues and debates are synoptic. This means you may be asked to make connections by comparing issues and debates across topics in psychology or comment on issues and debates within unseen material.

Can you identify ethical issues associated with theory and research within social psychology?

Can you comment on the practical and methodological issues in the design and implementation of research in social psychology?

Can you explain how theories, research and concepts within social psychology might be considered reductionist?

Can you compare theories and research within social psychology to show different ways of explaining and understanding memory?

Are you able to discuss whether theories, concepts, research and methodology within social psychology are scientific?

Are you able to discuss how obedience and prejudice may be affected by culture and gender?

Are you able to discuss the nature–nurture debate in the context of social psychology, in terms of which parts emphasise the role of nature and nurture or the interaction between them?

Do you understand how social psychology has developed over time?

Do you understand what is meant by social control and how research within social psychology may be used to control behaviour?

Can you know how the theories, concepts and research within social psychology can be used in a practical way in society?

Are you able to understand what is meant by socially sensitive research and explain how research in social psychology might be considered to be socially sensitive?

References

Burger, J. M. (2009) Replicating Milgram: Would people still obey today? *American Psychologist,* 64 (1), pp. 1–11.

Cohrs, J. C., Kämpfe-Hargrave, N. and Riemann, R. (2012) Individual differences in ideological attitudes and prejudice: Evidence from peer-report data *Journal of Personality and Social Psychology,* 103, pp. 343–361.

Milgram, S. (1974) *Obedience to Authority.* New York: Harper & Row.

Reicher, S.D. and Haslam, S.A. (2006) Rethinking the psychology of tyranny: The BBC prison study. *British Journal of Social Psychology,* 45, pp. 1–40.

Sherif, M. (1966). *Group Conflict and Cooperation: Their Social Psychology.* London: Routledge and Kegan Paul.

Sherif, M. Harvey, O. J., White, B. J., Hood, W. R. & Sherif, C. W. (1961) *Intergroup Conflict and Cooperation: The Robber's Cave Experiment.* Norman: University of Oklahoma Press.

Tajfel, H. and Turner, J. C. (1979). An integrative theory of intergroup conflict. In W. G. Austin and S. Worchel (eds) *The Social Psychology of Intergroup Relations.* Monterey, CA: Brooks/Cole Publishing Co, pp. 33–47.

Tajfel, H. and Turner, J. C. (1986). The social identity theory of intergroup behaviour. In S. Worchel and W. G. Austin (eds) *Psychology of Intergroup Relations.* Chicago: Nelson-Hall, pp. 7–24.

Cognitive psychology

Cognitive psychology is the study of the role of cognitive processes in human behaviour. Cognitivists study mental processes, such as perception, memory, attention, language and problem solving, in order to understand how we view, interpret and respond to our world. Cognitive psychologists investigate mental processes by examining people with cognitive impairments. By doing this, they are able to understand how damage affects processing ability. They also use experimentation and brain-imaging to gather information about the nature and location of cognitive modules.

In this topic you will learn about:

- the nature of human memory systems

- individual differences in memory and how memory changes with age

- the way in which experiments and case studies of brain-damaged patients are used to understand cognition, and the analysis of data

- a classic and contemporary study of human memory

- key issues around the topic of cognitive psychology that are of relevance to society today

- how to carry out a practical research exercise relevant to topics covered in cognitive psychology

- wider issues and debates in cognitive psychology (A level).

2.1 Content

Learning outcomes

In this section you will learn about theories of memory including:

- the multi-store model of memory

- working memory as a theory of short-term memory

- the nature of semantic and episodic memory as different long-term memory stores

- reconstructive memory including schema theory.

Introduction to cognitive psychology

Cognitive psychology is concerned with internal mental processes, such as language, memory, problem solving and thinking. An important development in the cognitive approach was the advent of the computer age. The computer gave cognitivists the metaphor for understanding the human brain and the terminology to explain cognition more easily. The computer analogy likens the brain to a computer; a storage system that receives information from our environment, processes the information, and gives an output. The computer hardware resembles the structural features of our brain and the software resembles the experience that we write into the program or system. Experimental cognitive psychology is the study of human mental functioning in a controlled laboratory setting, using experimental tests to determine functioning. Cognitive science is a field that is concerned with mimicking human cognition in a computer program, modelling computer simulations and offering computational models for various aspects of cognition. Cognitive neuropsychology is the study of patients with brain damage to determine the impact of the damage on capacity and functioning. These studies have been particularly important in understanding the cognitive function that we refer to as memory.

The multi-store model of memory (Atkinson and Shiffrin, 1968)

Richard Shiffrin, and his academic supervisor, Richard Atkinson, proposed a general theoretical framework for understanding human memory, often referred to as the multi-store model of memory. Atkinson and Shiffrin distinguished between the permanent structural features of memory and its **control processes**. The structural features of memory can be seen as similar to the hardware and built-in programs of a computer which cannot be altered by the programmer, which amount to the basic memory stores of human memory. The control processes involved in memory are seen as similar to programs that the programmer can write into the computer and which determine the operations that the computer can perform. These control processes involve the way we encode, rehearse and retrieve memories.

WIDER ISSUES AND DEBATES

Reductionism
This model has been criticised for being overly simplistic: that it underplays the interconnections between the different memory systems by proposing that the memory has distinctly different stores. Artificially breaking up the memory stores makes it easier to study memory experimentally, but this model can be criticised for being reductionist.

The structure of human memory

The multi-store model describes memory as consisting of three basic stores: a sensory register, short-term store and long-term store. A sensory experience (something we have seen, heard, touched, etc.) first enters the sensory register/memory where it is held for a brief moment before it decays. **Attended information** from the sensory register is then transferred to the short-term store. Information is held for around 30 seconds before it decays, unless **rehearsal** is used to maintain this information for a longer period of time. From short-term memory, information can be transferred to long-term permanent storage in the long-term store.

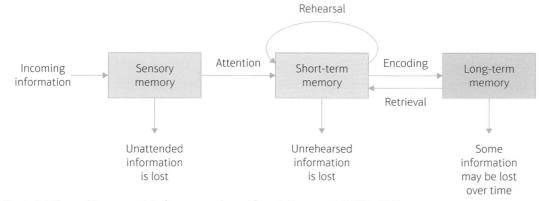

Figure 2.1 The multi-store model of memory, adapted from Atkinson and Shiffrin, 1968

Sensory register/memory

We experience our world through our five senses, and it is believed that we have a sensory register for each of these sensory modalities (seeing, hearing, touching, tasting and smelling). The visual sensory register has been widely researched using a **whole or partial report technique** (Sperling, 1960, 1963) in which a **visual array** of letters is presented via a **tachistoscope** for a brief moment and then a direction is given to recall the whole or a specific row of the array. Participants typically recalled on average 4.32 letters of the whole array. If a direction is given to recall a row of the array

Key terms

Control processes: conscious decisions about what to attend to from the sensory information in our environment.

Attended information: information that is given attention.

Rehearsal: consciously rehearsing and repeating items.

Whole or partial report technique: participants are asked to recall the whole array or part of the array, such as a line.

Visual array: an arrangement of digits or letters.

Tachistoscope: a device used to present visual information in a controlled way, typically to test sensory memory.

immediately after presentation, recall is reasonably precise, but this decays rapidly if there is a delay before the direction. Thus, the sensory register can hold only a limited amount of information for only a few hundred milliseconds before it is lost.

D	V	Y	Q
P	U	J	A
S	M	E	K

Figure 2.2 A visual array

Short-term store

Duration of short-term memory

The second structural feature of Atkinson and Shiffrin's memory model is the short-term store or 'working memory'. Information that is attended to enters the short-term store and is held temporarily for 15–30 seconds and then is assumed to decay completely unless it can be maintained through rehearsal. Peterson and Peterson (1959) investigated the duration of short-term memory using an **interference task** to prevent rehearsal. Participants were required to remember a single **trigram** of three consonants for intervals of 3, 6, 9, 12, 15 and 18 seconds. The trigram was read out and participants were then given a number from which they had to count backwards in threes (e.g. 679, 676, 673, etc). Correct recall of the trigram was likely after a short interval, but performance dropped rapidly after 15–18 seconds. Assuming that the interference task prevented rehearsal of the trigram, it can be concluded that decay occurs in the short-term store over a period of 15 seconds.

Capacity of the short-term store

Atkinson and Shiffrin assumed that the capacity of the short-term store was around five to eight items of information. However, Miller (1956) refined this figure to 'the magical number seven, plus or minus two'. We can therefore view the short-term store as a series of between five and nine slots in which information can be stored.

Encoding of short-term memory

The nature of information held in the short-term store does not depend on its input form, for example, we may register the image of a pineapple in its visual form, but it is held in verbal form as a short-term memory. Atkinson and Shiffrin believed that a memory trace in the short-term store was held in an auditory or verbal form because of the **phonological similarity effect**; letters and words of a similar sound presented to participants are more difficult to recall than dissimilar sounding letters and words. The similarity of sounds leads to confusion in the short-term store suggesting that the encoding in this store is primarily acoustic (auditory or verbal).

Retrieval from the short-term store

Retrieval of memory from the short-term store is largely based on a rapid sequential scan of the stored information. Rehearsal is important in maintaining information in the short-term store, increasing the strength of the memory trace and ultimately building up the memory trace in the long-term store. **Digit span** experiments suggest that we are able to maintain between five and nine items using rehearsal, and as more information is input into the store, older information or information with a weaker memory trace is knocked out (displaced) and quickly decays.

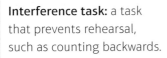

Key terms

Interference task: a task that prevents rehearsal, such as counting backwards.

Trigram: a set of three digits or letters.

Phonological similarity effect: similar sounding words and letters are acoustically confused in short-term memory, making them more difficult to recall.

Digit span: how many digits can be retained and recalled in sequential order without mistakes.

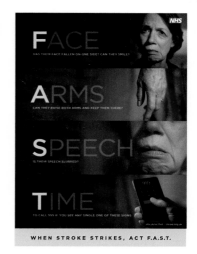

This mnemonic was created by the Department of Health to help people identify the symptoms of a stroke.

Transfer of information between short-term and long-term store

Atkinson and Shiffrin described the relationship between the sensory register and long-term memory as being important for identification of sensory information. In order to transfer information received by our sensory register to the short-term store, we must use our long-term memory to make sense of the information and assign it a verbal label. For example, we may register the image of a horse, but this cannot be stored as an auditory-verbal short-term memory until we have identified it as such using our long-term memory of what the object represents. Transfer of information from the short-term to long-term store can be as a result of rehearsal, although this would leave a relatively weak memory trace. According to Atkinson and Shiffrin, a more durable memory trace can be achieved by using a mental operation, such as a **mnemonic**, to increase the strength of transfer.

Long-term store

Retrieval from the long-term store

Atkinson and Shiffrin believed that long-term memories existed for all sensory modalities; we have memories for taste, sound, smells, etc. In the 1968 model, they proposed that multiple copies of a memory were retained in the long-term store. This proposition was largely based on the 'tip-of-the-tongue' phenomenon (Brown and McNeill, 1966), which demonstrated that people were able to accurately predict that they could recognise a correct answer even if they could not recall the answer at that moment in time. The individual may feel a correct answer is on the 'tip of their tongue' and may even be able to recall some features of the correct answer, such as the initial letter or its number of syllables. Atkinson and Shiffrin suggested that these results indicate that a long-term memory is not stored as one memory trace, but that multiple copies, in their various forms and fragments, are stored. When we experience 'tip of the tongue', we are retrieving a partial copy of the memory trace, and this partial copy retrieval can help us gain access to a more complete copy of the long-term memory through some associative process.

Taking it further

The next time you experience 'tip-of-the-tongue' consider what features of the to-be-remembered information you can recall; how many syllables it contains, what letter it begins with, what does it sound like, what is it similar to? Consider whether or not these fragments of a memory actually indicate that we have multiple copies of it, or something else.

Encoding in the long-term store

Encoding information into the long-term store can depend on the rehearsal process or some form of association between the new and pre-existing knowledge stored there. If information is linked to

---

Key term

Mnemonic: a system for remembering something such as an association or a pattern of letters.

Taking it further

The emphasis given to the role of rehearsal in memory has been criticised for ignoring other ways of transferring information to the long-term store. Fergus Craik and Robert Lockhart (1972) describe an alternative framework for memory called the Levels of Processing Approach. Investigate this alternative approach further and consider how this different theory of memory could be used to aid your own revision.

pre-existing knowledge it will make a search for the information far easier. This makes more sense as a random search of such a large store would be exhaustive. Atkinson and Shiffrin (1965) explain this based on their quizzing of a graduate student about the capital cities of US states. The student could not immediately recall the capital of Washington, but when he later recalled that the capital of Oregon was Salem, he immediately remembered that Olympia was the capital of Washington. When asked how the student remembered this, it was found that he had learned the capitals together. They were recalled as an associated pair that was semantically or temporally related.

Duration of long-term memory

The duration of long-term memory is potentially a lifetime. Bahrick et al. (1975) investigated what they referred to as Very Long-term Memory (VLTM) using a series of memory tests on the names and faces of students in their high school yearbooks. Four hundred participants between the ages of 17 and 74 years old were tested. They found that identification of names and faces was 90 per cent accurate within 15 years of leaving school and between 70 to 80 per cent accurate 48 years after leaving school. This shows that although memory deteriorates over time, long-term memory for faces and names is fairly resilient over the passage of time.

Capacity of the long-term store

The capacity of long-term memory is potentially infinite. Brady et al. (2008) showed participants 2500 objects over the course of 5.5 hours. They were then shown pairs of objects and asked to identify which of the two objects they had seen. When participants saw the original object paired with a very different object, identification was 92 per cent. When the object paired with the original was similar, the identification rate was 88 per cent, and when the original object was depicted from a different angle, identification was 87 per cent. This demonstrates that thousands of images can be maintained successfully in the long-term store.

Table 2.1 Summary of the memory stores

	Sensory register	Short-term store	Long-term store
Encoding	One register for each sensory modality: visual, auditory, haptic, olfactory, gustatory	Largely acoustic and verbal	Semantic and temporal
Storage duration	Limited – approximately 50 milliseconds to a few seconds	15–30 seconds	Potentially a lifetime
Storage capacity	3–4 items	5–9 items	Potentially limitless
Forgetting	Decay	Decay through displacement	Decay and interference
Retrieval	Scanning	Sequential search	Semantic or temporal search

Evaluation

Studies of patients with brain damage

Evidence to support the distinction, particularly between the short-term and long-term stores, comes from case studies of brain-damaged patients and experimental evidence from memory studies. Henry Molaison suffered amnesia following brain surgery for epilepsy, resulting in severe impairment to his long-term memory but his short-term memory was largely intact. This case study demonstrates that the short-term and long-term memory stores were differentially affected by the brain damage caused, perhaps because they are located in different regions of the brain. Similarly, Clive Wearing suffered long-term memory impairment following **encephalitis**, but his short-term store remained unaffected. In both cases the patient was unable to transfer information from the short-term store to the long-term store. Case studies such as these demonstrate the separation between short-term and long-term memory and support the distinction proposed by the multi-store

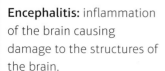

Key term

Encephalitis: inflammation of the brain causing damage to the structures of the brain.

model of memory. However, the subjects of case studies are unique and the nature of the brain injury sustained by each individual is equally unique, so we may not be able to generalise such a distinction based on individual cases alone. Despite this problem, amnesia research offers fairly convincing evidence for the distinction between short-term and long-term memory.

Case studies of brain-damaged patients that are used to support the multi-store model of memory can also be used to highlight the overly simplistic view of long-term memory. Clive Wearing, musician and chorus master, could not recall past events in his life, but he could remember how to play the piano and conduct an orchestra. Following a motorcycle accident that caused memory loss, Kent Cochrane (known widely as patient KC) could recall facts but showed severe memory impairment in remembering personal events in his life before the accident. These cases suggest that long-term memory is not one single unitary store, but that perhaps we have different long-term stores for procedural memory of practised skills and abilities, and other long-term stores for factual information and autobiographical events.

Memory for practised skills may be stored separately from stores for factual information.

WIDER ISSUES AND DEBATES

Ethical issues

Case studies of brain-damaged patients are often anonymised by using the initials of the patient rather than their full name, for example, until his death, Henry Molaison was only known as HM. This helps to protect patients' identities and maintains their right to privacy. In fact, the identity of Henry Molaison was fiercely defended by the researchers involved in his care. Despite being the most widely cited case study in the history of psychology, his identity was protected for over 55 years. However, in high-profile cases, such as Clive Wearing who was in the public eye, these individuals cannot be anonymised. This can lead to issues of privacy being violated as the research concerning the case is available within the scientific community and public arena.

Serial position effect

Compelling evidence for the existence of separate short-term and long-term memory stores comes from the **serial position effect** or primacy–recency effect. Murray Glanzer and Anita Cunitz (1966) conducted an experiment to investigate whether the position of a word in a list affected recall. They found that participants recalled more words from the beginning (primacy effect) and end (recency effect) of the word list, but recalled few from the middle of the list. It was thought that words recalled at the beginning of the list had the chance to be rehearsed, and memory for these words would have been strengthened and transferred to the long-term store. While the words at the beginning of the list are being processed, words in the middle of the list were filling up the slots in the short-term store. Words at the end of the list acted to displace the older memory trace for the middle words, leaving only words at the end of the list in the short-term slots.

> **Key term**
>
> **Serial position effect:** recall of information at the beginning and end of a list is higher than the middle of the list.

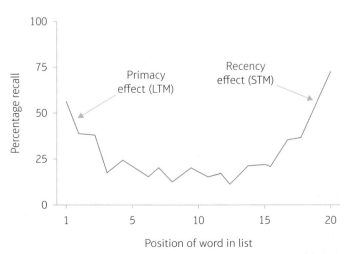

Figure 2.3 The serial position curve demonstrates the difference between short-term and long-term stores

Key term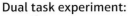

Dual task experiment:
experiments that involve
two tasks that either
compete with each other
for the same cognitive
resource because they are
similar tasks (two verbal
or two visual tasks) or
involve different cognitive
resources because they are
different tasks (one verbal
and one visual).

**WIDER ISSUES AND
DEBATES**

**An understanding of how
psychological knowledge
has developed over time**
Despite these criticisms,
the multi-store model
of memory proposed by
Atkinson and Shiffrin has
been a valuable framework
in understanding human
memory and heuristics
that has stimulated a huge
wealth of memory research.
Because of the development
of this model of memory,
better and more precise
theories of memory have
been proposed.

Coding

The difference in the type of coding used by short-term and long-term memory also indicates that
we have two separate memory stores. Alan Baddeley (1966) conducted a laboratory experiment
on the sequential recall of ten words in a list that were either acoustically or semantically related.
He found that semantically related words were more difficult to recall from long-term memory
compared to acoustically related words; 9.6 per cent of similar sequences were recalled as opposed
to 82.1 per cent of dissimilar words, suggesting that encoding in short-term and long-term stores
was different. This leads to the assumption that different memory stores exist independently of
one another. Additionally, similar sounding letters and words are less well recalled than dissimilar
sounding letters and words. This suggests that there is acoustic coding in the short-term store,
explaining why similar sounding phonemes are confused.

Alternative explanations

The multi-store model of memory has often been criticised for being an overly simplistic view of
human memory. In particular, it fails to address the dynamic nature of short-term memory and
our performance on **dual task experiments**. Dual task experiments show that we perform poorly
when trying to deal with similar tasks, but perform well when trying to do two tasks of a different
nature. For example, we tend to perform poorly when asked to do two verbal tasks or two visual
tasks together, but perform well when given one verbal and one visual task together. Dual task
performance cannot be explained by the short-term store, which assumes that capacity is unaffected
by type of task. A different explanation of short-term memory, proposed by Alan Baddeley and
Graham Hitch in 1974, can explain dual task performance and is seen as a more dynamic model of
short-term memory.

The multi-store model has also been criticised for the emphasis given to rehearsal in the transfer
of information from short-term to long-term storage. Although we do use rehearsal as a memory
strategy, it is not essential for permanent learning to take place. In fact, we are often able to learn
new skills and information without consciously trying to learn them. Using imagery is one such
example of a memory strategy that leaves a strong long-term memory trace without the need for
rehearsal. Craik and Lockhart (1972) offer an alternative explanation for the transfer of information
from the short-term to long-term store. They describe different levels of processing; structural,
phonemic and semantic, suggesting that the greater depth of processing we give information, the
more durable the memory trace formed.

Exam tip

When evaluating the multi-store model of memory it is important to use research evidence that
highlights the qualitative and quantitative differences between the short-term and long-term
stores. It is not enough to state that Miller (1956) found that the short-term store could hold
between five and nine bits of information, without contrasting this to the capacity of the
long-term store.

It is also very important to explain **how** the research supports or goes against the model.
Simply stating the research findings without linking back to the model is not effective
evaluation.

For example:

Point: Clive Wearing suffered amnesia which meant that he could not remember events from his
past or store new memories. However, he could hold information temporarily in his
consciousness.

Link: This supports the multi-store model of memory as it shows that his long-term store was
damaged but his short-term store was unimpaired. These stores must be independent of one
another.

Working memory model (Baddeley and Hitch, 1974)

Alan Baddeley and Graham Hitch first proposed the theory of working memory as a three-component short-term memory system in 1974. The idea of a working memory was not a new one; in fact Atkinson and Shiffrin (1968) used the label 'working memory' for the short-term store within their multi-store model. Baddeley and Hitch noted significant problems with the multi-store explanation of working memory because it was overly simplistic and emphasised the role of rehearsal as being critical to learning. Baddeley and Hitch set about trying to understand short-term memory as a complex and active working memory.

The model

In their original model, Baddeley and Hitch proposed three components for working memory: a central executive that would deal with the running of the memory system, and two slave systems to deal with verbal and visual information. Overall, working memory was seen as a limited capacity system only able to deal with a restricted amount of information temporarily while it could be manipulated or worked with.

A useful exercise to demonstrate working memory is to perform a complex calculation, such as 15 multiplied by 32 in your head rather than on paper. Performing such a mathematical calculation requires the temporary storage of the two initial numbers while retrieving the knowledge needed to conduct a multiplication. It is likely that two calculations are needed (10 multiplied by 32 and 5 multiplied by 32) and the solutions to these calculations will also need to be stored temporarily before addition is used to generate a solution to the sum. All of these processes are performed by the working memory.

The role of working memory is therefore to temporarily store and manipulate information being used. We rely on working memory for many functions, such as remembering telephone numbers and lists, comprehending sequences of words in the form of sentences, mental calculation and reasoning. However, working memory is fragile and frequently susceptible to distraction (someone talking to you while you are trying to remember a number), overload (a long list of items) and overwork (complicated calculations).

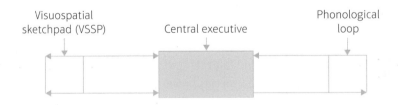

Figure 2.4 The working memory model

The central executive

The central executive was originally described as a limited capacity component involved in general processing. It was essentially seen as a **homunculus**, a little man, with a supervisory role in deciding how the two slave systems should function. It was also regarded as having limited capacity but with the ability to deal with different types of sensory information (**modality free**). In the early stages of the theory of working memory the role of the central executive was unclear and it was not until later that it became more defined as an attentional controller with the capacity to focus, divide and switch attention.

Key terms

Homunculus: a very small human.

Modality free: able to process different forms of information (acoustic, visual, haptic, etc.).

Psychology as a science

The central executive in memory is a largely theoretical concept with limited experimental support. Because it is abstract it is not directly testable and does not meet the criterion of being scientific as empirical data cannot be gathered.

The phonological loop

The phonological loop is a slave system that deals with the temporary storage of verbal information. The phonological loop was initially believed to have two components: the articulatory rehearsal system and the phonological store. The phonological store was only able to hold a limited amount of verbal information for a few seconds, but this could be extended if the information was subvocalised or refreshed using the articulatory rehearsal system.

The phonological store can explain the phonological similarity effect, where it is more difficult to remember similar sounding words and letters (man, cad, mat, cap, can) compared to words and letters that sound different from one another (pen, sup, cow, day, hot). However, this effect was not true of remembering words that had semantic (meaning) similarity (huge, long, wide, tall, large) or words that were semantically unrelated (thin, wet, old, late, strong). This demonstrates that the phonological store relies on acoustic encoding for storage (Baddeley, 1966a).

INDIVIDUAL DIFFERENCES

It can be claimed that the working memory model ignores individual differences in capacity and functioning of each subsystem, or at least fails to explore these individual differences. Yet we know that some people have a better short-term memory than others and, in many cases, poor working memory has been associated with dyslexia and Specific Language Impairment.

Key term 💬

Specific Language Impairment: Individuals whose language skills are much lower than other cognitive skills such as IQ and non-verbal abilities.

WIDER ISSUES AND DEBATES

Psychology as a science

Much of the research into working memory is experimental and laboratory based, involving the testing of specific hypotheses concerning the nature of short-term memory that have testable outcomes (e.g. word recall/accuracy). This research meets many of the criteria of being scientific because there is an emphasis on control, objectivity and replicability.

The articulatory rehearsal system was used to explain the word length effect, where short monosyllabic words (cat, rug, hat) were recalled more successfully than longer polysyllabic words (intelligence, alligator, hippopotamus). Essentially, longer words filled up the limited capacity of the articulatory rehearsal system resulting in the decay of words positioned earlier in the list. The longer the word the more capacity was used up and forgetting was more likely. It could also explain why there was deterioration in recall when rehearsal was prevented through articulatory suppression (repeating the word 'the' while learning a word list).

Subsequent research into the phonological loop has provided an understanding of why it may have evolved. Researching an Italian woman (VP) with an acquired phonological impairment, Baddeley found that she was unable to retain any vocabulary learned from a different language, suggesting that the phonological loop may have evolved for language acquisition (Baddeley, et al., 1988). Further research using children with **Specific Language Impairment** (SLI) demonstrated that they found it incredibly difficult to recall non-words (slimp, poot, dar, gep), and this correlated to the size of their vocabulary. This finding suggested that the phonological loop was necessary for language acquisition and that deficits in this component of working memory resulted in difficulty learning and comprehending novel language (Gathercole and Baddeley, 1996). Non-word repetition tasks are now a standard and widely used test for and indicator of Specific Language Impairment.

Visuospatial sketchpad (VSSP)

This slave system of working memory was described to temporarily hold and manipulate verbal and spatial (position/location) information. The VSSP can deal with visuospatial information either directly through observing images or by retrieving visuospatial information from long-term memory. The role of the VSSP is to maintain and integrate visual and spatial information from these different channels using a visual code.

Recent research has attempted to distinguish between the visual and spatial components of the VSSP using tasks that test memory span. Spatial span has been tested using the Corsi block tapping task, where participants are presented with a series of blocks on a screen that light up in a sequence that they have to repeat. Error frequency increases with the number in the sequence, suggesting a limited capacity to spatial memory.

We rely on visuospatial information in our long-term memory to remember our route home.

Exam tip

Describing the working memory model requires a straightforward recount of the facts about the explanation. The command word 'describe' means that you will need to write about the original model and each of the subcomponents in terms of their features (capacity, function, coding). The amount of detail will need to be guided by the mark allocation and available writing space. You are not required to evaluate the theory but you can use examples to help elaborate your description points.

You will be required to demonstrate your knowledge and understanding of this theory by being able to explain different situations; for example, how you may find it difficult to process two sets of visual or verbal information simultaneously. Try to use your knowledge of working memory to explain the following situation. Remember that the command word 'explain' means that you need to make a point (why it is difficult) and then justify your point (expansion or explanation).

Why it is difficult to process two conversations simultaneously, such as when you are talking on the phone and a friend is trying to tell you something at the same time.

Point: It is difficult to process both conversations because they are verbal and both utilise the phonological store.

Expansion: The phonological store has a limited capacity so is unable to cope with the demands of two tasks at once and results in poor performance in processing.

Evaluation

Evidence for separate visuospatial and phonological subsystems comes from both experimental research and neurophysiological evidence.

Neurophysiological evidence

Williams syndrome is a rare condition where individuals show normal language ability but impaired visual and spatial ability. Individuals with this condition are affected by the same phonological factors, such as word length and word similarity, as the general population, but perform poorly on Corsi block tapping tests. This offers clinical evidence for separate visuospatial and phonological subsystems. Interestingly, children with Williams syndrome were also found to have significant problems comprehending sentences with spatial prepositions (words that describe the position of an object in relation to another object, such as behind, underneath, against), suggesting an association between visuospatial memory and language acquisition (Phillips et al., 2004).

Further neurological evidence comes from the single case study of KF (Shallice and Warrington, 1974) who suffered short-term memory impairment following a motorbike accident that damaged the parietal lobe of his brain. KF had a digit span of one, suggesting a gross impairment in his phonological store, but his visual memory was intact. In contrast, Henry Molaison suffered from a gross impairment in his spatial memory with a relatively unaffected short-term memory for verbal information. This supports the proposal that working memory has two subsystems to deal with verbal and visuospatial information relatively independently. Neuropsychological case studies offer an insight into memory function but are limited to unique individuals with specific impairments so care should be taken when generalising these findings.

Evidence from neuroimaging

Neuroimaging has also offered some evidence for the localisation of the different subcomponents of working memory in the brain. Paulesu et al. (1993) demonstrated that different regions of the brain were activated when undertaking tasks that employed the phonological store and the articulatory rehearsal system. Using a PET scan, they found that the **Broca's area** was activated during a subvocal rehearsal task (remembering words) and the **supramarginal gyrus** was activated when the phonological store was being used. This research provides evidence for the phonological loop and its separate subcomponents. However, the exact location of the central executive has been difficult to find as it is largely diffuse across the cortex.

Experimental evidence

Dual task experiments require participants to perform two tasks simultaneously that involve one or more slave systems of working memory. Baddeley and Hitch (1976) conducted an experiment where participants had to simultaneously use a pointer to track the location of a moving light on a screen while imagining the capital letter 'F' and mentally tracking the edges of the letter and verbally saying whether the angles they imagined were at the top or bottom of the image. Participants could easily complete each task separately, but had difficulty performing the tasks simultaneously. This shows how two visual tasks both compete for the limited resources of the visuospatial sketchpad resulting in impairment in performance. However, when participants were asked to perform the visual tasks while undertaking a verbal task at the same time, performance was not affected because one task used the visuospatial sketchpad and the other task used the phonological loop. Dual task experiments offer support for separate visual and verbal slave systems because performance is affected by whether the tasks compete for the limited resources of the same or different slave systems.

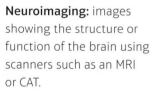

Key terms

Neuroimaging: images showing the structure or function of the brain using scanners such as an MRI or CAT.

Broca's area: an area of the left (typically) frontal lobe associated with the production of language.

Supramarginal gyrus: an area of the parietal lobe of the brain associated with the perception of language.

Research into separate visual and spatial memory systems

Recent research into the visuospatial sketchpad has been concerned with distinguishing between the visual and spatial components. Klauer and Zhao (2004) found that visual memory tasks were more disrupted by visual interference and spatial tasks more disrupted by spatial interference, offering evidence for separate components to the visuospatial sketchpad.

This separation of components was further supported by Darling et al. (2007), where 72 non-student participants were all presented with a series of 30 white squares positioned randomly on a black screen. In one of the squares was the letter 'p'.

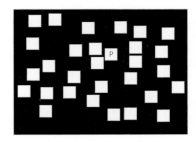

Participants had to recall either the appearance (font) of the letter 'p' or its location within a square on the screen. Participants then experienced either spatial interference by having to tap a sequence of keyboard keys in a figure of eight, or experience a visual disruption task in the form of a visual array of black and white flickering dots on the screen, before they saw the screen again.

The researchers found that the spatial interference task disrupted spatial memory but not memory for appearance, and that the visual disruption task affected, to a lesser extent, memory for appearance but not for location. This provides evidence for separate visual and spatial memory systems; however, visual memory often has to contend with an array of visual stimuli rather than just one category of visual information (the letter 'p'), so this experiment does not reflect everyday visual processing of images.

Figure 2.5 Darling et al. (2007) apparatus

Alzheimer's disease and the role of the central executive

Evidence for the coordination role of the central executive is far less extensive than research into the subsystems; nevertheless research with clinical patients suffering from **Alzheimer's disease** has shown decreased central executive function as the disease has progressed. Baddeley et al. (1991) conducted a series of dual task experiments on young, elderly and Alzheimer's patients using verbal and visual tasks together or separately. The performance of the Alzheimer group did not differ significantly from the other groups when performing a visual or verbal task but showed significant impairment when trying to do them together. According to Baddeley et al., the central executive is responsible for the coordination of the subsystems, so this impairment in performance demonstrates significant problems with executive functioning.

The episodic buffer

A significant limitation with the working memory model was its inability to explain why we could store only a limited number of word sequences in the phonological loop but could store far longer sentence sequences (up to 15 to 20 sentence units). It seemed that word sequences in the form of sentences could be bound together by meaning and grammar that could not be explained by the limited capacity of the phonological loop alone and this somehow related to information held in the long-term memory. A further problem with the original model was that it did not explain evidence from verbal span experiments that verbal and visual encoding could be combined. The model could not explain how the subcomponents could interface with each other or with long-term memory. Baddeley addressed this in 2000 with the addition of a fourth component called the **episodic buffer**. The episodic buffer was proposed as a limited capacity storage system that could integrate information between the subcomponents and feed into and retrieve information from long-term memory.

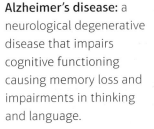

Key terms

Alzheimer's disease: a neurological degenerative disease that impairs cognitive functioning causing memory loss and impairments in thinking and language.

Episodic buffer: a subcomponent of the working memory associated with interfacing with long-term memory and integrating information from other subcomponents.

Taking it further

There is a huge wealth of experimental research into working memory, much of which involves laboratory research using specifically designed verbal and visual learning tasks. Consider how well this research represents everyday use of working memory and the implications of this for understanding everyday memory.

Explanation of long-term memory – episodic and semantic memory (Tulving, 1972)

Endel Tulving first made the distinction between **episodic** and **semantic** memory in a book where he aimed to reduce the ambiguity around the nature of long-term memory. He proposed that long-term memory could be divided into two memory stores: episodic memory (remembered experiences) and semantic memory (remembered facts). Tulving proposed that the dissociation between semantic and episodic memory was based on evidence that each store was qualitatively different in terms of the nature of stored memories, time referencing, the nature of associations between memories held in each store, the nature of retrieving or recalling memories held in each store and the independence of each store.

The nature of semantic and episodic memory

Tulving suggested that semantic memory represented a mental encyclopaedia, storing words, facts, rules, meanings and concepts as an organised body of knowledge. These memories are associated with other facts that link the concepts together (e.g. 'school and learning', or 'bird and nest') without autobiographical association. For example, the statements 'I know that June follows May in the calendar' or 'South Africa is a hot country' are memories of facts that have been learned at some earlier time.

Tulving described episodic memory as a kind of mental diary. Episodic memory receives and stores information about experiences or events that occur at a time in our life. These memories are linked to time and context.

Time referencing

Tulving believed that episodic memory was dependent on time-referencing: memories about events that happened to you are linked to the time in which they occurred. For example, recalling your first day at school is linked to the date this event occurred. However, semantic memory was detached from any temporal link, as factual information could be recalled without reference to when it was learned. For example, you can recall that Paris is the capital city of France without remembering when and where you learned that fact.

Spatial referencing

Input into episodic memory is continuous, as we experience a whole episode in some **temporal** frame of reference, such as experiencing a birthday party, whereas semantic memories can be input in a fragmentary way. We can piece factual information together that has been learned at different points in time; for example, you may learn that Emmeline Pankhurst formed the Women's Social and Political Union in 1903, and later learn that Emily Davison is thought to have thrown herself under the hooves of the king's horse on Derby Day. Both pieces of information can be stored independently and pieced together in a temporal form later on to understand key events in the suffragette movement.

Retrieval

Recall of episodic memory is dependent on the context in which the event was initially learned or experienced. It is this context that aids the retrieval of episodic memories. However, semantic memory does not seem to be dependent on the context in which it is learned, so it assumed that retrieval of semantic memories is similarly not dependent on context to aid recall. Retrieval from semantic memory can be based on inferences, generalisation and rational, logical thought.

Retrieval from semantic memory leaves the memory trace relatively unchanged from its original form, so we can recall a fact without interfering with that knowledge. However, Tulving believed that episodic memory was susceptible to transformation.

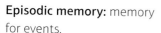

Are the stores interrelated?

Semantic memory can operate independently of episodic memory. For example, we do not need to remember a classroom lesson about equations to be able to use the equations we learned. However, episodic memory is unlikely to operate without semantic memory as we need to be able to draw on previous knowledge of objects, people and events that occur in order to understand them. Tulving argued that, despite this and although the two systems may overlap, they can be treated as separate independent stores.

WIDER ISSUES AND DEBATES

The use of psychological knowledge in society

The concept of **cue dependent recall** has been extensively researched in psychology. It has been established that we encode, alongside the memory, the context and the emotional state we experienced at the time of learning. These context and state cues can be used to aid recall of the original memory. Godden and Baddeley (1975) found that when scuba divers learned and recalled a list of words underwater or on land, they performed twice as well as when learning and recalling in different contexts. Kenealy (1997) found that participants recalled more when in the same mood as when they learned rather than a different mood. These state and context cues can be useful in everyday life, for example, using colour cues for revision of certain topics or imagining being in your classroom when taking an exam in a different context. State and context cueing has also been useful in the development of police interviewing techniques.

Studies involving divers have shown that recalling information in the same context in which it was learned improves performance

Table 2.2 Summary of differences between semantic and episodic memory

	Semantic memory	Episodic memory
Nature of memory	Mental encyclopaedia	Mental diary
Time referencing	Independent of time referencing Input can be fragmentary	Time and context referenced Input is continuous
Retrieval and forgetting	Retrieval possible without learning Not cued retrieval	Retrieval using cues which are encoded at the point of learning
Forgetting	Memory trace more robust and less susceptible to transformation	Forgetting due to retrieval cue failure Memory trace can be transformed/changed

Anoxic episode: lack of oxygen to the brain causing injury.

Evaluation

Brain damage

Evidence for the dissociation between semantic and episodic memory suggests that one store can be affected without affecting the other one. Amnesia patients are rich sources of information.

Ostergaard (1987) described a case of a 10-year-old boy with brain damage following an **anoxic episode**. Although his intelligence was intact, he suffered impairment to both his episodic and semantic memory. However, he did make educational progress and was able to store information in semantic memory. This offers some evidence for the independence of the two memory systems as Tulving suggested.

Support for the nature of episodic and semantic memory as separate long-term storage systems is also derived from case studies of KC (1951–2014). Following a serious motorbike accident, KC suffered specific long-term memory impairment to his episodic memory resulting in an inability to form or recall many personal events in his life; however his recollection of factual information was intact. This case study supports the distinction between the two long-term memory stores and indicates possible regions of the brain where the different types of memory are stored. Examining case studies of brain-damaged patients also points out a weakness in the model of long-term memory proposed by Tulving. Henry Molaison and Clive Wearing both suffered memory impairment that affected their ability to retain and recall long-term memory from episodic storage. However both men were still able to remember how to perform tasks, such as playing the piano, and could still learn new skills. This points to a further long-term store for remembering practised skills. Tulving (1985) outlined this additional store in subsequent reformulations of his idea, adding procedural memory for skills and abilities that we learn, such as learning the grammatical rules of language, or riding a bicycle.

INDIVIDUAL DIFFERENCES

The use of case studies of brain-damaged patients gives us an important insight into the nature of human memory, and the relative independence or links between the various memory stores and functions. However, the extent of such brain damage and the response of individual patients to that damage highlights important individual differences between these unique cases. Therefore it is important to acknowledge that care should be taken when generalising the findings of these unique case studies to our overall understanding of memory in the whole population.

A significant problem with describing long-term memory in terms of two separate systems is that it does not account for any interrelationship or continuity between each system. Clearly they work together when given an episodic memory task, such as learning a list of words, as a word can have a semantic feature (meaning of the word) and an episodic reference (when and where the word was remembered). This makes research into the separate stores problematic because they cannot be studied in absolute isolation from one another.

Additionally, experimental studies of learning word lists are problematic as evidence for either semantic or episodic memory because they do not take into account the 'guesses' that participants may make when recalling the list. If a participant makes an informed guess about a word that could have been on the list of words to remember, this would represent recall from semantic, not episodic, memory. The likelihood of semantic recall in an episodic memory test is high, which means that testing the separate stores independently becomes problematic.

Reconstructive memory (Bartlett, 1932)

Sir Frederic C. Bartlett (1886–1969) was one of the most influential cognitive psychologists of the last century; his most notable contribution was a collection of memory experiments published in his book *Remembering*. Contrary to much experimental research at the time, Bartlett insisted on representing memory in a real context. He stated that experiments should not just capture reactions, they should capture human beings. Bartlett believed that memory should not be divided into its constituent parts and treated as independent from other functioning, but rather should be studied in a special way to capture the relationship between memory and other cognitive processes.

Perception

Bartlett believed that in order to study memory, we must first understand what precedes it and what follows it. To understand perception as a precursor to what is remembered, Bartlett devised a series of experiments to test memory for shapes and objects. He found that participants often assigned verbal labels or names for each shape or object that they saw and that these names often shaped the representation of the object drawn afterwards. He concluded the perception of the shape or object determined how it was remembered.

INDIVIDUAL DIFFERENCES

How we perceive an object or event is based on individual interpretation. This interpretation is strongly influenced by our past experiences, knowledge we have learned and the attitudes and beliefs we possess. Therefore perception is an individual characteristic that is unique to every person.

Imaging

In order to understand what is remembered, Bartlett conducted a series of tests on imaging, as what is remembered is what is first imaged. Using ink blots, he asked participants to describe what they imaged in the pattern they saw. He noticed that participants often 'rummaged about' their own stored images to find one that would best fit the ink blot pattern they saw. Often describing the blot as a plant or animal, Bartlett suggested that the descriptions given were largely determined by the individual's own interests and experiences, and even the mood that they were in at the time. He coined the term 'effort after meaning' to describe how participants spent considerable effort in trying to connect a stimulus that they are given with some knowledge or experience they possess. Once the stimulus gains meaning for the individual, it can be more readily assimilated and stored.

Taking it further

Use the Internet and find some images of ink blots or projective tests. Try to verbalise what you see in the picture. This will demonstrate Bartlett's effort after meaning as you search for the meaning in the picture.

It is clear that perception is not simply the passive process of receiving an image, but an active construction of what we think we see using prior knowledge to guide the judgement. In Bartlett's follow-up experiments on memory, he employed the same philosophy to his research, moving away from artificial laboratory investigations and the use of 'non-sense' or random letters and words. Instead he used images of faces and stories that participants were required to describe or repeat. In his most famous experiment, Bartlett asked participants to read and recall a North American folk tale called 'The war of the ghosts'.

Remembering

Bartlett chose this folk tale for four reasons: it was culturally unfamiliar to participants so he could examine the transformations that the story may make when reproduced by participants, it lacked any rational story order, the dramatic nature of the story would encourage visual imaging, and the conclusion was somewhat supernatural and Bartlett wanted to see how participants would perceive and image this.

'The war of the ghosts' folk tale

One night two young men from Egulac went down to the river to hunt seals, and whilst they were there it became foggy and calm. Then they heard war-cries, and they thought 'Maybe this is a war party.' They escaped to the shore, and hid behind a log. Now canoes came up, and they heard the noise of paddles, and saw one canoe coming up to them.

There were five men in the canoe, and they said: 'What do you think? We wish to take you along. We are going up the river to make war on the people'.

One of the young men said: 'I have no arrows.'

'Arrows are in the canoe,' they said.

'I will not go along. I might be killed. My relatives do not know where I have gone. But you', he said, turning to the other 'may go with them.'

So one of the young men went, but the other returned home.

And the warriors went up the river to a town on the other side of Kalama. The people came down to the water, and they began to fight, and many were killed. But presently the young man heard one of the warriors say: 'Quick, let us go home: that Indian has been hit.' Now he thought: 'Oh, they are ghosts.' He did not feel sick, but they said he had been shot.

So the canoes went back to Egulac, and the young man went ashore to his house, and made a fire. And he told everybody and said: 'Behold I accompanied the ghosts, and we went to fight. Many of our fellows were killed, and many of those who attacked us were killed. They said I was hit, and I did not feel sick.'

He told it all, and then he became quiet. When the sun rose he fell down. Something black came out of his mouth. His face became contorted. The people jumped up and cried.

He was dead.

Key term

Repeated reproduction: a participant recalls information at increasing time intervals (e.g. after 10 minutes, a week, a month).

Each participant read the story twice and **repeated reproduction** was used to test the effect of time lapse on recall. Bartlett was interested in the form that the reproduced story would take, particularly after repeated reproductions. Twenty participants recalled the story after several minutes, weeks, months, and years; the longest time lapse was six and a half years. Bartlett found that the story became considerably shortened because of omissions made, the phrases used reflected modern concepts, and the story became more coherent in form. A number of transformations to the story were reported, particularly objects within the story were made more familiar – 'canoe' was changed to 'boat', 'hunting seals' changed to 'fishing'. Many participants did not grasp the role of the ghosts in the story, so simply omitted to mention them or rationalised their presence in some way.

Bartlett concluded that memory is reconstructed each time it is recalled. It is rarely accurate, and is prone to distortion, rationalisation, transformation and simplification. Even recall after several minutes elicited errors in recall, and these errors tended to be consolidated in subsequent reproductions. The process of remembering is constructive in nature and influenced by inferences made by an individual.

Psychology as a science

Bartlett's experiments had a distinct lack of control and standardisation in the procedures he followed. Participants were reasonably free to deliberate over the objects and stories presented to them. In one instance, he simply bumped into a previous participant after six and a half years and suggested he recall 'The war of the ghosts' story. The findings were qualitative; he described the nature of recalled information in a descriptive way. Therefore, his experiments can be criticised for lacking scientific rigour and being open to subjective interpretation.

A theory of memory

Based on the numerous experiments he conducted, Bartlett proposed a theory of **reconstructive memory**. Rather than viewing memory as a passive and faithful record of what was experienced, he viewed memory as constructive in nature. He proposed that previous knowledge was used to interpret information to be stored and to actively reconstruct memories to be recalled. Rather like using a note pad, in order to remember something we interpret an event and make brief notes on it. When it comes to recalling the event we actively draw on past experiences to reinterpret the notes, fill in the gaps and transform it into a coherent story. It is an imaginative reconstruction of events. Bartlett drew on the concept of schema to explain this.

Schema theory

Schemas are parcels of stored knowledge or a mental representation of information about a specific event or object. Every schema has fixed information and variable information. For example, a schema for going to a restaurant would contain knowledge of fixed events, such as being waited on, choosing from a menu, eating and paying for the meal, and variable events, such as what was on the menu and how much the meal cost. Bartlett argued that we do not remember all that we perceive. We therefore draw on our schema when we recall an event to fill in the gaps. This means that recall is an active reconstruction of an event strongly influenced by previously stored knowledge, expectations and beliefs.

Schemas are also used in recognition and interpretation of unfamiliar objects and events. This can explain the 'mental rummaging' Bartlett's participants experienced when trying to find meaning in the ink blots: effort after meaning (the effort we put into trying to find the correct schema that offers some meaning to an object).

> **Triggering a schema**
> Read the following passage:
>
> **'When the man entered the kitchen, he slipped on a wet spot on the floor and dropped the delicate glass vase he was holding. The glass vase was very expensive and everyone watched the event with horror.'**
>
> (Bransford, 1979)
>
> Now cover up the passage and write it down.
>
> Compare your passage to the original, do you notice anything different?
>
> You may have written down that the glass was broken. This is because the passage triggered your schema of broken glass because of the other details it contained – horror, wet spot, slipped, dropped. Yet it does not state in the passage that the glass broke; it was just your interpretation of the event.

> **Key term**
>
> **Reconstructive memory:** the idea that we alter information we have stored when we recall it, based on prior expectations/ knowledge.

Nature–nurture
Schemas are mental constructs that form the structural or hardware components of the human memory system and can be inferred to be biological structures or containment units (modules). However, the way in which schemas actually represent knowledge will vary between individuals and certainly across cultures. Because schemas represent stereotypical beliefs about an object or event, these will be affected by upbringing and so they are a product of nurture.

Evaluation

Bartlett based much of his research on story and object recall, but some have criticised his use of 'The war of the ghosts' story for having little relevance to everyday memory, and being a deliberate attempt to orchestrate evidence for his schema theory. However, Bartlett conducted his repeated reproduction experiments using eight different stories on different participants and found the same overall general shortening, transformation, familiarisation and omission. He also found similar effects on repeated and serial reproduction of pictures. Therefore, it can be argued that memory for any type of story or object is subject to the same memory errors.

Bartlett believed that schema had an effect at the recall stage of memory. That is, we actively reconstruct our memory when it is retrieved, and this retrieval process is affected by the schema we possess. However, others argue that sometimes schema have an influence at the point of learning because we draw on schema to comprehend a situation and make inferences about it.

A further criticism levelled at Bartlett is the overstatement of memory as inaccurate and flawed. This has led to a wealth of experimental research to demonstrate that eyewitnesses are unreliable when recalling witnessed events. Although we should maintain caution when using eyewitness testimony as a sole source of evidence in criminal cases, Steyvers and Hemmer (2012) argue that the experimental conditions of such research deliberately induce errors in recall; leading to the view that memory is unreliable. Their research demonstrates that in a real context without manipulated material, schematic recall can be very accurate. Therefore we should be cautious when assuming that eyewitness memory is completely unreliable.

> **Exam tip**
>
> Practise applying your knowledge of reconstructive memory to explain the following scenario.
>
> Mary was witness to a shoplifting incident at her local shop. She reported to the interviewing police officer that the shoplifter had stolen high-value items including coffee and alcohol. When viewing the CCTV footage, the police noted that the shoplifter had actually stolen low-value items: frozen chips, tinned beans and toothpaste.
>
> Using your knowledge of reconstructive memory, explain why Mary may have reported the incident inaccurately.
>
> Remember that it is important that you relate your knowledge of the theory to the details given in the scenario.

Individual differences in memory

Memory has been examined so far in terms of general theories that account for the majority of people. However, it should be acknowledged that there are individual differences in memory that make us unique.

The speed at which we can process information differs between individuals. This is known as 'processing speed'. You may have noticed that some people take longer to write notes from the whiteboard than others in your class. This is likely to be due to the speed at which they can process information and their short-term store capacity. Processing speed and capacity is affected by age too. Younger children have a shorter digit span than older children, suggesting that memory capacity increases with age. This evidence will be discussed later in the study by Sebastián and Hernández-Gil, 2012.

Schemas and autobiographical memory (episodic memory)

Bartlett's reconstructive memory theory suggests that we all have relatively similar schemas, but that these schemas can be heavily influenced by experience. This in turn affects the way we perceive information received by the senses and retrieve information held in memory. A teacher, for example, may perceive a simple cylindrical drawing as being a writing implement such as a pen, whereas a child may perceive it as an arrow or a drumstick. This experience-based perception will affect how the object is remembered. Similarly, the development of our schema will affect how we recall information.

It is also true that episodic memory is individual to the person as it is a collection of memories of their own life; an autobiography of personalised events. There are individual differences in autobiographical memory. In a large-scale investigation of 598 volunteer participants, Daniela Palombo and her colleagues (2012) conducted a Survey of Autobiographical Memory (SAM) designed to assess individual differences in naturalistic **autobiographical memory**. Using a design more commonly associated with measuring personality, they subdivided autobiographical memory into four domains: episodic memory (memory for events), semantic memory (memory for facts), spatial memory and prospective memory (imagination for future events). The questionnaire contained 102 items which participants scored on a five-point Likert Scale.

The findings suggested that the individuals who scored high or low on episodic memory also scored high or low on semantic memory. So we either have a good or poor memory overall.

Palombo et al. also found that men scored higher on spatial memory; this finding is consistent with other research indicating that men have stronger spatial ability than females. They also found that people who self-reported having depression scored low on episodic and semantic memory.

This survey gives a useful insight into self-reported accounts of naturalistic memory that could not be captured under laboratory conditions, and a useful insight into individual differences in autobiographical memory. However, it is possible that participants made inaccurate self-appraisal or lacked the insight to make accurate judgements of their own memory performance.

Developmental psychology in memory

Developmental psychology is a branch of the subject that investigates what happens to us as we age. Developmental psychology is concerned with both normal and abnormal behaviour as we grow up. For example, it is interested in how and when children learn language, but also when and why children may fail to learn language as they are expected. In memory research, dyslexia and Alzheimer's disease have been investigated in young and old participants.

Dyslexia

Dyslexia is a reading disorder defined as a problem in learning to recognise and decode printed words at a level that would be expected for the individual's age. This means that children with dyslexia find it difficult to read fluently and accurately, but have normal levels of comprehension (understanding). Dyslexia affects between 3 and 6 per cent of children (some estimate as many as 10 per cent) and is more prevalent in boys than in girls. It is characterised by having a particular difficulty with **phonology** which is critical for learning to read. The first indication of dyslexia is showing difficulty learning letter sounds and names, indicating a problem with learning to associate a word with its speech sound. This consequently leads to spelling and reading problems.

Children with dyslexia have a poor verbal short-term memory. Evidence for this comes from the phonological similarity effect (difficulty in remembering similar sounding words) and the word length effect (difficulty remembering sequences of long words compared to short words). So perhaps it is that children with dyslexia have an impaired short-term memory to deal with speech sounds.

- McDougall et al. (1994) divided 90 children into three different reading ability groups: poor readers, moderate readers and good readers, and found that poor readers had significantly lower memory

Key terms

Autobiographical memory: Like episodic memory, it is a memory for personal events.

Phonology: speech sounds.

Example items used in Survey of Autobiographical Memory

Episodic memory item: When I remember events, I remember lots of details.

Semantic memory item: I can learn and repeat facts easily, even if I don't remember where I learned them.

Spatial memory item: After I have visited an area, it is easy for me to find my way around the second time I visit.

Prospective memory item: When I imagine an event in the future, I can picture people and what they look like.

spans for words and slow reading rate. Good readers can articulate words quickly, leading to a greater number of words being represented phonologically in short-term memory. Poor readers sound out words more slowly, leading to fewer words being held in short-term memory. This basic inefficiency in phonological processing and storage may explain dyslexia.

Alloway et al. (2009) suggest that children with dyslexia have difficulty in processing and remembering speech sounds because of poor working memory. They cannot hold all of the speech sounds for long enough in working memory to be able to bind them together to form a word. They simply do not have the working memory capacity to store syllables for long enough to form them into a fluent word. Investigating 46 children, aged 6–11 years, with reading disability, she found that they showed short-term working memory deficits that could be the cause of their reading problems. Similarly, Smith-Spark et al. (2010) found that adults with dyslexia had unimpaired spatial working memory, but impaired verbal working memory, compared to a control group of non-dyslexic participants. They suggest that their results indicate a deficit with the phonological loop in dyslexic participants.

Research seems to conclude quite strongly that children and adults with dyslexia have an underlying cognitive impairment leading to a shorter memory span and difficulty processing and storing verbal information in short-term memory. However, it is difficult to establish exactly what role verbal memory plays in causing dyslexia, particularly because people with dyslexia present a range of sensory impairments in both the auditory and visual systems. Additionally, dyslexia is **comorbid** with other learning difficulties, in particular attention deficit hyperactivity disorder and other specific learning impairments. The interaction between dyslexia and other related difficulties makes it difficult to isolate phonological issues as a reason for reading impairment.

> ## Key term 💬
>
> **Comorbidity:** the presence of more than one disorder in the same person at the same time.

Alzheimer's disease

Alzheimer's disease is a progressive, degenerative, neurological disorder associated with ageing that will affect around one in twenty people, although the risk of development increases with age. It is the most common form of dementia and typically occurs after 65 years of age, but can occur as early as 40 years old. Alzheimer's is characterised by memory loss, concentration loss, confusion, and changes in mood that progressively become worse.

The normal ageing processes result in a loss of general cognitive functioning, but Alzheimer's disease appears to selectively impair certain cognitive systems rather than deteriorating cognition globally. In particular, Alzheimer's initially deteriorates the memory system for new events and information whereas older information is preserved. It also affects working memory; central executive functioning becomes impaired, making complex tasks more difficult to coordinate, and visuospatial processing becomes impaired.

A major characteristic of Alzheimer's disease is the inability to recall autobiographical information from episodic memory, thus it affects both short-term and long-term memory recall. The extent of the memory loss is associated with the depletion of brain matter, particularly in the hippocampus and temporal cortex. The greater the brain damage, the more significant the impairment; typically this increases with progression of the disease.

Loss of executive functioning results in a lack of general coordination and difficulty with attention. Baddeley et al. (2001) conducted a series of attentional tests on individuals with Alzheimer's and control participants, one involving looking for the letter 'Z' among easy and difficult distractor letters (letters that either looked like the letter Z or not), and a dual task procedure. They found that patients with Alzheimer's performed worse on the difficult distractor task and were even more impaired on the dual task. This suggests that dual attentional tasks are specifically impaired by the disease.

2.2 Methods

Learning outcomes

In this section you will learn about

- how to design and conduct experiments
- hypothesis construction
- experimental research designs
- problems that arise when conducting experiments
- controls that can be used to ensure reliable and valid research findings
- how to analyse and present quantitative data
- the use of statistical testing
- the use of case studies of brain-damaged patients in memory research, including the most famous case of Henry Molaison (HM)
- the use of qualitative data.

Experiments

Memory is difficult to observe or accurately measure using a self-report method, so cognitive psychologists often use experiments to objectively quantify the capacity and duration of each memory store. Traditionally **laboratory experiments** have been used to investigate memory, but increasingly **field experiments** are being used to understand memory in more everyday contexts.

Experiments are investigations where a variable is manipulated or altered and its effect can be measured, while maintaining control over other variables that might interfere with this situation. Experiments 'set up' a situation where participants are required to perform a task and the performance of this task is measured. The extent to which this task reflects real life or is conducted in a realistic situation depends on the type of experiment being conducted.

Figure 2.6 The experimental method

Aim

The aim of an experiment is a general statement about what area or topic is being researched. An aim typically begins with 'To investigate…'. The aim is a concise and to-the-point statement that directs the overall ambition of the study.

> **Example aims**
>
> To investigate whether the type of food given to cats affects their purring
>
> To investigate whether praise affects the time children spend washing dishes

Directional or one-tailed

The direction of the results can be predicted.

Non-directional or two-tailed

A change or difference is predicted, but not the direction it will go in.

Figure 2.7 Differences between hypotheses

> ### Key terms
>
> **Alternative hypothesis:** a statement that lays out what a researcher predicts will be found. This is also known as an experimental hypothesis when the research methodology adopted is experimental.
>
> **Directional hypothesis:** a directional hypothesis predicts the direction of difference or relationship that the result is likely to take.
>
> **Non-directional hypothesis:** a non-directional hypothesis predicts that a difference or relationship will be found, but not the direction that the difference or relationship will take.
>
> **Null hypothesis:** predicts no difference/relationship will be found or that any difference/relationship is due to chance factors.

Hypotheses

Experiments begin with a prediction of what is likely to happen in the investigation based on previous knowledge, research or theory. This prediction of a likely outcome is known as the experimental hypothesis. An experimental hypothesis is a type of **alternative hypothesis**. An experimental hypothesis is a clear and precise statement predicting the results of the experiment.

Sometimes we can be certain of the outcome of an experiment because, perhaps, there is strong evidence to suggest the outcome may happen, or it is based on a robust theory. In such cases a **directional hypothesis** will be predicted. When we are not certain of the outcome of an experiment, because there are conflicting theories or a lack of relevant evidence, a **non-directional hypothesis** will be predicted. A non-directional hypothesis predicts that a difference or relationship will be found, but not the direction that the difference or relationship will take.

Examples of experimental hypotheses

Directional hypothesis:

    Cats will purr for longer when they are fed tinned food compared to dry food.

    Children will spend longer washing dishes the more praise they receive.

Non-directional hypothesis:

    There will be a difference in the length of time a cat purrs when given tinned and dry food.

    Praise will affect the time children spend washing dishes.

A **null hypothesis** is a default prediction that is supported if there is a greater likelihood of the results occurring by chance. When we conduct research we often find some difference or relationship; it is rare we would find nothing, but sometimes the difference or relationship found is too small or insignificant to be due to anything other than chance variation. For example, if we are investigating whether praise affects a child's inclination to tidy their bedroom, it is unlikely that we will find no/zero effect of praise on bedroom tidying. However, the change observed in bedroom tidying may be too small or insignificant to be due to praise alone and could be due to chance.

Example null hypotheses

There will be no difference in the length of time cats spend purring when fed tinned or dry food. Any difference found will be due to chance factors.

There will be no effect of praise on the time children spend washing dishes. Any effect found will be due to chance factors.

Independent and dependent variables

An experiment always has an independent variable and dependent variable. The independent variable (IV) is the variable that is manipulated or changed by the researcher in order to demonstrate a difference between the experimental conditions. The dependent variable (DV) is the variable that is measured or the result of the experiment. The dependent variable measures any changes that occur because of the independent variable. This allows causality to be established (cause and effect).

Example IVs and DVs

'A researcher wished to investigate whether participants will recall more words from an organised list compared to a random list'

In this example, the researcher will have to change which list participants have to learn and recall from. This is manipulated by giving one set of randomised words and one set of organised words. The type of word list is the IV.

The researcher will then ask participants to recall the list of words and record how many words they remember. This is the measured variable or outcome of the investigation, so is referred to as the DV.

Operationalisation

Once the IV and DV have been decided, it is very important to make these variables precise and specific by operationalising them. This means deciding exactly how you are going to manipulate the IV and exactly how the DV will be recorded. Operationalisation of the IV and DV means that the study can be precisely replicated to check the conclusions are reliable. **Operational definitions** of the DV can increase objectivity in research; this is because the outcome is measured in the same way by all researchers, and the outcome is not open to interpretation. It also means that other psychologists can assess whether or not the researcher has conducted valid research.

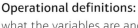
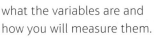

Key term

Operational definitions: what the variables are and how you will measure them.

Good and poor operationalisation

Poor operationalisation:

A researcher thought that children who came to school without a healthy breakfast had problems during literacy hour. The researcher decided to ask the children what they had for breakfast and split them into healthy and unhealthy breakfast groups. She then watched them read a book and decided how well they could read.

This is an example of poor operationalisation because the way in which the healthy and unhealthy breakfast groups are defined is unclear. It is also not clear how the researcher measured reading skill. A study such as this example would be difficult to replicate exactly to check for reliable findings. If more than one researcher was involved in the research, it would not be clear what is meant by reading skill, so they may reach different conclusions for the same child. A different researcher would not be able to assess how healthy breakfasts were defined or how reading skill was defined, so could not be certain that the study was valid.

Good operationalisation:

A researcher thought that children who came to school without a healthy breakfast had problems during literacy hour. The researcher asked the children and parents to make a record of what they ate for breakfast over the course of a week. A nutritionist was asked to categorise the breakfasts as health and unhealthy. Breakfasts with over the recommended meal allowance for salt, fat and sugar were defined as unhealthy. The researcher then timed how long a child took to read a story during literacy hour. All children read the same story out loud to the researcher, who timed the children and recorded any errors they made.

This is an example of good operationalisation because the IV (healthy and unhealthy breakfasts) are clearly defined and the DV (reading speed and errors) can be measured exactly without any ambiguity. This study is replicable and it would be easy for a different researcher to assess whether the definition of healthy and unhealthy breakfasts and reading ability were measuring what was intended.

Extraneous variable: a variable that may have affected the dependent variable but that was not the independent variable.

Confounding variable: a variable that affects the findings of a study directly, so much that you are no longer measuring what was intended.

Exam tip

When considering control, it is common to suggest that noise, temperature and lighting conditions might affect the dependent variable without carefully considering whether they are relevant extraneous variables. In extreme, these variables could affect research, but they would have minimal influence on the dependent variable in most studies. It is important to consider the nature and aims of the investigation before you decide which extraneous variables are likely to have an effect.

Experimental variables

Extraneous and confounding variables

An experiment should try to establish control over factors that may have an unwanted effect on the dependent variable. These other variables are known as **extraneous variables**. Sometimes an extraneous variable can influence the dependent variable and make it look as though the effect was from the independent variable; this is called a **confounding variable**. This variable confounds the results of the study in such a way that you are no longer measuring the effect of the IV on the DV.

Extraneous and confounding variables can be divided into two types: situational variables and participant variables.

Situational variables

An extraneous variable that might affect the results of a study could be found in the environment in which the study is conducted. Situational factors such as lighting, noise, temperature, other people, disturbances, time of day, etc., may all affect the results of a study so should be controlled or eliminated. Controlling extraneous variables means that they are held constant for all participants, so that the variable affects everyone equally. Eliminating extraneous variables involves removing the possibility of them occurring in the first place.

Participant variables

Participants themselves may affect the results of the study. Participants may bring different characteristics to an experiment that could have an effect on the dependent variable, such as level of motivation, personality, intelligence, experience, age and skills. It is fairly easy to control participant variables such as age and gender, but controlling motivation or experience may take more thought.

It is not necessary, and would certainly be far too time-consuming, to control for all situational and participant variables. It is only really necessary to control those variables that might have an unwanted impact on the dependent variable. For example, controlling the temperature of a room is not vital unless you are testing something where the temperature might affect performance.

Careful control

List some situational and participant variables that could affect the following studies and then consider how you would control or eliminate them.

- An investigation into sporting experience and the ability to shoot a hole in one with a basketball

- An investigation to see if rehearsal was a better memory technique to learn a list of digits than creating a mental picture of the digits

- An investigation to see if more cars stopped at a zebra crossing on a busy street for men or women

- An investigation into essay writing skills of history and art undergraduate students

- An investigation into alcohol and driving performance

Experimenter effects

Experimenter or researcher effects refer to the way an experimenter may influence the outcome of an experiment by their actions or mere presence. These may be subtle cues that may influence the way a participant responds in an experimental situation. Sometimes these can be obvious effects, such as a female researcher asking a male participant about his attitudes towards gender equality, or a young researcher asking an older participant what they think about youth culture. However, some experimenter effects are more subtle. The **Hawthorne Effect** is one such example where the mere presence of a researcher can have an effect on performance.

Closely related to this is the concept of demand characteristics. This is when the effect of the experimenter causes participants to alter their behaviour to meet the expectations (whether real or imagined) of the experimenter. Rosenthal researched this expectancy effect over many decades. Rosenthal found that psychology graduates who were told one set of rats were brighter than another set of rats resulted in the bright rats being able to learn their way out of a maze faster than the dull rats. With no actual difference between the two sets of rats, Rosenthal concluded that the students may have treated the rats differently, pressed their stopwatch earlier or reported false findings as a result of expectancy effects.

Experimenter effects may explain why a researcher finds a result that other researchers fail to replicate.

Experimental control

In experiments using human participants, a great many variables can influence outcomes. It is important to be able to identify these variables and then put into place controls to help prevent them having any effect on the experiment. Various control techniques have been established to help deal with these control issues.

Standardisation

Standardisation refers to making an experiment the same experience for all participants. Standardised instructions are a set of instructions given to all participants that can be used to eliminate experimenter effects because it removes the potential for the experimenter to give verbal or non-verbal cues to participants. Standardised procedures (stages of the experiment, timings, apparatus, etc.) ensure that all participants are treated in the same way (other than the change in condition due to the independent variable) so there is no variation in the way they experience the research that may affect the way they behave. Standardisation also improves the replicability of the experiment.

Double- and single-blind experiments

To control for demand characteristics, participants may be unaware that they are part of an experiment, or may have been deceived as to the true nature of the study. This is known as a **single-blind procedure**, where the participants are unaware of the study aim so it does not influence how they perform. To eliminate experimenter effects, independent researchers who are not told the aim of the study may be employed by an experimenter to conduct the study on their behalf. If neither the participant nor researcher knows the aim of the study, it is referred to as a **double-blind procedure**.

Experimental design

Once the independent variable has been operationally defined, the levels of the independent variable can be identified and the conditions of the experiment established.

Taking it further

In the exam you may be asked to identify extraneous variables associated with psychological research. Practise by assessing the extraneous variables and controls in the following research studies.

Identify:
- participant variables
- situational variables
- controls that the researchers used.

Studies:
- Godden and Baddeley (1975) scuba diver study of context dependent recall
- Schab (1990) chocolate cue research
- Pickel (1998) memory and weapon focus study

Try to find some more studies to assess.

Key terms

Control group: A group of participants that does not experience the experimental situation but acts as a baseline against which to judge any change.

Individual differences: natural variation in human characteristics.

Participant variables: natural variation in human characteristics.

Random allocation: participants are allocated to a condition of the study at random (names drawn from a hat).

Identifying levels of the IV and conditions of the experiment

For example: The effect of music (IV) on transcription speed and accuracy (DV)

Levels of the IV – Rock music or silence

Conditions of the experiment: Whether participants hear rock music while trying to transcribe verbally dictated information or transcribe in silence

The conditions of the experiment reflect directly the levels of the independent variable. More levels of the IV can be added, for example, classical music or popular music and therefore there will be more conditions involved in the experiment.

Note: Often one level of the independent variable is a **control group**, which receives no treatment. In the above example, the control group is the group that transcribes in silence. It is important to have a control group as a baseline comparison to determine the effect of the IV on the DV.

Participants recruited to take part will need to be allocated to one or both conditions of the experiment. There are several designs that can be used to achieve this: an independent groups design, a repeated measures design and a matched pairs design.

Independent groups design

This is when the participants are divided into groups and are only involved in one of the experimental conditions of the experiment. A strength of this experimental design is that participants are less likely to guess the aim of the investigation as they only take part in one level of the independent variable, they do not get to know about the other conditions. This means that the chance of demand characteristics or expectancy effects is somewhat reduced. However, it does mean recruiting twice as many participants because you need separate groups and there may be **individual differences** or **participant variables** between the participants in each group that make a comparison of the groups unreliable. One way of controlling for individual differences is to randomly allocate participants to one or other of the conditions. **Random allocation** means that it is probable, but not certain, that there will be an even distribution of participant variation because they all have an equal chance of being selected for each condition of the experiment.

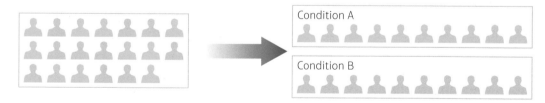

Figure 2.8 Independent groups design

Repeated measures design

This is when all participants take part in all conditions of the experiment. This resolves the problem of individual differences because the same participants are in all levels of the independent variable, so the participant's results in one condition are compared to the same participant results in a different condition. Fewer participants are needed for a repeated measures design, because they are used twice, so it is more economical than an independent groups design. However, the chance of participants displaying demand characteristics is greatly increased because they have knowledge of all conditions of the study, and are therefore more likely to be able to guess the aim of the study. There is also a problem of **order effects**; this is when the performance of participants in one condition is influenced by the previous condition of the experiment. Order effects include practice and fatigue; a participant may learn the task in the first condition so perform better in a second condition, or become tired and performance declines in a second condition.

One way of controlling for the effect of demand characteristics is to use a single-blind technique. To control for order effects, randomisation or counterbalancing can be used to ensure that participants experience the conditions in a different order. Randomisation involves selecting at random which of the conditions of the experiment a participant does first. This can be done by picking a card out of a hat. Counterbalancing involves the participants being placed into either a group that does Condition A then Condition B, or a group that does Condition B then Condition A. However, if the order effect (practice or fatigue) in one sequence order (AB) is not equivalent to the order effect in a different order (BA), a more complex counterbalancing technique may be required. The ABBA design is used to balance unsymmetrical order effects by getting participants to complete the conditions twice – A, B, B then A. The mean score for both conditions A and conditions B are then taken.

When there are more than two conditions in an experiment, a Latin square can be used to designate participants to one of the combinations of ordering. This means that, although order effects still occur, they are balanced out between each group.

A simpler way to overcome order effects is to leave a time gap between participants completing condition A and condition B. The effects of fatigue are likely to be reduced, although the same may not be true of practice effects depending on what the task is.

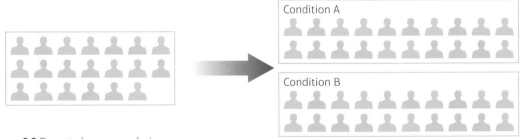

Figure 2.9 Repeated measures design

Matched pairs design

To overcome the problems associated with repeated measures and independent groups designs, a matched pairs design can be used. This is when different participants are assigned to each condition of the experiment (similar to independent groups) but they are matched on characteristics important to the study. These characteristics are often established by pre-testing and researching the lives and backgrounds of all the participants. This control ensures that the participants in each condition can be compared fairly. This can be achieved by matching all participants on important characteristics and then randomly assigning them to each condition. It is important to match participants on characteristics central to the aim of the study; it would not be useful to match participants on hair colour, for example, in a study of driving ability, the matching would have to concern driving experience, eyesight, reaction time, or other characteristics where any variation could affect the results.

A matched pairs design ensures that the conditions can be compared more reliably and that any difference found between the results of each condition is more likely to be due to the manipulated variable, so causation can be established. However, a matched pairs design is time-consuming and many participants have to be excluded from the study because they do not meet the matching criteria. It is also very difficult to match participants on all possible characteristics that could have an effect on the dependent variable. For example, if a study was conducted into the effect of an unhealthy breakfast on reading ability, it would be useful to match participants' educational level and

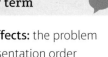

Key term

Order effects: the problem with presentation order of stimulus material. Participants may become practised at the test so improve performance or they may become tired so that performance deteriorates.

A	B	C
C	A	B
B	C	A

Figure 2.10 Latin square used to counterbalance conditions of an experiment

eyesight. However, there may be variables that are much more difficult to match, such as how many books a child has at home, the educational level of parents, how much time parents spend reading with their children, etc. Therefore a matched pairs design cannot be truly matched on all possible variables.

Which experimental design?

Which experimental design is being described in the following investigations?

1. An investigation to see if boys or girls are better at mathematics.

2. A study to test whether sport improved self-esteem divided volunteer participants into sporting and non-sporting groups and gave them a questionnaire on self-esteem.

3. Researchers investigated the difference in attitudes between identical twins.

Reliability

Reliability refers to the consistency of findings from research, and it is an important criterion for being scientific. For experiments, test-retest reliability is important.

Test-retest reliability

If findings are consistent, and can be considered reliable, we can trust that the finding will happen again and again. In order to achieve reliability, research must be replicable. This requires very tight control of extraneous variables that, if not controlled, could result in different findings when a study is repeated.

Validity

Validity refers to whether the study is measuring the behaviour or construct it intends to measure. Understanding validity is an important skill for both designing and evaluating research studies. There are two broad categories of validity; **internal validity** and **external validity**. Internal validity refers to how well the procedure of a study establishes a causal relationship between the manipulated independent variable and the measured dependent variable, or whether it has been confounded by uncontrolled extraneous variables. Internal validity can be ensured by using standardised procedures, controlling for order effects and individual differences, and avoiding demand characteristics.

A way of assessing internal validity is by examining **construct validity**. Construct validity is how well the measure of a behaviour being used is a useful indicator of what is supposed to be studied. For example, recall of a previously learned list of words may not be a useful measure of episodic memory because a participant may draw on semantic memory and make a good guess. If you are measuring what you intend to be measuring, then another way to assess internal validity is through **predictive validity**; the extent to which the performance on the measure can predict future performance on a similar criterion. For example, if a test of intelligence can accurately predict future academic success, then it has predictive validity.

External validity refers to how well research findings study can be generalised beyond the study itself, that is, to other situations or other populations. There are two main types of external validity; ecological and population validity. **Ecological validity** refers to the extent to which the research can be generalised to other situations, for example real-life or everyday situations. Memory experiments conducted in artificial environments with artificial tasks may not be generalised to everyday use of memory. **Population validity** refers to the extent to which research findings apply to other populations than those used as the sample. External validity can be improved by ensuring that the sample is representative of the population it intends to represent, and by making the context of the study as realistic as possible.

Exam tip

Understanding validity can be difficult, particularly as there are different types of validity that you will need to know. However, validity is important to know not just when you are designing your own research, but it can also be a useful tool to help you evaluate the research of others.

Key terms

Internal validity: the extent to which the outcome of the study is the direct result of the manipulated independent variable.

External validity: the extent to which the findings apply to other people and situations.

Construct validity: the extent to which the test measures what it claims to measure.

Predictive validity: the extent to which results from a test or a study can predict future behaviour.

Ecological validity: the extent to which the findings still explain the behaviour in different situations.

Population validity: the extent to which the findings can be applied to other people.

Objectivity

Being objective refers to the need to be impartial and judgement free. It is important that the dependent variable is measured objectively, so that the opinions or judgements of the researcher do not affect how the dependent variable is recorded. For example, imagine that you are asked to guess the length of a table. Your judgement will be based on your own opinion or belief about length, and will probably differ from the guesses of others. Your guesses and those of others are subjective and therefore unlikely to be either reliable or valid. However, if you use a ruler to measure the length of the table, your recorded answer is objective, and will be exactly the same as others who measure the same table using the same ruler. This is an objective measure of the table length, and therefore will be both reliable and valid.

Cognitive psychology studies concepts, such as memory, that cannot be directly observed and measured. Cognitive psychologists would agree that we cannot objectively measure mental processes, but we can objectively observe the data produced by experiments and neuroimaging techniques. If we conduct a short-term memory test that records a participant recall of five words, this is an objective measurement of short-term memory. If we use a PET scan to test brain functioning during a memory experiment, we can objectively observe regions of the brain that are active during the task.

Laboratory experiments

A laboratory experiment is conducted in an artificial environment where an independent variable is manipulated and its effect on the dependent variable measured in some way. Removing participants from their natural environment eliminates the potential for extraneous variables affecting their behaviour; exposing the objective truth by stripping away the context ensures a human characteristic can be studied in an objective and value-free way. An artificial context provides the researcher with the level of control over relevant variables necessary to achieve a more scientific approach and ensure **causality**.

However, laboratory experiments can be criticised for lacking ecological validity as behaviour is measured in an artificial environment and artificial way. This makes the findings of laboratory research unlike normal life so they may not apply to a real-life situation. Participants are often invited to take part in laboratory research, so they are aware of their participation which can lead to demand characteristics and expectancy effects. The presence of the researcher during the experiment may influence the behaviour or performance of participants, so experimenter effects are more likely to have an influence on the results.

Field experiments

A field experiment is conducted in a natural environment where the independent variable is manipulated and the dependent variable measured. Participants are tested where they would normally display the behaviour being studied; this may be a classroom, supermarket or high street, and they may not be aware that they are taking part in an experiment until it is over. This means that field experiments have greater ecological validity as participant behaviour will be more natural and the environment in which they are tested is more realistic. If participants are unaware of their participation in the experiment they will not show demand characteristics. However, because the research is not conducted in a controlled environment, there is greater chance of extraneous variables having an effect on the dependent variable. There may also be ethical problems if a participant is unaware that they are taking part, as they have not given consent and do not have a right to withdraw from the experiment. In such cases, the experimenter may choose to debrief them after the experiment and offer them the right to withdraw their data from the study.

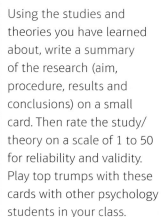

Taking it further

Using the studies and theories you have learned about, write a summary of the research (aim, procedure, results and conclusions) on a small card. Then rate the study/ theory on a scale of 1 to 50 for reliability and validity. Play top trumps with these cards with other psychology students in your class.

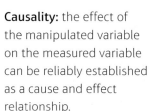

Key term

Causality: the effect of the manipulated variable on the measured variable can be reliably established as a cause and effect relationship.

WIDER ISSUES AND DEBATES

Psychology as a science
The laboratory experiment is considered to be the most scientific of the research methods that psychologists can use. It is characterised by a high level of control and standardisation. This means that the study can be repeated to check the findings are consistent. As such, laboratory experiments are highly reliable. However, they may lack validity because they do not reflect real-life behaviour.

Inferential statistics

Descriptive statistics, summary tables and graphs describe a data set, but to know whether there was a real effect of the independent variable on the dependent variable an inferential test of significance needs to be carried out. When data differs between two conditions (which it is likely to do as we rarely find no difference at all) we need to establish whether the effect is a real one or simply due to chance variation between the conditions. If there is a real effect we can accept the alternative hypothesis, but if there was no real effect we need to accept the null hypothesis. An inferential test of significance will indicate whether we should retain or reject a hypothesis.

Inferential tests rest on the concept of probability. Probability is the likelihood of an event occurring, so the probability of getting heads or tails on a single coin toss is 0.5 (or 50 per cent or one in two). When testing the probability of data we are actually testing the likelihood of the data (or rather difference between the data sets as defined by the independent variable) being due to random chance factors or something else. We use an inferential test to decide whether or not to accept the null hypothesis because it tells us whether the results were likely to be due to chance or not.

How small is small?

If the probability of the results is due to chance, we are assuming that the difference between the data is too small to be significant to show a real effect and the null hypothesis would be retained as the study conclusion. The question here is 'how small does the difference have to be to be too small?' In psychology it is generally accepted that the cut-off for making the decision about whether or not to reject the null hypothesis (and therefore make a judgement about whether the results are due to chance or not) is equal to or less than 0.05. This is expressed as $p < 0.05$. This means that we accept a 1 in 20 or 5 per cent probability that the results are due to chance. When we conduct an inferential test of significance it tells us whether we meet this 0.05 probability threshold or not. If the probability of the result occurring by chance is equal to or less than 0.05 we support the alternative hypothesis. However, if the probability of the result occurring by chance is greater than 0.05, we retain the null hypothesis.

If the inferential test is significant, we can support the experimental hypothesis because we are 95 per cent confident that our prediction is correct and the likelihood of the result occurring by chance is 5 per cent or less. If the inferential test is not significant, we accept the null hypothesis because we are less than 95 per cent confident that our prediction is correct and the likelihood of the results occurring by chance is greater than 5 per cent.

> ### Maths tip
>
> - Notice that nowhere so far is there mention of 'proving' the results. We simply cannot prove the results are true even after conducting a statistical test. We can only claim that the test reasonably supports the alternative hypothesis we are stating, or that we are not confident in our results so we are retaining the null hypothesis.

Levels of significance and error

Although 0.05 is the accepted level of probability in psychology, if the result of the inferential test is equal to or less than 0.1 (10 per cent or 1 in 10 probability of the result occurring by chance) it may still be reported and followed up with more research. However, at a 0.1 level of significance, there

Maths tip

Statistics and variables are linked when using an inferential test of significance, so it would be useful to refresh your memory on variables and hypotheses before reading this section. Pay particular attention to the types of alternative hypothesis and the null hypothesis.

Link

For quantitative data analysis including calculating measures of central tendency, frequency tables, measures of dispersion (range and standard deviation) and percentages, please see the Methods section of Topic 1: *Social psychology*.

is a chance that the alternative hypothesis is accepted when it should not have been. Accepting the alternative hypothesis when the results were really not significant and the null hypothesis should have actually been retained, is known as a **Type 1 error**. A type 1 error occurs because the level of significance is too lenient.

However, if the result of the inferential test is equal to or less than 0.01 (1 per cent or 1 in 100 probability of the result occurring by chance), it is this finding that should be reported as it is highly significant and therefore not likely to be due to chance. However, if we set 0.01 as the accepted level of significance in psychology we are likely to reject a number of alternative hypotheses when there was a real effect. Retaining the null hypothesis when there was actually a real effect is known as a **type 2 error**, and this occurs because the level of significance set is too stringent.

Inferential tests of difference

Different inferential tests are used on different types of data. The test you choose will depend on the following features:

- are you investigating a difference or relationship between variables?

- are you using a related or unrelated design?

- what type of data are you analysing?

The last feature refers to what type of data you will analyse. There are four different types of data, nominal, ordinal, interval and ratio.

Nominal level data

Nominal data is the most basic form of data you can gather because it does not tell you very much information about the data set or results. This is because the data gathered are categorical or grouped and the total number of values in each category or group is calculated. We know nothing about each value within the categories; we just know the category totals. For example, if you conducted a class survey on pet ownership, you are likely to gather data on how many students own a pet or not, or what types of pet the students in your class own.

The class will be asked whether they own a pet, and the frequency of pet owners or individuals without a pet will be calculated. We know very little about the individual differences in pet or non-pet owners, just the totals for each category. Similarly, if you divided the class into students under 1.85 metres tall and over 1.85 metres tall, and calculate the frequency in each category, you would have nominal level data. However, you would not know the actual heights of each individual student or their height in relation to one another.

Ordinal level data

Ordinal data tells us a little more information about the values in the data set. Ordinal data is data that are ranked into an order or position. For example, your school may collect house points and present a prize to the house with the greatest number of points at the end of the year. Each house will be placed in rank order of first, second, third, fourth. This data tells us about the position of each house, but it does not tell us how many points were achieved or the difference between each rank. So, the house in first place may have only ten points more than the one in second place, but the house in third place may be way behind second place with 100 fewer points. Ordinal data is often derived from arbitrary scales, such as grades for a test, or ratings of a characteristic such as attractiveness from 1–10. Because the scales are arbitrary, the intervals between each value are not equal in reality. The difference between a grade A and a grade B is not the same as the difference between a grade C and grade D, nor will someone rated as 5 on the attractiveness scale be half as attractive as someone rated as 10.

Key terms

Type 1/Type I error: when the null hypothesis is rejected and the alternative hypothesis supported when the effect was not real.

Type 2/Type II error: when the alternative hypothesis is rejected and the null retained when there was actually a real effect.

Matched pairs design

A matched pairs design is an independent groups design where participants in one group are matched on important factors, such as IQ, to participants in another group. For the purposes of selecting an appropriate inferential test, because the groups are matched, it should be treated as a repeated measures design.

Interval and ratio level data

With interval and ratio level data, you do know the differences between each value within a data set because a scale is used where the intervals between each value are equal. Typically interval and ratio level data are gathered using a recognised scale or tested psychological instrument. The only difference between interval and ratio level data is that ratio data will have an absolute zero. Measurements such as height in centimetres, speed in seconds and distance in kilometres are ratio level data because they start at zero on the scale.

For the purpose of selecting which inferential test to use, you will only need to decide between nominal and 'at least' ordinal level data (interval and ratio level data can be treated as ordinal level data).

You will only have to learn about a few inferential tests, so you can use this decision tree to work out which test you should use:

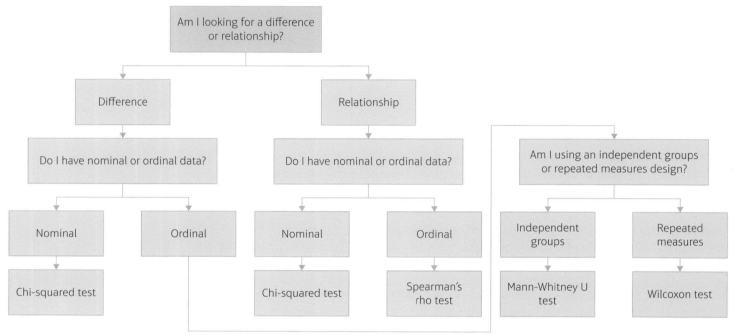

Figure 2.11 Inferential test options

Key terms

Repeated measures design: where all participants complete all conditions of the experiment.

Matched pairs design: where different participants are allocated to only one experimental condition (they do not do both) but are matched on important characteristics.

Wilcoxon Signed Ranks test

The Wilcoxon Signed Ranks test is used as a test of difference between two conditions when the data achieved is at ordinal level or above and the experimental design being used is a **repeated measures design** or **matched pairs design**.

Calculation procedure

1. Calculate the difference between the pairs of scores achieved by each participant on the two tests. In the example here, this is done by subtracting the column A score from the column B score.

2. Ignoring any plus or minus signs, rank the score differences.

3. Calculate the sum total of the ranks for positive differences and total sum of ranks for negative differences.

4. The smaller of these scores is referred to as the T value (the test statistic or calculated value of the test).

Maths tip

Assigning ranks to a set of scores literally means to give each score a position on a scale; position 1, position 2, etc. However, if you have scores of equal value, they cannot share the same rank position, but the positions need to be divided between them.

For example:

Rank position	1	2.5	2.5	4	5	6	7.5	7.5	9
Scores	3	4	4	7	8	9	10	10	13

Notice that the scores of 4 and 10 do not get a rank position of 2 and 3 or 7 and 8, the ranks are divided between them.

Table 2.3 An example of assigning ranks

Participant number	Number of words recalled from a non-categorised list	Number of words recalled from a categorised list	Difference	Rank of difference
N = 10	A	B	(B-A)	
1	8	11	3	4
2	7	7	0	
3	9	16	7	6
4	11	12	1	1.5
5	13	18	5	5
6	9	8	-1	1.5
7	8	16	8	7
8	5	17	12	9
9	13	11	-2	3
10	6	17	11	8

Sum of ranks for positive differences: 1.5+4+5+6+7+8+9 = 40.5

Sum of ranks for negative differences: 1.5+3 = 4.5

The smallest value is 4.5, so this is accepted at the calculated value of T.

In order to find out whether the calculated value of the Wilcoxon test is significant (showing a real difference in recall) we need to compare the calculated value of T=4.5 to a table of critical values for a Wilcoxon Signed Ranks test.

Table 2.4 Critical values for a Wilcoxon Signed Ranks test

	Level of significance for a one-tailed test		
	0.05	0.25	0.01
	Level of significance for a two-tailed test		
n	0.1	0.05	0.02
n=5	0	–	–
6	2	0	–
7	3	2	0
8	5	3	1
9	8	5	3
10	11	8	5
11	13	10	7
12	17	13	9

The calculated value of T must be equal to or less than the table (critical) value for significance at the level shown.

Suppose the hypothesis is that there will be more words recalled from a categorised list than a non-categorised list of words. This is a directional hypothesis, because the direction of difference between the conditions is predicted. This means that a one-tailed test is used. The accepted level of significance in psychology is 0.05, so will need to consult the first column until it reaches the row where n=9 (as 10 participants were used but N is the number of scores left ignoring those with 0 difference). The critical value we need to compare the calculated value to is 8. Now we need to consult the instructions below the table. 'The calculated value of T must be equal to or less than the table (critical) value for significance at the level shown.' This instructs us that the calculated value of T=4.5 must be equal to or less than the critical value of 11 to be significant at 0.05. Because 4.5 is less than 11, the result is significant and the alternative hypothesis can be supported.

One- and two-tailed tests

A one-tailed test is used because the direction of difference can be predicted and a directional hypothesis is stated. A two-tailed test is used when the direction of difference cannot be predicted and a non-directional hypothesis is stated.

Mann-Whitney U test

The Mann-Whitney U test is used as a test of difference between two conditions when the data achieved is at ordinal level or above and the experimental design being used is an **independent groups design**.

Calculation procedure

1. Use the Mann-Whitney U Test formula

Rank all of the scores as a whole group:

Position	1	2	3	4	5	6	7	8	9	10	11	12	13	14	15	16	17	18	19	20
Score	5	6	7	7	8	8	8	9	9	11	11	11	12	13	13	16	16	17	17	18
Rank	1	2	3.5	3.5	6	6	6	8.5	8.5	11	11	11	13	14.5	14.5	16.5	16.5	18.5	18.5	20

2. Now you will need to find the sum (total) of the ranks for both groups, so each group will need to be divided back into their original sets:

Number of words recalled from a non-categorised list Group A	Ranks	Number of words recalled from a categorised list Group B	Ranks
8	6	11	11
7	3.5	7	3.5
9	8.5	16	16.5
11	11	12	13
13	14.5	18	20
9	8.5	8	6
8	6	16	16.5
5	1	17	18.5
13	14.5	11	11
6	2	17	18.5
Sum total of ranks	75.5	Sum total of ranks	134.5

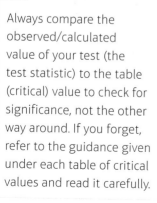

3. Now use the formulae to calculate Ua and Ub

Note that Ra is the sum total of ranks for list A and Rb is the sum total of ranks for list B

$U_a = N_a \times N_b + N_a \times (N_a +1) /2 - R_a$

$U_a = 10 \times 10 + 10 \times 11 /2 - 75.5$

$U_a = 100 + 110/2 - 75.5$

$U_a = 79.5$

$U_b = N_a \times N_b + N_b \times (N_b +1) /2 - R_b$

$U_b = 10 \times 10 + 10 \times 11 /2 - 134.5$

$U_b = 100 + 110/2 - 134.5$

$U_b = 20.5$

The lowest value of Ua or Ub is the U value taken. In this case the U value is 20.5.

The U value = 20.5, which is less than the critical value of 27 for a one-tailed test (which we will assume in this instance), therefore the results are significant.

Table 2.6 Critical values for a Mann-Whitney U test

n	1	2	3	4	5	6	7	8	9	10
1	-	-	-	-	-	-	-	-	-	-
2	-	-	-	-	0	0	0	1	1	1
3	-	-	0	0	1	2	2	3	3	4
4	-	-	0	1	2	3	4	5	6	7
5	-	0	1	2	4	5	6	8	9	11
6	-	0	2	3	5	7	8	10	12	14
7	-	0	2	4	6	8	11	13	15	17
8	-	1	3	5	7	10	13	15	18	20
9	-	1	3	6	9	12	15	18	21	24
10	-	1	4	7	11	14	17	20	24	27

Critical values of U for a one-tailed test at 0.05; two-tailed test at 0.1 (Mann-Whitney)

The observed value of U is significant at the given level of significance if it is equal to or less than the table (critical) value above.

> **Maths tip**
>
> The Mann-Whitney U test has several different critical values tables that can be referred to in order to determine significance. You will first need to decide which table to use by referring to the titles of each table:
>
> Critical values of U for a one-tailed test at 0.005; two-tailed test at 0.01 (Mann-Whitney)
> Critical values of U for a one-tailed test at 0.01; two-tailed test at 0.02 (Mann-Whitney)
> Critical values of U for a one-tailed test at 0.025; two-tailed test at 0.05 (Mann-Whitney)
> Critical values of U for a one-tailed test at 0.05; two-tailed test at 0.1 (Mann-Whitney)
>
> First, decide whether the hypothesis is directional (one-tailed) or non-directional (two-tailed). Next, decide on the level of significance to be used. This is typically 0.05, but you may be asked to refer to a significance level of 0.1 or 0.01.

> **Maths tip**
>
> It is critical that you show all of your calculations/ workings in the exam. Using the formulae, write down step by step how you are calculating the Mann-Whitney as shown above.

> **Maths tip**
>
> Remembering which test to use can be difficult, but imagery can help. Imagine Mr Mann, Mr Whitney and Mr Wilcoxon. Mr Wilcoxon is cross (x) because he has to do both conditions of the experiment (repeated measures design) which is taking up his time. Mr Mann and Mr Whitney are happy because they only have to do one condition of the experiment (independent groups design) and then can go home early.

In addition to gathering quantitative data, we can also gather qualitative data from research. Case studies are a research method where both qualitative and quantitative data can be gathered.

Case studies of brain-damaged patients and the use of qualitative data

Case studies of brain-damaged patients have been critical to cognitive psychology in order to investigate how brain injury affects cognitive functioning. Sometimes we can understand cognitive functions, such as memory, more in their absence, as is the case in brain-damaged patients.

Taking it further

A biography of the surgical procedure and subsequent memory loss has been depicted in a short film. You can find this online by searching for the key words 'Amnesiac Henry Molaison'.

Key terms

Temporal lobe: an area of the brain, called a lobe, situated below the ear.

Hippocampus: a structure of the brain responsible for learning, emotion and memory.

Anterograde amnesia: the loss of ability to make new memories, while memories before the injury remain relatively intact.

Retrograde amnesia: the loss of ability to recall events prior to the injury.

Henry Molaison (HM)

An invaluable case study was that of Henry Molaison who suffered brain injury as a result of a surgical procedure to relieve him from seizures caused by epilepsy.

Henry Molaison, known by thousands of psychology students as 'HM', lost his memory on an operating table in a hospital in Hartford, Connecticut, in August 1953. He was 27 years old and had suffered from epileptic seizures for many years. He was operated on by William Scoville, who removed a brain structure within the **temporal lobe** called the **hippocampus**. The procedure did reduce his seizures, but left him with severe memory loss.

Henry was quickly referred to two neuropsychologists, Wilder Penfield and Brenda Milner, to assess the extent of his amnesia. The hippocampus was known to be associated with consolidating memories so the removal of this structure was devastating and irreversible.

Having already established themselves by conducting memory research on other case studies of brain-damaged patients, Penfield and Milner realised that Henry was an ideal amnesia case because his injury was specifically localised and his personality and intelligence were virtually intact.

Taking it further

Penfield and Milner's research can be found by searching for the title 'Loss of recent memory after bilateral hippocampal lesions, on the National Center for Biotechnology Information website. Read the summary of the case of HM and other cases of amnesia.

Henry was assessed as having **anterograde** and **retrograde** amnesia. His anterograde amnesia resulted in an inability to form any new memories after the operation (he could not store memories for new names, faces, events or information). Despite this, he did learn new skills, although he had no memory of being able to learn them. His retrograde amnesia meant that he lost the ability to retrieve memories from 19 months to 11 years prior to the operation; he was 27 years old at the time of his surgery, so this meant he could only remember partial events after the age of 16 and virtually no events after the age of 25. His retrograde amnesia may not have been due to the surgery, but is likely to have been affected by epilepsy medication and the frequency of his seizures prior to the operation.

During his life, Henry was interviewed many times, and this qualitative information has informed an understanding of which cognitive functions were still intact and which were impaired. Following his death, HM's brain was gifted to psychological research; it was spliced into over 2 000 segments to map the human brain at the Brain Observatory in San Diego.

The use of qualitative data

Unlike quantitative data, which presents data as numbers and statistics, qualitative data presents descriptions of findings in prose. In cognitive psychology, memory research is often reported as quantitative data, but research using case studies of brain-damaged patients is often qualitative in nature, describing what functioning is intact or lost as a result of amnesia and gaining an understanding of the patient's subjective experiences. Qualitative data provides us with detailed accounts of a person's experiences, feelings and beliefs. Some argue that this is the essence of psychology, but others argue that it is at the expense of objectivity as qualitative data requires interpretation, which can be biased.

Taking it further

The case of Henry Molaison and his brain atlas can be found online at the Brain Observatory. You can also do an Internet search of the Science Museum to read one of the transcripts of an interview with Henry.

Qualitative research is not straightforward or mechanistic; quantitative research involves working through a step-by-step procedure resulting in data analysis, whereas qualitative research is defined by the nature of the investigation and the choices made by the researcher along the way. It is a process of making meaning from responses given by participants, and as such is open to the individual interpretation of the researcher. As a researcher establishes the themes that emerge from the discourse, they apply meaning to its content and reach subjective conclusions. This does not mean that the emergent themes found are invalid, but it is up to the researcher to explain and justify the emerging conclusions using evidence in the discourse.

Rather than following the hypothetico-deductive model, which proposes a hypothesis and then tests it, qualitative research is an inductive process whereby a research question is proposed and the answer emerges from careful decoding of the information gathered. Information can be gathered using a variety of methods, such as unstructured or semi-structured interviews, questionnaires with open-ended question types, group discussions, speech analysis and a literature review. The non-numerical information gathered is carefully transcribed and notes are taken on the emerging themes or ideas that run through the text. There is no single type of qualitative research, and no single way of conducting qualitative analysis. However, they generally follow a similar format.

Common to all qualitative research is the way it is used to understand how individuals make sense of their own experiences. Qualitative research aims to understand how people perceive their world and make sense of it. This results in rich descriptions based on what people disclose about themselves, the connections they make between events that happen and the meanings they attribute to them, and how they feel.

Qualitative analysis is idiographic; it does not claim any general rules that apply to other people, but only that the results are specific and unique to the individual involved. Although some research can claim that emergent themes are general to others, qualitative research is often based on small sample sizes and built up into a case study.

Once qualitative data has been gathered, transcriptions are made of the discourse and the researcher immerses themselves in the text, making notes on the feelings, beliefs and meanings given to experiences by the participants. Then the researcher reflects on these notes, checks that the notes reflect the content of the transcript and develops from these notes the emerging themes from the transcript. These themes are presented as conclusions with extracts from the transcript to support the interpretation given to them.

Evaluation

Qualitative analysis gathers rich descriptions based on meaning, which can often be missed when using quantitative methods. However, it is laborious and difficult to conduct because data analysis and transcription takes a lot of time. It does not follow any particular standardised format and has been criticised for being unscientific and highly subjective. Additionally, many argue that it is largely a descriptive rather than explanatory method. However, qualitative research goes beyond merely describing discourse, it is a process of comprehending the information, synthesising the material and theorising about why the themes exist. A strength of qualitative research is that it is very important when trying to understand some of the important issues in health and clinical psychology, such as how patients experience palliative care, or what caregivers believe could help them as carers for those with long-term illness. These big questions could not be addressed by simply administering a questionnaire which would be unable to address people's deeply held beliefs and feelings.

Types of qualitative methods

Content analysis (although some dispute this method as being truly qualitative as it quantifies qualitative material).

Discourse analysis

Grounded theory

Interpretive phenomenological analysis

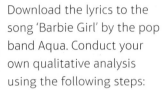

Taking it further

Download the lyrics to the song 'Barbie Girl' by the pop band Aqua. Conduct your own qualitative analysis using the following steps:

1. Read the lyrics through (without singing them!)

2. In the margin of each line, write a summary of the lyrical content, and consider the meaning of the lyrics.

3. Reflect on your notes, synthesise them and consider any overall message being delivered in the song.

Hint: Consider gender roles and themes of dominance and power.

4. Drawing together your themes, suggest possible reasons for these themes existing and present them using evidence from the lyrics in the song.

2.3 Studies

Learning outcomes

In this section you will learn about one classic study:

- Baddeley (1966b) on working memory

and three contemporary studies, from which you will need to choose one to learn about:

- Schmolck et al. (2002) on HM and other brain-damaged patients
- Steyvers and Hemmer (2012) on reconstructive memory
- Sebastián and Hernández-Gill (2012) on the developmental pattern of digit span.

WIDER ISSUES AND DEBATES

Psychology as a science

The independent variable in this investigation was the type of similarity between words in a list and the dependent variable was the recall of the list sequence from long-term memory. Baddeley operationalised the independent variable by giving the groups either a word list that was acoustically similar, semantically similar or a control list. He operationalised the dependent variable by measuring the accuracy of recall of the words in the correct sequential position. Importantly, he gave some participants a list of same frequency words as a baseline for recall comparison. This was to show the effect of semantic and acoustic similarity compared to dissimilar words. Any differences between the experimental and control lists were a result of similarity and not other factors affecting recall.

The influence of acoustic and semantic similarity on long-term memory for word sequences (Baddeley, 1966b)

Alan Baddeley, a prominent researcher in memory, wanted to test whether long-term memory and short-term memory were different or whether the emergent view of the time that memory existed on a continuum was accurate. However, investigations into short-term and long-term memory employed different research techniques, and Baddeley suggested that it would be impossible to tell whether short-term and long-term memory were different or the same unless the same research techniques were used on both. He set out an investigation to explore the effects of both semantic and acoustic coding in both long-term and short-term memory.

Aim

To investigate the influence of acoustic and semantic word similarity on learning and recall in short-term and long-term memory.

Procedure

A laboratory experiment was designed to test sequential recall of acoustically and semantically similar word lists. Three different experiments were conducted, but here we will focus on experiment three.

Experiment three

Four lists of 10 words were used:

- List A contained 10 acoustically similar words (man, can, cat, map, etc.)
- List B contained 10 acoustically dissimilar words that were matched in terms of frequency of everyday use to List A (pit, few, cow, mat, etc.)
- List C contained 10 semantically similar words (great, large, big, broad, etc.)
- List D contained 10 semantically dissimilar words that were matched in terms of frequency of everyday use to List C (good, huge, deep, late, etc.)
- List B and D acted as baseline control groups for List A and C.

The participants were men and women recruited from the Applied Psychology Research Unit subject panel and were assigned one of the four list conditions as an independent groups design.

Each list of 10 words was presented via projector at a rate of one word every three seconds in the correct order. After presentation the participants were required to complete six tasks involving memory for digits. They were then asked to recall the word list in one minute by writing down the sequence in the correct order. This was repeated over four learning trials. As it was not a test of learning words, but a test of sequence order, the word list in random order was made visible on a card in the room. After the four learning trials, the groups were given a 15-minute interference task involving copying eight digit sequences at their own pace. After the interference task participants were given a surprise retest on the word list sequence.

Table 2.7 Procedure order

Hearing test	Learning trials				Interference task	Retest
Listening and copying each word presented in random order from the list	Trial 1 Visual presentation of list followed by a 6 eight-digit sequence recall task, followed by recall of the list.	Trial 2 Visual presentation of list followed by a 6 eight-digit sequence recall task, followed by recall of the list.	Trial 3 Visual presentation of list followed by a 6 eight-digit sequence recall task, followed by recall of the list.	Trial 4 Visual presentation of list followed by a 6 eight-digit sequence recall task, followed by recall of the list.	Copying sequences of digits	Recall of the word list in the correct order.

Results of experiment three

Recall of the acoustically similar sounding words was worse than the dissimilar sounding words during the initial phase of learning (trial two in particular). However, recall of the similar and dissimilar sounding words was not statistically significant. This demonstrates that acoustic encoding was initially difficult, but did not affect long term memory recall. Participants found the semantically similar words more difficult to learn than the semantically dissimilar words and recalled significantly fewer semantically similar words in the retest.

Conclusion

The fact that participants found it more difficult to recall list one in the initial phase of learning suggests that short-term memory is largely acoustic, therefore acoustically similar sounding words were more difficult to encode. Later retest recall of list three was impaired compared to all other lists because they were semantically similar, suggesting that encoding in long-term memory is largely, but not exclusively, semantic.

Evaluation

Laboratory research, such as this, employs the use of experimental techniques that are not typical of the way in which we use memory in an everyday context; we do not often learn lists of random monosyllabic words. Therefore the ability to generalise these findings to everyday contexts is questioned. However, memory researchers would argue that in order to understand memory we need to remove the context in which normal memory is used and simplify the nature of the to-be-learned information in order to isolate the aspects of memory we are concerned with.

This experiment relied heavily on the role of rehearsal during the four learning trials in order for information to become established in long-term memory. The very concentrated nature of rehearsal is likely to have exaggerated this memory process with the result found being an artefact of the experimental procedure. Under normal conditions we would not be expected to use rehearsal in such a contrived way, so this study lacks **mundane realism**.

However, the study was scientific in that it was conducted in a controlled laboratory environment with a standardised procedure. Therefore the study can be regarded as replicable and the reliability of the results can be established. Due to the highly controlled nature of the experiment, Baddeley can also establish a cause and effect relationship between the independent variable (semantic or acoustic word list similarity, and the dependent variable (long-term memory).

> **Key term**
>
> **Mundane realism:** The extent to which the test used in an experiment represents a realistic activity.

Semantic knowledge in patient HM and other patients with bilateral medial and lateral temporal lobe lesions (Schmolck et al., 2002)

Case studies of brain-damaged patients have been invaluable in understanding the nature and function of human memory. Amnesia patients have been investigated in neuropsychological research to establish which regions of the brain are responsible for which stores and processes involved in encoding new and recollecting previously learned information. It is widely accepted that damage to the temporal lobe of the brain is associated with memory loss, in particular anterograde and retrograde amnesia, but often well-established long-term semantic knowledge is intact.

Aim

Heike Schmolck, Elizabeth Kensinger, Suzanne Corkin and Larry Squire attempted to investigate the effects of specific brain damage on semantic memory using case studies of brain-damaged patients compared to a control group of 'normal' participants. Specifically they wanted to test the relationship between semantic test scores and temporal lobe damage and to determine whether Henry Molaison (HM) was unique in the way the brain damage he sustained affected his memory compared to similar damage in other cases.

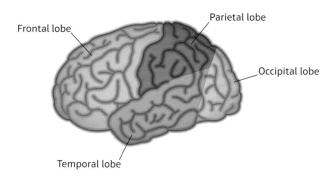

Figure 2.12 The lobes of the human brain

Procedure

Participants

Six participants with amnesia were compared to eight 'normal' control participants. The control group was matched for age (74 years old), sex (male) and education (12.4 years) to the amnesia patients (apart from one female). The six amnesia patients were divided into groups according to the level of brain damage they suffered. Two patients had brain damage largely restricted to the hippocampus (HF); three patients had suffered **encephalitis** resulting in large **medial** temporal lobe and **anterolateral** temporal cortex damage (MTL+) and Henry Molaison (HM) had medial temporal lobe damage with some **lateral** temporal lobe damage following surgery to resolve his epilepsy. All patients had suffered **bilateral** damage to varying degrees. A biography of each patient was compiled.

Apparatus

Nine tests were conducted over three to five different sessions with participants. Seven of these tests were from the Semantic Test Battery and two tests were constructed by the researchers. The tests were all based on line drawings of 24 animals and 24 objects. The 48 line drawings were further categorised into groups of eight domestic land animals, foreign land animals, water animals, birds, electrical household items, non-electrical household items, vehicles and musical instruments.

Tests

The nine tests were designed to measure semantic knowledge related to identifying, sorting or defining the line drawings. A further four semantic tests were conducted on some of the patients and control participants (HM only received test 10 of these additional tests).

Table 2.8 Test conditions

Tasks 1–4	Pointing to or naming a picture	Participants were asked to point to or name a picture when given the name or a description of the object.
Task 5	Semantic features	Participants were asked to answer yes/no questions about the physical and associated features of an object.
Tasks 6 & 7	Category fluency and sorting	Participants were asked to name or sort into categories as many examples within a category or class (living/non-living) of objects without a picture cue.
Tasks 8 and 9	Defining task	Participants were given the name or picture of the 24 less common objects and they were asked to provide a definition.
Task 10	Pyramid and palm tree test	Participants were given a target picture and two test pictures and asked which test picture went with the target picture. For example, a target picture of a saddle was presented with two test pictures of a horse and a goat, and participants were asked to say which test picture went with the target.
Task 11	Object/non-object discrimination task	Participants were asked whether the object presented to them was real or not.
Task 12	Colouring object task	Participants were asked to colour 28 line drawings of objects using appropriate colours from a selection of four coloured pencils.
Task 13	Nouns and verbs test	Participants were given a fill-in-the-gaps exercise designed to test knowledge of regular and irregular verbs and tenses. For example, 'A hoof is hard, in fact most _____ are hard'.

The percentage of correct responses was scored for all tests other than test 6, 8 and 9, which were recorded and transcribed and were given an accuracy rating of between 0 and 4 by the researchers. These transcripts were also assessed for errors in grammar, expression, confusion and word intrusions. **Inter-rater reliability** was established for the scoring.

Results

Tasks 1–9

Patients with damage restricted largely to the hippocampus (HF) were able to name, point out and answer questions about objects they were given with considerable accuracy. They were also comparable to the control group when asked to generate examples of a given category or give definitions of objects. Patients with damage to the medial temporal lobe and anterolateral temporal cortex (MTL+), performed less well at naming, pointing out or answering questions about objects. They also had considerable difficulty generating examples in a given category. Notably one MTL+ patient could not generate names of dog breeds despite previously being a dog breeder. They also had difficulty defining objects, often giving less detail which contained more errors; HM performed worst among these patients. Interestingly the MTL+ patients found it most difficult to identify and recall facts about living objects compared to non-living objects in all tasks.

When the participants were ranked in terms of their overall performance on these tasks, their rank appeared to correspond directly with the extent of their brain damage. In particular, damage to the anterolateral temporal cortex seemed to cause impairment in semantic knowledge.

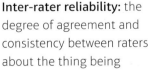

Key term

Inter-rater reliability: the degree of agreement and consistency between raters about the thing being measured.

Other semantic tests (test 10–13)

When asked to decide whether an object was real or not two of the MTL+ participants performed well, but one made eight errors. All MTL+ patients scored well on the colouring task. On the Pyramid and palm tree test, the MTL+ patients and HM scored either below the required 90 per cent accuracy or performed below the control group. The MTL+ group were able to produce regular plurals and verbs but performed less well at producing irregular verbs and plurals. In contrast, HM performed well on both tasks, suggesting that the difficulty with irregular items is associated with anterolateral temporal cortex damage.

Conclusions

The MTL+ patient data shows that damage to the anterolateral temporal cortex is consistent with a loss of semantic knowledge that results in a 'blurring' or overlap of conceptual knowledge that leads to confusion. This semantic knowledge is associated with the anterolateral region and is not associated with the medial temporal lobe. This is consistent with patients with **semantic dementia** whose impairment is restricted to the anterolateral temporal cortex and the medial temporal lobe is relatively unaffected. Additionally, **MRI scans** seem to suggest that the more progressed the disease, the greater the anterolateral damage.

HM – a special case

HM was similar to the MTL+ patients in tests of definitions suggesting that his impairment had a similar physiological basis. However, in many respects his semantic knowledge was in the normal range in other tests. Unique to HM was the large number of grammatical errors he made during these tests. The researchers suggest that his deficit in language production was unlikely to be related to his temporal lobe damage but due to other factors during his childhood. HM suffered from a seizure at age 10, was from low socioeconomic status and his schooling was interrupted. These factors could have contributed to poor language development.

The researchers conclude that the hippocampus is not involved in sematic knowledge because HF patients performed similarly to the control group. HM was less affected than the MTL+ patients, which leads to the conclusion that the anterolateral temporal cortex and not the medial temporal lobe is involved in semantic knowledge. The language impairment displayed by HM was unrelated to his neurological condition and probably due to his upbringing.

Key terms

Semantic dementia: a degenerative neurological disorder resulting in loss of semantic memory.

MRI scan: a brain scan that produces an image of the structure of the brain, a bit like an X-ray but with more detail.

WIDER ISSUES AND DEBATES

Nature–nurture

Schmolck et al. believed that HM's language impairment had developed due to causes other than the neurological impairment caused by his surgery, that it was perhaps due to nurture rather than nature. It is possible that his low socioeconomic status and interrupted education had a negative effect on his language development.

The following transcript was made of HM describing a motorcycle:

'… well…it can be…uh,… a motorcycle is…uh…maybe, … it's on two wheels…And it could be have 'cause my father used to ride one at one time…and he stopped himself because the doctor told him not to.'

It seems somewhat questionable whether these errors in grammar and form could be solely attributed to educational disruption and economy. However, the nature–nurture debate will never be resolved in this case because HM's language was not tested prior to the surgery.

Evaluation

Case studies of brain-damaged patients are rare and therefore small in number. The small sample size involved in this investigation limits the **generalisability** of the conclusions made. However, findings from semantic dementia, neuroimaging, **brain stimulation** and **unilateral lobectomy** all support the finding that the anterolateral and, in particular, the lateral temporal cortex is involved in semantic knowledge, strongly reinforcing the conclusion of this study.

Exam tip

It is easy to criticise research for its shortcomings without understanding the reason for such problems or trying to understand whether the problem is actually well founded. Answers in psychology are rarely agreed on, so it is important to discuss evaluation from alternative points of view rather than taking a single-sided or definitive approach. To be able to evaluate effectively and demonstrate a mature and considered approach to evaluation, it is worth considering these questions:

Is the criticism justified?

Is there any further support for or against the criticism being levelled at the research?

Does the criticism demonstrate the view of certain psychologists or groups of people? If so, could an alternative view be considered?

The special case of HM reported in this investigation was seen as a product of upbringing and events prior to his surgery for epilepsy. However, it could be argued that the individual differences found in this investigation demonstrate individual variation in neurology which may account for the differences between them. It is often the case that retrospective research, such as this study, cannot establish causal relationships between the injury sustained and the resulting impairments tested. The brain is adaptable and can compensate for injury. The findings of tests may reflect the ability of the brain to adapt to injury rather than the injury itself. However, prospective research is not possible as it would involve predicting those individuals who are likely to sustain such brain damage.

Also the stimuli that are common to many cognitive investigations used to test semantic knowledge, such as the line drawings used, lack mundane realism and may not tap into semantic knowledge as it is used in everyday life. Such research may be said to lack ecological validity, as the findings cannot be generalised to everyday use of semantic memory.

WIDER ISSUES AND DEBATES

Ethical issues

Doctor Scoville, the surgeon responsible for HM's surgery, was vilified for his reckless approach. However, the case of HM was fundamental to our understanding that memory is a distinct cognitive process, independent of language and thought. Damage to his hippocampus and temporal lobes enabled neuroscience to establish a location for memory in the brain. This is arguably the most important advance in our understanding of memory functioning and HM was the most researched individual in the field of neuroscience.

Key terms

Generalisability: the ability to apply findings to other people, situations and contexts.

Brain stimulation: the use of electrodes to stimulate regions of the brain and examine resulting behavioural or cognitive changes as a result.

Unilateral lobectomy: the surgical removal of parts of the brain from one hemisphere.

Reconstruction from memory in naturalistic environments (Steyvers and Hemmer, 2012)

Mark Steyvers and Pernille Hemmer investigated the interaction between episodic and semantic memory, and the reconstructive nature of memory recall. Previous research into reconstructive memory suggested that prior knowledge stored in semantic memory had a detrimental effect on recall, often resulting in false memories of an object or event. However, Steyvers and Hemmer argued that research focused on the fallibility of memory often derived its findings from laboratory-based investigations designed to deliberately induce these errors in recall. For example, asking participants to recall objects in a photograph of an office with no books or computer in the picture would deliberately induce a false memory for such items. Removing such highly probable items would only result in a high likelihood of such items being expected and subsequently falsely remembered. Rather than seeing the recall of books or a computer as a typical everyday error in recall, Steyvers and Hemmer argued that it is only an error because of the experimental manipulation of the environment (withholding objects from the image), and that this was not representative of naturalistic environments.

Therefore, rather than accepting that memory is prone to error, as much previous research concluded, they felt that these errors in recall could provide important insights into the nature and function of memory, and that memory should be studied in a more naturalistic way where environments were not manipulated to elicit certain responses.

Aim

The aim of the research was to investigate the interaction between episodic and prior knowledge in naturalistic environments. They wanted to see how prior knowledge (semantic memory) was used to reconstruct memory for photographs of normal everyday settings (episodic recall), such as a hotel, kitchen, and office.

Procedure

Initial testing

An important element of the investigation was to first assess prior knowledge, and therefore expectations, about the naturalistic scenes they would show participants. A random sample of 22 participants was recruited from an experimental participant pool at the University of California, Irvine. To assess prior expectations, one group of participants was required to list objects that they would expect to find in five naturalistic scenes (office, kitchen, hotel, urban and dining). Participants were required to enter their responses on a computer for at least one minute per scene. The frequency of objects named was recorded as a measure of prior expectation.

A separate group of 25 participants was shown 25 images of the five scenes; office, kitchen, urban, hotel and dining (there were five images of each scene), and asked to name all the objects they could see as a measure of perception. This initial testing was an important control to ensure that objects were not overlooked because they were not perceptible in the image.

The frequency of objects named in the expectation test and then identified in the perception test was recorded. The top ten most frequently recalled objects were analysed along with low frequency recall objects. Expectation of high frequency objects tended to be associated with iconic objects from each scene, such as television in a hotel room (22/22 participants), a table in a dining room (19/22 participants), and a computer in an office (20/22 participants). This prior testing suggested that people have good prior knowledge of each scene that seems largely representative of each naturalistic environment.

The experimental memory condition

Using the same experimental pool, 49 participants who had not taken part in either the expectation or perception test were randomly selected. Ten of the stimulus images from the prior tests were chosen to be used in the experiment (two from each scene that elicited the most objects named in the perception test). From these, two sets of five images, one from each scene, were formed. Participants only viewed one set of five images to avoid carry-over effects from viewing more than one image from the same scene type.

Participants were shown the five images for either 2 or 10 seconds to control for exposure duration. There were four possible trial time orderings, and participants were randomly allocated to one of these time orderings.

So, for example, one participant might see:

Set 1
The kitchen scene for 10 seconds
The hotel scene for 10 seconds
The urban scene for 10 seconds
The dining scene for 2 seconds
The office scene for 2 seconds

Exposure duration was manipulated to alter the extent to which participants used prior knowledge in episodic memory retrieval. It was thought that recall from short exposure duration of 2 seconds would rely more heavily on prior knowledge, as the event would have had little opportunity to be encoded as an episodic memory. It was also thought that the correct recall of objects not consistent with a scene (e.g. a microwave in an office) could only be recalled from episodic memory, and recall of objects that were missing from the image (e.g. a table cloth missing from the dining scene) could only be recalled using semantic memory/prior knowledge. The trials were randomised and participants were asked to carry out **free recall** of objects they remembered from each scene in their own time.

The researchers noted down all objects that were recalled by participants and the order in which they were remembered. Responses were normalised to remove plurals ('chairs' was treated as 'chair') and additional descriptive content ('silver car' was treated as 'car').

Table 2.9 Time orderings (duration of exposure in seconds)

10	10	10	2	2
10	10	2	2	2
2	2	2	10	10
2	2	10	10	10

> **Key term** 💬
>
> **Free recall:** recall of stimulus material in any order and without memory cues.

Results

Analysis of errors:

Recall of objects that were also listed in the perception test was recorded as accurate.

Table 2.10 Average recall rate

	2 second exposure duration	10 second exposure duration
Mean number of objects recalled during free recall	7.75	10.05

Steyvers and Hemmer used the initial analysis of high and low probability of recall rates for objects based on expectation to analyse the results. It was found that incorrect recall of highly probable objects was 9 per cent and incorrect recall of low probability objects was 18 per cent.

These error rates ran in contrast to previous research that suggested that error rates were high for high probability objects. However, this low error rate for high probability objects is unsurprising as they were likely to be present in the unmanipulated naturalistic scenes. This suggests that when participants are presented with scenes that are representative of naturalistic contexts and unmanipulated by experimental control, memory of such scenes is quite accurate. Where scenes do not represent real-life context accurately, such as a dining scene without a table cloth, the error rate increased to 19 per cent.

The effect of prior knowledge:

The effect of prior knowledge (semantic memory) was assessed by comparing the correct number of objects guessed in the expectation test, to those objects actually recalled in the two experimental conditions (2- and 10-second duration exposure). The cumulative accuracy of object guesses based on the expectation test was over 55 per cent from semantic memory under initial testing, and the actual recall in both conditions was much higher, over 80 per cent, suggesting that episodic memory played a significant role in recall.

Unsurprisingly, they found that longer duration improved recall overall; with short exposure to the picture, seven objects were correctly recalled on average compared with nine objects recalled with longer exposure to the picture.

Conclusions

It seems that in recall of naturalistic scenes, prior knowledge drawn from semantic memory can contribute to accurate recall in episodic memory tasks, when such scenes are unmanipulated. We draw on general knowledge as good guesses of what is expected to be seen in such contexts. Prior knowledge contributes greatly to recall of naturalistic environments, but this is not at the expense of accuracy; in fact we are more likely to notice novel items more readily than previous research might suggest.

Adopting a naturalistic approach to the study of memory has highlighted that prior research tends to be unrepresentative of everyday event recall; removing high probability objects from a familiar context will induce false memory and give a misleading view of memory as unreliable. When using untampered naturalistic contexts, guesses can be effective because of the high probability of the objects being present. This guessing frees up cognitive resources to be better spent focusing on novel and unexpected objects in a scene. In this sense, both recall of inconsistent and consistent objects is benefitted using a more ecologically valid approach.

Evaluation

Steyvers and Hemmer are strong advocates for increased ecological validity in memory research to be able to generalise findings to everyday use of memory. But they acknowledge that their research is not as naturalistic as it could have been. Using photographs rather than exposing participants to real environments, and using laboratory rather than real conditions. As such, this research goes some way to trying to establish greater ecological validity in the field of memory research, but does so without compromising generalisability and operationalisation of concepts.

Important controls were used in this investigation. A control during the memory experiment was that the participants only viewed one image from each of the five scenes rather than multiple images of each scene. This was to prevent interference from a previously viewed scene of a similar nature affecting subsequent recall. Time orderings were manipulated using a Latin square design, and participants were randomly allocated to one of the time ordering sequences.

This research has important implications for the way in which eyewitness testimony is viewed in the justice system. It suggests that contrary to previous research, prior knowledge from semantic memory can enhance recall of episodic events and even allow greater cognitive effort to be spent on recognising unexpected features of a context. This implies that eyewitnesses are effective when recalling from familiar contexts and effective at encoding novel features.

Sebastián and Hernández-Gil's (2012) study of the developmental pattern of digit span

Working at the University of Madrid, Mariá Victoria Sebastián and Laura Hernández-Gil examined the developmental pattern of digit span in the Spanish population to test the phonological loop component of working memory (Baddeley and Hitch, 1974). They set out to investigate the capacity of the phonological loop to understand whether it would differ in a Spanish population across different ages. Anglo-Saxon research concluded that digit span increased with age, so Sebastián and Hernández-Gil wanted to see whether the same developmental trend occurred in a different culture to assess whether Anglo-Saxon findings could be generalised using the same digit span procedure.

Aims

To investigate the development of the phonological loop in children between the ages of 5 and 17 years using digit span as a measure of phonological capacity. They also wanted to compare the findings to their previous research of adult, aged and dementia patients.

Procedure

A sample of 570 volunteer (or volunteered) participants were taken from schools in Madrid. All participants were native Spanish and impairments in hearing, reading and writing ability were controlled. Participants were divided into five different age groups and the average digit span was recorded for each age and age group. Tested individually, participants were read increasing sequences of digits to recall in the correct order. The digits were read out at a rate of one per second and the digit list increased one digit per sequence. The digit span for participants was recorded as the maximum digit recalled in the correct order without error.

Table 2.11 Example of digit span measure

Read out digits	Recall of digits in sequential order	Digit span
2 5 9 4 5	2 5 9 4 5	Correct
3 7 8 1 6 9	3 7 8 1 6 9	Correct
9 0 1 5 2 6 8	9 0 1 5 2 6 8	Correct Maximum digit span of 7
4 3 7 5 9 2 1 5	4 3 7 - 9 2 7 2	Errors and omission

Results

Table 2.12 Mean average (and standard deviation) digit span for each age and age group

	Age groups mean (SD) digit span
Preschool (5 years)	3.76 (.52)
Primary school (6–8 years)	4.34 (.58) aged 6–8 years
Primary school (9–11 years)	5.13 (.81) aged 9–11 years
Secondary school (12–14 years)	5.46 (.85) aged 12–14 years
Secondary school (15–17 years)	5.83 (.84) aged 15–17 years

The table shows clearly a developmental trend of increasing digit span with age. Children aged 5 years have a very low digit span that rises steadily until around 11 years old where it slows. The digit span between 15 and 17 years remains fairly stable.

Comparing the findings to previous research

Comparing the findings of this study to previous related research conducted by Sebastián and Hernández-Gil, they found that elderly participants had a significantly higher digit span compared to the 5-year-olds in this study, but it was not significantly different from other age groups. Patients with **advanced dementia** (AD) showed a similar profile (mean digit span 4.2). However, patients with **frontal variant frontotemporal dementia** (fvFTD) had a digit span that was significantly similar to the younger age group. Comparing the elderly group to the dementia patients showed no significant difference, suggesting that impoverished digit span was a consequence of ageing rather than dementias.

Key terms

Frontal variant frontotemporal dementia: a degenerative neurological disease that affects the frontal lobes of the brain.

Advanced dementia: the later stages of dementia where symptoms are more profound.

Consistent with Anglo-Saxon research, this investigation showed a continued increase in digit span over time in the Spanish population. However, the overall capacity of digit span was far lower in the Spanish population compared to the digit span of seven found in Anglo-Saxon studies. This decrease in phonological capacity could be accounted for by the nature of the Spanish language. Digits in Spanish tend to be two or more syllables (e.g. uno, cuatro, cinco, ocho), compared to the monosyllabic Anglo-Saxon numerals (e.g. one, two, three, four). This word (or digit) length effect means that it takes more time to sub-vocally repeat and rehearse Spanish words, taking up more space in the phonological loop, resulting in a lower digit span.

To further support the word length effect as an explanation for the difference in digit span, differences at each age was examined. As sub-vocal rehearsal does not appear until the age of 7–8 years, there should be no difference in digit span as a result of word length effect until after this age. This was found to be true as, before the age of 7 years, differences between Spanish and Anglo-Saxon counterparts were not found. At age 9 years, there is a noticeable difference in digit span, suggesting that word length effect occurs once sub-vocalisation appears in phonological development. However, unlike previous research, this study speculates that digit span in the Spanish population increases beyond the age of 15 years.

Conclusions

Digit span was found to increase with age; the starting point of this development occurs when children are able to sub-vocalise at around 7 years. Digit span in the Spanish population is significantly shorter than Anglo-Saxon culture, probably due to the word length effect associated with digits. Comparing the findings to research into patients with degenerative neurological disease and the aged population, it is possible to speculate from this research that poor digit span is a result of ageing rather than dementias.

Evaluation

Digit span experiments are measures of the phonological loop proposed by Baddeley and Hitch (1972). However, we rarely use verbal memory to memorise lists of digit in everyday life, other than when trying to rehearse a telephone number. Everyday verbal memory is used to hold sequences of words in order to comprehend sentences, master new languages or aid reading of complex information. Therefore it is open to question whether or not digit span experiments reflect everyday use of verbal memory. However, digit span tests have been reliably linked to performance in reading ability and intelligence, suggesting they are a good general measure of verbal memory. Digits, rather than word sequences or sentences, are also considered to be a culture-free and meaning-free way of measuring pure verbal memory. However, based on the cultural differences found, digits may not be the best culture-free determinant of verbal memory capacity.

Cultural differences in digit span have been reported by other researchers. Ellis and Hennelley (1980) reported poorer digit span in Welsh-speaking children compared to English children, largely because Welsh words for digits take longer to pronounce than English digit words. Longer digit spans have been reported in Chinese because the words for digits are short (Stigler et al., 1986). This research supports the finding that language and the phonological loop are interrelated.

A large sample size was tested in this study, allowing the findings to be considered reliable and generalisable to the Spanish population as a whole. The sample size gathered was important for this research because comparisons were made across different cultures. The study also excluded participants with any hearing, reading or language impairments, known to diminish digit span, which could have affected the results.

INDIVIDUAL DIFFERENCES

There are several individual differences that can be detected by digit span testing. Dyslexia, which is a problem with learning to recognise words at the level appropriate for age, is associated with a poor digit span (Helland and Asbjørnsen, 2004).

2.4 Key questions
Learning outcomes

In this section you will learn about one key issue of relevance in today's society. You will need to be able to:

- describe the key issue and its importance to today's society

- apply concepts, theories and research used in cognitive psychology to explain the key issue.

This section will describe an example of the key issue of how our knowledge of working memory can be used to inform the treatment of dyslexia as a reading disorder. However, you can choose your own key issue and relate it to theories, concepts and research used in the cognitive approach.

Can knowledge of working memory inform treatments for dyslexia?

Dyslexia is a reading disorder associated with poor or inefficient working memory. Children with dyslexia find it difficult to hold enough information in working memory to be able to blend sounds to form a word and find associating letters to sounds problematic. This results in slower reading and writing ability. They have particular phonological deficits too, meaning that they code phonology inefficiently in the brain, causing problems with short-term verbal memory such as difficulties with non-word repetition, rapid naming and learning a new language. Ultimately, the memory problems associated with dyslexia mean that skills associated with reading, writing, spelling and grammar are impaired.

These difficulties are often detected during preschool and early years education, and a number of classroom strategies have been identified in order to help students with dyslexia.

Interventions based on working memory

There are currently two main interventions used to help children with dyslexia in schools. One is a classroom-based approach that aims to alter the teaching and learning environment to better suit children with working memory problems. These classroom strategies are easy to implement by educators and can be used with all children to aid learning. The second is direct intervention to help children with literacy difficulties to improve their working memory. There are several types of direct intervention programmes, but all aim to help children practise and develop working memory using specific or a variety of tasks targeted at increasing processing speed and strategies for remembering.

Classroom strategies approach

Strategies used in the classroom to help children with dyslexia include:

- clearly stating lesson aims
- using checklists
- simplifying instructions
- highlighting or colour coding information
- using audio and visual materials
- avoiding asking a child to read out loud.

By simplifying and breaking down classroom tasks it avoids overloading the limited working memory capacity associated with dyslexia. Because dyslexia is also associated with slower processing speeds, avoiding lengthy periods of teacher talking and using alternative delivery methods can work better to prevent phonological loop overload.

Taking it further

Consider whether the introduction of PowerPoint® into the classroom has been of benefit to children with dyslexia. Make a list of the arguments for and against using PowerPoint® with children with a literacy impairment.

Taking it further

Using the classroom strategies listed on the previous page, design specific classroom objects, signs, devices or rules that could be used in any classroom environment. For example, vocabulary books could be used when new words are being taught, and the aims of the lesson could be written in short simple statements at the top of every worksheet.

Taking it further

Conduct an Internet search into specific memory improvement packages, such as Cogmed. Make a list of the strategies used to improve working memory described in this section and from your research. For each strategy, make a list of concepts, research and theories you have studied in cognitive psychology. You may find it useful to read through Baddeley's working memory model and developmental psychology and memory.

Spelling can be difficult for a child with dyslexia because they find it hard to associate a letter sound with the printed letter. Phonics is a literacy strategy that uses phonological rules to learn letter sounds and encourages sound blending. Mathematics can also be difficult for a child with dyslexia because they are required to take different steps to solve a mathematical problem, which can overload working memory. Each arithmetic step can be written down or verbally discussed to ensure that it is broken into stages.

Direct intervention programmes

Different intervention strategies have been designed to help children with literacy difficulties in schools by directly targeting memory skills. Some of these interventions are computer based and target a range of working memory skills, such as Cogmed, or target specific memory skills, such as the N-Back programme (Klingberg et al., 2005; Jaeggi et al., 2011). These programmes have been shown to enhance working memory with long-lasting cognitive gains and academic improvement in both Maths and English.

Are interventions effective?

In a review of dyslexia interventions, Snowling and Hulme (2011) commented that for dyslexia interventions to work there should be targeted training in phonological awareness, letter-sound recognition, and practice in reading and writing. However, children present different literacy difficulties, so it impossible to implement a 'one fits all' strategy. They also highlight that there is currently a delay in diagnosing literacy difficulties, which can sometimes be mistaken for attention problems, making early intervention difficult.

Dyslexia, like many learning impairments, can cause social and emotional difficulties, such as a loss of self-esteem and confidence. These aspects of the condition are not treated in intervention programmes per se, but should be addressed as much as memory enhancement techniques because they may not naturally recover with working memory improvements.

In conclusion, the evidence so far suggests that there are cognitive benefits shown from both classroom-based and direct intervention strategies, particularly early interventions; however the long-term gains and transferability of these benefits to daily tasks and activities is questionable.

2.5 Practical investigation

Learning objectives

In this section you will have to design and conduct a practical investigation using a laboratory experiment in an area relevant to the topics covered in cognitive psychology. In conducting the practical research exercise, you must:

- design and conduct a laboratory experiment to gather quantitative data on a topic in cognitive psychology

- make design decisions in your planning

- collect and present the data you have gathered using appropriate tables, graphs, descriptive statistics and a non-parametric tests of difference, and draw conclusions from your data

- consider the strengths and weaknesses of your experiment and suggest possible improvements that could be made

- use typical reporting conventions to document your procedure, results and discussion.

There are many laboratory experiments in cognitive psychology that you could replicate or modify. In this section you will follow an example of a laboratory experiment used to investigate the influence of acoustic similarity on short-term memory recall. Although you may choose a different area of cognitive psychology to investigate, this section will provide a worked through example of how to go about designing, conducting and discussing a practical investigation.

Before you begin planning your practical investigation, you should review the methodology section in this topic to familiarise yourself with key terms and concepts concerning laboratory experiments.

Aim

All research begins with an aim that is typically based on current theory or research into an area. The aim of this experiment is to investigate the effect of acoustic similarity on short-term memory. This is based on the theory that the short-term store uses acoustic encoding, so similar sounding words and letters are more difficult to sub-vocalise and encode, resulting in poor recall performance. It is important that you read around the topic before you plan your practical investigation to establish a rationale for your own aim.

Hypotheses

Your practical investigation should have an experimental hypothesis and a null hypothesis. Once you have read around the topic you are interested in, you will need to decide whether your experimental hypothesis is directional or non-directional. If prior research and theory indicates the likely direction in which your results will go, you must use a directional hypothesis, but if there are conflicting theories and research, it may be more prudent to use a non-directional hypothesis.

Before a clear hypothesis can be written, the independent and dependent variables should be defined and operationalised. This practical investigation is looking to see if acoustically similar or dissimilar sounding words (the independent variable) will have an effect on recall (the dependent variable).

WIDER ISSUES AND DEBATES

Psychology as a science
Science follows the hypothetico-deductive method. This means that in order to be scientific (objective, reliable and empirical) we must first propose a testable hypothesis and then conduct an experiment to gather empirical data that will support or refute this hypothesis. In this experiment, a clear hypothesis has been predicted and measures taken to collect data that can be used to test this hypothesis.

Experimental hypothesis

The experimental hypothesis for this practical investigation will be directional because prior theory and research indicates the direction of difference that is likely to be found between recall of acoustically similar and dissimilar sounding words, that is, more acoustically dissimilar sounding words will be recalled than acoustically similar sounding words.

Null hypothesis

Remember that your practical should also have a null hypothesis. For this practical investigation the null hypothesis is that there will be no difference in the number of acoustically similar and dissimilar sounding words, and any difference found will be due to chance.

Experimental design

When choosing an experimental design, it is worth considering the strengths and weaknesses of each. An independent groups design is a good design to select if you want to avoid **order effects** and **demand characteristics**, but it can mean that the individual differences between participants in each group may affect your results. A repeated measures design avoids individual differences, but has the problem of order effects and demand characteristics.

In this experiment the aim is to examine encoding in short-term memory which, unless affected by age, illness or a learning impairment, is relatively similar between participants. If the sample you select is fairly **homogenous**, individual differences should not be a significant problem. However, order effects are likely to be a problem if participants are asked to repeat the memory test, particularly immediately after one another, and they may guess the aim of the study if you are involved in both conditions of the experiment.

On balance, an independent groups design should work to avoid order effects and demand characteristics, and you can be reasonably assured that the individual differences in memory between participants is not going to impact on your results. However, to evenly distribute any individual differences in short-term memory span, participants can be **randomly allocated** to each condition of the experiment.

If you chose to use a repeated measures design for your experiment, it is worth considering using **counterbalancing** or **randomisation** of conditions.

Sampling

Selecting a sampling method involves considering your target population and using a sampling technique that draws out a representative sample of people. This means that you can confidently generalise your findings back to the target population. For this experiment, the target population is very large as it can involve any individual with a reasonably intact and unimpaired short-term memory. This means that it would be difficult and time-consuming to use a random or stratified sampling technique, so either a volunteer or opportunity sample would be more efficient.

The volunteer sampling technique encourages participants with a particular compliant nature. This would be a problem for social psychological research, but as cognitive processing is relatively unaffected by personality type and an independent groups design is being used, the volunteer sampling technique is probably more ethical than an opportunity sample. No one is being directly asked and put under pressure to participate.

Twenty participants will be selected from the first twenty who respond to an advert placed in a sixth-form common room, excluding anyone with short-term memory impairment.

Operationalisation

Operationalisation means that you need to make your independent variable and dependent variable specifically defined. The independent variable in this experiment is whether the words presented to participants are acoustically similar or dissimilar in sound. This will be operationalised by presenting one group of participants with ten monosyllabic words that rhyme (acoustically similar) or ten monosyllabic words that do not rhyme (acoustically dissimilar). The dependent variable will be the total number of accurately recalled words from the original list in a free recall memory test. It is very important that you operationally define both your independent and dependent variables.

WIDER ISSUES AND DEBATES

Psychology as a science

Operationalisation is very important to establish objectivity and reliability in psychological research. In this experiment operationalisation has been achieved by defining the type of words each group of participants will receive, and exactly what will be measured as an outcome. With good control over extraneous variables, it is possible to establish a cause and effect relationship between the IV and the DV in this experiment.

Controls

Situational variables

Because you are conducting a laboratory experiment, the environment will be reasonably well controlled already. However, it is worth considering any situational variables that are likely to have an effect on participants. In this experiment it would be important to control for any noise or interruptions that might affect learning and recall, so participants will be tested individually and a sign will be placed on the door to prevent interruptions. To prevent conferring, and therefore the potential for demand characteristics, all participants will be placed in a room, called out individually to do the memory test, and will be told not to return. The procedure will also be standardised to prevent experimenter effects occurring.

Participant variables

Although cognition is reasonably similar in the majority of people, individual differences are not likely to have a huge impact on your investigation. However, it is worth considering significant individual differences such as age and learning impairments. Once you have identified potential individual differences between your participants, you will need to either control them or eliminate them. In this practical investigation individual differences in short-term memory will be controlled by equally distributing them using random allocation of participants to the conditions of the experiment. However, a short questionnaire will be conducted prior to the experiment to check for any short-term memory problems by asking participants about their educational needs. There will, of course, be participant variables that are not controlled for, such as motivation. However, the experiment will be conducted in the morning to prevent any possible effects of fatigue that might occur later in the day.

Developing a procedure

A procedure should be a schedule of what happens, where, when and how. This ties into how you will control for extraneous variables and it is important that the procedure stays the same for all participants. In this experiment, participants will be read a set of standardised instructions by the researcher and asked to sit at a desk directly in front of a whiteboard and projector. To prevent

Example standardised instructions

Thank you for volunteering to take part in this memory experiment.

You will see a set of ten words appear one at a time on the whiteboard in front of you. Each word will appear for 3 seconds and you will need to learn as many as you can. Immediately after the tenth word, you will see a blank screen, this is a cue for you to write as many words as you can remember on the piece of paper in front of you. You may write them down in any order and you will have 1 minute to remember all the words that you can.

If you wish to take part, please sign the consent form in front of you. If you do not wish to take part, please let me know now. If you wish to leave the experiment, you are free to do so at any point. This is not a test of intelligence.

Do you have any questions you would like to ask before we begin?

demand characteristics, the participants will be told what they will be required to do, but not why they are doing it or what other participants will be doing. The words will be presented one at a time for a duration of 3 seconds per word. Participants will be given a pen and paper to recall in any order the words they have learned immediately after the words have been presented. They will be given 1 minute to recall the word list. This standardised procedure will mean that all participants will be treated in exactly the same way, and will minimise any experimenter effects.

Apparatus

Any research into memory typically involves participants learning something, whether it is a list of words, letters or digits, a set of images, or a simulated event. Your apparatus will depend on your aim, but it is worth considering the nature of the apparatus you ask participants to remember. A word list may seem fairly straightforward, but you need to remember that some words are easier to remember or more memorable than other words. It may be worth considering using a list of high frequency words, words of similar syllable length (particularly for short-term memory research) or using letters or digits instead.

This practical investigation uses monosyllabic words to ensure that each word takes up an equal amount of short-term storage capacity. The words have also been selected for being high frequency, so that each list is equal in familiarity and difficulty.

Table 2.13 Apparatus: word lists

Acoustically similar sounding words	Acoustically dissimilar sounding words
Cat	Pan
Mat	Ten
Hat	Mill
Lot	Hit
Hot	Gun
Dot	Dog
Cot	Get
Den	Hot
Pen	Bun
Hen	Pit

Ethical issues

Before undertaking any psychological research it is essential you consider the ethical implications of your research. Both the British Psychological Society (BPS) and British Education Research Association (BERA) guidelines should be consulted and adhered to as closely as possible, even for a small A-level practical investigation. Any research can make participants feel pressured, intimidated, embarrassed or concerned. It is important that ethical issues are given careful thought before proceeding with your experiment. If you are unsure whether your experiment will present any ethical issues, you may wish to conduct a pilot study on family and friends first and ask them how they felt during the experiment.

Valid consent

In this experiment, participants have been asked to volunteer for an experiment into short-term memory. This is clearly stated on the recruitment advertisement. However, participants will not be entirely aware of the full aim of the experiment until after they have completed the memory test. This means that, although consent to take part has been given, fully informed consent has not been achieved because the true nature of the experiment has been partially withheld. When deciding on whether to gain fully informed consent for your own experiment, it is worth considering whether knowledge of the aim will affect the performance of participants and whether the participants are likely to refuse to take part if they did know the full aim. It might be prudent to ask other people whether they would object to taking part in your experiment; if they would not mind, you may assume presumptive consent. Where possible, fully informed consent should be gained or otherwise fully justified, and no offer of incentives should be given for taking part in the investigation.

> **Example advert for a psychology experiment**
> We are looking for volunteers for a psychology experiment on memory. You will be asked to learn a list of words to remember and recall; this will measure your short-term memory. This is an experiment for my A-level practical investigation, which may be used in my exam.
>
> The study will take place in the psychology classroom on Monday morning. You will be required for most of the morning, but the actual memory test will take only 2 minutes. You will be tested

individually and no details of your memory score will be shared with any other participant. You will be told your memory score and the full aim of the study once you have finished. You may use your right to withdraw before, during and after the study has taken place. Any of your details will be destroyed following my A-level examination.

If you are interested in taking part, please place a note with your name and school email address in my pigeon hole.

Because the participants being recruited for this experiment are under the age of 18 years, it is necessary to gain consent from a parent or guardian of the child. In this experiment, details of parents/carers were gained from the volunteers and a consent form was sent out to parents with information about the experiment. You will also need to consider whom consent needs to be gained from if your participants are considered to be children. You should provide an information sheet for both parents/guardians and participants setting out the nature of your experiment.

Right to withdraw

In any psychological investigation, it is very important to offer participants a right to withdraw. This means that they can elect to leave the study before, during or after the experiment has taken place. If they withdraw from the study after it has happened, the participant's results should be destroyed. In this experiment, participants were offered a right to withdraw in the recruitment advertisement, the standardised instructions and debrief.

Example debrief

Thank you for taking part in this psychology experiment into memory.

You were given a list of ten words to learn and recall. The words you were given either rhymed or did not rhyme. This was to test whether dissimilar sounding words were more easily recalled from short-term memory than similar sounding words. Psychological theory predicts that, because we use rehearsal to hold information in short-term memory, we will be better at rehearsing dissimilar sounding words. Similar sounding words will be more difficult to rehearse because they can be confused.

Your memory test score was X out of ten, which is in normal range for this type of experiment.

This result will only be used for my A-level practical investigation. Your result will be anonymised and the data destroyed after the exam. If you feel uncomfortable with this, you may withdraw your results.

Do you have any questions?

Thank you for your time.

Risk

It is important to consider whether your participants will be protected from harm. Harm can be physical or psychological. Under no circumstances should you physically harm your participants, and you will have to think very carefully about whether they will suffer any psychological harm, even modest harm such as embarrassment or stress. In this experiment participants are reminded of their right to withdraw, the results were anonymised, and they were told that the test is not a measure of intelligence. It is also important that participants are given an opportunity to ask any questions they may have arising from the research. This can help alleviate any anxiety before the test and any embarrassment caused by the test.

Information sheet contents

The aim of the study

The type of data to be collected

The method of data collection

Confidentiality and anonymity conditions

Compliance with the Data Protection Act and Freedom of Information Act, how the results will be made available and details on destruction of data

The time commitment participants should expect

A right to decline or withdraw from the study without consequence

The possible risk to the participants

The nature of debriefing

How the data will be used and the benefits of the study

The name and contact details of the researcher and supervisor

(Adapted from the BPS Code of Conduct 2010)

Design decisions taken in this experiment

Aim: to investigate the influence of acoustic similarity on short-term memory

Experimental hypothesis – directional: more acoustically dissimilar sounding words will be recalled than acoustically dissimilar sounding words.

Null hypothesis: there will be no difference in the number of acoustically similar and dissimilar sounding words recalled, and any difference found will be due to chance.

Experimental design: independent groups

Sampling method: volunteer

Independent variable: whether participants receive a list of ten monosyllabic rhyming words, or ten monosyllabic non-rhyming words.

Dependent variable: the total number of accurately recalled words from the list.

Ethical issues: parental/guardian consent gained, participant consent gained but this was not fully informed. No psychological harm was anticipated. A full debrief was given.

Analysing the results

Gather together the results from the participants and present them in a raw data table, like the one in Table 2.14.

Table 2.14 A raw data table to show the recall of acoustically similar and dissimilar sounding words

Participant number	Total number of similar sounding words recalled	Participant number	Total number of dissimilar sounding words recalled
1	4	11	9
2	5	12	7
3	3	13	8
4	7	14	6
5	9	15	8
6	3	16	10
7	7	17	9
8	8	18	5
9	5	19	10
10	4	20	9

This raw data indicates that the highest number of words was recalled when the words presented were acoustically dissimilar and the lowest number recalled was from the acoustically similar list. The raw data seems to support the experimental hypothesis. However, raw data can be difficult to interpret and represents individual scores. To help interpret the findings, descriptive statistics can be useful to present a summary of the average score achieved in a data set. Measures of central tendency, such as mean, median and mode, and measures of dispersion, such as range and standard deviation, should be presented in a summary table, as shown in Table 2.15.

Table 2.15 A summary table to show typical recall score and distribution of scores between acoustically similar and dissimilar sounding words

	Acoustically similar sounding words	Acoustically dissimilar sounding words
Median of words recalled	5	8.5
Mode of words recalled	-	9
Mean number of words recalled	5.5	8.1
Range of words recalled	6	5
Standard deviation	2	1.6

The mode score for acoustically similar sounding words were 3, 4, 5 and 7, so is not a useful modal score to present. However, overall, the measures of central tendency suggest that more acoustically dissimilar words were recalled than similar sounding words. The measures of dispersion suggest that there was greater spread of results for the acoustically similar sounding words than the dissimilar sounding words, but this was only slightly greater. It perhaps suggests that some participants found it slightly easier or more difficult to recall the words than others within the acoustically similar word group.

> **Maths tip**
>
> All tables should be clearly labelled and titled to make it clear to the reader what the table represents and what the figures in the table mean.

The mean of words recalled seems to reflect the typical score achieved by participants in both conditions of the experiment, so this statistic can be graphically represented in a bar chart.

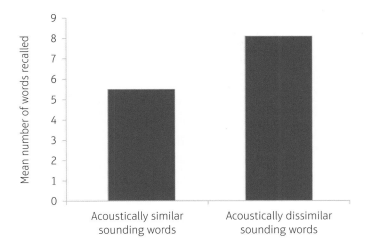

Figure 2.13 A bar graph to show the mean recall of acoustically similar and dissimilar sounding words

Drawing conclusions

From the data gathered and presented, it is important that you can draw conclusions from your findings. This can involve going beyond the findings and relating your data to the concepts under investigation. This practical investigation found that participants recalled fewer acoustically similar soundings words compared to acoustically dissimilar sounding words. The typical recall score achieved by participants given acoustically similar sounding words was, on average, three words fewer than for dissimilar sounding words. However, the distribution of scores suggests that there was a large degree of individual variation in recall for both groups, which was marginally greater for the acoustically similar words group. This demonstrates that some individuals found word recall easier and some more difficult than others.

Inferential test of significance

To determine whether the findings of the practical investigation are statistically significant, or just due to chance, you will have to run your data through an inferential test. For your practical investigation you will need to gather quantitative data that is at ordinal level or above, and therefore conduct either a Mann-Whitney U or Wilcoxon non-parametric test of difference. If you have used an independent groups design you will use a Mann-Whitney U test, or if you have used a repeated measures design you will use a Wilcoxon test.

This practical investigation used an independent groups design, so a Mann-Whitney U test was run on the data:

Mann-Whitney U test formulae

$$U_a = n_a n_b + \frac{n_a(n_a + 1)}{2} - \Sigma R_a$$

$$U_b = n_a n_b + \frac{n_b(n_b + 1)}{2} - \Sigma R_b$$

(*U* is the smaller of U_a and U_b)

Maths tip

All graphs should be clearly titled and both axes fully labelled.

If the Y-axis scale is particularly large, it is possible to start the axis at a greater number than 0, however, if the Y-axis scale is not set at zero, it should be indicated with two intersecting diagonal lines at the lower end of the Y-axis scale. This should be done to alert the reader that differences between the bars may appear exaggerated.

Do not present individual scores/raw data in a chart.

Table 2.16 Scores for each group: words recalled

Total number of similar sounding words recalled Group A	Rank	Total number of dissimilar sounding words recalled Group B	Rank
4	3.5	9	16.5
5	6	7	10
3	1.5	8	13
7	10	6	8
9	16.5	8	13
3	19.5	10	19.5
7	10	9	16.5
8	13	5	6
5	6	10	19.5
4	3.5	9	16.5
Sum total of points	89.5	Sum total of points	138.5

The sum of the ranks for group A and group B should be used in the following formulae:

$$U_a = N_a \times N_b + N_a \times (N_a + 1) / 2 - R_a$$
$$U_a = 10 \times 10 + 10 \times 11 / 2 - 89.5$$
$$U_a = 100 + 110/2 - 89.5$$
$$U_a = 65.5$$

$$U_b = N_a \times N_b + N_b \times (N_b + 1) / 2 - R_b$$
$$U_b = 10 \times 10 + 10 \times 11 / 2 - 138.5$$
$$U_b = 100 + 110/2 - 138.5$$
$$U_b = 16.5$$

This should be compared to a table of critical values for a Mann-Whitney U test.

Table 2.17 Critical values of U for a one-tailed test at 0.05; two-tailed test at 0.1 for a Mann-Whitney U test

n	1	2	3	4	5	6	7	8	9	10
1	-	-	-	-	-	-	-	-	-	-
2	-	-	-	-	0	0	0	1	1	1
3	-	-	0	0	1	2	2	3	3	4
4	-	-	0	1	2	3	4	5	6	7
5	-	0	1	2	4	5	6	8	9	11
6	-	0	2	3	5	7	8	10	12	14
7	-	0	2	4	6	8	11	13	15	17
8	-	1	3	5	7	10	13	15	18	20
9	-	1	3	6	9	12	15	18	21	24
10	-	1	4	7	11	14	17	20	24	27

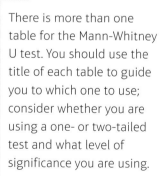

Maths tip

There is more than one table for the Mann-Whitney U test. You should use the title of each table to guide you to which one to use; consider whether you are using a one- or two-tailed test and what level of significance you are using.

The observed value of U is significant at the given level of significance if it is equal to or less than the table (critical) value above.

The calculated (observed) Mann-Whitney U-value is 16.5. This is less than the table (critical) value at $p \leq 0.05$ of 27, with N = 10, 10. Therefore, the result is significant at $p \leq 0.05$ for a one-tailed test. Therefore the experimental hypothesis can be supported. In fact the calculated (observed) value is less than the critical value for a one-tailed test at $p \leq 0.01$, meaning that the result is highly significant and therefore the difference between the recall of the groups is unlikely to be due to chance. This means that the likelihood of making a Type 1 error is reduced and the experimental hypothesis can be supported with confidence.

Making a statistical statement

Following your statistical test, it is important to make a statistical statement and support or reject your hypotheses. Your statistical statement should include the following information:

- the statistical test used
- the observed/calculated value
- whether a one- or two-tailed test was used
- the level of probability
- the number of participants
- the critical value used
- whether the calculated value was greater than/equal to/less than the critical value
- whether the result is significant or not
- which hypothesis it supported.

Discussion

A discussion section of a report will include a summary of the findings and how these relate to the wider concepts, theory and prior research related to the study. It will also include the strengths and weaknesses of the practical investigation and suggestions for possible improvements and new directions for the research.

In this practical investigation it can be concluded that there was a significant difference between recall of acoustically similar sounding and dissimilar sounding words; acoustically dissimilar sounding words were significantly less well recalled. This finding is consistent with theory which suggests that encoding in the short-term store is primarily acoustic, making similar sounding words difficult to sub-vocalise (rehearse) and maintain compared to dissimilar sounding material. This is also consistent with research conducted by Sperling (1963) who found that participants had difficulty remembering acoustically similar letters (B, D, T) compared to acoustically dissimilar sounding letters (F, L, M, X).

Critical evaluation

It is important to consider both the strengths and weaknesses of the practical investigation. For this, you will be better placed to judge the successes and failures with regard to your own procedure and outcomes. However, a number of general questions should be asked.

- Is the study ethical?
- Can you generalise the findings to others/different cultures/different eras?
- Is the study reliable?
- Is the study carried out in a natural or artificial environment?
- Is the task ordinary?
- Are the findings useful in real life?
- Is the research valid?
- Is there any conflicting evidence from other research?

Is the task ordinary?

This is a common question asked of much cognitive research conducted in laboratories using series of stimulus lists of words, letters and digits, seemingly unrelated to memory tasks that occur in ordinary everyday life. It is true that we are often required to draw on our memory for shopping

Maths tip

Use this statistical statement template to help structure your conclusion:

The calculated value of the _____ test was _____.
This was equal to/greater/less than the critical value of _____ for a one/two tailed test at $p \le 0.05$ with N = _____.
Therefore the result is/is not significant and the experimental/null hypothesis can be supported, which states that _____
_____.

lists, telephone numbers or random sequences. However, this is not a typical activity for memory to undertake and often takes a degree of conscious processing and effort. For this reason, the task used in this practical investigation may be criticised for not reflecting an ordinary use of memory.

However, the task was intended to investigate encoding in the short-term store in a way that actually measured short-term memory in its most pure form, unaffected by the meaningfulness of everyday material. In order to study memory this practical investigation had to remove the social context in which memory normally operates in order to remove variables that could potentially confound the research. This can be more easily understood by comparing psychology to biology as a subject. No one would criticise a biologist for collecting blood in a test tube to determine its blood group, yet a test tube is not a natural state for blood to exist. In order for the blood to be tested, it needs to be collected from the body and isolated from contamination. This experiment performed the same function to test encoding in short-term memory.

Suggestions for improvement

In addition to considering the strengths and weaknesses of you practical investigation, you should also refer to how your study could be improved. To do this effectively you will need to consider the weaknesses of your research and how these weaknesses could be overcome. Suggestions for improvement can be ambitious, but should not be impractical or impossible to achieve.

In this practical investigation the nature of the word lists were withheld from participants, resulting in a lack of valid consent being gained. This is a potential ethical weakness of the study that could have been improved by fully informing participants of the aim of the research. A pilot study could have been conducted where participants were told that they would receive either a similar sounding word list or a dissimilar sounding word list, and participants could have been asked later whether this knowledge affected their performance. This is a useful suggestion to improve the ethical problem with the practical investigation that is not impractical and would not ruin the research.

Writing up the report

Psychological investigations are written following a set of conventions for report writing as shown below.

Conventions of report writing

Abstract: a summary of the background theory/research, aims, hypotheses, method, results and discussion. This is a short paragraph overview of the entire report.

Introduction: an overview of related theories and research in the topic area. The introduction provides a rationale for the current investigation that links prior research to the study aims and hypotheses.

Method: a detailed account of the participants, sampling method, apparatus, procedure, controls and ethical issues.

Results: a detailed account of the data gathered and its analysis using descriptive and inferential statistics.

Discussion: conclusions drawn from the results analysis, reference to prior research, strengths, weaknesses and possible improvements for future research.

To complete your practical investigation, it is necessary and useful to follow these conventions when writing up your report.

2.6 Issues and debates (A level only)

In this section you will learn about issues and debates relevant to cognitive psychology. You will have already noticed that issues and debates have been mentioned throughout this topic. This section will draw together the main themes and ideas related to the cognitive approach as a whole.

Issues of social control

Psychology is largely concerned with how knowledge can be applied to the real world, and as such can have important applications in many areas of life, such as health, education and crime. However, we need to exercise care when applying knowledge in real life to ensure that it is not unwittingly directing the behaviour of others or encouraging social injustice. Using psychological knowledge can impact adversely on others, even if the application reflects dominant thinking at the time, this thinking may change practise or opinion. Memory research has been very influential in directing legal practise. Criminology is the application of memory research, used by police interviewers and the courts. One such theory has dominated legal practise for many years; that is the belief that eyewitnesses may not be reliable because their memory is reconstructive and prone to distortion. This has driven legal policy and police practise in an attempt to improve the reliability of testimony or ensure that eyewitnesses are not the only form of evidence used in court. This knowledge has effectively been used as a form of social control, dictating who can testify and under what conditions they can give accurate testimony.

Ethics

Experimental research

Cognitive psychology is largely based on experimental research into 'normal' participants with average memory ability. Although the full nature of experimental aims may be withheld from participants, to avoid the possibility of demand characteristics, most research gains participant consent and rarely involves deliberately violating the protection of participants by causing distress or anxiety. Some research may use deception by misguiding participants as to the true nature of the experiment, but will offer participants the right to withdraw from the research at any stage. In fact, most experimental research adheres very closely to the BPS ethical guidelines for research with human participants.

Case studies of brain-damaged patients

In case studies of brain-damaged patients, such as HM, participant confidentiality is maintained by ensuring that they are given pseudonyms to anonymise their identities. Research using individuals with brain damage is often criticised for violating a right to privacy; case studies of brain-damaged patients are rare and unique, which can result in them being over studied and their normal life impinged on by rigorous and intensive experimentation. This may be true of some cases where researchers may become overzealous in their research. However, Henry Molaison was reported to have enjoyed being tested and saw memory experiments as fun and challenging activities; this is perhaps because he had no recollection of any prior testing.

Practical issues in the design and implementation of research

Cognitive research often involves the use of laboratory experiments using tasks that lack mundane realism. The ecological validity of this research has often been debated, particularly when the findings are used to explain everyday memory or are applied to everyday contexts. However, laboratory

Ethical issues in recent research
More recent experimental research into memory has adopted more naturalistic methodology, such as the field experiment. This research can involve staging realistic events for people to witness and asking them to recall the event later on. These experiments may not ask participants for their initial consent to take part, but do gain consent after the staged incident and provide a full debrief after the memory test has concluded.

Socially sensitive research
Memory loss is a sensitive area for both the amnesia patient and the families concerned. Amnesia is a life-altering impairment that can cause an individual extreme distress because their intelligence remains virtually intact, leading to confusion and frustration about their loss of memory. However, this research is important for both psychological understanding and to benefit amnesia patient recovery.

experiments are often necessary to study memory in a vacuum that is devoid of variables that could affect the findings of the research, for example, the use of trigrams may not reflect ordinary information that we need to remember, but trigrams are necessary to study memory without the inference of meaning that we often associate with words or images. Ecological validity is often lost at the expense of internal validity.

Reductionism

Historically, the cognitive approach has tended to separate different cognitive functions, such as perception and memory, to make these cognitive processes easier to research and understand. Breaking up these areas of cognition into these separate parts can be considered to be reductionist as clearly what we remember is based on what we perceive in the first place, and to some extent perception is affected by previously stored knowledge. Bartlett recognised this in his theory of reconstructive memory, which can be considered as less reductionist than the other models of memory described in cognitive psychology. The multi-store model of memory can be considered as reductionist because it artificially fragments the short-term and long-term memory stores without discussing the interconnections between each store. Similarly, Baddeley and Hitch divided the short-term memory into slave systems for the purposes of studying working memory.

It has become increasingly acknowledged that in order to better understand memory and other cognitive processes we need to acknowledge the interplay between systems and stores. Research using brain-imaging has helped us to appreciate the interrelatedness of different parts of the brain when we perform cognitive functions, and amnesia patients have helped us understand that loss of functionality may not be a direct consequence of damage to a particular region of the brain, but an interaction between different regions.

Comparing explanations

Comparing explanations of memory can be done on many levels; such as the type of research used to support the explanation, whether it has practical application, the role of nature or nurture within the explanation, or whether its emphasis is on structure or function. As an example, the explanations of memory described in this section can be compared in terms of whether they emphasise the nature of memory as a series of structures or the way that memory is processed. The multi-store model views memory as a series of stores; the sensory store, the short-term store and the long-term store, so can be considered a structural model of memory because the focus of the explanation is on the architecture of the memory system. Similarly, Baddeley and Hitch also focus their explanation of working memory on what components of short-term memory exist. Although both theories of memory acknowledge the type of processes involved in the transfer and manipulation of information, this is second to describing how memory is represented as a structural system.

An alternative model

In direct contrast to these structural models is Bartlett's reconstructive memory. This explanation of memory does not attempt to describe the structure of memory, instead focusing on memory as a process or function. Reconstructive memory is a functional model of memory because it explains how stored knowledge affects perception and remembering as an active process of construction.

Psychology as a science

The cognitive approach is one of the most scientific perspectives in psychology because it largely adopts the scientific method. The dominant research method used is the laboratory experiment, which means that controls are used to establish causality between the independent and dependent

---

Case studies of brain-damaged patients

The use of case studies of brain-damaged patients can be very scientific because they use highly controlled experiments and brain-imaging techniques, however, these cases are rare and often the damage is unique to the individual, resulting in a lack of generalisability.

However, the cognitive approach can study concepts that are largely theoretical with no empirical evidence to support them, such as the working memory's central executive.

variables, and research has replicability. Studies within this approach employ the hypothetico-deductive experimental method, which investigates predictions in an objective way and, unlike the inductive method, ensures that hypotheses can be refuted or supported.

Nature–nurture

The cognitive approach emphasises the role of both nature and nurture within its explanations of cognitive functioning. Using the computer metaphor, the cognitive approach assumes that we are born with the hardware to have the capacity to perform certain functions, such as remembering. The approach also assumes that the experiences we have during our lives change what we remember and how we process information in the same way that a programmer alters the software of a computer. How our experiences affect cognition represents the role of nurture.

Reconstructive memory describes how we all represent knowledge as schema; these are universal mental constructs (nature) hardwired into our memory, but the contents of which are affected by how we are raised and what we experience as we develop (nurture).

How psychological knowledge has developed over time

The study of memory can be traced back many years, and each time that a new explanation is put forward, psychology develops a new understanding. The multi-store model was one of the first coherent theories of memory, and although now largely regarded as simplistic, it has been useful in understanding what memory might look like and has contributed to a better understanding of memory today. The multi-store model directly informed the development of Baddeley and Hitch's working memory and Tulving's semantic and episodic long-term memory. Similarly, within the working memory theory, a reformulation was done to fine-tune the explanation by adding the episodic buffer to explain the interrelationship between short-term and long-term memory. More recently there has been a resurgence of interest in reconstructive memory that has led to a wealth of studies conducted into eyewitness memory which continues to debate whether we can rely on such testimony in our courts.

The use of psychological knowledge within society

The most important use of cognitive psychology is its application of explanations and research in society. A general understanding of how memory works can be used in everyday contexts, such as using mnemonics to aid revision or chunking bits of information together to remember a telephone number. Understanding how memory works can also help in the treatment of learning impairments such as dyslexia; teachers can simplify and shorten instructions and information so that working memory is not overloaded. As there is no cure for memory loss, cognitive therapies, such as cognitive stimulation, have been used with dementia patients to practise memory tasks (remembering the date, people in a group) and reduce their confusion.

One of the most significant contributions of memory has been to our understanding whether eyewitness testimony can be relied on. There has been considerable research examining the factors affecting reliability of memory, such as whether age, anxiety or post-event information can affect our ability to accurately recall an incident and identify a perpetrator. This academic research led to the Devlin Report (1976) which called into question eyewitness reliability following a number of cases of false imprisonment based on witness identification. This has led to recent changes in the Police and Criminal Evidence Act Codes of Practice in the way eyewitnesses are asked to identify a perpetrator from a line-up.

HM

The case of HM is a useful example when considering the nature–nurture debate because his unique characteristics make it unclear which elements of his impairment are due to the surgery that caused his brain damage and which to the lack of schooling and seizures he experienced when growing up. Clearly the loss of his hippocampus (nature) resulted in severe amnesia, but perhaps his underperformance on certain tests could be a result of nurture.

Knowledge check

Content

In the content section you are required to describe, evaluate and apply your knowledge of four theories of memory.

To check your evaluation skills, refer to the introduction section of this book and review 'how to evaluate a theory'. Remember that you may be asked to consider issues of validity, reliability, credibility, generalisability, objectivity and subjectivity in your evaluation of theories.

Can you describe Atkinson and Shiffrin's (1968) multi-store model of memory and understand the difference between each store in terms of their capacity, duration, encoding and forgetting?

Are you able to apply the concepts used in the multi-store model of memory to explain how we remember and why we forget?

Can you evaluate the multi-store model of memory in terms of strengths and weaknesses?

Are you confident that you can describe the components of the working memory model (Baddeley and Hitch, 1974)?

Are you able to apply working memory concepts to explain dual task performance?

Can you evaluate the working memory model in terms of strengths and weaknesses?

Can you identify and distinguish between the episodic and semantic long-term memory stores?

Are you able to evaluate Tulving's (1972) distinction between the types of long-term memory in terms of strengths and weaknesses?

Can you describe Bartlett's (1932) theory of reconstructive memory?

Are you confident that you can apply your knowledge of schemas to understanding everyday memory and how memory can be affected by stored knowledge?

Can you evaluate reconstructive memory in terms of strengths and weaknesses?

Can you explain individual differences in memory in terms of processing speed, autobiographical memory and schemas?

Can you describe at least one developmental difference in memory by age (see Studies section for Sebastián and Hernández-Gil, 2012), dyslexia and Alzheimer's.

Methods

Are you able to describe how laboratory and field experiments are designed and conducted?

Can you identify and write independent and dependent variables and fully operationalise each?

Can you identify and write operationalised experimental (directional and non-directional) and null hypotheses?

Are you able to identify, describe and evaluate experimental designs (repeated measures, independent groups and matched pairs), explain order effects and how problems with each design could be controlled (counterbalancing and randomisation)?

Are you able to identify and explain extraneous variables (situational and participant) and understand the impact of confounding variables?

Can you identify and explain experimenter effects and demand characteristics and consider how these could be controlled?

Can you explain what is meant by the concepts of objectivity, reliability and validity, and understand the impact and control of these concepts within the scientific process?

> **For quantitative data, can you identify, calculate and understand the analysis and interpretation of measures of central tendency (mean, median and mode), measures of dispersion (range and standard deviation), and percentages? Can you draw, interpret and select appropriate table and graphical representations of quantitative data (frequency table, bar graph and histogram)?**

Do you understand the purpose of inferential tests, and the concept of probability?

Can you select an appropriate non-parametric test of difference (Mann-Whitney and Wilcoxon)?

Do you understand levels of significance ($p \leq 10$ $p \leq 05$ $p \leq 01$) and are you able to use these to interpret the results of an inferential test?

Can you compare observed and critical values on a critical values table to check whether results are significant?

Are you able to select an appropriate one- or two-tailed test according to the hypothesis and use this to interpret significance using a critical values table?

Can you explain what is meant by Type I and Type II errors and how the results of a statistical test may be vulnerable to these errors according to the level of significance adopted?

Can you describe, identify, draw and interpret normal and skewed distribution?

Are you able to describe the case of Henry Molaison (HM) as a case study of a brain-damaged patient, including how this case demonstrates individual differences in memory and the evaluations done of this case?

Do you understand what is meant by qualitative data, how qualitative data is conducted and interpreted and its strengths and weaknesses?

Studies

> **In the studies section you are required to describe, evaluate and apply your knowledge of one classic and one contemporary study of memory.**
>
> **To check your evaluation skills, refer to the introduction section of this book and review 'how to evaluate a study. Remember that you may be asked to consider issues of validity, reliability, credibility, generalisability, objectivity and subjectivity in your evaluation of studies.**

Can you describe the classic study by Baddeley (1966b): The influence of acoustic and semantic similarity on long-term memory for word sequences, in terms of its aim(s), method, procedure, results and conclusions?

Are you able to evaluate Baddeley's (1966b) study in terms of strengths and weaknesses?

Are you able to identify and describe the aims, method, procedure, results and conclusions of a contemporary study from the following list and evaluate the study in terms of strengths and weaknesses?

- Schmolk et al. (2002) Semantic knowledge in patient HM and other patients with bilateral medial and lateral temporal lobe lesions.

- Steyvers and Hemmer (2012) Reconstruction from memory in naturalistic environments.

- Sebastián and Hernández-Gil (2012) Developmental pattern of digit span in Spanish population.

Key question

Are you able to identify and describe a key question in cognitive psychology that is relevant to today's society?

Can you explain this key question using concepts, theories and research that you have studied in cognitive psychology?

Practical investigation

Have you designed and conducted a laboratory experiment to investigate an area of cognitive psychology?

Can you explain how you went about planning and designing you laboratory experiment, justifying your decision making for your choice of design, sampling, operationalisation and hypothesis construction?

Can you explain your control issues for experimenter effects and demand characteristics, and ethical considerations you had?

Can you describe and analyse (using measures of central tendency and dispersion) the quantitative data that you gathered for your laboratory experiment and how you presented your data (table and graphical representation)?

Are you able to explain, justify and interpret the non-parametric test of difference that you used on your data?

Are you able to draw conclusions from your descriptive data and inferential test (including critical and observed values, and level of significance)?

Remember that you may be asked to consider issues of validity, reliability, credibility, generalisability, objectivity and subjectivity in your evaluation of your practical investigation.

Can you explain the strengths and weaknesses of your laboratory experiment and suggest possible improvements that could have been made?

Are you able to write up the procedure, results and discussion sections of your laboratory experiment in a report style?

Issues and debates (A level only)

Remember that issues and debates are synoptic. This means you may be asked to make connections by comparing issues and debates across topics in psychology or comment on issues and debates within unseen material.

Can you identify ethical issues associated with theory and research within the cognitive approach?

Can you comment on the practical and methodological issues in the design and implementation of research within the cognitive approach?

Can you explain how theories, research and concepts within the cognitive approach might be considered reductionist?

Can you compare theories and research within cognitive psychology to show different ways of explaining and understanding memory?

Are you able to discuss whether theories, concepts, research and methodology within cognitive psychology are scientific?

Are you able to discuss the nature–nurture debate in the context of cognitive psychology, in terms of which parts emphasise the role or nature and nurture or the interaction between them?

Do you understand how cognitive psychology has developed over time?

Do you understand what is meant by social control and how research within cognitive psychology may be used to control behaviour?

Can you show how the theories, concepts and research within cognitive psychology can be used in a practical way in society?

Are you able to understand what is meant by socially sensitive research and explain how research in cognitive psychology might be considered to be socially sensitive?

References

Atkinson, R. and Shiffrin, R. (1968) 'Human memory: A proposed system and its control processes', in K. W. Spence and J. T. Spence (eds) *The Psychology of Learning and Motivation: Advances in Research and Theory*, 2, pp. 89–195, New York Academic Press.

Baddeley, A.D., and Hitch, G. (1974) 'Working memory' in G.H. Bower (ed.) *The psychology of learning and motivation: Advances in research and theory*, 8, pp. 47–89, New York: Academic Press.

Bartlett, F. C. (1932). *Remembering: A Study in Experimental and Social Psychology*, Cambridge, UK: Cambridge University Press.

Sebastián, M.V., and Hernández-Gil, L. (2012) 'Developmental pattern of digit span in Spanish population. *Psicothema*', 24 (2), pp. 183–187.

Steyvers, M. and Hemmer, P. (2012) 'Reconstruction from Memory in Naturalistic Environments' In Brian H. Ross (ed.) *The Psychology of Learning and Motivation*, 56, pp. 126–144, Elsevier Publishing.

Schmolck, H., Kensinger, E. A., Corkin, S. and Squire, L. R. (2002) 'Semantic knowledge in patient H.M. and other patients with bilateral medial and lateral temporal lobe lesions', *Hippocampus*, 12, pp. 520–533.

Tulving, E. (1972) 'Episodic and semantic memory', in E. Tulving and W. Donaldson (eds), *Organization of Memory*, pp. 381–402. New York: Academic Press.

3 Biological psychology

Biological psychology aims to make a direct link between the normal functioning of the body (your physiology) and behavioural studies. This topic explores different biological factors such as genes, the brain and hormones, and how they have been related to human behaviours such as aggression and drug taking. You will also explore how individual differences in biology such as brain damage caused by accidents, or differences in personality traits, can change elements of behaviour. As part of your understanding of this topic you will look at how evolution may explain certain aspects of human behaviour, as well as different research methods often associated with biological research in psychology.

In this topic, you will learn about:

- the role of the central nervous system and neurotransmitters in human behaviour
- the effect of recreational drugs on the transmission process in the central nervous system
- the structure of the brain and the role of brain functioning, evolution, natural selection and hormones as explanations of aggression
- how damage to the brain may be affected by individual differences
- Freud's view of personality and how individual differences are developed
- the role of evolution and hormones in human development
- methods for studying biological psychology
- a classic and a contemporary study
- key issues around the topic of biological psychology that are of relevance to society today
- how to carry out a practical research exercise relevant to topics covered in biological psychology
- wider issues and debates in biological psychology (A level).

3.1 Content
Learning outcomes

In this section, you will learn about:

- the central nervous system (CNS)
- the structure and role of the neuron
- the function of neurotransmitters
- the effect of recreational drugs on the transmission process
- brain structure and function as an explanation of aggression
- evolution and aggression
- Freud's psychodynamic explanation of aggression
- the role of hormones in aggression.

What is the central nervous system and how does it work?

The central nervous system (CNS) consists of the brain and spinal cord. It is the central processing and control point for all human behaviour. The brain processes all incoming information from the senses and is then responsible for controlling behaviour that may result from this information. The spinal cord connects the brain to the rest of your body, and allows messages to be passed from the body to the brain, and also from the brain to other parts of the body in order to get them to respond. The cells in the central nervous system are known as **neurons** and these cells communicate with around 1 000 other cells at a time in huge networks.

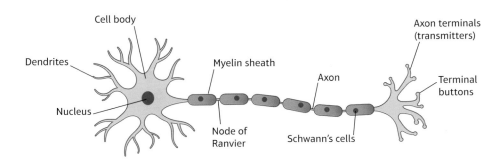

Figure 3.1 The structure of the neuron

Structure and role of the neuron

There are four main parts to the neuron as shown in the figure above.

- The **cell body** of the neuron contains the cell **nucleus**, which houses the genetic material for that particular neuron. The cell body also contains other materials that allow the cell to function, such as the **mitochondria**, which provide the neuron with energy.

- Attached to the cell body are **dendrites** that receive messages from other neurons in order to trigger an action potential (an electrical impulse) within the cell.

- Also attached to the cell body is the **axon**, an extension of the cell body that passes the electrical impulse towards the axon terminals. At the top of the axon, attaching the axon to the cell body is the **axon hillock**, which is where the nerve impulse is triggered from. Around the outside of the axon are layers of fatty deposits called **myelin sheath** that provide an insulating layer to the axon and help to speed up the rate of message transmission. There are breaks between the cells along the myelin sheath, which are known as **nodes of Ranvier**.

- At the very end of the axon are the **axon terminals**, and on the ends of these are **terminal buttons** (also known as **terminal boutons**). Action terminals pass nerve impulses from the cell body to the parts of the body that they control or activate – this could be another neuron, or it could be something like a muscle or a gland. These bulb-shaped structures contain tiny sacs called **vesicles** that store **neurotransmitters** ready for the next stage of neural transmission.

Resting membrane potential: the difference in electrical potential (meaning how 'ready' the neuron is for action) on each side of the cell membrane while the cell is at rest.

Excitatory postsynaptic potential: the temporary depolarisation of a neuron as a result of positively charged ions flowing into the cell that make it more likely to fire an action potential.

Inhibitory postsynaptic potential: changes in the polarisation of a neuron that make it less likely to fire an action potential.

Action potential: the electrical trigger that passes along the axon and stimulates the neuron to activate and release neurotransmitters as a result of synaptic transmission.

Synaptic gap/cleft: the tiny space between the dendrite of one neuron and the terminal button of another where chemical messages can be passed.

Presynaptic neuron: the neuron where a chemical message starts from.

Postsynaptic neuron: the neuron where a chemical message travels to.

Receptors: sites on the dendrites that are designed to bond to and absorb a specific type of neurotransmitter molecule.

Reuptake: the process by which unused neurotransmitter molecules are absorbed back into the presynaptic neuron and then destroyed by enzymes.

The action potential

The action potential refers to the actual method by which the nerve impulse passes down the axon of the neuron to stimulate the release of neurotransmitters. This is a tiny electrical impulse that is triggered by a change in the electrical 'potential' of the neuron itself.

Neurons have a **resting membrane potential** of about -70mV, meaning that the inside of the neuron has a slight negative charge in relation to the outside of the neuron. When a neuron receives a message from another neuron, this chemical message can either stimulate an **excitatory postsynaptic potential**, which means that it will slightly depolarise the neuron, reducing its charge, or it can hyperpolarise the neuron, increasing its charge and stimulating an **inhibitory postsynaptic potential**.

When a neuron has received enough excitatory messages, or at least more excitatory messages in comparison to the number of inhibitory messages, that are sufficiently strong to reach the neuron's own threshold, an **action potential** is triggered. This usually happens when the neuron's charge reaches approximately -55mV. The action potential sends an impulse along the axon of the neuron towards the axon terminals at the end of the neuron.

  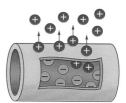 

1 When the neuron is at rest, the inside is negatively charged relative to the outside.

2 When the neuron is stimulated, positively charged particles enter. The action potential is initiated – the neuron is depolarised.

3 After a brief period, some positively charged particles are pushed outside the neuron, and the neuron moves back towards its polarised state.

4 The neuron has finally returned to its initial polarised resting state.

Figure 3.2 Synaptic transmission: how a message is carried by the neuron by action potential

Synaptic transmission

The cell's electrical impulse/action potential starts as small electrical impulses generated at the axon hillock, but once the message reaches the terminal button it turns into a chemical message. When the impulse reaches the axon terminal, the neuron can pass its chemical message to further neurons across the **synaptic gap** (also known as the **synaptic cleft**) – the space between two adjacent neurons. The neuron that is sending the message is referred to as the **presynaptic neuron,** while the one receiving the message is the **postsynaptic neuron**.

Each neuron is responsible for producing a certain chemical, or neurotransmitter, and when the action potential reaches the axon terminal, calcium channels will open – flooding the terminal button with calcium ions. Vesicles containing the neurotransmitter substance will then be released and travel down to the outer membrane of the terminal button, where the casing of the vesicle will fuse with the membrane. This allows the neurotransmitter to be released from its vesicles into the synaptic gap/cleft.

The **receptors** on the postsynaptic neuron are designed to bind to a specific neurotransmitter, and when they detect it the neurotransmitter molecule will then be absorbed by the postsynaptic neuron. Any neurotransmitter molecules that have not been absorbed by the receptors of the postsynaptic neuron will be destroyed by enzymes in the synaptic gap/cleft, or they will be absorbed again by the presynaptic neuron in a process known as **reuptake.** These reabsorbed molecules will be destroyed by enzymes within the neuron in order to 'turn off' the neuron in preparation for a future action potential.

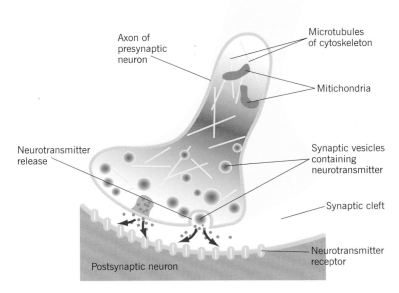

Figure 3.3 The synaptic cleft

The table below gives a summary of the functions of four of the most common neurotransmitters

Table 3.1 Functions of the most common neurotransmitters

Neurotransmitter	Function
Acetylcholine	Stimulates muscle contractions and has a key function in motor control and movement. It is also necessary for memory and other cognitive functions such as attention and wakefulness/alertness. Acetylcholine is also involved in expressions of some emotions such as anger and sexuality.
Noradrenaline	It is also a neurotransmitter associated with emotion, particularly in mood control. Noradrenaline is involved in functions such as sleeping and dreaming as well as learning.
Dopamine	A chemical precursor to noradrenaline so their functions are quite similar. Dopamine has been related to emotion and cognitive functions, as well as posture and control of movement. It has also been associated with reinforcement in learning as well as dependency such as addictions. Dopamine is used in hormonal regulation such as control of the menstrual cycle in women.
Serotonin	Serotonin is often most commonly associated with mood control, particularly in the **limbic system** in the brain. It is involved in many other functions such as feeling pain, sleep, regulating body temperature and hunger.

> **Key term**
>
> **Limbic system:** a set of structures in the brain associated with drives, emotions and mood.

The effect of recreational drugs on the transmission process in the central nervous system

Recreational drugs are those that are used in the absence medical grounds, but are taken by users for personal enjoyment. These are often referred to as psychoactive drugs because they alter brain function, which changes our mood, perception or conscious experience. Such drugs include caffeine, nicotine, alcohol, cannabis, amphetamines, LSD, cocaine and heroin, but there are others. It has long been recognised that the use of such substances leads to an altered state of consciousness, but only fairly recently has it been possible to investigate the effect of drugs on the nervous system.

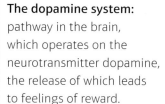

Key terms

The dopamine system: pathway in the brain, which operates on the neurotransmitter dopamine, the release of which leads to feelings of reward.

Nucleus accumbens: an area of the midbrain associated with the brain's reward system.

Ventral tegmental: an area of the midbrain associated with the brain's reward system and the origin of dopaminergic activity.

Euphoria: an intense pleasurable feeling often referred to as a 'high'.

Dysphoria: an intense dissatisfaction, anxiety or depression, discomfort and distress.

The brain contains a 'reward pathway', which when activated unsurprisingly causes us to experience a pleasant and rewarding feeling. This encourages us to repeat the behaviour that activated the pathway and is a key component in learning: if we do something that leads to the activation of this pathway we feel good and are likely to do it again. Being rewarded for specific behaviours has an adaptive function, for example, the reward or enjoyment we feel after eating high-calorie foods would ensure we store enough fat on our bodies, in preparation for periods of famine. Drugs hijack this reward system and produce pleasurable feelings without any adaptive function.

Drugs act by changing the way neurotransmitters operate in the brain. Most psychoactive drugs of addiction work on **the dopamine system**. For example, heroin increases the amount of dopamine in the reward pathways of the brain (the **nucleus accumbens** and **ventral tegmental** areas) by boosting the activation of dopaminergic synapses, causing an intensely pleasurable experience or feeling of **euphoria** while it lasts. However, the brain naturally reacts to the sudden increase in dopamine and reduces (or down-regulates) its own natural production of dopamine, so when the drug effects on the dopamine system wear off the person now has less dopamine than they would have for normal brain functioning. This causes an unpleasurable experience (**dysphoria**) and that motivates the person to take more heroin to stop them feeling bad and to reproduce the high they felt when they first took the drug. Repeated use of the drug causes further down-regulation of dopamine production; this makes the person physically dependent on the drug in order to avoid the negative experience of withdrawal, which is caused by the lack of dopamine now produced by the brain and so leads to addiction.

INDIVIDUAL DIFFERENCES

Although drugs have a common biological mechanism they have different effects on different people. This may be due to physiological differences between people in the way their brain chemistry works or it could be due to the mediating effect of the environment. In some cases the effect is determined by where the drug is taken, for example in situations where the user has never experienced drug taking, even taking the regular dose of drugs can lead to overdose. This is because the brain is conditioned to expect the increased levels of chemicals in some situations; this expectation causes a down-regulation of neurotransmitter release, making way for the sudden rush of chemicals caused by the drug. This explains why people who have overcome addiction will develop craving and will relapse when they return to places where they used to take drugs.

Table 3.2 The mode of action of recreational drugs

Drug	Mode of action
Alcohol	Has a depressant effect on the nervous system; it acts to inhibit neural transmission by increasing the action of GABA (an inhibitory neurotransmitter).
Opioids, e.g. heroin and morphine	Reduces GABA activity, which leads to overactivity of dopaminergic neurotransmission in the reward pathways of the brain.
Amphetamines, e.g. methamphetamines	Increases dopamine and noradrenaline in the synapse by changing the reuptake process so that it works in reverse. Amphetamines force the release of these neurotransmitters, can block reuptake, and in high doses can inhibit their breakdown by enzymes.
Cocaine	Increases activity in the dopamine pathway by blocking the reuptake of dopamine.
Nicotine	Targets aspects of the dopamine pathway increasing the amount and transmission of dopamine by blocking the enzyme that breaks it down. It also mimics acetylcholine and binds to nicotinic receptors.

How do these processes lead to addiction?

Withdrawal occurs when a drug is no longer active in our nervous system. This can result in withdrawal symptoms that are often unpleasant and can be dangerous. Withdrawal happens when the brain adapts to the changes imposed by the drug so that it no longer operates normally without the drug. This also leads to tolerance, where the user has to take ever-greater doses of the drug to get the same effect as on the previous occasions when they took it. The brain adapts to the high levels of dopamine caused by the drug and down-regulates its own natural production of it; this means that the baseline measure of dopamine is now lower than before, so in order to get the same 'high' the user now needs more dopamine and so more of the drug.

Brain structure

Historical overview

There is evidence that early humans understood some basic qualities of the brain. Fossil evidence shows **trepanning** was used in connection with migraines and epilepsy, indicating that 10 000 years ago humans had some ideas about brain functioning. Hippocrates, a Greek physician known as the father of medicine (born in 460 BC), was familiar with brain injuries and put forward the idea that each side, or **hemisphere**, of the brain served a distinct function. However there was little development in our understanding of the role of brain structure until in the early 19th century when the 'science' of **phrenology** was introduced by Franz Joseph Gall. This 'science' was mistaken in its belief that you could tell someone's character by mapping the bumps on their head, but it at least reflected the idea that behaviour was in some way linked to the brain.

One of the earliest cases that indicated a specific role for brain structure in governing behaviour was that of Phineas Gage, a railway worker in the mid-west of the USA. In 1848 he suffered an unfortunate accident when a tamping iron (an iron rod used for pushing explosives into drilled holes in rock in order to blow them up) set off the explosive and blew the iron rod up through Gage's face and out the top of his head. For the remaining 11 years of his life after the accident, his personality had a fundamental change; from being a reliable sort of person he became irresponsible and aggressive. His doctor concluded that the damage done to his brain, which included severing the **prefrontal cortex**, had led to the change in his character.

WIDER ISSUES AND DEBATES.

Generalising from case studies

There is a problem in generalising from single case studies because the case outcome may result from a unique set of variables, so other people in different circumstances with similar damage may have reacted in a different way from Phineas Gage. This may be because Phineas's change in behaviour was due to his individual reaction to the facial disfigurement suffered alongside the brain injury. Would his reaction have been the same without the damage? Psychology looks for confirming evidence from many sources, so might build a range of evidence from similar case studies and if enough agree then the findings would be regarded as reliable and generalisable.

Key terms

Trepanning: surgical intervention in which a hole is drilled into the skull to treat problems related to the surface of the brain.

Hemisphere: the brain is divided into two symmetrical halves, one on the left and one on the right, known as hemispheres.

Phrenology: the practice of mapping the bumps on a person's skull and using these to deduce aspects of their character.

Prefrontal cortex: the front area of the brain situated just behind the forehead.

Taking it further

Look at the work of Roger Sperry on split brain patients in the 1970s for a fascinating insight into how the hemispheres of the brain operate.

Lobes: specific locations in each hemisphere of the brain, frontal – is the front part, temporal is to the side and behind the ears, parietal is the top area and occipital is at the back of the brain (see Figure 3.4). Brains have eight lobes, four in each hemisphere.

Aphasia: a disturbance in the comprehension or production of language caused by brain dysfunction or damage, such as a stroke.

Lesion studies: investigations into the effect on behaviour of damage to specific areas of the brain.

The case of Phineas Gage was one of the first investigations into how the structure of the brain affects behaviour. A series of case studies of people who had suffered damage to their brain allowed physicians to start to 'map' the brain. This is not an easy task as superficially the brain appears to be one whole organ with little definition of specific areas beyond the two hemispheres. One example is the work of Paul Broca, a French neuroscientist and physician who treated stroke patients in the 19th century. His most famous case study was that of a patient known as 'Tan' (because he had lost the ability to say any word other than 'tan'). It was revealed through post-mortem examination that an area of Tan's brain had been damaged in the lower part of the left frontal **lobe**. This part of the brain, which came to be named Broca's area, is now known to be responsible for the motor control involved in speech production. Damage to this part of the brain would mean someone could understand speech but would not be able to articulate a reply.

Another part of the brain that was identified early is Wernicke's area. This is named after Carl Wernicke who was a German neurologist working in the late 19th century. Wernicke's area is situated at the rear of the left temporal lobe as it joins with the parietal lobe and is involved with the understanding of speech. Patients with Wernicke's **aphasia** typically can produce speech but it is meaningless; superficially it sounds like speech but it is essentially nonsense as these patients have a problem with language comprehension. Over the years psychologists have built a functional map of the brain using research such as this and the case studies you looked at in the memory section (in Topic 2) on the role of the hippocampus in memory. With modern neuroimaging techniques this task has become easier as we no longer have to rely on **lesion studies** to understand the link between a brain area and behaviour.

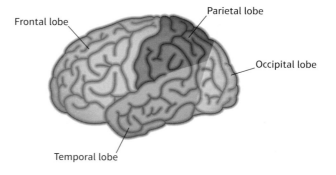

Figure 3.4 The structure of the brain

Explaining aggression

The Phineas Gage study showed that damage to the frontal lobes seemed to cause an increase in aggression; this was an early research finding showing a possible biological basis for aggression.

This could not initially be done under experimental conditions on humans for ethical reasons so typical studies into the biological structures that underlie aggression had to be done using lab animals, typically rodents and cats.

Studies show three different and specific types of aggressive behaviour in these animals:

- offensive behaviour, where they physically attack another animal
- defensive behaviour shown in response to threat of attack
- predatory aggression, which involves attacking another species to gain food.

Lesions/stimulation to different areas of the brain has been shown to activate behaviour associated specifically with one type of aggression. For example, stimulation of:

- the **medial hypothalamus** in a cat's brain produces offensive behaviour
- the **dorsal hypothalamus** produces defensive behaviour
- the **lateral hypothalamus** results in predatory behaviour (Flynn, Vanegas, Foote and Edwards, 1970).

WIDER ISSUES AND DEBATES

Psychology as a science

The use of animals in psychological investigations allows for scientific rigour to be applied. More control is possible as the animal can be genetically bred for a specific study and their environment carefully monitored. This removes the chance of extraneous variables affecting the outcome of the study, making the studies using animals extremely well controlled, enabling objective data gathering, leading to clear cause and effect conclusions being drawn. This level of control would not be possible with human participants because of ethical considerations.

Brain areas associated with aggression

The midbrain

The midbrain contains an area called the **periaqueductal grey matter (PAG)**, which links the **amygdala** (see below) and hypothalamus with the prefrontal cortex. It has a role in coordinating and integrating behavioural responses to perceived internal and external stressors such as pain and threat. Lesions to the PAG in rats that have recently given birth show an increase in aggression when the rats are confronted with potential threat in the form of unfamiliar male rats being introduced to the cage (Lonstein and Stern. 1998).

The amygdala

The amygdala is the centre for emotions, emotional behaviour and motivation. It integrates internal and external stimuli and every sensory modality has an input, which when combined gives us an instinctive feeling or reaction to the environment that will include aggression. The prefrontal cortex also connects to the amygdala and it is this connection that may lead to the expression of aggression.

The hypothalamus

The role of the hypothalamus is to maintain **homeostasis** through the regulation of **hormones**, including those that regulate sexual function. This is linked to aggressive behaviour in males via the production of **testosterone** (see later section on the role of testosterone and other hormones).

WIDER ISSUES AND DEBATES

Issues of social control

In the mid-20th century this knowledge was used to 'treat' aggressive mental patients by performing a prefrontal lobotomy, an operation that severed the connection between the limbic system and the prefrontal cortex. This was effective in reducing aggression but it also reduced all other emotional reactions too and is no longer regarded as ethical.

Key terms

Lesions: damage (either accidental or deliberate) to the brain that causes areas to die.

Stimulation: artificial activation of brain areas often through use of electrodes giving off small electrical charges.

Hypothalamus: area of the brain responsible for maintaining control of the body through release of hormones.

Medial, dorsal and lateral are signifiers of a specific part of something, medial being in the middle, dorsal at the back and lateral to the side.

Periaqueductal grey matter (PAG): an area of grey matter located within the midbrain. It plays a role in the modulation of pain and in defensive behaviour.

Amygdala: centre in the brain responsible for emotions, emotional behaviour and motivation.

Homeostasis: process that maintains the stability of the human body in response to changes in external conditions, for example temperature.

Hormones: chemicals produced by glands that are used to signal between organs and tissues.

Testosterone: principal male sex hormone and an anabolic steroid.

Cost–benefit analysis: method for deciding whether to approve a research proposal involving balancing the suffering of the animal (costs) against the quality of the research and the medical benefit from the knowledge (benefits).

Anterior cingulate cortex: surrounds the frontal part of the corpus callosum (the tissues that connect the two hemispheres of the brain) and connects to the prefrontal cortical area. It has several functions, including those governing autonomic behaviours, but has been implicated in such cognitive functions as reward anticipation, impulse control and empathy.

The prefrontal cortex

The prefrontal cortex is an area of brain that sits right behind the forehead. It is influential in governing social interaction and regulation of behaviour. The ability to delay gratification of an impulse is associated with this area. The prefrontal cortex has connections to the amygdala and to the hypothalamus. Damage to this area often leads to problems with anger management, irritability and impulse control.

Evaluation

Much work has been done to investigate aggression and the brain and laboratory research has required the use of specially bred animals. However, there are issues with the use of lab animals. There are always problems of generalisability across species and much of the experimental work to investigate the role of brain structure by selectively damaging precise brain areas has been carried out on cats and rodents, although human brains are much more complex than those of small mammals. However some researchers argue that the basics are the same between the species and therefore these experiments are worthwhile. There is some support for these findings from human case studies such as that of Phineas Gage. Blair, Colledge and Mitchell (2001) found that many patients with psychopathic behaviour patterns have very similar neurocognitive functioning to patients who have suffered damage to the amygdala.

Furthermore there are ethical considerations in the use of animals in research into human psychology. Some would argue that such research is immoral as the animals are harmed by these types of studies, for example through having parts of their brain lesioned. Others would argue that using animals for human benefit in this way is no different from using them for meat or keeping them as pets. Ethical guidelines now ensure that all studies using animals require a **cost–benefit analysis**, which clearly shows that any suffering caused to the animal is outweighed by the potential benefit to humanity.

WIDER ISSUES AND DEBATES

Reductionism

It could be argued that brain functioning as an explanation for aggression is reductionist. It reduces the production of aggressive behaviour and all that entails down to the working of specific neural circuits and ignores other possible causes such as social learning. There are cultures that show much higher than average aggression and cultures that show much lower levels. This is unlikely to be due to differences in brain structure but very likely caused by social learning.

The link between brain functioning and aggression has support from research into human cases such as that of Phineas Gage, however he is but a single case study and may not be representative of other humans. Other case studies support the findings though suggesting that the prefrontal cortex is genuinely linked to aggression. In a more scientific study of 41 convicted murderers, Raine et al. (1997) found lower activity in the prefrontal cortex and differences in the functioning of the limbic system in the brain scans of impulsive murderers.

Further research by Raine on prisoners in New Mexico supports the structural explanation: brain-imaging studies completed before release revealed reliable predictors for reoffending. Specifically reduced function in the anterior cingulate and smaller amygdala were found to be present in reoffenders.

The idea that there is a biological basis for aggression is consistent with the genetic explanation because our genetic blueprint builds our brain structures and therefore people with a genetic blueprint for aggression would have brain structures that predispose them towards aggressive responses. This could explain why, on average, males across all cultures tend to be more physically aggressive than females.

WIDER ISSUES AND DEBATES

Determinism

This argument is known as biological determinism, which is the view that your behaviour is predetermined by your biological makeup and that you as an individual have no free will or choice as to how you behave, so those people with smaller amygdala and low activity in the prefrontal cortex are destined to be aggressive. These ideas can be used as a defence for violence with the argument that the aggressive behaviour of some offenders could be genetically determined and/or the result of their biological makeup, as was the case in Raine's research (see Section 3.3, *Studies*). This could provide an excuse for some people to engage in violence, as they could say that their behaviour is beyond their control and therefore they are not responsible for their violent outbursts. This could limit their willingness to engage in treatments such as anger management programmes as they might believe them to be futile in the face of biological factors, ignoring the effects of nurture on their behaviour.

Take it further

There are several high-profile cases where a biological defence for acts of aggression including murder have been put forward, for example the Charles Whitman case. Do some research into this case and investigate how changes in his brain may have led to the killings he committed.

Evolution
What is evolution?

Evolution is the gradual development of different kinds of living organisms from earlier forms during the history of the Earth. This means that all species share some **genes** with each other because they all have common ancestors.

Evolution happens by **natural selection**. This is the process in which organisms better adapted to their environment are healthier, live longer and reproduce more frequently passing on the genes that made them reproductively fit to their offspring. For example, an animal, such as a giraffe, that depended on foliage from trees as their main source of food would be better adapted to that environment if they had the ability to reach more foliage higher up the tree. There is a variety of neck lengths, caused by series of random **mutations**. Every now and then a genetic mutation would occur causing a change in the organism, the giraffes that have slightly longer necks have an advantage over the shorter ones when searching for food, making them more likely to live to reproductive age. Because they were more reproductively successful, their alleles (versions of a particular gene) were passed on, and because the shorter-necked giraffes were unsuccessful, their alleles died out. Over time, the frequency of certain alleles in a population changes. This is known as **sexual selection**.

Evolution has been described as a 'series of lucky accidents' because successive mutations that conveyed some kind of adaptive advantage for the animal would come to dominate the gene pool. Evolutionary psychologists would argue that the mind evolved much like the body and that some aspects of human behaviour result from evolutionary adaptations that served a purpose in our ancestral past.

Key terms

Genes: a unit of heredity that contains DNA carrying information from one generation to the next. Each gene influences development by triggering the production of enzymes and proteins that are involved in the production of certain cells.

Natural selection: the gradual process by which heritable traits become more or less common in an environment.

Mutation: a change in the genetic structure of an animal or plant that makes it different from others of the same kind.

Sexual selection: a form of natural selection; individuals that are successful in attracting a mate out-reproduce others in the population.

Environment of evolutionary adaptedness (EEA): the conditions that prevailed in the environment at the time that a species was adapting in response to. In psychology we are interested in the development of behavioural characteristics 'hardwired' in the brain so the EEA we are interested in would be at the point when humans lived in hunter-gatherer groups.

The giraffe is one example of successful natural selection.

Supporting research

Support for this idea can be found in research that looks at current patterns of violence where sexual jealousy is often cited as a major cause of aggression between males and within couples (Harvey, Sprecher and Wenzel, 2004). Males may be biologically driven to protect their reproductive resources from male competition.

How does this explain behaviour?

The brain is the organ of behaviour. Just like any other physical part of our body it is built according to the genetic blue print we inherit from our parents. The structure and function of our brains have evolved to serve an adaptive function in the **environment of evolutionary adaptation (EEA)**.

In the EEA, successful humans were, like any other animal, those who were best suited to the environment in which they lived. Evolutionary psychologists look at fossil records in order to understand the EEA and speculate about the type of behaviour that would be adaptive. They then try to match that behaviour to current universal behaviours shown by modern-day humans in order to argue that the behaviour is genetically determined through our brain structure and chemistry. Examples of behaviour that can be explained within an evolutionary perspective include parental investment, mate choice and understanding emotions. Unlike our genetic makeup, our environment has undergone rapid change leading to a potential mismatch where we are stuck with 'hardwired' behaviour that would have served us well thousands of years ago but which can clash with the way we live now. For example, we have a predisposition to consume calorie-dense food. This served us well when we were foragers but not in modern society. It is now the driving force behind the obesity epidemic.

How does this explain aggression?

In evolutionary terms success is measured by the production of offspring that survive to reproductive maturity. In the EEA, successful males were physically bigger and stronger and so would be those most capable of providing food and protecting their mates and their offspring. Psychologically, males who were naturally more aggressive when their resources were threatened, or when out hunting, would also have had an adaptive advantage. Such men might also have been prepared to attack other humans and take their resources in order to provide for their families.

This gave them an advantage in terms of mate choice. Successful females chose mates who provided good genes, so big, strong men were favoured. Such men were also more likely to provide better resources in terms of food and protection, suggesting that those who displayed aggressive traits would be more successful than those who did not. Thus, competition for mates has driven masculine aggression.

This theory would also suggest that females would be less physically aggressive as it would be an evolutionary disadvantage for females – who spend long periods of time pregnant, breastfeeding and looking after vulnerable young children in order to ensure their survival – to put themselves and their children at risk by engaging in conflict and hunting. According to evolutionary psychology this has led to female aggression being less physically violent and more verbal and emotional in nature. Buss (1999) proposed that females would still be in competition for the best mates, but achieved victory by denigrating other females to potential mates so as to make these other women appear less attractive. This hypothesis has been tested experimentally and found some support.

If these ideas are valid then we might expect to see a physical difference in the structure and/or chemistry of the brains of males and females, which would lead to a greater expression of aggression in males. We would also expect to see a greater degree of aggression among males than among females and those animals to which we are more closely genetically related would show similar behaviour.

Evaluation

Male brains do have minor differences in structure compared to females, partially due to a much higher exposure to testosterone before and after birth. It has been argued that these differences are linked to typical male attributes and abilities such as spatial awareness and aggression, both of which would have conveyed an adaptive advantage in the EEA. There is a great deal of experimental evidence suggesting that testosterone levels are associated with aggression; for example Mazur

(1983) showed a marked increase in inter-male fighting around puberty when it is known that there is also a rapid increase in testosterone.

Ultimately any evolutionary theory is a 'post hoc' argument where the theory is developed to fit the facts. It is difficult to prove these ideas as they cannot be scientifically tested; there are limited fossil records for behaviour so although they make sense and can explain the observed facts they cannot be empirically tested as we cannot access the EEA.

Biological explanation of aggression as an alternative to Freud's psychodynamic explanation

Freud's psychodynamic explanation

Sigmund Freud

While biological psychology is often seen as a branch of psychology, with a very modern feel to it, Sigmund Freud's psychodynamic approach to understanding human behaviour was developed throughout his work during the late 19th and early 20th century and is often viewed as the beginnings of the movement towards psychology as we know it now. Freud began his medical education in Vienna in 1873. After qualification he worked for many years with another researcher called Josef Breuer, investigating the link between painful memories and physical illness known as 'hysteria'. It was here that he began to consider the relationship between the 'mind' and the 'body' as two separate things – the mental and the physical. His work then moved on to look more closely at the mind and how problems within the mind, that we may not even be consciously aware of, can manifest themselves in physical symptoms. So began his development of the psychodynamic approach to understanding human behaviour: 'Psyche' meaning 'mind' and 'dynamic' meaning 'active'. In 1923 Freud published his work *The Ego and The Id* in which he discussed the relationship between the mind and personality at length.

Freud's psychodynamic explanation of aggression begins with two innate drives that he believed were the motivation for all human behaviour: Eros (the life instinct) and Thanatos (the death instinct). The energy of Eros (known as libido) is focused on the preservation and enjoyment of life. This instinct has to balance out Thanatos, which is a drive towards death and destruction, initially directed towards the self. Human behaviour is seen as an interaction between these two opposing forces and consequently to prevent us from hurting ourselves; the energy of Thanatos will often be redirected away from the person and towards others, resulting in aggression. However, we know that humans are not uncontrollably aggressive all the time; this is due to something Freud referred to as **catharsis.** Catharsis is a way of satisfying our urges without resorting to violent impulses by watching violence or taking part in minor aggression such as playing video games or sports.

These two innate drives (Eros and Thanatos) form the first part of personality that all humans have from birth until the age of about two years: the **id**.

The id is the most primitive part of personality that is completely driven by the impulses of Eros and Thanatos with no thought for consequences. The id operates on the pleasure principle, demanding the immediate gratification of its urges. Then around the age of two years, a new aspect of personality emerges, which Freud termed the **ego.** This is driven by the **reality principle** and the urges of the id begin to be controlled and delayed. At this stage in the development of personality, the norms and rules of society are learned and, although the ego does not understand right from wrong, there is some appreciation of when and to what extent it is appropriate to show certain behaviours, such as aggression.

WIDER ISSUES AND DEBATES

Reductionism and determinism

This idea argues that human behaviour can be simplified to the evolutionary pressures that operated hundreds of thousands of years ago and that other factors such as social learning have little or no influence on complex behaviour like aggression, this is an example of reductionism.

It is also deterministic as it argues that we have little free will in whether or not we show aggression, we are programmed by evolution to respond in a fixed way that we cannot change. Some would argue that this provides an excuse for those who behave aggressively. Theories that suggest we are wired to behave in certain ways can be used as an excuse for socially unacceptable behaviour, for example such theories have been used to explain rape as an evolutionary strategy that would have been successful in the EEA, so some men may be genetically predisposed to use violence in this way.

Figure 3.5 Freud's theory of personality

At some time between the ages of three and six years, the third and final aspect of personality emerges: known as the **superego**. The superego operates as the **morality principle** and takes the role of the ego to the next level by developing an understanding of right and wrong. This means that the urges of the id are now not only delayed until an appropriate time or place, but also the child begins to feel pride for acting correctly (the ego-ideal) or feel guilty for incorrect behaviour (the conscience). At this point, aggressive impulses should be well controlled, assuming the superego is well developed in the individual.

Any issues in the development of either the ego or the superego could result in problems in managing the impulsive urges of the id and therefore aggressive behaviour could be frequent. Thankfully, for most people, the ego and superego are well developed, and the urges of the id remain in the unconscious mind and out of conscious thought so we are unaware of the violent urges we feel. The only time we may be at all aware of them is through the behaviours we show that act as catharsis, such as having a love of violent films or enjoying watching boxing.

Comparing Freud's psychodynamic explanation to a biological explanation

There are many similarities and also many differences between Freud's explanation for aggression and the biological explanation of aggression if we compare them. One very stark difference between the two theories is that there is much scientific evidence that has been gathered to support the role of biological factors in aggression, but there is a distinct lack of such evidence to support Freud's views. Raine et al. (1997) found that dysfunction in areas of the brain such as the prefrontal cortex and limbic system does seem to be associated with aggressive criminal behaviour.

With biological factors it is easy to design and conduct scientific studies that will allow a link to be established between biology and the behaviour, because we would be looking at objective data such as the amount of brain activity in different brain areas. With concepts in Freud's theory, for example, his ideas on the id, ego and superego, it is impossible to physically see these things, making the

Catharsis: the process of releasing negative energy in the mind.

Id: a part of the personality that acts on instinctive drives.

Ego: a part of the personality that attempts to satisfy the id within the restrictions of reality.

Reality principle: the rules of what is socially acceptable. The ego uses these principles to control the demands of the id.

Morality principle: the concept of understanding what is right from what is wrong.

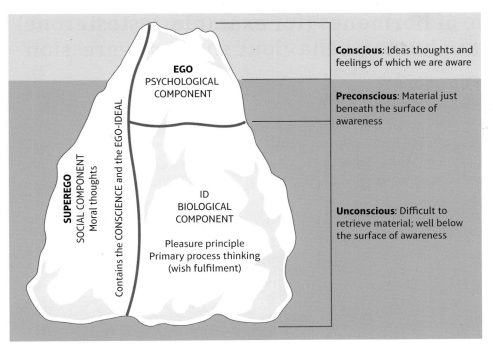

Figure 3.6 Freud's model of personality structure

design of scientific research to test his ideas very difficult. In fact, many scientifically tested studies into Freud's concepts actually contradict his claims. Evidence from an experiment by Bushman (2002) into the role of catharsis in controlling aggression actually found that participants who engaged in catharsis and vented their anger were more aggressive than those who did nothing after they had been deliberately angered by another person. Testing Freud's ideas scientifically is much more difficult than testing out biological concepts. It is possible to test biological factors objectively, because they are things that can be seen and measured, but Freud's concepts are more subjective and so far more difficult to test as they cannot be seen. The id, for example, is thought to reside almost completely in the unconscious mind – so that even the person is unaware of what it contains or feels.

WIDER ISSUES

Nature–nurture

We could compare the two explanations by looking at their position in the nature–nurture debate surrounding the development of aggression. Both Freud and biological psychologists would consider that whether a person becomes aggressive or not is down to internal factors that are, for the most part, beyond external control. Biological psychologists look at the role of genes and brain function in aggression, which are clearly factors of nature, while Freud considered the role of personality factors such as the id, ego and superego, which are naturally occurring elements of personality dependent on maturation. But both of these explanations would also agree that the development of aggression is not completely determined by nature. Brain damage can easily be caused by external factors such as abuse in childhood or a car accident, and the way that genes are expressed can be affected by the environment children are raised in. So while the cause of aggression by both genes and brain dysfunction are natural, the role of nurture cannot be completely ignored. Likewise, Freud felt that the development of the id, ego and superego could be affected by events that occurred during the first six years of life while the personality was maturing. This draws a similarity between Freud's theory and the biological explanation of aggression.

The role of hormones (for example, testosterone) to explain human behaviour such as aggression

What are hormones?

Hormones are chemical messengers that transmit information around the body. However, unlike neurotransmitters, they are carried in the blood and operate all around the body – not just in the central nervous system. This means they take longer to work than neurotransmitters and tend to be used to effect longer-term changes. They are produced and excreted by **glands** and the system of glands is called the **endocrine system**.

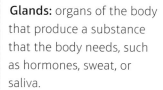

Key terms

Glands: organs of the body that produce a substance that the body needs, such as hormones, sweat, or saliva.

Endocrine system: the system of glands that secrete hormone messages around the body using the circulatory system.

Oxytocin: a hormone released by the posterior pituitary gland, which has been shown to increase trust between people.

Pituitary gland: the small organ at the base of the brain, which produces hormones that control the growth and development of the body.

Androgen: a chemical that develops or maintains male characteristics.

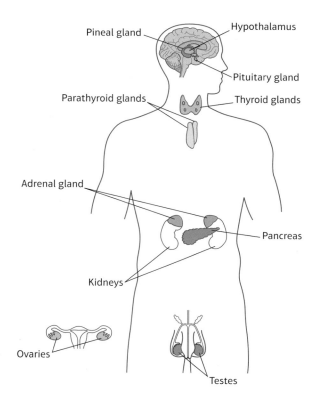

Figure 3.7 The endocrine system

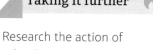

Taking it further

Research the action of other hormones such as corticosteroids on behaviour. This links the idea of stress from the environment with biological factors, such as hormones, effecting behaviour giving a more interactionist approach to aggression.

Hormones affect behaviour and cause physical changes in the body. For example, **oxytocin** is a hormone released by the posterior **pituitary gland**, which has been shown to increase trust between people.

Testosterone is an **androgen**; this means it is a chemical that develops or maintains male characteristics. We all have testosterone in our bodies but it is present in a much greater degree in the average male compared to females.

Antenatal exposure to testosterone has an organising effect on the developing brain, leading to increased spatial ability and (arguably) competitive aggression. There is also a critical period immediately following birth when testosterone sensitises certain neural circuits, for example, it stimulates cell growth in areas of the hypothalamus and amygdala (Naftoli, Garcia-Segura and Keefe, 1990), which later sets up the action of testosterone as an adult to effect aggression.

Studies that support this tend to come from research done on rodents. Typically male rodents will be **castrated** (which effectively stops the production of testosterone) and their behaviour will be compared with control rodents under various conditions, including threat and competition for mates. Castrated rodents show little or no aggressive behaviour, however, if their testosterone is replaced, for example, by injection, then they will show typical aggressive behaviour. Differences emerge according to the age of rodent at the time of castration. If the rodent is newborn, then testosterone injections have a limited effect on their aggression; whereas if they were over 10 days old the replacement testosterone quickly brings their levels of aggression back up to normal for uncastrated rodents (Motelica-Heino, Edwards and Roffi, 1993). Injecting **neonatal** female rodents with testosterone made them act much more aggressively when given testosterone as adults compared to control females (Edwards, 1968). This supports the idea that testosterone is implicated in aggressive behaviour and that the sensitisation of neural circuitry after birth is an important factor in the effect of testosterone release.

Testosterone influences aggressive behaviour by effecting changes in neurotransmission, but this is complex. For example, a modulating effect on aggression is produced by serotonin (a neurotransmitter associated with, among other things, mood regulation), increased activity of serotonergic synapses inhibits aggression and low levels of serotonin will increase aggression, (Goldman, Lappalainen and Ozaki, 1996).

Human studies generally support the link between testosterone and aggression: for example, boys are, on average, more aggressive than girls; boys have higher exposure to testosterone both pre- and post-natally (D'Andrade, 1966). Testosterone levels increase during the early teens and there is a strong positive correlation with aggressive behaviour and inter-male fighting (Mazur, 1983). However, correlation does not indicate causality and it might be that other variables such as socialisation affect these factors. However, there have been cases where convicted sex offenders have been castrated and this led to a removal of aggression and a loss of sex drive (Hawke 1951). This seems to lend support to the hypothesis that testosterone is influential in aggressive behaviour, but these studies lack appropriate scientific rigour such as having a control group and fully objective measures of aggression; current ethical standards would prevent such studies taking place.

Evaluation

Direction of causality is an issue here. It could be that raised levels of testosterone occur as an effect of being aggressive or achieving dominance – the **reciprocal model** of testosterone suggests that testosterone is an effect of dominance and not the cause of it. Mazur and Booth (1998) found that individual testosterone levels varied across the lifespan according to environmental status; for example being married decreased testosterone levels whereas divorce increased it. The same study, however, found support for the **basal model**, which suggests that testosterone causes a change in a person's aggressive dominance as it found that men with higher levels of testosterone were more likely to get arrested and to use weapons in fights.

Much of the research supporting the view that testosterone is linked to aggression has been conducted on small mammals, such as rodents, with some studies being carried out on primates; this limits the generalisability of the findings from experimental research. For example, the brain areas said to be affected by testosterone serve different functions across species: the **cingulate gyrus** in monkeys is associated with fear-induced aggression but in dogs and cats stimulation of this area leads to irritability.

Experimental research of this sort cannot ethically be carried out on humans. There are limited case studies of convicted sex offenders being castrated, which support the findings from animal research, but these cannot be regarded as representative of the general population since the perpetrators of such crimes are atypical.

Key terms

Castrated: to remove the testicles of a male animal or a man.

Neonatal: relating to babies that have just been born.

Reciprocal model: something cannot happen in one part of the relationship without it affecting the other.

Basal model: a model that suggests the testosterone is assumed to be a persistent trait that influences behaviour.

Cingulate gyrus: part of the brain, which is involved in emotion formation.

3.2 Methods

Learning outcomes

In this section, you will learn about:

- the use of correlational research in psychology

- types of correlation

- issues surrounding the use of correlations in psychology; cause and effect, other variables

- analysing correlational data, including the use of scatter diagrams, using Spearman's rho, and statistical significance

- other biological methods including brain scanning

- a twin and an adoption study.

Correlational research

Correlational research involves measuring two different variables in order to see if they are related in any way. Correlation studies do not tell you whether one variable caused another to change, but they are a way of looking to see if a relationship might exist between any two co-variables. Co-variables can be measured directly by the researcher, or they could be obtained from secondary data gathered from other sources. In biological psychology, co-variables might include measuring the number of genes a person shares (closeness of family relationship) and a behavioural characteristic such as the amount of aggression they show. By plotting scores on these two variables on a graph called a scatter diagram it is possible to see if any relationship exists between them.

> **Exam tip**
>
> Students often confuse correlation research with experimental research. However, there are differences between experimental and correlation research that need to be identified clearly. Experimental research involves establishing a causal relationship between an independent variable and dependent variable, whereas a correlation does not establish causality, it simply compares co-variables to see what relationship they have to each other.
>
> This affects the way that a hypothesis is written for each type of research method and the name given to the hypothesis. Because a correlation is not an experiment, the hypothesis is known as an 'alternate hypothesis' and not as an experimental hypothesis. A directional alternate hypothesis for a correlation will either predict a positive or negative relationship. A non-directional alternate hypothesis for a correlation will simply predict that a relationship will occur. The null hypothesis will predict no relationship. Compare this to the way in which an experimental hypothesis is written, specifically that it predicts a difference or a specific direction of difference.

When looking at correlational data, there are two types of relationship that may be seen: positive and negative. A positive correlation is seen when both co-variables increase, as one variable increases so does the other, and a negative correlation is shown when one variable increases while the other decreases. The most obvious way to see the relationship between any co-variables is to plot them on a scatter diagram (also called a scattergraph). One variable is plotted on the y-axis, and the other along the x-axis, and then the trend can be seen in the positioning of the dots on the graph where the corresponding points meet. For example, if a person scored 50 on a test of stress, and they also did a test of their aggression level and scored 125 on that, on the point at which those two points intersected on the scatter diagram you would place an x. You would then do the same for every other participant's scores on the stress test and aggression test, which would allow you to see if there was any link between the variables, once all the scores had been plotted.

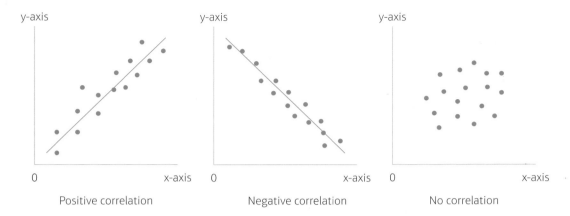

Figure 3.8 Positive, negative and no correlation

Evaluation

There are many issues associated with the use of correlational research in biological psychology. One key problem is that you can only see a relationship between two variables and it is impossible to tell which is the causal variable (made the other one change). In fact, it is possible that any relationship that seems to exist may merely be coincidental. In the previous example of stress and aggression, it could easily be shown that the more stress people experience, the more aggression they show, which would suggest a positive correlation. But from these two sets of scores we would not be able to tell if being stressed made you aggressive, or vice versa.

We would also be unable to tell if there was another factor, a third variable, that could have caused both an increase in stress and aggression. For example, the weather might have been very warm, which could have increased both stress levels and aggression separately from one another. Some biological psychologists would use correlations to test for genetic explanations for behaviour by measuring the amount of genetic similarity between two people, and the amount of similarity in their behaviour (concordance rate) and plotting these to look for a relationship. However there are many reasons why people who are closely related share the same behaviours that have nothing to do with their shared genes. For example if they live together, or share many of the same experiences, then we cannot ignore how this could influence them to show the same behaviours.

Correlations can often use secondary data (information gathered from the research of others) to investigate whether there seems to be any link or relationship between two variables to see whether further, more expensive research, may yield useful results. Researchers may believe that two variables are linked, but to start by conducting a large-scale experiment could prove costly if it quickly emerges that their initial idea was wrong. Starting with a correlation to see if a relationship seems to exist, and, if it does, then designing an experiment to see if the relationship is causal, may be much more cost-effective.

Analysing correlational data

Scatter diagram

When conducting a correlational study you will be looking for a relationship between two variables. One of the easiest ways to begin your analysis is by drawing up a scatter diagram to see if there seems to be any link between changes in the co-variables. If it seems as if the variables do show some kind of link, you can then go on to investigate this further by conducting an inferential test of significance. Here we are going to look at how to conduct a Spearman's rho test on the data gathered, and what this can tell us.

Consider for a moment that we have gathered some correlational data, for example in an investigation into the link between the number of hours of revision that students did for a test, and the mark they achieved on a test of the topic they were told to revise.

Table 3.3 Data on students' marks and hours of revision

Student number	Hours of revision	mark/20 achieved on the test
1	4	14
2	2	11
3	1	8
4	3	7
5	4	17
6	5	20
7	1	7
8	1	12
9	6	18
10	4	15

Below is a scatter diagram to illustrate this data and you can see from the trend line added that there appears to be a positive correlation between the two variables. However, the line does not suggest that the correlation is strong so to be sure that we can actually conclude that the number of hours of revision is related to the score achieved on a test, further investigation would be needed and this is where an inferential test would be useful. For this data, because we are conducting a correlation and the data gathered is best treated as ordinal, a Spearman's test would be most appropriate.

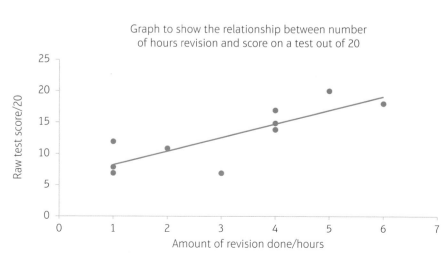

Graph to show the relationship between number of hours revision and score on a test out of 20

Figure 3.9 Scatter diagram to show a relationship

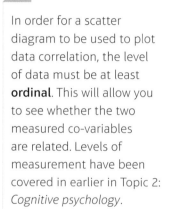

Key term

Ordinal data: a level of measurement where numbers are rankings rather than scores in themselves, for example a rank order for attractiveness on a scale of 1 to 5.

Maths tip

In order for a scatter diagram to be used to plot data correlation, the level of data must be at least **ordinal**. This will allow you to see whether the two measured co-variables are related. Levels of measurement have been covered in earlier in Topic 2: *Cognitive psychology*.

Spearman's rho

Spearman's rho is an inferential test that is used to see whether statistical data gathered in a correlation using ordinal data can be generalised from the sample used to the whole population. It can only be used to analyse correlational data, and only works where the level of data is ordinal, or can be reduced to ordinal (if it was originally gathered as interval or ratio data for example).

The formula to conduct a Spearman's calculation is

$$r_s = 1 - \frac{6\sum d^2}{n(n^2 - 1)}$$

where r_s represents the result of the test, d represents the difference between the ranked position of the scores on each row, and n represents the number of scored pairs gathered (in this case $n = 10$). The symbol $\sum$ means 'the sum of' or 'the total'. To illustrate how to do this calculation, work through this example below:

The first thing to do when calculating a Spearman's rho is to rank the scores of each of the two variables measured – in this case, the hours of revision and the raw mark achieved. For any ranks where there are a number of scores that are the same/tied, work out the mid-point of the ranks they would take up. For example, in the number of hours of revision, there are three people who did four hours revision who would take up position 3, 4 and 5 in the ranks, so they each get a rank of 4 and then the next rank available will be position 6 for the person who did three hours of revision.

Table 3.4 Data on students' marks and hours of revision with ranking

Student number	Hours of revision	Rank of revision hours	mark/20	Rank of mark	Difference in ranks (d)	d^2
1	4	4	14	5		
2	2	7	11	7		
3	1	9	8	8		
4	3	6	7	9.5		
5	4	4	17	3		
6	5	2	20	1		
7	1	9	7	9.5		
8	1	9	12	6		
9	6	1	18	2		
10	4	4	15	4		

The next step will be to work out the difference between the ranked positions of each pair of scores. The easiest way to do this is to take the second rank away from the first rank and then record this in the next column.

Table 3.5 Data on students' marks and hours of revision with ranking differences

Student number	Hours of revision	Rank of revision hours	mark/20	Rank of mark	Difference in ranks (d)	d^2
1	4	4	14	5	-1	
2	2	7	11	7	0	
3	1	9	8	8	2	
4	3	6	7	9.5	-3.5	
5	4	4	17	3	1	
6	5	2	20	1	1	
7	1	9	7	9.5	-0.5	
8	1	9	12	6	3	
9	6	1	18	2	-1	
10	4	4	15	4	0	

Link

The use of alternate, experimental and null hypotheses and the use of IV and DV in experiments can be found in the Methods section of Topic 2: *Cognitive psychology*.

The final thing to do with this data set is to square the differences in order to get rid of any negative figures and calculate the total of squared difference.

Table 3.6 Data on students' marks and hours of revision with ranking differences squared

Student number	Hours of revision	Rank of revision hours	Raw mark/20	Rank of raw mark	Difference in ranks (d)	d^2
1	4	4	14	5	-1	1
2	2	7	11	7	0	0
3	1	9	8	8	1	1
4	3	6	7	9.5	-3.5	12.25
5	4	4	17	3	1	1
6	5	2	20	1	1	1
7	1	9	7	9.5	-0.5	0.25
8	1	9	12	6	3	9
9	6	1	18	2	-1	1
10	4	4	15	4	0	0

Total d^2 = 26.5

This is now all of the information required to put into the formula and calculate Spearman's rho.

$$r_s = 1 - \frac{6 \sum d^2}{n(n^2 - 1)}$$

$$r_s = 1 - \frac{6 \times 26.5}{10 \, (10^2 - 1)} \qquad r_s = 1 - \frac{159}{10 \times 99} \qquad r_s = 1 - \frac{159}{990} \qquad r_s = 1 - 0.161 \qquad r_s = 0.839$$

Once the value of r_s has been calculated, we can then consider the calculated **correlation coefficient** to see how closely, if at all, the co variables are related. The coefficient is a figure between +1 and -1 that can tell you how strong any existing relationship is between the two variables. In this case, the calculated coefficient is 0.839, which suggests that there is a strong, positive correlation between the number of hours revision done by the students, and the mark they achieved for the test on that topic.

The next step is to look at whether this result is statistically significant, that is, whether the result is truly showing a relationship between the two variables. If a result is found to be significant it is possible to assume that the two variables are related in some way, but if the result is shown not to be significant then there is a high chance that any relationship seen is actually the product of something else such as sampling error.

In order to tell whether the results are significant it is important to understand the term '**statistical significance**'. When conducting research and analysing the data using descriptive statistics, such as measures of central tendency or dispersion, it is possible to observe trends in the data but it is unclear whether these trends are showing how one variable is actually affecting another in some way. Inferential statistical tests allow researchers to work out the probablility that their data is the result of an actual relationship existing between the variables rather than a coincidence. As psychologists, the generally accepted level of significance is 5 per cent, which means that there is a 95 per cent chance that the results are showing a true relationship. This is often expressed as $p \leq 0.05$, where p stands for 'the probability of the results being due to chance' – the probability of the results being due to chance is less than or equal to 0.05 or 5 per cent. Once the result of a statistical test has been calculated, this figure is known as the **observed value**.

Maths tip

The **correlation coefficient** is a number between +1 and -1 that represents how the movement of one variable is related to movement in another variable. A positive coefficient refers to a positive correlation, while a negative figure relates to a negative correlation. The closer to +1 or -1 the coefficient is, the stronger the correlation. The closer to 0 the figure is, the weaker the correlation. A coefficient of 0 indicates no correlation at all.

Key terms

Statistical significance: the probability that the data is a result of an actual relationship existing between the variables rather than a coincidence.

Observed value: the value given by a statistical test, such as rho for Spearman's. It is compared with the relevant critical value to see if a null hypothesis should be retained or not.

This value then has to be compared to a table of **critical values** to assess whether it is significant – these figures have been calculated by statisticians to enable us to more easily tell whether our data meets the criteria to be significant. The table below shows part of a critical values table for the Spearman's rho test, and in order for the result to be significant, the observed value needs to exceed the critical value in the table relevant to the study conducted.

Table 3.7 Critical values

n	Level of significance for a one-tailed test			
	0.05	0.25	0.01	0.005
	Level of significance for a two-tailed test			
	0.1	0.05	0.02	0.01
4	1.000	-	-	-
5	.900	1.00	1.00	-
6	.829	.886	.943	1.00
7	.714	.786	.893	.929
8	.643	.738	.833	.881
9	.600	.700	.783	.833
10	.564	.648	.745	.794

The calculated r_s must be equal to or exceed the table (critical) value for the significance at the level shown.

For the data above, the n value was 10 so the final row of the table would be of interest. If the original hypothesis was directional (one-tailed) then the critical value of interest would be the first column (0.564), whereas if the hypothesis was non-directional (two-tailed) then the critical value of most interest would be in the second column (0.648) as these relate to the 0.05 level of significance. The observed value of r_s in the above example was 0.839, and as this exceeds the critical values, regardless of whether the hypothesis was directional or non-directional, the result would be significant, meaning that the alternative hypothesis could be accepted and the null rejected. This means that there was an equal to or less than 5 per cent probability that the relationship that was found occurred by chance. In fact the calculated Spearman's rho value of 0.839 exceeds the critical values for a one- and two-tailed test at p 0.01, so we can be 99 per cent confident in the relationship found. This also means that there is less chance of a Type 1 error having been made.

Caution should be exercised when interpreting the results of a Spearman's rho test when a large sample size has been used because the greater the sample, the more likely you are to find that the results are significant, even if the correlation coefficient is close to zero. You should also check for outliers or extreme scores in the data. These may affect the correlation coefficient you calculate, and therefore whether the findings are significant or not.

Maths tip

A table of critical values for a Spearman's rho shows only positive values. When you compare the correlation coefficient from your test to the critical values in the table, you should ignore whether your coefficient is positive or negative to determine its significance. For example, if your coefficient is -0.5, you should ignore the negative (-) sign when you compare it to the critical value in the table to determine significance, but remember that it is negative when you interpret your findings and relate it back to the hypothesis.

Key term

Critical value: a statistical cut-off point. It is a number presented on a table of critical values that determines whether the result is significant enough for the null hypothesis not to be accepted.

Link

Levels of measurement (ordinal, interval, nominal) have been covered in the Methods section of Topic 2: *Cognitive psychology.*

Other biological methods

Brain-scanning techniques

CAT (Computerised Axial Tomography) scans

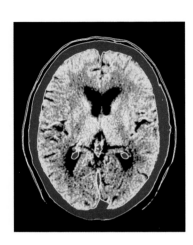

A computer processes the information from the CAT scan and the results are then passed to a radiologist to interpret.

CAT scans are sometimes referred to as CT scans (Computed Tomography) and can be used to take images of any part of the body including the brain. CAT scans of the brain involve passing X-rays into the head, but unlike a standard X-ray where the beam is focused on one specific area, multiple beams are passed around the head from different angles to gather more information. A standard X-ray may be used to investigate whether a bone is broken so a single beam focused on one area would be useful for this purpose, but when scanning something as complex as the brain, more information will be needed. The information from the multiple X-ray beams is interpreted by a computer and a detailed image of the structure of the brain can be seen. This is useful for detecting areas of brain damage following an accident or the positioning of tumours in the brain but it does not give any information about how the brain is functioning.

The use of X-rays in CAT scans can pose a risk to patients as they involve exposure to radiation and it is advised that they are only used whether the possible benefits in relation to diagnosis outweigh the potential risks. If the scan removes the need for exploratory surgery then this would be preferable, especially as unnecessarily having brain surgery could be much more risky for the patient. Pregnant women are advised not to have CAT scans wherever possible as there is some evidence that exposure to X-rays can cause damage to the unborn baby. The advantages of using CAT scans include the fact that they are very quick to conduct and can give accurate details of brain structure, which can help to guide clinicians in decision making regarding treatment or surgery. A CAT scan may help a surgeon to better plan a procedure before surgery takes place by being able to accurately see the layout of the brain structures before physically entering the skull. This may make the procedure faster and more efficient, reducing the risks associated with longer duration under anaesthetic for patients.

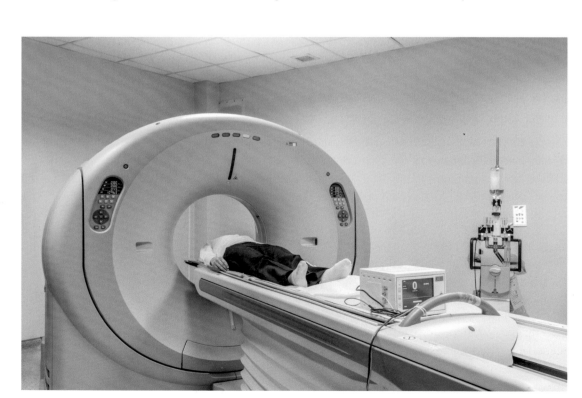

A scan can last from a few seconds up to 10 minutes depending on the body area being investigated.

PET (Positron Emission Tomography) scans

PET scans are a form of nuclear medicine procedure as they involve injecting the patient with a small amount of radioactive material in order to conduct the scan. Patients having a PET scan of the brain will be injected with a substance known as 'fluorodeoxyglucose' (FDG). This is a tracer substance where the radioactive atom is attached to glucose because the brain will use up the glucose as a form of energy. Once the tracer has been absorbed into the bloodstream, a task may be given to stimulate the brain (such as the task used in the Raine et al. study (1997)) and encourage activity. As the brain is working, the glucose will be used up and, as this happens, the radioactive atoms start to break down emitting positrons. During this process gamma rays are produced and it is these that the scanner picks up. High concentrations of gamma rays will be found in areas of high activity as a lot of glucose will have been used up there, while areas of low activity will have fewer gamma rays present. The image produced from this information is in colour with areas of high activity shown by warmer colours like red, and areas of low activity shown by cooler colours such as blue. PET scans can be useful for investigating areas of the brain that are not functioning normally, which could indicate damage or tumours.

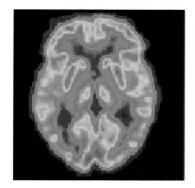

A PET scan.

PET scans detect areas of damage by indicating which parts of the brain are showing abnormal levels of activity, and this can help researchers to not only see where problems exist, but also predict what kinds of issues patients might face in relation to the brain activity being shown. These scans are, however, more invasive than other techniques such as CAT scans as they require the patient to be injected with a radioactive substance. Although this carries a low risk due to the very low levels of the substance involved, it is not advisable for patients to have too many of this type of scan unless absolutely necessary because it is unclear whether there may be long-term effects.

fMRI (Functional Magnetic Resonance Imaging)

Functional MRI scans are a relatively new procedure, designed in the 1990s to enable images of brain activity to be gathered without the use of radiation. The idea behind fMRI scanning is that brain activity is associated with blood flow in the brain and this activity is used to gather the information by the scanner to produce a picture. Because of its comparative safety in relation to other forms of functional scans, such as PET scans, which use radiation, fMRI scans are often the procedure of choice for psychologists researching brain activity. Having a functional MRI scan involves having your head placed inside a very large, very powerful electromagnet. Inside the magnetic field, the nuclei within hydrogen molecules in water align themselves with the direction of the magnetic field. As neural activity increases in the brain, blood flow increases in the active areas to keep up with the demand for oxygen. The oxygen is carried to the neurons in haemoglobin within red blood cells. Haemoglobin, when carrying oxygen, repels a magnetic field (diamagnetic), but when it has been deoxygenated it will follow the direction of the magnetic field (paramagnetic) and it is these changes that the scanner will detect to create an image. The scanner sends the information to a computer that is then able to create a map of activation to show changing levels of neural activity in different brain areas as tasks are being completed.

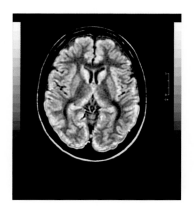

An fMRI scan.

Because of the use of high-powered magnetic fields in fMRI scanning, some people are unable to have these kind of brain scans. For example, anyone with a cardiac pacemaker or who has had recent metal surgical implants would not be able to have one of these scans. These scans are, however, non-invasive and do not involve any injections of radioactive substances so they do not have any of the potential risks associated with PET scanning. Anyone who is claustrophobic or unnerved by confined spaces or loud noises may become quite stressed during fMRI scanning procedures as they have to lie flat and still in a large tube for the duration of the scan. This can upset some people and therefore may not be suitable for all patients.

Using brain scanning to study human behaviour

In recent years psychologists have been using brain-scanning methods to make links between brain structures and activity, and a variety of human behaviours. An element of human behaviour of considerable interest has been aggression and researchers have been using different scanning techniques to explain aggressive behaviour. One example of such a study is Raine et al. (1997), featured in this topic. The researchers used PET scans to look at the brain activity of prisoners convicted of murder and then compared this to a matched control group of non-murderers. Using PET scans they were able to map abnormal brain activity in the murderers' group in areas of the brain associated with impulsivity and risk-taking behaviour, which may explain increased aggressive behaviour. Other research into violent video games has investigated how the brains of gamers process emotions to see if playing these games may change brain activity, making people more likely to become aggressive. Montag et al. (2011) used fMRI scans and found that gamers showed lower levels of activity in reaction to pictures of negative emotion than the control group did. This dampening of the brain's response to negative emotional stimuli may explain why there is a suggested link between playing a lot of these games and becoming more aggressive, as gamers may not find aggressive actions as 'serious' because their brains do not process them in that way.

> **Taking it further**
>
> There are many news stories making links between research into brain activity and a variety of human behaviours, but aggression is something that society finds particularly interesting. Try looking up news articles on this topic and see what other examples of studies you can find.
>
> These types of research studies are reliable as there is a wealth of evidence building up linking areas of the brain such as the limbic system and prefrontal cortex to aggressive behaviour. Brain-scanning techniques are objective ways of measuring the structure and function of the brain, increasing the reliability of the evidence. However, the evidence makes the assumption that these areas of the brain cause aggressive behaviour. Some might argue that being involved in violent behaviour may change the way the brain functions meaning it is the effect of violence not the cause. It is difficult to conclusively support either view because that would mean the brains would need to be scanned before showing tendencies towards violence and then compared with scans taken afterwards and we cannot accurately predict who is likely to become violent before it happens.

Twin and adoption studies

Twin studies

Twin studies provide psychologists with a unique design to test the influence of nature and/or nurture on human behaviour. Monozygotic, or identical, twins share 100 per cent of the same genetic material, while dizygotic, or fraternal, twins share only 50 per cent of the same genes like any two siblings. When investigating twins, psychologists are able to compare behaviour between a group of identical twins and a group of fraternal twins to see which group shared the most similarity between each set of twins.

The extent to which behaviour is the same between twins is known as the concordance rate. For example Gottesman and Shields (1966) studied twins over a 16-year period where one had been diagnosed with schizophrenia and found that in monozygotic twins 42 per cent of their co-twins were also diagnosed with schizophrenia, whereas in dizygotic twins only 9 per cent of the co-twins were diagnosed with the same illness. Because the concordance rate is higher in monozygotic twins than dizygotic twins in Gottesman and Shields (1966) study they concluded that there may well be a genetic element that could explain why people develop schizophrenia.

If the concordance rate was equally high (or low) in dizygotic twins for any behaviour then the researchers might assume that there was no significant genetic component at play and in fact experiential factors may explain the behaviour as twins are generally raised together and will have shared a similar upbringing. Coccaro et al. (1997) found in their study of male twins (182 MZ pairs; 118 DZ pairs) that there was a high chance that aggressive traits would be found in both twins suggesting that impulsive aggression could be at least partly due to genetic factors. They had their participants complete the Buss-Durkee Hostility Inventory, which is a 75-item questionnaire used to assess various emotional traits associated with aggression, and then compared the scores of each member of the twin pairs. It was found that a significant concordance rate was shown between twins for measures such as indirect assault suggesting an element of heritability in some features of aggression.

Adoption studies

Adoption studies, in principle, are the best method to allow psychologists to measure whether a behaviour is the result of nature or nurture. Groups of adoptees are studied and their behaviour is then correlated with their adopted families as well as their natural families. Adoptees share no genetic material with their adopted families, but they have shared an environment throughout their upbringing. On the other hand, adoptees will share 50 per cent of their genes with each biological parent, but have not lived with them for the majority of their life. If the behaviour of the adoptees shared more similarity with the adopted family, we might assume that the behaviour in question was more likely to be the result of the shared environment. But if the behaviour of the adoptees correlated more strongly with the biological family, and is not associated with the behaviour of the adoptive family, then it could be concluded that the behaviour being studied is caused by a biological component.

An example of this type of study from psychology would be research by Cadoret and Stewart (1991). Their research suggested that adopted boys were at an increased risk of attention deficit/hyperactivity and aggression as children if they had a biological parent who had been convicted of a crime in adulthood. They also found that the boys were more likely to be aggressive or have a diagnosis of attention deficit/hyperactivity if there were psychiatric problems in members of the adoptive family. This suggests that behaviour as complex as aggression can have a variety of causes and is not significantly attributable to nature or nurture.

Evaluation

There are many possible problems with using twin and adoption studies in psychological research. The main aim of these types of studies is investigating biological causes of behaviour, but it is virtually impossible to separate nature completely from nurture. It is rare, for example, for a child to be adopted by a family immediately from birth so an adoptee may have spent time living with their biological family before adoption took place, or could have spent time in foster care, meaning there are possible confounding variables affecting validity of the findings. Likewise, almost all twins will be raised together. Therefore it is problematic to assume that, just because MZ twins show a higher concordance than DZ twins for a behaviour, it must be genetic.

Monozygotic twins are likely to have a very similar life experience because they look so similar so this could well explain why their behaviour is more concordant than DZ twins.

Another issue associated with these research methods is that sample sizes can be limited, making generalisability difficult. It is not easy to recruit a large and diverse group of MZ and DZ twins, or adoptees and their parents, meaning that psychologists will find generalising from their samples problematic. A specific problem associated with adoption studies is that children who are being adopted tend to be placed with families that closely reflect the family background they came from. It may be unreliable to assume that any similarities between the adoptee and their biological family are the result of nature because the similarity could well be due to similar life events they have experienced.

WIDER ISSUES

Ethics

Gathering accurate and reliable information about people's life experiences, especially if they are related to something sensitive like an adoption, is also likely to be difficult. People may be reluctant to take part in a study that looks into their biological and adoptive families as it could be uncomfortable for them, or access to both families may be limited and therefore the information could be restricted. There are also ethical implications associated with using methods such as this to uncover possible influences on behaviours like aggression, as psychologists could be seen as labelling people as 'bad apples' because of their family history.

3.3 Studies
Learning outcomes

In this section you, will learn about one classic study:

- Raine et al. (1997) on brain abnormalities in murderers indicated by positron emission tomography

and three contemporary studies, from which you will need to choose one to learn about:

- Li et al. (2013) on abnormal function of the **posterior cingulate cortex** in heroin-addicted users during resting-state and drug-cue stimulation task
- Brendgen et al. (2005) on examining genetic and environmental effects on social aggression: a study of 6-year-old twins
- Van den Oever et al. (2008) on prefrontal cortex AMPA receptor plasticity being crucial for cue-induced relapse to heroin-seeking.

Classic study

Brain abnormalities in murderers indicated by positron emission tomography (Raine, A. et al., 1997)

Aim

A pilot study conducted by Adrian Raine et al. (1997) on 22 participants pleading 'not guilty by reason of insanity' (NGRI) and 22 controls found that there was a significant difference in activity of the prefrontal cortex. Specifically, the group of participants pleading NGRI showed prefrontal cortex dysfunctions compared to the 'normal' controls. From this, and other established research, Adrian Raine, Monte Buchsbaum and Lori LaCasse hypothesised that participants pleading NGRI would show brain dysfunctions in areas of the brain associated with violence. Namely, these were the prefrontal cortex, **angular gyrus**, amygdala, **hippocampus**, **thalamus** and **corpus callosum**.

Procedure

The participants consisted of two groups of 41 people: 39 males and two females in each group. The experimental group were 41 criminals with convictions for murder or manslaughter who were being tested to gain evidence to support a claim of NGRI. Of these: six had schizophrenia; 23 had suffered organic brain damage or head injury; three were substance abusers; two had an affective disorder; two had epilepsy; three suffered with hyperactivity and/or learning disability; and two were diagnosed with passive-aggressive/paranoid personality disorder. All participants in this group remained medication-free for two weeks prior to the PET scan.

The control group had been matched with the experimental group on age and gender. They were all screened for general health, which included a physical examination, access to their medical history and a psychiatric interview. Participants were excluded if they had a history of seizures, head trauma or substance misuse. Consent was obtained from all participants before the PET scan was administered.

All participants were given a continuous performance task (CPT) to complete, which consisted of a sequence of blurred numbers to focus on. Participants started the CPT as a practice trial 10 minutes before being injected with fluourodeoxyglucose (FDG). After a further 32 minutes on the CPT a PET scan was then completed to measure the metabolic rate in different areas of the brain in order to look at activity levels in those areas.

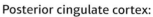

Key terms

Posterior cingulate cortex: lies behind the anterior cingulate cortex and has been linked with human awareness. It connects to multiple neural networks and is known to play a role in pain perception and episodic memory.

Angular gyrus: part of the parietal lobe associated with memory, language processing and attention.

Hippocampus: a structure of the brain responsible for learning, emotion and memory.

Thalamus: part of the brain associated with sensory perception and consciousness.

Corpus callosum: a band of nerve fibres that join the two hemispheres of the brain together and allow communication between the two parts.

WIDER ISSUES AND DEBATES

Ethics

Raine and his colleagues' research was approved by an ethics committee at the University of California, and all participants provided consent to take part. However, the murderers were taking part in the research to build up a case for claiming that they were not guilty by reason of insanity. This raises the question of whether the participants were under duress by their counsel to take part in the research. If the murderers were indeed mentally ill as they were building evidence to claim that they were, we should question their capacity to consent, especially as they were trying to establish that they were of diminished capacity and could not stand trial. Furthermore, the murderers were being referred for various psychiatric disorders such as schizophrenia, brain injury, substance abuse and personality disorders, likely to diminish their ability to give full consent to take part in the investigation.

Results

The key findings of the study were that support was found for the hypothesis: brain dysfunction in the NGRI group was in areas previously implicated in violent behaviour. Specifically, compared to the control group, murderers showed:

- lower activity in the prefrontal cortex (both lateral and medial areas)
- lower activity in parietal areas, especially the left angular gyrus and bilateral superior parietal regions
- higher activity in the occipital lobe
- identical activity in the temporal lobe.

In subcortical areas, murderers also showed:

- lower activity in the corpus callosum
- asymmetrical activity in the amygdala (lower in the left, but higher in the right)
- asymmetrical activity in the medial temporal lobe, including the hippocampus (lower in the left, but higher in the right)
- higher level activity in the right of the thalamus.

Conclusion

These brain differences have been associated with many behavioural changes that could be related to violent behaviour. For example, dysfunction in the prefrontal cortex has been linked to impulsivity, lack of self-control and an inability to learn from the consequences of behaviour. The hippocampus, amygdala and thalamus have all been related to learning and it has been suggested that abnormal activity here could result in criminals being unable to modify their own behaviour by learning from the consequences of their actions.

Evaluation

The sample used in the research has a number of strengths. It was the largest sample of severely violent offenders to be studied in this way and compared to matched controls, meaning there is good degree of validity in the findings. An effort was also made to eradicate possible effects of medication on brain activity by keeping participants drug-free for two weeks before the scan. The researchers also made an effort to rule out potential confounding variables such as the effect of whether participants were right- or left-handed and possible head injuries suffered. However, one problem with the sample is that it only represents a small number of severely violent offenders as those pleading NGRI are not representative and therefore it cannot be considered a representative explanation of violence. The study focused specifically on a subgroup of violent offenders, but the findings cannot be used as an explanation for other types of violent behaviour or indeed criminality as a whole.

The use of a PET scan provides reliable comparisons to be made between the groups as all participants were subject to the same procedure, allowing an objective measure of the difference in brain activity to be measured. However, the researchers themselves point out that there is some possibility in variation in the procedure for different participants as the images are often taken based on the location of certain brain landmarks within each individual.

One limitation of this type of research is that it is impossible to be sure that the brain dysfunction is directly related to the behaviour. There could be a number of possible extraneous variables that could interfere with these findings, such as social or situational factors that may contribute to either violent behaviour, brain dysfunction, or both. Therefore the research cannot conclude whether violence is due to biology or environmental influences.

The researchers were cautious about the findings. These did support their hypothesis, which was based on some preliminary findings, about whether there was a relationship between these patterns of brain dysfunction and violent behaviour. Some of the findings had not been shown in prior research so, to be sure that they were related to violent behaviour, additional research would need to be conducted.

WIDER ISSUES AND DEBATES

Issues related to socially sensitive research

Research into the biological causes of crime can be considered to be socially sensitive for a number of reasons. One is that research suggesting that criminality is biologically determined sends out a message that the offenders were not in control of their behaviour, and perhaps they are not criminally responsible. This idea would suggest that we decriminalise certain offences because the offender cannot be held accountable for their actions.

Another reason that this type of research is socially sensitive is because it could be suggested that violent offenders could be detected using diagnostic brain scans, so their future offending behaviour could be predicted and perhaps intervention strategies used to prevent violent crime. This would be a very frightening proposition, particularly as such research is correlatory, and it could be that changes in brain functioning is a result of violent offending rather than a cause.

Adrian Raine and his colleagues were insistent that criminal responsibility and using PET scans as a diagnostic tool were not the intention of the report, and neither should be pursued as possible ideas because the causality of the findings could not be established with any degree of certainty.

Abnormal function of the posterior cingulate cortex in heroin-addicted users during resting-state and drug-cue stimulation task (Li et al., 2013)

Aim

Li Qiang, Yang Wei-Chuan and colleagues aimed to investigate the relationship between chronic heroin use and changes in specific brain areas – specifically a part of the cortex directly next to the limbic system in the middle of the brain, called the cingulate cortex. They were specifically interested in the back most part of the cingulate cortex known as the posterior cingulate cortex (PCC) because of its connectivity to other regions of the brain. Previous studies had identified neural circuits involved in reward, motivation, inhibitory control and working memory all of which are implicated in addiction associated with other regions of the brain, but very little research had been done on the PCC. The researchers aimed to look specifically at the PCC and its functional role in relation to heroin addiction.

Procedure

The sample consisted of 14 heroin-addicted males with an average age of 35 years. All participants were recruited from a drug rehabilitation centre in China and had been using heroin for an average of 89 months. At the time of the study they were tested for opiate use and found to be clean of heroin and any other drug of addiction except nicotine. All were right-handed and none had a history of psychiatric disorder. They were all physically healthy and medically cleared to spend 40 minutes in a magnetic resonance imaging scanner. The matched control group of 15 males varied from the experimental group only in their substance misuse history.

All participants were required to undergo a session in the fMRI scanner, their resting state was tested where they had to focus their attention on a target for 5 minutes and do nothing else. This was immediately followed by the cue-induced condition where after a 10-second gap participants were exposed to 24 pictures of drug-related activity and 24 neutral pictures each shown for 2 seconds in a random order; between each picture presentation there was an inter-stimulus interval, which ranged between 4 and 12 seconds.

Data was analysed using statistical techniques designed to model brain activity in the two tasks over both conditions.

Results

The participants who had subsequently been addicted to heroin reported craving for heroin following the cue-inducing pictures. The researchers then looked at the brain scan images to see if there were significant differences in the brains of ex-addicts and the control group that could account for these cravings. The results of the heroin picture cue-induced task showed significantly different activation in specific areas of the PCC and between the PCC and other regions associated with the brain's reward system in the heroin group compared to the control group.

In the resting-state the relationship between different parts of the brain showed a stronger connectivity between the PCC and bilateral insula and between the posterior cingulate cortex PCC and bilateral dorsal striatum in chronic heroin users than in the control group. The insula is believed to be responsible for associating internal emotional states with decision-making behaviours, so could be more readily activated as a result of seeing the heroin picture cues as the behaviour pattern of craving and seeking drugs would have been established. Put simply, the ex-addict would have established a brain circuitry to respond to the urge to take a drug. The picture cues would have activated this pathway in the brain of an ex-addict, but not a healthy control. Abnormal dorsal striatum has been associated with drug-seeking behaviour, so the increased connectivity between the PCC and dorsal striatum might explain the abnormal reward and craving that is experienced by the ex-addict.

Furthermore, there was a positive correlation between the degree of connectivity between these regions of the brain and the length of time of heroin use; chronic users of heroin showing the greatest level of connectivity. This demonstrates that brain pathways associated with addiction, craving and the brain's own reward system become more established with increased length of drug use.

Conclusion

Activity in the PCC was significantly increased when heroin users were exposed to drug-related cues. This brain area is linked to visual orientation and reward processing, and is sensitive to unpredictable rewards. Heroin use alters the functionality and connectivity of the brain to reinforce addictive thinking, craving and drug-seeking behaviour, which becomes abnormally associated with reward.

This brain circuitry is activated when presented with a heroin cue. This may explain why ex-addicts are particularly susceptible to relapse if exposed to a drug stimulus that activates these areas of the brain. They also conclude that the PCC could be a useful indicator for the extent of brain damage caused by heroin use.

Evaluation

The samples were well matched as statistical tests across several measures such as nicotine use revealed no significant differences between them other than their history of substance abuse suggesting that the differences observed in the PCC were a result of heroin use only, although there could have been other factors that were not controlled in this investigation. The researchers also ensured that the ex-addicts were detoxified by conducting a urine analysis. This made sure the ex-addicts did not have morphine in their body during the investigation.

The sample size used in this research was small and limited to males from only one culture, suggesting that generalisability beyond this group may be unreliable. But the results are consistent with a range of other studies testing different brain areas that show similar differences in the reward centres of the brain associated with heroin use. Although only a small sample of participants were used, research using ex-addicts can have serious ethical implications. Exposing addicts to drug cues could have implications for relapse for the individuals concerned, particularly in the detoxification phase that they were currently in. However, all participants gave fully informed consent and the procedure was approved by two ethical committees.

Using scanning to measure activity in one specific brain area is difficult as the other areas will also be active and could cause the analysis to be less reliable. However the background 'noise' from other brain areas would have affected the heroin users and the healthy participants equally so the difference that was observed could be regarded as a genuine effect of heroin use.

The findings from this research helped to build a picture of the effect of long-term drug misuse and provide a marker of brain damage, which helps to measure the severity of the effect of drug addiction. They also helped to build a model of the brain structures associated with addiction.

Examining genetic and environmental effects on social aggression: a study of 6-year-old twins (Brendgen et al., 2005)

Aim

Much of the research into causes of aggression has focused on physical expressions of aggression, and occasionally researchers have also considered verbal forms of aggression. Mara Brendgen and her colleagues in this study were interested in the origins of social aggression: aggression characterised by socially manipulative behaviour such as ignoring others, spreading rumours or making threats to withdraw friendship. Social aggression can be both overtly and covertly expressed.

The researchers set out with three key aims:

1. To see if social aggression could be caused by genes or the environment

2. To see if social aggression shared the same cause as physical aggression

3. To see if one type of aggression leads to another type.

Procedure

Participants for this study were recruited from the Quebec Newborn Twin Study (QNTS) and all were pairs of twins born between November 1995 and July 1998. At the start of the study, 322 pairs of twins were tested, but complete data at all stages was only gathered on 234 twin pairs. Of these: 44 pairs were MZ males; 50 pairs were MZ females; 41 DZ males; 32 DZ females and 67 pairs were mixed-sex DZ twins. Data from the sample was gathered longitudinally at 5, 18, 30, 48 and 60 months, and then again at the age of 6 years and it is this final data that the researchers focused on in this study. The data gathered consisted of two ratings of each twin's behaviour – one by their teacher and one by their classmates. The ratings were gathered in the spring term of the school year to ensure that the twins were well known by those providing the ratings of their behaviour.

Teacher ratings were based on agreement with a series of statements taken from items on the Preschool Social Behaviour Scale (PSBS-T; Crick et al., 1997) and the Direct and Indirect Aggression Scales (Bjorkvist, Lagerspetz et al., 1992) such as 'To what extent does the child try to make others dislike a child' (social aggression) and 'To what extent does the child get into fights' (physical aggression). The scores given by the teachers for each statement was done on a 3-point scale (0=never; 1=sometimes; 2=often). Peer ratings of the twins were done by giving each child in the twins' classes a booklet containing photos of every child in the class. Every child was then asked to circle three pictures of children that they thought matched four different behaviour descriptions for example, 'Tells others not to play with a child' (social aggression), and 'Gets into fights' (physical aggression). Each twin was given a physical and social aggression score from the teachers' ratings, and any peer selections on the social or physical aggression descriptors that were made of each twin were also recorded.

Results

Initial findings from the study suggested that there was a much higher correlation between the ratings of MZ twin pairs on physical aggression than between same-sex DZ twin pairs. This was the case in both teacher and peer rating scores for the twins. On the other hand, scores for social aggression were roughly equally correlated in MZ and DZ twin pairs. These findings would suggest that in relation to the first aim, physical aggression may well be caused by genetic factors, whereas social aggression may be better explained by shared environmental factors. In relation to the second aim of the study, a correlation was found between physical and social aggression in the children that was best explained by genes rather than the fact that the twins shared the same environment. This could be the result of aggressive tendencies in general being the result of genetic factors, but the way these tendencies are expressed may be determined by environmental factors such as exposure to other people's aggressive behaviours. Finally, when looking at the third aim of the study, the data suggested that physical aggression may lead to social aggression, but not the other way around. They concluded that perhaps the expression of aggressive tendencies changes as children grow as they may learn more 'socially acceptable' ways to show aggression. As young children, they are only able to express aggression physically, but as their language and cognitive skills develop, so do their abilities to demonstrate aggressive behaviour in new ways.

Conclusion

The research concludes that there seems to be a strong genetic component to physical aggression but not social aggression, which is more likely due to environmental effects. Children who were physically aggressive were also more likely to display social aggression, probably because of an interaction between genes and environment. As children grow, they tend to become more socially aggressive because of social conventions on physical violence and developing different ways to express themselves.

Evaluation

The study benefits from taking measures of the twins' aggressive behaviour from two different sources: both teachers and peers. This would suggest that the researchers were validating their findings by looking at two different sources of information, which should eliminate or highlight any bias. The fact that the teachers and peers were in good agreement with each other also adds to the validity of the findings because it would suggest that neither peers nor teachers were giving a seemingly biased view of the aggressive behaviour of the individuals. A strength of the study could be seen in the potential for the research findings to be used to prevent the development of social aggression. If children are showing physically aggressive tendencies then dealing with this may prevent them later expressing this aggression socially. It could be used as an early indicator to parents or teachers that a child's behaviour could become problematic later on, allowing them to intervene early on rather than waiting until the behaviour has become a habit before tackling it. It would be much easier to challenge aggressive behaviour in a small child while they are still learning, than it would be to change the behaviour of an older child when they have already established a strong sense of their own personality and may be more resistant to change. One key criticism of the study is the small sample sizes when looking at the different groups being compared. This makes generalisation difficult because the chance of the sample being representative of the entire population would be very low. The reason for the small sample was a consequence of the way in which the study was conducted. Asking 6-year-old peers to provide ratings before they can read and write themselves, obviously meant that the researchers had to record the data with each child individually, which was a time-consuming process and resulted in the small sample achieved.

There could be many possible extraneous variables in the lives of this specific group of twins that may explain the aggressive behaviour shown. However, the researchers themselves justified this criticism by saying that the costs in time and effort associated with individually measuring the twins' behaviour across 409 different classrooms meant that selecting an assessment of moderating factors would have been extremely difficult. Another issue with generalising from this sample is that the age group being studied is very specific and it would be impossible to assume that aggression in other age groups will have the same cause. Research has found, for example, that physical aggression reduces when children start school (Nagin and Tremblay, 2001) while social aggression does not fully develop until later in childhood around the age of 8 years (Bjorkvist, Lagerspetz et al., 1992). This would suggest that aggression in children from an older age group may be characterised very differently.

Key terms

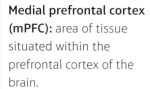

Medial prefrontal cortex (mPFC): area of tissue situated within the prefrontal cortex of the brain.

Physical dependency: a state where chronic and prolonged drug abuse results in a physical need for a drug in order to function, categorised through tolerance for the drug and withdrawal symptoms when the drug is absent.

Classical conditioning: a form of learning based on the association with an environmental event or stimulus with an internal response.

Paraphernalia: apparatus or equipment used for a particular activity.

Plasticity: changes in neural pathways and synapses, which are due to environment or behaviour.

Extinction: when behaviour that has previously been reinforced no longer produces reinforcement and is no longer repeated in response to the stimulus (unlearning).

Prefrontal cortex AMPA receptor plasticity is crucial for cue-induced relapse to heroin-seeking (Van den Oever et al., 2008)

Aim

To investigate the physiological basis of relapse to heroin by understanding the acute physical changes at the synapse that take place immediately after exposure to drug-conditioned stimuli in the **medial prefrontal cortex (mPFC).**

Background

One of the key indicators of addiction is the failure of the individual to remain abstinent from drugs once they are no longer **physically dependent** on the drug. This has been explained through the process of learning theory, particularly **classical conditioning**, where exposure to environmental cues associated with prior drug taking could lead to renewed addiction. For example, the items of drug **paraphernalia**, such as those used to smoke crack cocaine, were sufficient to cause severe craving for the drug and were enough for many people to relapse back into addiction even years after they last took the drug and there was no chance of them still being physically dependent on the drug.

The authors set out a case for the importance of understanding how the **plasticity** of the medial prefrontal cortex may be affected by drug taking and how this may be linked to learned cues.

By exploring what happens within the brains of drug users it may be possible to understand the mechanisms that change in response to drug use and that are subsequently implicated in relapse. Ultimately this may lead to a pharmacological treatment that could help reduce relapse rates.

Procedure

Male Wistar rats were used throughout the study, which consisted of a series of experiments with each subsequent one being designed to further investigate the findings of the last.

Initially the rats were conditioned to become dependent on heroin by the administration of the drug by intravenous infusion through a surgically implanted catheter in response to nose-poking behaviour. During this conditioning they were also exposed to environmental stimuli that acted as a trigger for the nose-poking behaviour. Once heroin dependent, they then underwent **extinction** training for three weeks in the same cages in which they were exposed to the drugs, or in their home cages, until they no longer showed drug-seeking behaviour (nose pokes in the holes that led to heroin). It was found that relapse was substantially more likely when the cues associated with drug taking during the conditioning phase were then present during the re-exposure phase.

The researchers established that learned cues associated with the drug-taking situation are powerful influences on relapse, so they then went on to explore the biological mechanisms that underlie this in a sequence of different investigations.

Taking it further

If you study biology or chemistry you could look at the original article, which precisely outlines the biochemical changes observed but which are not reported in exact detail here.

Investigation 1

This aimed to uncover a difference at the level of the synapse between the rats who had cues and had therefore relapsed and those who had not had cues.

The rats were then immediately euthanised, their brains dissected and areas of the medial prefrontal cortex (mPFC) examined microscopically using sensitive **mass spectrometry**.

Significant changes linked to **endocytosis** were observed in six proteins in the synaptic membranes of **AMPA receptors** of the rats exposed to the cues compared to the control rats. This demonstrated that cue-induced heroin seeking alters synaptic functioning and strength in the rat's brain.

This led to a further hypothesis that preventing the endocytosis of specific proteins will reduce cue-dependent heroin-seeking.

Investigation 2

In the next investigation the rats were injected with either an active **peptide** that would limit endocytosis or an inactive one (as a control) 90 minutes before they were exposed to a 30-minute session of relapse testing.

Those given the active peptide and exposed to cues showed significantly less nose-poking behaviour compared to those exposed to cues and given the inactive substance.

The rats were euthanised and slices of the mPFC were examined, as before.

It was found that those exposed to the cues and injected with the active peptide showed no difference in synaptic reactivity compared to those that had not been exposed to the cues. Rats that were exposed to the cues and given the control (inactive) peptide showed the same changes as before.

The active peptide stopped the endocytosis confirming the role of endocytosis on AMPA currents.

Investigation 3

The researchers then investigated the precise location of the effect of the endocytosis on cue-dependent drug seeking.

The active peptide was injected precisely into various areas of the rat brain.

It was found that the active peptide only decreased heroin seeking in the relapse trial when administered to the ventral (top part) areas. This led to the conclusion that cue-induced relapse to heroin seeking depends on minute chemical changes brought on by endocytosis in the ventral mPFC.

Investigation 4

The researchers then tested to see if this effect on the reduction of the impact of cues would be extended to naturally occurring reinforcers such as sucrose. Rats trained to nose poke for sucrose solution were tested in the same way as those trained for the heroin investigations. While it was found that cues did affect relapse, the administration of the peptide did not change this, suggesting that this effect is drug specific and does not stop operant reinforcers in general.

Results/findings

Environmental cues presented during drug taking will significantly affect the risk of relapse in previously dependent rats, if presented alongside the drug following extinction or abstinence so rats are no longer drug dependent.

Key terms

Mass spectrometry: analytical technique to identify the amount and types of chemicals present in a sample.

Endocytosis: the taking in of extra-cellular materials from outside a cell by fusing with its plasma membrane.

AMPA receptors: post synaptic receptors responsible for glutamate transmission (glutamate is the most prevalent neurotransmitter in the nervous system and the main excitatory one).

Peptide: chain of biological molecules containing 50 or fewer amino acids.

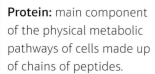

Key terms

Protein: main component of the physical metabolic pathways of cells made up of chains of peptides.

Operant conditioning: learning based on the consequence for the operator of the action performed, actions that are reinforced are repeated and learned.

This can be shown to be linked to brain plasticity in the mPFC where exposure to the cues changes the **protein** make up at the AMPA receptors.

Endocytosis leads to these changes. This can be blocked by the administration of a peptide. Blocking endocytosis stops cue-induced relapse especially when applied to the ventral areas of the mPFC. The peptide does not stop cues acting on other **operantly conditioned** reinforcers affecting learning.

Conclusion

Re-exposure to conditioned stimuli associated with prior heroin use, can act as a trigger to relapse. The cue in some way triggered a synaptic response that encouraged heroin-seeking behaviour to recover following a period of abstinence. This synaptic response can be blocked to prevent synaptic reactivity, suggesting a possible pharmacological treatment for those addicted to drugs.

Evaluation

The data for this study is gathered from rats so the validity of extrapolating their findings to model human addiction and relapse could be challenged. Arguably humans have much higher levels of choice in their decision making, involving more cognitive functioning than rodents do; so reducing relapse to the workings of basic neural circuitry present in rats may by misleading. Also, drug taking in humans can be a social activity rather than a purely physical experience so cannot be accurately modelled by animal studies.

However, rodents and humans are alike in having these same brain areas and it would be ethically impossible to investigate them using the highly controlled scientific studies conducted on animals because you would have to expose ex-addicts to cues that are likely to cause relapse and monitor their brain activity at the cellular level. Although some such studies have been conducted, for example Li et al., (2013) they must meet very stringent ethical requirements, they also tend to be very small scale with few participants and they are typically less invasive than research on non-humans. The findings cited in the paper are consistent with less experimental human research on the effects of cues on relapse.

This study is highly scientific in its use of specialised equipment to precisely measure changes at the molecular level, providing objective quantifiable differences in neuro-chemistry associated with the effect of cues on relapse.

This study is supported by others, such as Rogers et al. (2008), who found similar results, but only investigated the effect of cues and the biological substrate of heroin addiction. Other substances of abuse may act on different neural substrates, and indeed this study established that naturally occurring reinforcers like sucrose are not affected in the same way, thus potentially limiting the usefulness of the model of relapse presented here. However, the results have been shown to be consistent with other studies that involved cocaine (for example Peters et al., 2008).

It could be argued however that the model is useful because of the scale of the drugs problem. The US government estimates that relapse back into drug use is between 40 and 60 per cent, stating that drug addiction should be treated like any other chronic illness, with relapse serving as a trigger for renewed intervention.

> **Exam tip**
>
> Do not try to evaluate this study in terms of the ethical standards applied to human studies. Instead you could look at the ethical guidelines that govern animal research, bearing in mind the potential benefits conveyed by the findings. But if you think that the findings are not valid, or convey only limited benefits, then you could argue that the study is unethical.

3.4 Key questions

Learning outcomes

In this section, you will learn about:

- one issue of relevance to today's society

- the application of concepts, theories and/or research (as appropriate) drawn from biological psychology as an explanation of this issue.

What are the implications for society if aggression is found to be caused by nature not nurture?

Luis Suárez gained infamy in 2014 in Brazil after being accused of biting an opposing player for the third time in his football career. Footage appears to show Suárez bite the shoulder of Italian defender Giorgio Chiellini during a clash in the match between Italy and Uruguay on 24 June 2014. Chiellini lowered his top to the referee to reveal what appear to be teeth marks in his shoulder, but no action was taken during the game. However, Suárez later received a four-month ban from all football as punishment for his alleged actions. He is not the first player however to have an outburst of impulsive aggressive behaviour during a World Cup match. In 1998, the usually mild-mannered David Beckham was sent off after kicking out at Diego Simeone, and France's Zinedine Zidane received a red card during the World Cup Final in 2006 after headbutting Italy's Marco Materazzi in the chest. The key point about all of these actions is that they happened on impulse. They were not premeditated actions, but things that seem to happen 'in the heat of the moment'. Footballers are used to having to think quickly and react to situations as they arise on the pitch, so they are naturally very impulsive. But does this same impulsivity that creates successful footballers, also create aggressive individuals who are ticking time bombs of aggression if placed in the wrong situation?

It has been well established by research that aggression can have a biological cause, so one question to consider here is whether to blame people who find themselves in such a situation as this. If their aggression is caused by a biological factor that in many circumstances is actually a positive thing, can we treat them harshly when they use the impulse in a more negative way? Many would argue that the behaviour, regardless of its cause or intention, should be treated appropriately so behaving aggressively deserves punishment. In this case, just because they are footballers with successful careers based on their impulsive tendencies does not mean they should be treated leniently when they lash out.

David Beckham was ostracised by many for his outburst on the pitch as it was seen as out of character and, despite many praising his talents, they were outraged by his behaviour in this incident. Psychologists may argue that impulsivity is a behavioural trait that people learn to control by experiencing the urges in different social situations. But the World Cup, for any footballer, could prove to be such a high-pressure situation that the ability to control impulsivity is hindered. While normally able to channel the impulsive urges into their game, the stress felt in a match with high importance could interrupt this – causing an aggressive outburst.

An explanation for this could be gained from an understanding of evolution. Impulsivity is a survival mechanism, useful as an ability to think and act quickly and avoid threats. As we have evolved over time to live in large social groups, self-restraint has evolved as a way to allow us to successfully live with others. This impulse control mechanism is controlled by the actions of the prefrontal cortex, which is thought by many to be a highly evolved part of the human brain. Research by Raine et al. (1997) found evidence that violent behaviour (in this case, murder) was related to low levels of activity in the prefrontal cortex, suggesting violence is caused by poor impulse control.

Another concept we could use to explain this issue might be the influence of the hormone testosterone on aggressive behaviour. Evidence has found that high levels of testosterone may be linked with behaviour traits such as dominance and competitiveness as well as aggression. The above cases all refer to male sportsmen, and perhaps the same hormone that makes them driven to compete in sport, also makes them more prone to aggression.

Another explanation for this comes from research into expression of the MAOA gene often referred to as the 'warrior gene' because of its links with aggressive and impulsive behaviour. Research has found that people with a version of this gene that shows low activity, or low expression, may be more likely to react to provocation by showing aggression (McDermott et al., 2009). Other research has found that people with this 'low expression' version of the MAOA gene, who also have high levels of testosterone, are more likely to be aggressive, especially if they have suffered a poor upbringing.

The implications for society, if evidence suggests aggression is caused by nature rather than nurture, include the fact that if a person's biology is found to have resulted in them being aggressive, can we really find them criminally responsible for the result of their actions? Luis Suárez, for example, may not be able to control his impulsive reaction to perceived threats as he may have biological features that make this difficult. This would mean that punishing him could be seen as unfair as his biological make-up is beyond his control. Perhaps an emphasis should be placed on investigating whether violent individuals have any biological predisposition that may explain their behaviour, and then focus on helping them rather than punishing them. These biological factors may also change the way society views aggressive behaviour. If a person's biology causes the aggression then this is beyond their control, and therefore the suggestion might be that aggression is a form of illness or a symptom of a disorder. It even suggests that a person could be identified before they show aggressive behaviour, meaning that an implication of research in this area might be in developing mechanisms to predict aggressive behaviour in certain people in order to prevent the behaviour before it occurs.

WIDER ISSUES AND DEBATES

Free will vs determinism

Biological explanations suggest that whether or not people become aggressive is predetermined by biological factors that may be present. This means that an implication of this area of research is that it takes away the blame from individuals for their aggressive actions. It suggests that they cannot help the way that they behave as it is the result of the way that their brains function. This removes the element of free will in aggressive behaviour, but this fails to explain why not all people with the biological features become aggressive, or why some people will be aggressive without having any biological predisposition.

3.5 Practical investigation

Learning objectives

In this section, you will learn how to:

- design and conduct a correlational study, which could be linked to either the topic of aggression or attitudes towards drug taking
- analyse correlational data including conducting an inferential test (Spearman's rho)
- discuss significance levels
- produce descriptive statistics from the data
- produce an abstract of the investigation
- write a discussion section about the conclusions of the investigation.

Aim

Correlational research investigates the relationship between variables, specifically how strong a relationship it is and whether it is positive or negative. As this section of the course is about biological psychology, then you could look for a link between a biological variable and a behavioural one, in particular one relevant to aggression or to attitudes to drug taking.

All studies start with a research question; for example 'is there a link between the masculinity of a person and aggressive behaviour?'

Hypotheses and variables

In this case, your alternative hypothesis might be; 'there will be a significant positive correlation between masculinity and aggression.' This is a directional hypothesis because it is predicting the specific nature of the relationship. The null hypothesis is that there will be no relationship between masculinity and aggression and any relationship found will be due to chance.

The next stage would be to operationalise both co-variables, which means that you have to work out how they are to be measured exactly. For example, you could get participants to do a brain sex quiz that gives a score about masculinity of the brain, and then observe the person play a moderately violent video game that would allow you to get an aggression score. The aggression score will be calculated by how many characters in the game that they knock down, which will receive 1 point each time in the game. The hypothesis can now be refined to include an operational definition of the measured co-variables, for example there will be a significant positive correlation between a participant's masculinity score on a brain sex quiz and their scores on a moderately violent video game.

Design

Correlational designs measure two variables and then calculate the exact nature of the relationship between them. In this study, you would have to measure the masculinity of participants, then for the same people, measure their aggressiveness.

Controls

You should try to ensure that as far as possible you have controlled for other variables that could impact on either of your measures (brain sex score and aggressive acts in video game). For example, when brain sex is measured, all participants ought to be tested in the same way and their scores should be capable of objective measurement; for example you could use a computerised test that gives a masculinity score.

In measuring aggression you would need to make sure that all participants are equally proficient at the video game. This might mean that you have to invent one in order to control for prior exposure and practice, and that everyone participates with the game in exactly the same circumstances to rule out extraneous variables.

Finding a sample

Once you are satisfied you have the materials necessary to run the study you should recruit a sample of participants. The sample should be representative of the target population that you wish to apply your findings to, in this case the male general public. At the point of recruitment you must make them aware of the aims and nature of the study so as they can make an informed decision as to whether to participate or not. There are several methods available to gather a sample. In this practical example, an opportunity sample could be used as it is quick and easy to do, but because testing might take up quite a lot of time it might be better to get a volunteer sample of people who are willing to give up an afternoon; you could do this through advertising on workplace or college noticeboards or online. You should aim for about ten participants, in this case male participants. Although samples gathered using volunteer or opportunity sampling methods are not typically generalisable to the general population, in this investigation there will be certain ethical implications with asking participants to play a violent video game, so representativeness will be compromised for ethical reasons.

Ethics

It is important to deal with the ethical issues before the participants start the study.

They should be clearly informed as to the nature of the study, what you are investigating and what they will be required to do.

If and when participants consent to take part you should notify them that they are free to withdraw at any point and to take their data with them.

You should ensure that their data is kept confidential so that any information you get about the participant will not be shared with anyone else. You should keep their data anonymous by replacing names with a number, and any data should be destroyed in a reasonable time frame.

You must ensure that your sample participants are all able to give their consent and that no one under the age of 16 is included. For this investigation it is important that all participants are over the age of 16 because they will be asked to play a video game that involves some aggression. The video game must be age appropriate, and all participants must be informed that they will be expected to play this type of game before the study begins.

> **Example consent form**
> A consent form should have the following information:
> What the aim(s) of the study are.
> Exactly what they will be expected to do – in full detail so that participants can decide whether or not they want to take part.
> Any possible implications for the participant – in this example they will need to know the possible implications of playing an aggressive video game.
> A clear statement that the participant can withdraw at any point without consequence.
> A reassurance that their data will be anonymised and destroyed after a certain date.
> Who else will see the findings and how the information will be distributed.
> Your contact details and the details of your supervising teacher/school/college.
> The signatures of the researcher and participant.

Developing a procedure

Now you can set up the study. Think about what you will need in order to measure your variables and how you will get them. In this example, you might get all your participants to do the brain sex test while supervised to ensure that no other variables might affect their concentration and their ability to give it full attention. You would need to think through how to do this, for example, have all participants together working on a bank of computers so that less researcher time is needed.

As a researcher you will need to use a standardised procedure to gather your data, which you will then carefully write up in your report of the investigation. It must be detailed enough to allow for others to replicate what you did and test whether they too get the same results as you, so must include all instructions to the participants and a step-by-step run through of the study. For example, once the participants have been recruited, you could set up a time for them to come to the lab to establish their brain sex score. This could be all at the same time, or it could be separately. You would need to work out how you will measure aggression on the video game.

Pilot study

Before you conduct a study, it is worth doing a run through of the procedure using a pilot study. This will highlight any procedural and ethical issues that you may have overlooked in your planning. You will need to pilot the video game and the brain sex quiz, check your instructions are understood by all participants, your timings are appropriate, and that your venue is suitable for the study. A pilot study is a dry run rather than a measure of whether your variables work or whether the study is reliable or valid.

Example of possible procedure section of the report that is relevant to this example practical investigation

The study took place over one afternoon between the hours of 2 and 4 pm. Following the initial briefing and once participants had given their informed consent, ten volunteer participants (aged between 19 and 52 years old) were gathered in a lounge area in the university and were allocated a number. They were then shown into an IT room and each person was seated in front of a computer preloaded with a brain sex test. They were allowed as much time as they needed to complete the test. The fastest time was 25 minutes and the slowest was 42 minutes. The test was done in silence and was supervised by the researcher who recorded their score against their allocated number once they completed the test. The scores were calculated as part of the computer program.

Once each participant had completed the test they returned to the lounge area and were asked to wait until called. Refreshments were available while they waited. They were then shown into one of two small lab rooms. Each participant was seated alone at a laptop set up with a bespoke computer game that required them to do moderate acts of aggression to score points. They were supervised at all times by a research assistant who had minimal interaction with them other than to set up the game and input their participant number. The game offered a practice session lasting 3 minutes and then a 5-minute data-gathering session. All instructions appeared on the screen. The participant's score was logged by their number. Once the game was complete they met with the main researcher in another small room and were debriefed individually or in pairs, and reminded of their right to withdraw. Any questions they had were answered and they were offered the chance to see the results once available. They were thanked for their participation, asked whether they wished to offer any insights into their experience of the study and released.

Analysing results

Analysing correlational data requires that there are two scores from related sources; in this case, the source is each participant and the two scores are their brain sex measures and their aggression score from the video game. This data must be at least ordinal.

The data from the video game provided an aggression score for the participants between 0 and 20 where a low score represented low levels of aggression.

The data from the brain sex test was calculated by the computer program. A high score indicated a high level of masculinity. The maximum score possible was 100 and the minimum was 25.

The data should initially be tabulated as follows.

Table 3.8 Participant data for brain sex and aggression scores

Participant number and gender		Brain sex score	Aggression score
1	M	56	17
2	M	69	18
3	M	30	10
4	M	88	10
5	M	80	15
6	M	87	16
7	M	95	17
8	M	67	15
9	M	77	14
10	M	45	6

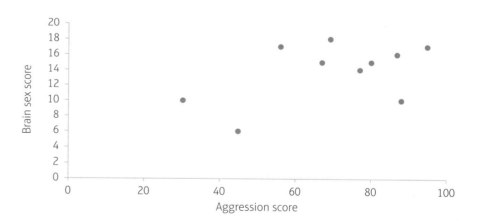

Figure 3.10 Scatter diagram to show the relationship between brain sex score and aggression score on video game

The scatter diagram above does not illustrate any definite linear relationship between the co-variables, but there is a slight trend from the bottom left to top right that could demonstrate a potential weak positive correlation.

By looking at the scatter diagram you can see the nature of the relationship and get a rough idea of its strength. However, to accurately gauge the strength of any relationship you will need to do a statistical test, and for a correlation you will need to conduct a Spearman's rho test. If you have gathered interval or ratio data, this will be reduced to ordinal level data when it is ranked during the procedure of the test.

The co-variables will need to be ranked and then the differences between the ranks for each co-variable calculated and the sum of rank differences found.

Table 3.9 Ranking of co-variables for brain sex and aggression scores

Participant number	Brain sex score (A)	Aggression score (B)	Rank A	Rank B	D = rank A-B	D^2
1	56	17	3	8.5	-5.5	30.25
2	69	18	5	10	-5	25
3	30	10	1	2.5	-1.5	2.25
4	88	10	9	2.5	6.5	42.25
5	80	15	7	5.5	1.5	2.25
6	87	16	8	7	1	1
7	95	17	10	8.5	1.5	2.25
8	67	15	4	5.5	-1.5	2.25
9	77	14	6	4	2	4
10	45	6	2	1	1	1
					ΣD^2	112.5

Calculating the value of r

Rank the scores on one of the variables giving 1 to smallest score and so on.

> ### Maths tip
>
> When ranking scores you might find it easier to keep tabs on what is happening if you write out your ranks first, so if you have 10 bits of data, write out the numbers 1 – 10 and then score them off as you allocate the rank, this is especially helpful when you have tied data. For example:
>
> | Number position | 1 | 2 | 3 | 4 | 5 | 6 | 7 | 8 | 9 | 10 |
> |---|---|---|---|---|---|---|---|---|---|---|
> | Scores for B | 6 | 10 | 10 | 14 | 15 | 15 | 16 | 17 | 17 | 18 |
> | Ranks for B | 1 | 2.5 | 2.5 | 4 | 5.5 | 5.5 | 7 | 8.5 | 8.5 | 10 |
>
> So the score of 6 gets ranked 1, and the scores of 10 get the average of the number positions they occupy, in this case the average of 2 and 3 number positions is 2.5, and the next score of 14 is given the rank of 4 and so on until the last rank of 10 is given to the highest score of 18.

- Do the same for the other group of variables
- Calculate the difference (D) between the ranks for each score
- Square each difference (D^2)
- Find the sum of the squared differences
- Count the number of participants (N)
- Find the value of r_s

Spearman's rho formula:

$$r_s = 1 - \frac{6\Sigma D^2}{N(N^2 - 1)}$$

Applied to this analysis:

$$r_s = 1 - \frac{6 \times 112.5}{10\,(10^2 - 1)} \qquad r_s = 1 - \frac{675}{10 \times 99} \qquad r_s = 1 - \frac{675}{990} \qquad r_s = 1 - 0.682 \qquad r_s = 0.318$$

The correlation coefficient (r_s) = 0.318

The final stage in the statistical analysis is to find the critical value appropriate to the data, this means using a critical values table for Spearman's rho.

The study had a directional or one-tailed hypothesis that there would be a positive relationship between the masculinity of brain sex and aggression scores, so a one-tailed test will be used. The minimum level of probability acceptable in psychological research is 0.05 level, and there were ten participants (N = 10). Using this information, the observed (calculated value of Spearman's rho of 0.318 is compared with the critical value on the table, which it has to be equal to or greater than if the result is to be considered significant.

Table 3.10 Extract from critical values table: Calculated r_s needs to exceed the table (critical) value for significance at the level shown

	Level of significance for a one-tailed test			
	0.05	0.25	0.01	0.005
	Level of significance for a two-tailed test			
n	0.1	0.05	0.02	0.01
4	1.000	-	-	-
5	.900	1.00	1.00	-
6	.829	.886	.943	1.00
7	.714	.786	.893	.929
8	.643	.738	.833	.881
9	.600	.700	.783	.833
10	.564	.648	.745	.794

In order to be significant the observed (calculated) value of r_s should have been 0.564 or greater. But it is not, so in this case we must accept the null hypothesis and reject the alternative hypothesis because the probability of the results occurring by chance was greater than 5 per cent. There is no evidence of a significant relationship between masculinity of the brain and aggressive responses to a computer game.

If our variables are positively related, then we should expect that participants who score low on one measure will also score low on the other, and similarly for those who score high. If they are negatively related, then we would expect that those who score low on one variable will score high on the other. So if the variables are ranked separately, high ranks for one variable should mean high ranks on the other if there is a positive correlation. If there is no correlation then there is simply a chance distribution of scores, so rank of score on one condition is unrelated to rank on the other.

Presenting findings

State whether the null hypothesis should be accepted or rejected based on the analysis of the data. Researchers must provide enough data to allow the reader to understand that decision. Raw data ought to be available although only as an appendix to the final report, however the descriptive statistics including tables and graphs must be included at the point of presenting findings in the results section of the report.

The conclusion of the inferential statistical analysis must also be stated in the following format:

The calculated value of the Spearman's rho test was r_s = 0.318. This was less than the critical value of 0.564 for a one-tailed test at p = 0.05 with N 10. Therefore the result is not significant and the null hypothesis can be supported, which states that there will be no relationship between masculinity and aggression, and any relationship found was due to chance.

Table 3.11 Significance of findings

r_s observed = 0.318	N = 10	p>0.05 (one tailed)	r_s crit = 0.564
Calculated statistic from the test done on your data	Number of participants contributing data	Probability of result being significant determined by comparing calculated statistic (r_s) with table value at specific level of significance. In this case, the result shows that the probability was greater than 5%	The critical value for n = 10 at the 5% level drawn from the appropriate table for Spearman's rank order correlation coefficient table of critical values.

Drawing conclusions

Once the data has been gathered and analysed you will be able to state whether you reject the null hypothesis or not.

You cannot be reasonably certain that a genuine relationship existed for this study because of the inferential test results, but this does not mean that other factors did not influence the data and therefore challenge the validity of any conclusions drawn.

In considering the findings of any investigation the researcher must examine the reliability and validity of the method and procedures used to gather data.

Validity

Were the variables truly a measure of the concepts being tested? In this case, was the brain sex test a true measure of masculinity and the video game a true measure of aggression? The use of the brain sex test could, however, challenge this measure as a valid reflection of masculinity as it is very superficial and ignores many other factors that influence masculinity, such as social roles and norms of behaviour. The computer game could also be challenged as lacking ecological validity in the way that it measured aggression, sitting at a screen and manipulating virtual characters for points does not necessarily translate into real-world aggressive tendencies, which are likely to be constrained by social regulations.

It could be argued that the number of times a character was hit in the game was merely a reflection of the rules of the video game and not an indication of aggression.

With any correlation, we cannot actually establish a causal relationship between aggression and masculinity as there might be a third variable that affects both co-variables that are not included in the analysis.

Reliability

Were the procedures used a consistent test of aggression and masculinity? The use of the standardised procedures and the objective measures in the example practical investigation increase the reliability of the data, so it is realistic to expect that the procedure could be replicated and that another researcher could consistently record and interpret the data on both measures in the same way as in this study.

However, there are still challenges, for example for some participants doing the brain sex test first might have alerted them to the goals of the study, which may have affected how they performed on the video game. Some students also had longer between the brain sex test and the video game, this might have relaxed them and so they did not operate at the same level of focused attention as others who did it straight away. Also, although the study ensured that no participant had prior knowledge of the game itself and all participants had the same amount of practice time, it might be that some participants were experienced gamers and had a higher generic skill that could have led to them scoring more points. This means that we measured gaming performance rather than consistently measuring aggression.

If the study had used a questionnaire to measure aggression then there might have been more issues with accepting the measure as reliable.

Generalisability

In the example study the sample size was small at only ten people and although a range of ages was tested, it might be that the sample is not representative. This could be especially true because it was a volunteer sample so those who came forward might represent only a certain type of person. Volunteers tend to have a more compliant personality, so perhaps could have altered their behaviour to meet the expectations of the researcher.

The amount and type of aggression displayed in different cultures and subcultures are very different. Some cultures nurture aggression while others actively prohibit it. Because this example practical investigation is based on a sample of participants who are from an industrialised Western culture, the study can be regarded as ethnocentric and the findings will not apply to other cultures. The study is also limited to explaining male behaviour, so cannot be applied to explain female aggression.

Writing the abstract

Once the research is complete and has been written up in the appropriate format the final job is to write the abstract. This is a brief summary of the aims, procedure, result and conclusions drawn from the study. It is designed to allow others to quickly assess whether the study is appropriate for their needs and whether to continue reading or to purchase the entire study.

For example: this study aimed to investigate the nature of the relationship between brain sex and aggression. Ten healthy participants measured the masculinity levels of their brain by using a psychometric test and then engaged in a moderately violent video game that enabled the expression of aggression. Their scores on the game were related to the measured masculinity score on the test. A non-significant positive correlation emerged ($p>0.05$) but this was felt to be due to flaws in the methodology, especially in the way the data was measured. Further investigations using more appropriate tests of aggression and masculinity would be necessary for firm conclusions to be reached.

Writing the discussion

The discussion section of a report should be where conclusions about the data are drawn from the data analysis. This is where the findings are explained with a wider context of background theories and previous research in the area. It is a section where the researchers suggest limitations and strengths of the investigation and possible improvements that could be made to the methodology used. A discussion section also offers practical uses of the findings and potential implications for the knowledge with a wider context such as organisations, education, clinical practice or society as a whole.

3.6 Issues and debates (A level only)

Ethics

Ethical issues in using animals in research

A great deal of research into the biology of behaviour has been done on animals. There are several reasons for this. One is that non-humans have simpler but similar central nervous systems so it is easier to see what is happening in an organism that has only a few thousand neurons than in humans who have 100 billion. For example, Eric Kandel (1965) demonstrated the neurobiology of basic learning in *Aplysia californica* (Californian sea slug), which has a nervous system of 20 000 well-defined and easy-to-map neurons.

A further reason is that it is possible to control the environment in which non-humans live, enabling rigorous controls to be used in experimental research, such as raising and keeping the animal in isolation to avoid any effects of socialisation. This would not be possible with humans for obvious ethical reasons.

It is also possible to conduct invasive procedures on non-humans such as lesion or in-vivo stimulation studies. For example Olds and Milner (1954) attached electrodes to different areas of the brains of male black-hooded rats: the rats could activate the electrode via a lever thus stimulating that brain area. As a result of this study they found a potential mechanism of addiction as the rats that had electrodes wired to their reward system (nucleus accumbens and ventral tegmental areas) pursued this activity to the exclusion of other normally rewarding behaviour like eating and sex. Clearly this was harmful to the rats and it would not be possible, ethically, to do this research on humans.

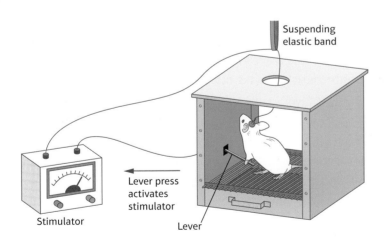

Figure 3.11 The apparatus used in Olds and Milner (1954)

Other research of this kind links to aggression lesions/stimulation to different areas of the brain, which have been shown to activate behaviour associated specifically with one type of aggression. For example, stimulation of the medial hypothalamus in a cat's brain produces offensive behaviour, stimulation of the dorsal hypothalamus produces defensive behaviour and stimulation of the lateral hypothalamus results in predatory behaviour (Flynn, Vanegas, Foote and Edwards, 1970).

There is a separate BPS code of ethics for psychological research using non-humans, which you can read about in Topic 4: *Learning theories*.

In this section, you will learn about issues and debates relevant to biological psychology.

You will have already noticed that issues and debates have been mentioned throughout this topic.

This section will draw together the main themes and ideas related to the biological approach as a whole.

Taking it further

Even with all the controls on research using non-humans there are still many animal rights organisations that regard such research as immoral and illegitimate, arguing it to be a case of 'speciesism', a form of prejudice similar to racism or sexism. This idea was popularised by Peter Singer in his 1975 book *Animal Liberation* in which he proposed that despite the differences between humans and non-humans both shared the capacity to suffer and so must be treated equally in situations where this might occur. You can find out more on the British Union for the Abolition of Vivisection (BUAV) website.

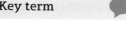

Key term

Artificial neural networks: computational models inspired by an animal's central nervous system (in particular the brain) that are capable of basic learning, generally presented as systems of interconnected nodes or neurones that can compute values from inputs.

As technology improves the way we can model and access the brain, the need for animal studies decreases. Sophisticated scanning techniques mean that we can now see what is happening under controlled conditions in a human brain, and **artificial neural networks** have been developed, which are capable of being lesioned to see the effect on the workings of the system.

Ethical issues in researching aggression with humans

Research involving human participants faces its own ethical challenges, for example the use of scanning techniques is not without cost to the participants. PET scans require the injection of radioactive dye to the bloodstream and most scans require the person to remain still for an extended period in a very enclosed space. This goes against the guideline of protection if a participant is subjected to repeated PET scans. Raine's study, for example, used PET scans. However, in the case of the control group the scans were being done for other medical purposes rather than just for the sake of the research, and in the case of the criminals they wished to gather evidence to help their case that they were not guilty of crime by reason of insanity. However, this raises a particular issue with consent and whether the murderers would have participated under duress.

One of the tenets of ethical research is that the participant should leave the study in the same state/condition in which they started. It could be argued that if they have undergone a brain scan they may leave with knowledge that changes their view of themselves. For example if the scan identifies brain structural differences associated with impulsive aggression the person may feel differently about themselves.

Issues of reductionism

Reductionism is the belief that complex things can be explained through the action of simple mechanisms.

It is argued that in order to fulfil the requirements of being scientific, reductionism is necessary because it reduces behaviour to a simple testable set of variables. However, this may be at the cost of validity as the bigger picture is ignored in favour of a simplistic and mechanistic explanation. Scanners can tell us which part of the brain is active when we perform an action but it cannot tell us what motivates us to perform the action in the first place.

Reductionist explanations, such as the nativist genetic view, suggest a lack of free will as heredity and chemical imbalances are thought to dictate our behaviour. Broader biological theories suggest that behaviour like aggression can be reduced to the action of chemicals in specific brain areas. Raine discovered that impulsive murderers had differences in the activity in various areas of their brains. The murderers, not the researchers, wanted to argue that this meant that they were somehow less responsible for their actions; indeed, they were trying to avoid the ultimate punishment for their crime by arguing that they were only guilty by reason of insanity and tried to prove this by showing that their brains operated differently from other people.

Such explanations neglect factors at other levels that interact with each other to produce the behaviour. In the case of aggression, looking at genetic inheritance can only be part of the picture; it has a part to play, but on its own can explain very few cases of aggression. However if you add genetic inheritance to an upbringing where aggression was regularly modelled in the family and cultural factors, such as approval of violence, there is a much more valid explanation.

Issues of socially sensitive research

Research into the topic of aggression is socially sensitive. This means that the findings have social consequences for individuals or groups of people beyond the setting of the study itself.

Socially sensitive research is likely to gain attention in the media because it has implications for society.

Neurological explanations for various types of behaviour are examples of such research. These include research studies that link genetics to homosexuality, intelligence and aggression.

You will be familiar with one of Adrian Raine's studies as it is the classic study detailed earlier in this topic. Raine's research is very socially sensitive as it went against the prevailing view that crime was a result of social and environmental factors imposed on the person, such as poor nurturing in childhood, rather than a result of individual differences in biology. For example, Raine's (1997) research found that the brain scans of people convicted of impulsive murder showed differences in the areas associated with impulse control. This suggests that a physical marker could be identified for this kind of crime, so it might be possible in the future to screen the population and identify future criminals.

This research caused controversy perhaps because in the past, research that has linked biology to behaviour has been used to justify extremist views and social policies, such as eugenics where individuals belonging to certain social groups were subjected to compulsory sterilisation (or worse) as an attempt to control the gene pool by removing undesirable genes.

One outcome of a neuro-criminological stance might be the medicalisation of criminal behaviour. If brain scans reveal differences that are associated with aggressive behaviour then perhaps it is a form of disorder or illness. This leads to issues about personal responsibility when crime is committed, where it could be claimed that such behaviour is beyond the control of the individual, but also leads to issues about what to do with such people. It could be argued that this is an ethical 'slippery slope' that could lead to pre-emptive action being taken to control the behaviour of people identified as having the biological markers for crime before any crime is committed.

Issues regarding the use of psychological knowledge in society

Psychological knowledge can be used to improve people's lives either by providing treatments or understanding for problem behaviour. Drug addiction is one area that has benefited from psychological knowledge. For example, understanding the physiological changes that underlie addiction to drugs has furthered treatments to the extent that some researchers (Van den Oever et al., 2008) are beginning to develop pharmacological treatments that may be used in the future to help avoid relapse.

Insight into to the contributory role of genes, hormones and brain structures on aggressive behaviour can also be beneficial to society, as by understanding the causes of such behaviour it is possible, in some cases, to avoid it. Research shows how aggression can result from the interaction between genes, hormonal factors and brain structures. This provides an explanation as to why some people may be more aggressive than others and potentially allows for predictions of risk to be made. This might, in the future, allow for those identified as at risk to experience a modified environment that reduces the risk of aggressive behaviour patterns developing, therefore benefiting both the individual and society.

> **Taking it further**
>
> Do some research on eugenics. This was a popular social movement in many countries in the early part of the 20th century. This will help you understand the extreme ways in which a biological explanation for behaviour can be used. You could start by looking at Sir Francis Galton's work on inheritance and intelligence.

Issues relating to psychology as a science

The biological approach is arguably the most scientific in psychology. It has as its subject matter physical aspects of behaviour that can be objectively measured. For example, changes in the chemical make-up of synapses can be measured by the use of sensitive mass spectrometry, which is a technique that can identify the amount and types of chemicals present in a sample of brain tissue based on their mass and charge. Such scientific techniques can serve to increase the credibility and status of psychology, making it more in line with the natural sciences of biology, chemistry and physics.

However, not all measures in biological psychology are completely objective, as you have seen in this topic the correlational method is a common technique that lacks some of the rigour of science in that clear cause and effect conclusions cannot be drawn. Ethically, sometimes this is all that can be established as to do full experimental research could require the manipulation of an aspect of human physiology, for example the control of hormone levels associated with aggressive behaviour in groups of babies to establish whether such hormones have an effect on their development.

The use of scientific techniques that identify and measure physical structures has led to a much deeper understanding of the central nervous system and has established facts about the foundations of behaviour, such as how synaptic transmission works and the role of the action potential.

However, this leaves psychology open to charges of reductionism as it seeks and identifies simple biological mechanisms that underlie complex human behaviours, such as aggression.

Issues relating to how our psychological understanding has developed over time

Physiognomy (judging someone's nature or character by their appearance) has been evident throughout history and it is only with recent scientific advances in brain scanning that the focus of biological explanations has shifted to the structure and function of the brain.

In the late 19th and early 20th centuries, explanations for criminal behaviour (including aggression) drew on Darwin's theories and include the work of Cesare Lombroso (1835–1909). Lombroso proposed that there was a physical 'type' of person linked to crime, and that such types represented a more primitive version of humanity, essentially uncivilised in nature, thereby linking a form of behaviour to a physical difference between people. Although Lombroso's specific ideas have been discredited, the idea that our genetic make-up plays a part in criminal behaviour has not. Recent studies, such as Barnes, Beaver and Boutwell (2011), do show that for lifelong persistent criminal behaviour there seems to be a strong genetic influence, but this is not manifested in physiognomy.

Sir Francis Galton, working around the same time as Lombroso, took a more scientific stance and photographed criminals to produce a composite picture of a 'criminal', thus identifying the physical characteristics associated with crime. Phrenologists related the role of brain structure to behaviour and personality by attempting to map behavioural characteristics to bumps on the head, supposedly caused by areas of the brain that differed in size. Such ideas now are regarded as pseudoscientific.

Early treatments for psychological conditions included trepanning, which is simply boring a hole in the skull with the intention of letting 'evil spirits' out. However, nowadays, trepanning is only done in emergencies to relieve swelling on the brain, and is based on reliable information from brain scans, such as CAT or MRI, that show clearly what is going on within the skull.

Thus you can see that the focus of research has changed over time: from very broad, obvious physiological differences, such as in Lombroso's studies, to less obvious brain structural differences

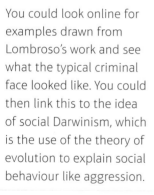

Taking it further

You could look online for examples drawn from Lombroso's work and see what the typical criminal face looked like. You could then link this to the idea of social Darwinism, which is the use of the theory of evolution to explain social behaviour like aggression.

that led to the study of the formation of bumps on the skull, to modern brain-scanning techniques, such as those used by Raine.

Issues related to the nature versus nurture debate

Theories within the biological approach tend to have their roots in the nature side of the debate, as it often focuses on the role that genetics plays in programming the way biological structures develop in the brain and/or in influencing the release of hormones. This can be seen in the genetic studies that suggest a role for heredity in aggression, such as that of Brendgen et al., (2005) who found a high concordance for physical aggression in MZ twins compared to DZ twins.

The nature side of the debate encompasses the evolutionary explanation of human behaviour by proposing that aspects of human behaviour are biologically determined. This is because genes that programme for such behaviour convey an adaptive advantage for the individuals who possess them, which leads to those genes surviving and being passed on through the generations. This includes behaviour such as male aggression, because a clear adaptive advantage can be proposed for it. However, because the genome changes very slowly compared to the environment, these genes are still present, as they do not convey any disadvantage for males who have them. However, such explanations can be criticised because they cannot be subjected to direct scientific testing as the conditions in which the genome developed no longer exist.

An extreme version of this view of genetic determinism ignores the role of nurture that is provided by the environment as the person grows and develops. As you can see in the section on socially sensitive research, this can be detrimental both to individuals and to society. Furthermore, no sensible psychologist would take such an extreme stance. The brain continues to develop throughout life, especially during childhood, and its structure is affected by experience, showing how nature and nurture are interactive. Research on rats, in which they are allocated to an enriched or impoverished environment for an extended period and then measures taken of their brain density, has repeatedly shown that those given the enriched environment have greater cortical density than those in the poor environment, thus showing that nurture affects our biology. Post-mortem studies comparing the brain density of college-educated individuals with that of less well-educated individuals found more dendrites on the nerve cells of college-educated individuals, suggesting a similar environmental effect can be found in humans (Jacobs et al., 1993). McGuire et al., (2006), established differences in the hippocampal areas (involved in consolidation of spatial memory) in licensed London taxi drivers compared to matched controls, showing how lifestyle contributes to changes in brain structure.

An interactionist approach to this debate is therefore supported by the evidence rather than a nature or nurture view.

Issues of social control

Social control can result from knowledge about the role of biological factors in behaviour, such as aggression and addiction, because knowing what causes problematic behaviours can mean that people may strive to predict which people will go on to develop certain traits. If research into brain dysfunction, such as the studies of Adrian Raine, uncover biological determinants of aggressive behaviour, researchers may try to use this to scan people early on in life to find out who is at risk. With this knowledge, there is a possibility that people could be labelled as potentially violent, leading to unfair treatment. If we know who will become violent, we may try to control them to prevent the behaviour developing, so they may be subjected to potentially unnecessary monitoring or therapy.

Unethical treatments, such as prefrontal lobotomies, have been used to control antisocial behaviour, based on weak evidence about the role of the prefrontal cortex in controlling behaviour. Despite the limited evidence available, during the 1940s and 1950s in the USA 20 000 such operations took place, often with poor outcomes for the patients. Another way in which biological knowledge has been used to control people is through the chemical castration of males, which involves giving antiandrogenic drugs (male hormone blockers). These reduce the sex drive and some US courts have sentenced male sex offenders to undergo this therapy. Some would argue that this is an excessive punishment that unfairly affects the minds and bodies of those to whom it is applied, but others state that it allows men convicted of sexual crime to avoid prison. A study into the effects of one such drug found that, when taken for a year, it successfully reduced sexually deviant behaviour in males, and that there were no lasting side effects from taking the drug (Gagne, 1981).

However, as there is no research suggesting that any of these biological factors are definitive causes of aggression, this form of control and monitoring may be unfairly administered. In 2014, researchers at the University of Lincoln reported that they had been trying to develop a genetic test to predict aggressive behaviour in dogs. The research aimed to help predict which dogs may be a risk, to help owners manage their animals' behaviour better and to prevent accidents. This would be a positive application of this knowledge, so the argument might be that issuing forms of 'social control' in relation to predicting aggression do not have to be considered a negative.

Practical issues in the design and implementation of research

Brain scans are incredibly complex methods of data collection that are becoming more popular in biological research as the methods are developed further. Many argue though that while brain-scanning techniques are hailed as objective measures of brain structure and function, they are heavily flawed and may not tell us what they claim to. When scans take images of the brain, the scanner picks up lots of information that it then has to collate and interpret to create the image that can then used by the researchers. Often brain activity is widespread during different activities, for example reading a book may require the use of a variety of different brain areas rather than just one 'reading' brain centre. This means that when we look at very complex behaviours, the images are unlikely to show only one brain area as being active, and if it did, this would probably be very unreliable. Consider Raine et al's., (1997) study into impulsive murderers in which many different brain regions showed 'abnormal' levels of activity. However, when comparing this study to other similar studies, the role of the prefrontal cortex is highlighted as being important in this kind of impulsive aggression, but we have no way of knowing whether this is just a small part of a much larger brain activity pattern associated with this type of behaviour. Simply because the findings have been supported by other brain-scanning studies does not automatically make the findings more reliable. There is a possibility that some of these supposed patterns of activity associated with behaviours such as aggression occur purely by chance. When the scanners are sifting through a vast amount of information about the structure and function of brain areas, using the same scanners with the same interpretation mechanisms will undoubtedly yield similar results, but if the scanning method itself is flawed, the evidence gathered has no reliability.

Knowledge check

Content

Can you explain the role of the central nervous system (CNS) and neurotransmitters in human behaviour, including the structure and role of the neuron, the function of the neurotransmitters and synaptic transmission?

Can you describe the effect of recreational drugs on the transmission process in the central nervous system?

Are you able to describe the structure of the brain and explain the role of different areas of the brain (for example the prefrontal cortex) in governing human behaviour?

Are you confident that you can evaluate the link between brain functioning and aggression?

Can you evaluate the link between brain damage and human behaviour, including aggression?

Can you define evolution and explain the role of evolution in human development?

Are you able to apply your knowledge of evolution and natural selection to explain human behaviour, including aggression?

Are you able to explain Freud's psychodynamic approach to understanding human behaviour with reference to the id, ego, superego, catharsis and the importance of the unconscious?

Can you apply Freud's theory of personality to explain individual differences in the development of human behaviour, including aggression?

Can you compare Freud's psychodynamic explanation to a biological explanation of aggression?

Can you evaluate the role of hormones (for example testosterone) in the development of human behaviour, in particular aggression?

Methods

Are you able to explain the use of the correlational research method in biological psychology and compare co-variables to see what relationship they have to each other?

Can you identify the types of correlation – positive and negative – and how to use a scatter diagram to see them?

Can you evaluate correlational research in terms of the issues surrounding their use in biological psychology, including determining cause and effect, and the influence of other variables?

Are you able to analyse and draw conclusions from correlational data, including using scatter diagrams and inferential statistical testing (Spearman's rho)?

Do you understand levels of significance and are you able to use these to interpret the results of an inferential test?

Are you able to identify levels of measurement (ordinal, interval, nominal) in order to select an appropriate inferential test?

Can you compare observed and critical values on a critical values table to check whether results are significant?

Can you identify and write operationalised alternate, experimental (directional and non-directional) and null hypotheses?

In the content section, you are required to describe, evaluate and apply your knowledge of mechanisms within the body and how they affect human behaviour such as aggression and drug taking.

To check your evaluation skills, refer to the introduction section of this book and review 'how to evaluate a theory'. Remember that you may be asked to consider issues of validity, reliability, credibility, generalisability, objectivity and subjectivity in your evaluation of theories.

Link

For information on levels of measurement, alternate, experimental (directional and non-directional) and null hypotheses, and independent and dependent variables, please see the Methods section of Topic 2: *Cognitive psychology*.

Can you identify and write independent and dependent variables in experiments and co-variables in correlations and fully operationalise these?

Are you able to explain the use of control groups, randomising to groups and sampling?

Can you describe and explain the use of other biological research methods, including CAT scans, PET scans and fMRI?

Can you describe and explain the use of brain-scanning techniques to investigate human behaviour such as aggression?

Can you describe and evaluate one twin study, for example Gottesman and Shields (1966), and one adoption study, for example Cadoret and Stewart (1991)?

Studies

In the studies section, you are required to describe, evaluate and apply your knowledge of one classic and one contemporary study of biological psychology.

To check your evaluation skills, refer to the introduction section of this book and review 'how to evaluate a study'. Remember that you may be asked to consider issues of validity, reliability, credibility, generalisability, objectivity and subjectivity in your evaluation of studies.

Can you describe the classic study by Raine et al. (1997), Brain abnormalities in murderers indicated by positron emission tomography, in terms of its aim(s), method, procedure, results and conclusions?

Are you able to evaluate Raine et al's. (1997) study in terms of strengths and weaknesses?

Are you able to identify and describe the aims, method, procedure, results and conclusions of a contemporary study from the following list and evaluate the study in terms of strengths and weaknesses?

- Li et al. (2013). Abnormal function of the posterior cingulate cortex in heroin addicted users during resting-state and drug-cue stimulation task.

- Brendgen et al. (2005). Examining genetic and environmental effects on social aggression: A study of 6-year-old twins.

- Van den Oever et al. (2008). Prefrontal cortex AMPA receptor plasticity is crucial for cue-induced relapse to heroin-seeking.

Key question

Are you able to identify and describe a key question in biological psychology that is relevant to today's society?

Can you explain this using concepts, theories and research that you have studied in this topic?

Practical investigation

Have you designed and conducted a correlational study to investigate an area of biological psychology?

Are you able to link your study to aggression or attitudes to drug use?

Can you justify your choice of research questions or hypotheses?

Can you justify your choice of design and sampling method, and explain the ethical considerations?

Can you describe and analyse the quantitative data that you gathered for your study and how you presented your data (table and scatter diagram)?

Are you able to explain, justify and interpret the non-parametric test of difference (Spearman's rho) that you used on your data?

Are you able to draw conclusions from your descriptive data (strength/direction) and inferential test (including level of significance)?

Can you produce an abstract of the research method and a discussion section that includes conclusions?

Are you able to write up the procedure, results and discussion sections in a report style?

Issues and debates (A level only)

Can you identify ethical issues associated with theory and research within the biological approach?

Can you comment on the practical and methodological issues in the design and implementation of research within the biological approach?

Can you explain how theories, research and concepts within the biological approach might be considered reductionist?

Can you compare theories and research within biological psychology to show different ways of explaining and understanding aggression?

Are you able to discuss whether theories, concepts, research and methodology within biological psychology are scientific?

Are you able to discuss the nature–nurture debate in the context of biological psychology, in terms of which parts emphasise the role of nature or nurture, or the interaction between them?

Do you understand how biological psychology has developed over time?

Do you understand what is meant by social control and how research within biological psychology may be used to control behaviour?

Can you show how the theories, concepts and research within biological psychology can be used in a practical way in society?

Are you able to understand what is meant by socially sensitive research and explain how research in biological psychology might be considered to be socially sensitive?

> Remember that issues and debates are synoptic. This means you may be asked to make connections by comparing issues and debates across topics in psychology or comment on not upon issues and debates within unseen material.

References

Brendgen, M., Dionne, G., Girard, A. et al. (2005). Examining genetic and environmental effects on social aggression: A study of 6-year-old twins. *Child development*, 76, pp. 930–946.

Gottesman, I. I. and Shields. J. (1976a). A critical review of recent adoption, twin, and family studies of schizophrenia: Behavioral genetics perspectives. *Schizophrenia Bulletin*, 2, pp. 360–401.

Li, Q., Yang, W.C., Wang, Y.R., Huang, Y.F., Li, W., Zhu, J., Zhang, Y., Zhao, L.Y., Qin, W., Yuan, K., von Deneen, K.M., Wang, W. and Tian, J. (2013). Abnormal function of the posterior cingulate cortex in heroin addicted users during resting-state and drug-cue stimulation task. *Chinese Medical Journal* (Engl), 126(4), pp. 734–739.

Raine, A., Buchsbaum, M and LaCasse, L. (1997). Brain abnormalities in murderers indicated by positron emission tomography. *Biological Psychiatry*, 42, pp. 495–508.

Van den Oever, M. C., Goriounova, N. A., Li, K. W., Van der Schors, R. C., Binnekade, R., Schoffelmeer, A. N., Mansvelder, H. D., Smit, A. B., Spijker, S. and De Vries, T. J. (2008), Prefrontal cortex AMPA receptor plasticity is crucial for cue-induced relapse to heroin-seeking. *Nature Neuroscience*, 11, pp. 1053–1058.

Learning can be defined as a process that leads to relatively stable behavioural change. When we learn, we change the way we see our environment, the way we interpret information and ultimately the way we interact or behave. Learning theories are associated with the behaviourist approach and the work of pioneering psychologists such as John B. Watson (1878–1958), B.F. Skinner (1904–1990) and Albert Bandura (born 1925) who believed that the focus of psychology should be on observable behaviours, as internal moods or thoughts are too subjective and untestable. This approach dominated early 20th-century psychological research.

In this topic, you will learn about:

- the three learning theories that explain the acquisition of behaviour – classical conditioning (learning by association), operant conditioning (learning by consequence) and social learning theory (learning through observation and reinforcement)
- how learning theories can explain the acquisition and maintenance of phobias and how the approach can offer practical treatment solutions for phobias, for example systematic desensitisation
- how individuals differ because of different learning experiences and environmental influences, for example the role of rewards and punishments
- the use of observations and content analysis as research methods, and issues surrounding the use of animals in laboratory experiments
- classic and contemporary studies of human and animal learning
- key issues in the relevance of learning theories to today's society, such as whether or not airline companies should offer treatment programmes for fear of flying
- wider issues in psychology including ethics, reductionism, the nature–nurture debates and psychology as a science
- how to carry out a practical research exercise relevant to the psychology of learning theories.

4.1 Content
Learning outcomes

In this section, you will learn about:

- the main features of classical conditioning and Pavlov's (1927) experiment with salivation in dogs
- the main features of operant conditioning and the properties of reinforcement
- behaviour modification including shaping behaviour
- the main features of social learning theory
- Albert Bandura's Bobo doll experiments
- how learning theories explain the acquisition of and maintenance of phobias
- treatments for phobias based on theories of learning.

Learning theory has its basis within behaviourism, an approach or perspective within psychology that emphasises 'nurture' – the importance of understanding how behaviour is shaped by the environment around us – rather than biological mechanisms within us (nature). By noting how behaviour is shaped by environment rather than biology such theorists emphasise the way in which a human baby is effectively 'tabula rasa' – a blank slate, which external forces can then shape and mould accordingly.

Classical conditioning

Classical conditioning is learning by association. When we pair a new stimulus with an existing stimulus-response link, we learn to associate the two stimuli and respond in a similar manner to both. For example, think about the following familiar scenario. Your cat anticipates being fed when you take a can of cat food from the cupboard. This can be explained by the process of classical conditioning as follows.

The first part of the process involves a naturally occurring stimulus that will automatically elicit a response in an organism. Food is an **unconditioned stimulus (UCS)** for your cat and salivation in response to the presentation of food is an **unconditioned response (UCR)**. No learning is required here as salivation is an automatic response to the presentation of food. At this point of the conditioning process, there is also a **neutral stimulus (NS)** that produces no effect as yet – the sound of an opening can of cat food. There is, however, no innate reflex response to this sound. According to the theory, the neutral stimulus must be paired with the UCS to evoke a response.

If the neutral stimulus (NS) and the unconditioned stimulus (UCS) are repeatedly paired with each other an association is formed. The neutral stimulus now becomes the **conditioned stimulus (CS)** and the unconditioned response (UCR) becomes the **conditioned response (CR)**. Therefore, your cat salivates when it is presented with its food. If the sound of the opening can is paired multiple times with the presentation of its food, the sound alone will eventually trigger the conditioned response in your cat, as it will have learned that its food will be coming soon.

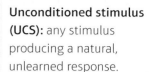

Key terms

Unconditioned stimulus (UCS): any stimulus producing a natural, unlearned response.

Unconditioned response (UCR): a response that is occurs naturally without any form of learning (a reflex action).

Neutral stimulus (NS): an environmental stimulus that does not of itself (without association) produce a response.

Conditioned stimulus: (CS): a stimulus that has been associated with an unconditioned stimulus so that it now produces the same response.

Conditioned response (CR): a behaviour that is shown in response to a learned stimulus.

Pets learn to associate the sound of the tin being opened and/or the sound of their bowls to know they will be fed, which conditions them to come running.

Stimulus generalisation and discrimination

In classical conditioning there is a tendency for the conditioned stimulus (CS) to produce the same behaviour to a similar stimulus after the response has been conditioned. Using our current example, your cat may come running to any tin being opened in the kitchen – tinned pineapple, baked beans and not just cat food! Generalisation here suggests that the stimulus triggering a reaction does not have to be the exact one involved in the process of learning, but that the more similar it is, the more likely it will produce a conditioned response. It is also possible that discrimination can occur, meaning that over a period of time, learning only occurs in response to a specific stimulus. For example, that your cat may only respond to a can opening at a certain time of day or your cat only responds to a tin of food but not a glass jar.

Links to the evolutionary approach

The ability to generalise has important evolutionary implications. If our ancestors ate red berries while foraging and this made them seriously ill they may have thought twice before eating some purple berries. Although the berries are slightly different, they are also similar and could therefore cause the same negative consequences. Such cautious behaviour would have helped to ensure their survival. Similarly, discrimination may also have proved useful to our ancestors' survival. If they took the risk of eating the purple berries and they produced no negative consequences, they would be able to make a similar distinction in future and provide the hunter–gatherers with another valuable food source so enhancing their own survival.

Exam tip

To practise making stimulus response associations and to help you split the process down, consider the following examples. Take each of them, and see if you can identify the separate components of classical conditioning. You might represent this either as a cartoon or simply as a table. You need to identify Unconditioned Stimulus (UCS), Unconditioned Response (UCR), Neutral Stimulus (NS) Conditioned Stimulus (CS) and Conditioned Response (CR) for each scenario.

Scenarios:

At home, whenever someone flushes the toilet, your shower becomes very hot, causing you to jump out of the way of the very hot water. As this continues over time, you begin to jump back to avoid the very hot water whenever you hear the toilet being flushed.

You are a very young infant. You are taken into a laboratory. An experimenter shows you a white rat before sounding a loud startling noise. This continues. You start to become unhappy at the sight of any white rat.

Walking home from college your route takes you past a house where there is a large dog. It barks loudly at you. This unnerves you. So you take a different route home, past a smaller dog that is not so loud.

Lois and Laurence are brother and sister. Every time they go into the kitchen they get hungry.

In the exam, it will be important to show your understanding of these terms and how they apply to situations. Practise applying the components of classical conditioning to different scenarios. Your use of these terms and their correct application to the scenario given illustrates your understanding of key components of the principle of classical conditioning.

Extinction and spontaneous recovery

As the first term extinction, suggests, this is the removal (death) of a behaviour. Thinking of our cat example, if the conditioned stimulus (the sound of a can opening) is continually presented without any food being paired with it, the cat will gradually learn to disassociate the two stimuli – and so will not salivate on hearing a can opening. However, this association may not be entirely lost.

If the tin is once again paired with the food following extinction, the cat will quickly learn to associate the food with the tin. This accelerated form of learning is known as spontaneous recovery and means that extinction is not the same thing as 'unlearning'. While the response may disappear, it has certainly not been eradicated.

Pavlov's (1927) experiment with salivation in dogs

Ivan Petrovich Pavlov, a Russian physiologist, and winner of the Nobel Prize in Physiology or Medicine in 1904, had a principal interest in studying digestive processes. Yet he also made what could be described as one of the most profound contributions to psychology, specifically to learning by association and classical conditioning theory. His landmark discovery came as a result of his experiment with salivation in dogs.

Pavlov found that when a dog encounters the stimulus of food, saliva starts to pour from the salivary glands; saliva is of course required, to make food easier to swallow and also contains enzymes to break down certain compounds in the food. While carrying out his experiments, Pavlov became involved in studying reflex reactions as he observed that the dogs drooled and produced saliva without the proper stimulus. Pavlov hypothesised that the dogs were reacting to the lab coats of his assistants. Each time the dogs were presented with food, the assistant presenting the food was wearing a lab coat. In essence, the dogs were responding as if food was on its way in the presence of a lab coat.

In a sequence of experiments, Pavlov then tried to establish how the two phenomena were linked. Pavlov created a soundproofed lab to see if the presentation of precise stimuli would evoke a response in conditions that ensured no direct contact between the dogs and experimenter. Pavlov knew that food (UCS) would lead to salivation in the mouth of an animal (UCR). Pavlov then used a neutral stimulus – an item that in itself would not elicit a response – for example a metronome. Over several learning trials the dog was presented with the ticking of the metronome immediately before the food appeared. If the metronome was ticking in close association with their meal, the dogs learned to associate the sound of the metronome with food. After a while, just at the sound of the metronome, they responded by drooling. Pavlov concluded that environmental stimuli that previously had no relation to a reflex action, for example the sounding of a metronome could, through repeated pairings, trigger a salivation reflex and that through the process of associative learning (conditioning) the conditioned stimulus leads to a conditioned response.

Having established the existence of this associative learning, Pavlov wished to establish the reliability of his findings. He set out to see if the same system of learning would work with neutral stimuli, for example the presentation of a vanilla odour, and a visual test involving a rotating disc being seen prior to food being given. Pavlov went on to pair a further neutral stimulus with the conditioned stimulus, for example, a shape or colour (CS2) with the sound of a metronome (CS1), and found that higher order conditioning was possible. He also found that dogs showed stimulus generalisation to sounds of a similar tone, but were able to discriminate between sounds that were of a quite different tone. The more similarity there was between a new neutral stimulus and the conditioned stimulus, the greater the amount of drooling from the dog.

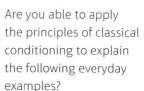

Taking it further

Are you able to apply the principles of classical conditioning to explain the following everyday examples?

- When you hear the national anthem at a world class event, does it have any effect on you?

- When someone blows up a balloon, why might you flinch as it increases in size?

- When you walk into a doctor's or dentist's surgery, how do you feel when you detect the clinical smell of disinfectant?

Psychology as a science

Psychology's status as a science has been the subject of debate. A common argument against psychology as a science suggests that it does not have a common or established set of ideas accepted by the discipline, unlike more traditional sciences such as chemistry or physics. Against this, however, the scientific methods used by psychologists are often cited as an example of why psychology should be categorised as a science. Scientific methods refer to the use of observation, experimentation and the scrutiny of data to support proposed theories. Therefore research should focus on observable, measurable phenomena.

John Watson, founder of behaviourism as an approach in psychology, proposed a manifesto, 'Psychology as the Behaviorist views it' (1913), that set out how psychological research should be conducted using a scientific methodology and principles. He stated that only directly observable behaviour, not consciousness, should be the topic of investigation and rigorous scientific methods should be used.

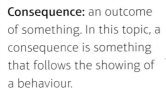
Key terms

Consequence: an outcome of something. In this topic, a consequence is something that follows the showing of a behaviour.

Instrumental learning: the term Edward Thorndike originally gave to the form of learning where the consequence of a behaviour dictates the further repeating of it.

Law of effect: created by Thorndike, suggesting that behaviour with a nice consequence following it will lead to replication of behaviour. Behaviour with an unpleasant consequence following it will lead to it being withdrawn.

Operant conditioning

Operant conditioning involves learning through **consequence**. Through operant conditioning, an association is made between a behaviour and a consequence for that behaviour. Put simply, if we get punished for a particular behaviour, according to the theory it is likely that we will not repeat that behaviour in future. However, if we show a behaviour that is followed by a positive experience – maybe praise or some physical reward – it is likely that this behaviour will be repeated.

For example, when a laboratory pigeon taps a blue button with its beak, it receives a food pellet as a reward. However, when the pigeon taps a red button it receives a mild electric shock. As a result of learning these consequences, the pigeon learns to press the blue button but avoid the red button in future.

It was Edward Thorndike (1911) who originally labelled this form of learning **instrumental learning**. His research involved what he called the puzzle box. This was a box, in which he placed a kitten; it had to solve a puzzle in order to escape the box to receive a food reward. Initially, he observed that the kitten would climb everywhere around the box – quite randomly – and accidentally hit the latch to open the door. Once the kitten opened the door it was given food. However after several learning trials the kitten escaped faster. So the kitten had learned by trial and error learning (not by insight) that finding and opening the latch to get out meant it was rewarded by food. Thorndike termed this the **Law of effect** stating that a response followed by a pleasant consequence, for example being rewarded, tends to be repeated while one followed by an unpleasant consequence, for example punishment, tends not to be repeated. Moreover, according to Thorndike's Law of Exercise, all things being equal, the more often a response is performed in a given situation, the more likely it is to be repeated.

Positive and negative reinforcement

B.F. Skinner renamed instrumental conditioning as operant conditioning. Skinner was a true scientist at heart, and felt that he could not study something that was not directly observable, such as the mind. He believed that to understand human behaviour, it was necessary to apply scientific principles and methods. He felt the description operant conditioning was more appropriate as with this form of learning you are 'operating' on or being influenced by the environment.

Skinner started his research in the 1930s, using lab experimentation with his 'Skinner Box' (see illustration below) – which was essentially a box that could dispense food and electric shocks to animals such as rats or pigeons. Skinner created the **ABC model of operant conditioning** to explain how learning works:

- antecedent: the Skinner box would present a stimulus (lights / noise) that triggers a behaviour

- behaviour: a response made by the animal that can be observed (measured) as an outcome of the antecedent

- consequence: the reward / punishment following the behaviour (shock / food).

The stimulus-response association is only repeated or learned if the consequence of the pairing is a positive one. A negative consequence would weaken the stimulus-response link.

Therefore, if the rat or the pigeon is given something pleasurable like a food pellet following a desired behaviour, for example lever pressing, they are more likely to repeat this behaviour in future. This is known as positive reinforcement. On the other hand, negative reinforcement is the removal of something unpleasant in response to the desired behaviour. This will also increase the likelihood of the behaviour being repeated, in order to avoid the unpleasant stimulus. Therefore if a rat or a pigeon is given an electric shock until a lever is pressed, they are more likely to press the lever again to avoid electric shocks in future.

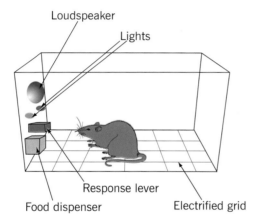

Figure 4.1 A Skinner box

In summary, both positive and negative reinforcement produce repeated behaviour. Punishment on the other hand, weakens the behaviour by presenting something unpleasant or painful whenever the behaviour is shown. Therefore if a rat presses a lever and is given an electric shock, it will stop pressing the lever to make sure it does not get another electric shock in future. Like reinforcement, punishment can be both positive and negative.

Positive punishment (P+) – is adding an aversive stimulus that will reduce the showing of a behaviour. For example, a child behaves badly at a party. The parents shout at and scold the child. This reduces the showing of a behaviour by presenting an unpleasant stimulus (shouting and scolding) when the behaviour occurs.

Negative punishment (P-) – The removal of a liked/desirable stimuli to reduce the showing of a behaviour. For example, if a dog jumps on a person to greet them but the person walks away just as the dog jumps, they are removing their attention from the dog, and so will reduce the frequency of jumping in the future.

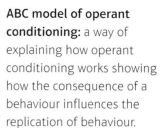

Key term

ABC model of operant conditioning: a way of explaining how operant conditioning works showing how the consequence of a behaviour influences the replication of behaviour.

Exam tip

It is important to notice how the words *positive* and *negative* are used in this context. They have a particular meaning. These are used in the mathematical sense – of adding to or taking away. So punishment and reinforcement can be both negative and positive in terms of the stimulus provided (good things can be added or taken away).

Taking it further

Dog training is often based on the principles of operant conditioning. Look at the following examples and identify whether it is positive reinforcement, negative reinforcement, positive punishment or negative punishment.

- You give your dog some doggie chocolate every time he sits to your command 'sit'.

- Your dog jumps on you very excitedly every time you return home. You remove your attention from your dog by turning your back and not fussing over it every time it jumps in this manner.

- You sound an air horn every time your dog barks excessively.

Key term

Token economy: a treatment method that provides secondary reinforcement for a desirable behaviour that can be saved up or exchanged for a primary reinforcer.

WIDER ISSUES

Practical issues in the design and implementation of research

Psychologists like Pavlov and Skinner chose to study animals for a number of reasons. Undoubtedly, humans and animals share many biological characteristics, which allow researchers to draw conclusions from one species to another. Moreover, animals allow researchers a higher degree of experimental control and objectivity compared to human participants. Indeed, Pavlov's and Skinner's experiments, which were generalised to humans have made a huge contribution to the understanding of human behaviour. Others however criticise animal research for its lack of generalisability, suggesting that extrapolating from one species to another is problematic. In biological terms, evolution has created very specific demands for each species and, with it, its own set of unique behaviours. There are also significant brain differences between humans and non-human animals. Validity is also an issue given that animals are studied in an artificial laboratory setting. Researchers need to be aware of such issues when looking to extend the results gained from animal studies to humans.

Types of reinforcer

In operant conditioning there are two types of reinforcer that increase the likelihood of a behaviour being learned. Primary reinforcers occur naturally and satisfy basic human needs such as food, water and shelter. Secondary reinforcers, on the other hand, only strengthen the behaviour because they are associated with a primary reinforcer, for example money can be used to buy food, accommodation, clothing and so on.

To give these types of reinforcer a practical context, a **token economy** is based on the principles of operant conditioning. It has the aim of trying to encourage desirable behaviour through a system of reward, and reduce undesirable behaviour through withdrawal of reward (punishment). The tokens used in such a system are secondary reinforcers as it is these that will be exchangeable for primary reinforcers. The tokens are only given in return for showing the desired behaviour. The more tokens saved, the better the reward. Therefore through selective reinforcement, desirable behaviours are encouraged and undesirable behaviour extinguished. Token economies have been implemented in institutions such as schools and prisons. For example, students may be allocated tokens for good behaviour such as good attendance, punctuality, high test scores, etc. These can then be exchanged for items in the school shop or perhaps a school trip.

In some high security prisons, inmates are given credits for taking part in constructive activities such as going to the library, cleaning or learning to play an instrument. The credits can then be used to purchase tobacco, toiletries or time on the telephone.

WIDER ISSUES AND DEBATES

Issues of social control

Token economies provide a context for us to understand primary and secondary reinforcers. They have been used rather controversially in treatment of various abnormal behaviours. For example Paul and Lentz (1977) investigated the effectiveness of operant conditioning by reinforcing appropriate behaviour with 84 schizophrenic patients. Patients were given tokens as rewards when they behaved appropriately and these could be exchanged for luxury items. They found that the token economy reduced some schizophrenic symptoms, such as bizarre motor behaviours, for example rocking and blank staring, and was also successful in improving interpersonal skills and self-care skills. However they were not effective in treating the cognitive symptoms of schizophrenia, such as delusions and hallucinations, nor hostile behaviour such as screaming and swearing. They found that 11 per cent of token economy patients required drug treatment, compared to 100 per cent in their control group and concluded that operant conditioning is an effective means of treating people with chronic schizophrenia.

Paul and Lentz's study raises an important issue of social control. Some may argue that it is not morally correct for one person to control the behaviour of another and that this experiment violated the patients' basic human rights. The patients in this study had their rights to their personal properties and their freedom of choice with regard to treatment options constrained by the token economy. It is also possible that the token economy was for the benefit of the psychiatric staff by making the schizophrenic patients more manageable, rather than for the patients themselves, and so it also raises questions about the therapeutic goals of the treatment.

Schedules of reinforcement

While it would be easy to agree that the consequence of a behaviour will determine if the behaviour is shown again, the situation is somewhat more complicated than this. This is because when and how often you reinforce behaviour can also have a very big impact on the strength and likelihood of a behavioural response. Put very simply, a schedule of reinforcement is a 'rule' that dictates the situations in which a behaviour will be reinforced. It is quite possible that in some situations a behaviour might be reinforced every time it is seen (**continuous reinforcement**), although more realistically in the context of day-to-day life, a behaviour might be reinforced some of the time (**partial reinforcement**). Interestingly, a behaviour that is acquired through partial reinforcement might take longer to learn, but is more resistant to extinction. The four schedules of partial reinforcement are:

1 Fixed interval – the rewarding of a first correct response only after a preset amount of time has passed. For example, a rat in the Skinner box gets a food pellet for pressing the lever only after a 30-second time delay. Learning takes longer, but the response rate of the animal is higher towards the end of the learning. Interestingly also with this form of schedule there is a scalloping effect (a dramatic drop off in response immediately after reinforcement).

2 Variable interval – the rewarding of the first correct response after a set amount of time has passed; after which a new time period is set. Learning is still noticeable and the scalloping effect noticeable in fixed interval reinforcement is not seen here.

3 Fixed ratio – where a response is reinforced only after a specified number of responses, for example providing a food pellet to a rat after it presses a lever eight times.

4 Variable ratio – a response may be reinforced after a set number of correct responses is given. After this has been achieved, the number of correct responses in order for reinforcement to be given changes. Skinner argued that this form of schedule is good for maintaining behaviour.

Key terms

Continuous reinforcement: the desired behaviour is reinforced every time it occurs.

Partial reinforcement: the desired response is only reinforced some of the time.

Key term 💬

Successive approximations: rewarding behaviour for acting in a way that gets closer and closer to the desired behaviour.

WIDER ISSUES AND DEBATES

The use of psychological knowledge within society

The token economy has been a particularly successful example of where applications of operant techniques have been used in society. The token economy has been used in psychiatry, clinical psychology and education using patterns of reward to shape behaviour. Some token economies may take tokens away as punishment for undesirable behaviour, such as aggression. Ayllon and Milan (1979) reviewed a number of such programmes and found that they were successful for promoting certain behaviours, for example keeping rules and control over aggression. Research suggests, however, that the benefits of token economies are relatively short-lived and tend not to generalise beyond the institution itself. This raises a question over the rehabilitative value of token economies.

Behaviour modification (including shaping behaviour)

To modify means to change something. Behaviour modification is a therapy that has its theoretical basis in operant conditioning and the experiments of B.F. Skinner. The ideas behind behaviour modification are to:

- extinguish undesirable behaviour (by removing the reinforcer)
- replace original behaviour with a desirable behaviour and reinforce it.

Skinner was fascinated with trying to understand how more complicated behaviours could be learned over and above showing behaviour to get a pellet of food. Skinner developed the theory further to include the idea of behaviour shaping or what he referred to as 'the method of **successive approximations**'. In Skinner's system, at the start of a behaviour-shaping exercise, very general desired behaviours related to what you want to see are rewarded. Once this behaviour has been shown, the rewards become more selective so that only behaviours a little closer to the exact desired behaviour you wish to see are reinforced. This is in many ways a step-by-step process, gradually getting closer and closer to the desired behaviour change.

Behaviour modification has been used in a variety of contexts. It can be used as a mode of therapy to treat Attention Deficit Hyperactivity Disorder (ADHD), Obsessive Compulsive Disorder (OCD) and autism. The target behaviour is identified and then rewards are given for behaviours that gradually get closer to the target. For example, a therapist working with a child with autism, might use rewards to reinforce good behaviour and gradually become more selective in the distribution of rewards to encourage specific or problematic behaviour for the child.

Taking it further 🏳

Consider whether you have been part of a token economy in school or at home. How did you earn the tokens? What could they be exchanged for?

Exam tip

Separation anxiety is a common complaint among dog owners. Their dogs become destructive when left alone and show signs of anxiety when their owner prepares to leave the house. How could you use behaviour modification to counteract this negative behaviour so that a dog is calm and non-destructive when left alone?

Try to consider the following points:

- What clues may owners give to their dog that they are shortly going out? How could you counteract this?
- How would you change a dog's fearful, anxious mood to a pleasant, relaxed one instead?
- How could you change the anxiety about being left alone by using something the dog loves?
- How could you gradually accustom a dog to being alone?
- Should the owner make a fuss over the dog when they return?

Evaluation

What was accidentally observed by Pavlov is now a universally accepted principle in psychology. It has in many ways remained unchanged since it was formulated by Pavlov and remains one of the most important principles in psychology's history. It formed the basis for what would become known as the behavioural or learning approach.

Pavlov greatly influenced John Watson and B.F. Skinner, and continues to inspire psychological research to this day. Between 1997 and 2000, more than 220 articles appeared in scientific journals citing Pavlov's research on classical conditioning. Pavlov's contributions to psychology have helped shape the discipline and are likely to continue to shape our understanding of human behaviour well into the future.

A major strength of operant conditioning is that it can explain a wide assortment of behaviours, from addiction to language acquisition. A substance or activity can become addictive if it is rewarding; that is, if it is pleasurable or enjoyable. Skinner would argue that a child's correct utterances are positively reinforced. For instance, a child says 'juice' and the parent smiles and gives the child some juice as a result. Obviously, the child will find the outcome of saying this word rewarding and this in turn will aid the child's language development. The theory of operant conditioning also has practical applications. Token economies have been used successfully in psychiatric hospitals, schools and prisons.

Both classical and operant conditioning lay claims to being scientific. Concepts can be defined, precisely measured and controlled, as illustrated by both Pavlov's and Skinner's laboratory experiments on animals. As only observable behaviour is measured, it could be argued that this is an objective measure. Moreover, such experiments can be replicated – allowing for reliability to be assessed. However, this controlled environment is not a natural way to observe behaviour. The contrived and artificial nature of such experiments questions the ecological validity of the findings and the extent they can be applied to real-life settings.

A number of criticisms can be levied against learning theories. Of particular significance is that of reductionism: reducing all behaviour to learning through association or reinforcement. Both theories greatly underestimate the role of biological factors, including genetic differences and instincts, on behaviour. It could be said that Skinner's observations only account for observable behaviours and do not account for any unobservable behaviours, for example mental and emotional states, such as anger or happiness, making his explanations limited and oversimplified.

Some would argue that a major weakness is the use of animal research on which a large proportion of the theories are based. This raises the issue of extrapolating findings from animals and applying them to humans. Animals obviously have different anatomy and physiology and their day-to-day experiences are very different from humans; for example, animals do not reflect on their learning experiences with logic, patience or feelings like humans do. A fundamental difference between a rat and a human is language. A human can stop a behaviour simply by being told that no more rewards will be given. For a rat, this is obviously not an option and so it will continue to press a lever for a food pellet a long time after the food has stopped.

The use of laboratory experiments with animals in classical and operant conditioning also raises a number of ethical issues. It could be argued that Pavlov's research, for instance, caused unnecessary suffering to the dogs in his experiment. This needs to be weighed against the benefits of the research and whether or not the ends justify the means. Others may argue that the research was justified as it furthered our understanding of behaviour.

WIDER ISSUES AND DEBATES

Reductionism

Learning theorists, such as Skinner, would be very happy to explain all behaviour as an outcome of previous learning. In a sense he, like other learning theorists, would argue that we are organisms that behave the way we do due to the sum of our experiences. This is known as reductionism.

Taking it further

- In what way could Skinner's view be deemed reductionist? Remember to justify your point. (Explain why this would be the case.)

- Take one of the following behaviours: phobia, schizophrenia, depression. While learning theories may explain these conditions through maladaptive learning, list other possible explanations for the cause of the condition with a short explanation for each.

Self-efficacy

An important factor in the development of social learning theory is the concept of **self-efficacy.** Bandura argued that in addition to requiring a role model in order to imitate behaviour, its final reproduction relies not just on reward, but on the child's own self-confidence and belief to imitate the behaviour. Bandura viewed self-efficacy as 'the belief in one's capabilities to organize and execute the courses of action required to manage prospective situations'. It is an individual's belief in their ability to succeed in a particular situation or task.

Both theories can be viewed as strongly deterministic with behaviours largely being governed by environmental forces. If individuals are largely the product of their environment, it suggests that they cannot control their own actions and in turn cannot be responsible for them. Moreover, it has potentially sinister implications, allowing for others to control the behaviour of an individual through conditioning mechanisms, raising further ethical issues linked to social control. Skinner, however, viewed this as potentially positive as behaviourist principles could be used to create a better world.

Social learning theory
Origins

Social learning theory differs from the principles of learning already examined earlier in this topic. For social learning theory behaviour is explained not by the simple association between a stimulus and response (classical conditioning); nor is it explained by how a consequence of an action can dictate if a behaviour is shown again (operant conditioning). Rather, social learning theory is learning through observation and is largely attributed to the work of Albert Bandura (born 1925). Proponents of the approach believe that humans and animals learn by observing the others around them and subsequently imitating or copying the behaviour. Individuals that are observed are called models. Mineka and Cook (1988) observed rhesus monkeys raised in captivity, who originally showed no fear of snakes but did show alarm after watching the anxious reactions of wild monkeys in the presence of snakes. Similarly, children are surrounded by many **role models**, such as parents, peers, teachers and television characters. On a daily basis, these models provide examples of behaviour to the children to observe and replicate.

Behaviour is more likely to be copied if the observer can identify with the role model and the observed behaviour is reinforced in some way. Effective role models are typically the same sex as the observer and/or can be admired for having status/power. Similarly, an observer is more likely to reproduce the model's behaviour if the consequences are rewarding rather than resulting in punishment for the role model. For example, if a younger sibling is watching their older sibling eat their lunch and they get praised for using a knife and fork, they are more likely to copy this behaviour. They are unlikely to copy eating behaviour that has previously been punished, for example an older sibling eating their lunch with their mouth open. This process is known as **vicarious reinforcement** and essentially means learning from the successes or mistakes of others.

Children may learn to fear things such as the loud noise of a balloon bursting, through watching the reactions of siblings.

Social learning 'stages'

Bandura theorised that social learning would only occur if the following four criteria were met.

Attention

Bandura argued that one of the required conditions for effective **modelling** was 'attention'. This illustrates a clear cognitive element to his theory, and one that could result in behaviour being copied or not. Attention must be paid to the role model or else learning will not take place. Attention could depend on many factors such as the distinctiveness of the behaviour being modelled and also factors within the person observing a model, such as their level of arousal. Bandura proposed that a child is more likely to attend to role models who are similar to themselves and so are more likely to attend to the behaviour of people of the same sex.

Retention

Having focused on the modelled behaviour the individual must then retain or store what they have attended to. Imagery and language assist in the process of retaining information. Humans store the behaviours they observe in the form of mental images or verbal descriptors, and are then able to recall these later when reproducing the behaviour.

Reproduction

The third of the four criteria involves simply the showing of the modelled behaviour – the reproduction of what has been observed. Again here Bandura made it clear that factors such as the physical capabilities of the individual, as well as their own self observation of reproduction were factors that affected the showing of the behaviour. If the behaviour is beyond our capabilities then it cannot be reproduced.

Motivation

The final process refers to the 'incentive'. If a reward is offered, we are more likely to reproduce the behaviour. Intrinsic motivation refers to the doing of an activity where there might be inherent satisfaction rather than some physical outcome. For example, a young boy imitates his dad's behaviour. The young person 'feels good' about his copied behaviour because he feels it makes him more like his dad.

Extrinsic motivation refers to a motivator that is not so much a feeling or view, but rather something tangible, something that has a separable outcome, for example a sportsperson receiving a trophy or medal for their performance.

Vicarious reinforcement as the name suggests, is a form of motivation that does not directly reward the individual themselves. In its simplest form this could involve, for example, a child witnessing another child showing a good behaviour. The observing child witnesses the well-behaved child getting a reward. Notice here the observing child does not get a reward themselves – the reward is vicarious. But the observing child thinks – 'if I act like that I could get a reward too!'

> ### Key term
>
> **Modelling:** a way of learning by imitating the behaviour of others.

> ### Exam tip
>
> It is important to explain Bandura's theory in both 'breadth' and 'depth'. You need to explain both the underlying assumptions, for example imitation, modelling and vicarious reinforcement, as well as the four stages above. This will demonstrate sound understanding to the examiner.

> ### Taking it further
>
> - It is common for children to be fearful of going to the dentist. A recent review of this problem suggested that dentists are forced to treat the dentally anxious child with methods that do little to reduce the anxiety of the child and in some cases may often lead to their anxiety increasing.
>
> - How could a dentist apply social learning theory to reduce dental anxiety in children perhaps by means of a preventive method?

INDIVIDUAL DIFFERENCES

Bandura's theory of social learning accounts for individual differences in behaviour concepts such as self-efficacy and modelling. Self-efficacy refers to how an individual feels about their capabilities to succeed at a particular task and is therefore a purely individual concept. An individual will not copy a behaviour unless they feel they have the capabilities to do so. Modelling is also influenced by individual differences. For modelling to be effective, the role model must be competent, powerful and relevant in the eyes of the observer. Similarly, in vicarious learning, the rewards received are also individual to the observer. In essence, according to Bandura's theory, the individual decides which behaviours they will copy.

WIDER ISSUES AND DEBATES

Comparing learning theories: nature–nurture

All learning theories assume that our behaviour is determined by the environment we live in, which provides stimuli to which we respond. Moreover, the environments we have been in in the past have caused us to learn to respond to stimuli in a particular way. Learning theorists disregard internal mental processes when explaining behaviour as it is sufficient to know which stimuli elicit which responses. Learning theorists also believe that individuals are born with a small number of innate reflexes (stimulus-response links that do not require learning). Complex behaviours are therefore the result of learning through interaction with the environment.

Evaluation

As with other learning theories, a strength of social learning is its commitment to scientific research methods. The theory is based on laboratory-based research methods that ensure reliability and allow inferences about cause and effect to be made. This can also be viewed as a weakness as the studies have taken place in rather artificial settings, bringing into question the generalisability and ecological validity of the research. Unlike classical and operant conditioning, social learning theory does allow for individual differences and acknowledges that cognitive and motivational factors can influence behaviour as factors as reflected in the four processes suggested by Bandura – through attention, retention, reproduction and motivation.

The theory has also made a significant contribution to the psychology of aggression and gender development and has formed the basis for a range of treatments such as phobias. Modelling-based therapies, for example, can be used with children or adults, who may find behaviour therapies using direct conditioning difficult. Typically, modelling therapies involve learning through the observation and imitation of others. Having a positive role model can give individuals something to aim for, allowing them to change their behaviour in line with their role model. This role model may be the therapist or someone the individual already knows.

Social learning theory sits on the nurture side of the nature–nurture debate, suggesting that the environment is the dominant influence on behaviour. For example, in the psychology of attraction there appear to be many similarities in what men and women perceive as attractive attributes in the opposite sex. Men tend to rank youthfulness and signs of fertility as highly attractive, whereas women select status and resources as the most attractive features. It is possible that such differences are learned via the process of social learning, but it could equally be the case that evolutionary demands have favoured certain features over time. Social learning theory obviously ignores such factors and other biological influences on behaviour. Although social learning theory appears on the surface to be less deterministic than the other learning theories, the approach generally does not acknowledge the influence of free will. While cognitive and motivational factors may appear to offer freedom of choice in behaviour, it should be stressed that an individual's motivation is the product of prior learning and that therefore the choice over their actions are not free. This approach can also be accused of reductionism by breaking down highly complex behaviours to merely observational learning.

Albert Bandura's Bobo doll experiments

Aims

Albert Bandura, Dorothea Ross and Sheila Ross aimed to investigate whether exposure to aggression would influence behaviour. They hypothesised that children exposed to aggressive role models would imitate the aggression shown. Children exposed to non-aggressive role models would not show such high levels of aggression. They also believed that there would be a gender difference with boys expected to show more imitated aggressive behaviour than girls.

Procedure

Bandura's participants were 72 children from the Stanford University Nursery School; 36 boys and 36 girls with a mean age of 52 months. The children were split into eight experimental groups (six in each) and a control group of 24 children. Half the children in the experimental groups observed an aggressive role model, the other half saw a non-aggressive role model. Bandura then split the groups again so that half of the subjects in the non-aggressive and aggressive conditions saw a same-sex role model. The other half saw a role model of the opposite sex.

The control group did not experience the presence of a role model. Their behaviour would simply be observed when the children were allowed to play with toys in the final condition.

In order to control for baseline levels of aggression (physical, verbal, aggression inhibition and aggression towards inanimate objects) participants were rated on each of these characteristics on four separate 5-point scales. The children in each group were then matched for aggression so that the groups were similar.

Children were initially brought into a room, and asked to sit at a small table. They were instructed on how to play with various implements such as potato prints and stickers in order to create a scene. Elsewhere in the room there was another table with a tinker-toy set (a construction set), a mallet and a 'Bobo' doll. A Bobo doll is an inflatable plastic toy about three-feet tall painted to look like a clown. The doll has a weight in the bottom so when it is hit, it will fall down and then immediately spring back up. The Bobo doll was a well-known television character at the time and was known as an object to be punched.

The children were individually brought into the room by the experimenter and, soon after, a model was also brought into the room. The child was placed in one corner of the room and shown how to draw a picture. The model, on the other hand, was taken to the opposite corner and seated at the table containing the toys. The experimenter then left the room. The child could only watch the model and overheard the experimenter say to the model that it was 'their' play area and the child had no access to it.

In the aggressive conditions – the model would initially (for about one minute) play with the tinker toys, before then turning to the Bobo doll and for the remainder of the time act aggressively towards it.

The model made distinctive aggressive acts towards the Bobo doll:

- The model laid the Bobo doll on its side, sat on it and punched it again and again on the nose.

- The model picked up Bobo, picked up the mallet and hit the doll on the head.

- The model then threw the Bobo doll in to the air and kicked it around the room.

This set of behaviours was repeated three times. In between these behaviours, verbal statements were used:

- hit him down
- sock him on the nose
- throw him in the air
- pow

- kick him
- he sure is a tough fella (non-aggressive)
- he keeps on coming back for more (non-aggressive).

In the non-aggressive conditions, the model simply sat in the corner of the room playing quietly with the tinker toys and ignoring the Bobo doll.

After a period of ten minutes, the child was taken to another room and given a selection of toys to play with. After two minutes, the child was told that the toys were not for them but for other children, and that the child could play with any toys that would be found in an adjoining room. This situation was set up to provoke mild aggression arousal in the children.

Table 4.1 Toys used in the Bobo doll experiment

Aggressive	Non-aggressive
Bobo doll	Cars and trucks
Mallet with peg board	Tea set
Dart Guns (2)	Farm animal plastic models
'Tetherball'	Dolls (2)
	Crayons and paper
	Bears (3)

In the next room there were a range of toys categorised as aggressive and non-aggressive for the purposes of the experiment.

Participants would spend 20 minutes in this room. The behaviour of the participant was observed through a one-way mirror through interval sampling (observing the behaviour at regular time intervals).

The behaviours of the participants were scored according to three types of imitative behaviour that the children displayed.

1 Imitative verbal aggression – the participant repeated word/ phrases that the model said (for example, 'hit him down', 'throw him in the air', 'pow', etc.).

2 Imitative non-aggressive verbal statements – the participant repeated non-aggressive statements said by the model (for example, 'he sure is a tough fella').

3 Imitative physical aggression – the participant re-showed acts of physical aggression shown by the model (for example, sitting on the Bobo doll and punching the nose, kicking the Bobo doll).

Bandura also noted other categories of behaviour shown by the children:

- Mallet aggression – the participant used the mallet to hit other objects, not just the Bobo doll.

- Acts of non-imitative physical or verbal aggression (statements or actions of aggression that were not originally modelled to the children) – so aggression towards other objects other than the Bobo doll. Or statements such as 'shoot the Bobo', or 'knock over people'.

- Aggressive gun play – the participant aimed the gun at imaginary objects around the room and 'shoots'.

Observations of any behaviour that constituted non-aggressive behaviour (sitting quietly not playing with objects at all) were also made.

Results

Table 4.2 Mean number of 'imitative physical aggressive acts' (physical and verbal aggression copied from the adult model)

	Aggressive adult role model		Non-aggressive adult role model		Control group
	Female model	Male model	Female model	Male model	
Female child	5.5	7.2	2.5	0.0	1.2
Male child	12.4	25.8	0.2	1.5	2.0

Table 4.3 Mean number of 'non-imitative aggressive acts' (physical and verbal aggression directed at targets other than the Bobo doll)

	Aggressive adult role model		Non-aggressive adult role model		Control group
	Female model	Male model	Female model	Male model	
Female child	21.3	8.4	7.2	1.4	6.1
Male child	16.2	36.7	26.1	22.3	24.6

Not surprisingly, those participants in the aggressive model condition tended to display a lot more aggressive acts – both physical and verbal. This was quantitatively established since mean scores from participants in the aggressive condition compared to those in the non-aggressive and control conditions varied considerably.

What was interesting in this study was that imitation was not just linked to aggressive acts. Indeed one-third of the participants in the aggressive condition also demonstrated non-aggressive verbal statements.

Key observations from the data:

- Partial imitation of the model's behaviour, as illustrated for example by the use of the mallet, was significantly different between conditions. Also, sitting on the Bobo doll was significantly more common in the aggressive condition compared to the non-aggresive and control conditions.

- Participants in the aggressive condition were more likely to display non-imitative aggression.

- The original assumption that boys would be more aggresive than girls was only partially confirmed. Boys showed more imitative physical aggression (including acts of aggression, more aggressive play and use of aggressive language) following exposure to a male model than girls. Females exposed to a female role model showed more imitation of verbal aggression and non-imitative aggression than the boys.

- Bandura felt that when looking at the results for non-aggressive and control conditions, the male model had a greater effect over the behaviour of the participants than the female model.

- Girls spent more time playing with dolls, the tea set and doing colouring activities. Boys spent more time with guns. But most importantly, those particpants – whether male or female, who were in non-aggressive conditions spent double the amount of time sitting quietly in the room not interacting with play equipment at all.

Conclusions

Bandura concluded that if a child was exposed to an aggressive model, it is likely that they would imitate their behaviour. Boys were more likely to imitate the same-sex role model (more so than girls).

Taking it further

One really good way to evaluate a study is to refer to other studies that may offer additional support for the findings and conclusions. Moreover, you can also offer a counter-argument or perspective that might suggest different causes for the participants' behaviour. Consider the following.

Phillips (1983) observed that homicide rates in the USA increase in the week following major boxing matches.

Williams et al. (1981) conducted a natural experiment in a small, remote town in British Columbia, Canada following the introduction of television into the town. They looked at children's behaviour from before television was introduced and after. They found that physical and verbal aggression increased following its introduction.

During the Vietnam War, the FBI reported that rates of homicide increased in the USA among all age groups (Archer and Gartner, 1984).

- How do these studies offer additional support for Bandura's Bobo doll study?
- Could there be other explanations for these findings apart from social learning theory?

Evaluation

Bandura's study has undoubtedly made a huge contribution to our understanding about how children learn to acquire behaviours through observing those around them. Bandura has received an Association of Psychological Science (APS) lifetime achievement award and was also named in the top five most eminent 20th-century psychologists by the *Review of General Psychology*.

Following the publication of Bandura's findings that children exposed to aggression will initiate the behaviour, there was substantial debate in 1960s' America, from lawmakers to broadcasters, regarding the effects of television violence on children's behaviour. This debate continues to this day. Although there is significant experimental evidence to suggest that media aggression can influence behaviour, the findings of research employing different methodologies do not support such a link being made, particularly in the long term.

Bandura's laboratory experiment has a good degree of control and can be easily replicated. Moreover, the study did not rely on a sole observer and only agreed behaviours between observers were used, so good inter-rater reliability (the degree of agreement between two different raters of behaviour was 0.90) was found. Furthermore, Bandura's later research obtained similar findings showing the influence of modelled behaviour on aggression. The study does therefore have reliability.

However, Bandura's study has attracted a number of criticisms, particularly in relation to its research methodology. First, Bandura only studied the immediate impact of observing the aggressive actions of a role model. What could the long-term changes in behaviour be? We are unable to answer this question as the participants were never followed up. Bandura, by his own admission, has trained individuals to be aggressive but we will never know if any of the children applied this learned behaviour beyond the study.

Secondly, the internal validity of the experiment is questionable. The Bobo was an object designed to be punched. Indeed Bandura reported some children actually passing comments before the study such as 'Ok mum there is the doll we have to hit'. This strongly casts doubt on the overall validity of behaviour shown by the children, and questions whether it was 'observational learning' that was really the cause of the behaviour change in the study. These demand characteristics weaken the integrity of the study.

Moreover, it could be argued that the aggressive behaviours displayed by the children were a result of obedience. They copied the adult because they interpreted their behaviour as instructions; the children were therefore simply trying to please adults as this was the behaviour expected of them.

The study has also been criticised for its cultural bias, evident in the selection of the participants. The children all attended the nursery at Stanford University and as a result represented only the upper-middle class white population of the time; it therefore lacks generalisability. It is perhaps likely that these children were more inclined to be compliant and responsive to the model's behaviour during the experiment.

Finally, Wortman, Loftus and Weaver (1998) argue that the study by Bandura was unethical and morally wrong, suggesting that the participants were 'manipulated' to respond in an aggressive way. Indeed they argue that the children were 'trained to be aggressive' as a result of the methods of the study; for example agitation and dissatisfaction were incited through the taunts given and the fact that they were not allowed to play with certain toys.

Bandura (1965) Bobo doll experiment with vicarious reinforcement

Aim

Unlike the original Bobo doll study, in this variation, Albert Bandura arranged for the children to watch a televised model exhibit novel verbal and physically aggressive behaviour to investigate whether children would be more aggressive when they viewed a model rewarded for their aggression. The study was to investigate the role of vicarious reinforcement.

Procedure

The 33 male and 33 female participants (all from Stanford University Nursery School) were randomly allocated to one of three conditions (11 boys and 11 girls in each):

1 Model rewarded for aggressive behaviour

2 Model punished for aggressive behaviour

3 No consequences (control).

The children followed a researcher into a room. They were told that before they could go to a 'surprise playroom' they would have to wait while the experimenter dealt with some business. While they were waiting they might want to watch some television. The television was showing a programme about five minutes long in which a model exhibited aggressive behaviour. Depending on the condition, the model was rewarded, punished or, if in the control group, there was no response at all to their aggression. In the film, initially the model walked up to the Bobo doll and ordered him to 'clear the way'. The model then stared at the doll. The model then showed four distinctive aggressive responses along with verbal statements (that were not considered to be in the child's normal verbal repertoire).

1 The model put the Bobo doll on its side and sat on it, punching its nose and saying 'pow right in the nose, boom, boom'.

2 The Bobo doll was then allowed to come back up again before the model hit it on the head with a mallet, accompanied by the statement 'sockeroo… stay down'.

3 The model kicked the doll about the room, and this was interspersed with the comment 'fly away'.

4 The model threw rubber balls. Every time the model hit the Bobo doll with the balls the model would shout 'bang'.

This order of behaviour was repeated twice during the programme.

In the closing scene of the programme the model was either rewarded or punished (or nothing happened).

Conditions of the experiment

Model rewarded condition: A second adult walked up to the model with a soft drink and some sweets. The adult then stated to the model that he was 'a strong champion' and that the aggressive behaviour was seen as deserving 'considerable treats'. While the model was eating the sweets and drinking the soft drink the second adult made further comments that positively reinforced the aggressive behaviour.

Model punished condition: The second adult was seen walking towards the model shaking his finger disapprovingly, stating they there, you big bully. You quit picking on that clown. I won't tolerate it'. As the model drew back from the second adult, he tripped and fell. The second adult sat on the model and hit him with a rolled up newspaper, reminding him of how bad his aggressive behaviour was. The model then run off cowering, and the second adult said 'if I catch you doing that again, you big bully, I'll give you a hard spanking. You quit acting that way'.

No consequence (control) condition: The same film was shown as in the previous two conditions. However the closing scene of this film included no form of reinforcement.

Following the exposure to the closing scene, the child participant was taken to another room. In it was a Bobo doll, a mallet, three balls, a peg board, dart guns, some plastic farm animals and a dolls' house with dolls and furniture. For a total of ten minutes the children were observed in this room, with behaviour being recorded every five seconds. Two observers recorded observations, but neither had any knowledge of which condition the children were assigned to.

Results

Bandura's results showed that children were more likely to imitate aggressive behaviour if the model was positively rewarded. Bandura's original belief that boys would perform more imitated responses than girls was also supported.

Evaluation

The criticisms levied at Bandura's earlier study can also be applied here. Bandura himself acknowledged that mere exposure to a model does not provide sufficient conditions for observational learning to take place. The majority of children did not reproduce the behaviour exhibited by the model even when positive incentives were presented, suggesting that the children's motivations and previous experiences prior to observation may have influenced their response to the model. Moreover, the way in which the stimuli were presented to the observers may affect the degree to which they imitate the behaviour. A lengthy or complex sequence of observation could mean that children only attend to part of it. Furthermore, younger children are more likely to imitate physical aggression than verbal aggression because, given their age, they have more capacity to imitate motor actions than verbal actions. Boys performed more imitated aggression than girls in line with the findings of the original Bobo study. Bandura suggested that this reflects willingness on the boys' part to exhibit aggression rather than identifying with a particular role model. Such behaviour is dependent on the different reinforcement histories experienced by girls and boys. Girls are more likely to be negatively reinforced for displaying aggression than boys.

WIDER ISSUES AND DEBATES

How psychological understanding has developed over time
The effect of violent media on behaviour has been a hotly debated topic since the 1950s. In recent years, a significant amount of psychological research has focused on the links between violent behaviour and video games. Many media reports of mass shootings have questioned whether the killer's actions were a result of playing a violent shooting game. There are numerous studies suggesting a link between playing violent video games and aggression over the years. For example, Anderson and Dill (2000) conducted two studies into violent video game effects on aggression. Their first study found that real-life violent video game play was positively related to aggression and delinquency, particularly for individuals who were male and who typically displayed aggressive characteristics. In the second study, laboratory exposure to a violent video game increased aggressive thoughts and behaviour in participants. However many of these studies have been criticised for only examining short-term effects and ignoring the background of participants. Moreover, there are differences in how aggression is measured and a bias towards publishing studies that show positive results, that is, showing a significant link between video games and aggressive behaviour.

Learning theories and phobias

Phobias can be defined as 'an overwhelming and debilitating fear of an object, place, situation, feeling or animal' (NHS, 2015). A phobia is an anxiety disorder, a complex behaviour, that when compared to a fear has more far-reaching effects on the individual both emotionally and socially. It is estimated by the NHS (2015) that approximately 10 million people in the UK have a phobia of some kind.

Phobia can be split into three kinds:

- specific phobia: a phobia of animals, for example snakes; inanimate objects, for example heights; illness, for example cancer

- social phobia: for example fear of eating in public places, public speaking

- agoraphobia: a fear of places of assembly, for example crowded areas.

Some people suffer with claustrophobia which is a fear of confined spaces.

> **WIDER ISSUES AND DEBATES**
>
> **Different ways of explaining behaviour**
> Phobias can be explained in a number of ways, including learning theories (such as the ones we have seen earlier in this topic). However, there are also other factors that may contribute to the development of a phobia including our underlying biology (for example our genetic make-up) and our personality. Both the psychodynamic and cognitive approaches have attempted to offer explanations via unconscious fears and distorted thinking.

Our focus however is to examine how the three learning theories may explain how phobias are acquired and maintained via classical conditioning, operant conditioning and social learning theory.

Classical conditioning as an explanation for phobias

Put very simply this is the pairing/associating of a neutral stimulus (which could be an object, a situation or an event) with an unconditioned stimulus, which of itself leads to an unconditioned response. A loud noise such as a door slamming (unconditioned stimulus) will make most people jump (unconditioned response). If a person heard the wind howl (neutral stimulus) prior to a door slamming (which makes them jump) it is possible that they would come to fear the wind, anticipating that a loud noise would always follow.

Later in this topic, you will learn about the single case experiment of 'Little Albert': a classic study that demonstrates how a phobia of rats can be acquired through the process of classical conditioning through the pairing of a loud noise and the presentation of a white rat.

Naturalistic observations have also demonstrated that classical conditioning is a mechanism through which fears and phobias develop. Dollinger, O'Donnell and Staley (1984) compared child survivors of a severe lightning-strike to a control group and found that the survivors group demonstrated more numerous and intense fear of thunder, lightning and tornadoes. However, not all phobias can be linked back to a conditioning experience and some would suggest that the notion of classical conditioning in phobias only has modest support. Kleinknecht (1982) studied a group of members of the American Tarantula Society. Among those who reported being afraid of tarantulas, none reported a direct traumatic experience associated with classical conditioning. Hekmat (1987) investigated a group of students with various animal phobias and concluded that only 23 per cent of these reported direct conditioning experiences. Similarly, DiNardo et al. (1988) studied 16 dog phobics and noted that 56 per cent of them reported conditioning experiences.

Operant conditioning as an explanation for the maintenance of phobias

As we have already seen, operant conditioning can explain increases and decreases in response behaviour in relation to different reward and punishment conditions such as positive reinforcement, negative reinforcement, positive punishment and negative punishment. Operant conditioning has been linked to **social phobias** such as social anxiety disorder. For example, if you were scared of social situations such as parties, one way of dealing with it would be to avoid or escape from such anxiety-provoking situations. These actions would lessen or remove the unpleasant anxiety symptoms experienced. In other words, these avoidance behaviours become rewarding and in line with the theory, reinforces the avoidance behaviour and makes it more likely to occur in future. Similarly, if you were pressured to go to the party by friends, despite your reservations, and experienced a panic attack while there, one coping mechanism might be to escape immediately from the situation. This will again lessen the feelings of anxiety and will once again reward escape behaviour by the quick reduction of anxiety. These avoidance and escape behaviours demonstrate negative reinforcement. The removal of unpleasant emotions leads to an increase in avoidance behaviour. This explains why phobias are maintained and difficult to treat.

Social learning theory as an explanation for phobias

Bandura (1986) reminds us that learning can occur from observing others and in particular 'observing the consequences of others' behaviour'. Taking a common phobia such as arachnophobia (fear of spiders), it would seem that the key aspects of social learning theory in its application to phobias are as follows.

- Observation: a child watches an older sibling respond to finding a spider in their bed. The older sibling might run out of the bedroom, they might scream, show their fear and shake.
- Vicarious reinforcement: the parents might well then try to make the older sibling feel better by comforting them.
- Imitation: sometime later the observing child finds a spider in their bed. They repeat the behaviour they had witnessed earlier. They scream, shout, and shake.
- Reinforcement: the observing child's parents provide comfort – and while it might console the child it reinforces the fear.

A number of studies have offered support for vicarious reinforcement. Mineka and Zinbarg (2006) describe a case study of a boy who developed a significant vomiting phobia after witnessing his grandfather vomit while dying. His phobia was so severe it caused him to contemplate suicide on one occasion when he felt nauseous and feared being sick. Similarly, Dubi et al. (2008) observed toddlers aged 15–20 months show fear and avoidance behaviours to both 'fear-relevant', for example a rubber spider or snake and 'fear-irrelevant' objects, for example a rubber mushroom, following their observation of negative reactions from their mothers. They concluded that the maternal modelling impacted on young children's fear and avoidance behaviour.

> **Taking it further**
>
> - Research five different types of phobias. List them and outline their key characteristics.
> - Do you think that you could learn a phobia? Explain your answer.
> - Could there be another reason for why a phobia develops? Explain your answer.
> - If phobias are the product of learning, how would the learning approach explain phobias of objects/situations that you have not experienced?

Treatments for phobias

A proponent of learning theories would argue that a phobia is simply the result of 'maladaptive learning', so to treat it you simply need to focus on observable behaviour change and the unlearning or deconditioning of the maladaptive behaviour associated with the phobia. A learning theorist does not assume that there is an internal or biological cause for the behaviour and will therefore ignore any mental or physical causes for the phobia.

Treatments for phobias based on learning theories fall into two main categories:

- exposure treatments (based on classical conditioning)

- modelling.

You will need to know about systematic desensitisation as one treatment for phobias and a further treatment of your choice.

Exposure treatments

Systematic desensitisation

This technique is based on the idea of reciprocal inhibition, that is, that you cannot be anxious and relaxed at the same time. Phobias are thought to be acquired through maladaptive learning, in a sense a learned response to a particular stimulus. So the basis of this treatment is that just as you can 'learn to fear' something you can unlearn the fear by relaxing when in contact with the phobic object. The therapist and client initially agree on a target aim for the therapy (for example being able to handle an insect) and the client is taught relaxation techniques. Over several sessions, depending on the strength of the phobia and the client's ability to relax, the client is exposed to the object of their phobia until the client is desensitised to the object. The process can either be in vivo (being exposed to a real object) or in vitro (literally 'in glass' through an imaginary exposure to object).

Systematic desensitisation involves four key processes.

- Functional analysis: a conversation between therapist and client to identify the nature of the anxiety and the possible triggers.

- Develop an anxiety hierarchy: working jointly, the client and therapist create a hierarchy of fear from the least anxiety-provoking situation to the most. It is important that the client has input here and that they determine the speed at which the treatment progresses and the stages of hierarchy they progress through.

- Relaxation training: the client is taught how to relax using methods that suit them best. For example, deep breathing exercises or visualisation imagining being in a peaceful setting.

- Gradual exposure: working through the agreed anxiety hierarchy, the phobic object is slowly and gradually introduced according to the scenarios agreed in the hierarchy. The therapist always works at the speed agreed by the client.

Figure 4.2 A typical anxiety hierarchy from the least fearful to the most fearful situation

Systematic desensitisation has proven effectiveness as a form of treatment. Most studies report that individuals receiving systematic desensitisation therapy improve more than a non-treatment group. For instance McGrath et al. (1990) found that 75 per cent of individuals with phobias respond to the therapy. Systematic desensitisation is also an appropriate form of treatment. Behavioural therapies require considerably less time and effort in comparison with other therapies. It is also possible for people to administer the therapy themselves via computer simulations. The therapy does not pose any significant ethical issues as the techniques employed, such as the fear hierarchy and relaxation techniques, ensure that the client is not exposed to any high anxiety situations.

Systematic desensitisation has a number of limitations, however. Firstly, it can only treat certain anxiety disorders. Situations or objects have to be clearly identifiable for the therapy to work so systematic desensitisation would be inappropriate for someone with general anxiety disorder who worries about numerous imprecise situations. Moreover, systematic desensitisation appears to be less effective at treating phobias that have an underlying survival component, such as fear of the dark, or dangerous animals. One possible explanation for this is that these deep-rooted fears may have enabled our ancestors to survive by keeping them out of danger. It is thus very difficult to remove such fears deep within our evolutionary past.

Overcoming a fear of heights is one example of a phobia that could be treated through systematic desensitisation.

Flooding/Implosion

The **flooding** technique was devised by Thomas Stampfl in 1967 and involves the phobic being physically placed in a situation with their feared object/situation for a prolonged period of time with no means to remove themselves from that situation. Through continual exposure to the feared stimulus, the client will eventually see it as less fear-producing. The key to the effectiveness of this treatment is that the feared stimulus must be quickly presented, continuously, and in a situation where escape is not possible.

Implosion is effectively the same process except that instead of placing the person physically in a situation with the phobic stimulus, they are asked to imagine it. Both techniques aim to remove the maladaptive (phobic behaviour). According to Wolpe, the therapy works via the process of reciprocal inhibition, which has both a psychological and biological component. It suggests that two incompatible psychological states cannot occur simultaneously, for example anxiety and relaxation. When an individual is anxious, the activation of sympathetic nervous system inhibits the action of the parasympathetic nervous system. The deep muscle relaxation exercises that are involved in the therapy increase parasympathetic activity and therefore reduced sympathetic activity and in doing so reduce arousal.

The key to flooding is the rapid exposure to the feared object and situation rather than more spaced presentations. This facilitates the extinction, perhaps because the person becomes too physically exhausted for the conditioned response to occur, or perhaps it prevents avoidance responses developing. A significant advantage of flooding is that it is much faster than other therapies. A major disadvantage is that the therapy runs the risk of increasing the strength of the conditioned response to the feared object/situation rather than extinguishing it. Moreover, it is questionable whether flooding is an ethical treatment for people with phobias. Joseph Wolpe (1973) notably carried out an experiment in which he took a girl who was afraid of cars, and continued to drive her around for several hours. While at first hysterical, she eventually calmed down. But two issues for psychologists arise here: firstly, the issue of ethics and the morals surrounding the treatment of a phobic by putting them purposefully into a situation of great distress; secondly, the issue of social control. Is it right for a therapist to control the behaviour of a client?

Although some clients are reported to improve following implosion therapy, other clients acquire more anxiety. Barrett (1969) used implosion therapy for the treatment of snake phobias in college students. In one student, the images of snakes became associated with having her eyes shut (as she did during treatment). She then consistently pictured snakes when she shut her eyes, resulting in insomnia and could not attend lectures. The literature and research on implosion is mixed. It is obviously very difficult to determine the results of different implosion therapies due to the different practitioners involved and the variety of problems their clients face.

> **Key term** 💬
>
> **Implosion:** prolonged exposure to the phobic situation or experience by imagining the feared stimuli.

> **Taking it further** ↗
>
> Imagine you are a psychologist treating someone for a phobia of flying via systematic desensitisation. Looking at the key features of the treatment, design a treatment plan to reduce or eliminate their anxiety when flying. The therapies advocated by the learning theories approach only focus on observable symptoms of the phobia or fear.
>
> Investigate how other approaches you have studied might treat phobias. Suggestions might include the cognitive and the biological approach.

Modelling

Although its origins are in social learning theory, this treatment incorporates a cognitive element to the behavioural treatments of flooding and systematic desensitisation. It aims to treat phobias by using vicarious reinforcement. A person with a phobia of a snake sees another person (for example an older sibling, or parent) interacting happily, and without fear, with the snake.

The fundamental idea behind this is that if the phobic person sees another person acting in a relaxed and stress-free way around the phobic stimulus, then the phobic will vicariously learn that the stimulus will not harm them. Thus their fear will be reduced. This is famously illustrated by Mary Cover Jones's Little Peter experiment. Peter was a three-year-old boy who was afraid of rabbits. Cover Jones treated Peter's fear through direct conditioning and modelling. Each day Peter and three other children were brought to the laboratory for a play period. A rabbit was always present during a part of the play period and Peter observed the other children interacting playfully and fearlessly with the rabbit. New situations requiring closer contact with the rabbit were gradually introduced. It became apparent that Peter showed progressive improvement from almost complete terror at sight of the rabbit to a completely positive response by allowing the rabbit to nibble his fingers. This study was undoubtedly a defining landmark in behavioural therapy and clear evidence of how behaviour could be studied and manipulated in the laboratory via conditioning processes.

> **Exam tip**
>
> The application of learning theory to treatment illustrates your understanding of the topic. It is important that when you are asked about a therapy in the context of learning theory, you can explain the underlying principles, for example classical and operant conditioning or social learning, as well as describing how the therapy works/progresses. Try to use the appropriate learning theories terminology in all of your explanations.

Developmental psychology

Social learning theory can explain how children learn their gender identity from observing the world around them. Firstly, a child is more likely to imitate someone perceived as similar to themselves and therefore is more likely to model the behaviour of a same-sex role model. Through the process of vicarious reinforcement, if this behaviour is reinforced the child will be motivated to imitate it in future, or if it is punished they will avoid it. In turn, these models will respond to the child's gender-related behaviour by reinforcement or punishment.

Beverly Fagot (1978) carried out an observational study of toddlers playing at home with their parents and noted the praise and punishments received. She found that boys were reinforced for playing with gender appropriate toys and punished for playing with dolls, so lending support to the idea that gender role behaviour is learned from the child's environment. The American anthropologist Margaret Mead (1935) studied three tribes in Papua New Guinea and there discovered significant differences in gender roles. Among the Arapesh, both men and women were peaceful and avoided warfare. Among the Mundugumor both men and women were warlike and among the Tchambuli the men decorated themselves while the women worked. This offers strong evidence for the role of observational learning in gender development.

Fagot's study was obviously carried out in the 1970s and it is possible to argue that gender socialisation has changed greatly in the last 30 to 40 years. Neither can social learning theory account for cognitive influences on gender development such as preparedness to imitate a role model. In addition to cultural differences there are also similarities in gender behaviours throughout the world, which would suggest the influence of biology or genetics at work.

A child is more likely to be reinforced for gender-appropriate behaviour and either punished or ignored for gender-inappropriate behaviour.

4.2 Methods
Learning outcomes

In this section, you will learn about:

- the use of the observational research method in psychology including the gathering of both qualitative and quantitative data (including tallying, time and event sampling)

- types of observation: participant, non-participant, structured, naturalistic, overt and covert

- the use of content analysis

- the use of animals in laboratory experiments where results can be related to humans

- inferential statistics, levels of measurement, reasons for choosing the chi-squared test

- comparing observed and critical values to judge significance

- the chi-squared test

- analysis of qualitative data using thematic analysis (including evaluation in terms of validity and reliability

- psychology as a science including: replicability, reliability, validity, reductionism, falsification, empiricism, hypothesis testing and use of controls.

Human research

Using the observational research method in psychology: qualitative and quantitative data gathering

Many research methods use observation, for example laboratory experiments and case studies; however observations as an actual research method involve observing as the main way of obtaining data and where there is no independent variable to manipulate. All data is therefore gathered by simply observing. The researcher has to then determine what type of data they would like to collect using the observation method, **quantitative data** or **qualitative data**. Quantitative data is where the data gathered can be counted or expressed numerically, for example the number of aggressive acts observed. Qualitative data, on the other hand, cannot be expressed numerically but is concerned with words, texts, ideas and themes.

Data collection in observational research might include tallying, where observers write down when and how many times certain behaviours occurred. They may also take notes during the observation session and review them later to try to determine behavioural patterns from the notes. Alternatively they may use audio or video recordings.

An example of a tally chart is shown in Table 4.4, where a researcher is interested in observing if men and women drive different size cars. Once they are ready for the observation they simply 'tally' or note down in the appropriate cell each time they see a person in a certain category, so for example, if you saw a female driving a small car, you would make a tally in the cell in which female/small car link.

The categories for observation need to be clear and unambiguous. In larger scale studies, observers need training to ensure that they understand the operational definitions of behavioural categories.

Key terms

Quantitative data: numerical data.

Qualitative data: descriptive data

Table 4.4 An example of a tally chart

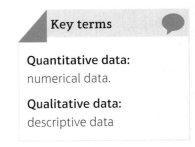

	Male	Female
Small car	I I I	I I I I I I
Large car	I I I I	I I

Training and standardisation of observers is important where more than one observer is making an assessment.

Due to the potential volume of data to be recorded researchers often use sampling to gather information; this can be via time sampling or event sampling. Time sampling involves making observations at different time intervals, for example every 30 seconds, and recording what is observed. This may not always be representative as certain behaviours can be missed if they are only recorded at certain times. Event sampling involves recording a certain behaviour every time it happens, for example ticking a box every time someone displays a particular behaviour. A problem with this approach is that if too many instances of the behaviour happen at once, the researcher may not be able to record all instances.

Taking it further

Practise this skill by seeing if you can conduct an observation in your institution. Look at whether there is a gender difference in book-carrying behaviour. Do males and females carry books differently? This idea is based on a published piece of research by Jenni and Jenni (1976).

- First create a table similar to Table 4.4.
- Now agree where on the body constitutes 'by side' and 'in front'
- Identify a location to make the observation and how long the observation will last for.
- Carry out the observation. Remember you do not want to be noticed, so blend in to the background.
- Tally each time you see a male or female carrying books in a particular way (by their side or in front).
- Once complete, total up the number of tallies in each cell.
- What initial conclusion can you draw?

Types of observation

Observations fall into two broad categories – structured and naturalistic.

Naturalistic observation involves observing the behaviour of participants within their own environment. The situation has not been created by the researcher and so allows them to gain a real insight into a person's behaviour.

Structured observations are staged observations and are normally carried out within an environment in which the researcher has some control, such as a laboratory. Subsequent behaviour can be observed behind a one-way screen. Structured observations are set to record behaviours where it would be difficult to gain information from naturalistic observations. A positive aspect of structured observations is that numerical data can be generated and so information is gained. Good structured observations will have a naturalistic feel and so natural behaviour can be observed while gaining numerical data. However, it can be difficult to ensure that all observers interpret the same information from structured observations and so it is important that there are a few observers to validate the study. Structured observations are more reliable than naturalistic observations as the coding systems used allow for replicability.

These observations can be **non-participant observations** or **participant observations**. The first type refers to the observer not being part of the situation, whereas in the latter the observer is also a participant. The obvious advantage of participant observations is that there is no stranger

Key terms

Non-participant observation: a form of observation where the researcher observes behaviour of others but does not form part of the group they study.

Participant observation: a form of observation where the researcher takes an active role in the situation being observed.

observing the behaviour, which could impact on how participants behave. It may also reveal data that might be missed by other methods. However, by taking part it may be hard to record notes of the observations. Non-participant observations are therefore limited in terms of validity as the presence of an observer has the potential to change participants' behaviour. However, they do allow researchers the opportunity to concentrate on recording data.

Observations can also be **overt** or **covert**. Overt observations are where the person being observed is aware that they are being observed whereas covert observations mean the participants are unaware they are being observed. An advantage of overt observations is that informed consent can be obtained and participants can also be informed of their right to withdraw. Covert observations are more problematic on ethical grounds as participants are unaware they are taking part. However, this is also an advantage as participants are unlikely to change their behaviour in a presence of an observer, thus making the observations more valid, which is not the case with overt observations.

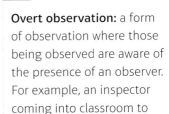

Key terms

Overt observation: a form of observation where those being observed are aware of the presence of an observer. For example, an inspector coming into classroom to observe teacher/pupils.

Covert observation: a form of observation where the participants do not know they are being observed. For example, you making an observation of behaviour in your student area, while simply sitting in one of the seated areas.

Exam tip

Most research techniques involve the researcher 'making an observation'. For example, in a lab experiment the researcher could observe for a change in behaviour due to the manipulation of a specific variable; here observations are used as a technique to gain data. Remember that observations as a research method are subtly different – they simply involve the researcher simply watching behaviour – there is no manipulation of any variables.

- In order to show your understanding of the different types of observation method, be ready not only to outline what is involved, but also give examples to illustrate your understanding – this could be with reference to specific studies that might have used the same methods.

- Remember to explicitly state which type of observation you are describing or evaluating. Ethical and methodological issues that apply to one type of observation type may not apply well to a different type. For example, participant observations affect the behaviour of those being observed, but this may not be true of non-participant observations.

- Use the grid in Table 4.5 to help discriminate between different evaluation points for each observation type. Remember that not all evaluation points will apply equally to each.

Table 4.5 Types of observation

Type of observation	Ethical issues	Subjectivity	Reliability and validity	Observer effects
Naturalistic				
Structured				
Participant				
Non-participant				
Covert				
Overt				

Content analysis

Content analysis is typically used as a research tool for analysing the content for the incidence of certain words, images or concepts within material, typically advertisements, books, films, newspapers, etc. For example, a researcher may use content analysis to observe instances of gender stereotyping in children's books. Categories would therefore be agreed in advance. In this particular instance the researcher may examine instances where males and females show stereotypical behaviour and where males and females show non-stereotypical behaviour. A researcher would therefore go through the selected material and tally or count the number of times that each of these categories occur. The researcher may also use qualitative analysis in their content analysis to examine the meanings and relationships of words, concepts and pictures and then make inferences about the messages contained within them. In content analysis it is vital that the content to be analysed is coded into clear and manageable categories so that appropriate conclusions can be drawn.

Evaluation

A clear advantage of content analysis is that it is an unobtrusive method where there are rarely ethical issues associated with the research, as data is collected from existing sources rather than live participants; nevertheless, researchers should respect confidentiality. The content analysis may also offer the opportunity for a fresh interpretation of existing data, which may not be achieved via other methods. It is very useful for analysing historical material and documenting trends over time. Reliability can be easily assessed as the content analysis can be easily replicated using the same categories.

Content analysis does, however, rely on the personal interpretation of the researcher and therefore involves an element of subjectivity or bias. There are also potential issues of internal validity as the categories used should represent what they intend to measure, otherwise the data will not be valid. Content analysis is a purely descriptive method. It describes what is there, but may not reveal the underlying motives for the observed pattern ('what' but not 'why'). The content analysis may be limited by the availability of material. Furthermore, observed trends in the media may not accurately reflect reality, for example dramatic events usually receive more coverage than less dramatic events.

Animal research
The use of animals in laboratory experiments

As we have seen so far, researchers within the 'learning approach' mirrored their methods heavily on natural sciences, particularly those earlier on in the development of this approach; for example, the use of lab experiment conditions, in which a variable (independent variable) is manipulated to see its effect on resulting behaviour of subjects. Learning theorists such as Pavlov and Skinner made significant use of experimentation on non-human (animal) participants. We will now consider the arguments for and against animal research.

The use of animals in psychological research sparks much debate and controversy on practical and ethical/moral grounds.

Arguments for the use of animals

Rats are heavily used in psychological research because of the speed at which they produce offspring: a rat's gestation period is typically 22 days and therefore large samples can be bred in short time frames. Also when investigating a characteristic across generations, for example aggression, the researcher does not have to wait so long for such results to become apparent.

It is argued that laboratory experiments have a degree of internal validity as animal participants are naive about what is happening, since behaviour is unlikely to change due to demand characteristics that are likely in humans.

Experimentation using animals offers researchers a higher degree of control compared to humans. For example, animals can be caged in a way that humans cannot, and you can isolate variables from animals in ways that would be more difficult for human participants.

While unnecessary pain must be avoided, pain and distress is permitted, which is not the case for human participants, for example Skinner gave electric shocks to animals in his 'Skinner box'. However, animal research is heavily regulated and controlled by legislation to ensure that correct housing and treatment is provided. Laboratories also undergo regular inspections to check the welfare conditions of animals being studied.

Animal research has provided significant insight into vital areas of medical research including drug treatments, transplants, surgical techniques and cloning. Animal research has made a hugely significant contribution to what we know about the brain and nervous system. Conditioning techniques have been used successfully in therapeutic settings.

From an evolutionary perspective, humans share common ancestry with other animals, particularly primates, and therefore animal research gives valid information on human processes. We share basic nervous system structures and functions that mean that we are able to generalise to some extent from animals to humans.

From an ethical perspective, the utilitarian argument would suggest that the suffering of a small number of animals is justified because it helps a significant number of people; moreover some would argue that we have a moral obligation to our own species to advance knowledge and reduce suffering. Gray (1991) would argue that animal research is justified if it furthers this cause.

Arguments against

Most people would argue that animal research is not credible and lacks ecological validity. Lab-based animal research produces behaviour that is different from animals' natural behaviour, for example drug addiction studies. Moreover, there are just too many differences between humans and animals. Consider a simple example of this: a newly born mouse in terms of development and hormonal influence is equivalent to a seven-week-old foetus – so can comparisons really be made? Extrapolation may also reduce the validity of the research. Generalisations between animals and humans are also guilty of anthropomorphism (where animals are mistakenly attributed with human qualities).

Human and animals are just very different. There are differences in human and animal evolution and our genetic make-up. We act differently both cognitively and emotionally. Our behaviour and thought processes are subject to many more variables such as, for example, cultural context/social norms and language. Physiologically our brains differ from animals; humans have a much larger cortex proportionally than any other animal. This therefore suggests that generalising from animals to humans has questionable value.

A researcher should avoid pain and discomfort for the animals unless the findings have a significant benefit for humans. The problem is that the benefits of research are not known until after the study, so it is possible that their use in the study has limited effect. This does raise wider ethical issues. Others point to the inconsistency in continuity argument. If animals are so similar to humans why should they therefore not be afforded the same ethical considerations as us?

From a moral perspective the utilitarian argument would suggest that the research gives human suffering priority over animal suffering. Singer (1975) viewed this as a form of discrimination, which he termed speciesism. It could be argued that animals have the same rights as humans and we have a moral obligation to protect them. No amount of regulation can justify animal research.

Ethical issues regarding the use of animals in laboratory experiments

There are many ethical issues that emerge from using animals for research and these differ from the ethical standards applied to human research. Legislation that protects the rights of animals in scientific research has advanced significantly since the days of Pavlov and Skinner. The Animals

(Scientific Procedures) Act (1986) covers all animal research. It relates to 'any scientific procedure that may cause pain, suffering, distress or lasting harm to a 'protected' animal.' Protected animals comprise all non-human vertebrates and a single invertebrate species (the octopus). Psychologists are expected to comply with this act. They are also directed to follow the Animal Welfare Act (2006), which discusses more general duties of care towards animals.

The British Psychological Society (BPS) clearly states that permission to perform animal procedures regulated under the 1986 Act will not be granted unless the researcher can justify the costs to the animals in relation to the likely benefits of the research. This restricts someone from simply using animals in experiments because there is a curious interest. It has to be shown to have some potential value in undertaking the research.

When permission to perform a regulated procedure is requested, the researcher is also required to demonstrate that consideration has been given to the three 'R's (Russell and Burch, 1959) to minimise pain and distress for animals:

- replacing animals with non-sentient alternatives whenever possible (animals that show no signs of intelligence or self-awareness)

- reducing the number of animals used

- refining procedures to minimise suffering.

To maximise protection of the animals, all animal research must be licensed, with each project given a new licence. This licence will specify the species and number of animals to be used. It is only granted once it has been decided that the benefits of undertaking the research outweighs any cost to the animals. Individuals undertaking the research are also required to have a personal licence, which is only given after training to ensure they are competent to perform the procedures. They are required to seek to minimise any pain, suffering or distress that might arise, given the requirements of the experimental design. Whatever procedure is in use, any adverse effects on animals must be recognised and assessed, and immediate action taken whenever necessary. The licensed researcher has responsibility to make sure this happens.

Taking it further

Search for 'BPS Animal research' online to read more about best practice when working with animals for research.

Taking it further

Investigate the work of Seligman (1967) and his research into learned helplessness. What ethical issues do you think arise here in the use of animals in his research? Do the benefits of his research outweigh the costs? Discuss your answer, and justify your views.

Link

For information on levels of measurement including nominal, ordinal, interval and ratio data see Topic 2: *Cognitive psychology*.

Analysis of data

Reasons for choosing a chi-squared test

There are different reasons why the chi-squared test can be chosen:

- where you have a hypothesis that is predicting a difference or an association. For example, a researcher may predict that boys and girls will show differences in the toys they choose to play with at nursery

- where your level of measurement is **nominal**. For example, the researcher could use two categories here – 'stereotypical' and 'non-stereotypical' toys

- where your participant design is **independent measures**, that is you have at least two different groups being studied, for example boys and girls.

Carrying out a chi-squared test (χ^2)

This is a test for difference or association where two or more independent sets of data are compared to see if they are different/related. It is used with nominal data, when the results are gathered in groups/categories. This test is used to gather occurrences within each group or 'frequency data'. Chi-squared tests can be used to question differences or common ground between two groups.

It is important not to translate numbers into averages or percentages here; use the total number to gain a reliable result. Using a chi-squared test requires you to put the data into a contingency table.

Consider a worked example. A researcher may be interested in testing if four-year-old children show stereotypical choices in the toys they play with at nursery.

Table 4.6 Children and toy choice: a worked example

	Stereotypical toy	Non-stereotypical toy	Row total
Girls	8 (Cell A)	12 (Cell B)	20
Boys	17 (Cell C)	3 (Cell D)	20
Column total	25	15	40 (Overall total)

Formula for a chi-squared test

$$\chi^2 = \Sigma \frac{(O - E)^2}{E}$$

Chi-squared is calculated as follows.

Step 1: Place the data gathered from the observations into a contingency table like the one above. This is a 2 x 2 contingency table as there are two rows and two columns. It is possible to have other variations such as a 3 x 2 table depending on your research design.

Step 2: Calculate 'expected frequency' for each cell using the formula:

$$\text{Expected frequency } (E) = \frac{\text{row total} \times \text{column total}}{\text{Overall total}}$$

Therefore:

Cell A = 12.5   Cell B = 7.5   Cell C = 12.5   Cell D = 7.5

Step 3: Subtract expected value (E) from observed value for each cell (O) O–E

Cell A = 8 – 12.5 = –4.5   Cell B = 12 – 7.5 = 4.5   Cell C = 17 – 12.5 = 4.5   Cell D = 3 – 7.5 = –4.5

Step 4: for each cell $(O–E)^2$

Cell A = 20.25   Cell B = 20.25   Cell C = 20.25   Cell D = 20.25

Step 5: for each cell $\frac{(O - E)^2}{E}$

Cell A = 20.5 / 12.5 = 1.62   Cell C = 20.25 / 12.5 = 1.62
Cell B = 20.25 / 7.5 = 2.7   Cell D = 20.25 / 7.5 = 2.7

Step 6: Add all the values from the previous stage to get the observed value (χ^2)
1.62 + 2.7 + 1.62 + 2.7 = 8.64

Step 7: Calculate degrees of freedom (df)
(rows – 1) × (columns – 1)
(2–1) x (2–1) = 1

Step 8: Look up critical value in the table below using the degrees of freedom and considering whether you have a directional (one-tailed) or non-directional (two-tailed) hypothesis.

In this example, at a significance level of $p = 0.05$ with a one-tailed test (we have a directional hypothesis because it can be predicted that boys and girls toy choices will be stereotypical), the critical value is 2.71.

Step 9: Compare observed and critical value. If the observed is *equal* to or *greater* than the critical value, it is significant.

Table 4.7 Critical values table for a Chi-squared test

Degrees of freedom (df)	Levels of significance (one-tailed test)		
	0.05	0.025	0.01
	Levels of significance for a two-tailed test		
	.10	0.05	.02
1	2.71	3.84	5.41
2	4.60	5.99	7.82

Link

For information on thematic analysis see the Methods section of Topic 1: *Social psychology*.

In this instance as the observed value of 8.64 is greater than the critical value of 2.71, we can reject our null hypothesis and support our alternative hypothesis and conclude that boys and girls differ in their choice of stereotypical and non-stereotypical toys. If the observed value was less than the critical value the reverse would be true and we would have to reject the alternative and accept the null hypothesis in that toy choice was based on chance.

Scientific status of psychology

The argument over whether or not psychology is a science is long standing. Whether you see it as a science or not depends on how you define science. Generally most commentators in this area look at the key features of what constitutes a science, including theory construction, processes and methods, and formulate a view in relation to this.

We will now consider the research process in psychology that can help us examine the scientific status of psychology.

Hypothesis testing and falsification

You will have carried out practicals as part of your psychology course and noticed that psychologists, much like natural scientists, assert predictions before conducting the research proper. These predictions are called hypotheses. The writing of a hypothesis is basically a statement of what you expect to happen/find out. If a psychologist fails to support this hypothesis then it may require modification. Based on the hypothetico-deductive method, it can be more important to test a hypothesis to determine whether it is supported or not by evidence, than for knowledge to emerge from research (inductive method).

Karl Popper (1935), a philosopher of science, proposed that the only way to prove a theory was to look for disproof rather than proof. He called this falsification and used the analogy of seeing white and black swans. He suggested that no number of sightings of white swans can prove the hypothesis that all swans are white. However, the sighting of one black swan would be enough to falsify the statement that all swans are white. The latter statement is truer therefore, as we can be categorically correct in stating that not all swans are white, but we can only claim to be correct in saying that all swans are white. Psychology researchers aim to falsify statements/assertions of others. If they gain similar results then the idea is supported, but if they derive different results the idea can be falsified. It works on the basic idea that it is more scientific to evidentially prove an idea wrong that to prove that it is right.

Objectivity and control

Science dictates that the data gathered from experimentation should be objective and measurable and not influenced by the views and expectations of the researcher. Control is therefore important in gathering such data and observations should take place under controlled conditions, such as a laboratory, and dependent and independent variables should be clearly defined. It is possible to argue that the learning theorists had objectivity and control in their research. Others claim that psychologists cannot measure human behaviour objectively as humans (unlike subject matter of the physical sciences) react to the researcher and therefore factors such as demand characteristics are hard, if not impossible, to eliminate.

Empiricism

Based on the ideas formulated originally by John Locke, empiricism can be defined as the view that all knowledge is based on experience. Scientific research should therefore be based on directly observable phenomena. The main method of scientific enquiry is therefore experimentation. It could be argued that psychologists strive for empiricism via experimentation. This is clearly evident in the work of learning theorists such as Pavlov, Skinner and Bandura. Careful control over variables in a lab environment ensures that a cause and effect relationship can be established by seeing the effect of an independent variable on a dependent variable. Such methods involve standardised procedures that aid replicability.

Replicability

If a study is conducted initially in a particular way then later another researcher repeats it exactly as described it should produce the same results. So if after conducting the study again different results are derived, the study is not that replicable. Some psychologists, such as Skinner, have conducted studies that have very high levels of control, and precise standardised procedures, which help in subsequent replication of their work. Replication is central to developing scientific theory.

Reliability

Reliability means consistency. An aspect of scientific methodology and assessment is in how reliable is the data derived or conclusions drawn. Is there consistency in findings in a research area? We would not take medication that has only proved successful for one person; we would expect it to reliably treat many people, otherwise it could be a one-off finding. Reliability is necessary to make wider claims that apply to the population and not just one person. Therefore science can be regarded as a nomothetic (general) approach, because it tries to explain wider behaviour using theories that apply to the general population and not just unique individuals – as an idiographic (individual) approach might adopt.

Validity

Put simply, to be valid means to be true. Does a study or a test measure what it intends to measure? A scientific study will be one where the results are due to the manipulation of an independent variable to see the effect on the dependent variable. If a researcher can create an environment in which this can be engineered, a study would be said to have internal validity. External validity refers to the application of the study findings to other settings, for example a study performed in a lab might not easily generalise its findings to a real-life environment (ecological validity).

Reductionism

A typical aspect of the scientific approach is to focus on one small area in isolation rather than to look at the whole area. This is driven mainly by the fact that in order to use empirical testing an area of examination must be small enough to study. Therefore complex issues might have to be reduced to very small constituent parts in order to be studied without establishing interconnections between areas. It is possible to argue that many of the learning theorists we have studied have been reductionist as they have only investigated behaviour in terms of learning alone and have failed to consider the emotional and cognitive elements. This is a debate among psychologists between reductionism and holism – studying an organism as a whole rather than the sum of its parts.

> **Link**
>
> For more information on validity please see the Methods section of Topic 2: *Cognitive psychology*.

> **Taking it further**
>
> Look at the work of Pavlov, Skinner and Bandura. In what ways was their thinking and their research studies to support their assertions reductionist? Give examples.

4.3 Studies
Learning outcomes

In this section, you will learn about one classic study:

- Watson and Rayner (1920) Conditioned emotional reactions

and three contemporary studies, from which you will need to choose one to learn about:

- Capafóns et al. (1998) Systematic desensitization in the treatment of fear of flying
- Becker et al. (2002) Eating behaviours and attitudes following prolonged exposure to television among ethnic Fijian adolescent girls
- Bastian et al. (2012) Cyber dehumanization: Violent video game play diminishes our humanity.

Watson and Rayner (1920) Conditioned emotional reactions
Aim

John Watson and Rosalie Rayner wanted to see if they could condition a phobic response to a white rat in an infant. Using the principles of classical conditioning, they wanted to investigate if a human child could learn to be afraid of a previously neutral stimulus, which initially caused no fear response, and whether this reaction would be generalised to similar objects.

Procedure

Using a single case experiment, Watson and Rayner selected one child, 'Albert B', a nine-month old infant chosen for his 'stolid and unemotional' character. Watson and Rayner initially tested Little Albert's responses to various stimuli, such as a dog, a mask, a white rat, cotton wool and burning newspaper. Little Albert did not response adversely to any of them until they struck a hammer on a four-foot pole hanging from the ceiling. They noted that initially Albert showed a startled response. On the second hitting of the pole, the same thing occured and his lips began to pucker. On a third hitting of the pole the child broke down in a crying fit.

The actual conditioning of a phobia did not start until two months later, when Little Albert was 11 months old. Before conditioning took place they presented Albert with a white rat. No fear reaction was noted. Indeed he tried to reach out for it as it roamed around him. It was only in later trials, when Watson hit the steel bar suspended from the ceiling behind Albert's back when he touched the rat, that Albert demonstrated fear. At first, Albert was shocked but did not cry. But following seven more conditioning trials Little Albert began to crawl away quickly at the sight of the white rat.

Seventeen days after the conditioning tests began, Watson and Rayner noticed evidence of stimulus generalisation. Watson presented Albert suddenly with a rabbit. He leaned away as far as he could, whimpered and burst into tears. Albert also showed an adverse reaction to other stimuli that Watson and Rayner presented; a dog, a seal skin coat and a Santa Claus mask.

Towards the end of the study, Watson relocated the investigations to a lecture room, to observe the effect of surroundings on the child's responses. This would have allowed the researchers to control

WIDER ISSUES AND DEBATES

Ethical issues

Watson and Rayner were aware that their research could cause harm, and Watson notes a considerable reluctance in deliberately conditioning a fear reaction experimentally. Little Albert was selected because he tended to not show extreme emotions, and barely cried. It was this character that could have made him more resilient and less prone to the distress that would be involved in the conditioning trials. This, however, does not make the experiment any more ethical as the infant endured many conditioning trials where his fear reaction was strengthened over time. His mother withdrew him from the experiment before he could be deconditioned, so it is possible to speculate that the child spent his life with a phobia of white rats. However, theoretically, as it took so many conditioning trials for Little Albert to develop his fear, it is likely that his reaction would not have persisted for any significant length of time in his life. It is also known that Little Albert died young from a childhood illness.

for potential **context effects** in the experiment. One could argue that conducting the experiment in the same room could make the effects of conditioning specific to a particular environment. However, the researchers noted that fear reactions were still evident in in Albert in the lecture room. Thirty-one days into the experiment, Little Albert was taken from the hospital by his mother.

Results

The study confirmed that a phobia of an object that was not previously feared could be learned. If a neutral stimulus (in this case, the white rat) is associated with an unconditioned stimulus (the loud bang) which naturally triggers an unconditioned response (fear), successive introductions of the white rat together with a loud bang would lead to a stimulus association being formed. The presence of the rat (now a conditioned stimulus) resulted in fear (now the conditioned response). Stimulus generalisation was observed as Albert transferred his feared response to other animals and objects that were broadly similar to the white rat. In this study, Albert's fear response lasted for 31 days after the emotional tests were carried out, although the reaction became weaker towards the end. It was not possible to test Albert's fear response over a longer period of time, as he left the hospital.

Conclusion

Watson and Rayner concluded that an infant could be classically conditioned to develop a fear of a white rat. They also proposed that, since the fear reaction was present one month after the initial association, such conditioned emotional responses have the potential to last a life time. Objects similar to the feared stimulus can also elicit a feared response.

Evaluation

Watson's research makes a notable contribution to the understanding of the acquisition of human behaviours through the principles of classical conditioning. It also highlights the importance of the role of the environment in the shaping of our behaviour. Furthermore, a strength of Watson and Rayner's study lies in its scientific methodology. The researchers employed a degree of control in observing the stimulus-response link. For instance, they measured fear in Little Albert before the conditioning took place to act as a baseline comparison. They also conducted the study in another room to eliminate the effect of context as an extraneous variable; if they had not done this the researchers could not have been sure whether Little Albert was fearful of the white rat or just the room in which he was conditioned. Behaviours shown at every stage were copiously documented, ensuring potential replication. As a result of the methodology employed, the reliability of the study could be assured.

Many would criticise this study for a lack of ecological validity. This is because the location of study was largely a laboratory-like environment; in addition the tasks given to Little Albert were not necessarily those that would be expected to confront him in normal everyday life.

Although ethical guidelines as we know them today did not exist at the time of Watson and Rayner's research, the study can still be criticised on ethical and moral grounds. It could be claimed that the psychological and the physical well-being of the Little Albert was neglected by the research because he was quite obviously distressed by the conditioning process and the researchers were unable to decondition his phobia. Fridlund et al. (2012) suggest that Albert was not as healthy as Watson described.

They claim that Albert had suffered hydrocephalus since birth (an accumulation of cerebrospinal fluid in the brain) and presented a convincing argument that Watson knew about the child's condition.

Key term

Context effects: the surrounding environment influences how an event is perceived.

Taking it further

Use an Internet search engine to research the original footage of the Little Albert experiment.

If Fridlund et al. are correct about Albert's health, this casts serious doubt over Watson and Rayner's findings and raises further ethical and moral questions about their approach.

A significant problem in generalising from the research is that the case study is of one individual child. One of the reasons why Watson and Rayner selected Little Albert as a research participant was for his unemotional character. Therefore, Little Albert may not be representative of individuals of the same age and gender and this could invalidate the findings.

Finally, the research could be criticised for cultural bias. Albert and the researchers themselves represent one culture (USA). This would have influenced their design of the study and their subsequent analysis of results. As a result there is a question over the generalisability of their findings to other cultures.

WIDER ISSUES AND DEBATES

Nature–nurture

One of the oldest debates in psychology surrounds the influence of environmental factors versus the influence of genetics in determining/constructing behaviour. Watson and Rayner's research is interesting in that we would assume there to be a natural feared reaction to hearing a loud noise – surprise. However the study shows that such a natural reaction can be adjusted, to become associated with certain items. This study therefore raises important questions with regard to the nature–nurture debate: might it be more productive to see behaviours through a composite explanation (an interaction) of both nature and nurture – rather than nature or nurture?

Capafóns et al. (1998): Systematic desensitization in the treatment of fear of flying

Aim

Juan Capafóns, Carmen Sosa and Pedro Avero aimed to validate the effectiveness of systematic desensitisation as a treatment for a fear of flying, and to assess the therapeutic success of systematic desensitisation when applied to this type of specific phobia.

Procedure

Participants were recruited for the study using a media campaign, which informed them of the opportunity to take part in a free-of-charge intervention programme aimed at treating fear of flying. In total, 41 participants came forward and 20 of these (8 males and 12 females) were randomly assigned to the treatment group (the group that would be subject to systematic desensitisation therapy. The remaining 21 (9 males and 12 females) were assigned to a control group (waiting for systematic desensitisation therapy). Various diagnostic scales were used to assess participants' fear of flying, in particular the IDG-FV (a Spanish general diagnostic information tool on the fear of flying). Three key questions in the IDG-FV were allowed measurement before and after treatment.

Other measures for assessing the dependent variables pre- and post-treatment included three other fear of flying scales (EMV scales):

1 fear displayed during the flight

2 fear of flight preliminaries – situations preliminary to the actual flight, for example going to the airport, obtaining boarding card, etc.)

3 fear without involvement – this contains four elements not directly related to flying, for example seeing a plane.

There were also two EPAV scales (Scales of Expectation of Danger and Anxiety) that measured the occurrence of catastrophic thoughts, such as the fear of the engine catching fire, or wing falling off, and additional measures of subjective physiological anxiety.

The researchers additionally recorded the participant's actual physiological arousal using measures of heart rate, palm temperature and muscular tension.

All participants were interviewed individually and completed the IDG-FV. They later came back to watch a video of a plane trip (showing a person from the time she packed her case to her arriving by plane at her destination). Just before watching the video there was a **habituation** session involving a period of time during which the participant could become acquainted with the situation. It was here that the participants' heart rate, temperature and muscular tension were measured for a period of three minutes prior to the showing of the video. The participants were asked to 'feel as involved as possible' in the video.

At the end of the video, an interview appointment was made for presenting the treatment to be followed (in the case of the treatment group), or for the next assessment session (in the control group subjects). In both cases the interval between the pre- and post-test sessions was approximately eight weeks. For the treatment group this involved two one-hour sessions a week with between 12 and 15 sessions in total. The session used traditional training techniques of breathing, **progressive muscle relaxation** and imagination. The treatment combined in vitro (imagined situations) and in vivo elements (exposure to real-life situations). It systematically used the technique of stop thinking and of brief relaxation in natural situations where the phobic stimulus was present. After eight weeks, the treatment and control group were invited back to retake the questionnaires and simulated video test.

Key terms

Habituation: the process by which a response to a given stimulus is seen to decrease with repetition.

Progressive muscle relaxation: in each session the therapist focuses the client on tensing and relaxing one particular muscle group to create awareness of tension and relaxation.

Results

The table shows three different measures taken before and after systematic desensitisation (or no therapy) in the treatment and control groups. Before any treatment began, the scores between both groups were fairly similar, suggesting that there was little differences between them and that they were a fairly homogenous sample.

Table 4.8 Some of the pre and post-test results

Mean (SD)	Pre-test		Post-test	
	Treatment condition	Control group	Treatment condition	Control group
Fear during flight EMV Scale	25.6 (4.2)	26.05 (3.67)	13.25 (7.97)	25.81 (4.8) $p<0.001$
Catastrophic thoughts EPAV Scale	10.30 (4.17)	9.76 (4.92)	5.0 (2.64)	9.67 (5.61) $p<0.01$
Objective physiological measures: heart rate	1.04 (0.09)	1.07 (0.1)	0.99 (0.04)	1.31 (0.09) $p<0.01$

For the control group the 'mere passing of time' without any form of treatment did not lead to any reduction in the participants' assessment of their own fear of flying or objective measures of arousal. Yet for the treatment group (with the exception of two participants) there were significant arousal reduction in the participants' self-reporting of their levels of fear as well as in objective physiological measures.

Of the scores they obtained using the scales and objective physiological measures, they found that there was a significant reduction in fear measures following systematic desensitisation; many of these changes were highly significant. In fact only 10 per cent of those treated with systematic desensitisation showed no significant reduction in fear measures.

Conclusions

Capafóns et al. concluded that given the lack of improvement in the control group and the significant improvement of the experimental group, systematic desensitisation is an effective treatment for decreasing or eradicating fear of flying. He noted however, that systematic desensitisation is not infallible given that 10 per cent of participants were incorrectly classified. This suggests that future research should look at why the therapy was successful and why it was more or less successful in certain patients.

Exam tip

Remember that 'not significant' does not mean that no difference was found, in this case between pre- and post-test analysis. It just means that there was a 5 per cent greater likelihood that the results were due to chance.

You also need to consider what 'difference' is being investigated. If the analysis suggests no significant difference between two therapies, for example, it suggests that the therapies had a similar success rate. Students often mistake 'non-significant' findings as being worthless findings. This is sometimes not the case; you need to examine what the difference being examined is before making a judgement. If, for example, one therapy is cheap and one is expensive, a non-significant difference between them could help the NHS direct resources to the cheaper therapy if there is no difference in terms of effectiveness.

Evaluation

A strength of this study is in its application of a scientific method of assessment. Measures of fear and anxiety were achieved through quantifiable data, such as the use of scales to assess fear of flying, and objective measures such as heart rate and body temperature to determine the fear response; many of these scales were also validated for reliability.

The use of a control group is also advantageous as it acts as a baseline comparison between the two groups. This allows researchers to analyse differences between the groups in terms of the dependent variables and test for statistical significance, giving the researchers more confidence in their overall findings.

Undertaking the research within a consistent, laboratory-based environment meant that every participant experienced the initial stages of the study in the same way. Such standardisation in procedure would minimise the effect of any extraneous variables affecting the study. Of enormous benefit is the practical application of the findings. If participants benefit significantly from the therapy then this would suggest it should be offered as one of the main methods for treating fear of flying and, in doing so, bring significant personal, social and economic benefits as individuals are not prevented from flying on business or to visit distant relatives.

The study is somewhat limited due to the small sample size of 41 people. This causes a problem of generalisability: an ability to apply conclusions from the study to a wider population. To address this issue, researchers could increase the size of the sample in future and perhaps look for consistency of findings with other groups of participants, possibly in other regions or countries. In addition, one of the main methods for assessing fear of flying was conducted by means of interview questioning. This, while being quite a logical assessment, could be seen to limit the validity of the responses given. This is because techniques such as interviews rely on self-reporting (that is, a respondent stating their view/answer). Where, as in this study, closed-ended questions are used and especially where preset responses are given, as in the case of the IDG-FV system used in the study, respondents often choose a response that 'best fits' rather than accurately describing their view. Validity of response is limited, as the respondent's true view might not be 'best matched'.

The study also raises some ethical questions. While the control group offers useful comparisons, it is not acceptable to deny them the treatment. This ethical problem was lessened by the fact that the control group were placed on a waiting list for treatment.

Becker et al. (2002): Eating behaviours and attitudes following prolonged exposure to television among ethnic Fijian adolescent girls

Aim

Dr Anne Becker and her colleagues aimed to investigate the effect of prolonged exposure of television on attitudes to eating and eating behaviours in Fijian adolescent girls.

Procedure

This **naturalistic experiment** made use of a **prospective multi-wave cross-sectional** design, using two separate samples of adolescent females from Nadroga, Fiji. The first sample of 63 girls was studied in 1995, several weeks before the introduction of television to Fiji. A second different sample of 65 girls was studied three years later in 1998. The study involved a combination of qualitative and quantitative methods to investigate the impact of culture on the participants' feelings and attitudes, and eating behaviours. The key question was: would exposure to television, which introduced images and programmes from the developed world (mainly the United States), have an effect on the traditional values and eating habits associated with Fijian culture, namely a preference for a robust body, the encouragement of robust appetites and a widespread vigilance for and social response to weight loss? Moreover, dieting and exercise have been traditionally discouraged by Fijian culture.

Initially, both groups completed a modified version of the **EAT-26 survey** that investigated bingeing and purging behaviours. The use of this survey was important as this self-reporting method allowed researchers to obtain quantitative data about the participants' attitudes towards eating. Each response was scored, and a score of 20 was deemed high. The significance of this score is that it indicates that the person is completing the test views themselves, and has attitudes towards eating that are deemed necessary to elicit further intervention – thus there is a concern that the eating attitude is disordered. Separate questions were asked about subjects such as household ownership and television viewing. Those who initially responded highly (above 20) on the EAT-26 survey were then asked to take part in a semi-structured interview.

In the second sample in 1998, further questions were added on body image and dieting as well as questions to determine any disparities between themselves and their parents concerning diet and weight. A varied subset of 30 girls from the original 65 with a range of disordered eating habits and behaviours were followed up with an interview that included probing, open ended-questions aimed at investigating practices concerning weight and diet.

Results

Two significant differences were noted between the groups of girls studied in 1995 (before television was introduced) and 1998 (after television was introduced). Firstly, the percentage of subjects with an EAT-26 score of more than 20 had more than doubled (growing from 12.7 per cent in 1995 to 29.2 per cent in 1998). Secondly, the proportion of the sample that used self-induced vomiting as a means of weight control increased from 0 per cent in 1995 to 11.3 per cent in 1998. Body dissatisfaction increased, with significantly more 1998 respondents reporting that they thought they should eat less.

Key terms

Naturalistic experiment: a type of experiment that occurs in a natural setting (and where the independent variable is not being manipulated by the experimenter).

Prospective design: a study that begins at the starting point of a change and tracks development over time, looking forward rather than looking back (retrospective).

Multi-wave: where there are several different measurements being used in the study.

Cross-sectional: (research that looks at a group of individuals within a set period of time (as opposed to longitudinal research where the same individuals are examined over a prolonged period of time).

EAT-26 Survey: A widely used self-measure assessment of characteristics/behaviours associated with eating disorders.

Qualitative data derived from the study followed several themes:

- an admiration for characters seen on television (a tendency for women to imitate role models by changing their behaviour, choice of clothing or hairstyle): 83 per cent of the sample interviewed felt that television had influenced the way they and their friends looked at their bodies, with 77 per cent stating that television had influenced their body image

- a belief that eating less might actually improve their career prospects with 40 per cent of participants interviewed justifying their desire to eat less or lose weight as a means of improving career prospects or becoming more useful at home. In addition, 30 per cent of those interviewed indicated that television characters served as role models concerning work or career issues

- an awareness of generational differences towards eating, with parental generations feeling that the girls should eat more, while the younger girls had a desire to eat less.

Conclusion

From this study Becker concluded that in Fiji, (which until the late 1990s had no form of organised visual media communication), the introduction of television influenced changes to eating attitudes in women, which ran counter to the traditional attitudes towards eating and body image that had previously dominated within that culture.

Evaluation

A strength of Becker's study is that it illustrates good reliability of findings. This would be because Becker draws similar conclusions about the influence of the media to previous studies (Lee, 1998; Furnham and Husain, 1999), yet is the first to examine media influence on disordered eating attitude in a media-naive culture. As a result, such research has practical application and can be used to press for more regulation of extreme body forms (size zero models) in the various types of visual media in society. Becker's study furthermore has a high level of ecological validity, because the study examines a naturally occurring event. As a result, the impact can be assessed in the wider context of conflicting cultural values.

While the study holds significant strengths, issues of validity of diagnosis are apparent. The EAT-26 survey provides indicators of eating attitudes, not a formal clinical diagnosis. As a result, the disordered eating attitudes and behaviours observed cannot necessarily be equated with the presence of an eating disorder. The issue of self-induced vomiting and its association with eating disorders is a western phenomenon, and does not take account of the Fijian historical and cultural background, which might not associate these behaviours with body dissatisfaction.

A further criticism could be made with relation to the samples. While the participants in the two samples used in the cross-sectional design were matched as closely as possible, these were not directly comparable and there was the possibility of a cohort effect. As a result, comparisons between the two groups are problematic. There were also only 63 or 65 in each sample; therefore they may not have been representative of the whole Fijian population, which was around 85 000 at the time of the study.

Other variables, such as developing consumerism or peer group influence, could also increase disordered eating habits. The respondents not only made explicit references to how television had influenced them, but also to how their peers' views of what was admirable in television characters affected them. Thus peer influence may have been a mediating factor on body image.

Despite Becker's claim that the Fijian society was virtually absent of eating disorders, she recorded high scores on the questionnaire equating to eight girls at the beginning of the study. Only an additional 12 girls scored high on the questionnaire three years later. So although this increase was statistically significant, it is perhaps misleading to conclude that the media had a significant influence on the girls' eating behaviour.

The use of psychological knowledge within society

The Becker study clearly claims that the watching of television by a media-naive society has the potential to change behaviour (as measured by level of body dissatisfaction and disordered eating attitude) – even where cultural beliefs are historically well grounded and resilient in older generations. The influence of the media in this study shows that visual imagery is a powerful force in changing a person's view of their body and levels of satisfaction towards it. Such research therefore can be used to inform future debates about the nature and size of models in fashion and television shows as well as images broadcast within popular music videos and films. Learning theory informs us that imitation is possible from role models. If models in the media are idolised, then their body form is likely to be imitated by younger generations. Psychological knowledge can be used within society to greater regulate this area, ensuring that images broadcast are realistic and promote health rather than limit it.

Bastian et al. (2012): Cyber-dehumanization: Violent video game play diminishes our humanity

Aim

The negative effects of violent video games have been well documented (Anderson and Bushman, 2001; Dill, Brown and Collins, 2008; Anderson et al., 2010). But before 2011 it had not been so well documented whether violent game play could have dehumanising effects on those who played the games. Brock Bastian, Jolanda Jetten and Helena Radke wanted to investigate to what extent the games affected participants' perception of their own humanity as well as that of their co-players.

Procedure: Study 1

This research had two parts.

Using *Mortal Kombat* as the violent game, and *Top Spin Tennis* as the non-violent video game 106 undergraduates (74 women and 32 men aged between 17 and 34) were randomly assigned to either the violent or non-violent condition. They played their two-player game for a period of 15 minutes with a dividing wall between players so they could not see each other or be affected by another's game playing. Participants were then were given a questionnaire to complete. The questionnaire included questions concerning how enjoyable the game was, how exciting and how frustrating it was. The questions were framed using a 1 to 7 Likert-type scale rating. Using a separate scale, participants were asked to assess their own level of 'humanness'.

Results: Study 1

They found that participants in both conditions found the games equally frustrating, but *Mortal Kombat* was rated as more enjoyable and significantly more exciting. They also found that the mean score for self-humanity was lower in the violent game condition (3.74) than the non-violent game (4.35), and mean score for others' humanity lower in the violent game condition (4.43) compared to the non-violent game (4.93). Even when factors such as gender, enjoyment and frustration were accounted for in their analysis, the findings were still statistically significant.

Bastian's predictions about the effects of violent games on perceptions of humanity were confirmed. He found that playing a violent game, as opposed to playing a game with little or no violence, resulted in reduced perceptions of an individual's humanness as well as that of their opponent.

Procedure: Study 2

While Study 1 showed clear links between video game violence and dehumanised perceptions of oneself and of an opponent, Bastian felt that several questions remained unanswered. Firstly, the characters in *Mortal Kombat* are clearly not human. Could it have been that reduced levels of humanness were reported because the participant simply saw themselves as another character in the game?

Or was it that simply the act of placing a person in a situation of conflict against another leads to a reduction in our perceived level of humanness. Could playing the game actually induce the participant to view themselves negatively (that is, they feel bad after playing the game) and thus negatively assess themselves after the game?

The second study aimed to overcome the limitations of the first one and seek answers to these questions. First, participants played the games not as opponents but as co-players. Secondly, the assessment system measures of stated self-esteem and mood were incorporated into the assessment system. Finally, participants played *Call of Duty 2*, a violent first-person shooter game where the player experiences the action through the eyes of the character, with computer characters that are more humanlike. Using 38 undergraduates (28 women, 10 men with an average age of 20), participants were randomly assigned to the *Call of Duty 2* condition or the *Top Spin Tennis* condition. Participants played for a period of 20 minutes as co-players. After playing they were then asked as before how frustrating, enjoyable and exciting the game was. They then had to rate themselves and the other person on the same measure of humanness in Study 1, specifically focusing on their own experience of the video game, and then the view of the other person.

Results: Study 2

Study 2 shows that the playing of a violent game did reduce a person's own self-reported perception of their humanness when playing both first-person shooter games and acting collaboratively rather than against a co-player. The study further illustrated that engaging in violent games does not necessarily make us feel bad, or see ourselves more negatively, but it might affect how 'human' we feel. Indeed the simple playing of a violent game also does not affect our perception of the humanness of others – this is only affected when the other person is an opponent not a co-perpetrator. The study indicated that there are many variables needing to be accounted for in understanding the complex effect of video games and dehumanisation, and that future research in this area will add weight to the conclusions.

Conclusion

In Bastian's own words: the studies have provided a means by which we can understand the effects of violent video games on behaviour, our emotions and the way we think. Furthermore, the study provided the first empirical evidence that people might perceive themselves as less human when playing violent games. In addition to this the research has shown the following.

(A) People do view themselves as less human when engaged in violent game play compared to equally competitive non-violent game play. This is further noted to be the case when the opponent is a co-player or even a computer-generated character.

(B) When engaged in acts of violence towards other co-players our view of their humanness is also affected, more so than when the co-player is an opponent in a non-violent game play.

Thus the Bastian et al. study contributes further to previous research in the area on dehumanisation, and as people increasingly spend longer periods of time playing online games the likelihood and possibility of such experiences dehumanising the players is greater. This could suggest that repeated exposure to such dehumanising experiences might result in radical changes in self-perception and perception of others.

Evaluation

The Bastian et al. study very clearly has real-world application. Computer gaming is very popular, and with computer animation becoming ever more realistic, and the consoles becoming more affordable, questions need to be asked about its effect on behaviour. This is because it contributes to a widely held and heated debate on the effects of violent computer games and particularly the effects that prolonged exposure can have on its audience, especially children. Studies like this have led to and helped justify the use of age certification of games.

Furthermore, the Bastian et al. research results concur with previous research in the area on the video game effect. Studies conducted by notable authorities such as Anderson and Bushman (2001); Anderson, Gentile and Buckley (2007); and Anderson and Bushman (2007) all show negative impacts and effects on behaviour through video gaming. As a result, this adds to the academic impetus of the present research of Bastian et al. and his unique drive to examine dehumanisation in this process, which had not been examined previously.

A problem with concluding that video gaming causes dehumanisation of self and others is that the participants playing the games were actually also victims of game violence, either by another player or by a game avatar. It is perhaps because they were victims that the scores of self-humanity were reduced following playing the violent games.

This study was ethically appropriate on many grounds. This is because individuals were fully informed in their decisions to take part; the study itself holds limited if any deception, and the research team illustrated their competence as researchers throughout. As a result the research ensures that the moral standards expected in psychological research are maintained.

However, the Bastian et al. research illustrates problems of generalisability because the study used a small and biased sample. Between the two studies, the majority were women. As a result it is arguable that this gender bias (gynocentric result) might produce findings that are not globally representative of a typical computer gaming population. Furthermore, questions of validity can be raised with Bastian's research, such as with the rating scales that the researchers used. Bastian himself admits that participants might have been compelled to rate themselves less human or more negatively given the context in which they were studied. However, participants indicated that they did not suspect that the research concerned a link between video game violence and dehumanisation.

WIDER ISSUES AND DEBATES

An understanding of how psychological understanding has developed over time

The Bastian et al. study illustrates clearly (as do other related pieces of research in the area) that gaming does have an effect on individuals, and this study specifically suggests that gaming would seem to lead to a reduction in the way in which we rate our humanness. Although computer games have been available in basic forms for 20 to 30 years, it is really only in the last 10 years that consoles have been produced with increasingly life-like forms and perspectives.

It was not a focus of psychological interest 40 years ago but gaming is now at the forefront of psychological research. Psychology therefore cannot be a static science, but one that changes with the ebb and flow of social behaviour and interest. As gaming becomes an ever-popular pastime for individuals, psychologists must continue to research into the potential effects on users. A better knowledge of the effects of gaming can lead to a fruitful discussion of how to change and develop them in the future.

4.4 Key questions

Learning outcomes

In this section, you will learn about:

- 'fear of flying' as a key question of relevance to today's society
- how this key issue can be linked to and explained by learning theories.

Should airline companies/airports offer treatment programmes to passengers with a fear of flying?

Fear of flying in society

Fear of flying includes fear of travel by air, or just of sitting in a plane – even when stationary.

It is estimated that one in six of us are fearful of flying. While fear of flying is a distinct phobia in itself, it may also be associated with other phobias and anxiety disorders such as a fear of heights (acrophobia) or claustrophobia (a phobia of confined spaces). When individuals are asked about why they fear flying the most common explanation is fear of crashing; however, other explanations include not being in control, fear of having a panic attack and – increasingly – fear of hijacking.

Following the 11 September 2001 terror attacks on the twin towers of the World Trade Center in New York, passenger miles on the main US airlines fell by between 12 per cent and 20 per cent, while road use jumped. Professor Gerd Gigerenzer, a psychologist specialising in risk behaviour, estimated that an extra 1595 Americans died in car accidents in the year after the attacks. The change is widely believed to have been caused by passengers opting to drive rather than fly; this was a behavioural change induced by fear of flying. Statistically speaking, travelling long distances by car is more dangerous than travelling by plane. Gigerenzer ascribed these extra road deaths to people's poor understanding of risk and danger.

Aerophobia receives more attention than many other phobias because air travel is often unavoidable in modern society. Many business people need to fly on a regular basis in the course of their everyday work. Thus fear of flying would prevent them from travelling on work-related business and can also prevent people going abroad on holiday or to visit family and friends overseas. The fear therefore has significant economic, social and emotional consequences and raises the question: should airline companies/airports offer treatment programmes to passengers with a fear of flying? For example, easyJet offers a 'Fearless Flyer course' and Virgin Atlantic offers a 'Flying Without Fear course', which are both designed to help passengers overcome their fear of flying. In 2011, Manchester Airport introduced a psychologist, offering free therapy sessions in the Terminal One departures lounge.

Explaining the issue using learning theories

It is widely accepted that the way that we acquire a fear or phobic response is the same way as Pavlov conditioned his dogs to salivate at different stimuli. We learn to associate a neutral stimulus with the fear response via classical conditioning. For example, it is possible that a person may become fearful of flying because they experienced turbulence on a previous flight, causing them to experience stress and anxiety. The next time a person considers taking a flight they exhibit a similar fear response. According to the theory of classical conditioning, prior to experiencing turbulence, flying was a neutral stimulus (NS) and fear the unconditioned response (UCR). After the unnerving experience of turbulence, flying now becomes conditioned stimulus (CS) as it has now become associated with the anxiety experienced during the turbulent flight. Anxiety has therefore become the conditioned response (CR) to flying.

A fear of flying can also be acquired through operant conditioning by repeatedly reinforcing the avoidance of a mildly fearful situation. For example, if a man has a relatively minor fear of flying and his wife agrees to drive or take the ferry instead of flying, the person's fear of flying has been reinforced and may develop into a full blown phobia. The fear can also be maintained by operant conditioning process through negative reinforcement. When a person is confronted with the object or situation of their phobia, they tend to get anxious and avoid the object/situation. The avoidance behaviour reduces this anxiety and therefore becomes negatively reinforced and the phobia is maintained. A person with aerophobia will therefore avoid flying and such actions would lessen or remove the unpleasant anxiety experienced.

Finally, we do not need to experience fear directly in order to become fearful of flying. Observational learning or social learning theory could also explain the situation. A person may witness news reports of a plane crash on the television, which may trigger feelings of anxiety and thus the fear is reinforced vicariously. Alternatively, they may have observed a parent or the reactions of another person on board a flight when turbulence occurred and this may be sufficient to induce a fear response to flying.

Treating fear of flying via the learning theories approach

Unsurprisingly, the methods used to treat aerophobia are based around 'unlearning' the fear response: typically using classical conditioning principles where fear is substituted with the response of relaxation. This is known as **reciprocal inhibition**. Those who fear flying may be taught several calming techniques such as deep breathing and progressive muscle relaxation. In progressive muscle relaxation the client is told to relax. It is progressive in the sense that it proceeds through all the

Key term 💬

Reciprocal inhibition: two contrasting emotions cannot co-exist – you cannot be relaxed and scared at the same time.

major muscle groups, relaxing them one at a time so the client eventually experiences total muscle relaxation.

Systematic desensitisation is another technique that can be used to treat a fear of flying as discussed earlier in the topic. The client is required to form a list of issues that begin with the least feared, such as looking at a photograph of a plane, through to the most fearful situation such as actual take-off and landing. This hierarchy is then worked through with the therapist, while using some of the relaxation techniques mentioned above. As seen earlier, Capafóns et al. (1998) concluded that systematic desensitisation is an effective treatment for fear of flying.

Many of the fear of flying courses run by airlines claim to have a 92 to 98 per cent success rate and utilise some of the learning techniques mentioned above, in addition to using techniques from the cognitive approach, which aim to challenge the negative thought processes associated with flying.

Fear of flying courses have been criticised for being expensive and difficult to access outside large cities. As the courses are largely sponsored by airlines there is concern that they have not been subjected to rigorous evaluation. **Virtual reality exposure therapy** offers an alternative treatment option. This involves clients being exposed to a computer-generated three-dimensional virtual aeroplane rather than an actual aeroplane. Rothbaum et al. (2000) studied participants with a phobia of flying who were given four sessions of anxiety management training followed by either virtual reality exposure (VRE) therapy or standard therapy (an actual aeroplane), or a control group. A post-treatment flight immediately after treatment measured participants' willingness to fly and anxiety during the flight. The results found no differences between VRE and standard therapy. Six months after treatment, 93 per cent of VRE participants and 93 per cent of standard therapy participants had flown. This suggests that VRE therapy and traditional therapy for fear of flying are equally effective.

Key term

Virtual reality exposure therapy: a method of therapy using virtual reality technologies to treat phobias and anxiety disorders.

Taking it further

Investigate easyJet's 'Fearless Flyer course' and/or Virgin Atlantic's 'Flying Without Fear course'.

- Can you identify the underlying learning theory principles involved in the courses?
- What other strategies are involved? To which psychological approach do they belong?

4.5 Practical investigation

Learning outcomes

In this section, you will learn:

- how observational data is collected
- how quantitative and qualitative data can be analysed
- to analyse research findings using a chi-squared test
- how to present your qualitative and quantitative findings in an appropriate format
- how your practical observation can be linked to and explained by learning theories.
- to critically evaluate your practical observation

Observing gender differences in behaviour on public transport

Observational research allows psychologists to collect quantitative and qualitative data. In this section, we will work through a practical example of an observational study of prosocial/polite behaviour in men and women on public transport such as a bus or a train. As we have already seen, Bandura suggested that children observing an aggressive role model will later replicate this antisocial behaviour. Through conducting an observational study you will be able to investigate whether social learning theory may also explain the modelling of more prosocial behaviours in society. As part of your studies in psychology you will be required to conduct two observations (one quantitative and one qualitative) or one observation that gathers both qualitative and quantitative at the same time. Through conducting an observational study you will be able to investigate whether social learning theory may also explain the modelling of more prosocial behaviours in society.

Within psychology, observations can be used as a technique within an actual experiment or as an overall research method. Bandura for example, used observation as a technique within his experiment. In this instance we will be using observation as an actual research method.

Prosocial behaviour can be defined as any behaviour that is intended to benefit another.

Hypotheses

The aim of your research is to investigate gender differences in behaviours on public transport such as prosocial behaviours or politeness. In quantitative observational research, it is important that the prosocial behaviours you are observing can be clearly measured. In formulating your hypothesis, you will need to decide whether to select a directional (one-tailed) or non-directional (two-tailed) hypothesis. Generally speaking, if researchers are unsure of the effect, they will use a non-directional hypothesis. If, however, they have an idea of which way the research will go, perhaps through the results of previous studies that have been done, then they will use a directional hypothesis. Whatever hypothesis you choose, it is very important that it is clearly testable.

Background and links to learning theories

Social learning theory can be used to explain gender differences in society. It suggests that we learn gender-appropriate behaviours from the people around us, for example parents, teachers, siblings, peers and the media. These role models show us how to behave and also reinforce gender-appropriate behaviours through rewards and punishments. The theory can therefore explain stereotypes in society such as women being kind, helpful and perhaps being more polite and friendly to people on the whole. These behaviours may be modelled and rewarded in females more than males. Eagly (2009) suggested that women and men both engage in prosocial behaviours, equally. However, women tend to engage in more communal and relational prosocial behaviours whereas men tend to display more agentic prosocial behaviours, meaning that men engage in prosocial acts to gain status or to show their strength to others. Similarly, a study by Leslie, Snyder and Glomb (2013) examining workplace donations to charity suggested that women donated more than men. This may therefore suggest that women will show more helpful and polite behaviours on public transport than men, for example giving up a seat, helping with a pram, polite interactions with drivers and fellow passengers or making way for fellow passengers to squeeze through on a crowded bus.

Because the background literature and research on gender and prosocial behaviour is mixed, a non-directional hypothesis will be put forward: there will be a difference in the number of males and females who thank the bus driver before alighting.

Planning an observation

In planning your quantitative observation you will need to think about the statistical test that you will use later to analyse your data. In this instance, you have participants who are distinguished by category – male and female. They can only be in one of these categories so the data in unrelated.

Before conducting your observation you will have a few design decisions to make. You will more than likely be undertaking a naturalistic observation as you will be observing participants in a natural setting. You will need to decide when and where you will undertake your observations. This will include factors such as which bus or train route, the day of the week, the time of day and the duration of your journey. All of these factors will influence how many passengers there will be and the type of passenger travelling. This example practical observation will be a naturalistic observation of people on a bus, so the sampling technique used to recruit participants will be opportunity sampling.

You will also need to consider the type of behaviour you are going to observe. Do not overcomplicate – stick to one observable behaviour that you can focus on and count easily. For instance, you may decide to measure polite behaviour by whether or not bus passengers thank the driver before alighting.

Other behaviours could include assisting other passengers, giving up a seat or making way for others on a crowded bus. Once you have decided which prosocial behaviours are suitable to investigate on a bus journey, you will need to draw a chart so that you can tally each time a passenger displays such behaviour.

Table 4.9 Example of an observation record

	Male	Female
Thanking the bus driver		
Giving up a seat on the bus		
Helping a passenger with a pushchair		

As you will be able to count up the instances of polite or prosocial behaviour occurring, you will be able to tally the observations – this is quantitative data that can be tested for significance with an inferential statistical test. Your observation can also use qualitative data by writing down what you observed in more detail; for instance, what passengers actually said, or annotating your observations in more detail in your notepad about whether the bus driver was male or female, the age of participants whether there was eye contact.

Pilot study

Before you conduct your observation, you may want to give it a 'dry run' via a pilot study to address any potential problems and test out your observational criteria. For instance, where is the best position to observe behaviours? If you are observing interactions with the driver, it would pay to sit closer to the front. You may want to see how long the journey needs to be to give you enough data. At busy times such as rush hour can you observe everyone?

Controls

You might want to consider recruiting someone to help you, for example with one of you observing male passengers and your friend, female passengers. You would however need to consider factors such as inter-rater reliability (the degree of agreement between two or more observers) to ensure you are both being consistent in your observations. Your observation is likely to be covert (participants are unaware they are being observed) but it could be worth checking if passengers pay attention to your note taking and become suspicious, which could pose a confounding variable for your observations.

Ethical considerations

Observations in public places are considered an ethical place to observe people because you might well be expected to be observed by others in your day-to day interactions. This would include public transport, such as buses and trains. As you are not collecting names or any other personal data, only the gender and the observed behaviour, you will not be contravening ethical guidelines.

Analysing quantitative data

This practical investigation example has collected the data on an hour's bus journey between 3.00 and 4.00 pm on a Thursday afternoon. In all, 51 passengers were observed, 24 females and 27 males. It tallied the number of males and females on whether they thanked the bus driver not.

Maths tip

A pilot study is not used to test whether an investigation is valid or reliable, it is only used to check that apparatus, timings, and so on work correctly. A pilot study is a useful opportunity to ask participants whether they felt uncomfortable, suspected anything was going on or felt their behaviour was influenced in any way.

Summary of design decisions
- Naturalistic observation method
- Non-directional hypothesis
- Covert observation
- Inter-rater reliability
- Event sampling and qualitative data collection

You could present your data as follows in preparation for a chi-squared test.

Table 4.10 Presentation of data

	Male	Female	Total
Thanked the bus driver	11 (cell A)	18 (cell B)	29
Did not thank the bus driver	16 (cell C)	6 (cell D)	22
Total	27	24	**51**

The table shows that 11 males and 18 females thanked the bus driver when alighting, whereas 16 males and 6 females did not thank the driver on alighting. This is known as a two-by-two contingency table, which is suitable for nominal data.

From analysing the table, you will see that there is a fairly equal frequency of male and female participants observed on the bus journey. There is also a small difference in the number of male and female passengers who thanked the driver.

What do the results suggest in relation to the initial hypothesis? Is the difference significantly large? It is difficult to tell if the results are significant or due to chance, so an inferential test can help to determine if we can accept our experimental hypothesis and reject our null hypothesis.

Carrying out a chi-squared test

The chi-squared test is the most appropriate statistical test in this circumstance as the study is predicting a difference, it is using related data and we have nominal level data.

The following procedures apply to conducting a chi-squared test:

1 You first need to calculate the expected values against the observed values. The observed values are the ones in our contingency table – 11, 18, 16, 6. The expected values need to be calculated for each cell in our table by working out how the data would be distributed if there were no differences in the pattern, that is no difference between males and females in thanking the bus driver. This is done by using the totals for each row or column.

Expected value = row total × column total / overall total

Cell	E = row × column/total
A	29 × 27 / 51 = 15.35
B	29 × 24 / 51 = 13.65
C	22 × 27 / 51 = 11.65
D	22 × 24 / 51 = 10.35

2 You will now need to take the expected value (E) from the observed value (O) for each of the cells and square the result. Then you divide that result by the expected value (E). Finally add the four results to find the overall chi-squared result.

Cell	
A	$(11-15.35)^2$ / 15.35 = 1.23
B	$(18-13.65)^2$ / 13.65 = 1.39
C	$(16-11.65)^2$ / 11.65 = 1.62
D	$(6-10.35)^2$ / 10.35 = 1.83
Total	**= 6.07**

3 Find the critical value for chi-squared by first calculating the degrees of freedom (df). This is done by multiplying (rows-1) × (columns-1) of your table. In our two-by-two contingency table, this means our df =1.

Compare the overall observed value against the critical values table. For a one-tailed hypothesis, with df=1, the critical value at a significance level of ($p<0.05$) is 2.71. As the observed value of (6.07) is greater than the critical value in the table (2.71), the result is significant and the null hypothesis can be rejected. This means that there is less than a 5 per cent probability that the difference in prosocial behaviour displayed by males and females is due to chance. The direction of this difference can be established by examining the cells/totals. In this case, females travelling on the bus were more likely to thank the bus driver and males were not.

df	Level of significance for a one-tailed test					
	0.10	0.05	0.025	0.01	0.005	0.0005
	Level of significance for a two-tailed test					
	0.20	0.10	0.05	0.025	0.01	0.001
1	1.64	2.71	3.84	5.02	6.64	10.83
2	3.22	4.61	5.99	7.38	9.21	13.82
3	4.64	6.25	7.82	9.35	11.35	16.27
4	5.99	7.78	9.49	11.14	13.28	18.47
5	7.29	9.24	11.07	12.83	15.09	20.52

The observed/calculated value must equal or exceed the critical value to be significant at the level shown.

Type 1 and Type 2 errors

A problem for inferential statistics can be Type 1 and Type 2 errors. In psychology, it is common practice to use a significance level of 5 per cent or ($p<0.05$). However sometimes we may accept or reject the null hypothesis when we should not have. A Type 1 error involves rejecting a null hypothesis that is in fact true. Typically, this error is made when the level of significance is set too leniently or at a higher level such as 10 per cent or ($p\leq0.10$). This runs the risk of accepting our results as significant when they are not. A Type 2 error, on the other hand, involves accepting a null hypothesis that is not true. This is more likely when we set our significance level too stringently or at a lower level such as 1 per cent or ($p\leq0.01$).

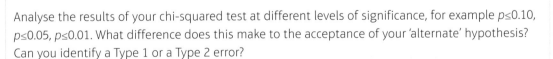

Taking it further

Analyse the results of your chi-squared test at different levels of significance, for example $p\leq0.10$, $p\leq0.05$, $p\leq0.01$. What difference does this make to the acceptance of your 'alternate' hypothesis? Can you identify a Type 1 or a Type 2 error?

Analysing qualitative data

Unlike quantitative data, qualitative data can be hard to summarise in a chart or graph. Typically, the analysis of qualitative data involves recognising repeated themes. The technical term for this type of approach is thematic analysis. Braun and Clarke (2006) outline a five-phase approach to the structure of a thematic analysis as follows.

Phase one – Familiarisation with the data – while on the bus journey, you may have noticed in your observations that when males and females thank the bus driver they do it in a different manner. Male passengers were observed to say 'Thanks mate' or 'Thank you driver'. They were also more likely to engage in 'small talk' with the driver before alighting, for example 'What time does your shift finish?' Females, on the other hand, were more likely to say thank you followed by a simple departure greeting such as 'goodbye' and were more likely to make eye contact with the driver when alighting. Therefore, you have begun to notice things or themes that might be relevant to the research question.

Phase two – Generating initial codes – a label or a code is the given to any specific categories identified such as 'Thank you with familiarity', 'Thank you with no familiarity', 'departure greeting', 'Smalltalk', etc.

Phase three – Searching for themes – in this phase a researcher would seek out themes on the basis of initial labels/codes for some meaning. In our example, 'implied familiarity' could be one such category suggesting that passengers make 'small talk' with the driver or call them mate.

Phase four – Reviewing themes – here, the researcher tries out these categories. This could mean collecting another set of data to see if future observations fit within them. If the research suggests that it does, then this could mean it is a topic area for the researcher to investigate further.

Phase five – Defining and naming themes – the researcher has clearly defined their themes, which allows them to select information and analyse it against the themes.

Finally, a report is produced in relation to the categories identified, which tells a story about the emerging themes identified.

Unlike quantitative data, qualitative data presents observations, thoughts, etc. that are not always easily counted. It does, however, provide much richer detail on the complexities of human interaction and behaviour. Nevertheless, it is sometimes difficult to select patterns and draw firm conclusions. Qualitative analysis is also more likely to be subjective, perhaps reflecting the personal viewpoints and background of the researcher.

Conclusions

The outcome of the inferential test informs the overall conclusion of the observation. In this instance, the chi-squared test would suggest the results of the experiment are significant so the null hypothesis is rejected and the experimental hypothesis accepted – females are more polite than males on public transport.

In drawing conclusions in relation to the qualitative data, you will need to look at the themes in the observation. You could also illustrate how themes are demonstrated by providing specific examples to support your interpretation. For example if you observe more 'small talk' with the driver and male passengers, you could provide specific quotes or observations to back this up.

Evaluating the practical investigation

In evaluating your overall observational study you will need to consider its validity, reliability, generalisability and credibility.

Validity

In considering the validity of your observations you need to consider the setting in which it took place. Undertaking a naturalistic observation is real life and would suggest that a certain degree of validity. You will also need to consider how objective or subjective your observational categories are. In the case of observing 'thank you', this is a relatively objective measure as it does not involve any kind of judgement. Qualitative data on the other hand can reflect the personal view or interpretation of the observer. What is seen as 'small talk' for instance involves more interpretation on the part of the observer.

One way of improving the validity of qualitative data is respondent validation. There are many different forms of respondent validation but one way of checking your interpretation of your results is to gain feedback from participants in your sample. This is difficult in naturalistic observation but a researcher could interview regular users of public transport to ascertain their views on the interpretation of results. This allows interviewees to cast a critical eye over the findings and comment on them in relation to their own opinions, feelings, and experiences. If participants are generally in agreement then this affirms the validity of your interpretation. Triangulation is another method for ascertaining reliability and validity of both qualitative and quantitative investigations. It refers to the use of more than one approach in the investigation of a research question. The use of a single research method may suffer from the limitations associated with that particular method, triangulation therefore offers the opportunity to check results and in doing so provides increased confidence in the findings if similar results are gained via other methods. Again, there are many ways of triangulating research methods and data. Investigator triangulation, for instance, uses one or more researchers to gather and interpret data. Therefore, in checking the validity and reliability of this observational study, a researcher could check the results with another researcher or another bus to see if they achieve similar results. Similarly, methodological triangulation utilises one or more than one method for gathering data. A researcher may use a questionnaire with bus passengers to ascertain their views on politeness on public transport to see if they correspond with the research question.

Reliability

How easy is it for you or another observer to repeat the study and would it lead to similar findings if the study was conducted on another bus? Or in another town? Or at another time of day? This can only be determined by repeating the observation numerous times and comparing the data. For qualitative data, reliability is harder to assess due to its subjective nature. However, triangulation, (mentioned in the paragraph above) could be one possible method for assessing reliability. Other methods available to researchers are inter-rater reliability and the test-retest method. If there are two or more observers, inter-rater reliability gives a measure as to how much agreement there is between researchers when conducting an observation. If researchers are in agreement about the behavioural categories, and note similar observations in similar circumstances, this would suggest there is reliability. However, a lack of consensus may mean that the behavioural categories used may need to be revised to ensure reliability. Alternatively, in the test-retest method, a researcher could conduct the observation and then conduct it again a day, week or month later on the same bus route to see if similar results are achieved.

Generalisability

In assessing if you can generalise from your observations you will need to consider your sample. The time of day at which you conducted your observations may affect the sample achieved. The ages of the participants also need to be considered. An equal distribution of ages within the sample will minimise bias. For instance, a larger proportion of retired people on the bus may result in more polite interactions being observed as such participants may be less time pressurised and hold more traditional values of respect and politeness.

Credibility

In summary, how credible is your experiment? Science would suggest that the credibility of the research is dependent on how the research meets the scientific principles mentioned earlier in the topic such as replicability, measurable phenomena, etc. At the very least, you should weigh up the overall strengths and weaknesses of your study. On one hand, a naturalistic observation is a valid form of measurement. However, your observation is likely to be carried out at a certain time of day and therefore it will influence the sample achieved, which can pose potential problems when generalised to other populations and situations. A number of repeated observations may be required to assess its overall effectiveness.

Observations at a station at 6.30 pm may include more commuters who at the end of a long day may be potentially less polite.

4.6 Issues and debates (A level only)

In this section, you will learn about issues and debates relevant to learning theories. You will have already noticed that issues and debates have been mentioned throughout this topic. This section will draw together the main themes and ideas related to the learning theories approach as a whole.

Ethics and socially sensitive research

Research in this approach tends to involve the use of animals. In conditioning experiments, rats, birds, dogs and monkeys have been used to investigate how stimulus-response links are formed. Laboratory reared animals have been used extensively, which raises the ethical issue concerning the nature of using adverse stimuli. To test the concept of negative reinforcement, Skinner electrified the floor of a cage or box that would be turned off when the animal pressed a lever. This procedure deliberately exposed animals to adverse stimuli. Conditioning a rat to press a lever to dispense food at a signal (light or sound) is not adverse in itself, but in order for the animal to have sufficient motivation to press the lever, some degree of food restriction is necessary. This means that an animal's food may be restricted before the conditioning trial, which contravenes the ethical guideline of food deprivation.

The most contentious research in the learning theories approach was conducted by Watson and Rayner (1920). In this study, they deliberately distressed Little Albert in order to condition a phobic response. This caused harm, and was exacerbated by the fact that his mother withdrew him from the study before he could be desensitised to the white rat. We will never know whether his phobia of rats would have persisted into adulthood because Little Albert died at the age of six from a childhood illness. Albert Bandura has also been criticised on ethical grounds for deliberately exposing children to aggressive models, and for causing distress to the children by frustrating them when they were told that they could not play with the toys in a room.

Treatments that are based on learning theories can be regarded as socially sensitive because the control of the client's behaviour is managed directly by the therapist. Aversion therapy, for example, involves associating a behaviour with a negative stimulus, such as taking an emetic drug to cause feelings of nausea when smoking cigarettes or drinking alcohol. In the past, aversion therapy was also used as a treatment for homosexuality. This treatment has negative consequences for the individual concerned, and concerns judgements about what is acceptable or unacceptable behaviour in society.

Practical issues in the design and implementation of research

The most significant practical issue when using animals in conditioning research is with the generalisability of the findings to humans. Although humans and animals have the same biological basis to their nervous system, it can be argued that animals do not have self-awareness so would respond very differently from humans in conditioning experiments. The ability of humans to be aware of being conditioned means that they grasp the nature of the aims of an experiment and will respond accordingly by displaying demand characteristics.

Reductionism

The learning theories of classical and operant conditioning explain learned behaviour as a result of stimulus-response connections being formed. These basic units of learned associations form together to explain the acquisition of complex behaviour, which is a highly reductionist approach. Explaining human behaviour as a set of learned responses makes the study of behaviour less complicated, because each stimulus-response link can be isolated and causation can be ascertained;

however, this is only a partial explanation because it ignores the role of other factors that affect how and what we learn. Bandura's social learning theory partially addresses this because it takes into account both the behavioural and cognitive factors associated with learning through observation and imitation.

Comparisons between ways of explaining behaviour using different themes

Learning theories can often be used to explain the same human behaviour, for example phobias can be explained through association, reinforcement or imitation. We may associate a dog with fear after being bitten or startled, avoiding or escaping a growling dog (demonstrating negative reinforcement), or watching another person show a fear response to a dog. Although one theory may be a more likely cause in a particular situation, you should consider which one is the most appropriate or likely in a given situation. For example, observational learning can explain why someone might begin to use heroin, but classical and operant conditioning explain why someone would continue to use the drug for its rewarding and pleasurable effects.

Psychology as a science

The behaviourist approach is perhaps the closest that psychology has come to a paradigm, with the endeavour to be scientific as an underpinning principle. The Behaviourist Manifesto set out clear rules about what could be studied and should be studied in a scientific way. Behaviourists create testable hypotheses and collect empirical data using objective methods. Behaviourists are principally concerned with only observable behaviour that can be scientifically studied and objectively recorded (for example, lever pressing). As internal processes and activities such as thinking, perception and memory, cannot be observed or objectively measured, they should not be studied.

Culture and gender

Learning theories are based on the role of nurture, which is concerned with what we learn from our environment rather than what is innate. Therefore, different cultures will have different experiences that impress on a developing human; specific behaviours familiar to a culture will be observed and specific behaviours that are deemed acceptable will be reinforced. For example, American culture is argued to be more aggressive than other western cultures, which may be explained by aggression being reinforced or observed from role models. Huesmann (1999) found that students in a Detroit high school were more accepting of aggression if they had been born in America, compared to students who emigrated to America, particularly if they had emigrated after the age of 11 years.

Learning theories can also be used to explain gender differences. Male and female children are treated very differently by others and strongly socialised according to their gender. Children observe stereotypical male and female behaviour and are encouraged through reinforcement to adopt behaviours appropriate to their assigned gender. Gender inappropriate behaviour may be ignored or even punished.

Nature-nurture

Although many gender-appropriate behaviours can be attributed to learning, many are determined by our biology, in terms of the sex we are born with and the evolution of gender-specific traits, such as male aggression and female nurturing. Cross-cultural research of gender roles demonstrate variation. For example, the Aka people of central Africa have interchangeable gender roles; females hunt and males look after the children. This suggests that gender roles are learned rather than biologically determined. The learning theories of classical and operant conditioning lie firmly on the nurture side of the nature–nurture debate, largely because they consider it unscientific to investigate cognitive processes or innate influences on behaviour.

An understanding of how psychological knowledge has developed over time

Learning theories have contributed to a phenomenal wealth of psychological knowledge over the course of more than a century. Much of this knowledge has remained the same; the principles of classical conditioning, operant conditioning and social learning theory remain the same, but the areas of human life in which learning theories apply have altered. Behaviourism was dominant at the beginning of the 20th century, but was overshadowed by the cognitive revolution of the 1950s. Today behaviourism is used in a more applied manner, and known as behaviour analysis. Behaviour analysis uses the principles of learning theories in a practical context and has been particularly successful in the treatment of autism and other clinical disorders.

Issues of social control

Learning theories are based on deterministic principles, which believe that all behaviour can be shaped by environmental forces; essentially proposing that human behaviour can be manipulated and therefore be subject to social control. B. F. Skinner, a radical behaviourist, published works discussing how societies could exercise control over their citizens by using schedules of reinforcement. This extreme view is rejected by most, and viewed as akin to the biological eugenics proposed by Hitler. Learning theories are important when considering that a number of psychological therapies employing behaviourist principles are used to manage the behaviour of vulnerable individuals. With the power in the hands of the therapist, the behaviour of a client is directly and deliberatively altered to conform to what is considered to be 'normal', or acceptable, in society or to ensure the client's well-being. Flooding is a therapy that forces people to confront anxiety provoking situations, or objects from which they cannot escape. This treatment is based on the principles of classical conditioning, and can be viewed as a distressing form of social control. Token economy programmes have in the past been employed in prisons to manage the behaviour of prisoners, with no actual therapeutic benefit. These programmes can be regarded as a form of social control.

The use of psychological knowledge in society

Learning theories have been used in many areas of real life – education, advertising, clinical and prison settings – to shape desired behaviour. In schools, teachers often employ a rewards system, such as stars for good work, which positively reinforces behaviour. John Watson moved into advertising and applied the learning theory principles to shape consumer behaviour; classical conditioning is a popular marketing strategy used to associate products with pleasurable feelings for consumers. This could also be regarded as a form of social control because our consumer behaviour is being influenced by companies wishing to make a profit. In a clinical setting, learning theory principles have been used to treat individuals with anxiety, phobias, autism, eating disorders and other mental health issues.

Knowledge check

Content

In the content section, you are required to describe, evaluate and apply your knowledge of three learning theories – classical conditioning, operant conditioning and social learning theory. You should also be able to explain individual differences in learning behaviour and how these theories link to developmental psychology.

Learning theories contain an array of technical terms. Check your understanding of these terms by testing yourself against the key terms glossary.

- Can you explain the process of classical conditioning? Can you define what is meant by the following terms – neutral stimulus (NS), unconditioned stimulus (UCS), unconditioned response (UCR) and conditioned stimulus (CS)?
- Can you explain the processes of stimulus generalisation and discrimination in classical conditioning?
- Can you define the terms extinction and spontaneous recovery?
- Are you able to describe and evaluate Pavlov's (1927) classic study of classical conditioning of salivation in dogs?
- Can you explain the process of operant conditioning?
- Can you distinguish between negative and positive reinforcement? And positive and negative punishment?
- Can you distinguish between primary reinforcers and secondary reinforcers?
- Can you apply the principles of operant conditioning to a token economy programme?
- Can you explain a schedule of reinforcement and define the terms fixed interval, variable interval, fixed ratio and variable ratio?
- Can you apply the principles of operant conditioning to behaviour modification therapy?
- Can you evaluate classical and operant conditioning
- Can you describe and evaluate social learning theory?
- Can you explain the concept of self-efficacy?
- Can you define and describe four key criteria for social learning – attention, retention, reproduction and motivation?
- Can you describe and evaluate Bandura's original Bobo doll study?
- Can you outline Bandura's (1965) later Bobo experiment on vicarious reinforcement?
- Can you describe how classical conditioning and social learning theory can explain the development of a phobia?
- Can you explain how phobias can be acquired and maintained via operant conditioning?
- Can you explain the process of systematic desensitisation as an exposure treatment?
- Can you distinguish between flooding and implosion as therapeutic techniques?
- Can you explain how modelling aims to treat phobias via vicarious reinforcement?
- Are you able to evaluate behavioural treatments?

Methods

- Are you able to explain what is involved in observational research?

- Do you understand the difference between quantitative data and qualitative data?

- Can you define the terms time sampling and event sampling?

- Are you able to describe how participant observation and non-participant observation is conducted?

- Can you distinguish between naturalistic observations and structured observations? And overt and covert observations?

- Can you explain how a content analysis can be conducted?

- Can you evaluate the strengths and weaknesses of using animals in psychological research?

- Can you explain the main reasons for using a chi-squared test for testing significance?

- Can you explain possible methods of analysing qualitative data?

- Are you able to identify, explain and evaluate the main issues and debates in considering the scientific status of psychology?

Studies

> **In this section of the topic, you are required to describe, evaluate and apply your knowledge of one classic and one contemporary study of learning theories.**

- Can you describe the classic study of Little Albert by Watson and Rayner (1920) in terms of its aim, method, procedure, results and conclusions?

- Are you able to evaluate the Little Albert study in terms of strengths and weaknesses?

- Are you able to identify and describe the aims, method, procedure, results and conclusions of a contemporary study from the following list and evaluate the study in terms of strengths and weaknesses?

  o Capafóns et al. (1998) Systematic desensitization in the treatment of fear of flying.

  o Becker et al. (2002) Eating behaviours and attitudes following prolonged exposure to television among ethnic Fijian adolescent girls.

  o Bastian et al. (2012) Cyber dehumanization: Violent video game play diminishes our humanity.

Key questions

- Are you able to identify and describe a key question in the psychology of learning theories that is relevant to today's society?

- Can you explain this key question using concepts, theories and research that you have studied in this topic?

Practical investigation

- Have you planned and conducted an observational study to investigate an area of behaviour linked to learning theories?

- Can you explain why you have chosen a directional or non-directional hypothesis?

- In planning your observation, can you justify the categories you having chosen for recording quantitative data on behaviour?

- Can you describe in detail how you would collect and analyse qualitative data from your observation?

- Can you explain any potential areas bias in your observation that may affect the reliability and validity of your observational study?

- Quantitative data can also be analysed via thematic analysis to pick out repeated themes in your observations, for example gender differences in polite behaviour when the bus driver is thanked. This may provide richer detail from your observations.

- Can you construct an appropriate table and/or bar chart to present your quantitative data?

- Are you able to explain, justify and interpret the non-parametric test of difference that you used on your data?

- Are you able to draw conclusions from your descriptive data and inferential test (including critical and observed values, and level of significance)?

- Can you suggest an appropriate method to representing any qualitative data gathered from an observation?

- Can you evaluate your observational study in terms of its strengths and weaknesses paying particular attention to issues of reliability and validity? Can you suggest possible improvements that could have been made to any future observational study in this area?

> Remember that you will be expected to evaluate your observational study in terms of reliability, validity and overall credibility. Be sure that you know what these terms mean before you apply them within the context of your study.

Issues and debates (A level only)

- Are you able to discuss the nature–nurture debate in the context of learning theories, and their emphasis on the nurture side of the debate?

- Are you able to discuss whether theories, concepts, research and methodology within the learning theories approach are scientific?

- Can you comment on the practical and methodological issues in the design and implementation of research within the learning theories approach, for example the use of animal studies?

- Can you identify ethical issues associated with learning theories and where it may be viewed as socially sensitive?

- Can you identify any issues of social control within the research on learning theories?

- Can you demonstrate how the theories, concepts and research within the psychology of learning theories can be used in a practical way within society?

- Can you define the term reductionism and explain how it relates to theories, research and concepts within the learning theories approach?

- Can you compare theories and research within learning theories to demonstrate different ways of explaining and understanding behaviour?

- Can you explain how the learning theories approach has developed over time?

- Are you able to discuss cultural issues within the context of the learning theories approach?

References

Bandura, A. (1965). Influence of models' reinforcement contingencies on the acquisition of imitative responses. *Journal of Personality and Social Psychology*, 1 (6), pp. 589–595.

Bandura, A., Ross, D. and Ross, S. A. (1961). Transmission of aggression through the imitation of aggressive models. *Journal of Abnormal and Social Psychology*, 63 (3), pp. 575–582.

Bandura, A., Ross, D. and Ross, S. A. (1963). Imitation of film-mediated aggressive models. *Journal of Abnormal and Social Psychology*, 66 (1), pp. 3–11

Bastian. B., Jetten. J., Radke. H.R.M. (2012) Cyber-dehumanization: Violent video game play diminishes our humanity. *Journal of Experimental Social Psychology*, 48, pp. 486–491.

Becker, A.E., Burwell, R.A., Gilman, S.E., Herzog, D.B., and Hamburg, P. (2002). Eating behaviours and attitudes following prolonged exposure to television among ethnic Fijian adolescent girls. *British Journal of Psychiatry*, 180, pp. 509–514.

Capafóns, J.I., Sosa, C.D., Avero. P. (1997). Systematic desensitization in the treatment of fear of flying. *Psychology in Spain*, 2 (1), pp. 11–16.

John B. Watson, J.B. and Rayner. R. (1920. Conditioned emotional reaction. *Journal of Experimental Psychology*, 3(1), pp. 1–14.

Understanding examination questions

You will learn all about psychology during your course; the challenge is being able to demonstrate your knowledge in the examination. This requires the ability to understand the nature of the question being asked as this will determine what approach you take to answering it. Examination questions include different elements that you will need to unpick to be able to plan your answer.

Examination questions test both your skills and psychological knowledge. The psychological knowledge that you need to learn is spelled out in the specification. This includes learning about concepts, theories, studies and research methodology.

How you present this knowledge in your answer will depend on the skill that is required of you. This will be indicated clearly in the examination question as a command word.

To recap, the examination question will indicate a command word that will tell you what skill you will need to draw on to present your knowledge in an answer. Below is a table of command words and the skill that they relate to. For each command word and skill there is an explanation of how you should present your answer.

There will be a mixture of short answer and extended writing questions in the examination, so it is important to understand the types of command words associated with each type of question and the demands it will make of your answer.

Short response questions

Short answer questions will typically range from 1–4 marks depending on the skill required.

Command word	Skills needed	Answer required
Define List State Name Give	Remembering/recall of small amounts of information from what you have learned	Typically you will need to provide a short answer of a sentence or less drawing on factual information that you have learned.
Identify	Recall and understanding	Key factor(s) will need to be picked out from a given stimulus.
Explain why… Explain how…	Recall, understand and apply knowledge	The command word 'explain' requires you to demonstrate understanding of the point, and a justification or expansion that links to the point being made. 'Explain how' questions will require you to write a chronologically correct answer where each point logically follows on to the next stage of the process.
Suggest A 'suggest' question may be followed by a strong hint to use your knowledge of theories/research/concepts to answer this question.	Application of knowledge and understanding	This command word implies that the answer will not have been directly taught, but can be answered through application or translation of existing knowledge to a new situation.
Analyse	To inspect and question, examine or appraise	This command word expects you to examine something (text or figures) to understand the meaning relayed by the material. You will need to break down the features of the material, examine each feature carefully and identify how they are related/differentiated. Typically, there will be more guidance in the question that will give you direction. This could also be an extended response question.
Plan/design	Creative skills, application and understanding	This command word will typically relate to the planning of methodology related to a context. A step-by-step approach should be taken for the proposal that includes justifications regarding decision making where relevant.
Calculate	Mathematical skills	The mathematical content of the course will demand calculation that can be done using a calculator, using formulae or mental maths. Workings should be shown where possible.

Command word	Skills needed	Answer required
Describe	Recall and understanding	Typically, this requires recall of factual knowledge where you will have to give an account of a theory, study, method, concept or process. The amount of detail needed will be indicated by the marks allocated for that question.
		If you are required to describe a process, it is logical to order the process as a sequence of events/factors.

Longer extended writing responses

Extended writing questions will have between 5 and 15 marks allocated, and typically will occur later
on in each paper and towards the end of each topic.

Command word	Skills needed	Answer required
Assess	Understanding, application and evaluation skills	This command word will require a two-step process:
		1. You will need to identify the relevant and important features that apply to the knowledge asked of in the question.
		2. Then you will need to make a judgement or draw a conclusion from the relevant points you have identified.
Evaluate	Judgement and evaluation skills	This command word expects that an answer will weigh up strengths and weaknesses of knowledge and draw on relevant evidence and counter evidence to support or contradict that knowledge. This information must then be reviewed, summarised and formed into a conclusion or judgement.
Discuss	Understanding, evaluation and application skills	This command word is commonplace in higher education and requires that the relevant material for the question is identified as an issue, argument or problem. Once identified, all aspects of the argument should be explored using reasoned understanding and knowledge relevant to formulate a conclusion.
		Often a 'for and against' approach is useful as it balances both sides of an argument or problem.
Compare	Understanding, evaluation and judgement, application skills	Beyond simply describing each aspect of the material, comparison involves looking at how each element differs from or is similar to each other element and can be centred around issues and debate themes.

Preparing for your exams: AS Paper 1 and 2 /A level Paper 1

Advance planning

- Plan well in advance the content you need to revise for your paper. This will be different depending on whether you are doing the AS level course or the A level course.
- Draw up a timetable for your revision and try to keep to it. Spread the topics equally over the timetable and leave enough time to recap your revision notes in the week before the exam. Write all your exam dates and times on the timetable.
- Identify topics you are less confident about. Spend more time on these topics and revise them several times. Use the knowledge check sections at the end of each topic to help you.
- Try using cue cards, spider diagrams and highlight the main points or key concepts using colour.
- Familiarise yourself with the layout of the paper and make use of practice questions.

AS level Paper 1 and 2 overview

AS level Paper 1	Time: 1 hour 30 minutes	(Weighted 50% of the AS level)
Section A: Social psychology	A mixture of short answer questions and one extended response question (8 marks)	29 marks
Section B: Cognitive psychology	A mixture of short answer questions and one extended response question (8 marks)	29 marks
Section C: Social and/or Cognitive	An extended response question	12 marks
	Total marks =	70 marks

AS level Paper 2	Time: 1 hour 30 minutes	(Weighted 50% of the AS level)
Section A: Biological psychology	A mixture of short answer questions and one extended response question (8 marks)	29 marks
Section B: Learning theories	A mixture of short answer questions and one extended response question (8 marks)	29 marks
Section C: Biological and/or Learning theories	An extended response question	12 marks
	Total marks =	70 marks

All questions are compulsory. Both papers require the use of a calculator. Statistical tables and formulae are provided at the beginning of each paper.

A level Paper 1 overview

A level Paper 1	Time: 2 hours	(Weighted 35% of the A level)
Sections ABCD: Social psychology, cognitive psychology, biological psychology and learning theories	Answer a mixture of short answer questions and one extended writing question (8 marks) for each section	70 marks split fairly evenly between sections (between 16–18 marks for each section)
Section E: Issues and debates	Answer two extended response questions (between 8–12 marks).	20 marks
	Total marks =	90 marks

All questions are compulsory. The paper requires the use of a calculator. Statistical tables and formulae are provided at the beginning of the paper.

Sections A and B (AS level) and sections A, B, C and D (A level)

The questions will target your knowledge of concepts, theories, studies, research methods, key issues and practical investigations. At least 10 per cent of each paper will ask you to demonstrate your mathematical ability, and around 30 per cent will test your knowledge of research methodology. Very few questions will ask you to simply recall knowledge that you have learned. The emphasis will be on how you apply your knowledge to explaining novel scenarios, how well you can assess and evaluate psychological knowledge, and how you can analyse and interpret information. You will be presented with sources that relate to theories, studies or methodology, and asked to apply your knowledge to interpret or critique each source.

Each 8-mark extended response question will require you to discuss, assess or evaluate psychological knowledge. 'Assess' questions require you to consider and review appropriate psychological knowledge, make a judgement and form a conclusion. 'Evaluate' questions require you to consider psychological knowledge, weigh up the strengths and weaknesses of the factors and reach a reasoned conclusion.

'Discuss' questions require that you explore the argument or stimulus being presented and consider contrasting views.

Section C (AS level only)

Section C may comprise an 'evaluate' question. It may also involve a 'to what extent' style question; this will often present a scenario and you will be asked to apply your psychological knowledge in a balanced way to explain the scenario and reach a reasoned conclusion. If the question includes the phrase 'with reference to the context', you must draw on relevant context from the scenario within your answer. You should aim to spend around 20 minutes planning and writing your answer.

Section E (A level only)

Section E questions cover issues and debates in relation to the psychological approaches you have covered over the course of your first year of study. These questions can be 'assess', 'evaluate', 'discuss' or 'to what extent' questions. Plan your response carefully and consider developing your arguments in a comprehensive, clear and organised way. You should aim to spend around 30 minutes planning and writing your answer.

Sample answers with comments

This is an example of a short answer question that requires you to apply your knowledge of theories and research in social psychology to unseen material.

Poppy has just started an apprenticeship at a hairdressing salon. She really wants to begin to learn how to cut hair, but she has to sweep the floor and tidy up for the first few weeks. When the manager of the salon is not present Poppy is reluctant to perform these tasks, but when the manager is present she performs these tasks to a good standard.

Question: *Explain Poppy's behaviour using your knowledge of social psychology.* **(4 marks)**

Student answer

Poppy is being obedient to authority because the manager of the salon has legitimate authority and status. Agency theory would predict that Poppy may be reluctant to sweep the floor and tidy up when her manager is absent because she is acting in an autonomous state. However, when her manager is present, she will surrender her freewill and act as an agent for the manager because Poppy has been socialised to be obedient to authority, which is an evolutionary mechanism to maintain social order. Milgram's research can also be used to explain why she is obedient as his variation studies showed a higher level of obedience when the authority figure was present in the room compared to when he gave orders over the phone. Distance or immediacy was a situational factor that affected obedience in this research, and can also be used to explain the difference in Poppy's behaviour. Similarly, social impact theory can be used to explain Poppy's behaviour as the psychosocial forces of strength and immediacy apply to this situation. Poppy's manager has strength in terms of her credibility and status in the salon, and when she is immediate proximity, Poppy is more likely to be compliant. When she is absent from the salon, Poppy is less likely to be compliant because she is distant and the impact reduced.

This is a strong answer that is focused on the scenario and accurately applies a good breadth and depth of knowledge to answering the question. The answer draws on two theories of obedience: agency theory and social impact theory, carefully selecting the relevant parts of each theory to explain the scenario. The answer also draws on carefully selected research in terms of Milgram's variations studies to apply to the scenario.

Importantly, the answer addresses both compliance and non-compliance in the explanation, so offers a full account.

Reference to evolution may seem to drift off the point, but actually this is the explanation needed to answer this question. Social impact theory is referred to in a largely descriptive manner, but the answer cannot be criticised for this because the theory is descriptive in nature rather than explanatory.

The answer does well to continually refer to the scenario, rather than offer a generic description of explanations and research. The answer also maintains focus on 'explaining' rather than evaluating knowledge. There is also good consideration of the marks available, so the answer is balanced in terms of content within the time and mark allocation constraints of the question.

This is an example of a data response question where you will have to apply your knowledge of methodology and data analysis to answer short response questions on unseen material.

Lesley had noticed that boys appeared to be aggressive when trying to solve difficult mathematical problems. She asked the English teacher to rate aggression in the same students and compared them to her own ratings of these students.

Question: *Complete the table and calculate a Wilcoxon Signed-Ranks test.* **(4 marks)**

Student	A. Teacher rating in a mathematics class	B. Teacher rating in an English class	Differences (B – A)	Rank of differences
1	9	4	-5	4
2	6	9	3	2.5
3	5	6	1	1
4	8	2	-6	5
5	7	7	0	
6	4	4	0	
7	6	3	-3	2.5
Sum of positive ranks				3.5
Sum of negative ranks				11.5
				T = 3.5

Table 1 Data from the investigation.

This answer is complete. The rank of differences has been correctly calculated, omitting the equivalent scores which gained a rank of zero. The procedure for calculating the entire Wilcoxon Signed-Ranks test will be at the beginning of the examination paper. This section should be referred to carefully when asked to calculate any mathematical or statistical process.

This answer correctly establishes the total rank score for positive differences and the total rank score for negative differences. Take care here, because it is easy to assume that you simply count the number of ranks rather than the sum of ranks.

Using the calculation process, this answer correctly identifies that the T statistic for the Wilcoxon Signed-Ranks test is the lowest of the positive and negative scores.

Lesley decided to adopt a directional hypothesis because she predicted that boys would be more aggressive in her mathematics class.

Question: *Explain whether Lesley should accept or reject her experimental hypothesis.* **(3 marks)**

Student answer

The calculated value of T = 3.5, which is not less than the critical value of 0 for a one-tailed test at p 0.05 with N = 5. Therefore the experimental hypothesis cannot be accepted and the null hypothesis should be retained.

This answer is clear, precise and succinct. The answer is a statistical statement answering all aspects of the question using the calculation procedure required. The answer gains credit for establishing a non-significant finding and rejecting the experimental hypothesis, further credit for the justification of this as the calculated value not being less than the critical value and credit for identifying that the N = 5. This means that the response successfully identifies that N is not the number of participants but the number of ranks ignoring zero differences.

Question: *Explain why Lesley's findings could be regarded as subjective.* **(2 marks)**

Student answer

Lesley may have used a different way of rating aggression to the English teacher. This could be because she did not operationalise what she meant by aggression, or that each teacher interpreted aggression differently. Lesley could have interpreted a student banging a desk as aggressive, whereas the English teacher may have interpreted the same behaviour as frustration.

This is a strong answer that has correctly identified issues with why Lesley's data may be subjective, and suggested detailed reasons for this being the case. This is exemplified further, and therefore offers more response than demanded by the mark allocation. Although caution should be maintained when considering mark allocation, in short answer questions, offering a little bit more detail should work in a student's favour because it is not too time-consuming.

Section C (AS level only)

This is an example of an extended response question that requires application of knowledge of a specific psychological theory to an unseen scenario.

Young children or individuals with memory difficulties, such as dyslexia or Alzheimer's, often struggle to process lots of information at one time. In a classroom setting, they may find it difficult to write down lots of information from the whiteboard or process lengthy instructions.

Question: *To what extent can the working memory model be used to explain one of these difficulties experienced in the classroom?* **(12 marks)**

Student answer

Dyslexia is a developmental learning difficulty that is defined as problems with the printed word that would not be predicted from the chronological age of the individual. Individuals with dyslexia often find it difficult to read passages of text fluently and struggle learning words phonetically. This can be explained by working memory because short-term memory is used when decoding words and putting word sounds together; individuals with dyslexia have a poor working memory. This may account for difficulties in the classroom, because lengthy instructions and information on a whiteboard can overload the impaired capacity of working memory.

This is evidenced by the finding that people with dyslexia often cannot remember as many long words compared to short words, because they have a limited working memory which is filled up quickly by longer words compared to shorter words which take up less capacity. This was concluded by research which showed that poor readers were less able to remember words compared to good readers. It was suggested that good readers can read quickly and so retain more words compared to poor readers who were slower and therefore could only retain a few words due to working memory's limited and temporal nature.

Because of the temporary duration of working memory, Alloway suggests that individuals with dyslexia often struggle to learn new words using phonetics or sounding out, because they cannot hold the speech sounds for long enough to be able to put them together to form a whole word. Additional research into learning impaired participants found that individuals with dyslexia found it difficult to store verbal information but did not show impaired spatial memory. This supports the working memory distinction between the two different slave systems of the phonological loop and the visuospatial sketchpad.

Research seems to strongly suggest that working memory can be used to explain developmental issues concerned with dyslexia, but this research is far from conclusive. It could be that individuals with dyslexia have an underlying cognitive impairment that manifests as a difficulty with word span, rather than the difficulty being the cause of dyslexia itself. The link between working memory and dyslexia is also problematic to investigate as dyslexia is often co-morbid with other impairments of the sensory system, both visually and verbally. This can make it difficult to establish causality as it could be that memory difficulties are caused by an interaction between dyslexia and other specific learning impairments.

Individuals with dyslexia may find long passages of writing and lengthy instructions difficult to process and retain because of other underlying cognitive impairments unrelated to short term memory issues, and because dyslexia can be often comorbid with attentional problems, it could be that a child lacks the concentration to manage lengthy scripts rather than have a working memory impairment.

However, intervention programmes aimed to teach children with dyslexia strategies to improve their working memory have been to some extent successful, providing evidence for the role of working memory in dyslexia. This finding should be considered in light of difficulties assessing intervention programmes, such as the strategies adopted, which differ greatly between programmes, and the lack of long term effectiveness.

In conclusion, there is strong evidence to support the role of working memory in explaining the difficulties that an individual with dyslexia can experience in the classroom. However we cannot discount the potential influence of comorbid conditions and lack of long term evidence that strategies used to improve working memory show long term improvement.

This is a rather lengthy but comprehensive essay that directly answers the question, uses good evidence and shows a reasonable balance between arguments for and against the role of the working memory as an explanation for dyslexia. This could have been improved by reducing the content that lacked specific reference to the question such as in paragraph three, which is rather loosely linked to the title of the essay and did not directly address the scenario of the classroom difficulties described in the question stem. Although good, this essay is a little long.

The knowledge is accurate and demonstrates very good understanding of psychological knowledge, and there is a logical argument formed throughout the essay. Competing ideas are expressed well and strengthened by continued reference to the question, which keeps the essay on track.

The final paragraph of this essay is important as it clearly signposts a conclusion and summarises the arguments in a balanced and reasoned way. There is no need to come to a firm conclusion one way or the other, as in psychology this is rarely the case. This conclusion would have benefitted from clearly linking the counterargument to the title of the essay.

Section E (A level only)

This is an example of an extended response question which requires you to assess a situation and come to a reasoned conclusion.

Question: *Assess whether case studies of brain-damaged patients should be used to investigate memory.* **(20 marks)**

Student answer

Case studies of brain damaged patients, like Henry Molaison, are often used in the study of memory because they can demonstrate how damage to specific parts of the brain are involved in memory function. The loss of these functions can inform us about how memory works and where functionality can be located in the brain.

Henry Molaison suffered catastrophic memory loss following a surgical procedure to relieve his epileptic seizures. As a result, he could no longer form new memories following the operation (anterograde amnesia) or recall past memories from up to 11 years prior to the operation (retrograde amnesia). This case study demonstrated that the hippocampus was important in the formation of new memories but did not affect retrieval of semantic knowledge.

Schmolck et al (2002) investigated the memory ability of other patients with varying degrees of brain damage, finding that damage to the anterolateral temporal cortex is associated with a loss of semantic knowledge, and the extent of such damage is linked to the extent of loss of function. This research has implications of treatment and strategies to help cope with memory loss.

However, there are issues associated with the use of case studies of brain damaged patients that question whether they should be used as a research tool to investigate memory. One such issue concerns the ethics of using these patients. Amnesia patients can be regarded as vulnerable participants as they do not have the complete capacity to give fully informed consent or, potentially, the right to withdraw and understand the implications of their participation. Some argue that amnesia patients are not protected from harm because they are exposed to a battery of cognitive tests and interviews that they may not comprehend or find challenging.

Paragraphs 1–4: This description is a useful introduction into the use of case studies of brain-damaged patients, and satisfies the descriptive element of the question, offering background information regarding knowledge gained from such research. This can be taken as a 'for' argument for using such methodology.

Further, this can be regarded as socially sensitive research because it can harm not only the individual, but the family that suffer the burden of care and loss of family member. Deficits in memory can result in an individual not being able to function normally in everyday life, and may result in residential care that, if under investigation, can expose families to further distress. Although confidentiality is provided by researchers often by anonymising the participant, this may not be possible in high profile cases, such as that of Clive Wearing who was already in the public eye.

Despite the ethical issues involved in case studies of brain damaged patients, there can be positive outcomes. The wife of Clive Wearing formed a charity to raise awareness of amnesia, and research findings can be used to help formulate treatments for patients.

Whether amnesia patients should be used to study memory also raises methodological issues. It is often the case that amnesia patients are only investigated after they have suffered a trauma or injury, so researchers cannot be absolutely certain of their memory abilities prior to their memory loss. These retrospective studies cannot reliably establish a link between the damage and the loss of function, often instead relying upon family accounts and interviews with the patients themselves. Although Henry Molaison was known to the medical profession for his epilepsy prior to his surgery, it is still unsure whether aspects of his retrograde amnesia were a result of the surgery or prior epilepsy medication and seizures. In fact, his poor grammatical ability was attributed to his school absence and low socioeconomic status, although this cannot be proven.

The recent development of brain imaging techniques has allowed more conclusive evidence to be formed concerning the location of brain structures implicated in memory.

This has allowed researchers to pinpoint the brain damage in a variety of patients and associate this damage to loss of memory ability quite specifically. However, such research can be regarded as reductionist as it often fails to acknowledge the interrelations between different brain structures and regions involved in memory.

A further issue is the lack of generalisability from case studies of brain damaged patients to normal individuals. With only a limited number of unique individuals who suffer from amnesia, nomothetic theories of memory function are not appropriate and so can be argued to be unscientific. Although it could be argued that the qualitative information gathered from such individuals offer rich and detailed accounts of memory functionality which could not be achieved by experimentation on normal individuals.

There are a range of arguments for and against the usefulness of case studies of brain damaged patients to study memory. Ethical issues are important, but it can be shown that despite these problems, research goes to great lengths to protect amnesia patients and maintain high ethical regard. Despite extensive research and published work into his case, the identity of Henry Molaison was only revealed after his death. His case remains and continues to be one of the most important in the advancement of knowledge in the field of neuroscience. Methodological concerns also question the use of case studies of brain damaged patients, although it could be argued that even the small glimpses into memory that have been obtained have not been achieved by any experimental research over the past century.

Paragraph 5–7: Relevant ethical issues are described and related to research, although some could have been developed better in terms of the implications of these problems for the individual and family.

Paragraphs 8–10: Useful commentary concerning methodological issues is discussed with some counterargument development. This is useful as it is rarely the case that poor or bad research is conducted without some procedures to ameliorate the problems or justification for doing it.

The final paragraph draws together the ethical and methodological issues and is presented in a balanced and considered way, reaching a sensible and just conclusion based on the evidence presented. The response would have benefitted from clearer signposting of this conclusion, but the answer does refer back to the original question of the essay, which maintains its focus well.

5 Clinical psychology

In this topic, you will learn about different explanations for mental health disorders and the different ways of treating them.

In this topic, you will learn about:

- the diagnosis of mental disorders
- classification systems for mental health
- the symptoms and treatment of schizophrenia, anorexia nervosa, obsessive–compulsive disorder and unipolar depression
- a classic and contemporary study for each of the above mental health disorders
- key issues around the topic of clinical psychology that are of relevance to society today
- how to carry out a practical research exercise relevant to topics covered in clinical psychology
- wider issues and debates in clinical psychology (A level).

5.1 Content

Learning outcomes

In this section, you will learn about:

- the diagnosis of mental health disorders
- classification systems used to diagnose disorders including the DSM V (you may wish to study DSM IV-TR instead) and the ICD-10
- issues with using these systems in terms of their reliability and validity
- the symptoms and features of schizophrenia, the function of neurotransmitters and one other biological and one other non-biological explanation of schizophrenia
- one other disorder from anorexia nervosa, obsessive–compulsive disorder and unipolar depression: the symptoms and features of your chosen disorder, one biological and one non-biological explanation for this disorder
- individual differences in mental health disorders
- how mental health disorders can affect development.

An introduction to clinical psychology

Clinical psychology is concerned with abnormal behaviour. It seeks to define what makes behaviour abnormal, and then to diagnose what the problem is so that it can be treated. Psychiatrists take a note of the symptoms their patient is suffering from and how long they have had them, plus information about their general health, and any social or psychological problems they have. Using this information, they can decide what disorder the person is suffering from and give them appropriate treatment.

Even among psychologists there is disagreement about the causes of abnormal behaviour. Depending on what approach the psychologist comes from, they will have a different view of the causes of the mental disorder, the reasons why that person has that disorder, and so what the correct treatment should be given.

Diagnosing mental health disorders – the four 'Ds' of diagnosis

One of the biggest issues for clinical psychologists is the point at which a behaviour that is displayed by an individual becomes so 'abnormal' that it requires clinical diagnosis and possibly treatment. One method used by clinicians is to refer to the four Ds: deviance; dysfunction; distress and danger.

Deviance

Clinicians look at the extent to which the behaviour is 'rare' within society. If the behaviour is considered rare enough, and 'deviant' from the norm, then this could suggest that a clinical disorder is present.

Dysfunction

If the behaviour is significantly interfering with the person's life then a mental illness may be present. The clinician should discuss with the patient all aspects of their everyday life to assess the extent to which the problematic behaviour is disturbing this. Although there may be no obvious day-to-day impact of the behaviour, the clinician should look carefully into all aspects of the patient's life because disturbances could be present in areas that are not immediately obvious.

Distress

This feature of the diagnostic decision is related to the extent to which the behaviour is causing upset to the individual. This should be treated in isolation from other features of the four Ds because the patient may be extremely distressed by their current situation but still able to function completely normally in other areas of their life. The subjective experience of the patient is very important here because the patient may be facing a great deal of difficulty in their life but be feeling no distress, and similarly someone else may be very distressed by something that others may view as trivial.

Danger

The patient's behaviour has to be assessed under two key elements of danger: danger to themselves and danger to others. If the person's behaviour is putting their own life or other people's lives in considerable danger then this may indicate that an intervention is needed. This could be considered on a scale of severity because many people engage in behaviour that could be considered dangerous, but if the problematic behaviour is extremely risky and not being addressed then a diagnosis may be necessary.

Some researchers have also considered that there may be a possible fifth 'D' – 'Duration'. Many behaviours may be seen as deviant, dysfunctional, distressing and dangerous in the short term, but if they persist then this is where the problem may be seen as a symptom of an illness that requires psychiatric attention.

Exam tip

These four dimensions of diagnosis can be used as a tool to decide whether behaviour is 'abnormal' and therefore worthy of further investigation and diagnosis. Do not get confused between this initial diagnostic process, and the classification systems in the next section. The DSM and ICD are actual diagnostic tools used by clinicians to decide what disorder, if indeed any, is present based on the symptoms shown by the patient.

'Patient' and 'client'

The terms 'patient' and 'client' are used synonymously to refer to a person who either voluntarily or involuntarily receives treatment from medical and psychological professionals. Typically, individuals are referred to as a 'patient' if they are receiving biological treatments, and 'client' if referring to individuals receiving psychological treatments. The term 'service user' is also used in the same context.

WIDER ISSUES AND DEBATES

Issues of social control

Many people have argued that clinicians have a lot of power in the diagnoses of mental health problems because there can be serious implications for patients once they have been labelled as 'mentally ill'. For example, in the treatment of disorders, it is possible to treat patients against their own consent if they have been sectioned under the Mental Health Act and are deemed to be at risk to themselves or others.

Evaluation

There are many possible issues with using these four 'dimensions' of behaviour to make a decision on the level of abnormality shown by the individual. One of the most serious is likely to be the potential for subjectivity in the interpretation of the individual patient's experience. The clinician must take into account how the person is coping with the behaviour being discussed because what is considered to be dysfunctional by one person will be seen differently by another.

There are also issues of reliability as the decision of whether the behaviour requires further diagnosis relies on what is discussed between the patient and the clinician. To be reliable, the clinician should ensure they explore all four of the above issues with every patient to be sure that everyone is measured in a standardised way. Reliability also requires that any decision over the level of 'deviance' shown by an individual is based on a standardised measure.

There are standard tests to assess symptoms of many disorders and these should be used where possible rather than making a personal judgement about the patient's symptoms. Another issue with the concept of 'deviance' is that there is an argument that some problematic behaviours are not actually that rare, depression, for example, is very common, so it is important that clinicians weigh up all four of the diagnostic dimensions above to consider whether the individual requires further psychiatric care.

Key term

Clinical interview: the process of evaluating a client by gaining important personal information about them regarding their health.

WIDER ISSUES AND DEBATES

Practical issues in the design and implementation of research

The diagnostic process is often conducted through **clinical interviews** with patients by clinicians. These are unstructured or semi-structured interviews. Consider the nature of un/semi-structured interviews in terms of reliability and validity, and how these issues may relate to gathering information from patients about their symptoms in order to diagnose them correctly. There are also problems with the self-report method generally. For example, whether patients tell the truth, withhold or embellish answers when giving self-report data to the researcher/clinician. This could seriously affect the validity of the diagnosis reached. It is not just the patient's responses that can lead to misdiagnosis. A clinical interview is guided by the clinician's questions, and if they focus on one particular set of symptoms, their diagnosis may be different from a clinician who focuses on a different symptom.

Taking it further

Look into these concepts further by searching for and reading the article 'Conceptualizing Psychiatric Disorders Using "Four D's" of Diagnoses'. Illustrate how the four 'Ds' might be used in the diagnostic process.

Classification systems

Mental disorders are described as a collection of symptoms by the medical profession just like other illnesses. The World Health Organization originally compiled a list of mental disorders in a publication called the *International Classification of Diseases* (ICD) in 1948. Four years later, the American Psychiatric Association established its own way of helping professionals reach a diagnosis, in a publication known as the *Diagnostic and Statistical Manual of Mental Disorders* (DSM). Both versions have been continually revised over the years with the current (fifth) version of the DSM published in June 2013 (DSM V). The ICD is currently in its tenth version and undergoing revision for release in 2017.

Reliable diagnoses are essential for guiding treatment recommendations, to ensure that a patient receives the correct treatment for their condition and an accurate prognosis can be given.

Because mental health disorders do not have obvious measurable physiological signs, like raised blood pressure or a high temperature, diagnosis often depends on the interpretation of behavioural symptoms and this is not an exact science so there are always issues of reliability and validity that surround diagnosis. The classification systems, such as DSM and ICD, describe clusters of symptoms that define disorders that have been derived from clinical practice, field trials and pooled expertise and, if applied properly, should lead to better-quality diagnoses. However, this does not mean that they are universally accepted and there are many influential critics of these systems.

WIDER ISSUES AND DEBATES

How psychological understanding has changed over time

There are several different types of mental disorder, although they are generally grouped under certain headings according to their main symptoms. The foundations for such classification systems were developed in the late 19th century by Emil Kraepelin in his *Compendium der Psychiatrie*, first published in 1883, in which he argued that psychiatric disorders were fundamentally physical in nature and should be studied as a branch of medical science. He believed , like many medical disorders, that it is possible to classify specific mental health disorders by their symptoms and therefore diagnose them and predict their course. European doctors such as Eugen Bleuler (who first coined the term 'schizophrenia') further developed the system in the early 20th century. The system is constantly under review by the psychiatric profession because it is important to have a reliable and valid way of diagnosing mental health disorders in order to ensure that correct treatments are provided.

DEVELOPMENTAL PSYCHOLOGY

The latest version of DSM reflects developmental and lifespan considerations beginning with disorders thought to reflect developmental processes, that is, those that occur early in life such as neurodevelopmental disorders and those on the schizophrenia spectrum come first, followed by those that are more commonly developed during adolescence, such as depression. This highlights the understanding that some psychiatric illnesses occur during certain periods in our development.

Taking it further

It has been argued that the DSM V has been influenced by the interests of big pharmaceutical companies, which has led to the classification of some types of behaviour as abnormal where a drug has been developed to treat the disorder. In order for the drug to be prescribed (and therefore profitable) there needs to be a diagnosis and in order for there to be a diagnosis the behaviour has to be classified as a disorder. Conduct a literature or Internet search and see if you can find some evidence for this view.

International Classification of Diseases (ICD)

ICD-10 is not only concerned with mental health disorders (MHDs) but with all diseases; it contains a section (F), which is specific for MHDs. Within that section it groups each disorder as being part of a family, for example mood (affective) disorders is the family that includes depression in all its forms, for example, bipolar and any other mood disorder. These disorders are coded F (for the section of the system) followed by a digit to represent the family of MHDs, in this case 3, which is then followed by a further digit to represent the specific disorder, (F32 is depression whereas F31 is bipolar disorder).

Further categorisation comes at the next digit that follows a decimal point where the type of depression is represented (for example, F32.0 is mild depression). Finally, very specific categorisation can be added after another decimal point followed by further digits (for example, F32.0.01 is mild depression with somatic (physical) symptoms, for example pain, whereas F32.0.00 is mild depression without somatic symptoms). This coding allows the clinician to go from the general to the specific and to convey their diagnosis to others in an easy and systematic way.

The clinician can use the system to guide their diagnosis through a clinical interview with the patient. This requires expertise on the part of the clinician as mental disorders are often not clear in their presentation. However, it does provide a basis on which to make a judgement, giving details of likely symptoms for each disorder and their severity and duration, allowing diagnosis to be made. In some cases the diagnosis will be tentative or provisional, but sometimes a confident diagnosis can be made as the patient clearly presents with the symptoms that fit the description in the ICD manual.

Taking it further

The ICD-10 is available online on the World Health Organization website.

The diagnostic and statistical manual of mental disorders (DSM V)

The DSM V adopts a similar system of grouping disorders into 'families', with linked disorders grouped together, to enable the clinician to go from a very general diagnosis to a specific one with guidance provided about the likely combination of symptoms and their severity. Again, the clinician would use the manual in combination with a range of information gained through clinical interview and medical records.

WIDER ISSUES AND DEBATES

Cultural differences

There is not perfect agreement between the European ICD and the American DSM, which means that the diagnostic systems – even when used appropriately – might lead to different diagnoses. This challenges the idea that it is possible to have a universal diagnostic system. However, the recent revision of the DSM to DSM V has been written with the goal of harmonising the two systems because it was recognised that, even with the intention to identify identical patient populations, diagnosis using DSM IV did not always agree with ICD-10; therefore we should expect that reliability between the two systems will improve. The recent edition of DSM has also sought to make diagnosis accurate for people from all cultural backgrounds. In the previous DSM IV-TR, 'culture-bound' syndromes were represented in a chapter that dealt with mental health disorders found in other cultures, but now the DSM V takes a more integrative approach with greater cultural sensitivity. It is now recognised that some cultures exhibit and explain symptoms differently from other cultures, for example panic attacks may present themselves as a difficulty breathing in one culture, but unexplained crying in another. Distress is also expressed differently across cultures, for example, the symptoms listed under social anxiety now include a 'fear of offending others' to represent the Japanese expression of anxiety in addition to the typical western expression of 'fear of harming oneself'. These symptoms have now been addressed in the new DSM to ensure that cultural manifestations of symptoms are acknowledged. Additionally, clinicians are now encouraged to take the cultural background of the patient into account using the cultural formulation interview guide.

DSM IV-TR

DSM IV was originally published in 1994 and updated to DSM IV-TR in 2000, and was described as a 'multiaxial tool' because of its five axes or chapters. Axis 1 described the major clinical syndromes, or mental health disorders such as schizophrenia and anxiety disorders. Axis 2 described the symptoms related to personality disorders. Axis 3 described medical conditions, such as brain damage or HIV, that could be used to explain or mediate the onset of clinical issues. Axis 4 described psychosocial and environmental problems that could be implicated in the onset or course of a mental health disorder; for example, bereavement, loss of housing or employment could trigger depression. Axis 5 contained a scale to assess global functioning of an individual. Clinicians could use this scale to assess how well an individual was able to go about normal activities such as washing, dressing and socialising. The functioning score given to an individual helped with diagnosis and was also used to assess the need for treatment and type of treatment necessary.

Reliability and validity of diagnoses

Reliability of diagnosis

Reliability of diagnosis refers to the extent to which clinicians agree on the same diagnosis for the same patient. Diagnosis is complex, especially as the same symptoms can occur across different disorders, such that two clinicians might see the same symptoms but assign their cause to different disorders. This would suggest that the diagnosis is unreliable. Ward et al. (1962) studied two psychiatrists diagnosing the same patient and found that disagreement occurred because of inconsistency of the information provided by the patient (5 per cent), inconsistency of the psychiatrists interpretation of symptoms (32.5 per cent) and inadequacy of the classification system (62.5 per cent). This research suggests that the main reliability issue at the time was with the diagnostic tool being used.

For the system of diagnosis to be reliable it needs to pass an **inter-rater reliability** test. This involves showing two or more clinicians the details of a person's case history and assessing the level of agreement between them. If all the clinicians (raters) agree on the same diagnosis then we can say that the system of diagnosis has high inter-rater reliability.

Tests on the early diagnostic systems showed typically low inter-rater reliability; for example, Beck (1954), found that the same set of symptoms were only diagnosed as the same disorder in about half of cases, suggesting low reliability. However, over the years as the systems have developed, further studies showed that reliability has improved. For example, Brown (2001), tested the reliability and validity of DSM IV diagnoses for anxiety and mood disorders and found them to be good to excellent. There are still some disorders, however, for which a reliable diagnosis is harder to obtain, for example, post-traumatic stress disorder (PTSD) has a high degree of symptom overlap with other psychiatric disorders and may be underdiagnosed as a result.

Patient factors

Unreliable diagnosis may occur because of patient factors. Information provided by the patient to the clinician may be inaccurate because of problems with memory, denial or shame. These psychological factors, along with specific issues such as disorganised thoughts, psychopathy or manipulative tendencies, can make diagnosis difficult and likely to differ between clinicians.

Clinician factors

The unstructured nature of the clinical interview can lead some clinicians to focus on certain symptom presentation, for example nightmares, while others may follow a different course of questioning, for example a traumatic past event. This can lead to different information being gathered about a patient and result in different diagnosis. In the example, the first clinician may diagnose a depressive disorder and the second post-traumatic stress disorder.

Clinicians also use their subjective judgement according to how they interpret the symptoms a patient presents. This is largely dependent on the background, training and experience of a clinician. For example, a clinician with psychodynamic training may emphasise the importance of early childhood experience and mistake hallucinations for a past trauma, while a medically trained psychiatrist might explain hallucinations as a consequence of excess dopamine in the brain.

A diagnosis may be reliable because different clinicians agree on it, but this does not mean that it is valid. Read about Rosenhan's research as the classic study in Section 5.3 of this topic. He found that there was high inter-rater reliability in diagnosing schizophrenia from the same set of symptoms, but the diagnosis was not valid because the people receiving the diagnosis were not mentally ill.

> **Key term**
>
> **Inter-rater reliability:** the degree of agreement and consistency between raters about the thing being measured.

The introduction of tighter clinical interviews and diagnostic classification systems have improved the reliability of diagnosis and limited the subjective interpretation brought about by clinician judgement.

Race and culture are also issues in diagnosis. Behaviour that is common in one culture could be interpreted as symptomatic of a disorder in another, or if the patient is of a culture different from that of the clinician they may be less likely to share their symptoms because of a sense of cultural shame. The boundary between what is considered normal and what is not varies across cultures for different types of behaviour. Some cultures feel that the more medicalised form of diagnostic systems widely in use overemphasise the separation of mind and body. For example, China has developed its own system based on the ICD but including other categories such as neurasthenia or weakness of the nerves, which is one of the most frequent diagnoses made in China.

Culture-bound syndromes are a good example of this. These are disorders that are found in only one culture, such as ghost sickness, which occurs among people belonging to Native American tribes. The symptoms are recognised in the culture as indicating a specific disorder that is not recognised universally. Ghost sickness symptoms include an obsession with death, nightmares, loss of appetite and feelings of suffocation and terror. There are many examples of culture-bound syndromes that challenge the use of the DSM and ICD, as these are intended to be scientific and universal systems for diagnosing mental health disorders, but do not contain those specific to one culture, viewing them rather as a localised manifestation of anxiety or depression. This ignores the experience of those people in that culture, preferring to try to manipulate their experiences as being symptomatic of a recognised disorder expressed in a culturally specific way.

Validity of diagnosis

Even if the diagnosis can be said to be reliable, to be of any use the diagnosis must also be valid. It must genuinely reflect the underlying disorder, because the consequences of misdiagnosis can be very serious. As diagnosis leads to treatment, the wrong treatment at best might delay recovery and at worst make the person's condition much more severe. Clinicians can establish validity in a variety of ways.

- **Concurrent validity** could be checked by looking at another diagnostic tool such as comparing the DSM with the ICD. If there is broad agreement about which symptoms constitute which disorder, we have broad concurrent validity. Interestingly, the recently published DSM V has referred consistently to the coding used in the ICD showing strong agreement between these two instruments.

- **Aetiological validity** can be established by examining what is known about the causes of the disorder and matching them to the person's history; for example, if there is a known genetic component to a disorder, the clinician could look for a family history to support their diagnosis.

- **Predictive validity** should also be examined. This is where the future course of the disorder is known and can be applied to the person, so the diagnosis can be checked against the outcome in order to see if it is valid; for example, if the patient genuinely has depression then an improvement might be expected within eight weeks if they are prescribed antidepressants.

Issues that affect reliability and validity centre on the interpersonal exchange between client (or patient) and clinician in the diagnostic interview. The clinician may be affected by **implicit biases** in their interpretation of the information given to them. For example, a clinician might be more ready to diagnose a female patient with depression – because depression is more prevalent in the female population – so is more likely to see the same symptoms as being consistent with depression in females and might be less likely to give the same diagnosis to a male. This could be exacerbated if the clinician is a different gender from the patient.

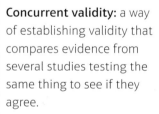

Key terms

Concurrent validity: a way of establishing validity that compares evidence from several studies testing the same thing to see if they agree.

Aetiological validity: the extent to which a disorder has the same cause or causes. Aetiological validity exists when the diagnosis reflects known causes, such as a family history, in a disorder that is known to have a genetic cause.

Predictive validity: the extent to which results from a test such as DSM, or a study can predict future behaviour.

Implicit bias: a positive or negative mental attitude towards a person, thing, or group that a person holds at an unconscious level.

According to Aboraya et al. (2006), these clinician variables include their training and perception of presenting symptoms with more focus on the acute symptoms and perhaps overlooking other symptoms as a result. This is further exacerbated by patient variables, such as their current state during the diagnosis. Their mood, memory and levels of shame associated with their symptoms can all lead to inaccurate information being provided to the clinician.

Additionally, many disorders are **comorbid** with each other, making a valid and reliable diagnosis difficult; for example, the majority of those suffering with depression also have anxiety disorders.

Exam tip

Questions on this topic might ask for you to discuss reliability and/or validity issues that relate to diagnosis. You could develop a pros and cons list to help you prepare. For example, under the pro heading you might state that the reliability of diagnosis is improving as the diagnostic systems are reviewed and refined regularly in light of research. Under the con heading you could state that the diagnostic system is only as good as the clinician who uses it and there is still room for clinician subjectivity to affect the reliability of the diagnosis.

Arguments for diagnoses being reliable/ valid	Arguments for diagnoses being unreliable/ invalid

---

Schizophrenia

Schizophrenia refers to a spectrum of psychological disorders that are characterised by abnormalities involving distortions of thought, perception and emotion; and social withdrawal. Positive and negative symptoms of schizophrenia have been differentiated between by researchers.

Symptoms

Positive (Type 1) symptoms add to the experience of the patient. These include delusions, hallucinations, disorganised thinking and/or speech and abnormal motor behaviours. Negative (Type 2) symptoms subtract from normal behaviour. The behaviours persist longer and result in a huge burden of care compared to positive symptoms. These might include a lack of energy and enthusiasm, poverty of speech, poor motivation and social withdrawal.

For a diagnosis of schizophrenia to be given by a clinician, the presenting patient must have described two or more of the key symptoms above having been present for a high proportion of the last month. Of the symptoms described by the patient, at least one of them must be **delusions, hallucinations, disorganised thinking/speech, disorganised behaviour** or **catatonia,** or **negative symptoms**.

Clinicians must be careful to consider other issues in the patient's life to make an accurate diagnosis. If a patient is also displaying signs and symptoms of disturbed mood, such as mania or depression, then the symptoms of schizophrenia must have existed before the disturbed mood for schizophrenia to be diagnosed. Also, the clinician must take into account whether the patient has any brain damage or substance misuse issues that could account for the altered behaviour.

Key terms

Comorbidity: the presence of more than one disorder in the same person at the same time.

Delusions: beliefs that are contrary to fact.

Hallucinations: perceptual experiences that occur in the absence of external stimulation of the corresponding sensory organ.

Disorganised thinking/ speech: an inability to make connections between thoughts, resulting in incomprehensible language and ideas that seem loosely connected.

Disorganised behaviour: behaviour that is not necessarily expected in the situation, or that changes rapidly and is out of context.

Catatonia: various motor disturbances characterised by abnormality of movement and behaviour.

Negative symptoms: symptoms that mean the person has 'lost' an element of normal functioning.

Key terms

Grandiose delusions: the individual believes they have remarkable qualities such as being famous or having special powers.

Persecutory delusions: the individual reports believing that others are 'out to get them' and trying to harm them in some way.

Referential delusions: the individual holds a belief that certain behaviours or language from others is being directed at them personally.

Avolition: a psychological state characterised by a general lack of motivation to complete usual, self-motivated activities such as work.

Taking it further

Search the Internet for video footage of two classic cases of schizophrenia in Gerald and Heather. Observe their behaviour and identify what symptoms of schizophrenia they present.

Conduct an Internet search for different types of delusions and hallucinations associated with schizophrenia and make a note of some examples.

Delusions

These are beliefs held by the individual that, despite not being true, cannot be changed by others even where clear evidence can be demonstrated that challenges the belief. Examples of common delusions held by people with psychotic disorders include **grandiose delusions** where the individual believes they have remarkable qualities such as being famous or having special powers, **persecutory delusions** where the individual reports believing that others are 'out to get them' and trying to harm them in some way, and **referential delusions** whereby the individual holds a belief that certain behaviours or language from others is being directed at them personally. One very specific example of a delusion would be thought insertion where the individual believes that their thoughts have been implanted by some kind of external force over which they have no control.

Hallucinations

These are experienced in the same way as the perception of an external stimulus would be, such as hearing or seeing something around you, but can happen without any actual stimulus being present. For example, a person with a psychotic illness may hear voices talking to them that are not really there, or see people in front of them when there is no one there. Hallucinations can occur in any sensory modality, however it is thought that the most common type of hallucination associated with schizophrenia are auditory hallucinations (hearing things that are not there). The hallucination must be experienced when the patient is fully awake and conscious to be classified as an actual symptom of disorder.

Disorganised thinking/speech

Disorganised thinking is best diagnosed from speech where ideas are loosely connected, or in severe cases, completely unconnected. In very severe cases the person's language may be completely incomprehensible because they are unable to make any connections between their thoughts – this may be referred to as 'word salad', which is a metaphor for the way individual words are tossed together during speech. Disorganised thinking/speech will mean that the person randomly skips from topic to topic during conversation, and will answer questions with bizarre statements that do not seem to fit.

Abnormal motor behaviour/grossly disorganised behaviour (including catatonia)

The behaviour of individuals will be categorised as abnormal for many different reasons, but any motor movement that severely affects their ability to cope with daily life is categorised as grossly disorganised. This ranges from fidgeting to childish 'messing about' or even dressing bizarrely. Within this category of symptoms is included catatonia, which is described as a significant decrease in the individual's responsiveness to the environment. They may sit completely still in odd postures, or refuse to speak to others, or even show continued, repetitive movements such as foot-tapping or hair-twirling that has no real meaning.

Negative symptoms

Of all psychotic disorders, negative symptoms are most usually associated with schizophrenia above any other. Two of the most common negative symptoms shown are diminished emotional expression, and **avolition**. Diminished emotional expression is characterised by the patient showing less and less emotion in their general use of non-verbal communication, such as facial expressions, eye contact and physical gestures. Avolition is a behavioural state characterised by a general lack of motivation to complete usual, self-motivated activities such as work. Symptoms in this category are negative because they represent a reduction in normal functioning.

Features of schizophrenia

Prevalence and onset

The likelihood of a person developing schizophrenia is somewhere between 0.3 and 0.7 per cent depending on factors such as their racial/ethnic background, where in the world they live, and their country of birth. There are also some gender differences in prevalence, for example, males are more likely to develop a higher proportion of negative symptoms and have a longer duration of the disorder, which are both associated with poor prognosis. Episodes of psychosis associated with schizophrenia tend to appear between late adolescence and mid-thirties, with the peak of onset being around early to mid-twenties in males, and late twenties for females. Often the episodes develop gradually over a period of time and may not be obvious at first. Patients who show psychotic episodes earlier than in late adolescence appear to be more likely to have worse prognosis over the long term.

Prognosis

It is very difficult to predict the course of illness in patients with schizophrenia – approximately 20 per cent of those diagnosed will respond well to treatment, with a small number regaining a good quality of life. However, a large percentage will remain chronically ill, requiring regular treatment and interventions to support them. Doctors, as yet, have not found a way to be able to accurately predict what an individual's prognosis will be after diagnosis.

Other features

Alongside the core symptoms associated with schizophrenia listed above, there are other common features associated with diagnosis of the disorder. For example, many patients will show general cognitive functioning deficits in areas such as working memory, language functioning and speed of information processing. Mood abnormalities are also common. Many patients describe periods of low mood similar to those experienced in depressive episodes, as well as inappropriate displays of mood such as laughing for no reason.

Biological explanation of schizophrenia: the function of neurotransmitters

It is a long-established idea that schizophrenia may, at least in part, be explained by an increase of certain neurotransmitters in areas of the brain. The key neurotransmitter thought to be associated with psychosis is dopamine. Very early on in the development of research in this area, it was noted that patients who had abused large amounts of the drug amphetamine often showed positive symptoms of psychosis, such as hallucinations and delusions. Randrup and Munkvad (1966) raised dopamine levels in the brains of rats by injecting them with amphetamine. The rats' behaviour changed, becoming more stereotyped, aggressive and isolated, showing that changing the dopamine levels resulted in psychotic-type behaviour consistent with that shown in patients with schizophrenia. By investigating the action of the drug they have found that amphetamine acts on the brain in a way that increases the level of the neurotransmitter dopamine. This sparked the beginning of the development of the dopamine hypothesis of schizophrenia. In 1967, a paper published by J.M. Van Rossum made a significant link between overstimulation of dopamine receptors and schizophrenia.

As research methods used to study the brain develop, so do biological theories that centre on the workings of the brain. The most recent version of the dopamine hypothesis centres on hypersensitivity of certain dopamine receptors (D2 receptors) in the brain, which mean that patients with the disorder are likely to 'overreact' to the presence of the neurotransmitter. Research by Lieberman et al. (1987) states that about 75 per cent of patients with schizophrenia show new symptoms or an increase in

WIDER ISSUES AND DEBATES

Use of psychological knowledge in society

The dopamine hypothesis emphasised to society that schizophrenia is an illness with a physical cause and therefore encouraged a change in opinions about treating those with mental health problems. The change in attitude towards medical treatment for disorders like schizophrenia has led to improvements in the understanding of how drugs can be used to alter brain chemistry. Antipsychotic medications are now a well-established treatment for schizophrenia. This medication has enabled many individuals suffering from schizophrenia to regain a good quality of life and has prevented many having to be hospitalised.

Amphetamine: a drug that stimulates the central nervous system. Its effects include increased activity and energy, as well as appetite suppression and difficulty in sleeping.

Methylphenidate: a psycho-stimulant drug that acts on the central nervous system. It is used medically to treat attention-deficit hyperactivity disorder (ADHD) in children and adolescents.

Antagonist: drugs that produce an antagonist effect bind to the receptor sites on neurons to prevent the substance from being absorbed in large quantities, therefore reducing the effect of the neurotransmitter.

psychosis after using drugs such as **amphetamine** and **methylphenidate**, which mimic the action of dopamine in the brain. However, only a small proportion of people who regularly use these drugs suffer from psychotic symptoms, which suggests that there is something different about how some people's brains react to dopamine that may explain the development of schizophrenia. This is supported by the fact that post-mortem examinations on the brains of people who have had schizophrenia show a higher density of dopamine receptors in certain parts of the brain (cerebral cortex) than do patients not suffering from schizophrenia (Owen et al. 1978), suggesting that they are more sensitive to the action of dopamine than people who have not had schizophrenia.

WIDER ISSUES AND DEBATES

Ethical issues

Drugs to treat schizophrenia have been well developed since the 1970s, but this is only possible through trials that have investigated the effects of different forms of medication. Many people have raised concerns about the ability of patients with psychotic illnesses such as schizophrenia to give informed consent regarding their participation in research. Someone who has lost touch with reality may not be able to consider all of the implications involved in their taking part in drug trials and this can cause problems with the ethics of such research.

Recent research has found that the amount of receptors may only account for about a 6 per cent increase from what is normally found in the brain: People diagnosed with schizophrenia may have a higher number of D2High receptors (Seeman, 2013). These receptors have a higher affinity to dopamine, which means they are more likely to bind to the neurotransmitter when it is present in the synapse, accounting for the higher degree of sensitivity shown by the brains of people with schizophrenia to dopamine-type drugs.

Evaluation of the neurotransmitter theory

Evidence to support the dopamine hypothesis as an explanation for schizophrenia comes from the fact that many traditional antipsychotic medications used to treat schizophrenia act by reducing the effect of dopamine by blocking dopamine receptors. However, there are many problems with this research as a support for the theory. Firstly, not all patients with schizophrenia respond to treatment with these drugs. Alpert and Friedhoff (1980), for example, found that some patients show no improvement whatsoever after taking dopamine **antagonists**. Secondly, more modern antipsychotic drugs, called atypical neuroleptics, do not necessarily only work by blocking dopamine receptors. For example, drugs such as clozapine not only block dopamine D2 receptors, they also block serotonin receptors, and they are just as effective as the older neuroleptics.

The advantage of these newer drugs is that they have fewer side effects for the patients so perhaps it is overly simplistic to assume that schizophrenia is merely the result of hypersensitivity to dopamine. Even more problematic for this explanation is evidence that has found that clozapine can actually increase dopamine levels in some parts of the brain, which would contradict the dopamine hypothesis completely.

Parkinson's is a degenerative disease associated with low levels of dopamine in the brain. People with Parkinson's disease often suffer from tremors or shaking of the limbs and head. To alleviate these symptoms, they are often prescribed L-Dopa, a medication known to be a dopamine agonist. When establishing how much L-Dopa to prescribe, patients can suffer the symptoms of schizophrenia, such as hallucinations and delusions, because their medication dose is too high. This indicates that dopamine is involved in Type 1 symptoms. Similarly, schizophrenia medication can cause Parkinson's-like symptoms of shaking when the dose is too high and the reduction of dopamine is too great.

Another issue to consider is whether the increase in levels of and sensitivity to dopamine is the cause of schizophrenia, or whether developing the illness changes brain chemistry in a way that results in this. Evidence can only be gathered from the brains of patients with schizophrenia after they have been diagnosed so it is unclear whether the brain was like this prior to diagnosis or not. It is also problematic that many patients who have been diagnosed as schizophrenic will have been given antipsychotic medication to treat their symptoms. Dopamine antagonists can cause **up-regulation** where the number of dopamine receptors increases, which can also increase levels of dopamine detected in the body. As schizophrenia is a relatively rare disorder it would be extremely difficult to test the brains of a sample of people and then monitor them to see if there were changes later if they were diagnosed with the illness. We have no way to predict who will develop schizophrenia. Post-mortem studies have shown that patients with schizophrenia who have taken antipsychotics for some time have elevated levels of dopamine, which are not found in the brains of those who have not received medication, suggesting that there may be up-regulation (Haracz, 1982).

WIDER ISSUES AND DEBATES

Reductionism

The dopamine hypothesis is a reductionist explanation as it explains a disorder that has many complex features, such as schizophrenia, by the smallest possible 'unit' of explanation – an imbalance of a single neurotransmitter. This ignores the complex interrelationship between neurotransmitter levels and other biological, psychological and social factors that may influence whether an individual develops the disorder. Brown and Birley (1968) found that 50 per cent of schizophrenic patients reported a major life event in the three weeks prior to relapse, suggesting that social conditions may trigger schizophrenia relapse. Although this does not directly propose that social triggers cause schizophrenia, it does indicate that we should be looking beyond the synaptic level when explaining schizophrenia.

The biochemical explanation can also successfully explain negative symptoms of the illness, which other explanations can sometimes struggle to account for. A reduction of dopamine in the **mesocortical pathways**, which links to the **mesolimbic system** (including the reward pathway in the brain associated with motivation to repeat behaviours), can lead to flattened affect, lack of motivation and the depressed mood state of individuals with schizophrenia. Schizophrenia often co-occurs with depression and also with substance abuse with some estimates showing a 50 per cent risk rate of substance misuse in sufferers of schizophrenia. The fact that these symptoms can be accounted for by changes in concentrations of dopamine in different areas of the brain, further supports the idea that the neurotransmitter is related to the illness.

DEVELOPMENTAL PSYCHOLOGY

Schizophrenia is a disorder that can be explained through the process of development. The two biological explanations for schizophrenia dealt with here (neurochemicals and genetics) could be used to discuss issues in developmental psychology. The neurochemical balance in the brain is something that could be affected by many things including the genes you have from conception, prenatal factors such as maternal illness, and chemical exposure such as drugs used throughout life. Other risk factors that have been linked with schizophrenia are prenatal exposure to infection or lack of nutrition (Opler and Susser, 2005). Schizophrenia develops in late adolescence and early adulthood, so it is of importance that developmental psychologists establish what biological, social or emotional changes occur during this period of life that could account for its onset.

Exam tip

Both the dopamine hypothesis and genetic explanation are examples of biological explanations for schizophrenia so they share many similarities but you should be able to use them as two separate theories. Make sure that you can distinguish between the two explanations clearly, but also think about how you can use similar points to evaluate them both, for example, they both ignore social/external factors.

Psychology as a science
There is a great deal of objective data to support biological explanations of schizophrenia. Evidence comes from studies using brain scans, blood tests, genetic testing, etc., all conducted using reliable equipment, meaning that the actual data is highly credible. Many of the studies are conducted in laboratories where it is possible to isolate and measure specific factors. There is also a great deal of evidence to demonstrate reliability by replicating the findings from previous research and building on evidence gathered as techniques develop further. For example, early research such as that by Gottesman (1991) found basic evidence of genetic causes for schizophrenia, but more contemporary research such as Egan et al. (2001) has developed from this to isolate specific genes associated with developing the illness.

Key term

Concordance rate: the probability that if one twin/family member has a certain characteristic (such as schizophrenia) then the other twin/another family member will also have it.

One other biological explanation: genetics

Another biological explanation for schizophrenia is that there is evidence of a strong heritable factor in the development of the disorder. The risk of developing schizophrenia at some point in your lifetime for the general population is less than 1 per cent. If you have a second degree relative (for example, aunt/uncle, niece/nephew) with the illness, that risk increases to between 2 and 6 per cent. If you have a first degree relative (for example, parent, sibling, dizygotic twin) with schizophrenia, the risk increases even more significantly to between 6 and 17 per cent. However the biggest risk seen was in people who had an identical or monozygotic twin with schizophrenia, where there was a 48 per cent chance that they would be diagnosed with the illness too (Gottesman, 1991). The greater the degree of genetic relatedness, the higher the risk of developing the disorder, suggesting a strong genetic element to schizophrenia.

Evaluation of the genetic explanation

Family studies like this have established that there does appear to be some inherited component in the development of schizophrenia, as lifetime risk goes up when the level of genetic similarity with a sufferer increases. However, research has failed to isolate a single recessive or dominant gene that seems to cause the illness (Tamminga and Schulz, 1991). Many researchers believe that a disorder as complex as schizophrenia probably results from the expression of multiple genes rather than a single gene. Harrison and Owen (2003) reported that recent research has suggested that up to six different genes may be involved in susceptibility to developing the disorder. Other research has put forward the argument that the causative influence of genes on schizophrenia could be the result of the genes' effect on the functions of synapses and the circuitry in the brain (Harrison and Weinberger, 2004). Family studies can also be criticised for failing to acknowledge that the incidence of schizophrenia in families may be a result of environmental influences. Research into dysfunctional family communication patterns and schizophrenic relapse rates indicate that schizophrenia may be a result of stress caused by negative emotions within families.

The evidence is clear that a genetic component is probably involved because of the dramatic rise in the risk of developing the disorder as the genetic relationship to a sufferer increases. However, a major flaw in the genetic explanation for schizophrenia is that there is clearly more to it than genes as even in MZ twins the **concordance rate** is only around 40–50 per cent. As these twins are genetically identical we would expect the concordance to be 100 per cent if the illness was purely attributable to genetic factors.

It is important to note here that research such as that by Gottesman (1991) has found that in DZ twins the concordance rate is only around 17 per cent, while in MZ twins it is 48 per cent. Both sets of twins will have shared prenatal and post-birth environments, but MZ twins share 100 per cent of the same genes while DZ twins only share 50 per cent. The fact that MZ twins show such an increased concordance suggests that genes must play a significant role in the development of schizophrenia. In comparison to other siblings, where the concordance found was 9 per cent in Gottesman's (1991) research, concordance rates in twins are increased. This could be accountable to a higher risk of birth complications in twins than in other pregnancies or the possibility that MZ twins are raised more similarly than DZ twins or siblings and are more likely to experience identity confusion (Joseph, 2004), products of environment and upbringing rather than genetics.

Family and twin research has indicated that the greater degree of family relatedness, the higher concordance for schizophrenia, but it fails to control for environmental influences. Adoption studies remove this problem because they examine concordance of children that have been separated from their biological parents, thereby removing the influence of the environment. Tienari et al. (2000) found that almost 7 per cent of adoptees with schizophrenia had a biological mother with the same disorder, compared to only 2 per cent of schizophrenic children born to mothers without schizophrenia. According to the researchers, this small difference could only be a result of genetics. However, it is not the case that adoptees are randomly placed, in fact they are selectively placed with families of similar background and to families that are often aware of the mental health of the biological parents.

An alternative biological theory: neuroanatomical theory

In 1919, Kraepelin first suggested that schizophrenia was a 'brain-based' illness, but there was a limited opportunity to test out this theory because it was impossible to study the brains of those diagnosed with schizophrenia until after death. Since the 1980s when there were advances in the use of brain-imaging techniques in research, psychologists have been interested in whether schizophrenia had any anatomical components. There is a lot of research that has found that patients with schizophrenia have enlarged ventricles in the brain – these are cavities in the brain that contain cerebrospinal fluid. Johnstone et al. (1976) used CAT scans to compare the brain structures of a group of schizophrenic patients, and a group of matched controls, and found that those with schizophrenia had significant enlargement in ventricular areas.

It has been found that enlarged ventricles are most associated with negative symptoms of schizophrenia, and also with patients who have the worst outcomes. There is a wealth of evidence to support this explanation of schizophrenia. For example, Giedd et al. (1999) found that patients with early-onset schizophrenia showed significant developmental increases in ventricular size throughout a longitudinal study using MRI scans of their brain at various intervals. There was a significant increase in the size of ventricles throughout adolescence as the disorder progressed, and there was a relationship between the severity of negative symptoms measured in the patients and the increase in ventricle size. However, criticism of this explanation is that it is difficult to identify cause and effect as brain abnormalities may be the result of developing schizophrenia rather than the cause of the illness.

WIDER ISSUES AND DEBATES

Nature–nurture

Biological explanations of schizophrenia ignore any role of external influences on the development of the disorder. Social factors have been implicated in explanations for schizophrenia, which could account for some biological factors that have been uncovered. For example, research has found higher rates of schizophrenia in deprived areas, and in these areas there may also be increased levels of drug use due to exposure to such behaviour. Drugs have been implicated in changes in brain chemistry that may be associated with developing the disorder and so the social context the patient lives in could be the ultimate cause of the illness. The **diathesis-stress model** of mental illness would argue that schizophrenia develops in those who have a biological predisposition to developing the illness due to genetic, neurochemical or neuroanatomical factors, but who also have some kind of environmental trigger. This theory suggests that there is no single explanation for mental illness, but rather the cause is actually a combination of factors, which therefore refutes the biological view.

INDIVIDUAL DIFFERENCES

Symptoms of schizophrenia are very diverse and not the same for everyone. Some might argue that the biological view of schizophrenia is unlikely to be a complete one as there are likely to be different factors associated with developing the disorder that may account for the various subtypes and presentation of symptoms.

Key term

Diathesis-stress model: a theory that explains behaviour through a mixture of biological and environmental factors. A dormant genetic disposition could be triggered by an environmental life event.

One non-biological explanation: cognitive theory

The cognitive explanation of schizophrenia begins by attributing Type 1 (positive) symptoms of schizophrenia to biological causes. The experience of hallucinations and delusions is thought to be associated with biological factors, such as increased dopamine levels, but when the patient tries to make sense of this experience they begin to experience other symptoms of the illness. This is where the cognitive explanation can help us understand the disorder. When the patient experiences a hallucination they may look to others to confirm what they think they have seen or heard, but when others cannot confirm this the patient may become wary of them and feel they are keeping information from them.

This can then, in turn, create further delusions of persecution or paranoia as the patient can feel that others are deliberately denying the experience they believe they are having. Therefore, many of the symptoms of schizophrenia are seen as a mistaken attempt by the patient to understand the experiences resulting from abnormal biological functioning in the brain.

Frith (1979) published work suggesting that schizophrenia results from the patient's increased 'self-awareness' whereby there is an inability to filter out unnecessary cognitive 'noise' created by internal information processing. As part of our general, day-to-day experience we ignore many cognitive processes that go on at a level beyond our conscious awareness. We do not consciously process every thought, decision, or perception because this would become exhausting, and is not really necessary. But he argued that schizophrenic patients are unable to ignore these minor processes, and as such they experience an increased level of cognitive awareness that they cannot make sense of. Imagine, for example, having the experience of being told to check your watch to make sure you are not late for work. We may unconsciously keep checking our watch when we know we are due to arrive at work soon, but often this would not be something we would actually think about. Someone with schizophrenia may experience this 'thought' as a voice telling them to check their watch because they might be late. For most of us, this thought would go unnoticed, but to a person with schizophrenia this might be experienced as an external voice telling them what to do. When they try to make sense of this and cannot, this can then lead to further delusions and worsening symptoms.

An alternative cognitive theory: social drift theory

Evidence has suggested that schizophrenia is more prevalent in lower social classes in society and this has been explained by the social drift hypothesis. This theory suggests that the symptoms of schizophrenia make it difficult for patients to hold down jobs, achieve well in education, and maintain relationships and so they often drop down into lower social and economic classes in society. Consequently, there are greater concentrations of people with schizophrenia in the more deprived areas than there are in more affluent areas in society. People with schizophrenia also drift into the more urban areas because they can gain better access to support services than is possible in rural areas. For example, there is generally more cheap housing, food kitchens and social service provision available in cities than in small towns or villages, which can encourage people with schizophrenia to drift into these different societal areas.

Evaluation of the cognitive theory of schizophrenia

Research evidence has supported the idea that cognitive deficits are often associated with schizophrenia. For example, Gold and Harvey (1993) report that people with schizophrenia often score lower on tests of attention, memory and problem solving, than similar people without the disorder. Research by McGuigan (1966) identified that immediately before episodes of auditory hallucination were reported, some schizophrenic patients showed activation of the vocal centres, which may suggest that they misinterpreted their own 'inner voice' as belonging to someone else. This is supported by McGuire et al. (1996) who discovered that during hallucinations, the part of the brain in the temporal lobe responsible for identifying and monitoring 'inner speech' recorded reduced activity. This suggests that the individuals might have been experiencing an internal conversation, but were more likely to perceive the voice as belonging to someone else. These findings support Frith's explanation as it suggests that patients with schizophrenia were unable to distinguish their own thoughts, that is, they had perceptual problems.

Evidence from Corcoran et al. (1995) has found that patients with schizophrenia also show deficits in tasks requiring 'theory of mind', which is the cognitive skill associated with the ability to read and interpret the intentions of other people's behaviour. This means there is a strong evidence base behind the claim that schizophrenia has a cognitive cause.

However, one criticism of this explanation is that, although the explanation focuses on the cognitive processing of the patient and how this may result in symptoms of psychosis, the underlying cause of the cognitive processing deficits is often attributed to biological factors. For example, in a book by Beck et al. (2009) the researchers summarise the effect of dopamine reduction on **'cognitive loading'** meaning that reduced levels of the neurotransmitter cause the brain to struggle more in processing information. This leads to **cognitive insufficiency**, and sets the person on the pathway to developing psychosis. This suggests that there is a pre-existing biological risk factor, which then affects the person's cognitive abilities. If there is a significant stressor in the individual's life, this will lead to continuing decline in cognitive processing, which could result in schizophrenia. Thus, although focusing on cognitive explanations for the disorder, separating out the biological factors is not easy and ultimately the explanation may be rooted in biology.

Sitskoom et al. (2004) found that the cognitive deficits found in patients with schizophrenia were also found in relatives of the patients who did not have the disorder. This suggests that there may be some genetic component underlying the cognitive deficit that is triggered in some people and not others.

Another criticism would be that there is no easy way to measure whether the cognitive impairments seen in schizophrenic patients are the cause of the illness, or whether they are actually the effect of having schizophrenia. There may in fact be a combination of factors associated with developing schizophrenia and the cause of the illness could be a combination of all of these. This brings us back to the diathesis-stress model of mental illness mentioned earlier in the topic.

WIDER ISSUES AND DEBATES

Nature–nurture

Biological explanations of schizophrenia suggest nature has the biggest influence on developing the illness, while social explanations would focus more on nurture as the cause. These two opposing views are part of a fundamental debate underpinning work in clinical psychology in relation to whether disorders are something that develop due to internal factors mostly beyond our control, or whether mental health problems stem from external factors. The cognitive explanation of schizophrenia suggests that the disorder is rooted in nature as the ability of the brain to process information will be best explained by biological factors. However, cognitive psychologists often talk about 'stressors' triggering the underlying problem, and these are usually external/environmental issues. This may suggest that there is a combination of factors that must be present in order for a person to develop schizophrenia. The diathesis-stress model would suggest schizophrenia develops as a result of an interaction between biological vulnerability and environmental stressors. This could explain why not everyone who has the genes associated with schizophrenia goes on to develop it (for example, only 48 per cent concordance rate in MZ twins), and why there are more diagnoses of schizophrenia in city-dwellers (for example, increased social stress).

Taking it further

Look into the effects of expressed emotion as an explanation of schizophrenia to see how external factors in the family may be seen as causal variables in the development of schizophrenia.

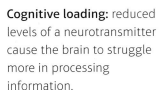

Key terms

Cognitive loading: reduced levels of a neurotransmitter cause the brain to struggle more in processing information.

Cognitive insufficiency: deficits and difficulties in processing information. These include problems with attention and slow processing speed.

Exam tip

It is important to learn the command words associated with essay writing for the examination. The command word 'discuss' will require you to consider contrasting views, in this topic the contrasting explanations of schizophrenia. However, the command words 'assess' and 'evaluate' require that you consider the relative strengths and weaknesses and come to a judgement or conclusion. Example questions to practise are:

Discuss two different explanations for schizophrenia.

Assess the contributions of the biological approach in understanding schizophrenia.

Evaluate one psychological explanation for schizophrenia.

Treatments for schizophrenia
Biological treatment: drug therapy

The frontline treatment offered to patients with schizophrenia is often antipsychotic medication that can help to alleviate the symptoms associated with a psychotic episode, such as delusional thoughts and hallucinations. These symptoms can adversely affect the quality of life for patients and make accessing other forms of treatment difficult, so the drugs are offered to try to control these symptoms. In the 1950s the first antipsychotic drugs were developed, which are now known as 'typical' antipsychotics. These include drugs such as chlorpromazine, haloperidol and fluphenazine. These had many reported side effects that patients found unpleasant, which led to the development of 'atypical' antipsychotics in the 1990s. Examples of these drugs include clozapine, risperidone and olanzapine. The atypical drugs seem to have fewer reported side effects while still being effective, making them preferable for many patients. One of these drugs, clozapine, has been shown to be highly effective in treating the positive symptoms of hallucinations and other associated psychotic symptoms including some negative symptoms such as emotional withdrawal (Brar et al., 1997) even in people who have not previously responded to treatment with other drugs.

Antipsychotic drugs work by helping to reduce the level of dopamine in areas of the brain associated with the symptoms. Their primary mechanism of action (the way they work in the brain) is through the blocking of dopamine receptors in those areas of the brain, which effectively prevents the dopamine binding to the receptors in the synapse and therefore depolarises the neurons, calming them down.

All antipsychotic drugs seem to share this same mechanism of action, and specifically they act by blockading mostly D2 receptors within those areas. There is also evidence that the newer atypical antipsychotics do not bind to the receptors quite so tightly, and that they also block 5-HT2A receptors, which are serotonin receptors. It is thought that it is these differences in action that somehow help to reduce the side effects associated with the use of atypical drugs as opposed to typical antipsychotics (Seeman, 2002). These drugs can be given in tablet form, or in some cases they can be administered by injection by a nurse, especially if there is a risk that the patient will not comply with the treatment regimen themselves.

Figure 5.1 The action of D2 antagonist drugs in reducing positive symptoms of schizophrenia by blocking the D2 receptors

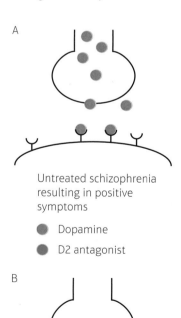

A

Untreated schizophrenia resulting in positive symptoms

- Dopamine
- D2 antagonist

B

Treatment for schizophrenia by D2 antagonists resulting in reduced positive symptoms

WIDER ISSUES AND DEBATES

Ethics

If a patient is detained under Section 3 of the Mental Health Act (1983), treatment can be given without their consent if it is deemed necessary. Drug therapy is one of only three treatments that can be given in this way and some would argue that this breaches ethical guidelines. However, for treatment to be given without consent the patient's current state of mind must be considered, that is, if they are putting themselves or others in danger. In fact, in some cases, it could be argued that the patient's symptoms could mean that they are unable to know what is best for them and so receiving treatment forcibly may be the most positive course of action.

Evaluation of drug therapy

One major criticism of the use of drug therapy to treat schizophrenia is the fact that these drugs can have quite serious side effects for some patients. Side effects can include drowsiness, blurred vision and rapid heart rate. Atypical antipsychotics have reported side effects such as weight gain and metabolic changes, which could increase risk of diabetes and high cholesterol. Typical antipsychotics are also associated with disturbances of movement and posture such as tremors and muscle spasms. Patients who use typical antipsychotics in the long term can end up with a condition called **tardive dyskinesia**, which causes involuntary muscle spasms that commonly occur around the mouth and can affect speech, but which can be irreversible.

WIDER ISSUES AND DEBATES

Issues of social control

There is a great deal of debate over whether some forms of medication have sometimes been used to make patients with abnormal behaviour more manageable. Many of the older, typical antipsychotic drugs made patients very passive and therefore easier for staff in institutions to control, which may have made the drugs open to abuse in busy wards. As such, drug treatments that have these effects have been regarded as pharmacological straitjackets. There is also a lot of opposition to the use of drugs to treat mental illness because pharmaceutical companies are argued to be more interested in making money from the drugs they produce rather than actually helping the patients who take them. More should be done to help treat patients long term and help them avoid side effects associated with the use of antipsychotic drugs.

Research has found that many patients will stop taking their medication because of severe side effects, which has serious consequences for the effectiveness of this treatment (Lieberman et al., 2005). One of the most effective antipsychotics is clozapine, which generally has fewer side effects than other similar drugs. It is this reduction in side effects that may explain its effectiveness, as patients are more likely to be drug compliant if they experience fewer adverse effects. However, clozapine has been found to increase the risk of patients developing **agranulocytosis**, which reduces the white blood count and increases the risk of infections. For this reason, patients on clozapine must have blood tests every two weeks to monitor their blood count.

Research by McEvoy et al. (2006) compared the time taken to discontinue treatment with four atypical drugs. The patients had already stopped taking another atypical drug earlier on in their treatment because the drugs were not working. They found that of the four drugs that were offered to the patient group to try, the most effective was clozapine because patients in this group continued taking this drug considerably longer than any of the others. The assessment of symptoms taken after three months of taking the new drug also showed the most improvement in the group taking clozapine.

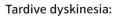

Key terms

Tardive dyskinesia: involuntary muscle spasms that commonly occur around the mouth and can affect speech.

Agranulocytosis: an acute condition resulting in a reduced white blood count, which increases risk of infections.

Exam tip

A useful structure to consider when evaluating any therapy or treatment is to think of the effectiveness, ethics and limitations of the treatment. By covering these three elements you will be able to give an overall discussion of critical evaluation relating to each treatment. You should try to consider as much evidence as you can to illustrate these three points, as this will help you to explain yourself clearly in the exam, using examples. Remember, evaluation should involve both strengths and weaknesses, and you will have to reach a conclusion/judgement.

WIDER ISSUES AND DEBATES

Issues of social control

In the late 1930s, Ugo Cerletti used electroshocks to induce seizures in animals, and this was later used to treat people with schizophrenia.

Electroconvulsive therapy (ECT) involves electrodes (paddles) being placed on one (unilateral) or both (bilateral) sides of the head (unilateral is typically administered to the non-dominant hemisphere) and a determined current of electricity is passed through the brain to induce a grand mal seizure. This procedure is followed approximately twice a week over the course of up to 12 sessions. The induction of seizures caused injury to patients, leading to the use of body restraints, mouth guards, muscle relaxant and anaesthesia.

During the 1960s, ECT was criticised by the antipsychiatry movement for being a barbaric treatment for patients with behaviours that staff found difficult to deal with. As such, it was seen as a form of social control to keep troublesome patients docile and easy to handle. The way in which ECT was claimed to have been used as a form of social control is portrayed in the film *One Flew Over the Cuckoo's Nest*.

Objections to the use of ECT largely saw it fall out of favour for the treatment of schizophrenia, and it is now typically used to stabilise mood disorders. However, recent guidelines for the use of ECT for schizophrenia have suggested that it could be an effective treatment for immediate relief of catatonic symptoms resistant to drug treatments. There have been a number of studies and meta-analyses conducted to examine the effectiveness of ECT for schizophrenia, some of which argue that it could be an effective treatment in conjunction with antipsychotic medication. However, conclusions have been mixed and some argue that research tends to lack the blind assessment necessary to establish effectiveness.

Psychological treatment: family therapy

The purpose of family therapy, or family intervention, is to help the whole family to support the individual who has been diagnosed with a mental illness. Living with someone who has experienced or is experiencing psychosis can be very difficult. Family therapy aims to develop a support network within the family and also to build up a collaborative relationship between the family and the professionals who will be providing treatment for the patient. The NICE (National Institute for Health and Care Excellence) guidelines for treating schizophrenia state that family therapy should be offered to patients during their course of treatment, and there is a great deal of evidence that it can help to reduce relapse rates and increase treatment compliance in patient groups.

One important feature of family therapy in schizophrenia is to encourage the family to talk openly about the symptoms being experienced by the patient. Here the patient themselves will be encouraged to explain what they experience as an 'expert' on schizophrenia. The family will also be educated on the causes of the illness so as to break down any concerns about 'blame' for the development of the psychosis. It is important that the whole family understands the illness to have a better understanding of the behaviours shown, such as learning that the symptoms cannot be controlled by the patient during an episode of psychosis.

Drug therapy is also likely to be part of the treatment given and the family will be offered information on how the medication works and what side effects to expect. Another important feature is that, as well as focusing on understanding the illness, family members are encouraged to talk about other day-to-day concerns they have. For example, it may be frustrating to live with someone who is no longer taking care of their own personal hygiene, which could lead to family members getting angry with the patient, but by discussing the different viewpoints and considering how the family can work together to solve problems they are all facing, everyone is given a chance to state their views.

The motivation for including family members in the treatment process is that the demands of living with someone with a serious mental health problem like schizophrenia can be very high. The challenging behaviour caused by the symptoms can be emotionally draining, and people might feel embarrassed or ashamed about talking to other people outside the family about the person with schizophrenia. Family therapy aims to give them the opportunity to air their concerns in a supported environment and work together to find solutions, or at least develop understanding that will reduce the negative emotions. This in turn will help to make the patient feel more supported in the home and this is thought to have a big impact on the chances of treatment being successful.

Evaluation of family therapy

It is important to understand that family therapy is not a treatment for schizophrenia per se, and will not cure the disorder, but it is a therapy to help families cope with the disorder, create a more manageable family environment, offer support and encourage medication compliance. Research by Goldstein and Miklowitz (1995) reviewed studies into the effectiveness of family therapy and found that a lot of evidence suggested that family interventions combined with medication were much more effective in reducing relapse rates than medication alone. However, they also pointed out that the level of effectiveness in family interventions was determined by the type of intervention offered. Other studies have compared the effectiveness of family therapy with other forms of psychological therapy in treating schizophrenia. One meta-analysis by Pilling et al. (2002) compared the effectiveness of family therapy with CBT as a treatment for schizophrenia and found that there were some differences in the effects of each type of therapy. Family therapy was effective in reducing relapse rates for episodes of psychosis, as well as improving the compliance with the medication prescribed.

Family therapy shows family members how to deal with the disruptions of the disorder, and helps them to understand the disorder better.

Family therapy relies heavily on the whole family being open and honest, as well as being willing to work with the therapists in supporting the patient. Not all families, or even all family members, will be willing or able to commit to this, which could account for the drop-out rates associated with family therapy. On its own, family therapy is not an effective therapy as it is an intervention for support for the family and to ensure the patient takes their medication. However, in combination with medication, which is the preferred treatment for schizophrenia, evidence has shown very positive outcomes for patients. The aim of family therapy is to achieve long-term maintenance of mental health. It is not designed to relieve symptoms but to reduce expressed emotion and prevent relapse, through medication compliance and support. One of the biggest limitations of family therapy is that, despite evidence of its effectiveness, it is not widely available on the NHS. Patients who could benefit from the therapy may not have access to it. One of the key outcomes of family therapy is reduced relapse rates and this could vastly improve the quality of life of many patients diagnosed with schizophrenia and could save the NHS money, as fewer relapses mean that fewer patients will be admitted to hospital at considerable expense.

Unipolar depression

Major depressive disorders are from the family of mood disorders, which means that they affect how we feel about ourselves and the world around us. The two main groups of mood disorder are unipolar depression and bipolar disorder. Bipolar disorder is characterised by manic and depressive phrases, whereas unipolar depression is characterised by a persistently low mood, among other symptoms. Unipolar depression is not a single type of disorder but has several subtypes classified by severity, length of occurrence and whether it has psychotic or other features.

Unipolar depression can be reactive, a response to adverse life events, or it can arise out of the blue for no observable reason. This is called **endogenous depression;** it has no apparent environmental trigger and is most probably linked to internal biological factors.

Symptoms

There is no reliable physiological test for depression so diagnosis relies on the clinician's expertise.

There is a range of symptoms that cover **emotional**, **somatic**, **motivational** and **cognitive** changes experienced by someone with depression.

Taking it further

Family therapy is a well-established therapy with many different uses, one of which is in the treatment of schizophrenia. To find out more about the wider issues involved in the use of family therapy in this way visit the Mental Health Care website and search for family therapy. There is lots of information about how the sessions work, the background of the approach to therapy, as well as the rationale behind this type of therapeutic approach.

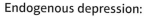

Key term

Endogenous depression: linked to internal biological factors rather than being caused by an environmental trigger such as a stressful event.

According to the DSM V depression can be diagnosed by the presence of five or more symptoms for a two-week period, one of which must be depressed mood or loss of interest or pleasure. The other symptoms are; significant weight loss or gain; changes in sleeping patterns; observable psychomotor agitation; fatigue; feelings of worthlessness or excessive inappropriate guilt; loss of concentration and recurrent thoughts of death or suicidal ideation.

Additionally the symptoms must cause significant distress or impairment to the person's life and must not be attributable to the effects of a substance or to another medical condition. Furthermore, the occurrence of the symptoms cannot be better explained as being due to a disorder from the schizophrenic spectrum and the sufferer has never had a manic or hypomanic episode.

Features

Unipolar depression can strike at any age, but is more likely in young adulthood. The course of the disorder varies in its severity. Some people may appear to be functioning well and some may go into remission within a few months of the onset and then remain symptom-free; however, for some (especially those with personality disorders and/or high anxiety) the symptoms can be severe and long lasting, with few periods of remission.

The risk of developing major depression is affected by temperament; specifically **neuroticism** is a well-established risk factor especially when combined with stressful life events. Risk is increased by having negative events in childhood and having a first degree relative with the disorder.

You are more likely to get depression if you suffer from another disorder and this is likely to adversely affect your recovery from depression; such other disorders include substance misuse, **borderline personality disorders** and anxiety. Comorbidity is also common with panic disorder, OCD, anorexia nervosa and bulimia.

Major depressive disorder is associated with high mortality, generally through suicide, but also when it affects the course of other illnesses. Suicide is higher in male sufferers but is attempted more frequently by females. It is more likely when the person is single, lives alone and has strong feelings of hopelessness.

Unipolar depression has a high **prevalence rate** although this varies across cultures. This may be due to cultural differences in the diagnosis and reporting of depression rather than a simple link between the culture and the disorder. The DSM estimates the rate at 7 per cent for the USA but states that this is higher in those aged between 18 and 29 and there is a much higher incidence in females with the female sufferers outnumbering males by at least a two to one ratio.

A person suffering with depression is often consumed by self-directed guilt and makes negative statements about themselves and their abilities.

Link

Before reading this section you might benefit by revising the section on neural transmission in Topic 2: *Biological psychology*.

Biological explanation

Biological explanations for depression focus on genetics, abnormalities in neurotransmitter systems and on the role of hormones. Explanations also include anatomical changes in brain areas such as the prefrontal cortex and limbic system, with research more recently investigating the role of the hippocampus. You will need to know only one biological and one psychological explanation for depression.

Taking it further

While only one of the biological explanations is covered in detail here you could opt to research any of the others, for example, you could look at the role of genetics and theories that suggest that depression evolved in some people as an evolutionary adaptation.

WIDER ISSUES AND DEBATES

Reductionism

Biological explanations can be challenged in terms of them being reductionist. They tend to simplify very complex behaviour such as depression to a mechanical and simplistic explanation, such as the activity of a few neurones, the expression of a certain set of genes or a lack/surfeit of some neurotransmitters. Attributing entirely to a biological explanation ignores other factors that may be equally influential or the interaction between these factors.

Key terms

Serotonin: a chemical created by the body that works as a neurotransmitter. It is responsible for managing moods.

Noradrenalin: (also known as norepinephrine) is a catecholamine hormone and neurotransmitter with multiple roles including maintaining concentration.

Receptor sites: areas on the postsynaptic neuron that allow neurotransmitters to lock onto the membrane.

Down-regulation: homeostatic mechanism where the brain produces less of something in response to an increase.

The role of neurotransmitters

The monoamine hypothesis proposes that depression results from a chemical imbalance in the monoamine neurotransmitters in the brain, more specifically **serotonin** and **noradrenaline**. It was noticed in the 1950s that drugs that decreased these amine neurotransmitters brought about symptoms of depression, so it was assumed that depression was caused by low levels of these neurotransmitters, particularly serotonin. Drugs were developed that increased their availability in the synapse and which then alleviated some of the symptoms.

However, although the levels of noradrenalin and serotonin increase within hours of the administration of these antidepressant drugs, the symptoms often do not improve for a period of up to six weeks in some cases. This challenged the simple monoamine hypothesis and led to a more complex alternate explanation, which suggested that the low levels of noradrenalin and serotonin led to changes in the neuro-circuitry of the brain, specifically causing an up-regulation in the sensitivity of the **receptor sites** on the synapses in relevant pathways. Because of the low levels of serotonin and noradrenalin there is too little stimulation of postsynaptic receptors. Therefore, in order to compensate more receptors are made, but when more of the neurotransmitter becomes available through the administration of antidepressant drugs, there is a **down-regulation** where the receptors are desensitised. This can account for the delay in the effect of the drug as this process interferes with alleviation of the symptoms.

More recent theories have refined the idea that depression results from a pathological alteration in receptor sites caused by too little stimulation by monoamine neurotransmitters. They now look in more detail at the interaction between serotonin and noradrenalin. In this explanation, serotonin controls the levels of noradrenalin so when there are low levels of serotonin, the levels of noradrenalin are affected. If these are too low then the person will experience feelings of depression, if too high then they may experience mania (as in bipolar depression).

> **Alternative explanations for depression – cortisol**
>
> Depression is consistently associated with abnormalities in the neuroendocrine system. The hypothalamic-pituitary-adrenal system is responsible for modulating the body's response to stress through the release of cortisol from the adrenal cortex. An important brain structure in this system is the hippocampus. The hippocampus controls the levels of corticotrophin-releasing hormone (CRH), which leads to the production and release of cortisol by the adrenal cortex. Usually a negative feedback mechanism will switch off the production of CRH, but in cases of severe stress and depression this does not work, leading to consistently high levels of cortisol in the blood. This adversely affects the hippocampus, which leads to more CRH being released causing a vicious cycle with the release of more stress hormones.

Evaluation

Most evidence for the role of serotonin and noradrenaline in depression comes from drug research. From this we know that serotonin mediates mood, and low levels of serotonin may account for depression. MDMA (ecstasy), an illegal recreational drug, works by increasing the amount of the neurotransmitter serotonin into the synaptic gap and is associated with feeling of euphoria (intense happiness). Many antidepressant drugs work to block the reuptake of serotonin so it is available in the synaptic gap to be taken up by the postsynaptic receptors, which elevates mood. With strong biological evidence for low levels of serotonin being the cause of depression, some researchers still believe that antidepressants cause a placebo effect, which may explain mood improvement in many patients (Kirsch et al., 2002).

Similarly, evidence for the role of noradrenaline has been found through the use of antidepressant medication to increase the amount of noradrenaline at the synaptic level. Versiani et al. (1999) used a double-blind trial of noradrenaline reuptake inhibitors (NRIs) and a placebo drug to find a marked mood improvement in depressed patients with NRIs compared to a placebo. Antidepressants known to increase noradrenaline levels have been shown to be just as effective as those that increase serotonin levels (Andreoli et al., 2002). However, NRIs are not always successful for all depressed patients, and seem to be more effective with endogenous than reactive depression types.

Drug research can be problematic in that just because a drug is effective in treating a disorder, it does not mean that it can indicate the cause of the disorder. This is known as treatment aetiology fallacy, because we assume that if a treatment is effective in reducing symptoms, the target of that treatment must be the cause of the disorder. This is simply not the case. Just because serotonin and noradrenaline levels can be treated with medication does not mean that they are the cause of depression. Although they may be biological correlates of depression, it does not prove that they cause it.

Recent research has cast doubts over the role of serotonin in depression. Mariana Angoa-Pérez and her colleagues (2014) bred mice lacking the gene for tryptophan, an enzyme that is the precursor of serotonin production, found that the mice did not show any signs of depression in a battery of tests, nor were they responsive to antidepressant medication. Even when put under stress the mice did not respond any differently from normal mice. This evidence suggests that the cause of depression must be more than low levels of serotonin, and that other factors must be involved. However, we should be cautious when generalising the findings from animal studies to our understanding of human depression.

A recent meta-analysis by Sullivan, Neale and Kendler (2000) of family, twin and adoption studies investigating the role of heredity in major depression found that there is a familial transmission of depression consistent with the figure of 40 per cent increased risk of developing the disorder when a first degree relative has it (DSM V statistic). This could indicate a genetic vulnerability to neurotransmitter dysfunction.

One non-biological explanation: a cognitive behavioural theory

Operant conditioning

Behaviourist theories explain depression as a result of environmental factors causing faulty learning, which leads to set behavioural responses. For example, Lewinsohn (1974) proposed that depression occurs because of a lack of **positive reinforcement** from the environment. The person either does not engage with the social environment, or they lack the social skills to engage with the social environment in a way that leads to reinforcement; for example, if they are socially awkward they might have their attempts at conversation ignored. This lack of reinforcement leads to the feelings of worthlessness and withdrawn behaviour associated with the symptoms of depression.

Learned helplessness is another behavioural explanation, based on research by Maier and Seligman (1969 and onward) on dogs. Dogs exposed to inescapable electric shocks learned to give up trying to escape and did not take the opportunity to escape when it was subsequently offered. This behaviour reflects the symptoms of depression such as the inability to initiate coping strategies. Research based on this showed depletions in neurotransmitter levels in the dogs consistent with those associated with depression. The value of animal research into a complex human behaviour like depression could be challenged as humans have much higher levels of cognitive functioning and might be expected to behave differently but the research has been successfully replicated on humans. However, not all dogs responded in the same way; if the behaviour were purely learned then we would expect all dogs to respond to the same environmental stimuli in an identical way. This led to the development of a cognitive element to the explanation that is more specifically related to humans.

Cognition

Abramson (1978), refined the behaviourist explanation to include a cognitive element, specifically the **attributional bias** of the person in response to failure. People with a **maladaptive** attributional style tend to put more emphasis on fault within themselves as a causal factor for their failure. Specifically they internalise failure in a way that suggests they cannot change and that will affect everything they do. This is known as an internal, stable and global attribution of failure. Non-depressed people are more likely to blame failure on external factors, a temporary blip or something specific only to that event.

For example, if a student gets a poor score on a test and they have a maladaptive attributional style, they might think 'I am stupid, I cannot do tests, I will fail every test I take'.

This is a faulty cognition and it could lead to feelings of learned helplessness, so the person withdraws from the situation in order to avoid further failure; they then lack positive reinforcement and can fall into a downwards spiral towards depression.

Beck (1967, 1976) focused on a more cognitive-based explanation arguing that depression and depressed mood is a product of pessimistic **schema** we hold about how the world works. **Negative schema** develop during childhood as a result of early trauma and unhappy experiences leading to a cognitive triad of beliefs in people about: themselves, seeing themselves as worthless and useless; their environment, which they see as overwhelming and full of obstacles; and their future, seeing it as hopeless.

When confronted with stress, people with these negative schema about themselves, the world and the future, apply faulty logic in their interpretation of the event. These can be described as cognitive distortions.

Key terms

Positive reinforcement: a rewarding outcome for behaviour.

Attributional bias: how we habitually locate causes for events, for example internal cause suggests that we are responsible for what happens to us, but external would suggest that events are beyond our control.

Maladaptive: behaviour that we commonly exhibit that is bad for us.

Schema: core information and beliefs about how we think about the world.

Negative schema: habitual ways of thinking that are self-critical and damaging.

Table 5.1 Examples of cognitive distortions

Cognitive distortion	Example
Polar reasoning (also known as 'all or nothing' thinking)	Unless everything is absolutely perfect it is considered a dismal failure, e.g. a student gets an A instead of an A* and feels worthless as a result.
Selective abstraction	Ignoring good stuff in favour of focusing on small negative things that can be interpreted negatively. Success is ignored and the person recalls only failure, e.g. a student gets 8 A*s and a D and they focus on the D grade, which is magnified in their mind.
Overgeneralisation	One tiny aspect of an experience is extrapolated from in order to form a belief about what happened, e.g. failure on one essay means that failure on the course is inevitable.

Cognitive distortions change perception and trigger anxiety and negative emotions, which in turn trigger behaviour consistent with the symptoms of depression such, as passivity and helplessness.

Beck continued to develop his theory over the years and now believes that there are two types of schema that operate in depression. One is a negative interpersonal schema, which is a generalised representation of self–other relationships developed during childhood through interaction with attachment figures; a schema like this might lead to an unrealistic view of relationships, such as needing to have everyone like them. The other is a schema based on personal achievement characterised by failure to achieve goals. Life events, such as a string of unhappy experiences, therefore have an impact on our cognitive architecture leading towards the formation of **depressogenic schema**.

Evaluation of the cognitive theories

The main problem with the behaviourist model of depression such as Lewinsohn's is that it fails to explain the root causes of depression: might the poor social interactions or the isolation that limits a reinforcing experience be a cause or a symptom of depression? Similarly the learned helplessness view cannot explain why someone would become suicidal because it predicts a passive acceptance of the situation rather than an active wish to die, a symptom of depression. Also it is not possible to explain cases of endogenous depression by this route because behaviourist theories require an environmental contribution and this is not obvious in some cases of endogenous depression.

The cognitive behavioural approach answers some of these issues by suggesting that a pessimistic explanatory style leads to depression; but, it is not clear how this develops and although it may be a factor in the maintenance of the symptoms, it might not be the primary cause.

Beck's cognitive view has been supported by a lot of research, such as that by D'Alessandro (2002), who found that students' negative views about their futures were strongly associated with an increase in depressed mood. Those with dysfunctional beliefs about themselves who did not get into their first choice of college then doubted their futures and developed symptoms of depression; this is consistent with the application of cognitive distortion linking to a negative belief about the future.

Lewinsohn et al. (2001) researched adolescent depression and found that when stressed, dysfunctional attitudes rather than environmental factors (as would be suggested by the learned helplessness model) was the strongest predictor of adolescent major depressive disorder. There are many other studies that show a link between negative thinking and depression, but there is little evidence that conclusively shows that the negative thinking was present before the onset of depression as is suggested by Beck's theory. It also fails to explain the gender bias, with women suffering more frequently than men, as there is no evidence that suggests females have more negative schema than males do.

Key term

Depressogenic schema: dysfunctional thoughts and beliefs contributing to the symptoms of depression.

It has been argued however that negative thinking is in fact perfectly reasonable. This has been termed depressive realism, with the view that people with good mental health are actually less realistic (or pessimistic) in their thought processes and view the world with rose-tinted glasses. A depressed person is just a realist.

Whether faulty thinking is a causal factor or not, it still leads to an effective form of therapy in the form of cognitive behavioural therapy with many studies showing it to reduce symptoms, for example Kuyken et al. (2007), suggesting that there must be some validity to the theory.

Rather than looking for an explanation from one explanatory perspective it would make sense to take a combined view. The diathesis-stress model for depression might argue that those with a biological vulnerability to depression, or with a certain personality type or who have been exposed to adverse early experience, will when exposed to sufficient environmental stressors become depressed. For some vulnerable individuals because of their history very little, if any, input is required from the environment. Others, however, never become depressed no matter how much stress they encounter. Taking an **eclectic** view can explain individual differences in experience and onset of depression.

Individuals may be more vulnerable to depression if certain life events occur that trigger a genetic predisposition. Brown and Harris (1978) studied depressed women in an area of London. They found that major life events tended to occur before an episode of depression. They also established that certain factors, such as lack of external employment, having young children, and chronic life difficulties contributed to depression. However, it is difficult to establish a causal relationship because depression may precipitate loss of employment or other major life difficulties.

> ### Key term
>
> **Eclectic:** using a broad range of sources/ explanations.

Treatments for depression
Biological treatments: drug therapy

Antidepressant drugs are the most common intervention for depression. These have been developed over time to target specific neurotransmitters. They are prescribed to quickly treat the symptoms of depression and to prevent relapse.

They work by increasing noradrenalin and serotonin in the brain and are often used in conjunction with other therapies aimed at treating the cause of the disorder. Antidepressants are agonists and increase noradrenaline or serotonin by either blocking reuptake of the chemical or preventing the enzyme that breaks down the chemical in the synapse. In both cases this causes the neurotransmitters to be available in the synapse for longer, thereby increasing the activity on the affected neural pathways.

Selective serotonin reuptake inhibitors (SSRIs)

Doctors often start by prescribing an SSRI. These medications are safer and generally cause fewer negative side effects than other types of antidepressants, and are less likely to lead to serious effects if overdosed. SSRIs include fluoxetine and work by blocking the reuptake of serotonin by blocking the transporter cells. This means that serotonin is left in the synapse to have a greater effect for longer.

Serotonin and norepinephrine reuptake inhibitors (SNRIs)

These were developed to work in a similar way to SSRIs by blocking the reuptake of both serotonin and norepinephrine but there is no evidence that they are more effective. For some individuals they may be the best choice for safety and tolerance issues. An example of an SNRI medication is duloxetine.

Tricyclic antidepressants

Tricyclic antidepressants, such as imipramine, block the reuptake of serotonin and noradrenaline so they remain in the synapse for longer and have a greater effect. These are older medications and tend to cause more severe side effects and more serious consequences if overdosed than do newer antidepressants. Therefore, these are not normally prescribed as a first choice but only when SSRIs have proven ineffective. These work by stopping the reabsorption of noradrenalin and serotonin.

Monoamine oxidase inhibitors (MAOIs)

MAOIs – such as tranylcypromine – may be prescribed as a last resort when other medications have not worked, because they can have serious side effects. These drugs work by stopping the enzymes that break down amine neurotransmitters in the synapse, thus making them available for longer. Using MAOIs requires a strict diet because of dangerous (or even deadly) interactions with foods that contain tyramine, such as certain cheeses, pickles and wines. They must not be taken in combination with many common drugs or with SSRIs.

Other medications may be added to an antidepressant to enhance antidepressant effects, for example, combining two antidepressants or medications such as mood stabilisers or antipsychotics. Anti-anxiety and stimulant medications might also be added for short-term use.

Evaluation

Drugs may treat the symptoms of depression but not the cause and for this reason they are often combined with other forms of therapy. They do, however, provide most people with relief from debilitating symptoms, which allows them to access and benefit from other types of therapy such as cognitive behavioural therapy (CBT).

Drugs can relieve the symptoms of depression relatively quickly. The Royal College of Psychiatrists reported that 50 to 65 per cent of people treated with antidepressants showed improvement compared to only 25 to 30 per cent of those treated with a placebo, showing that most people will benefit. This also shows that drugs are not effective for a substantial minority of people with depression and in some cases, especially where there is a risk of suicide, electroconvulsive (ECT) therapy might be required. ECT is particularly appropriate if there is an immediate threat of harm to oneself, as antidepressants can take several weeks to reduce symptoms.

However, there are common side effects that may make the drugs unpalatable. These include nausea, insomnia, blurred vision, dizziness and sexual dysfunction. These side effects should reduce over time if the patient persists with the drug. The older types of drug are dangerous if taken in overdose and even SSRIs have been linked to suicidal ideation in young people. This means that patients should be monitored regularly and have their prescriptions changed or dosage modified.

The minimum recommended prescription is usually six months, but it has been shown that a short course of CBT is very effective as a first-line treatment for mild to moderate depression. However, resourcing issues might lead to an over-reliance on drug treatments.

Drug trials are expensive and are often funded by drug companies with a vested interest in proving that a drug that has cost them millions of pounds to develop is an effective treatment. Some would argue that prescribing the drugs does little to treat the disorder. For example, a longitudinal study in Holland found that 76 per cent of depressed patients who did not take any antidepressant drugs recovered and never relapsed. A similar study in Canada found that people got better quicker without antidepressants. The World Health Organization has found that non-medicated patients with

Taking it further

Investigate electroconvulsive therapy (ECT), also known as electric shock therapy, as a treatment for depression. It is often used as a treatment of last resort for those with severe depression who do not respond to medication.

Consider the arguments for and against the use of ECT, including side effects, consent, effectiveness compared to 'sham ECT' or drug treatments.

WIDER ISSUES AND DEBATES

Ethics
Critics argue that drug treatment is being overused as an easy way to treat people with problems and that those people would be better off with an alternate therapy, which might help them take control and treat the cause of the issues rather than become dependent on a chemical 'cure'.

depression enjoyed better health than those who took antidepressants. The benefits of medication are therefore not conclusive.

Psychological treatment: cognitive behavioural therapy for depression

Cognitive behavioural therapy (CBT) is the first-line psychological treatment for depression and for anxiety disorders, especially for those with mild to moderate symptom severity. It is designed to achieve quick and lasting results with treatment consisting of weekly or fortnightly sessions lasting about an hour for a period of about three months (although this does depend on the nature of the depression).

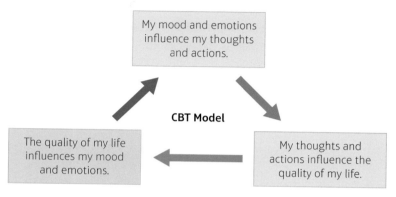

Figure 5.2 The CBT model

CBT is an active and directive therapy, first developed by Aaron Beck (1967), with the focus being very much on the 'here and now' of the client's life. Consistent with the cognitive theory it aims to challenge the irrational beliefs that may be at the root of the depression. It combines aspects of behavioural therapy with cognitive restructuring and problem solving. It can be delivered as a one-to-one therapy, as group therapy or more recently as a computerised therapy (iCBT).

The therapist helps the client recognise faulty cognitions that the client uses to process information about the world and encourages them to challenge these cognitions.

Clients are encouraged to keep a daily mood diary and to do exercises (homework) outside the sessions and then reflect and report back on their effectiveness. Typically the course of treatment will start with an education phase, where the client learns about the relationships between thoughts, emotions and actions. They can be taught techniques, such as thought catching where they analyse events that have happened, and map the emotional response that follows the thought that was associated with the event. This then allows the therapist to help the client to challenge the thoughts triggered by the event.

For example, the activating event might be a chance encounter in the street with an acquaintance who does not respond to your greeting and keeps on walking. The negative thought that follows could be that you are unlikeable and that the person deliberately snubbed you; this triggers an emotional response of sadness and unworthiness, which then goes on to cause you to withdraw from other social situations. The therapist would help you to identify these irrational thoughts (thought catching) and explore other more rational explanations thus disputing the negative belief that leads to the depressive behaviour.

The behavioural aspect of the therapy comes through hypothesis testing using a behavioural action plan. The client is set work to do outside therapy that is aimed at changing the experiences they are having and therefore challenging their negative beliefs about themselves. In this case, they could be set a task to socialise with someone and, hopefully, a positive experience would boost their self-esteem. Therapists only set tasks that the client can engage with successfully because failure at a task would be a major setback that would deflate self-esteem.

Evaluation

CBT is an evidence-based therapy, meaning that it has been widely tested with empirical evidence that has led to it being widely recommended by various agencies across the world, for example, the National Institute for Health and Care Excellence in the UK.

This therapy does not carry side effects with it so it could be regarded as more ethical than drug treatment if it works just as well. Early studies, such as by Elkin et al. (1989), found that it was marginally less effective than active drug treatment with clinical management, but as it is less invasive it might be more preferable to drugs. A recent large-scale study conducted in the UK found that, for people who do not respond well to drug treatment, CBT is an effective add-on treatment, leading to improvement in symptoms for 55 per cent of the CBT group compared to 31 per cent receiving the usual treatment alone (Otto & Wisniewski, 2012).

Embling (2002) also found that CBT was an effective treatment and was able to isolate certain personality variables that appeared to impact on the outcome of therapy, specifically perfectionism and **sociotrophy**. This indicates that a 'one size fits all' approach to therapy is inadvisable as certain types of therapy work better for certain types of people. It is most useful for those with good communication skills who are capable of rational thought.

A negative point is that this therapeutic view essentially blames the person for their disorder because it is their thoughts that cause it; this could have ethical implications for how the person feels about themselves. But CBT aims to give people the tools to enable them to deal with the disorder themselves rather than to passively take drugs for extended periods. Although it is based in the 'here and now' and does not seek to explore issues from the past that might have influenced the onset of the disorder, it does aim to change how the person thinks about such things. In this way, it is possible to argue that it aims to do more than just manage the symptoms. However, some have argued that it is too simplistic to deal with complex issues and that a better approach would be to use more psychoanalytic techniques to investigate the root cause of the disorder.

> **Key term** 💬
>
> **Sociotrophy:** a personality trait characterised by dependence on relationships with other people and an excessive need to please others.

Anorexia nervosa

Anorexia nervosa is an eating disorder characterised by persistent low body weight in the sufferer.

Symptoms

There are three criteria that must be met for a diagnosis of anorexia nervosa to be given.

- Criterion A: restriction of energy intake resulting in body weight being significantly below what would be expected based on the patient's age and height. This will be different for adults compared with children or adolescents. In adults, low body weight can be categorised as having a BMI measuring 18.5kg/m², so a weight significantly below this would be a BMI of 17kg/m² or less.

- Criterion B: an intense fear of gaining weight or participating in persistent behaviour that will interrupt the gaining of weight even though current body weight is very low. For example, sufferers might take up excessive amounts of exercise to prevent weight gain.

- Criterion C: distortion in body image where the body weight is hugely overestimated and the patient is unable to accept the severity of the low body weight. There may also be an emphasis on body weight in the patient's views of themselves, leading to poor self-image or an overuse of body weight in self-evaluations.

Significantly more females are diagnosed with anorexia than males.

Taking it further

Diagnoses of anorexia nervosa are considerably more common in females than they are in males. Consider what reasons there may be for this. Do you think that there may be some biological factor that makes females more susceptible to the behaviours that are symptomatic of the illness? Or could it be that there is some social element of being 'female' that makes women more prone to these behaviours?

Interestingly, the incidence of male anorexia is rising. What factors do you think account for this rise?

Key term

Amenorrhoea: lack of menstruation.

Features

Two subtypes of anorexia were defined by ICD-10-CM: Restricting type; and binge-eating/purging type. Patients with restricting type will have shown weight loss (or weight-gain prevention) through dieting, excessive exercise or fasting in significant periods within the past three months. Patients diagnosed with binge-eating/purging type will have shown recurrent bouts of binge-eating behaviours alternated with purging, such as self-induced vomiting, or the misuse of laxatives, diuretics or enemas, during the past three months.

Anorexia nervosa is usually diagnosed during adolescence or early adulthood, and onset before puberty or after age 40 is rare. Significantly more females are diagnosed with anorexia than males, with some estimating that diagnoses may occur in a ratio of 10:1 female to male. Onset of the disorder often appears to coincide with a significant life stressor such as starting university or leaving home. Although not symptoms of the disorder itself, there are physical effects associated with anorexia that occur as a complication of the illness, and these can be problematic for patients. For example, **amenorrhoea** (lack of menstruation) can occur in females as a result of low body weight, and vital sign abnormalities may be present as a result of lack of nutrition. There are some cultural features of the diagnosis of anorexia, with prevalence seeming to be higher in high-income countries that are highly industrialised such as the USA, Europe, Australia, New Zealand and Japan.

Biological explanation: genetics

There is recent research evidence that suggests that there may be an inherited factor involved in the development of anorexia nervosa. Research by Grice et al. (2002) was one of the first studies to find evidence of a genetic link in anorexia. The study followed 192 families where one member had received a diagnosis of anorexia nervosa, and at least one other member had been diagnosed with anorexia nervosa or another form of eating disorder such as bulimia nervosa. Initial findings did not show any significant genetic evidence for developing anorexia, until they focused on a subgroup of 37 families where at least two relatives had been diagnosed with the restrictive-type of anorexia. In this sample there was strong evidence for a susceptibility gene/genes on chromosome 1 as similar markers were found in the afflicted pairs/groups in each family.

Research published in 2013 (Scott-Van Zeeland et al., 2013, which is a key study mentioned later in this topic) has found a more specific genetic link to the disorder. It found that, when comparing 152 different genes in a sample of women with anorexia nervosa, and another group without the disorder, there were significant differences in and around the EPHX2 (Epoxide Hydrolase 2) gene between the two groups. The EPHX2 gene is associated with production of an enzyme (Epoxide Hydrolase 2) that metabolises cholesterol suggesting that the disorder may, at least in part, be caused by disruption in how the body processes cholesterol, which could affect both mood and eating behaviour. Other evidence cited to support this finding comes from observations that often patients with anorexia have higher cholesterol than expected considering many of them are severely malnourished and that, in some cases, such as in some patients with depression, weight loss can actually lead to an increase in cholesterol levels (cited in a press release from The Scripps Research Institute, 2013). The next step in this area of research, which is still quite new, will be to consider how these genetic factors actually cause and maintain the behaviours associated with anorexia nervosa.

It is highly possible, as with many psychological disorders that are very complex in terms of their symptoms and causes, that there may be a number of genes associated with the development of anorexia nervosa. Research published in 2014 (Boraska et al., 2014) has found variants in many different gene markers in a very large sample of participants with anorexia nervosa from multiple countries around the world. However, none of the findings proved individually significant in the samples chosen, so further research is needed to consider whether these markers are actually involved in developing the disorder.

Evaluation

Research in this area is still very new, and anorexia itself is a disorder where little is really understood about where it comes from. Although some evidence does exist to support a genetic explanation, it is still emerging and it is not clear about the extent to which genes can explain the cause of the disorder. Many people believe that, as for many psychological disorders, there may actually be multiple factors that work together to cause the illness. Perhaps having certain gene markers increases a person's risk of developing the illness, but other societal or cultural factors may then trigger the illness. There is evidence that people with relatives with eating disorders, such as anorexia nervosa and bulimia nervosa, have an increased risk of eating disorders and other psychiatric disorders such as major-depressive disorder and obsessive–compulsive disorder (Lilenfeld et al., 1998). This could be used as evidence to support a genetic component in the disorder. However, it cannot be ignored that many of these family members will have spent a great deal of time in the same environment and so the influence of external factors on the development of abnormal eating behaviours or associated mood or anxiety disorders could equally account for the onset of these symptoms. Perhaps the behaviour patterns are being learned through observation of the diagnosed individual.

It is very difficult to separate out the biological explanation as a cause of anorexia nervosa as opposed to being a result of the disorder. The evidence can show a relationship between genes, neurotransmitters and neurodevelopmental factors and the development of anorexia, but the causal factors are difficult to determine as anorexia is such a complex disorder. The biological explanations are also complicated by the fact that it is well documented that poor diet and malnutrition can cause biological changes in the body, making the direction of effect difficult to determine. In relation to prenatal factors and genes, it is difficult to separate what effects there may be of maternal health and diet in a woman with anorexia on her developing foetus, and the genetic factors she may pass on to her unborn child. This means that there could be a difficulty in determining whether the fact the disorder runs in families is the result of genetics or prenatal factors.

Biological explanation: neurotransmitters

Research evidence from Bailer et al. (2005) found that patients who had recovered from a diagnosis of the binge/purge form of anorexia showed increased levels of serotonin in the brain. This was strongly related to measures of anxiety in the women, showing that both increased serotonin and anxiety symptoms persist even a year following recovery. There has been a suggestion that the serotonin rise may increase levels of anxiety, and this increased anxiety may trigger the binge/purge form of anorexia. Research has also associated increased activity in dopamine receptors in patients recovering from anorexia nervosa. Kaye et al. (2005) documented increased dopamine receptor activity in areas of the basal ganglia, an area of the brain known to be associated with learning from experience. It is thought that overactivity in this area may interfere with the patients' ability to seek or respond to pleasurable activities such as eating. It may also interrupt the ability for patients to react to the negative feedback associated with their health such as the image of their emaciated body or symptoms associated with malnutrition. Kaye later (2011) reported that in women with anorexia nervosa, increased levels of dopamine activity increased anxiety, whereas in 'normal' controls the increased dopamine induced feelings of pleasure. This may suggest why women with anorexia often experience high levels of anxiety associated with food, something that most people would find pleasurable.

Evaluation

Much of the recent research into neurotransmitter levels is conducted in highly controlled conditions using high-tech equipment such as brain scans (predominantly PET and fMRI). This means that the evidence is very credible and reliable due to its objective nature. An example of a control measure taken is that in research by Bailer (2005); for example, the patients were studied a year into recovery to be sure that malnutrition was not a confounding variable and poor nutrition has been associated with changes in serotonin activity. A major criticism of research in this area is that the altered levels of neurotransmitters could easily be a result of poor nutrition rather than a cause. For example, a paper by Haleem (2012) suggested that serotonin production was associated with a restrictive diet. Tryptophan, an amino acid that is a precursor to serotonin, is only available through diet, so a restricted diet will reduce levels of tryptophan, and consequently is likely to reduce levels of serotonin found in the brain. When stored levels of serotonin are reduced, the brain may compensate with up-regulation, which consequently increases the levels of activity. This is therefore suggesting that the high level of serotonin activity is actually the result and not the cause of anorexia. Another problem is that drugs that are used to treat other disorders associated with high levels of serotonin and dopamine, such as SSRIs and neuroleptics, are found to be much less effective in treating anorexia nervosa, which suggests that the cause of the illness is unlikely to be purely related to neurotransmitter levels.

WIDER ISSUES AND DEBATES

The use of psychological knowledge in society

Research into biological factors is developing all the time as new techniques become available. The genetic explanation is still very new and research in this area is still quite limited. But as new methods develop, the research is becoming more conclusive and will continue to grow. An interesting application of this area of research is the way biological research into anorexia has changed society's views of the disorder. By considering it as an illness, much as other psychiatric illnesses are beginning to be seen, we encourage people to treat sufferers with more compassion. It also helps to change the views on treatment of eating disorders by challenging the view that people with anorexia 'just need to eat'. In the US for example, health insurance companies are now being forced to reconsider their categorisation of anorexia nervosa to allow patients to claim money for treatment.

One non-biological explanation: sociocultural theory

It has long been felt that anorexia nervosa is more likely to occur in social and/or cultural groups that place a great deal of emphasis on the ideal that 'slim is beautiful'. Research has found, for example, that anorexia is more likely to occur in dance or modelling students compared to other female university students because these groups value the slim body image as part of their image as 'dancers' and 'models' because it is seen as more normal for their body size to be smaller than other groups (Garner and Garfinkel, 1980). It is also well documented that working in occupations where there is a strong emphasis on body weight increases the risk of developing eating disorders such as anorexia, with diagnoses being considerably higher in occupational groups such as professional dancers, models and elite athletes. Research has even highlighted the 'female athlete triad' of 'anorexia, athletics and amenorrhea' to illustrate the association seen between these three features in young women participating in intense levels of physical activity (Rackoff and Honig, 2006). Schwartz, Thompson and Johnson (1982) conducted a review of Miss America beauty pageant competitors from 1959 to 1978 and found that over that 20-year period the average weight of contestants decreased, but at the same time, in America, the actual average weight of females was slightly increasing. The body size of the women in the pageant became gradually slimmer, while at the same time, the average body size of 'normal' women was increasing. This would suggest that the body type that was being hailed as 'ideal' and 'beautiful' was actually incongruent with reality, which could make women see themselves as unfairly 'fat' compared to these images. Garner et al. (1980) also found that over a 10-year period from 1970 to 1980 the number of diet articles in women's magazines hugely increased, suggesting a societal preoccupation with the need to lose weight.

INDIVIDUAL DIFFERENCES – CULTURAL EFFECTS

The cultural images and influences mentioned above are something we are all exposed to, but not everyone develops anorexia nervosa. This suggests that other factors must make some people more vulnerable to these images than others. Research has found that there are personality factors associated with diagnoses of anorexia. For example, evidence has shown that patients with anorexia score highly on measures of 'perfectionism' – a trait associated with serious concern over making mistakes. A person with this trait may be more likely to be influenced by these images and ideals and then go on to develop anorexia.

Anorexia was first diagnosed in western cultures, such as the USA and Europe, and was quite rare in eastern cultures. However, its diagnosis has increased worldwide since the mid-1970s, which coincides with the increased reach of western values into eastern cultures through the media (Iancu et al.,1994). This would suggest that cultural values may have a significant impact on the development of eating disorders, such as anorexia nervosa, as a method of trying to achieve this 'ideal' body type of slimness.

Evidence from Hoek et al. (2005) on the island of Curaçao where it is seen as culturally acceptable to be overweight, has found that the overall incidence of anorexia is much lower. In fact no cases were reported at the time in the majority black population, but the incidence rates in the minority group of white/mixed race population were comparable with that of the United States. This would suggest that the influence of cultural ideals is strong as even when immersed in a culture where a larger size is seen as acceptable, the cultural norm of a smaller body size may still have an effect on the individual's mental health.

A case study reported by Willemsen and Hoek (2006) considered the case of a black Antillean woman from Curaçao in the Caribbean where previous findings suggested anorexia did not occur. The culture in Curaçao values a larger body size and, while living there, the woman put on weight in order to become more attractive to gain a partner. When the relationship started to encounter problems she lost weight in a bid to become less attractive. When she emigrated to the Netherlands, the woman continued to lose weight to 'fit in' with the cultural ideals of the slimmer body type and then developed anorexia nervosa. This would provide some support for the influence that cultural ideals can have on body image and the development of eating disorders.

Anorexia and cognitive factors
Patients with anorexia tend to demonstrate cognitive distortions in the way they view themselves and their body size, which are thought to impact on their body image. Evidence has found that patients with eating disorders in general tend to overestimate their own body size in relation to other people, and often aspire to a body weight that is lower than normal weight control participants (McKenzie et al. 1993).

The issue of 'size 0' models (referring to the US size 0, which is equivalent to a UK size 4) has been an issue for many eating disorder campaigners as they argue that the image portrayed that 'fashion is for slim people' and 'people are usually this size' alters girls' own body image because they compare themselves to this ideal. When the average UK female is a size 14–16 there is plenty of room for a negative comparison to be drawn. When considering the fact that 'plus-size models' start from a size 12, the modelling industry certainly seems to offer an altered view of the reality of female body size and, for a vulnerable person, this could be a contributory factor to developing an eating disorder.

'Size 0' mannequins portray an unrealistic body image and have been associated with the rise of eating disorders.

Social learning theory

Social learning theory suggests that we learn through the observation of those we consider to be role models and then go on to imitate the behaviours they show when we find ourselves in a position where we can. Models and other famous figures may be seen as role models to young men and women and therefore the image that they display through the media could easily influence others. The concept of vicarious reinforcement is also important here because the positive responses given to these famous figures for their looks can teach young people that these body images are something to aspire to.

Evaluation

Although there is compelling evidence for the effect of cultural ideals on body image, and that this can possibly lead to the development of eating disorders, there are many people who are not influenced by these ideals to the extent of developing the disorder. This would suggest that sociocultural factors may simply be one of a number of risk factors that combine to cause the anorexia rather than an explanation in itself. For example, sociocultural factors may only influence the body image of certain people who already have a predisposition to develop the disorder such as, as the result of biological factors. Other evidence to support the sociocultural explanation for anorexia comes from the fact that diagnoses of anorexia have increased hugely since the 1950s, which marked the beginning of the change towards slimmer models and the preoccupation with body image and dieting in the media. In recent years, more males have been diagnosed with anorexia, which coincides with changes in 'men's magazines' to include more diet, fitness and body image articles. Both of these factors would suggest that there is a relationship between changes in cultural views and increased diagnoses of anorexia.

Despite all of the compelling evidence to suggest that sociocultural factors influence the development of anorexia, the illness is still quite rare in society and as these images are something we are all exposed to we must assume that other factors also combine with sociocultural factors to cause anorexia. Cognitive and personality factors may be a risk factor that, when combined with media images and cultural ideals, increase the likelihood that an individual will become anorexic.

Exam tip

Much of the evidence above in the description of the sociocultural explanation of anorexia could also be used to support the view put forward by this approach. This means that you can use the evidence both as description of factors associated with cultural transmission of the 'norms' of society, but also as evaluation to support the view. For example, Hoek et al. (2005) shows how cultural factors may have a direct effect of the development and diagnosis of an eating disorder such as anorexia. What is important is the way that you use the information. If you describe the research as an example, it will be considered to be descriptive. Whereas if you clearly indicate that the research is evidence, it can be used as an evaluation.

Treatments for anorexia nervosa

Biological treatment: drug therapy

The National Institute for Health and Care Excellence (NICE) state that drugs should not be used as a primary or only treatment for patients with anorexia nervosa, and there is very little (if any) evidence that states that drugs are a useful treatment for anorexia. However, many patients with anorexia may suffer from comorbid conditions (conditions occurring at the same time as the eating disorder) for which drug therapy may be very effective. Common comorbid conditions include depression and anxiety including obsessive–compulsive behaviours. Currently, the two types of drugs most commonly used in the treatment of anorexia nervosa are selective serotonin reuptake inhibitors (SSRIs) and olanzapine. SSRIs are a form of antidepressant that work by blocking the reuptake of serotonin in presynaptic neurons, therefore making more serotonin available in the synapse. This means that more serotonin can be passed to the postsynaptic neuron, increasing the levels of serotonin.

Olanzapine is an atypical antipsychotic drug, which is also used to treat anxiety, and is thought to block absorption of dopamine and serotonin in certain pathways in the brain. It is felt that in patients with comorbid conditions such as depression and anxiety, the use of medication to treat these symptoms may enable the patient to benefit more readily from the psychological therapies that are so effective in treating anorexia. For example, a patient who is anxious about their weight gain, which is necessary to treat their eating disorder, is less likely to drop out of a therapy programme if their anxiety can be treated with drugs.

Evaluation

Patients with anorexia nervosa often have poor physical health due to malnutrition, and it is not uncommon for anorexic patients to suffer quite serious heart problems and poor cardiac functioning. This can mean that prescribing medication may be too risky as some of these drugs can cause cardiac side effects. The potential risks would need to be considered carefully by the clinician and the patient and these risks would need to be outweighed by the possible gains in relation to the treatment outcomes for the patient.

Another problem is that many patients taking SSRIs and olanzapine find that they gain weight when they start taking the medication. While this would be a desired outcome for patients with anorexia nervosa, the patient may find this a difficult side effect to cope with because of the nature of the illness they have. This may make it hard for patients to continue taking the medication and explain why patients with anorexia are not effectively treated with medication alone.

Very little evidence exists that suggests drugs are an effective treatment for anorexia nervosa. Ferguson et al. (1999) did a comparison between 24 patients taking SSRIs and 16 patients treated on the same ward who were not taking SSRIs. They found that there was no significant difference between them in terms of age or body weight, but most importantly there was no difference in terms of their clinical symptoms or reports of anxiety. This suggests that the use of the drugs had no significant impact on the patients' treatment outcomes. However, Kaye et al. (2001) published evidence that in a double-blind study comparing outcomes for patients given fluoxetine with patients given a placebo, those on fluoxetine were much more likely to stay on the medication up to a year into their outpatient treatment. They also found that those who continued taking the fluoxetine had much lower relapse rates, measured by increased body weight and improvement in symptoms.

Jensen and Mejlhede (2000) reported case studies on three patients who were treated with 5 mg of olanzapine each day. In each case positive effects were reported in relation to the patients' body image, and they make suggestions for further study into the usefulness of the drug in treating anorexia. They suggest that the antipsychotic effect of the drug makes the patient's body image more realistic.

WIDER ISSUES AND DEBATES

Psychology as a science
Drug therapies are scientifically developed treatments for mental health disorders based on good scientific research, including large-scale, double-blind randomised control trials before they become passed for use. This means that the drug has performed better than a placebo in reducing symptoms, that possible side effects are well recognised and the risk of their development can be assessed for each individual offered the treatment.

However, they also commented that the first two months of treatment with olanzapine were difficult for patients as it can take this long for the drug to take effect and reported side effects included hunger and weight gain, which one patient reported as difficult to deal with.

Much of the evidence supporting positive effects of drug treatment for anorexia nervosa comes from small-scale studies with limited samples and, looking at the 'big picture', there is no evidence that any drug is an effective treatment for anorexia on its own. Much of the success evident in the research could be attributed to the psychological therapy that patients receive alongside their medication.

Psychological treatment: cognitive behavioural therapy

A form of cognitive behavioural therapy has been developed for use specifically with certain eating disorders. Enhanced cognitive behaviour therapy (CBT-E) is used in the treatment of anorexia nervosa as well as other eating disorders as it is aimed specifically at tackling the thoughts and behaviours associated with disordered eating behaviour. The advantage of CBT-E over other modified forms of cognitive behavioural therapy used in patients with eating disorders (for example CBT-BN for bulimia nervosa, and CBT-BED for binge eating disorder) is that the mechanisms in enhanced cognitive behavioural therapy are comprehensive enough to be used to treat the changing patterns of disordered eating that are common in patients with eating disorders over time. The therapy is conducted on a one-to-one basis between the client and therapist, and courses of about 20 sessions will be advised for most people initially. Clients who are significantly underweight will be indicated to complete 40 sessions.

Initially a detailed interview takes place, usually over two separate sessions, to allow the therapist to assess the patient's suitability for treatment using CBT-E at the current time. The therapist will also explain the treatment process to the client and allow them to ask questions if necessary. For the therapy to be effective, any possible barriers to treatment must be removed at the outset. This means if there are other factors in the client's life that could impact on treatment success, these can be dealt with before therapy begins.

Treatment takes place through four defined stages as shown in Table 5.2 below.

Table 5.2 The four stages of enhanced cognitive behavioural therapy

Stage	Preparation for treatment and change
Stage 1	This stage of treatment takes about four weeks with two sessions held per week to encourage rapid change in the client's behaviour. Two important procedures are implemented in this phase – 'weekly weighing' with the therapist, and 'regular eating'. Clients are educated about the disorder and they will also learn about the treatment programme so that they know what to expect. It is important during this first stage that the patient is positive about the treatment and motivated to progress because the therapy will only be effective if they are willing to make the necessary changes.
Stage 2	This stage is quite brief consisting usually of two appointments, one week apart. The therapist and client will meet to discuss the progress being made in stage one and 'taking stock' of how the patient is currently. Good progress can be praised to boost motivation, while poor progress can be discussed to uncover possible reasons for why things are not going well.

Stage	Preparation for treatment and change
Stage 3	This is the main stage of the treatment phase where clients will usually have eight appointments once a week to tackle the factors that are involved in the maintenance of the eating disorder. This will involve dealing with the client's body image, their dietary rules, and any event-related changes in eating. Dealing with body image will usually look at certain behaviours likely to lead to body dissatisfaction such as constant body checking, as well as the triggers that make them 'feel fat'. Dietary rules are explored to consider the impact that rigid and restrictive rules are having on the client's quality of life, and any foods they currently avoid are gradually introduced to the diet. It is also important that external events that impact on major changes in eating are considered and tackled at this stage in treatment.
Stage 4	Clients are encouraged to look to the future and consider factors that need to be managed to prevent relapse. Usually clients will have three appointments about two weeks apart at this stage. The therapist and patient will draw up an agreed plan that is personalised for their specific circumstances. Clients are also encouraged to consider their own mindset so that they do not see any relapse as 'failure', and instead think of it as a 'lapse' that they can address. A post-treatment review appointment will then be made about five months later where the client will be able to discuss any setbacks or issues.

Evaluation

One possible issue related to the use of CBT-E is that the client has to be motivated to change so this is a form of therapy that will not be effective for everyone. The initial stage of the treatment, however, does allow for the client to spend time learning about their disorder before they enter the full treatment phase so it will be important that the therapist recognises signs that the patient is not yet ready. The benefit of any form of CBT is that it is flexible and can be adapted to suit the needs of the patient. For example, there is a version of CBT-E that is designed specifically for patients with extremely low body weight. The most commonly used form of enhanced CBT is only effective for patients with anorexia nervosa whose eating disorder is not maintained by clinical perfectionism, low self-esteem or interpersonal problems. However, there are other forms of CBT that can be used with these patient groups and this can be identified early on in the treatment process.

Research from Pike et al. (2003) compared the effectiveness of CBT and nutritional counselling as outpatient treatments given to patients with anorexia nervosa following hospitalisation. In the 33 patients followed by the researchers, the relapse rates of those receiving CBT was considerably lower (22 per cent) than those receiving nutritional counselling (73 per cent). Byrne et al. (2011) considered the effectiveness of CBT-E in treating patients with the full range of eating disorders in an outpatient clinic is Australia. They found that two-thirds of patients in the treatment group showed significant improvement in symptoms both in relation to eating behaviour and also other general psychopathology. The strategies taught in CBT-E are probably more suited to treating older patients with anorexia nervosa who have more opportunity to access treatment independently and may be living away from the family. The strategies are designed to enable the patient to take control and monitor their own thinking and behaviour. For patients who still live at home, family therapy may be more effective as it deals with the effects that anorexia can have on the family, not just the individual.

Obsessive–compulsive disorder

Obsessive–compulsive disorder is a common mental disorder that can have a major impact on a person's life. The World Health Organization has it ranked among the top ten most disabling illnesses in terms of impaired quality of life and loss of earnings. Most people may experience OCD-type symptoms at some point in their lives, usually in times of stress, but these are not as severe or pervasive as suffered by those diagnosed with the disorder. Checking things and fear of contamination are among the most common types of OCD.

> ### Taking it further
>
> Diana was about eight years old when she first began to display symptoms of obsessive compulsive disorder. She developed a fear of stepping on the cracks in the pavement and felt physically uncomfortable if she did it. The symptoms continued into adulthood and at their most extreme, she feared that she might harm her own children in her sleep by strangling them with their dressing gown cords. This led to ritualised behaviour of removing the cords from the dressing gowns and tying them in knots to prevent her from doing so. Diana felt terrified and permanently exhausted by her compulsions so sought help from her GP. She was prescribed antidepressant medication which enabled her to sleep and eat well again. This gave her the strength to go on and access cognitive behavioural therapy to overcome the disorder. She is now working at OCD-UK and is helping others suffering with the disorder.   *Source: NHS Choices.*

Symptoms

Obsessive–compulsive disorder (OCD) is characterised by the presence of obsessions and/or compulsions.

Obsessions about germs or contamination can lead to excessive and repeated hand washing.

The diagnostic criteria as listed in DSM V are as follows:

- The **obsessions** cannot be ignored or suppressed and cause anxiety and/or distress. The sufferer may try to combat the obsession by the performing of compulsive behaviour that is not realistically connected to the obsession.

- The obsessions and/or **compulsions** are time-consuming (take up more than one hour per day) and/or cause clinically significant distress or impairment to daily life.

- The symptoms cannot be explained by substance use or another medical condition or other mental disorder such as generalised anxiety disorder.

- The clinician must determine if the individual has good or fair insight into their disorder and recognises that the obsessive–compulsive beliefs are definitely or probably not true, or if they have poor insight and believe their obsessions–compulsions are probably true, or, no insight and are completely convinced that their compulsions/obsessions are definitely true.

- They should also find out if the individual has a current or past history of a **tic disorder** as this can affect the severity of the disorder.

Features

The prevalence rate for the disorder is between 1.1 and 1.8 per cent of the population. Females are more frequent sufferers as adults although males are more commonly affected as children.

For most people the age of onset is late teens or early twenties, but it is possible for it to be earlier or later and for 25 per cent of male sufferers it started before the age of 10. Generally the symptoms develop gradually, but in some cases they can be acute right from onset.

The risk is greater for people with higher negative emotionality, and those who tend to internalise issues. It is also more frequent in those who suffered physical and sexual abuse in childhood. There may be a genetic risk as the rate of OCD among first-degree relatives of adults with OCD is approximately twice that of those whose family have no history of the disorder.

OCD occurs across cultures at a similar rate and shows a similar age of onset and comorbidity with other disorders. There is a similar symptom structure involving cleaning, hoarding, taboo thoughts and symmetry, however there are regional differences suggesting that cultural factors can affect the nature of the symptoms.

Exam tip

Symptoms and features are different aspects of the disorder. Symptoms refer to the behavioural, cognitive, emotional and social manifestations of the disorder in the afflicted individual. Features refer to other details concerning the disorder such as prevalence, onset, risk factors, comorbidity and prognosis.

Biological explanation: neuroanatomical

Prevailing theories suggest that OCD is a biological disorder due to faulty functioning in the circuitry of an area of the orbitofrontal cortex (see Figure 5.3).

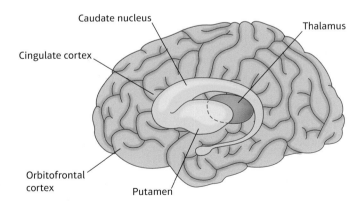

Figure 5.3 The orbitofrontal cortical loop in OCD

As with all biological explanations there are several potential influences; genetic, structural differences and biochemical make-up. In this section, the focus will be on a structural explanation, although there is likely to be an interaction between all these factors.

Tourette's syndrome: a disorder characterised by unwanted and uncontrollable noises and movements (tics).

Taking it further

The biochemical explanation focuses on the serotonin system and argues that a dysregulation in this system leads to the development of OCD symptoms. This is largely due to evidence that SSRI drugs (that stop the reuptake of serotonin from the synapse, thus increasing serotonergic activity) are effective in reducing the symptoms. Further research has implicated the dopamine systems in the production of the symptoms of tics and **Tourette's syndrome**.

Brain structure

The dominant view is that sufferers have faulty neuro-circuitry that links the orbitofrontal cortex to the thalamus. A key part of the circuit is the caudate nucleus, which normally inhibits the action of neurones that dampen the activity of the thalamus, acting as a kind of brake for thalamic activity. In OCD, the caudate nucleus is overactive, which impedes the dampening function, leading to an overactive thalamus. The overactive thalamus causes a cascade reaction in the orbitofrontal cortex which, via the cingulate gyrus, connects to the caudate nucleus, thus increasing its stimulation and causing a loop of hyperactivity. Hypothetically, the hypothalamus might be hardwired to produce primitive cleaning and checking behaviour, and the role of the orbitofrontal cortex is to alert the brain when something seems odd, causing anxiety, which promotes checking behaviour consistent with the obsessions and compulsions in OCD.

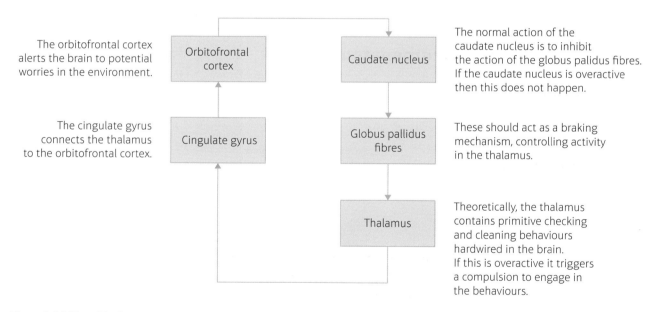

Figure 5.4 OCD and brain structure

Evaluation

Perhaps the most conclusive support is for the structural explanation, for example Menzies et al., 2007, found that scans of people suffering from OCD compared to healthy controls showed differences in the amount of grey matter in brain areas, including the orbitofrontal cortex, suggesting a physical difference in the areas implicated in this explanation. Other scanning studies show abnormally small caudate nuclei in sufferers of OCD. When people with OCD are shown objects that bring on their symptoms, such as a dirty piece of clothing in someone with a cleaning compulsion, activity increases in the orbitofrontal cortex, the caudate nucleus and the anterior cingulate (McGuire et al., 1994). Furthermore, surgical lesioning of the cingulate gyrus is a successful intervention for most patients for whom other treatments have not worked; this would break the loop of hyperactivity suggested by this model. While this evidence seems compelling it should be remembered that scanning is as yet, imprecise; for example it cannot detect decreased metabolic activity, and the changes in activity of some small areas or circuits could be missed when areas around them show no change. Further research is necessary before any firm conclusions can be drawn.

Support for the biological explanation comes from research that shows a genetic link because it suggests that physiological factors underlie the development of the disorder in many people. For example, twin studies typically (although not inevitably) show a higher concordance rate in MZ twins compared to DZ. Furthermore, family studies back this up, but in many cases sufferers have no family history at all, suggesting that genes alone cannot be an explanation; although this does not necessarily exclude other biological causes.

Promising research comes from animal studies such as that of Feng et al. (2007) who has bred mice to show symptoms consistent with OCD (excessive grooming and anxious behaviour), when a targeted gene is missing. This gene is one that is expressed in the brain areas associated with planning and initiation of action, showing a clear link to the formation of compulsions. However, although humans and mice share 97 per cent of their DNA, there is still a massive difference in how these genes are expressed. Extrapolation to humans may therefore be unreliable, but there are findings from human research, which suggest that there is a genetic marker for early onset OCD (Murphy et al., 1997).

When the disorder is present in the children of sufferers it is found that their symptoms differed from those of their parents. This suggests that the cause of OCD is unlikely to be social learning – leading us back towards a biological cause. This idea is supported by findings that show antidepressants that alter the chemistry of the brain, especially those that raise serotonin levels, relieve the symptoms of OCD, suggesting a physical cause for the disorder. However, there is an issue with the direction of causality here: we cannot conclusively state whether serotonin levels are a cause or an effect of the disorder. Further problems with this evidence centre on the fact that, for many sufferers, although the drugs can have an almost immediate effect on the serotonin levels in the brain, there is no relief from the symptoms for up to 12 weeks, suggesting that the role serotonin plays is more complex than that of a simple cause and effect.

WIDER ISSUES AND DEBATES

Comparisons between ways of explaining behaviour using different themes
Psychological explanations focus on the workings of the mind. The following section will focus on how the way our minds process information can lead to the development of OCD symptoms.

However, there are other non-biological explanations, such as the behaviourist approach, which suggests that the sufferer learns to associate non-threatening items with fearful stimuli such as negative thoughts or experiences (classical conditioning) but manages this fear through performing rituals that reduce the anxiety (negative reinforcement), thus maintaining the obsessive–compulsive behaviour.

A psychodynamic explanation would suggest that OCD is the result of ego defence mechanisms operating, such as isolation, where the person experiences unwanted thoughts that they do not wish to own up to; these become compulsions that they are incapable of managing. Another defence mechanism is reaction formation where the person reacts against undesirable wishes and desires by doing the opposite. These desires are often sexual in nature.

WIDER ISSUES AND DEBATES
Nature–nurture
Most psychologists would agree that a simple nature or nurture cause for any aspect of behaviour is unhelpful. Every person may have biological structures in common with other people but no-one is the same; the brain is shaped by its environment and the environment is shaped by the brain of the person experiencing it. The two things are interdependent and inseparable.

One non-biological explanation: cognitive theory

Cognitive explanations centre on faulty information processing as being at the root of the disorder. The perceptions or thoughts we have about our experiences will trigger an emotional response, which then triggers behaviour to deal with the emotion. If we change the original perception then what follows will also change. An influential theorist in this area is Paul Salkovskis, who has been developing and refining cognitive models of OCD for many years. The following summary is based on his work.

In the case of OCD, early childhood experiences could cause a general negative belief system about how the world works, for example, the world is full of threats. This leads to intrusive thoughts (obsessions) in response to events that happen. These thoughts are misinterpreted and made important, causing anxiety. To deal with the anxiety the person adopts counterproductive behaviour such as thought suppression, or they feel compelled to perform neutralising rituals (compulsions) that give temporary relief; this serves to reinforce the faulty thought pattern at the root of the sequence. Unless a link in this sequence is broken, it becomes self-perpetuating.

One further theory is that a lack of confidence in memory may explain checking behaviours, for example, it is not that the person does not have a memory for checking that they turned the oven off, it is that they do not trust their recall and feel compelled to check again. Woods et al. (2002) conducted a meta-analysis of studies that aimed to test how memory relates to checking and found that those suffering from OCD had a slightly worse memory for recalling stimuli that had been presented, but crucially they felt that their memory was inadequate compared to those who do not have OCD.

Another idea is that people with OCD may be hypervigilant (Williams et al., 1997). This means they are constantly scanning for threats in the environment and have an attentional bias towards potential threat; these threats form the basis of their obsessions. The detection of threat then triggers anxiety, which in turn triggers compulsive behaviour designed to reduce the anxiety level. Rahman (2004) reports a case study showing that someone with OCD centred on blood could, due to hypervigilance, recall all the times in her past that she had come into contact with blood.

Evaluation

Therapy based on a general cognitive explanation is used successfully in many cases, suggesting some validity behind the explanation. Van Balkom et al. (1996) found it to be just as effective as a drug treatment, which lends support to the view that the cause of the OCD may lie in faulty cognitive function, because if it were purely biological then the drugs would have been a more effective treatment. The Pediatric OCD Treatment study (POTS, 2004), compared treatments in a randomised investigation and found that CBT was more effective than drug treatment but that there was a minor improvement when CBT was combined with the drug therapy. This suggests that when CBT is done well it is the most appropriate treatment for children and adolescents.

Further support comes from studies that show what happens when sufferers try to engage in thought suppression in order to block the obsessions: rather than this stopping the cycle it suspends it temporarily, for example, Salkovskis and Kirk (1997) conducted a diary study of people with OCD. On some of the days of the study they were told to deliberately suppress the obsessive thoughts but on others they were allowed free rein. It was found that the frequency of intrusive thoughts was much higher on the days they tried to suppress them.

Superficially the theory seems to be a good explanation, supported by diary studies and other forms of self-report data, which show that sufferers have faulty cognitions that may be at the root of the disorder. Therefore it has face validity; however, it could be argued that the explanation suffers from the direction of effect issue. There is no evidence that the faulty cognition precedes the onset of symptoms.

A more eclectic explanation would involve combining the cognitive with other theories in order to increase its explanatory power; for example, a fuller explanation might involve the orbitofrontal cortex hyperactivity loop, which affects how the person processes information.

> **Exam tip**
>
> When asked to evaluate a theoretical explanation for a disorder you can gain points by comparing it to other explanations and explaining why the theory being discussed is better or worse at explaining the disorder. But you must ensure that the focus of your point remains on the theory in the question and that you do not start to evaluate the alternate theory.

Treatments for OCD
Biological treatment: drug therapy

The recommended treatment for someone with mild to moderate OCD is generally a short course of CBT. However, in those with more severe symptoms, or those who did not respond to the CBT, drug treatment is the next option. Different drug treatments have been made available to treat the considerable anxiety that is felt as a result of OCD.

Anxiety is regulated in the brain by GABA. This is an amino acid that acts to lower physiological arousal and return the body back to a resting state following a period of heightened arousal or anxiety. Benzodiazepines (such as Valium) are anti-anxiety medications that work to increase the effectiveness of GABA in regulating anxiety and returning the body back to a normal state of arousal. An alternative drug treatment is beta blockers. These drugs relieve the physiological effects of anxiety by blocking the stress hormones that are released into the bloodstream by the adrenal glands. These hormones normally have physiological effects such as increased heart rate and respiration. Beta blockers prevent the physiological response occurring and also help to reduce obsessional thoughts that lead to compulsive behaviour.

The most common treatment for OCD today is antidepressant medication, particularly those drugs that act on the levels of serotonin at the synapse (for example, selective serotonin reuptake inhibitors).

Antidepressant drugs that raise serotonin levels are used, for example fluoxetine or sertraline. These drugs increase serotonin by blocking its reuptake from the synapse back into the releasing neuron, so making more serotonin available for longer and thereby increasing activity on serotonergic pathways.

The dosage used to treat OCD is higher than that used to treat depression. It usually takes time for the drug to take effect, which can be up to 12 weeks. If no benefit is felt by that time the drug or the dosage will be changed or augmented with another drug being prescribed alongside.

Evaluation

There are often transient side effects associated with the drugs, such as nausea and headache. In some rare cases there can be an increase in anxiety, leading to self-harm and increased risk of suicide, so active monitoring of the person is always required. It is recommended that a family member or a friend keeps an eye open for changes in behaviour and alerts the person if necessary.

Soomro et al. (2007) used individual randomised controlled trials using antidepressants for the treatment of OCD. Comparing an SSRI antidepressant drug with a placebo, they reviewed 17 studies (3 097 participants), which showed that drugs were more effective than a placebo in reducing the symptoms of OCD. However, it was reported that adverse effects of taking SSRI medication included nausea. Koran et al. (2002) found that antidepressant medication had a long-term effect compared to a placebo and was better at preventing relapse over an 80-week trial.

In some cases where SSRIs have not been effective, a tricyclic antidepressant may be prescribed to augment the treatment, but these carry more serious side effects and can impact badly on people with other problems, such as heart conditions.

Key term

Refractory OCD: obsessive–compulsive disorder that is difficult to treat.

Drugs are often used in combination with CBT and they have been shown to increase the effectiveness of CBT. The prescription of drugs needs to reflect individual differences between patients that affect the outcomes of drug treatment, especially when it concerns **refractory OCD**. Research indicates the type of treatment most suited to a specific person. For example, SSRIs in combination with an antipsychotic drug like fenfluramine in low doses are more beneficial to those who have refractory OCD with a chronic comorbid tic (Goodman et al., 1993).

Drug treatments alone cannot treat most people with OCD effectively; they are most effective when combined with other forms of therapy such as CBT. The POTS study found that CBT was superior to drugs when the CBT was effective, but that adding drugs to the CBT improved the outcome where the CBT was perhaps less effective. However this was only relevant to children and adolescents and did not look at the more severe cases. Ravizza et al. (1995) found that SSRI drugs were not effective for 40 per cent of people.

Drugs carry side effects, which may put people off taking them, thus limiting their effectiveness, but careful monitoring and flexible prescribing may be able to overcome this. The drug must be taken for an extended period, probably about 12 months, and if improvements have been made only then can the dose be reduced as they move to a maintenance dose or the medication is discontinued. However, studies show that stopping the drug carries a very high risk of relapse, suggesting that the therapy is, in some cases, effective.

Drug treatment has to be sensitive to individual differences; for example, Brody et al. (1998) found that differences in the metabolism in the right compared to the left orbitofrontal cortex predicts whether the person will respond better to CBT or to drugs. Given that most diagnosticians do not have access to this information, which can only be gained by advanced scanning techniques such as positron emission tomography (PET), it suggests that treatment prescription might be a bit 'hit and miss'.

WIDER ISSUES AND DEBATES

Ethics

There are surgical interventions available to treat OCD. The NHS has set up a centre to treat refractory OCD, which aims to help people for whom more mainstream methods have not been effective. One of the techniques that has been developed recently is deep brain stimulation. In this technique, a surgeon implants electrodes in the brain and connects them to a small electrical generator in the chest. Deep brain stimulation does not permanently destroy neural tissue, as surgery does; instead, it uses electricity to modulate the transmission of brain signals. There are fewer side effects and recent small-scale studies show this to be effective for about two-thirds of patients.

Another surgical intervention to treat OCD is neurosurgery. This involves the destruction (ablation) of small amounts of brain tissue within the areas known to be implicated in the symptoms of OCD. This has been estimated to be effective in about half of the people treated but risks include seizures, personality changes, and more transient side effects associated with surgery and anaesthesia.

The ethical issues of psychosurgery are huge. This is especially true when the surgery is irreversible, however such interventions are only offered as a last resort and as knowledge increases about the structure and function of the brain such surgeries can be more effective and may become more mainstream.

Ablation techniques are only used as a treatment of last resort but do bring relief to those with severe refractory symptoms. Typically those offered the surgery will have an extended history of failed treatments so it might offer a 'ray of hope' to those who have tried everything else. As knowledge develops about the specific neuro-circuits involved then we can expect this treatment to be refined and be offered more widely, although at present it is largely experimental.

Similarly, deep brain implants although not irreversible and with fewer side effects, other than those associated with the surgery involved in implanting the devices, are still in the early stages of research; with improved knowledge from clinical trials specific targets for the implant will be found and there is already an improving picture of the effectiveness of this intervention emerging from small-scale trials.

Psychological treatment: cognitive behavioural therapy

Cognitive behavioural therapy combines elements of the cognitive approach with conditioning from the behaviourist. It is the first choice treatment for OCD and a brief course is recommended by the National Institute for Health and Care Excellence (NICE) in the UK for most cases of moderate severity. It is goal oriented and short term (about three months). It is possible to have a purely cognitive therapy based on changing thought patterns or a behaviourist one based on systematic desensitisation. In practice, however, most therapists combine the two approaches.

The aim of cognitive therapy is to identify and modify patterns of thought that cause anxiety and, in doing this, change how the person responds.

In OCD, intrusive thoughts cause beliefs that activate the negative emotion of anxiety; the goal of the therapy is not to remove the intrusive thoughts but to change the belief they trigger. This is achieved by asking the client to recall a recent episode that triggered intrusive thoughts and then examining the meaning of the thoughts. The therapist helps the client to challenge the meaning by exploring what makes them anxiety provoking. This is done in a graduated way, starting with thoughts that are least anxiety provoking and encouraging the client to test the belief that the thoughts activate until they no longer automatically generate anxiety.

For example, the intrusive thought might be that they have been contaminated by contact with a public toilet. This might mean that they would contaminate anyone they came into contact with, which then might lead to ritualised washing behaviour. By examining and testing the belief about contamination and transmission it will lose its power.

Exposure and response prevention therapy (ERPT) is a behaviourist treatment that requires the person to be highly motivated to get better as it involves facing their fears. The client is active in the treatment where they have to keep confronting the fears identified as triggering a compulsion without engaging in the compulsive behaviour. The therapy takes between 14 and 16 weeks on average and consists of regular sessions with a therapist, lasting about an hour on average, and a lot of home practice.

The first stage is to develop a hierarchy of situations that provoke obsessional fears, starting with the least anxiety-producing situation, and either engaging with it directly or through imagining, and then resisting the compulsion to perform the ritual that it triggers for a set period of time. For example, the client may have a fear of contamination, and their least-feared situation might be shaking hands with someone. They would be asked to shake hands and then wait for a short time initially, but longer later, before they engage with the ritual.

The client should record their anxiety levels and thoughts as they do this. At the end of the set time they may complete the ritual or they could choose not to perform it at all. This process should be repeated several times a week until the client can engage with the trigger without anxiety. After that the next most fearful situation would be tackled, for example, touching a clean bin, and the process is repeated.

The client is trained to monitor their anxiety levels in order to record how they feel accurately and to notice differences as they emerge. This therapy is estimated to be effective in reducing symptoms in the majority of clients.

Taking it further

Research CBT on the Internet. You will find training programmes that you can look at, which will give you more depth about the different elements. You will also find video clips that show CBT in action when working with patients with specific OCD symptoms.

Evaluation

In evaluation, ERPT would not be effective for clients that do not have compulsions. Masellis et al. (2003) found that a substantial proportion of clients (up to 44 per cent) only suffer from obsessions. They also found that up to 75 per cent of OCD clients also suffer with comorbid depression, which lessens the effectiveness of ERPT. Having persistent depressive symptoms at the end of therapy was found to be a strong predictor of relapse and suggested that a combined cognitive therapy with drug treatment would be more beneficial.

The therapy has been promoted as the first choice by NICE as it has been shown to be effective in reducing symptoms, and it can be applied flexibly; for example, as group therapy or online, with a therapist monitoring the completion of worksheets and an activity plan. It is cost-effective and time-limited, showing an improvement in more than 50 per cent of cases. Its effectiveness is increased when combined with drugs.

The therapy is ethical as it allows the person to take control of their own treatment because they identify the specific issues to work on, however, it may be uncomfortable for them as they have to face up to their fears and habituate to them. Unlike drug treatments, it does not have any side effects.

The success of the therapy relies on a good interpersonal relationship between the client and the therapist, perhaps because a high degree of motivation is required. This means that tests of its effectiveness are confounded by the therapist effect as the success of the therapy depends on more than just the nature of the therapy. This was supported by the POTS (2004) study (see Key studies section). It was found that one centre in the study testing the effectiveness of therapy for children and adolescents achieved more effective results in its delivery of CBT compared to the other, despite using the same treatment as prescribed by the CBT manual. It was proposed that this was because of a therapist effect.

Exam tip

When you need to use studies to evaluate something such as the effectiveness of a treatment it is important to be able to link the findings directly to the thing being evaluated. This does not involve a long explanation of the study's procedure and you could waste time if you did this. You will know a lot about the POTS study because it is a key study, but if using it in the context of an 'Assess the effectiveness of one psychological therapy' type question you do not need to go beyond the findings because you are using the study as evidence in your judgement.

5.2 Methods

Learning outcomes

In this section, you will learn about how research is conducted in clinical psychology including:

- the HCPC guidelines for clinical practitioners
- longitudinal, cross-sectional and cross-cultural methods, meta-analysis, and the use of primary and secondary data
- the use of case studies and an example case study in clinical psychology
- the use of interviews and an example interview study in clinical psychology
- quantitative data using descriptive and inferential statistics
- qualitative data and analysis using thematic analysis and grounded theory.

Health and Care Professions Council (HCPC) guidelines for clinical practitioners

Professionals who work in clinical practice, that is, those who deal directly with patient groups, have to register with the HCPC, which is a regulatory body that exists to monitor a variety of professions including practitioner psychologists. There are standards that professionals have to demonstrate in order to remain registered with the HCPC.

Character

Registrants have to provide credible character references from people who have known them for at least three years to give an idea of the character traits they have that make them suitable for the role. This standard also considers any criminal cautions or convictions given to the professional and whether they affect their suitability to practise.

Health

People on the register must provide information every two years when they re-register about their general health. They are required to provide information on any health issues that they have only if they are likely to affect their ability to practise safely. If a professional feels at any time that their health is impairing their ability to practise then they must limit or stop their work and declare this to the HCPC.

Standards of proficiency

For each profession there is a set of specific expectations for the ability to practise effectively. For practitioner psychologists these include Professional autonomy and accountability, and Formulation and delivery of plans and strategies for meeting health and social care needs. Professionals must be able to demonstrate and use these skills throughout their practice. For practitioner psychologists there are specific requirements within each standard to be demonstrated by practitioners in different areas of psychology, for example clinical psychologists and forensic psychologists.

Taking it further

To find out more about these standards, search online to find the complete list of proficiencies for practitioner psychologists.

Taking it further

To read the whole list including guidance on all 14 standards in this area search for Standards of conduct, performance and ethics on the Health and Care Professions Council website.

Standards of conduct, performance and ethics

There is a list of 14 guidelines that practitioners must adhere to in their clinical practice. These include points such as maintaining confidentiality in work with service users, and only acting within the limits of their own knowledge and skills, referring on to others where necessary.

Standards for continuing professional development

Professionals are expected to take part in and document regular training that they undertake to develop their own practice. This will include training events that they will attend, evidence of how they have changed their practice and an evaluation of the effectiveness of these changes. It is important for practitioners to keep up to date with current trends in clinical practice.

Standards of education and training

Standards of education and training is a set of minimum levels of qualification specified before people can register to practise in different areas of health and care professions. For any practitioner psychologists, registrants must be able to evidence at least a master's degree with BPS qualification in the area of practice they will be working in, but for some practices a doctorate degree will be required. This is the case for clinical psychologists. The HCPC also sets out standards for training courses to ensure that any registrants who attend will be able to meet the required standards for proficiency expected for their area of practice.

Standards for prescribing

These standards set out safe practice for prescribing medication by health and care professionals. This also includes the required knowledge and training to be able to prescribe within professional practice.

Researching mental health

One way to uncover causes of mental health problems is to investigate the impact of different treatment methods and find out how disorders progress in patients, all of which have a huge effect on the outcomes of patients. Depending on the purpose of the research there are many different methods available to psychologists in this area. Some of the most common include longitudinal studies, cross-sectional studies, cross-cultural methods and meta-analyses. The decision about which is most appropriate will depend on the research aims and whether the researchers require primary or secondary data.

Primary and secondary data

Primary data is information that the researchers gather themselves directly from a group of participants, while secondary data relies on evidence that has been gathered by other researchers by accessing other peer-reviewed articles or public access statistics. Gathering primary data is more time-consuming because they have to collect it themselves and the researchers may face many ethical considerations in working directly with patient groups. However, relying purely on secondary data means that the researchers have no way of knowing how reliable or valid the original research actually was. This could mean that conclusions are drawn from data that was originally flawed, especially if multiple types of secondary data are being used. Typically, research using secondary data eliminates research studies that are considered to be unreliable or flawed in some way, or at least comment on this in their analysis.

Longitudinal studies

Longitudinal research takes place over a long period of time, and often involves comparing a single sample group with their own performance over time, which means that developmental or time-based changes can be seen through the patterns of measurements. In mental health research, clinicians may be interested in monitoring changes in symptoms in a patient group undergoing a certain treatment. In this case, measurements may be taken of the symptom expression and severity over a specific time period at certain intervals. This should allow psychologists to see if there is any reduction in the symptoms to assess how effective the treatment is.

Evaluation

The advantage of using longitudinal research in clinical psychology is that, as patients often have very different symptoms and experiences even when suffering with the same illness, there is no difficulty in making comparisons between different people that could be affected by individual differences. It is also the only way of being able to reliably measure the effect of time on the behaviour in question, which is very important when considering whether treatments actually have the ability to significantly improve a patient's quality of life in the long term.

However, one of the major problems is that the research clearly has to go on for a long period of time. This can lead to several issues. One is that patients may drop out, die or not be able to be contacted, reducing the sample size and making the final outcome less valid. Another problem is that by the time meaningful data can be used to draw a conclusion in the study, the data may be irrelevant. Clinical psychology is a fast-paced area of research with new ideas and treatments being developed all the time, especially in relation to biological factors and drug treatments, so research that publishes findings years after it was started could be outdated.

Cross-sectional studies

When researchers want to take a quick 'snapshot' of behaviour in a given population they will usually use a cross-sectional design rather than waiting for longitudinal data to be gathered. In cross-sectional research the investigators will usually use a large group of people in the sample, so as to get a good 'cross-section' of the whole target population, and then draw conclusions from the data gathered from them. For example, researchers may want to know about the experience of people at different ages suffering from schizophrenia, but rather than conducting time-consuming and expensive research using a longitudinal design, they could take a sample of participants of different ages at the same time and investigate them.

Evaluation

The advantage of this is that the data is drawn together much more quickly, meaning that the conclusions drawn can then be used and acted on more rapidly. It is also much more likely that the results will be more valid as they will be reported at the time when they have most application rather than several years later.

The major drawback of this research is that the comparisons being made will be between different groups of people, therefore individual differences are likely to have a significant effect on the conclusions drawn. With cross-sectional studies there may be issues with cohort effects whereby the results of the research could be attributed to the effects of being raised in a particular time and/or place. This may have an impact on some research into abnormal behaviours, for example in studies into different age groups suffering from anorexia, not all of the groups would have been exposed to the same cultural ideals and images. This may make each group unique, and therefore affect any study into the development of anorexia, as the groups are not comparable because they were subject to the different social and cultural ideals of their time.

Cross-cultural methods

Cross-cultural research involves taking samples from different cultural groups to draw comparisons about the similarities and differences between them to consider how culture may impact on the behaviour in question. There are many reasons why this may be relevant in clinical psychology. For example, there may be questions over whether the experience of patients suffering from schizophrenia is the same in different cultural groups, whether the same symptoms are shown in all cultural groups, or whether treatments are equally effective across cultural groups.

Evaluation

By taking measurements in one cultural group, and comparing the same measurements taken in a different cultural group, it allows the researchers to gain an understanding of how culture plays a role in the validity and reliability of diagnoses in clinical psychology. Cross-cultural research can also identify elements of abnormal behaviour that can be attributed to purely biological factors. This is done by identifying universal trends in behaviour that seem to remain unaffected by cultural variation.

Cross-cultural research can also reduce the level of ethnocentrism in psychological studies and conclusions and improve generalisability of research.

WIDER ISSUES AND DEBATES

Culture

An advantage of cross-cultural methods is that they aid clinicians' understanding of the cultural factors they should take into account when diagnosing and treating patients from different cultural groups, especially when the culture of the patient is different from their own. Doctors who diagnose and treat patients who are not from their own cultural groups must be encouraged to refer to this cross-cultural evidence in order to understand the subjective experience of the patient. The disadvantage is that in conducting research across cultures there is likely to be a conflict between the cultural values of some or all of the participants and those of the researcher. Because of this, the conclusions drawn may lack validity if the interpretation of the patients' behaviours does not take into account their own cultural backgrounds.

Meta-analysis

Meta-analyses involve looking at secondary data from multiple studies conducted by other researchers and drawing the findings together to make overall conclusions. A meta-analysis is typically conducted when there is a huge body of psychological research where firm conclusions cannot be drawn without comparing this research, or where the research findings may be inconsistent. The researchers will seek out studies from a variety of places, cultures and times, which have all tested the same area, with the aim of bringing the findings together. Doing this means they can more easily consider a large amount of information gathered from a huge overall sample size rather than having to go out and gather primary data. In clinical psychology, researchers have conducted meta-analyses in many different areas, such as effectiveness of therapies and treatments across different patient groups. As such, meta-analysis focuses on effect sizes. This means that a meta-analysis of research looking at the effectiveness of CBT will focus its analysis on the size of the effect of CBT found by all of the research gathered.

Evaluation

The benefit of meta-analyses is that conclusions can be drawn from a vast array of different areas and a huge overall sample, very quickly and at much less cost than would be involved in conducting all the studies themselves. They also do not have any of the ethical concerns associated with conducting research on participants first hand.

However, a major disadvantage is that the researchers do not have involvement in gathering the data directly, so there may be undisclosed issues of reliability and/or validity in the methods of data gathering of which they are unaware. There is also the possibility of publication bias impacting on the validity of meta-analyses. Research that produces null effects may not be published and therefore would be ignored by meta-analytic research, which generally focuses on peer-reviewed publications. This would mean that the evidence produced by meta-analyses is often biased against research where no effect has been found. Some researchers may choose to include unpublished work in the analysis to make their data more valid, but then there is an increased risk of using that data as it has not been scrutinised by peer review in the same way.

The use of case studies

Case studies involve studying individuals or small groups with some kind of unique characteristic or experience. Researchers involved in conducting case studies will use a variety of different research methods to gather information on the group, and then **triangulate** the data to draw conclusions. In clinical psychology these case studies may be of people with rare symptoms or individuals taking part in a specific therapy. Often the evidence gathered from case studies will be qualitative, allowing an in-depth analysis of the group being studied. This allows the conclusions gathered to be highly valid for the sample being studied. In clinical psychology this will mean that a full understanding of the patient's problems can be assessed and all the factors that may have an effect on them can be taken into account.

Example case study

One case study by Lavarenne et al. (2013) referred to a session known as the 'Thursday group' – a group of patients, most of whom suffer from schizophrenia or schizoaffective disorder, who meet every week. The purpose of the group is to support the patients by giving them some structure to help them cope with their illness, and encourage a sense of connection with others for a group who are generally quite isolated in everyday life. There are ten members of the group who are referred from various local out-patient and in-patient services in the local area. The group is currently made up of members who have been attending for between 3 weeks and 22 years. The sessions themselves are never recorded but, immediately afterwards, the group leaders note down key points about the patients' behaviour, expressions and comments. The case study reports on one specific session with six patients present, which was just before Christmas, where the group members were facing a break of more than seven days before their next meeting because of the holidays. The key theme the leaders noted in this session was that of 'fragile ego boundaries' – a breakdown in the line that people draw between the real and the unreal, or their own thoughts and those of other people. They suggested that the group may be reacting to the potential change in routine by having a break from the group for more than the usual one week.

Evaluation

Research like this provides a brilliant insight into the behaviour of the patients involved, but this is very reliant on the interpretation of the researcher. In the Lavarenne et al. (2013) study there is also a concern that the memory of the group leaders may be inaccurate as they do not record the

Key term

Triangulate: to take multiple pieces of information and draw them together to make an overall conclusion.

sessions. If they recall something incompletely or inaccurately, or interpret information in a subjective way, there is a risk that the conclusions drawn could be unreliable or invalid. Another concern with research like this is that a small group of participants is unlikely to represent the whole target population and, therefore, the population validity of the research could be extremely limited. The six patients in attendance at the 'Thursday group' in the above study are unlikely to represent all patients with psychotic illness so the usefulness of the results is questionable.

The use of interviews in clinical psychology

Interviews involve verbal questioning of patients to gather information from them. Interviews can be structured, involving a specific list of questions, semi-structured, involving a range of themes to explore, or unstructured, where the direction of the conversation can be decided along the way.

One area that is often studied using interviews is depression.

Link

For quantitative data analysis using both descriptive and inferential statistics please see the Methods sections of the following topics:

Chi-squared: Topic 4: *Learning psychology*

Spearman's rho: Topic 3: *Biological psychology*

Wilcoxon and Mann-Whitney U: Topic 2: *Cognitive psychology*

Thematic analysis: Topic 1: *Social psychology*.

Example interview study

Research reported by Vallentine et al. (2010) used semi-structured interviews to gather information from a patient group on their experiences as part of a psycho-educational group treatment programme. The patients were 42 males detained in Broadmoor high-security hospital, most of whom had received a diagnosis of schizophrenia or a similar disorder. They were part of a programme aimed at helping them understand and cope with their illness, and several measures were taken to assess the impact of this on their symptoms. The aim of the interviews was to understand their experience better, but also get information about how the group could be improved in the future. Following the interviews, a content analysis was conducted on the data gathered to pick out key themes in the responses. Four core themes were identified in the data: 'what participants valued and why', 'what was helpful about the group', 'clinical implications' and 'what was difficult/unhelpful'. Some of the key findings were that patients valued knowing and understanding their illness, and the group sessions allowed them not only to understand their own symptoms, but also how other people's experiences were similar. Many also reported increased confidence in dealing with their illness, which made them more positive about the future.

Evaluation

Gaining information from interviews allows patients to fully explain their own point of view, which should help the researchers to understand their perspective more clearly. Using semi-structured or unstructured interviews allows more detail to be gained from the patients, however, it also means that there is a lack of reliability in the way the data is gathered because the questions are not standardised. The researchers in Vallentine et al. (2010) recorded their interviews to allow them to play back and check the accuracy of the data they report on. This means that they can check the reliability of the interpretation using the themes by having another researcher to also code the data.

Grounded theory

Grounded theory is a method devised by Glaser and Strauss in the 1960s for developing theory from research evidence. This method of data gathering and analysis generally focuses on qualitative research (although not exclusively so) and does not begin in the traditional scientific way of developing hypotheses that are then tested and adapted by research. Instead, research is conducted to gather information about something of interest and the theory emerges gradually from the data as it is gathered and analysed. This is known as an inductive method.

The researcher must first identify the area of behaviour they are interested in, and where they can gather information on this from. For example, Nathaniel (2007) was interested in nursing practice, and began by gaining information from nurses. As data is gathered, 'codes' and 'categories' can be drawn out from what they have seen. The researchers will begin by coding everything in some way until they begin to see patterns. As the theoretical concepts begin to become apparent, these codes may become more specific but initially they are likely to be very broad. As the researchers gather their evidence they will 'memo' their work, adding comments to try to develop the clarity about what the data is showing them. This can help them to identify the links between different concepts that are emerging from the data. Once clear theoretical concepts have become obvious, the researchers will start to selectively code only the relevant data they gather, and they will move to sampling that gathers more evidence to support what they are already beginning to see. For example, once they know what information they need to develop their understanding of the emerging concepts, they will work out who they need to talk to next to get this information. Once a clear theoretical concept has developed, the researchers can then review other literature and develop the theory in more detail.

Evaluation

An advantage of using this type of method to develop theory is that the evidence is integrated into the theory, therefore the theory itself should have a good degree of validity. However, this could be compromised if the data that was gathered to develop the theory was problematic in some way. For example, if the researchers were in any way biased in their gathering or interpretation of the data, the theory would be based on a subjective opinion and not actually 'grounded' in evidence. By selectively sampling data as the theory begins to emerge, some people might argue that the researchers are 'forcing' the data to support the theory they think is emerging. By doing this they may unintentionally miss crucial evidence that could contradict the concepts they believe they are starting to see. There may also be issues in the reliability of the conclusions drawn if it is possible that another person conducting the same research or coding the same data could come to a very different conclusion about the theoretical concepts. This type of research is likely to take a very long time to gather and analyse the information that is coming in, especially in the early phases when the researchers are unclear about exactly what they are looking for. While conducting the initial coding of every piece of information, they will need to try to interpret the viewpoint of all of the information as well as trying to decide how the data should be coded. Doing this will inevitably take a lot of time, and also a lot of skill on the part of the researcher.

Grounded theory in clinical psychology

Grounded theory is particularly useful in clinical psychology where researchers are interested in the beliefs, opinions and experiences of service users of the NHS or mental health professionals. This is because it is unlikely that a researcher could propose possible themes/codes prior to asking the service user; instead they emerge from the analysis.

5.3 Key studies
Learning outcomes

In this section, you will learn about one classic study:

- Rosenhan (1973) On being sane in insane places

one contemporary study:

- Carlsson et al. (2000) Network interactions in schizophrenia – therapeutic implications

and two contemporary studies from your chosen disorder, from which you will need to choose one to learn about:

Depression

- The PHQ-8 as a measure of current depression in the general population (Kroenke et al., 2009)
- Combining imagination and reason in the treatment of depression: a randomised control trial of internet-based cognitive-bias modification and internet-CBT for depression (Williams et al., 2013)

Anorexia nervosa

- Evidence for the role of EPHX2 gene variants in anorexia nervosa (Scott-Van Zeeland et al., 2013)
- Imagining one's own and someone else's body actions: Dissociation in anorexia nervosa (Guardia et al., 2012)

Obsessive–compulsive disorder

- Quality of life in OCD: Differential impact of obsessions, compulsions, and depression comorbidity (Masellis et al., 2003)
- POTS team (Paediatric OCD Treatment Study) including March et al. (2004) Cognitive Behavior Therapy, Sertraline and Their Combination for Children and Adolescents with OCD.

Classic study
On being sane in insane places (Rosenhan, 1973)
Aim

The background of this study was to answer the question 'can the sane be distinguished from the insane?' Inspired by the antipsychiatry movement, David Rosenhan wanted to challenge the diagnostic system for mental health, which puts the emphasis on the individual as the source of the symptoms used to classify disorders, as opposed to the environmental context in which the symptoms arose. Rosenhan thought that diagnosis was invalid and affected by observer bias, causing the clinician to see behaviour as symptomatic of an underlying disorder rather than something that arises in a certain context. He devised a test of the system to see if sane people could be admitted to a psychiatric institution and if, once admitted, they would be detected. He also wanted to find out what life was like in a psychiatric hospital and raise awareness about conditions.

Procedure

Eight pseudopatients – including Rosenhan himself – were recruited for the investigation, three women and five men. One was a psychology graduate student, three others were psychologists and the others were a housewife, a painter, a psychiatrist and a paediatrician. None of the pseudo-patients had any history of mental health problems.

They each had to phone the admissions office of one of 12 hospitals representing a range of good and bad, old and new institutions across five states in the USA and make an appointment because they were 'hearing voices'.

At the initial admission meeting they reported hearing the words 'empty', 'thud' and 'hollow'. Each pseudopatient gave a false name in order protect themselves in the future. For those whose profession was psychology related they also gave a fake job, but everything else they disclosed to the staff was true including significant life events and family relationships. All were admitted to the institutions with a diagnosis of schizophrenia except in one case where the patient was admitted with manic depression with psychosis.

Once admitted the pseudopatients stopped feigning symptoms and behaved normally, answering all questions from staff and patients honestly except about being part of a study. Once settled in they observed life on the ward, were friendly and cooperative, and recorded their experiences by taking notes. They had to try to convince the staff of their sanity in order to get out. They had daily visitors who indicated that they were all behaving normally.

Results

All of the pseudopatients were diagnosed as having a serious mental health disorder on minimal symptoms. Their sanity was never detected by the staff and they were discharged with a diagnosis of schizophrenia in remission. Their average stay in hospital was 19 days with the shortest being 7 days and the longest 52 days.

Patients did, however, suspect that the pseudopatients were sane. One asked whether the researcher was a journalist. In three hospitals where records were taken, about one-third of the patients challenged the pseudopatients.

The staff treated the researchers in a way that was consistent with their diagnosis and frequently pathologised normal behaviour, for instance note taking was referred to as 'writing behaviour', pacing the corridors due to boredom was interpreted as nervousness, and waiting outside the lunch hall early was labelled by one clinician as 'Oral-inquisitive syndrome'.

A central finding was about the depersonalisation of the patients by the staff. When contact was initiated towards the nurses by the pseudopatients, in 71 per cent of the times they were ignored; eye contact was made only 23 per cent of the time, with verbal responses in only 2 per cent of the cases. This was even worse when the contact was directed towards senior staff. Of 185 reasonable questions directed towards the staff, none were answered.

Conclusions and follow up

When the results were published some institutions reacted with a challenge as they did not believe that their systems would be so easily fooled. Rosenhan agreed with one leading hospital to do a similar study and set up a test: every staff member who dealt with admissions had to rate all patients in terms of the probability that they could be pseudopatients. Over a three-month period 193 patients were admitted, and of those 41 were thought to be fake by at least one staff member and 19 of those were classed as fake by two members. In fact, Rosenhan sent no pseudopatients to the hospital. This confirms his initial results that there is unreliability in the diagnostic process.

Rosenhan was concerned about the effect of the label conferred by diagnosis on the way the person was subsequently treated by the staff in the institutions. He contended that the diagnostic label changed the perception of the person so that all their behaviour was interpreted within the context of the label. He argued that this could lead to a self-fulfilling prophecy as the person is then treated in a way that is consistent with the label and their behaviour in response to this is interpreted as being consistent with the label thus confirming the validity of the label.

He compared the reaction of the staff in the institutions to being approached and asked questions by the pseudopatients, with the reaction of academic staff in a university when approached and asked a similar question by an apparent student and found that, in all cases, the academic staff responded with courtesy to the person, which was a complete contrast to the experience of the pseudopatients in the hospital.

Evaluation

There are ethical issues connected with this study. The only permission that was gained was for Rosenhan's own admission and even then it was only with the hospital administrator and the chief psychologist in one institution; none of the other staff in any of the other hospitals were aware of the ruse. It could be argued that their actions affected the amount of attention given to those who were genuinely ill. However the testimonies of the pseudopatients suggest this was not true as the staff had very limited contact with the patients. This was measured as an average of 6.8 minutes per day per pseudopatient to include admission, discharge and all medication, suggesting that this was not the case. Arguably the breach of ethical guidelines is justifiable in the public interest.

The sample of hospitals used is generalisable in that there was a variety of type of institution, from research and teaching hospitals to private ones and older shabbier hospitals; these were spread over a wide geographical area, so the findings were not limited to one type of hospital or one area. However, it was only tested in one culture and can only tell us about the diagnostic and treatment provided in the USA in the early 1970s.

The pseudopatients were able to provide an account of the quality of care in a psychiatric institution, which included a general lack of respect and occasional mistreatment of patients. Caretaking behaviour such as giving drugs to the patients was done, but there was no checking that this was having an effect. The pseudopatients disposed of their drugs but also noticed that so too did many patients, and yet none of the staff noticed. Rosenhan argued that this was due not to malice but to the system in which the care was given.

A recent attempt at replication by Lauren Slater for her book *Opening Skinner's Box* supported Rosenhan's findings, as she found that when she presented herself at nine emergency rooms reporting hearing a voice saying 'thud' she was diagnosed with depression with psychosis and prescribed antipsychotic and antidepressant medication. This was challenged by Spitzer et al. (2005) who sent a detailed vignette based on Slater's account of her methodology to 431 psychiatrists who were asked to make a diagnosis: 73 responded and 86 per cent of these categorically ruled out the diagnosis Slater claims she was given. One-third would prescribe antipsychotic medication but none would prescribe antidepressants. Spitzer claims that this and Rosenhan's research is flawed and sensationalist, causing great harm by creating doubt about the treatment of mental health.

Taking it further

Why not investigate the issues surrounding Spitzer's criticisms further? This is well documented but you could begin by searching for 'Opening Skinner's Box causes controversy'.

Network interactions in schizophrenia – therapeutic implications (Carlsson et al., 2000)

Aim

The aim of this research was to review studies into the relationship between levels of neurotransmitters, especially dopamine and glutamate, on symptoms of schizophrenia. The researchers considered that there were two main 'camps' in relation to neurochemical explanations for schizophrenia: those that focus on hyperdopaminergia (high levels of dopamine), and those that look at hypoglutamatergia (low levels of **glutamate**). This has implications for treatment of schizophrenia because drugs that change brain chemistry are the leading treatment given to patients with schizophrenia, but they are not effective for everyone. Many of these drugs act on reducing levels of dopamine, but the researchers consider that if other neurotransmitters are implicated in the cause of schizophrenia, then other drugs may have to be tested for effectiveness. One of the considerations made by the researchers is that most patients using antipsychotic medication complain about the impact that side effects associated with the drugs have on their quality of life. One priority they suggest is to work to produce drugs that reduce levels of relapse but also reduce negative side effects for the patients.

Literature review of research and current theory

This study reviews research from a variety of sources investigating neurochemical levels in patients diagnosed with schizophrenia, as well as studies into drugs known to induce symptoms of psychosis. It has been well documented that high levels of dopamine are related to psychosis, and the researchers here cite evidence from brain scans providing further evidence to support this view, for example, Abi-Dargham et al. (1998), and Breier et al. (1997).

This study also looks into evidence from studies on the use of recreational drugs known to induce psychosis. Many previous studies have linked amphetamines (which increase levels of dopamine) with schizophrenia, but there is other research linking the use of phencyclidine (PCP or 'angel dust') with psychosis. The researchers also draw on evidence from studies into the effectiveness of drugs used to treat schizophrenia and the method of action they have on the brain to support the hypothesis that there may be other neurotransmitters associated with schizophrenia.

Results

One of the key findings in this review is that there is a lot of research evidence supporting the role of low levels of glutamate in the development of psychotic symptoms. Research has found that **phencyclidine** (PCP) acts as an antagonist of a glutamate receptor subtype referred to as NMDA receptors. This means that the drug inhibits the action of glutamate, reducing its actions in areas of the brain. Use of PCP is found to be more likely to result in psychosis in users, even more so than research has suggested in users of amphetamine. In fact, some research cited in the study has found a relationship between levels of glutamate and dopamine production: reduced levels of glutamate seem to be associated with increased dopamine release. Carlsson et al. also state that they have reviewed evidence suggesting that 'Glutamate failure in the **cerebral cortex** may lead to negative symptoms [of schizophrenia], whereas glutamatergic failure in the **basal ganglia** could be responsible for positive symptoms'.

Evidence from studies into antipsychotic effectiveness has found that clozapine is a highly effective drug treatment for schizophrenia, with fewer reported negative side effects. Clozapine has been shown to have both **antidopaminergic** and **antiserotonergic** functions, meaning that it reduces levels of dopamine and serotonin in the brain. It is also a drug shown to be highly effective in

---

Key terms 💬

Glutamate: as a neurotransmitter, glutamate is involved in the activation of neurones, enabling neural transmission to take place.

Phencyclidine: (aka PCP; Angel dust) is a drug originally created as an anaesthetic because it induces 'numbness', but is no longer used for this purpose because of its other effects. These include hallucinations, loss of touch with reality, and changes in mood, often making the user feel as if they are 'not in control' of their actions.

Cerebral cortex: the outer layer of the brain.

Basal ganglia: situated within the base of the brain, this is a group of three structures associated with the coordination of movement.

Antidopaminergic: blocking the activity of dopamine.

Antiserotonergic: blocking the activity of serotonin.

Key term

Hypoglutamatergia: reduced levels of glutamate.

Exam tip

This article was published as a review of research that summarised secondary data from evidence gathered by other researchers and considered this in relation to the most up-to-date theories of schizophrenia. This is a key study for you to be able to report, but does not follow the standard process for reporting research such as APRC because it is not actually reporting on any one single study. Spend time considering the best way to report this research so that you cover all of the key elements being reported.

Arvid Carlsson – Biography

Carlsson is a Swedish scientist best known for his work into the effects of dopamine in the brain and particularly for his research into the relationship between dopamine and Parkinson's disease. Born in 1923, Carlsson was awarded a Nobel Prize in Physiology or Medicine in 2000 along with Paul Greengard and Eric Kandel for their work on neural transmission. You can find out more about Carlsson on the official website of the Nobel Prize.

patients who have previously not responded to treatment. Because of the relationship between serotonin and glutamate, a suggestion is made that this evidence could infer that some 'difficult to treat' patients with schizophrenia may belong to a subgroup whose disorder may be better explained by **hypoglutamatergia**.

Conclusion

The key conclusion drawn in this review is that further research needs to be conducted in developing drugs to treat schizophrenia that avoid negative side effects, possibly by considering the role of other neurotransmitters in the development of the disorder. There are currently a number of compounds reported to be in development that reduce dopamine levels without risking the very low levels of dopamine associated with negative side effects such as tremors. Considering all of the evidence, the researchers suggest that schizophrenia may have different types that could be caused by abnormal levels of different neurotransmitters and not just dopamine. This is assumed to have serious implications for the future of treatments developed for schizophrenia.

Evaluation

Researchers in this study have relied on a great deal of secondary data from a variety of different studies, which means that the reliability and validity of the research itself can be brought into question. There is no way of knowing how valid or reliable the original study was and therefore basing further conclusions about therapeutic options for schizophrenia could be problematic. However the advantage of this study using the secondary data is that it allows a larger amount of information to be brought together quickly and provide an overview of the core findings in this area. It would take a great deal of time to gather this amount of information first hand, but drawing together the evidence in this way allows a mass of information to be used to draw more valid conclusions. Much of the evidence used within this review comes from very reliable methods, such as PET scans, which take objective measures of the activity in different areas of the brain.

WIDER ISSUES AND DEBATES

Psychology as a science

The evidence cited in this article focuses on scientific methodology such as brain scans. Scanning techniques such as PET scans produce highly objective data using very precise methods. These are extremely scientific methods that offer a strong evidence base to the biological explanations of behaviours such as schizophrenia.

An advantage of this research is that the aim of helping to develop more effective treatments for schizophrenia is extremely beneficial for patients for whom the current antipsychotic medications are ineffective. A large percentage of patients do not respond quickly to the current medications and consequently it can take a while to develop a treatment regimen that is effective. For some, this never happens. The results of this study suggest that there are newer drug compounds that may provide the answer to this problem by working on levels of other neurotransmitters as well as dopamine.

The PHQ-8 as a measure of current depression in the general population (Kroenke et al., 2009)

Aim

The aim was to assess the validity of a shortened version of a questionnaire based on the DSM IV criteria as a measure of depression in a large-scale population study. The authors point out that depression is among the leading causes of decreased productivity in the population and that the prevalence rate is well studied by large-scale national studies. These have typically involved the use of a structured psychiatric interview, which is time-consuming and difficult to administer to large numbers of people. Kroenke developed the PHQ-9, a nine-item questionnaire based on the criteria for diagnosing depression from the DSM IV. This was proven to be successful and it led to a shorter version being developed. The PHQ-8 does not include an item that relates to suicidal thoughts and self-injury, as this was not deemed necessary to measure depression reliably, although it has obvious relevance in a diagnostic interview. It aimed to test whether a simple measure based on the PHQ-8 would be an accurate reflection of depression in the population, specifically if a score on the PHQ-8 of 10 or more would reliably indicate the presence of depression.

Procedure

The Behavioural Risk Factor Surveillance Survey (BRFSS) is a large-scale random dial national telephone study conducted in the USA by state health departments and the Centre for Disease Control and Prevention to gather data that measures the current health issues and investigates factors associated with the development of ill health. It includes three sections: the first is a section of core questions asked in all cases, the second section concerns specific topics of interest, for example, asthma, and the third section includes state-added questions, which in this case included the topic of depression.

The PHQ-8 is standardised to be similar in the way the questions are asked to other aspects of the BRFSS. The items strongly reflected the DSM criteria but in this case asked the respondent how many days in the last 14 they had suffered with the specific symptoms. This was then converted to a score of between 0 and 3 per item, where a high score represents most days. The score for each item is then totalled to give a score out of a possible 24, this allows a classification to be made regarding depression status with a score of 10 and above representing clinically significant moderate depression.

The BRFSS included a Quality of Life survey and also gained socio-demographic information as well as whether the respondent had ever been diagnosed with depression.

The survey had a high compliance rate with 74.5 per cent of those approached participating. This equated to 198 678 people: of whom 61.6 per cent were female, the majority were non-Hispanic white people, 58 per cent were in employment, 61 per cent college educated and 60 per cent currently married. Of the sample, 18 per cent had received a diagnosis for depression prior to the survey and 12 per cent a diagnosis of an anxiety disorder.

Within the depressed section of the population a higher proportion were female than male, non-white, less educated, unemployed and under the age of 55.

A comparison was made between respondents scoring 10 and above on the PHQ-8 and other measures, such as depression status.

Results

It was found that there was a large degree of agreement between measures of depression. For example, it was as good a predictor of items on the quality of life measure such as number of days of impairment in the last two weeks in terms of mental health, physical health and limited activity in people compared to the usual diagnostic process.

Using the 10 and above cut-off point was as successful in measuring depression as using a diagnostic algorithm (step-by-step procedure for reaching a diagnosis). There was very high degree of concordance between those scoring below 10 and no diagnosis of depression.

Conclusions

When compared to other measures, the PHQ-8 yielded similar prevalence rates; this suggests that it is a good way to investigate large-scale samples quickly and efficiently. For example, this study shows that it is possible to measure depression using a simple-to-administer self-report questionnaire that could be postal or web based.

Evaluation

This study validates the use of the PHQ-8 as a way of measuring depression in populations. This is useful because it is relatively easy to administer, so that there is less intrusion into the lives of the respondents, meaning that they are more likely to comply with requests for information. Yet it still gives accurate data necessary for producing a clear picture of the health of the population, allowing efficient resource allocation. Such studies also give indicators of risk associated with the development of disorders and may be influential in developing prevention strategies.

Despite a very large sample, the sample was limited to those with phones and this might exclude members of the population more likely to have depression (low income, perhaps no telephone) so could overestimate the effectiveness of the PHQ-8 for those outside of the sample and therefore not be a fair measure within the entire population.

Furthermore, because the measure focuses only on symptoms from the last 14 days it might be measuring the effect of events in the respondent's life rather than genuinely measuring depression. However, it demonstrates good construct validity as it was measured against other measures of depression; although the concordance rate is not perfect on all measures, this suggests it is just as good at measuring depression in large-scale surveys as any other measure but is quicker and easier to administer.

Combining imagination and reason in the treatment of depression: a randomised control trial of internet-based cognitive-bias modification and internet-CBT for depression (Williams et al., 2013)

Aim

The aim was to test remote forms of CBT and to see if imagination-based cognitive bias modification would impact positively on iCBT outcomes. CBT is the first line of therapy for moderate depression, but there is often a delay before treatment can be offered due to lack of resources. Because people with depression have a tendency to use negative and/or threatening appraisals to deal with ambiguous information this study aimed to see if pre-treatment aimed at adjusting appraisal bias would impact positively on outcomes following a course of iCBT.

Procedure

The sample was recruited from online applications delivered via a clinical and research unit in Sydney, Australia. Applicants were screened and those selected were given a diagnostic interview over the phone. The 69 participants were randomised into either a control group (31 people formed the waiting list control – WLC, who were given the treatment after the study) or a treatment group of 38 people.

Baseline measures were taken for both groups consisting of the following.

- Primary measures were taken using Beck's Depression Inventory (BDI) and the Patient Health Questionnaire Depression Scale (PHQ-9) to measure depression. Kessler's psychological distress scale was used to index distress. Interpretation bias was measured using the Ambiguous Scenarios Test for depression and an electronic version of the Scrambled Sentences Test.

- Secondary measures were based on the World Health Organization Disability Assessment Schedule II, the State Trait Anxiety Inventory and the Repetitive Thinking Questionnaire. There was also a short questionnaire designed to provide an evaluation of the treatment.

The treatment group underwent a 20-minute daily treatment of Cognitive Bias Modification using imagery for the first week followed by the iCBT programme, which lasted a further 10 weeks. No face-to-face contact was made between the therapist and the participant. The iCBT was a well-tested programme, which had been previously validated in clinical trials; it consisted of six online lessons and regular homework with supplementary resources offered.

All baseline measurements were then repeated and treatment commenced for the control group.

Results

Pre-treatment tests showed no significant differences between the groups at the outset.

After the first week of CBM I training there was a reduction in the depression scores and the distress scores in the treatment group with clinically significant changes evident in seven of the treatment group compared to only two in the WLC group.

Analysis at week 11 showed significant reductions in all primary measures for both the treatment group and the WLC but the reductions were much larger in the treatment group where 65 per cent of participants in this group showed clinically significant change compared to only 36 per cent of the WLC group.

The therapy was evaluated as easy, logical and good by the participants.

Conclusions

Rapid symptom reduction was achieved after one week of daily 20-minute sessions with minimal effort from the participant; there was no homework. The changes shown in the Ambiguous Scenarios Test for depression scores showed the CBM I treatment to be quick and effective in changing the negative appraisals, which may have helped reduce other depressive symptoms, distress, disability and anxiety, and as a result made the iCBT more effective.

Evaluation

The study is based entirely on self-report data and this might have issues of unreliability due to human inconsistency in their answers, however the measures used were well established and tested to ensure their relevance and validity. The self-report data allows for a quick and easy comparison to be made and substantially reduces the cost of the investigation in terms of time and man power needed to do the equivalent interviews.

The study does not show which component had the most impact – the CBM I or the iCBT, nor does it really tell us what the CBM I actually did; rather than have a direct effect on depression it could act as a motivation booster at the outset of therapy leading to more adherence to the iCBT programme, or it could enable the generation of more positive possible outcomes from the behavioural tasks proscribed by the CBT making it more effective. However the change in depression scores found after week one indicates a positive outcome on depression even without the iCBT.

The study does show that computer-based therapy is effective very quickly, which means that people in need of therapy can access it very quickly rather than waiting until a therapist is available. This study suggests that up to 65 per cent of people with depression could benefit, although there is no information available as to the long-term effectiveness.

Evidence for the role of EPHX2 gene variants in anorexia nervosa (Scott-Van Zeeland et al., 2013)

Aim

The aim of this study was to investigate genetic variants associated with the development of anorexia nervosa.

Procedure

DNA samples were taken from a group of 261 patients diagnosed with anorexia nervosa, and 73 controls without the disorder, all of whom were female. Another group of 500 DNA samples from anorexic patients and 500 DNA samples from non-sufferers were taken from the Price Foundation sample repository for further comparison. The researchers investigated 152 candidate genes previously suggested to be associated with feeding behaviour, dopamine function, serotonin signalling and other biological mechanisms that could have a relationship with developing anorexia nervosa. Information was also gathered from the participants originally recruited for this research using data from various psychometric tests, such as Beck's Depression Inventory, as well as information about lifetime Body Mass Index (BMI).

Results

The initial sequencing phase of the study suggested that variants in two genes (ITPR3 and EPHX2) would be worth further investigation from more in-depth methods. The next phase of testing indicated that the most significant variants between the patients with anorexia and the controls were in the EPHX2 gene, which led to further analysis. On further investigation, those participants with anorexia, who also had the anorexia nervosa associated EPHX2 gene variants, showed the highest scores on a measure of depression (Beck's Depression Inventory) and lowest BMI scores.

The EPHX2 gene is associated with the body metabolising cholesterol, and other research has previously found that patients with anorexia often show high levels of cholesterol despite being malnourished. This would support the concept of variants in this gene being related to having anorexia. The EPHX2 gene is expressed in areas of neural tissue related to feeding behaviours and anxiety, both of which are behaviours associated with anorexia nervosa. For example, it has been found that there are high levels of expression of the EPHX2 gene in the paraventricular nucleus of the thalamus, which has been associated specifically with food and water intake, and the stress response. It has also been found that, in rats, this area of the brain is related to weight gain.

WIDER ISSUES AND DEBATES

Reductionism

The research laid out here provides strong evidence of genetic material linked with the development of anorexia. This would provide a strongly reductionist explanation for a disorder that has a very complex set of symptoms and features. Although some might argue that the evidence here is very credible and clearly suggests that genes can be implicated in the development of the illness, others would suggest that simply suggesting genes are to blame, especially in the face of compelling evidence from sociocultural explanations, is to take a very limited view of the disorder.

Conclusion

The evidence gathered from this study suggests that variants in the EPHX2 gene may increase the risk of developing anorexia nervosa. This gives rise to future research because currently very little is known about the biological causes of anorexia.

Evaluation

The information gathered in this study has added to the developing body of research helping to understand the origins of anorexia nervosa, which is an understudied disorder from a biological perspective. Much of the older research on this disorder has focused on sociocultural factors, as there was a preoccupation with this explanation. This research may suggest a temporal change in the move towards a more scientific understanding of the disorder. The advantage of the methods used in this study is that they are very reliable as the researchers were measuring gene variants using highly standardised methods and equipment. Another advantage is that the sample sizes used are quite large throughout all stages of the study, so there is a reasonable amount of validity in the conclusions drawn. However, all of the patient samples came from females, and although most anorexic patients are female, an increasing number of males are diagnosed, which means there is a lack of population validity in relation to the entire target population.

A possible problem with research like this is that we are still in a position where very little is actually known about the actions of many genes and therefore, although a relationship has been seemingly uncovered, the explanation for how this gene is implicated in anorexia is still not understood. Consequently a lot of the explanation provided about the role of the EPHX2 gene, which has been gained from animal research among other things, is guesswork with little reliable evidence to support it.

Imagining one's own and someone else's body actions: Dissociation in anorexia nervosa (Guardia et al., 2012)

Aim

The aim of the study was to continue previous research by the same team that had found that patients with anorexia nervosa found it difficult to gauge their own body size and misjudged their ability to fit through a 'door frame' that was clearly big enough for them. This study wanted to test this phenomenon further by considering whether this perceptual problem extended beyond the individual to other people; would they also misjudge the body size of other people in the same task?

Procedure

Participants were a group of 25 female patients from a clinic for eating disorders in Lille, France, all of whom met the DSM IV criteria for anorexia nervosa, and another 25 healthy, female controls who were all students. Each group was matched for age (mean approximately 24 years old) and level of education (around 13 years of education after primary school). In the anorexic group, 12 were diagnosed with restricting type, and 13 were diagnosed with binge/purge type. The BMI and shoulder width of each group is shown in the table below to give an indication of their actual body size:

Table 5.3 BMI and shoulder width of two groups of females

	BMI (mean kg/m²)	Shoulder width (mean cm)
Anorexia nervosa group	15.6	37.7
Control group	22.1	41.5

A door-frame shape was projected onto a wall to give the illusion of an opening that the participants could possibly walk through. In total, 51 different width shapes were projected onto the walls varying from 30 cm wide to 80 cm wide. The projections were presented in a random order, and each one was presented four times to each participant. Every participant, tested alone, was asked to predict if they could walk through each 'door frame' at normal speed without turning to the side (first person perspective). They were then asked whether another female researcher standing in the room could fit through the frame (third person perspective). The researcher had a similar BMI and shoulder width to the control group.

Results

Supporting previous findings, the group of patients with anorexia showed a significant overestimation of body size in themselves, judging that they would be unable to fit through door frames that were considerably bigger than their actual body size. However, the same was not found in the judgements of whether the researcher could pass through. Here they were much more accurate in predicting the body size of the 'other person' in relation to their ability to pass through the 'frame'. The evidence from the control group found that they showed no significant difference in their ability to accurately predict the 'passability' of either themselves or the 'other person'. Interestingly, the researchers also found a correlation between the 'passability' judgements made by the anorexia nervosa group and their pre-illness body weight/size.

Conclusion

Evidence in this study suggests that the patients have not adapted their internal body image to take into account their 'new' body size after developing the disorder. They suggest that the brain still perceives the body to be a larger size despite visual information that would contradict this. It was also discovered that patients who had lost weight in the six months before the study was conducted showed a greater difference between their own and the 'other person' passability perceptions – and there was a positive correlation between amount of weight lost and amount of difference between the two measures of passability. This would suggest that when anorexics lose weight their central nervous system cannot update the body image schema quickly enough to provide an accurate representation of current body size. This might explain why patients with anorexia continue to see themselves as bigger than they are and strive to continue to lose weight because their brain does not perceive their current size accurately.

Evaluation

One criticism that could be made is that the sample used in the study is limited in terms of size. Only 25 participants were studied in the experimental group and 25 in the control group so this is perhaps not sufficient to support a generalised conclusion that anorexia nervosa affects one's own body size perceptions and not that of others.

> ### Research methods: generalisability
> A small sample size such as this study on 25 anorexic patients compared to 25 controls, all of whom were female, provides very limited data from which to generalise to the target population. Although many anorexics are female, not all are, and males are not represented at all in this research. Likewise, the evidence from only 25 patients in one clinic is unlikely to represent all patients suffering from anorexia as they are all from the same area and they were all relatively young. Older patients, or patients from different cultural groups, may be seriously underrepresented.

The sample could also be criticised for being all a similar age and all female, however the majority of sufferers with anorexia are young females so the sample is appropriate for many of the target population. Another criticism is that the experimenter used in the third person perspective condition had a body size that more closely matched the control group than the patient group. This may have meant that the control group had an advantage at estimating her ability to pass through the 'frame' projected on the wall. However, the researchers themselves identified that in order to get a 'third person' who had a similar body size may involve having patients with anorexia nervosa judge the body size of another person with the disorder. This carries with it ethical concerns in relation to making judgements of the body size of people who already have body image-related issues.

The study may lack validity in the sense that making a visual judgement of a person's ability to pass through a virtual door frame is different to actually attempting to walk through the projected shape. A better test of this may be to project the frame onto the wall and then observe the participant's approach to the 'opening' to see whether they walk as if they can fit through it, or if they begin to turn or slow down as if they will be unable to pass through. This would allow a more realistic idea of the body image the participant holds in their mind.

Quality of life in OCD: Differential impact of obsessions, compulsions, and depression comorbidity (Masellis et al., 2003)

Aim

To investigate the separate impact of features of OCD and to understand the effect of comorbid depression on the life experience of OCD sufferers. The authors point out that OCD is the fourth most frequently occurring mental health disorder and that compared to schizophrenia and depression there had been little examination about how the disorder impacts on the quality of life of sufferers. This study aimed to see the differential impact of obsessions or compulsions on quality of life; it has been assumed that the compulsive behaviour has most effect as it involves getting stuck in routines such as repetitive hand washing that the person does not feel they can avoid, and many therapeutic interventions focus on this aspect. It also wanted to unpick the effect of comorbid depression as estimates show depression co-occurs in between 31.7 per cent and 60.3 per cent of OCD cases. Their hypothesis was that the severity of the symptoms of OCD would impact on quality of life and that in cases where depression is comorbid quality of life would be negatively affected.

Procedure

There were 43 participants aged between 18 and 65 (average 34.9 years) years old, of predominantly European ethnicity, diagnosed with OCD using DSM IV criteria recruited from the Toronto area of Canada. Those with schizophrenia, bipolar disorder or substance misuse were excluded.

Several measures were taken from each participant.

1 the Yale-Brown OCD Scale (Y-BOCS) was used to assess the level of OCD symptoms, this is a 10-item scale using a 5-point Likert measure where 0 equates to no symptoms and 4 to severe, for example:

How much of your time is occupied by obsessive thoughts?

None	Less than 1 hour a day	1–3 hours a day	3–8 hours a day	More than 8 hours per day
0	1	2	3	4

2 The illness intrusiveness rating scale (IIRS) is a measure of quality of life that asks about the interference of symptoms across 13 life domains important to quality of life, for example, diet, work, and recreation. It uses a 7-point Likert scale where a low score indicates little interference.

3 The Beck Depression Inventory was also used to measure symptom severity of depression. This is a 21-item multiple choice questionnaire relating to symptoms of depression.

All participants completed all three measures and the researchers used these as a basis for investigating relationships between the data. Specifically they were testing to see if any of the clinical or demographic data they had gathered predict the scores achieved on the IIRS.

The results were as follows.

- Demographic data yielded no significant results in that age, marital status, education level, age of onset or gender did not affect severity of symptoms, so no one type of person was more likely to suffer more.

- Scores on Y-BOCS significantly correlated with scores on IIRS.

- Severity of depression predicted high scores on IIRS.

- Separating the obsessive element from the Y-BOCS showed that this significantly predicted high scores on IIRS.

- Separating the compulsive element from the Y-BOCS did not predict high scores on IIRS at a significant level.

Conclusions

Obsessive thoughts, images and impulses are more associated with distress than compulsions, which can be regarded as strategies used to reduce distress brought on by obsessions. However, the current treatment often focuses on treating the compulsions, which might not alleviate distress as effectively as treatments that focus on the obsessive elements. One study found that between 17 per cent and 44 per cent of OCD patients only have compulsions (Stavrakaki and Vargo, 1986) and 75 per cent of patients seeking help for OCD also have depression, arguably then behaviourist-based therapy such as Exposure and Response Prevention Treatment could be used. So this current study indicates a need for therapy to refocus on obsessions and on alleviating symptoms of depression to get a better outcome for sufferers.

Evaluation

This study relies on self-report data, which may be criticised as a potential source of unreliability because it depends on honesty and consistency on the part of the respondent. However, the measures taken here are all from well-tested, widely used, valid scales that indicate that the data used here is reliable and potentially objective. There may be an issue in measuring depressive symptoms as these fluctuate and it might be that this measure is not quite as reliable as other measures. The authors suggest that a longitudinal design might be better where the symptoms of depression are tracked over time and linked to the quality of life measure in this way.

A further issue is that other comorbid anxiety disorders are not controlled for here and there is no investigation as to the impact that these might have on the quality of life data. It is well known that other anxiety disorders are common among OCD sufferers.

The study has useful application in that it has highlighted an issue with the current offering of therapy suggesting that there should be more focus on a cognitive therapy as opposed to a behaviourist one. This kind of finding is useful in planning resource allocation because it provides evidence about likely effectiveness of different forms of therapy.

POTS team (Paediatric OCD Treatment Study) including March et al. (2004) Cognitive Behavior Therapy, Sertraline and Their Combination for Children and Adolescents with OCD

Aim

The aim was to see if CBT on its own is more or less effective than a drug treatment or if having CBT and drug treatment combined is more effective in treating young people with OCD. Statistics show that 1 in 200 young people have OCD and that between 33 per cent and 50 per cent of adult sufferers developed OCD in childhood. This study was funded by the National Institution for Mental Health in the USA in order to find the best early intervention.

Procedure

A volunteer sample of 112 children and adolescents aged between 7 and 17 years (average age 11.7 years) were recruited from among those who had been diagnosed with OCD using DSM IV. The severity of their symptoms were measured using the **Children's Yale–Brown Obsessive–Compulsive Scale** (CY–BOCS) and only those with a score of 16 and above on this scale were included. Children who were comorbid with other disorders such as Tourette's and major depression were excluded in order to avoid interaction effects. Children with **ADHD** were accepted as long as they were on **stimulant medication** and were stable. The children were not on any anti-obsessional medication at the outset.

Allocation to one of four conditions was done randomly using a computerised system. The conditions were: drugs-only, placebo-pill only, CBT-only and combination of CBT and drug. All the children were interviewed and their baseline measure taken using the CY–BOCS using independent evaluators. The study lasted 12 weeks and each child had a specialist psychiatrist to monitor their progress and offer support throughout.

The drugs-only condition and the placebo conditions required the children to attend weekly for the first six weeks of the study and then every other week (nine times in total). The dose would be established and changed as necessary during the clinical session; during the week their parents would monitor that the medication was taken and they kept a medication diary. Any adverse reactions would result in the medication being changed or stopped.

The CBT-only condition required 14 clinical sessions over the 12-week period. The therapy was standard based on the CBT manual and involved psychological education, cognitive training, mapping OCD target symptoms and exposure and response ritual prevention. Each session involved the setting of goals, a review of the previous week, therapist assisted practice, homework and monitoring. The manual was used flexibly according to the developmental stage of the child.

The combined condition was the drug and CBT sessions, time linked and provided simultaneously. It was not felt necessary to include a CBT and placebo comparison.

The participants were assessed again at weeks 4 and 8 and finally at week 12 by independent evaluators trained to a reliable standard. This process was strictly supervised and reviewed to establish reliability.

Key terms

Children's Yale–Brown Obsessive–Compulsive Scale: a self-rating scale used to measure depression in children and adolescents.

ADHD: a syndrome of behaviours including inability to sustain attention, impulsivity and restlessness.

Stimulant medication: drugs prescribed to treat ADHD that change neurotransmitter levels and increase focus.

Results

Of the 112 starters, 97 participants completed the study. All conditions showed improvement at 12 weeks as measured on CY–BOCS, however the placebo improvement was not significant. In the CBT-alone condition, 39.3 per cent entered remission (measured as a drop below 10 on the CY–BOCS) compared to 21.4 per cent in the drugs-alone condition. However, this figure rose marginally in the combined condition.

Table 5.4 Average drop in symptoms as measured by CY–BOCS in each condition

	CBT alone	Drug alone	Combination	Placebo
Baseline measure	26	23.5	23.8	25.2
Final measure	14	16.5	11.2	21.5
Difference	−12	−7	−12.6	−4.7

Conclusion

The study showed a clear effect of CBT leading to a higher improvement rate than drugs, suggesting that the first line of treatment should be CBT. Minimal gain can be added by including the drugs where effective CBT is provided, however it may be that the drug can compensate for less effective therapy. But these drugs require careful monitoring as SSRIs have been linked to suicidal ideation in young people. This study however showed that the treatment was well tolerated.

Evaluation

The study was conducted over three centres and run by two universities in tandem. There were some differences in the results in that one centre had better results on the CBT-only and this might be due to a therapist effect with one centre perhaps being more proficient at CBT; however all participating centres used the CBT manual in order to maintain consistency in treatment.

The sample was large and representative of the target population with a low drop-out rate (87 per cent completed the study). Analysis of the sample in each condition showed no difference between them so the differences in outcome cannot be attributed to individual differences between each target group.

All participants gave full written consent as did at least one of their parents. The fact that each one had an assigned psychiatrist to monitor and support them is a further ethical benefit. Those on the drug were regularly checked and dosages changed as necessary, thus protecting them from harm. Everyone in the placebo condition was offered the therapy on completion of the study.

The assessors were blind to the condition the participants were in so they could not be biased in their evaluation of improvements. The participants in the placebo condition were unaware that the drug was not active and neither was the therapist. The assessors were trained and monitored in order to ensure reliability in the measure of change and the scale used to assess change was a well-recognised, valid and reliable one.

All of the above combine to make this a well-controlled study, which provides a sound evidence base on which to evaluate the effectiveness of common therapies.

5.4 Key question
Learning outcomes

In this section, you will learn about one key issue of relevance in today's society. You will need to be able to:

- describe the key issue and its importance to today's society

- apply concepts, theories and research used in clinical psychology to explain the key issue.

This section will describe an example of the key issue of how mental health issues are portrayed in the media. However, you can choose your own key issue and relate it to theories, concepts and research used in the social approach.

How are mental health issues portrayed in the media?

According to Time to Change, an organisation set up to influence public attitudes to mental health issues, the way mental illness is portrayed and reported in the media is incredibly powerful in educating and influencing the public.

Signorielli (1989) found that 72 per cent of characters with a mental illness depicted in prime-time television were violent. Other studies found them to be unemployable or if employed, failing at work. A New Zealand study that conducted a thematic analysis of mental illness on television found danger/aggression, unpredictability, incompetence and childlike to be common themes, with the overall portrayal of mental illness as 'outstandingly negative'.

Discussion of the issue using concepts, theories and research drawn from clinical psychology

The mass media is the primary source of information for most people about mental health disorders, yet it contains misinformation and the inaccurate use of terminology. It teaches conventions on how to treat people with a mental health issue through consistent and recurrent messages that present a very negative and biased view of mental illness. Diefenbach (1997) analysed the content of prime-time television in the USA over a 2-week period and found that 32 per cent of programmes had at least one character with a mental illness and that these characters were ten times more violent than the general population of television characters, with 50 per cent of violent offences being committed by someone with a mental health disorder. Granello and Pauley (2000) found that intolerant attitudes towards those with mental illness were significantly and positively related to amount of television viewing.

In a content analysis of how mental illness has been portrayed in 50 years of Hollywood films, Lopez Levers (2001) found that mental illness is largely portrayed as passive, pathetic or comical, but is most frequently depicted as dangerous; requiring restraints or invasive procedures. These depictions of mental illness do not reflect the reality of mental illness within society today, but demonstrate how stereotypical views of mental illness are used in film iconography. In fact, mentally ill people are more likely to be the victims of violence than the perpetrators. However, these media depictions have been shown to affect public attitudes towards mental illness; a third of the public still believes that someone with a mental health issue is prone to violence (*Attitudes to Mental Health*, 2013).

In a review of media depiction of mental illness for the American Psychological Association (Tartakovsky, 2009), it was said that the media portrays depression as a chemical imbalance. Although this media image removes the view that depression is some moral failing on the part of an individual, it does perpetuate the idea that neurotransmitters are a significant factor associated with depression and can be cured by a wonder drug. Of course, there is research to suggest that serotonin is implicated in depression; but the improvements shown by serotonin drug research may suffer from publication bias.

Exam tip

It is best to start a key issues answer with a question and then seek to answer it. The issue chosen is up to you but it should be something of general interest that lends itself to a psychological discussion or explanation.

Other research suggests that providing a medical cause for disorders such as schizophrenia will reduce the blame associated with the disorder but does not change the prejudices linked to schizophrenia, such as unpredictability and danger (Penn et al., 2003); in fact, they found that it made people given this explanation more likely to avoid those with the disorder in future.

Wahl (2000) conducted a content analysis of articles dealing with OCD and found that although most were fairly accurate depictions of the disorder there were several that linked it to stalking behaviour thus confusing it with obsessive behaviour and spreading misinformation.

The media image of depression as a female disorder seems consistent with the statistical prevalence of mood disorders among women. However, the idea that depression is a female disorder may simply reflect the potential over-diagnosis of the illness in the female population perpetuated by stereotypes.

If diagnosis carries a stigma with it then people who need help might not seek it for fear of being labelled. This can impact on the course of the disorder as for some illnesses an early intervention is very beneficial. Research by Brown and Bradley in the USA (2002) suggests that 25 per cent of people with a mental health issue do not seek treatment and suggest that stigma is a primary cause of this.

Rosenhan's study shows how normal behaviour can be misinterpreted as symptomatic of a disorder once the label has been applied. If the information about mental health is negative, then the behaviour of those labelled with the disorder can be interpreted as negative. If the only examples of people with mental health issues are frightening and linked to violence, then these are the labels that will be applied.

One further issue of relevance here is the potential alienation of people suffering from mental health disorders; if people believe that those with mental health disorders represent a threat they will be less likely to interact with them. This might then rob them of the positive reinforcements to be gained by social interactions, which can act as a protective factor, possibly lessening the severity of the course of the disorder by providing social support and motivation to comply with treatments and to not give up.

Media exposure to mental health issues can help to ameliorate some of the negative attitudes and stereotypes that exist in society, remove the belief that individuals with mental health issues are a threat and help to portray a more positive image that could lead to more rational attitudes among the public. On the other hand, positive representations in the media can help to change attitudes; recent celebrity stories of mental health issues provide examples of successful people who the public can relate to, which helps to counter the negative views. For example, Stephen Fry (UK actor and comedian) talked about living with bipolar disorder and has become a supporter for mental health charities including the Time to Change campaign, which is run by the charities Mind and Rethink Mental Illness and works to change attitudes towards mental health. By using social learning theory effectively in this way, through the use of high-profile models either talking about their own experiences, or supporting other people with mental health issues, public opinion is changing.

Mental health campaigns such as 'Time to Change' work hard to raise awareness and to normalise mental health issues such as publicising the 'one in four' which reminds people that one in every four people will experience mental health issues at some time. It has also offered guidance for television programmes portraying mental illness to allow a sensitive and accurate portrayal to take place.

By increasing the sources of information about mental health and involving high status persons in doing so the message becomes more powerful and persuasive. It makes mental health more mainstream and less scary for people.

This is demonstrated in some recent research into public attitudes to mental health that found a significant decrease in intolerance over the last few years (*Attitudes to Mental Health*, 2013). This report gathered 18 years of survey data regarding the public perception towards mental health and suggested that attitudes (particularly women's attitudes) to mental health issues have improved markedly since 1994.

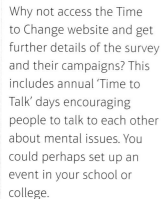

Taking it further

Why not access the Time to Change website and get further details of the survey and their campaigns? This includes annual 'Time to Talk' days encouraging people to talk to each other about mental issues. You could perhaps set up an event in your school or college.

5.5 Practical investigation

Learning outcomes

In this section, you will learn how to:

- conduct a summative content analysis on a topic in clinical psychology
- gather data from two sources relevant to answering a specific research question about attitudes to mental health
- perform a summative analysis based on data from two sources
- explore ethical issues associated with this type of research.

Summative content analysis

A content analysis is a technique used to quantify qualitative data. Over recent years several different types of content analysis have emerged.

- Conventional content analysis involves the coding of categories that have emerged from a review and analysis of the raw data.

- Directive content analysis is when the initial coding categories that are used in the analysis are derived from previous theory or research. This means that they are initially predetermined categories, although they may be revised as the raw data is analysed. This type of content analysis is typically used to extend or develop knowledge about an existing topic.

- Summative content analysis involves counting the frequency of key words/terms or content in the data. These key words can be determined before or during the analysis of the raw data. Then the frequency of the key terms are further assessed in terms of the context; who said the key word, in what way was it said, to whom, for example.

You will need to conduct a summative content analysis, which follows roughly the same process as a conventional content analysis, but you will need instead to consider the type of key words of interest to your topic of investigation. You will first need to calculate the frequencies of key word use within the content of two sources: this is known as the manifest content. Then you will need to go beyond superficial analysis of the manifest content and interpret the key words in the context of the two sources, this interpretation will give rise to the meaningful latent content.

For example, you might seek to analyse the content of news articles on the same topic but from media aimed at different audiences such as comparing *The Sun* with *The Times* on their coverage of key words associated with mental health issues. In this practical investigation example, a summative content analysis will be conducted on two films that depict mental illness.

WIDER ISSUES AND DEBATES

Issues related to socially sensitive research

You should think about the possible impact of your findings on different groups in society if there is any chance that your conclusions could be socially sensitive. For example, if you found that certain cultural groups have more negative attitudes than others, it might be detrimental to them to make this public.

You should also ensure that you do not overstate and sensationalise your findings, perhaps check them with a more experienced researcher, especially as the data and the categories are your own subjective interpretation of the content of the material being analysed.

Research question

First of all you must have a research question that can be answered using this method. This must be about attitudes towards mental health issues. For the purposes of illustrating the method we will ask whether media depictions of mental health issues and treatment have changed over the years.

Sample

This then allows us to select our sample materials for analysis. For instance we could look at the depiction of mental health in popular mainstream films about the subject from different eras, but you could use any source; they do not have to be of the same type so you could compare a print source with a film-based source. You need to select two sources.

A quick Internet search showed that there is a range of films to choose from, for example *One Flew Over the Cuckoo's Nest* and *Girl, Interrupted* both deal with mental health issues and therapy but one film was made in 1975 and the other in 1999. Or you could look at the differences between a film from 1960, *Psycho*, and another from 1999, *Fight Club*, both of which depict cases of dissociative identity disorder.

Whatever source you decide to use, it will be easier for your analysis if you transcribe the qualitative data into text form, unless it is already done for you of course. This can be a laborious process because even a small amount of content can take a long time to transcribe. If you are using a film source, try to restrict your analysis to a five- or ten-minute clip.

Defining keywords

From the research question we would then formulate a hypothesis: there will be a greater number of negative references to people with mental disorders in an older film compared to a more recent film. This will allows us to see whether media depictions of mental disorders have changed over time.

Deciding what key words to use in your initial manifest content analysis can be done before or during a review of the text. In this practical example, we are looking to see how mental illness is depicted in films, in particular the references made to derogatory terms about people with mental illness.

Analysis

Once the film material has been transcribed, the content needs to be reviewed and the frequency of the key words can be counted and compared across each film. Remember that the predetermined key words can be modified or added to once your review begins.

It is important to ensure the validity and reliability of your summative content analysis, so an expert could be consulted, for example in the field of clinical research, to check the validity of the key terms, and multiple coders could be used to assess the same material. If there is a good level of agreement between the coders, inter-coder reliability can be established.

Once the frequencies of key words have been calculated you need to go beyond this superficial analysis and consider the context in which they key words were used. In this practical example the people involved in the dialogue and the direction of the communication will be considered for latent content analysis; this will involve examining whether the word was spoken by a patient to another patient, by a patient to a health professional, by a health professional to a patient, and other directions of dialogue.

Key words

The key words associated with negative attitudes towards mental illness can be explicit or euphemisms.

Loony

Nutcase

Crazy

Dangerous

Has a screw loose

Lost their marbles

Mad

Insane

Cuckoo

Psycho

Schizo

Loopy

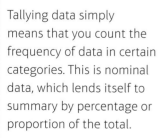

Maths tip

Tallying data simply means that you count the frequency of data in certain categories. This is nominal data, which lends itself to summary by percentage or proportion of the total.

Table 5.5 below is an example coding sheet to record the frequency of key words and subsequent latent content analysis.

Table 5.5 Types of communication used between characters

	Crazy	Loony	Nutcase	Mad
Patient to patient	111111	1	1111111	111
Patient to mental health professional	11		111111	
Mental health professional to mental health professional	1111	1111111	1	11111
Mental health professional to patient	1	1111111111	111	11
Patient to relative/friends	11	11	1	
Relative/friends to patient	1		1	1
Other (specify relationship)		To taxi driver 1	By taxi driver to patient 11	

This data could then be converted to tables of percentages describing the data – for example, for equal status communication.

Table 5.6 Types of communication used between characters – shown as percentages

	Crazy
Patient to patient	36%
Patient to mental health professional	12%
Mental health professional to mental health professional	24%
Mental health professional to patient	6%
Patient to relative/friends	12%
Relative/friends to patient	6%
Other (specify relationship)	0%

You could then translate this to a chart showing the data graphically.

Types of communication used between characters

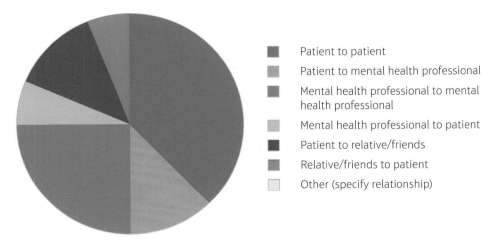

Figure 5.5 Types of communication used between characters – shown as a diagram

Drawing conclusions

This technique is very time-consuming to do properly, but can be flexibly applied across a range of different materials. It provides an objective account of the meaning of communications that might not otherwise be evident, which can reveal deep latent issues. When you begin to interpret the latent content of the material, it is important to examine relationships, trends and comparisons between the sources that can be used to explain what is going on within the film. Try to justify your interpretations with evidence from the data.

An analysis of one source in this example practical investigation reveals that the use of the key word 'crazy' was used in greater frequency between patients and between mental health professionals. This suggests that stereotypical notions of mental illness were being transmitted not only casually between patients as a form of everyday communication, but also between health professions – suggesting that stereotypes of mental illness were institutional terms of reference. However, this key word is not directed at the patient by a mental health professional suggesting some level of professionalism or perhaps clinical guidelines on the use of stereotypical language in front of patients. This interpretation should be compared with the other source to see if the same frequency of key word and pattern of communication exists.

Evaluation

To evaluate your practical investigation it is useful to consider the strengths and weaknesses of using a qualitative method like summative content analysis. This method of analysis examines how the key words are used in the film but during the quantification process the actual meaning and context of these key words may be lost. For example, during the film one patient says the key word 'screw loose' to another patient. However, on closer scrutiny of the context of the film it is clear that he is using the euphemism to describe how the patient is viewed by health professionals. In the next line of the film, the patient makes it clear that the other patient is not mentally ill at all. This demonstrates how meaningfulness is lost when using research methods that quantify qualitative data.

Because you are evaluating your practical investigation you may wish to consider issues of generalisability of your sources, inter-coder reliability, validity, credibility, objectivity and subjectivity. You should also consider possible changes that could be made to improve your practical investigation.

WIDER ISSUES AND DEBATES

Ethics

As you are not dealing with actual people in the investigation then the usual guidelines of protection from harm and withdrawal do not apply. However, you must ensure that the information you analyse is not private or confidential and is in the public domain or you have explicit permission from those whose material it is you are analysing, or those featured within it if not publically available.

You should also think about the possible impact of your findings on different groups in society if there is any chance that your conclusions could be socially sensitive. For example, you might find that certain cultural groups have more negative attitudes than others; it might be detrimental to them to make this public.

You should also ensure that you do not overstate and sensationalise your findings, perhaps check them with a more experienced researcher, especially as the data and the categories are your own subjective interpretation of the content of the material being analysed.

5.6 Issues and debates (A level only)

In this section, you will learn about issues and debates relevant to clinical psychology. You will have already noticed that issues and debates have been mentioned throughout this topic. This section will draw together the main themes and ideas related to the clinical approach as a whole.

Ethics

Clinical trials are an essential part of testing the effectiveness of therapies and ascertaining possible side effects, but they are not without ethical issues for the participants. Such people may be vulnerable and great care must be taken to ensure that no unnecessary harm is done. For example, these trials must be well controlled in order to ensure that the evidence found is reliable and generalisable. This is likely to involve the use of single-blind trials in which patients may or may not be given a placebo, in order to control for expectation effect. The patients who do not receive treatment might be denied a therapy that could improve their condition or quality of life. This is dealt with by putting them on the treatment as soon as the trial is complete, assuming that the results support the effectiveness of the therapy.

Practical issues in the design and implementation of research

When conducting research in clinical psychology psychologists may prefer to focus on qualitative data from case studies and interviews because of the variety of possible factors involved in each individual's experience of their illness and treatment. The issue with this is that, in comparison to quantitative data, the data can be difficult to analyse and the conclusions drawn are at risk of being unreliable and subjective. This may be a concern for clinical psychologists as they will have to weigh up the advantage of having more valid data about each patient, with the chance that the data gathered will have limited reliability.

Reductionism

Isolating mental health to a biological process in the brains of those who experience disorders is a contentious issue. It simplifies a complex behaviour by focusing on purely biological factors such as neurotransmitters and pathways in the brain at the expense of understanding the interrelationships between biology and environment. This leads to biological treatments designed to alter brain structure or chemistry. Many would argue that it is not appropriate to treat mental health in this way because it ignores the influence of environmental and other factors, which do not lend themselves to a medical intervention. Recent therapies, such as family therapy, recognise the importance of communication and relationships within the family as a mediating factor for triggering relapse of mental illness. This approach is less reductionist because it does not only focus on one component of mental illness, but instead looks at the wider social, emotional, communication and family support involved.

Comparison between ways of explaining behaviour using different themes

Clinical psychology considers explanations for mental illness from many different approaches, which means that the same behaviour is explained using a variety of themes. A common theme for most disorders is the use of biological factors such as genes and brain chemistry to explain the origins of illnesses. However, different disorders will have various other factors that could explain their development. For example, there is credible evidence to support sociocultural factors as an explanation for anorexia but the same factors could not be used to explain the origins of disorders such as OCD. Clinical psychologists can also use two different methods of categorising and diagnosing mental illnesses using the DSM or the ICD. These take a slightly different route to achieving the same ends by exploring the same behaviour in slightly different ways.

Psychology as a science

There has been a consistent drive in clinical psychology to apply the systems used to treat issues with physical health to mental health issues. This has meant that the medical model dominates clinical psychology with its diagnostic system and drug treatments. This is a highly scientific model, which builds theoretical explanations through the use of empirical research methods for the causes of disorders and develops treatments based on these explanations. For example, biological theories for depression have been developed through the manipulation of neurotransmitters and observation of the effect. Clinical psychology has also progressed the development of brain-imaging techniques, now used in research to investigate the relationship between brain structure and function and behaviour.

Culture

This issue is linked to ideas of social control because the definition of abnormal behaviour and the classification of such behaviour as a diagnosis is culturally determined. Although the scientific medical model would argue that mental health disorders are universal in the same way that other physical disorders are, this can be challenged by the existence of culturally specific disorders and by differences in the diagnostic criteria that exist between the American DSM and the European ICD systems.

The new DSM V has been specifically designed over the past ten years to ensure that individuals from all backgrounds can be diagnosed using the manual. This has been developed from extensive cross-cultural research that has identified the different symptoms associated with mental illnesses and adding those variations to each mental disorder category. The DSM V also now includes guidance on how to conduct a clinical interview with someone from a different culture.

Nature–nurture

Throughout psychology the causes of behaviour have been debated as to whether they stem more from biological forces (nature) such as genes, brain structure or biochemistry or from environmental factors driving changes in behaviour. This argument can easily be applied to clinical psychology where all disorders have competing explanations, some of which are nature based or biological and some of which are psychological and focus more on nurture. Most psychologists would argue that this is a false debate because there is a constant interaction between nature and nurture, which combines to create behaviour. For example, the diathesis-stress model proposes that a genetic vulnerability towards a mental health problem interacts with social and psychological factors to create a maladaptive reaction when an environmental trigger is experienced.

An understanding of how psychological knowledge has developed over time

The first edition of the DSM, DSM I was published in 1952 as a way to categorise mental health problems based on the symptoms. Over the past 60 years, a further four versions of the DSM have been published, which reflect the changing understanding of the symptoms and causes of these illnesses. For example, the DSM IV was developed to assess patients' behaviour on five different axes to help devise a conclusive diagnosis. But the development of DSM V based on work with a number of leading clinicians moved away from multi-axial diagnosis and instead focuses on cross-referencing symptoms to take them from a general diagnosis to a more specific diagnosis. The newer versions of DSM are also making attempts to include more culture-bound syndromes suggesting a move away from the view that this tool is a way to diagnose illnesses in 'western cultures,' which do not apply similarly across all cultures. Another area of historical change is in the development of treatments for mental disorders. For example, older medical treatments for schizophrenia came in the form of typical antipsychotics such as chlorpromazine and haloperidol but the reported side effects led to the development of atypical neuroleptics like clozapine and olanzapine, which have fewer side effects and are more likely to be used regularly by patients as a result.

Issues of social control

Is there exertion of control by society over the behaviour of the individual or group of people? This includes abnormal behaviour such as is defined by the 4Ds and therefore applies to people experiencing mental health issues. By labelling behaviour as abnormal it leads to diagnosis, which pathologises the behaviour. Some would argue (for example, those in the anti-psychiatry movement) that this forces people to conform to the standards set by society and if they do not, then they must receive treatment that will normalise their behaviour, such as antipsychotic drugs prescribed to people with schizophrenia or other psychoses. It might be argued that if we did not label the behaviour as abnormal and did not seek to apply a diagnosis to it, then people would be free to behave how they liked. Others, however, would argue that antipsychotic medication is critical for alleviating the distress associated with schizophrenia and enabling quality of life to be restored.

The use of psychological knowledge in society

There are negative issues within clinical psychology, such as how social control can be exerted through the misuse of diagnoses and treatments, and there are issues with the reliability and validity of diagnoses suggesting that the system is not perfect. But there can be no doubt that clinical psychology has made a major contribution to society in terms of providing effective treatments for disorders that seriously impair the lives of those who experience them. In addition, it has led to wider acceptance of those with mental disorders as understanding increases about their causes. Successful treatments have led to relief of symptoms enabling people who once might have been consigned to a mental institution to live in the community. It could be argued that the development of pharmaceutical drugs has been the most significant contribution to society in the last 100 years. Before the development of medication to treat mental illness, patients would probably have been institutionalised and subject to physically invasive and aggressive treatments, such as electroconvulsive therapy, insulin coma therapy and lobotomy. These earlier treatments caused significant injury and the possibility of death.

Issues related to socially sensitive research

Studying mental health issues can most certainly be considered an area of socially sensitive research. The research involves labelling people with an illness in order to then investigate the possible causes or treatments for the illness. There could possibly be negative outcomes for the patient from taking part in research in this area. One example of this would be in research into anorexia nervosa such as the study by Guardia et al. (2012) where the patients were being asked to compare their body size to that of another person. A common symptom of anorexia is low self-esteem and encouraging them to actively compare their body size to others may further harm their vision of themselves having a negative effect on self-esteem.

Knowledge check

Content

In the content section you are required to describe, evaluate and apply your knowledge of mental health issues and ways of treating them.

> To check your evaluation skills, refer to the introduction section of this book and review 'how to evaluate a theory'. Remember that you may be asked to consider issues of validity, reliability, credibility, generalisability, objectivity and subjectivity in your evaluation of theories.
>
> Can you describe the process of diagnosing mental disorders with reference to the four 'Ds': deviance, dysfunction, distress and danger?

Are you able to explain the ICD and DSM IV-TR or DSM V classification systems used in the diagnosis of mental health disorders?

Can you explain individual differences in mental health disorders due to cultural differences?

Do you know how clinical psychologists assess the reliability of diagnoses of mental health disorders?

Are you confident that you can explain how clinicians establish the validity of diagnoses of mental health disorders?

Can you explain the influence of cultural differences in the diagnosis of mental health disorders, and how these can affect reliability and validity?

Can you describe the positive and negative symptoms and features of schizophrenia, including thought insertion, hallucinations, delusions and disordered thinking?

Can you describe and evaluate the function of neurotransmitters as a theory or explanation of schizophrenia?

Can you describe and evaluate one other biological theory or explanation of schizophrenia, such as genetic or neuroanatomical theories?

Are you able to describe and evaluate a non-biological theory or explanation of schizophrenia, such as cognitive theories?

Are you able to apply your knowledge of biological explanations (genetics and neurochemicals) for schizophrenia to discuss issues in developmental psychology?

Can you describe and evaluate two treatments – one biological and one psychological – for schizophrenia?

Can you describe the symptoms and features of one other mental health disorder, such as anorexia nervosa, obsessive–compulsive disorder (OCD) or unipolar depression?

For your chosen disorder, can you describe and evaluate a biological theory or explanation for it?

For the same disorder, can you describe and evaluate a non-biological theory or explanation for it?

Are you confident that you can describe and evaluate two treatments – one biological and one psychological – for this same disorder?

Methods

Do you know and understand the Health and Care Professions Council (HCPC) guidelines for clinical practitioners?

Can you distinguish between primary and secondary data and evaluate their use in researching mental health?

Are you able to identify, describe and evaluate research methods used in clinical psychology, including longitudinal studies, cross-sectional studies, cross-cultural methods and meta-analyses?

Are you able to describe the use of case studies in clinical psychology with reference to a case study, such as the Lavarenne et al. (2013) research into schizophrenia, and evaluate the usefulness of the results?

Can you describe the use of interviews in clinical psychology with reference to an interview study, such as the use of semi-structured interviews by Vallentine et al. (2010), and evaluate the reliability of this method?

Are you able to analyse and draw conclusions from quantitative data, including using both descriptive and inferential statistical testing (chi-square, Spearman's rho, Wilcoxon and Mann-Whitney U)?

Are you confident you can use thematic analysis and grounded theory to analyse and interpret qualitative data?

Studies

> In the studies section you are required to describe, evaluate and apply your knowledge of one classic study and two contemporary studies, one of which must be on schizophrenia and the other on another disorder such as depression, anorexia or OCD.
>
> To check your evaluation skills, refer to the introduction section of this book and review 'how to evaluate a study'. Remember that you may be asked to consider issues of validity, reliability, credibility, generalisability, objectivity and subjectivity in your evaluation of studies.

Can you describe the classic study by Rosenhan (1973) On being sane in insane places, in terms of its aim(s), method, procedure, results and conclusions?

Are you able to evaluate Rosenhan's (1973) study in terms of strengths and weaknesses?

Can you describe the contemporary study by Carlsson et al. (2000) Network interactions in schizophrenia – therapeutic implications, in terms of its aim(s), method, procedure, results and conclusions?

Are you able to evaluate the study by Carlsson et al. (2000) in terms of strengths and weaknesses?

Are you able to identify and describe the aims, method, procedure, results and conclusions of a contemporary study from the following list and evaluate the study in terms of strengths and weaknesses?

Depression:

- Kroenke et al. (2009) The PHQ-8 as a measure of current depression in the general population.

- Williams et al. (2013) Combining imagination and reason in the treatment of depression: a randomised control trial of internet-based cognitive-bias modification and internet-CBT for depression.

Anorexia

- Scott-Van Zeeland et al. (2013) Evidence for the role of EPHX2 gene variants in anorexia nervosa.

- Guardia et al. (2012) Imagining One's Own and Someone Else's Body Actions: Dissociation in Anorexia Nervosa.

OCD

- Masellis et al. (2003) Quality of life in OCD: Differential impact of obsessions, compulsions, and depression comorbidity.

- POTS team including March J.S., et al. (2004) Cognitive behavior therapy, Sertraline and their combination for children and adolescents with OCD.

Key question

Are you able to identify and describe a key question in clinical psychology that is relevant to today's society?

Can you explain this key question using concepts, theories and research that you have studied in clinical psychology?

Practical investigation

Have you designed and conducted a summative content analysis to compare attitudes towards mental health?

Can you justify your choice of research question and/or hypothesis?

Can you justify your choice of design and sampling method?

Can you describe and analyse the quantitative data that you gathered for your study (from at least two sources) and how you presented your data?

Can you explain the ethical considerations involved in content analysis?

> Remember that you may be asked to consider issues of validity, reliability, credibility, generalisability, objectivity and subjectivity in your evaluation of your practical investigation.

Issues and debates (A level only)

> Remember that issues and debates are synoptic. This means you may be asked to make connections by comparing issues and debates across topics in psychology or comment on issues and debates within unseen material.

Can you identify ethical issues associated with theory and research within the clinical approach?

Can you comment on the practical and methodological issues in the design and implementation of research within the clinical approach?

Can you explain how theories, research and concepts within the clincial approach might be considered reductionist?

Can you compare theories and research within clinical psychology to show different ways of explaining and understanding behaviour?

Are you able to discuss whether theories, concepts, research and methodology within clinical psychology are scientific?

Are you able to discuss the nature–nurture debate in the context of clinical psychology, in terms of which parts emphasise the role or nature and nurture or the interaction between them?

Do you understand how clinical psychology has developed over time?

Do you understand what is meant by social control and how research within clinical psychology may be used to control behaviour?

Can you show how the theories, concepts and research within clinical psychology can be used in a practical way in society?

Are you able to understand what is meant by socially sensitive research and explain how research in clinical psychology might be considered to be socially sensitive?

References

Carlsson, A., Waters, N., Waters, S., Carlsson, ML. (2000). Network interactions in schizophrenia - therapeutic implications. *Brain Research Reviews*, 31, pp. 342–349.

Guardia, D., Conversy, L., Jardri, R., Lafargue, G. et al. (2012). Imagining One's Own and Someone Else's Body Actions: Dissociation in Anorexia Nervosa. *PLoS ONE*, 7 (8): e43241.

Kroenke, K., Strine, TW., Spitzer, RL. et al. (2009). The PHQ-8 as a measure of current depression in the general population. *Journal of Affective Disorders.*, 114(1–3), pp. 163–173.

Lavarenne, A., Segal, E., Sigman, M. (2013). Containing psychotic patients with fragile boundaries: a single-session group case study. *American Journal of Psychotherapy*, 67(3), pp. 293–307.

Masellis, M., Rector, N.A., Richter, M.A. (2003). Quality of life in OCD: Differential impact of obsessions, compulsions, and depression comorbidity. *Canadian Journal of Psychiatry*, 48, pp. 72–77.

March, J.S. (2004). Cognitive-Behavior Therapy, Sertraline, and Their Combination for Children and Adolescents With Obsessive-Compulsive Disorder. The Pediatric OCD Treatment Study (POTS) Randomized Controlled Trial. *JAMA: Journal of the American Medical Association*, 292, (16).

Rosenhan, D. L. (1973a). On being sane in insane places. *Science*, 179, pp. 250–258.

Scott-Van Zeeland, A.A., Bloss, C.S., Tewhey, R., Bansal, V., Torkamani, A. et al. (2013). Evidence for the role of EPHX2 gene variants in anorexia nervosa. *Molecular Psychiatry*, 19(6), pp. 724–732.

Vallentine, V., Tapp, J., Dudley, A., Wilson, C., Moore, E. (2010). Psycho-educational groupwork for detained offender patients: Understanding mental illness. *Journal of Forensic Psychiatry and Psychology*, 21(3), pp. 393–406.

Williams, A. D., Blackwell, S. E., Mackenzie, A., Holmes, E. A., and Andrews, G. (2013) Combining imagination and reason in the treatment of depression: A randomized controlled trial of internet-based cognitive bias modification and internet-CBT for depression. *Journal of Consulting and Clinical Psychology*, 81(5), pp. 793–799.

6 Criminological psychology

Criminological psychology specialises in using psychological knowledge to understand antisocial behaviour and what factors contribute to such behaviour. This knowledge is then used in a variety of settings, including assisting the police to gain information from witnesses, within the courtroom and after sentencing to treat offenders. An interest in criminological psychology may result in a career as a forensic psychologist or working within a legal setting or the probation services.

The area of criminological psychology is important to psychologists as well as the general public. Crime rates and antisocial behaviour are often heavily represented in the media. Understanding antisocial behaviour and those who commit it will help to reduce this behaviour.

In this topic, you will learn about:

- explanations of crime and antisocial behaviour
- how to gather information about crimes and understanding the offender
- treatments used with offenders to reduce future crime
- factors that can affect the outcome of criminal cases, including eyewitness testimony and decisions made by jury members
- research methods for studying criminological psychology
- a classic and a contemporary study
- a key issue around the topic of criminological psychology that is of relevance to society today
- how to carry out a practical research exercise relevant to topics covered in criminological psychology
- wider issues and debates in criminological psychology (A level).

6.1 Content
Learning outcomes

In this section, you will learn about:

- biological and social explanations of crime
- techniques used by the police during interviews
- why people commit crimes
- how forensic psychologists treat offenders
- whether eyewitness testimony is reliable
- what factors can influence jury decision making.

Understanding criminal behaviour

Understanding the factors that can make it more likely for an individual to commit a crime or act in an antisocial way is critical to controlling or preventing such behaviour in the future. The Crime and Disorder Act (1998) defines **antisocial behaviour** as 'Acting in a way that caused or was likely to cause **harassment**, alarm or distress to one or more people not of the same household as the person acting in this way.' Antisocial behaviour can include drunken behaviour, making hoax calls, being excessively noisy and not controlling animals, in addition to causing criminal damage, taking drugs and intimidating other people.

The terms 'antisocial' and 'criminal' have different meanings but are often used interchangeably. Psychologists aim to understand the circumstances of the individual to consider, on an individual basis, what changes need to be made for that person.

This then allows psychologists to look for patterns that are more prevalent among the offending population.

Psychologists seek to explain antisocial behaviour from a number of different perspectives. These can be categorised into two separate groups: biological and social factors. It is important to note that these factors can influence a person's behaviour and make it more likely that they will commit an offence. These factors are not **causal factors**, that is, ones that definitely make the person act in a criminal or antisocial way.

Biological explanations

When looking at the biological causes of antisocial behaviour, it is often the causes of aggression that are discussed, which in turn can result in antisocial behaviour, including crime. The biological causes of this can be considered in terms of brain structure or hormones, or can be the result of personality types.

WIDER ISSUES AND DEBATES

Nature–nurture

The 'nature–nurture' debate is one that considers whether an individual is predetermined to act in a specific manner as a result of genetics, hormones and other biological factors or whether influences outside the individual direct future behaviour. The 'nature' argument indicates that an individual will engage in criminal behaviour as a result of internal factors, which can be difficult to change, and in some cases such as genetic influences, not possible to change at all. The nature argument could therefore seem to suggest that an individual is predetermined to act in a specific manner as a result of their biological make-up.

Brain injury

One biological explanation of crime investigates the relationship between offending behaviour and damage to the brain as a result of injury. A brain injury may be caused by an accident or illness. 'Traumatic' brain injury occurs directly as a result of a trauma on the brain, such as being involved in a car accident, falling and injuring the head or being assaulted in the head. Brain injury can also be caused by long-term alcohol or drug use. Alcohol has a toxic effect on the central nervous system (CNS) and interferes with the absorption of vitamin B1 (thiamine), which is an important brain nutrient. As drunkenness can impair balance or decision making, it also contributes to an increase in falls or accidents that injure the brain.

The consequences of a brain injury are dependent on the area of the brain that has been injured, as different parts of the brain are responsible for different skills. The personality of an individual may change as a result of a brain injury, or the person may start to behave in a way that is untypical of them pre-trauma. Sometimes the behaviours that people engage in can be reckless or involve aggression towards others. For example, an injury to the amygdala (see below) may result in an increase in impulsive behaviours or irritability and aggression.

Williams et al. (2010) found that 60 per cent of the 196 prisoners they investigated had received some form of traumatic brain injury due to falling, car accidents and sports activities. They noted that adults with traumatic brain injury were relatively younger at entry into prison systems than those without brain injury and reported higher rates of repeat offending. They suggested that these injuries affect development of temperament, **temperance**, social judgment and control impulses. The injury may also contribute to a greater level of risk-taking behaviour, making it more likely an individual may become involved in antisocial activity. They went on to conclude that impairment in these areas of development could contribute to criminality.

Key terms

Antisocial behaviour: acting in a way that causes, or is likely to cause, harassment, alarm or distress to one or more people not of the same household as the person acting in this way.

Harassment: acting in an aggressive or intimidating manner to another person.

Causal factors: factors that definitely make the person act in a criminal or antisocial way.

Temperance: abstinence from drinking alcohol.

Taking it further

The nature–nurture debate has been discussed in relation to the behaviour of humans for many years. The topic is also well researched in criminological psychology. As technology becomes more advanced and we have access to scanning techniques, there is more information about the nature side of criminal behaviour.

Apply the nature–nurture debate to what we now know about offending behaviour.

Evaluation

When reviewing the influence of brain injury on criminal behaviour, other comorbid conditions should also be considered. Many offenders have a history of substance misuse, may have pre-existing personality disorders or have been exposed to violence as a child, all of which are known to increase criminality. It is therefore a complex process trying to determine which of a multitude of factors may contribute to offending behaviour. It is not as simple as concluding that offenders with a brain injury have done so as a result of the brain injury, particularly in the presence of other possible influencing factors.

Kreutzer et al. (1991) were unable to prove or disprove a cause and effect between traumatic brain injury and violence. In their investigation of 74 patients, they found that 20 per cent had been arrested pre-injury and 10 per cent post-injury. Most arrests occurred after use of alcohol or other drugs. The study concluded that criminal behaviour might be a result of post-injury changes, including poor judgement. Substance abuse, traumatic brain injury and crime were indeed interconnected, the researchers said, but they did not go so far as to conclude that the brain injury causes criminality and violence. Rather, they believed that substance abuse, which was most common among those younger than 35 years old, led to legal difficulties and traumatic brain injury. Following further research, Kreutzer et al. (1995) concluded that without the presence of a substance use history, traumatic brain injury was not a risk factor for criminal behaviour.

Amygdala

As noted earlier, the amygdala may become damaged as a result of a brain injury. The amygdala is an important part of the brain when considering human behaviour. As the amygdala is responsible for controlling human emotions, damage to this area of the brain can result in a person presenting as unemotional or they may react excessively to their emotions as they cannot reduce them. Evidence using brain-scanning techniques suggests the brain of a **psychopath** works quite differently from that of a non-psychopath. Smaller amygdalae have been found among individuals diagnosed with psychopathic personalities as well as those having higher levels of aggression (Pardini et al., 2014). It was noted that such behaviours were evident from childhood. The conclusion from their study was that individuals with smaller amygdalae were three times more likely than those with larger amygdalae to exhibit aggression, violence and psychopathic features three years later. They therefore suggest that amygdala size can predict future violence.

Sham rage

In 1925, Cannon and Britton introduced the term 'sham rage' to describe an emotional state found in animals. They severed neural connections to the cortex of cats (creating 'decorticate cats'). The decorticate cats, when provoked, exhibited the emotional behaviour normally associated with rage and aggression, as demonstrated by erect hair, growling and the baring of teeth.

They called the behaviour 'sham rage' as it occurred without the cognitive influence or inhibitory control of the cerebral cortex. After much research, it is now understood that the source of the rage came from the temporal region, specifically the amygdala. When this was **ablated**, the animals became much more placid; if the area was stimulated, aggression would be displayed. This has led to the acceptance that the amygdala plays a particularly important role in the production of hostile behaviour.

Raine study

Adrian Raine has dedicated his career to looking at the brain structure of offenders. One of his well-known studies conducted with colleagues in 1997 found significant differences in the brain structure of murderers and control participants. They particularly noticed a difference in the functioning of the amygdala within the two populations.

Key terms

Psychopath: a type of personality disorder that affects how a person interacts with others.

Ablate: remove or destroy the function of an organ or body tissue.

Link

For further information on the study by Raine et al. (1997), please see the Studies section of Topic 3: *Biological psychology*.

They studied 41 murderers who had pleaded 'not guilty by reason of insanity' (NGRI). These participants had a range of mental illnesses, including schizophrenia. The study included a matched group as a control. All participants had a tracer injected into their body. The tracer attached itself to glucose molecules, which would show brain activity in different areas of the brain in a PET scan (positron emission tomography). They completed a task lasting approximately 30 minutes that targeted different areas of the brain.

The results showed lower levels of glucose metabolism in the prefrontal cortex of the murderers' brains. This area of the brain has been linked with impulsivity. There were also differences in the amygdala and the hippocampus (responsible for learning). Abnormal functioning in these areas could explain why the non-control participants in the study had all committed murder.

WIDER ISSUES AND DEBATES

Reductionism
Focusing solely on the amygdala and its role within aggression underplays the complex nature of the brain. Many parts of the brain work simultaneously, affecting our behaviour. To ignore the interrelations between the amygdala and other parts of the brain is therefore reductionist.

Evaluation

It is possible that a person may have a smaller amygdala yet not act in a psychopathic way. James Fallon is a neurologist who has looked at the brains of many individuals using MRI scans. He has shown an ability to identify those brains that belong to psychopathic individuals. However, in 2006 he infamously identified one brain in particular as psychopathic, but was in fact incorrect. The brain he looked at on a scan was actually his own.

Sham rage studies conducted on animals can be largely criticised for lacking generalisability to humans. Animals, unlike humans, do not have the capacity to inhibit their aggression with higher order thinking, so sham rage studies could be argued to apply only to animals. However, Narabayashi et al. (1963) conducted psychosurgery on human patients with aggressive behaviour by severing their amygdala from the remaining **limbic system** and found a mood-stabilising effect in the majority of patients over time.

This shows that while there may be brain structures that contribute to the likelihood of aggressive behaviour in individuals, there may be others (Fallon, for example) who have the abnormalities, yet do not act in a callous or unemotional way. Brain structure cannot, therefore, be the only factor that makes psychopaths who they are, or that the structural abnormalities that lead to psychopathy do not necessarily lead to aggression and criminality.

Robert Hare has been influential in assisting the understanding of psychopathy and how to identify psychopathy among the general population. He has devoted his professional career to researching how such individuals think and respond in different situations. His book *Snakes in suits: When psychopaths go to work* (Babiak and Hare, 2006) demonstrates how psychopaths are not just found among a criminal population. Some traits of a psychopath, including callousness and a lack of empathy, arguably make individuals suitable for high-level management positions. A typical lack of fear and need for stimulation often entices psychopaths to engage in extreme sports such as skydiving.

Key term

Limbic system: a set of structures in the brain associated with drives, emotions and mood.

Taking it further

There has been recent interest in the career pathway of psychopaths, as not everyone with psychopathic traits go on to become criminals. Using the work of Babiak and Hare (2006) research the possible career choices that people with the characteristics of a psychopath may make. For example, consider which careers may be most suited to someone who experiences little fear, or likes to have high levels of stimulation in their work.

XYY syndrome

Humans have 23 pairs of chromosomes, giving a total of 46 chromosomes. At conception the embryo receives 23 chromosomes from the mother's egg and 23 chromosomes from the father's sperm. Pairs 1 to 22 are identical or nearly identical; the 23rd pair consists of the sex chromosomes, which are either X or Y. An XX pair will result in a baby being female, and an XY will result in a male.

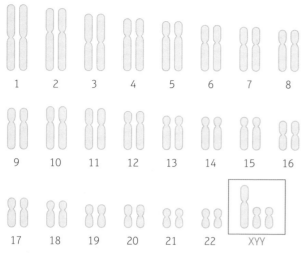

Figure 6.1 A visual representation of XYY syndrome

XYY syndrome is a genetic condition that occurs when a human male has an extra male (Y) chromosome within the 23rd pair of chromosomes, instead of the usual two (XY). They therefore have a total of 47 chromosomes. This occurs in 1 in 1000 male births. It is not an inherited condition, but occurs randomly at the time of conception.

Many men with XYY do not even know they have an extra chromosome. Most boys with XYY will have a normal development although some may grow faster and taller than usual. Some studies have shown they may have a slightly lower level of intelligence, although still within the normal range, and some may have behaviour problems and be easily distracted.

XYY syndrome has previously been thought to make men overly aggressive and lack empathy, leading to it being known as a 'super-male' syndrome.

Evaluation

Determining the rate of XYY among a criminal population requires skilled staff and is resource intensive. It is therefore not practical to look at the genetics of all male offenders to determine if they are XYY. As such, we are unlikely to know the true extent of the prevalence of XYY.

Theilgaard's study shows a small presence of XYY men among a criminal population. This suggests that it cannot be the only reason for criminal behaviour among men. Other factors must also contribute to male criminality or we would expect the rate of XYY to be 100 per cent. She found that men with XYY are likely to have lower levels of intelligence. The higher than expected number of XYY men in the offender population, therefore, may be a consequence of the learning difficulties associated with the condition, rather than XYY itself.

Women also engage in criminal behaviour, including violent crime. As women do not have Y chromosomes, XYY fails to account for criminal behaviour among women.

Other genetic explanations for criminality

There are a number of other explanations that can be used to explain aggressive behaviour or criminality, involving the influence of genetics and the environment on the individual. Twin studies are an effective way to attempt to separate these influences because of the similarities in genetic information among twins.

Twin studies: monozygotic twins (MZ) share all of their genetic information while dizygotic twins (DZ) share 50 per cent. If MZ twins are more alike in terms of aggressive behaviour than DZ twins, then this is likely to be due to genes rather than environment. Slutske et al. (1997) have shown there is some higher incidence of conduct disorder in twins when compared to singletons.

Adoption studies: one problem when studying twins is that twins will often be brought up together in a similar way, so it is hard to say whether the concordance rates are caused by genetic or environmental factors. Adoption studies help to determine if a change in environment results in the same behaviours. If this happens, it would suggest the behaviour is due to genetics. In 1997, Hutchings and Mednick studied male adoptees and discovered that 85.7 per cent of the males with a criminal or minor offences record had a birth father with a criminal record. They also noted that young male adoptees without a criminal record had a criminal father 31.1 per cent of the time. This suggests a link between criminal behaviour and genetics.

The family concentration of antisocial behaviour could be explained by a genetic influence. It can also be explained by non-genetic, social transmission of antisocial behaviour within families (the nurture debate).

WIDER ISSUES AND DEBATES

Nature–nurture

Comparing concordance rates between monozygotic and dizygotic twins who share the same environment indicates whether a behavioural characteristic, such as criminality, is due to nature or nurture.

If the concordance rate between MZ and DZ twins is the same for criminality, meaning they commit the same amount of crime as their twin, it would indicate that criminality is due to nurture. However, if the concordance rate is higher for MZ than DZ twins, it would suggest a genetic influence (nature).

Adoption studies provide an opportunity to explore the influence of nature and nurture on the behaviour of twins as they are raised separately.

Personality

Our personality makes us who we are as individuals. It explains our interests, how we interact with others and our overall outlook on life. Hans Eysenck has looked extensively at the personality traits of an individual; the enduring characteristics that make us who we are and influence our decisions and behaviour. He examined the dimensions of **extraversion** (E) and **introversion** (I), **neuroticism** (N) and **stability** (S), and **psychoticism** (P). He argued that the differences in people's personalities could be reduced to these dimensions, which related to the underlying functioning of the individual's nervous system. He also suggested that the three characteristics of psychoticism (P), extraversion (E) and neuroticism (N), which he thought were influenced by our biology, could explain criminality. He described this as the PEN personality.

Eysenck (1990) proposed the **arousal theory** to explain the causal roots of the three dimensions of personality. He explained extraversion in terms of cortical arousal via the **ascending reticular activating system (ARAS)** within the brain. Activity in the ARAS stimulates the cerebral cortex, which in turn leads to higher cortical arousal. Introverts are characterised by higher levels of activity than extraverts and so are more cortically aroused than extraverts. This means that introverts require less external stimulation or arousal, explaining why they are less outgoing and risk-taking. Extraverts, on the other hand, are characterised by underactive ARAS, so require greater amounts of external stimulation.

Key terms

Extraversion: behaviour is outgoing, sociable and active. Individuals want excitement and may become easily bored.

Introversion: individuals are typically reserved and reflective. An introvert is more likely to prefer solitary to social activities.

Neuroticism: emotional instability associated with anxiety, fear, depression and envy.

Stability: an individual is emotionally calm, unreactive and unworried.

Psychoticism: individuals lack empathy, are aggressive, impersonal and cold.

Arousal theory: individuals are motivated to act in a way to maintain a certain level of physiological arousal. When arousal levels drop below our personal optimal level, we engage in stimulating behaviour to increase arousal.

Ascending reticular activating system (ARAS): a system that transmits messages to the limbic system, triggering the release of hormones and neurotransmitters.

Eysenck also explained neuroticism in terms of activation thresholds in the sympathetic nervous system (limbic system). This includes the hippocampus, amygdala and hypothalamus, and is where emotional states such as fear and aggression are regulated. It is responsible for the fight-or-flight response in the face of danger. Neurotic individuals have greater activation levels and lower thresholds within the limbic system. They are easily upset in the face of very minor stresses. However, emotionally stable people are calm under such stresses because they have lesser activation levels and higher thresholds.

Eysenck provided a biological explanation for the personality trait of psychoticism in terms of hormones such as testosterone and enzymes such as monoamine oxidase (MAO). Although there has not been a lot of research done on psychoticism in comparison with extraversion and neuroticism, the current research shows that people who show a psychotic episode have increased testosterone levels and low MAO levels.

Eysenck believed that a criminal personality displayed the following three personality dimensions.

- High P scores are aggressive, antisocial, cold and egocentric.

- High E scores are sociable, active, lively and sensation-seeking. They need more stimulation from their environment.

- High N scores are anxious, depressed and react very strongly to aversive stimuli and have a high degree of instability.

Evaluation

A number of studies have supported aspects of Eysenck's theory and found individuals who reported higher levels of delinquency also scored higher on P, E and N. However, studies of 'official' delinquency, such as comparing convicted offenders with non-offenders, do not produce such consistent findings.

Rushton and Chrisjohn (1981) investigated delinquent, rather than criminal behaviour. Their study showed clear support for a relationship between high delinquency scores and high scores on both extraversion and psychoticism. They did not, however, find support for a relationship between delinquency scores and the dimension of neuroticism, leading them to suggest there are key differences between the three personality dimensions.

Boduszek et al. (2013) investigated personality traits in predicting violent offending within a sample of **recidivistic** inmates from a high-security prison in Ireland. They found that higher levels of extraversion predicted a greater probability of committing a violent criminal act. In contrast, Farrington et al. (1982) has shown that E scores are less associated with criminal convictions than the other two personality traits.

The contribution of each of the three factors to criminality has varied in different studies. This makes it difficult to determine accurately which of the factors has the greatest influence on criminal behaviour.

Personality disorders

A personality disorder (PD) is when an individual's way of thinking, feeling or relating to others differs significantly from that of a person without a personality disorder. A PD is a clinical diagnosis. It reflects extremes in people's personalities. PD can be diagnosed through official classifications

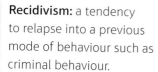

Key term

Recidivism: a tendency to relapse into a previous mode of behaviour such as criminal behaviour.

such as Diagnostic and Statistical Manual of Mental Disorders (DSM-IV) and International Statistical Classification of Diseases and Related Health Problems (ICD-10). These provide clear guidance for professionals to follow to ensure that there is consistency in the diagnosis given to people with the same symptoms. Psychopathy is a personality disorder. Others include the following.

- **Narcissistic**: a need to be admired, thinks they are the most important and will exploit others to get what they want.

- Antisocial: often aggressive, ignore rules and does not care about others.

- **Paranoid**: distrust of others, suspicious, takes criticism very personally and can bear grudges.

Michael Stone (2007) undertook research to look at the relationship of certain PDs to violent crime. Using personal interviews and looking at media reports of offenders convicted of such offences, he was able to assess the offenders to see if they had a PD. He made the following findings.

- Antisocial and paranoid PDs are the most common PDs among violent offenders.

- Psychopathy was also common.

- Narcissistic traits were high though not all were severe enough to get a diagnosis of narcissistic PD.

- Instrumental (as opposed to impulsive) murderers who killed their partners were strongly associated with narcissistic PD.

- Men committing serial sexual homicide usually show psychopathy.

- Mass murderers usually show strong paranoid traits.

- Many had more than one PD.

Evaluation

Eysenck's explanation of personality is somewhat simplistic and fails to consider that a person's reactions or behaviour may differ depending on the situation. It does not consider the potential for biological issues such as brain injury to contribute to why an individual may be more extravert and less inhibited, or social explanations for criminality.

Personality explanations suggest that a person's personality does not change, and therefore may suggest that their behaviour cannot change. Most personality types are consistent over time, but individuals may learn techniques to manage parts of their behaviour that cause them or other people difficulties. Many people are not fully aware of their own personality traits, although they can be quite accurate in describing themselves.

Personality research is frequently based on self-report data. This creates the potential for information given by the individual to be flawed, as they may be displaying response bias or may not want the researcher to delve into their personality (social desirability bias). As a result, the findings of the studies are less reliable.

Some studies have shown personality to be a contributory factor, rather than a causal factor, for aggression. Such studies also tend to give consideration to social or biological factors. These studies help to place an importance on personality, but within the context of wider influences. These studies are therefore supportive of other research that has attempted to explain criminality from alternative perspectives.

Personality disorders can sometimes be mistaken for symptoms of specific mental illness and vice versa. It is therefore important that a professional assesses personality to make sure the person can be given the correct support to manage the behaviours they present.

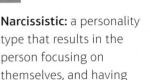

Key terms

Narcissistic: a personality type that results in the person focusing on themselves, and having a need to be admired by others. It can lead to the exploitation of others.

Paranoid: a personality type that results in a distrust of others and suspiciousness. A paranoid person takes criticism very personally and can bear grudges.

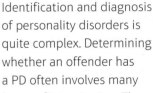

Taking it further

Identification and diagnosis of personality disorders is quite complex. Determining whether an offender has a PD often involves many hours of interviewing. The diagnostic tools used for this task are therefore heavily reliant on self-report information. What difficulties would this present to psychologists in terms of the reliability of their findings?

Serotonin: a chemical created by the body that works as a neurotransmitter. It is responsible for managing moods.

Dopamine: a neurotransmitter. It is a chemical messenger that helps in the transmission of signals between neurons in the brain.

Anabolic steroids: synthetic forms of testosterone. They promote the growth of body muscle and strength in users.

Exam tip

When asked to provide an explanation of a crime, be wary of saying factor X causes someone to become a criminal. All of the factors presented are those that may influence behaviour. It is not possible to be too definite as there are many other influences that may be just as valid an argument.

Neurotransmitters

An alternative biological explanation looks at the functioning of the brain, specifically the presence of neurotransmitters and their influence on behaviour. Neurotransmitters are chemicals that trigger a response in the brain (see Topic 3: *Biological psychology*). Examples include serotonin and dopamine, which are both thought to influence aggression levels.

Serotonin is considered to be the body's natural 'happy chemical'. It helps to relay messages from one part of the brain to another and can help to regulate mood. Low levels of serotonin can be linked with increased aggression. Serotonin also plays a role in inhibiting impulses, other than aggressive ones. It is therefore believed that serotonin can inhibit our impulsive response to stimuli, so low levels of serotonin may result in an over-reaction in emotional situations, which may include aggression.

Dopamine plays a key role in learning and in the brain's reward system. It is produced in response to rewarding stimuli such as food, sex and certain drugs. Lavine (1997) found that an increase in dopamine levels through the use of amphetamines was associated with an increase in aggressive behaviour, suggesting that higher levels of dopamine correlate with higher levels of aggression. Dopamine has also been shown to serve as positive reinforcement for aggression, that is, being aggressive generates increased dopamine in the brain, which activates the brain's reward system.

Evaluation

Evidence for the role of neurotransmitters in aggression comes from correlation studies that suggest a link between serotonin and dopamine and aggression. Cleare and Bond (1997) found that even in males with no history of psychiatric problems, low serotonin levels correlate with levels of aggression and hostility. Couppis and Kennedy (2008) found that dopamine levels in mice would increase and act as a reward during an aggressive act. This could mean that the increased levels of dopamine are not a cause of aggression but a consequence of it.

WIDER ISSUES AND DEBATES

Psychology as a science

Much of the evidence of the effects of neurotransmitters has been documented via the use of correlational studies. These studies show that there is a relationship between two variables, in this case the effect of biology on aggression. It is not possible from these studies to conclusively say that biological factors cause aggression. Such theories fail to take into account the cognitive part of humans; that we have the power to think and reason prior to acting, rather than just being the sum of structures within our body.

For psychology to be seen as scientific, it is argued that the cause and effect relationship between variables should be determined. This is not possible within correlational studies, and therefore questions the scientific nature of psychology.

Hormones

Testosterone is a male hormone. Women produce some testosterone, but in much lower quantities than men. Elevated levels of testosterone are associated with higher levels of aggression (see Topic 3: *Biological psychology*). The age at which men are most likely to be involved in violence is between the ages of 15 and 25. It may be more than coincidence that this is also the time when men have the highest levels of testosterone. Studies have shown that individuals using **anabolic steroids**, synthetic variants of testosterone, are more likely to engage in violent acts (Beaver et al., 2008). As the use of steroids elevates the presence of testosterone in the body, this further supports the relationship between testosterone and aggression.

Dabbs et al. (1995) took saliva samples of adult male prisoners to test levels of testosterone. They found that those with the higher levels of testosterone had a history of violent crime, whereas those with low levels of testosterone had committed only non-violent crimes. They also found that individuals with higher testosterone levels were more likely to be involved in direct confrontations with others while in prison and generally broke more prison rules.

Castration is a process that significantly reduces the production of testosterone. Animal studies have documented a reduction in aggressive behaviour in animals following castration. Albert et al. (1986) found this among rats, and also noted that there were fewer attempts to display social dominance among the rats that had been castrated.

WIDER ISSUES AND DEBATES

The use of psychological knowledge in society

Testosterone studies have typically used animals as subjects due to the ethics restricting the use of human participants in studies that may cause harm to the individual. These studies provide information about the effect of testosterone on behaviour, as demonstrated within animals.

Rats and other animals have significant biological differences from humans. As a result, these biological differences may influence the outcome of the studies. Generalising the findings of animal studies to humans must be undertaken cautiously for this reason, giving consideration to the type of animal used in the study and how similar they are to us.

Evaluation

When considering testosterone and violent behaviour, studies only suggest a relationship with aggression, rather than with violence or other criminality. Violence, however, is not always the result of increased aggression. For example, some individuals use violence in order to achieve a specific goal, such as a hired hit man killing someone for money, not because they are angry with the victim. It is therefore not possible to consider testosterone levels as a full explanation of all violent behaviour.

Males who use anabolic steroids, which are known to increase levels of testosterone, are more likely to be involved in violent crime (Skårberg, 2010). In 11 studies examining the relationship between blood and saliva testosterone levels and involvement in criminal activity, all 11 showed a positive but modest correlation in testosterone-related offences (Ellis, 2000). A study into domestic violence found that male offenders had higher levels of saliva testosterone than males with no domestic violence history (Soler et al., 2000). Elevated levels of testosterone, however, may be as much a result of violence as they are a contributor. Thus the cause and effect relationship cannot be fully established.

Social explanations

Social explanations of crime cover the 'nurture' element of the 'nature–nurture' debate, suggesting that as individuals, we are influenced by factors around us, making us who we are. In the context of criminal behaviour, the nurture argument would suggest we are influenced by what we observe in the world around us, including the people and other influences to whom we are exposed, and it is these influences that steer us either towards or away from criminal behaviour.

Labelling and self-fulfilling prophecy

Social explanations in relation to criminality include **labelling** and **self-fulfilling prophecy**. Labelling occurs when general and broad terms are used to describe members of a group. This often happens when a group of people, who are grouped together by a shared interest or characteristic, see

DEVELOPMENTAL PSYCHOLOGY

The biological approach provides multiple explanations for criminality, all of which result in individuals developing differently to others. XYY chromosomes inherited at conception cannot be changed and, from the outset, result in potentially differing development. Other biological explanations are the result of changes since birth, such as acquiring a brain injury, including damage to the amygdala. Throughout our lives, we are subject to hormones or neurotransmitters, the proportion of which can also result in individual differences in behaviour. This is particularly true for testosterone, which seems to have a greater influence on aggressive behaviour in adolescence and early adulthood stages.

Key terms

Labelling: this occurs when general and broad terms are used to describe members of a group.

Self-fulfilling prophecy: a stereotype that leads someone to act in a manner consistent with the stereotype.

Key terms

Stereotype: an overgeneralised belief about someone or something typically based on limited information.

Prejudice: dislike or unfair behaviour based on false or misguided opinion.

Discrimination: the practice of treating one person or group differently from another in an unfair way.

another group as inferior. This creates a majority (superior) group and a minority (inferior) group. As 'inferior' group suggests, the description often has negative connotations. Labels are often based on **stereotypes**. Once a label has been ascribed to an individual or group of people, they may be treated according to that label.

Robert Merton (1948) described self-fulfilling prophecy as 'a false definition of the situation evoking a new behaviour, which makes the originally false conception come true'. In other words, a person or group may assume that, at some point, an individual will behave in an antisocial way, perhaps because of previous antisocial behaviour or due to a stereotype. The individual is labelled and treated in accordance with this false belief, is possibly considered suspicious and kept under a high level of surveillance with the expectation of antisocial behaviour, or offered no encouragement towards more positive activities. This gives the individual little opportunity to change or disprove the label that they have been assigned. The individual internalises and subsequently lives up to the expectation of the label and fulfils the prophecy of being criminal.

DEVELOPMENTAL PSYCHOLOGY

The self-fulfilling prophecy helps to explain the development of some individuals because it is more likely that a label will be assigned and subsequently internalised as a young person is forming their own sense of identity. At this point in development, there is a greater vulnerability to the internalisation of others' beliefs about them.

Youths acting in an antisocial way strengthens stereotypes, which can lead to a self-fulfilling prophecy.

The stereotype of groups of youths acting in an antisocial way has received a lot of attention following the riots that occurred in London, Manchester, Birmingham and other areas of the UK in the summer of 2011. The young age of some of those involved dominated media reports, and any youth in the area faced suspicion. In reality, there were many other people involved in the riots, not just young people. A stereotype can influence our attitudes towards the other person or group, resulting in **prejudice**. If behaviour changes to the other group as a result of the stereotype, this is known as **discrimination**.

Robert Rosenthal and Lenore Jacobson's 1968 study explained the impact of self-fulfilling prophecy within an academic setting in San Francisco, USA. They wanted to find out if teachers would react differently towards particular students it they were told that some students would learn more information and more quickly than other students. Some students were labelled as being academic 'bloomers' and therefore had great potential. In fact, students were allocated to this group randomly, not according to their level of intelligence. Rosenthal and Jacobson ran the study for a year, allowing them to observe if the teachers treated the 'bloomers' differently. IQ scores were measured for all students at the start and end of the year to measure for educational performance. The study found that the IQ of students who had been identified as 'bloomers' was significantly higher than the non-bloomers, despite the 'bloomers' not necessarily being those with the highest IQ at the start of the study. They concluded that the teachers' expectations of the students influenced their behaviour towards them, and it was this behaviour that influenced the change in IQ scores. This indicates that the beliefs of teachers can result in their prophecies about the students' education coming true.

The self-fulfilling prophecy

The diagram below explains the self-fulfilling prophecy in detail. It is sometimes known as the Pygmalion Effect and explains better performances by people when greater expectations are placed on them. Pygmalion was a character from Ovid's poem 'Metamorphoses'. Pygmalion fell in love with a statue he had carved. The film *My Fair Lady* reflects a more recent account of the Pygmalion Effect and the self-fulfilling prophecy.

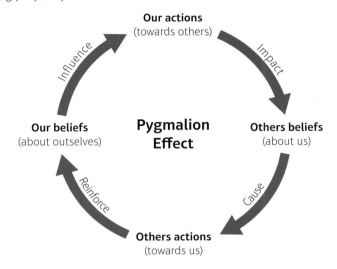

Figure 6.2 The self-fulfilling prophecy

Exam tip

Diagrams are helpful ways to remember key facts about a theory or explanation when revising. They can also be used within exams as long as they are fully explained and demonstrate your understanding of the theory or explanation.

INDIVIDUAL DIFFERENCES

Self-fulfilling prophecy as a theory of criminality can highlight individual differences in the development of criminality because some people are exposed to the type of labelling associated with criminal behaviour, whereas others are not. Not all individuals live up to the expectations of others around them and therefore do not respond to the self-fulfilling prophecy, particularly individuals with high self-esteem, greater autonomy and less regard for the opinions of others. Some people may actively resist the labels given to them and work to overcome the labels that have been assigned to them. For example, a child may come from an antisocial family, where various members of the family have been involved in crime. Others may expect the child to also engage in criminal behaviour and treat them according to these expectations. The child, however, may not internalise these expectations and may engage in activities that are of a non-criminal nature.

When a label is applied to a person, they can begin to see themselves in that way and believe they are expected to behave in a particular way. As they believe they should act in a specific way, they do, and therefore fulfil their own prophecy. This is a result of being given a specific label. In the case of Rosenthal and Jacobson, it included the label of 'bloomer'. For those individuals the label was positive and brought about a positive result, but if the label is a negative one, the outcome may also be negative.

Evaluation

The Rosenthal and Jacobson 1968 study was well controlled and helpful in explaining learning processes, but it has a number of significant issues. It was an unethical study as it allowed some students to receive less attention than others, interfering with their education. Additionally, the teachers were deceived about details within the study. While this study is not related to criminal behaviour, it demonstrates how individuals internalise the expectations of those around them.

Taking it further

Have you ever stereotyped someone based on their appearance or interests? Or has someone done this to you?

Reflect on how this affected the behaviour of the person whom you stereotyped, or your behaviour due to being labelled.

Jahoda (1954) provided support for the self-fulfilling prophecy and the application of labels to children in relation to antisocial behaviour. He studied the Ashanti people from Ghana, who name boys according to the day they were born. The Ashanti have expectations for the personality of the boys born on each day. For example, 'Monday' boys are considered quiet and placid, and 'Wednesday' boys are thought to be aggressive and short-tempered. After looking at five years of records at a local juvenile court, Jahoda found that nearly 22 per cent of violent offences were committed by boys born on Wednesday, but only 6.9 per cent by boys born on Monday. This suggested to him that cultural expectations about the boys' natures and their explicit labels led to them being treated differently according to their day of birth (for example, the boys born on Wednesday would have been treated with greater suspicion). As a result, many have conformed to the label set by their own namesake.

WIDER ISSUES AND DEBATES

Nature-nurture

The self-fulfilling prophecy rests on the nurture side of the nature–nurture debate as it does not take into account biological factors that could predispose an individual to criminality. Using both nature and nurture is a better way of explaining criminality. This is because it may be better to understand that some people are innately vulnerable and so predisposed to antisocial behaviour but they can also be affected by environmental factors, which increases their risk of engaging in criminal activity.

Madon et al. (2004) looked at self-fulfilling prophecy in a natural situation within the family home. They investigated whether parents' expectations about their child's alcohol use had any self-fulfilling effect on that child's future drinking behaviour. She found that there was a positive correlation between parents who overestimated their child's alcohol use and actual alcohol use a year later. Those children whose parents expected them to drink more alcohol did actually drink more when re-interviewed the following year. The study showed that there was a greater influence on the child's drinking behaviour when both parents overestimated their child's alcohol use. If both parents expected their child to drink alcohol, the child was more likely to do so. They did not find a similar significant difference in outcome when either one or both parents underestimated their child's alcohol use. This suggests that negative self-fulfilling prophecies may have a greater effect on behaviour than positive ones.

There is no proven direct link between an individual's IQ levels (Rosenthal and Jacobson, 1968) or drinking alcohol (Madon et al, 2004) to criminality. There is limited research in the area of self-fulfilling prophecy and crime, with the exception of Jahoda (1954). These studies provide an explanation of academic and antisocial behaviour from which estimations can be made about the potential influence of the criminal-related expectations of others and subsequent behaviour.

The ethical and moral issues surrounding research into self-fulfilling prophecy and antisocial behaviour are so great that it prevents experiments in this area. This will make it unlikely that self-fulfilling prophecy as a cause of antisocial behaviour can be proven (or disproven). As a result, it is only possible to suggest a correlation between self-fulfilling prophecy and antisocial behaviour. There may be other variables influencing the behaviour of the individual in these cases.

Much of the research into the self-fulfilling prophecy has been in education, investigating the teacher–child relationship. Other relationships may not have the same effect. This makes the application of self-fulfilling prophecy to other behaviours, such as criminality, limited. It is also very difficult to study self-fulfilling prophecy because it is by definition a false belief. Beliefs are often studied using self-report measures, which rely on individual insight, self-disclosure and honesty.

All research undertaken demonstrates a correlation between antisocial behaviour and self-fulfilling prophecy. This link cannot be accepted as a causal link as other variables may also influence behaviour, including biological factors. Self-fulfilling prophecy fails to account for other factors that may influence an individual's behaviour. It excludes peer pressure, politics, biological factors and social or economic circumstances. These other variables may also increase the likelihood that an individual will engage in antisocial behaviour.

Self-fulfilling prophecy does not take into account how an individual learns the antisocial behaviour they are expected to carry out. An alternative theory to explain crime is that of social learning theory, which does consider the influence of observing antisocial behaviour on the individual. This suggests that the self-fulfilling prophecy explanation cannot be the only social explanation for such behaviour, and that other factors must also be present in order for an individual to engage in such behaviour.

Social learning theory

Social learning theory is a social-cognitive theory that explains criminal behaviour as being the result of modelling such behaviour from observing it via the media or watching other people.

An individual cannot learn offending behaviour via social learning theory without observing someone commit a crime, either directly such as a peer or indirectly through watching crime-related television programmes. The individual must be motivated to reproduce the observed behaviour, which occurs as a result of **vicarious** or self-reinforcement. If an individual watches a criminal getting away with an offence or reaping the rewards, this may act as vicarious reinforcement for the observer. On television, antisocial behaviour and criminality are often glamorised and violence can be committed by 'good guys'. These role models may provide vicarious reinforcement, particularly in the absence of punishment and with only the sanitised effects on the victims shown. Social learning theory highlights the importance of the cognitive thinking processes of a person, someone may choose not to commit a crime immediately after observing it; the behaviour can happen much later. If news or crime programmes document some of the negative consequences of committing an offence, this may work towards encouraging an individual not to try the offence to seek a positive outcome.

> ### Exam tip
>
> Social learning theory is a topic that you will have studied before so you should be familiar with it by now. Do not assume, however, that the examiner knows that you are familiar with the topic. Your answers need to be as fully elaborated on as for a topic you have only just been introduced to. For example, this may include elaborating on the stages of social learning theory by applying them to the topic of crime, rather than simply listing them or describing them without making reference to crime.

DEVELOPMENTAL PSYCHOLOGY

Social learning theory is a developmental theory of criminality because it is concerned with the acquisition of antisocial behaviour (in addition to other behaviours) as part of the process of socialisation that occurs in childhood, adolescence and early adulthood. It does not pinpoint a particular age-related change associated with criminality, but describes how the values of a society or culture are internalised as a product of how someone is raised. During our development, we achieve or acquire various abilities at certain ages, such as levels of reasoning and morality. As children develop, exposure to aggressive or antisocial role models can affect how children internalise these behaviours. A persistent exposure to antisocial role models may have an accumulative effect throughout development.

Evaluation

The possibility of finding direct evidence for the role of social learning and antisocial behaviour in actual families is virtually impossible. Research in this area has therefore concentrated on the influence of violent media on aggressive behaviour. Studies into violent media have adopted a range of research methods to investigate its effects. Tannis MacBeth Williams (1986) used a natural experiment to investigate the introduction of television to a small community in British Columbia, Canada. Of the 16 young people that she studied, she found that after only two years of receiving television, these children were twice as aggressive as two control groups she studied in nearby

Link

Social learning theory has been covered in detail in Topic 4: *Learning theories*, so it is only covered here in relation to criminal behaviour.

Key term

Vicarious: learning through the consequence of another person's behaviour.

Why might this be an example of vicarious learning?

communities who had been brought up with television in varying amounts. This might offer some evidence for social learning theory as an explanation of criminality, although Williams herself suggested that increased aggression was more likely to be a result of the increased value placed on materialistic lifestyles than the violence that they were exposed to in television programmes.

Correlations have also been conducted to establish whether there is a relationship between watching violent media and aggressive behaviour. In a **meta-analysis** of correlational studies, Comstock and Paik (1994) concluded that many reported a positive correlation between television violence viewed and aggressive measures of behaviour recorded, with an overall correlation coefficient of +0.19. This correlation is not particularly strong, and is significantly affected by the large sample sizes used in some of the studies, which tend to make findings appear significant when they are not. It is also worth considering that correlations only show relationships between measured variables, therefore do not establish causality, measure other variables that could have an effect on aggression nor indicate the direction of possible causality; it could be that aggressive children seek out and prefer violent programmes.

There may be the influence of a third, unmeasured variable, such as social class. Children from lower socio-economic status watch more television than those in higher socio-economic groups, and are also more likely to be delinquent (Flood-Page et al., 2000). Other factors such as individual motivation, personality characteristics such as sensation seeking (Slater, Henry et al., 2004) and biological factors may also account for criminality.

Experimental evidence for social learning theory and aggression has focused on the behaviour and play of children following exposure to aggression (for example Bandura, 1961, 1963, 1965). Bandura found that children were more likely to copy aggressive acts if motivated vicariously by what would be regarded as a role model. This was particularly noted for boys. However, it can be argued that children are naive individuals and therefore do not fully appreciate the consequences of their behaviour. We therefore need to be cautious in applying the findings of child experiments to the decision making of non-naive adults. Experimental evidence can also be criticised for only examining the short-term effects of exposure to aggressive role models as the long-term effects have not been established. Although a child may imitate the behaviour of an aggressive television character the next day at school, it is unlikely that they will grow up and continue to display aggression as a result.

Social learning theory maintains that behaviour is not copied if a negative consequence for the criminal is observed. The high number of repeat offenders is not supported by this theory. Repeat offending may be better explained by the frustration–aggression theory in which frustration at not being able to achieve a goal is likely to result in aggression.

What we can conclude from the research into social learning theory and antisocial behaviour is that there is no convincing evidence that criminality is a result of observational learning, particularly as a result of observing violent media. Despite a phenomenal amount of research conducted using a range of research methods, there is no unequivocal evidence that links exposure to violence with aggression or antisocial behaviour. All the research indicates is that the relationship between exposure to violence and aggression is neither simple nor straightforward.

Key term

Meta-analysis: a research method where a researcher examines the results of several previous studies rather than conducting new research with participants.

WIDER ISSUES AND DEBATES

Comparisons between ways of explaining behaviour using different themes

There have been many explanations of criminality presented from a psychological perspective. Biological and social explanations both have their value in understanding why some individuals become aggressive or commit offences. These explanations look at very different aspects of human behaviour. Research is continuing in each of these areas, to explore the various factors why individuals engage in such behaviour.

Taking it further

Conduct your own Internet search for evidence for social learning theory and criminality. There are many studies that investigate the influence of media violence and antisocial behaviour using a variety of research methods, such as cross-sectional, longitudinal studies, laboratory, field and natural experiments, observations and surveys. Consider the weaknesses of these research methods and apply this knowledge to criticising the conclusions drawn from such research.

How does a psychologist understand the individual offender?

The role of a psychologist is often that of a 'consultant', helping to guide the work of other professionals such as the police. This can be through indirectly observing and reviewing the work practices of others, using psychological theories to inform any decision or suggestion they make. Additionally, in many situations the psychologist may speak to the offender directly, asking them questions to find out what influenced the individual to act in the way that they did. Once again, an understanding of psychological theories and approaches is essential to make sure that the work completed by the psychologist can be relied on as accurate.

Some of the key areas in which psychologists assist in understanding the offender are via:

- police interview techniques
- individual psychology formulation.

Interviewing

The cognitive interview is a specific way of asking a suspect (or witness) questions about an incident. It is designed to maximise the accuracy of the information obtained. If inaccurate information is taken during a police interview, the wrong person may be charged with an offence, leading to a wrongful conviction. This also means that the actual offender has got away with the crime.

Interviews can occur weeks after an incident, which can affect the amount of information a victim or witness recalls

Psychologists have worked with the police to develop the cognitive interview using their knowledge of how memory works and how there is a social tendency to want to please people in certain situations. It is based on two principal concepts of cognitive psychology.

1 Memory of an event is based on a number of associations and, therefore, there will be several means by which a memory can be cued.

2 Retrieval from memory will be more effective if at the time of retrieval the context surrounding the original events can be reinstated.

WIDER ISSUES AND DEBATES

Psychology as a science

Laboratory-based research within eyewitness testimony is commonly used. This creates an artificial situation in which participants undertake tasks to determine their ability to recall artificially created film clips of crimes. The laboratory setting is very controlled to minimise extraneous variables affecting the findings of the research. In removing all other variables, and creating such a controlled setting to undertake the task, the study and its findings cannot be considered ecologically valid. The participants might generate significantly different results if they were to observe a real crime, and be affected by all the additional variables present in a real-life situation that have been controlled for within a laboratory setting.

There are four main techniques used within the cognitive interview, as guided by Geiselman et al. (1985).

1 **Reinstate the context at the time of the event**. Encouraging witnesses to recall specific cues, such as how they felt, the weather, smells, time of day, etc. helps to put the person back in time to the incident and may improve recall accuracy. This supports cue-dependent recall.

2 **Report everything**. Allowing the witness to freely recall a narrative of the situation gains an initial account, without interruption. There is then scope for the interviewer to ask further questions to clarify significant moments in turn for more detail. Witnesses may exclude details they feel are irrelevant or trivial, especially if they do not fit into their existing schemas for that type of event. Unimportant detail can act as a cue for key information about the event.

3 **Change the order in which the event is recalled**. As we tend to remember situations in the order in which they happened, we are more likely to reconstruct a story and draw on existing schema. This can be inaccurate as a result. Recalling events in reverse order can help a person to avoid skipping over information that they have taken for granted, as it interrupts schema activation – what we would expect to see – and can help to prevent story formation.

4 **Change perspective**. Trying to adopt the viewpoint of a different witness, for example a prominent character in the incident can encourage recall of events that may otherwise be omitted. Cueing the person to specifically focus on a different element of the situation can increase accurate recall. It has to be made clear that the witness only reports what they know, and not what they think the other person would have seen.

This approach will minimise the extent to which witnesses can use prior knowledge or expectations to fill in any gaps they may have, which can result in reduced accuracy. In order to ensure accurate information is obtained, the police officer undertaking the interview needs to ensure that they do not ask 'leading questions' that provide a hint about a desired answer.

Does the cognitive interview work?

Edward Geiselman and colleagues (1985) compared their developed cognitive interview with a standard interview technique, using 51 volunteer participants from a wide demographic background. Participants watched two films of violent crimes and 48 hours later were interviewed by trained police officers using either a standard interview or a cognitive interview. There was also an interview undertaken under hypnosis.

The results showed a significant increase in the number of correct items recalled using the cognitive interview. The difference noted in the number of confabulated items (items of descriptions made up by participants to fit the story) was not statistically significant, and was low in all conditions. The findings were as follows.

Table 6.1 Findings from different types of interview

Average number of items recalled	Hypnosis interview	Cognitive interview	Standard interview
Correct items	38.77	39.46	29.56
Incorrect items	5.90	7.30	6.10
Confabulated items	1.00	0.70	0.40

They concluded that the increased retrieval using the cognitive interview was due to the guided approach to interviewing, which encouraged participants to remember the crime. Although participants recalled more information, it was not more accurate than the standard interview.

Exam tip

When reporting the results of a study, either to support an argument you are making or when simply discussing one of the named studies, it can be helpful to provide specific numbers or measurements that were found in the study. When quoting numerical data, accuracy in the numbers is critical.

Other studies have shown a positive effect on recall when using the cognitive interview in more ecologically valid settings, such as in relation to real crimes. Fisher et al. (1989) found that after training, detectives gained as much as 47 per cent more useful information from witnesses to real crimes compared to when they had been using standard interview techniques. It has also been shown to be more useful than a standard interview that does not use the four components when interviewing children as young as 5 years old (Holliday 2003).

Evaluation

The cognitive interview has been proven to be very successful in increasing the amount of information about crimes that can be obtained from eyewitnesses. However, it is possible that other factors such as individual differences may have affected how much information was recalled. It is also possible that asking a witness to consider another perspective may result in speculation, despite instructions not to. Further research needs to be undertaken to establish if all four components of the cognitive interview are required or if one component has a greater contribution to success than another.

While the cognitive interview is helpful in increasing the accuracy of recall, it requires specialist training in order to be used effectively. This training and expertise can be costly to police divisions who want to use this approach, both in terms of training their staff and using specialist staff to undertake these interviews. Using this approach is not always helpful at the scene of the crime when it is important that immediate information is obtained in order to try to catch the perpetrator. The crime scene can be chaotic and busy, which is not always conducive to undertaking a structured interview approach.

WIDER ISSUES AND DEBATES

An understanding of how psychology has changed over time
Research into the effectiveness of the cognitive interview in supporting the recall of accurate testimony has provided positive results. As a result, the use of the cognitive interview is now an important part of police interview strategies. This has created a change in the way officers interview witnesses to events. A revised cognitive interview, called the enhanced cognitive interview, now includes additional memory enhancing interview techniques and questions that validate the knowledge elicited by the witness. Fisher et al. (1989) found that the enhanced cognitive interview yielded 45 per cent more correct witness information than the original cognitive interview when used on 16 undergraduate participants. Although the overall benefits of the enhanced cognitive interview are yet to be established in reliable research, it does place greater demand on the interviewer than the original cognitive or standard police interview.

Ethics in interviews
To ensure the interview process remains an ethical one, it is important that interviewers are mindful of the need to remain impartial and open-minded to the information a witness may present. This will help to avoid the interviewer asking leading questions, often without realising, to gain information that may support their own assumptions about the event. Modern policing has moved away from 'interrogation' techniques, which is a more aggressive approach using psychological manipulation, to a more thorough, supportive interview process. They aim to gather the truth rather than to seek confessions or confirmatory testimony. The use of deception in interviews, where police may have provided intentionally ambiguous information or made false promises in order to seek confessions, are not practices followed within the British legal systems. Such behaviour can lead to the increase of false confessions and wrongful convictions. Any information within interviews needs to be given freely and willingly in order to be considered valid.

Taking it further

Ethics should underpin all of the work of a psychologist. This applies when conducting research but also within clinical practice, for example, when working with individuals such as eyewitnesses. It is important for psychologists to achieve their aims, providing the techniques to gain accurate information, but it is also important that these are achieved in a supportive, ethical way.

When being interviewed, witnesses are likely to be distressed at what they have seen. Witnesses can be of any age, so may not be adults, and therefore it may be necessary to think about how you would need to work differently with them, for example consent, etc. What are the key ethical issues to be considered when interviewing all witnesses? Does anything different need to be done when interviewing younger witnesses, or other vulnerable witnesses, such as those with lower levels of understanding?

Psychological formulations

Psychologists are often asked why an individual committed a crime. This may be as part of the court process to decide if the individual was capable of committing the offence and to help decide their risk of reoffending. They will often be asked similar questions when working with offenders after they have been convicted. Usually, this is to help decide if the individual is safe to be released into the community, if they were given a prison sentence.

Psychologists might also undertake a **psychological formulation** to assess what influenced an offender's behaviour and to be able to ensure the chance of future similar offending is minimal. This is a way of making sense of a person's difficulties, by looking at their relationships, biological and social circumstances, life events, and how they have interpreted the events that have happened to them. It is almost like getting a personal story of the offender so that a psychologist can understand how it all links to their offending. A formulation draws on all available psychological theories to understand behaviour. Any psychological treatment is based on a formulation, where the treatment aims to support the offender to develop skills in areas that the formulation shows they need more support. Whenever any new information is gained, it can be helpful to add this to the formulation.

Psychologists will invariably undertake formulations that differ from each other and between offenders. There is no one fixed way of undertaking a formulation. The British Psychological Society (BPS) has issued some guidance that helps to reduce the variability, and therefore make formulations more reliable. The Health and Care Professions Council (HCPC) support this guidance.

An example of a partially completed, simple formulation is shown opposite. Other formulations may be simpler or more complex than the example shown, depending on the different factors that are considered to be relevant to the individual and their offending. The formulation shows how this individual hit someone in a pub and the thoughts, feelings and physical symptoms they had while doing so. The individual received a criminal conviction for assaulting the person in the pub.

The formulation shows some of the background factors that may have influenced the individual's decision to hit the person in that specific situation. This includes the fact that some of their triggers may have been present in the situation: alcohol and a crowded place. They may have felt a little out of control. The size of the person who threw the drink may have also been a factor. Their early experiences suggest that this person has been brought up to use violence to deal with situations, rather than talk about them. The situation may have triggered past memories of being bullied when younger. The individual's core beliefs, which are thoughts that drive us all in our behaviour, suggest that it is important for him to make sure people do not take advantage of them. This is likely to be driven by their past experiences, possibly within the family or due to being bullied. This is someone who believes that violence is a way to resolve situations. All of these thoughts are likely to have influenced the individual's decision to hit the person who threw the drink over them.

The formulation shows that while the offence itself may seem impulsive, spontaneous or out of the blue, as we start to understand the background of the individual it helps psychologists to see some of the important factors that may have contributed to and influenced the individual choosing to hit the person in the pub.

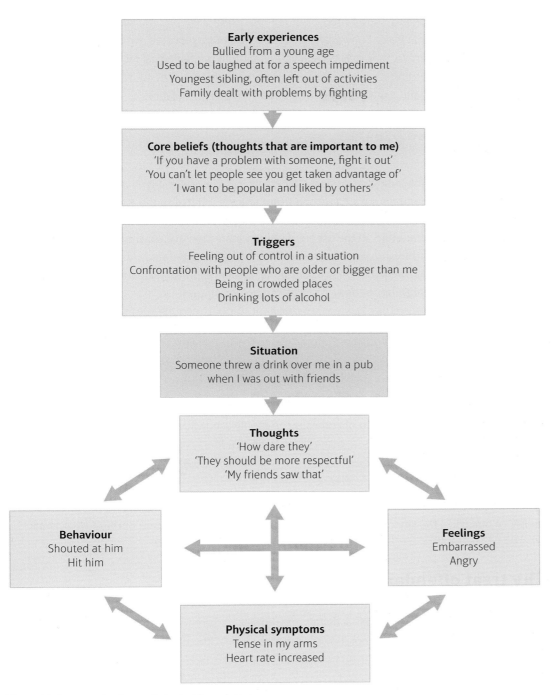

Figure 6.3 An example of a psychological formulation

Evaluation

Formulations, particularly when done in diagrams, can help to simplify a lot of complex information and to explain the factors influencing the offender's behaviour to other professionals. This can help professionals to make decisions about the individual's future. Most importantly it is a useful way of explaining to the offender themselves what led them to committing the offence. This can help them to understand how to manage future situations. Undertaking a formulation with a person can be an important first step in supporting them to make changes to their behaviour.

When undertaking formulations, it can be difficult to gain all the information about the individual. Such information relies on the offender being able to remember all the events that may be significant in their lives and being willing to share this information with a psychologist.

A formulation can include any known medical or mental health diagnosis. However, some individuals might have a disorder that is not known, and therefore cannot be reported, which may be influencing their behaviour. For example, they may be unaware that there is a biological factor, such as serotonin levels, that could be contributing to their behaviour. As such, the range of information that the psychologist can access and use within the formulation limits a formulation.

WIDER ISSUES AND DEBATES

Reductionism

When understanding the individual as a whole person, it is important not to be reductionist, that is, oversimplifying or fragmenting what is important to an individual to the extent that it does not accurately represent the person. It is easy to say that one factor influences a person's behaviour, without giving consideration to all the other influences that may have contributed. For example, we may spend so long thinking about how a person's background or family life has modelled antisocial behaviour that we fail to think about other influences, such as financial motivation or biological factors contributing to the behaviour. Psychological formulations can be criticised for being reductionist because they can overly simplify or compartmentalise factors that may have contributed to the person's behaviour, and perhaps miss out important factors or underplay the interconnection between each factor.

How do we treat offenders?

Punishment for offenders convicted of crimes is commonly used within the criminal justice system. This may include being sent to prison, being given fines or undertaking community punishments. Over the past two decades, there has been an increase in the inclusion of treatment for offenders in addition to being punished for their offence.

The majority of treatment focuses on psychological techniques and behavioural treatments. A number of biological treatments have also been identified. The effectiveness of these treatments varies by treatment.

Why treat offenders?

Punishment teaches offenders that there are consequences to their offending behaviour. It aims to act as a deterrent by restricting their activities and, if they are sent to prison, removing access to the community. Punishment does not, however, directly teach offenders how to act in a different way. Some offences may be committed because the offender is lacking in skills to deal with different situations or because they have learned to associate offending with certain positive outcomes. As a result, punishment cannot be the only solution to reduce reoffending.

Treating offenders aims to identify problem behaviours and the root causes of such behaviours, and to teach offenders non-offending ways to deal with their problems. The treatment is predominantly undertaken by **forensic psychologists** or staff trained in the skills required to provide the treatment to the offenders. If the staff are not psychologists, they are usually supervised by psychologists.

Offenders may receive treatment in the community or in prisons. The principles for each treatment are the same, irrespective of where the treatment is delivered. The extent of the treatment may differ depending on the severity of the offence and the risk of future reoffending.

Offence-related treatment is classified into three distinct groups:

- Cognitive-behavioural therapy (CBT)
- Behavioural treatments
- Biological approaches.

Cognitive-behavioural therapy

Cognitive-behavioural therapy (CBT) is a treatment option that helps the offender to develop insight into their thoughts and feelings and how these influence their behaviour. CBT works on the premise that for every situation we experience, we have thoughts about that situation (the cognitive part of CBT). We will also have emotional reactions to the same experience. Our thoughts will then influence our behaviour and how we react to the situation (the behavioural part). It is possible to change an offender's reactions to the same experience by developing their awareness of their own thoughts, and changing their thoughts to ensure their reaction in the same situation is more **prosocial**. It also works to encourage the offender to consider alternative ways they could act in situations that are not criminal. The offender may undertake CBT on an individual basis, with the therapist, or in a group setting with other offenders and a therapist guiding the discussions.

CBT has a sound theoretical basis in treating offenders because the way a criminal thinks has been firmly linked to their offending behaviour (Beck, 1999). Criminals have been shown to display distorted thinking such as displacing the blame of their crime onto the victim or another source external to themselves, justifying their offending, misinterpreting social cues as potential threats and having schema related to self-dominance and personal entitlement. These distorted ways of thinking are assumed to be learned, so CBT aims to help offenders identify and restructure these faulty patterns of thinking, develop victim empathy and challenge their tendency to self-justify their offending.

Evaluation

CBT is not a form of counselling, and therefore does not focus on overcoming emotional reactions to difficulties in the past, as counselling often does. The focus is mainly on the present thinking of the offenders, at the time of the treatment, although it does acknowledge past thoughts and experiences. CBT does not work immediately. It requires a commitment from the offender in order for it to be effective. As a talking therapy, it requires the offender to talk to the therapist about their thoughts and experiences so that the therapist can help them to understand their reactions to different situations and consider alternative thoughts and behaviours.

CBT has been shown to be effective in helping to treat many emotional difficulties, in offenders and non-offenders. In a meta-analysis of 20 group-oriented CBT research studies, CBT was found to reduce recidivism up to 30 per cent more than control groups that did not receive CBT (Wilson, Bouffard and MacKenzie, 2005). Other meta-analyses of CBT have also found it to be more effective than behavioural techniques in reducing reoffending (Pearson et al., 2002). However, some of the studies within each meta-analysis showed a greater effect than others, so it is not yet certain what aspect of the therapy works on what type of offender. There may be variables that moderate whether the effect of CBT on reoffending rates is small or large in bringing about changes in criminal thinking. In a review of 58 CBT studies, careful scrutiny of possible moderator variables such as type of offender in the programme, methodology of the study and nature of the intervention, revealed that only the amount and quality of the CBT programme affected the likelihood of success (Lipsey, Landenberger and Wilson, 2007).

Key term

Prosocial behaviour: behaviour that takes account of the welfare of others and avoids harming others deliberately.

WIDER ISSUES AND DEBATES

Gender

There is a prevalence of data regarding male offenders, as these represent the highest proportion of convicted criminals within the UK. Explanations for offending, such as elevated testosterone levels or XYY syndrome, help to explain male offending, but do not explain why females commit offences.

Similarly, structured treatment programmes have been designed with men in mind, and therefore may not reflect the needs of female offenders; thereby making them less effective for female offenders completing such treatments. Consequently, less is known about the factors influencing women and how to address their treatment needs.

Anger management

A common application of CBT for offenders is that of anger management, endorsed by Raymond Novaco since the 1970s. Novaco describes anger as a strong emotion that has an impact on a person's physiology, behaviour and cognition. Anger management teaches relaxation techniques to deal with the physiological response to anger (for example, increased heart rate), cognitive restructuring to retrain thought patterns and time out or assertiveness training to deal with the behavioural element of anger. There are three steps involved.

1 Cognitive preparation

Offenders identify situations that provoke anger so they can recognise when an aggressive outburst is likely to occur. Thought patterns are challenged. For example, if they become angry when laughed at, they might work through alternative conclusions such as that people are laughing at the behaviour and not at them. They also consider the negative consequence of their anger on others.

2 Skill acquisition

New coping skills are learned to help deal with anger-provoking situations, such as relaxation, avoidance, or social skills such as assertiveness and conflict resolution. As anger is a normal emotion experienced by everyone, offenders are not taught to be fearful of becoming angry. Instead the emphasis is on giving the offender skills so they can control their anger.

3 Application practice

Offenders role-play a variety of scenarios to practise new skills to control anger. These are conducted in controlled environments so that the offenders feel safe and untrained individuals are not exposed to risk of harm.

Anger management programmes can be used in prisons or with offenders who are serving a probationary period in the community. The courses are usually conducted in small groups and last for approximately ten sessions, although some can last for a number of months.

Offenders may be asked to complete anger diaries on a regular basis. Table 6.2 is an example of what an anger diary may look like. They will complete this every time they feel angry. With support from the therapist, they will start to recognise their triggers for anger and be in a position to evaluate which anger management techniques are effective for them in specific situations. The anger diaries may have additional columns added to them as they become more insightful throughout their treatment. This adopts a scaffolding approach to learning, to avoid giving the offender too many expectations at the start of the therapy when they are likely to need to develop their understanding before they can use these skills.

Table 6.2 Example of an anger diary

Date	What happened when I started to feel angry (Trigger)	What physiological symptoms did I have?	On a scale of 1–10, how angry did I feel (10 being very angry)	What did I think about the situation?	How did I deal with the situation?
Tues 1st July	Someone bumped into me and I spilt my cup of tea	Heart racing Fast breathing	5 / 10	'How dare he?' 'He did that on purpose'	I shouted at him and told him to make me another cup of tea

> **Exam tip**
>
> There may be tables or other diagrams within an exam paper that you are asked to comment on or interpret. You may simply be asked to report findings from the table. To ensure that you carry out the correct task, it is important to read the question carefully, to identify the 'command word' within the question that will tell you what you need to do.

Evaluation

Anger management is only effective for those offenders who have problems with anger control. Not all offences, even violent ones, are committed because the offender was unable to control their anger. Before attending a treatment for anger, offenders will be interviewed to assess if this would be a suitable treatment for them. It has also been shown to be effective only for those motivated to change their behaviour, who are committed to the programme (see Section 6.3, *Studies*, Howells et al., 2005).

Ireland (2004) assessed 50 young male prisoners on an anger management course and 37 control prisoners. It was found that 92 per cent of the prisoners showed an improvement in their management of their anger, suggesting such programmes are effective. It is possible, however, that offenders may be dishonest on psychometric assessments measuring anger and may try to show that they have either improved their anger management skills or minimised the anger they experienced in the first place. This remains a difficulty with any intervention that relies on self-reporting data, and is not exclusive to the treatment of offenders. For offenders, however, there may be a greater 'incentive' to lie, including looking good for parole (if in prison) or trying to have their restrictions reduced by demonstrating that they are no longer a risk to the public.

Behavioural treatments

Social skills training

Evidence suggests that the way an offender interacts with others can increase the potential for a situation to become hostile and therefore result in offending. Additionally, developing positive social skills will provide the offender with skills that can be used proactively in the community in different situations, including trying to obtain employment and dealing with future problems.

Typically CBT incorporates aspects of social skills training, problem-solving skills and assertiveness training. CBT as a treatment package is used to encourage offenders to consider their existing social skills and to develop these and other social skills.

One social skill that is focused on is assertiveness. This involves communicating in a confident, non-confrontational way to minimise conflict and increase the likelihood the offender will be responded to positively. This will encourage an offender who may usually interact with others in an aggressive way, by communicating in a forceful, threatening or intimating way, to consider how to do so in a more assertive way instead. They will be encouraged to practise the techniques introduced within such treatments and reflect on how successfully they used the skills. Such treatment provides a supported approach to developing skills that, by giving greater guidance, is more effective than simply telling the offender what they should do. The offender will learn from personal experience how beneficial it may be to be polite in a situation. It also helps them to feel more confident in being able to use the skills. The offender is then more likely to continue to use the skills in the future.

Offenders can be trained on general thinking skills and decision making, such as getting them to stop and think before they respond, considering other ways of responding to situations and helping them to reflect on the consequences of their decision making. They can also receive problem-solving training to help them deal with conflict that they may experience.

Evaluation

Pearson et al. (2002) reviewed the impact of social skills training on reoffending rates. They found that CBT programmes in general had a positive effect on reducing reoffending. However, it is difficult to assess the effectiveness of specific CBT techniques, such as social skills training, problem-solving and assertiveness training, because they are often used alongside other techniques. In a careful analysis of the techniques used within 58 CBT programmes, cognitive skills training and interpersonal problem solving were found to have a modest positive effect (respective effect sizes 0.2, 0.4) on reducing recidivism.

Taking it further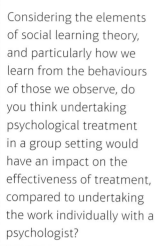

Considering the elements of social learning theory, and particularly how we learn from the behaviours of those we observe, do you think undertaking psychological treatment in a group setting would have an impact on the effectiveness of treatment, compared to undertaking the work individually with a psychologist?

Specific treatment packages that focus on problem-solving skills in juvenile offenders have produced mixed findings. The Enhanced Thinking Skills programme (McGuire, 1995) helps juvenile offenders to learn critical reasoning skills, problem solving and self-control. It is a 20-session programme specifically focused on the cognitive skills that younger people may not have developed, which may have contributed to the offending behaviours. Initial research findings suggested that the programme lowered juvenile recidivism in low-, medium- and high-risk offenders (Friendship et al., 2002), however a reanalysis of the data did not show any significant effect in reducing reoffending (Falshaw et al. 2003). A later study found that significant effects were only shown after one year, but reoffending rates after two years were not improved by the programme (Cann et al., 2003), suggesting that cognitive training may only have short-term effects.

Biological treatments

Diet

A lesser-used approach to treating offenders relates to biological interventions. The reason for such interventions being used less is due to the limited research evidence to support them. Diet is one consideration for a biological treatment for aggression. This suggests that minerals, vitamins or essential fatty acids play a critical role in human behaviour, with a deficit in any of these areas increasing the potential for an individual to act in a violent manner. Low blood sugar levels have been noted to result in increased irritability, although the evidence is often confounded by other variables, such as drug-taking behaviours or a lack of clarity as to the type of antisocial behaviours researchers are observing to determine any correlation between sugar levels and aggression.

Evaluation

Benton (1996) looked at Peruvian children aged 6–7 years old and monitored their irritability while playing a deliberately frustrating computer game. After monitoring their blood sugar levels, he reported there was an increase in irritability when there were moderate falls in levels. However, he concluded that the likelihood of this irritability to translate into aggressive behaviour depended on other factors such as provocation and their own social skills, suggesting diet was not the only influencing factor.

When looking at the effect of diet on behaviour, it is necessary to consider how diet can affect hormones within the body, which in turn influence behaviour, rather than the diet having a direct effect. There are many other variables that may contribute to violence, which are not accounted for by diet. Benton identified provocation and social skills as two excluded from consideration in this treatment approach. Others include the influence of others, previous experience and the individual's interpretation of the situation.

Gesch et al. (2002) undertook a study in a young offender's institution. A total of 231 male prisoners signed a consent form, supported by a prison officer, to receive either a daily vitamin, mineral and essential fatty acid supplementation (active group) or **placebo**. The participants were not told if they were taking placebo medication or the vitamin. The trial had to conform to the normal operations of the institution where participants would leave for reasons such as parole or requirements of cell space. Thus, participation varied from a minimum period of two weeks to nine months in both baseline and supplementation groups. The average time spent on supplementation was 142 days for the placebo group and 142.62 for the active group. No individuals were withdrawn as a result of ill effects from supplementation. Participants were debriefed about their participation by written report.

Measures of antisocial behaviour were recorded throughout the experiment, looking at disciplinary records, including serious incidents of violence, and minor occasions of non-compliance with the

Diet changes

Diet can be easily changed by the inclusion of multi-vitamins in a person's diet. This is a form of treatment that can be easily implemented with minimal cost. However, it is necessary to understand the person's dietary levels prior to starting them on any such treatment, and this requires the skills of medical professionals, which can be costly.

Key term

Placebo: an inactive substance often used as a control in a study to see the effect of a drug.

prison regime. Dietary intake was recorded, and a baseline measure of anger, anxiety and depression was obtained for all participants prior to commencing the study.

They found that the average number of 'disciplinary incidents per 1 000 person-days' dropped from 16 to 10.4 in the active group ($p<0.001$), which is a 35 per cent reduction, whereas the placebo group only dropped by 6.7 per cent. Violent incidents in the active group dropped by 37 per cent, and in the placebo group only 10.1 per cent. They found no significant difference in self-reported levels of anger, anxiety and depression between the active and placebo groups. They concluded that antisocial behaviour in prisons, including violence, are reduced by vitamins, minerals and essential fatty acids with similar implications for those eating poor diets in the community.

Hormone and drug treatments

Individuals may be placed on hormone treatments or be given other drugs as a means of treating aggression. There are a number of key treatments provided that aim to address the hormone imbalances identified as contributing to aggression.

Dopamine

High levels of dopamine have been found to increase aggression and, among adolescents, Conduct Disorder. Dopamine affects the reward systems in the brain, which results in aggressive behavior. Aggression activates the release of dopamine and generates rewarding feelings in the individual. The individual then continues to act in an aggressive way as it makes them feel good. The role of dopamine in aggression has been demonstrated in studies using amphetamines, a chemical that when consumed, increase levels of dopamine. Studies have found that when participants are given amphetamines, there is a corresponding increase in their levels of aggression.

In order to reduce dopamine-related aggression, it is necessary to reduce the level of dopamine in the brain. This can be achieved via the use of dopamine antagonists. These are chemicals that reduce dopamine activity in the brain, which in turn reduces aggressive behaviour. Evidence supporting the importance of dopamine in aggression comes from studies using antipsychotics, such as risperidone, which reduce dopamine levels in the brain. Risperidone is typically used to treat schizophrenia, and also works to reduce irritability. It works by blocking the receptors in the brain on which dopamine acts. This prevents excess dopamine activity, which then has a positive effect in reducing aggression.

LeBlanc et al. (2005) undertook a randomised controlled trial to investigate the effect of risperidone on aggression among adolescent boys diagnosed with either Conduct Disorder or Oppositional Disorder. Both conditions result in aggressive behaviour. All participants had below average levels of IQ. The randomised control trial resulted in the 163 boys being allocated to either a placebo drug or a dose of risperidone (taken orally). The study found that after six weeks, those who were treated with risperidone displayed a 56.4 per cent reduction in aggressive behaviour when compared to the placebo group. A reduction in aggression was also noted in the placebo group (21.7 per cent). An aggression score was calculated, which rated the level of aggression among the participants before and after the drug treatment. There was a clinically significant reduction ($p<0.001$) in the aggression score among the risperidone group at the end of the six weeks compared to the control group. They concluded that risperidone is effective in reducing symptoms of aggression among boys with disruptive behaviour disorders. As the risperidone decreases dopamine levels in the brain, this leads to the conclusion that reducing dopamine can lead to decreased aggression.

A study by Couppis and Kennedy (2008), however, found that dopamine might be a consequence of aggressive behaviour rather than a cause (see *Neurotransmitters* page 372). As such, to treat aggression with a treatment method that addresses the consequence of aggression may not address the underlying reason for the aggression.

WIDER ISSUES AND DEBATES

Issues of social control
The treatment of aggression via the use of drug treatments can be argued to be a form of social control. In prescribing hormone or drug treatments this can change the behaviour of the individual, to more closely match the expectations of those of the general population.

Maths tips

Interpreting levels of probability is very important. In this study the statistical significance was $p<0.001$, which means that the probability of the reduction in symptoms in the risperidone group compared to the control group being due to chance was less that 0.1 per cent or less than 1 in 1000. This does not mean that risperidone was 99.9 per cent effective, it means that the difference found between the groups was very unlikely to have been due to chance factors, and highly probable to have been a result of the risperidone.

Key term

Hyperprolactinaemia:
abnormal blood levels of
prolactin, associated with
spontaneous lactation,
menstruation, infertility and
erectile dysfunction.

Link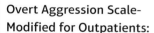

For more information
on the role of serotonin
in aggression, see
Neurotransmitters on
page 372 and Topic 3,
Biological psychology.

Key term

**Overt Aggression Scale-
Modified for Outpatients:**
a rating scale that is used
to identify the level of
aggression presented by
an individual within the
past week. The scale is
completed by people who
know the individual well.

WIDER ISSUES AND DEBATES

Individual differences

Risperidone is associated with a number of adverse side effects, such as a rash, vomiting, anxiety, sleep disturbance and **hyperprolactinaemia**, among many others. It is therefore questionable whether risperidone should be used to treat aggression, particularly in young male offenders. Pharmacological interventions, such as risperidone, should only be used after careful diagnosis, in conjunction with psychological therapy, and where aggression seems to be the most pervasive symptom. Because individuals with serious aggressive behaviour are often involved in other treatment programmes in addition to receiving medication, it is often difficult to establish whether the medication alone is effective in reducing symptoms.

Serotonin

Serotonin is responsible for maintaining mood balance.

Serotonin levels can be increased by the drug treatment selective serotonin reuptake inhibitors (SSRIs). SSRIs are a form of antidepressant medication. After carrying a message in the brain, serotonin is usually reabsorbed by the nerve cells. This is known as 'reuptake'. SSRIs work by blocking (inhibiting) this reuptake. This results in more serotonin being available to pass further messages between neurons.

Fluoxetine is an SSRI. Coccaro and Kavoussi (1997) investigated the influence of fluoxetine on impulsive aggressive behaviour among a sample of personality-disordered individuals with a history of aggression but who did not have major depression, bipolar or schizophrenia. A number of behavioural rating scales, including the **Overt Aggression Scale-Modified for Outpatients**, were used to monitor the level of aggression displayed by the participants over a three-month period. A placebo group was used as a comparison group. The study found that fluoxetine resulted in a sustained reduction in scores on irritability at the two-month stage and aggression at the third month of treatment. This was not observed in the placebo group. This suggested that fluoxetine, as an SSRI, had a positive effect in reducing aggression among impulsive aggressive individuals with personality disorder.

In a recent review of 62 sexual offenders in Whatton prison (Hocken and Winder, 2012), the 32 offenders taking fluoxetine reported reduced frequency of sexual thoughts and excitability. However, the side effects of drowsiness, constipation and nausea were reported (Lievesley et al., 2012).

Testosterone

Testosterone is a hormone found in both men and women, but in greater levels in men. It plays a key role on the development of male reproductive tissue and is required to maintain muscle strength and bone density. Elevated testosterone has been documented among individuals with a history of aggression.

The administration of the female hormone medroxyprogesterone acetate (MPA), which decreases the functioning of testosterone, has been investigated as a way of reducing testosterone levels in males. This chemical agent, referred to as an anti-androgen, acts by breaking down and eliminating testosterone and inhibiting the production of luteinising hormone through the pituitary gland, which in turn inhibits or prevents the production of testosterone. It also produces significant side effects, including breast enlargement, osteoporosis and depression. This makes it more likely an individual will decline such treatments or result in higher rates of non-compliance following initial agreement to treatment.

The use of psychological knowledge within society

Medroxyprogesterone acetate (MPA) has typically been applied to male sexual offenders as a means of reducing sexual aggression thought to be the result of elevated testosterone levels. The use of anti-androgen medications to reduce sexual drive and consequently sexual behaviour could be classified as a form of chemical restraint, a practice of using specific hormonal agents to restrict sexual freedoms and behaviours.

The use of such chemical interventions, particularly involuntarily, as forms of restraint carry a negative ethical connotation. This form of hormone has limited effectiveness in reducing sexual aggression and its application as a treatment of sexual aggression within the UK is now limited.

Loosen, Purdon and Pavlou (1997) found that the administration of MPA resulted in marked reductions in outwardly directed anger among all eight participants within their study. However, the participants were non-aggressive men so their findings have limited application to aggressive individuals.

Evaluation

Much of the guidance for the use of hormone treatment, specifically in relation to risperidone use, provides guidance that medication alone should not be the treatment plan. The use of drug treatments should form part of a wider intervention that also teaches individuals to recognise and manage their aggression. This suggests that drug treatment on its own is insufficient to treat aggression.

It is often necessary for prolonged drug treatment before an effect on behaviour can be observed. For example, it can take up to four weeks for SSRIs to have any noticeable effect on the individual. This can affect the medication compliance, with the potential for people to not take the medication consistently if they do not see any effect. This then reduces the effectiveness of drug treatment. There can also be physical side effects of hormone treatment. This means the treatment might not be suitable for everyone displaying aggression, due to ongoing medical conditions or because the side effects are too severe to warrant the continued use of the medication.

Research studies investigating the effect of drug treatments on aggression often use placebo-controlled trials, in which the participants do not know which group they have been allocated to. This reduces the likelihood of demand characteristics, making the data more reliable.

Ethics

Drug treatments used for aggression and sexual deviancy have been used in forensic-psychiatric institutions to treat offenders with mental health issues. Improvements in behaviour or reductions in symptoms are often assessed by clinical experts or through self-reports. Pharmacological treatments are voluntary in this country, so are only prescribed with the consent of the patient. However, there is concern over the nature of such consent within forensic-psychiatric institutions, and in other countries voluntary consent is not required.

What influences the accuracy of eyewitnesses?

Eyewitnesses are those individuals who see an event such as a crime occurring. The police, who will document everything that the person saw, usually interview them. An eyewitness is likely to be required to attend court so that they can tell the judge and jury what they saw during the event. Unfortunately our memories are not as accurate as we might want or expect them to be, and can be affected by a number of different factors, all of which influences how reliable we are in court.

Witness factors

Jury members tend to trust the evidence given by eyewitnesses more than by scientific experts. In *Cognitive psychology* (Topic 2), you learned about how our memory functions. You also looked at how it can malfunction, making jury faith in eyewitnesses flawed. Reconstructive memory explains that perception and recall are influenced by expectations and previously stored knowledge.

Stress and arousal

Eyewitnesses are placed under great emotional stress when witnessing an event, however serious it is. Research has suggested that our performance, for example remembering information, is impaired as we get too aroused/stressed. This is known as the Yerkes-Dodson Law (1908), as shown in Figure 6.4 below. As we become stressed about a situation or event, our performance in that situation will eventually decline. There is an optimum amount of arousal we need to be successful but it is very easy to go beyond this. Being too relaxed in a situation will also not help our performance. If a witness is too relaxed, and experiencing low arousal, their recall of the event may be less accurate, and therefore more unreliable.

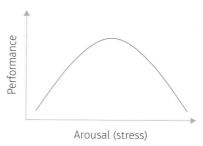

Figure 6.4 Diagram to show Yerkes-Dodson Law

WIDER ISSUES AND DEBATES

Practical issues in the design and implementation of research
The laboratory studies included in this section are discussed in relation to their validity in measuring the true arousal of a real eyewitness. The Yerkes-Dodson curve shows that students undertaking research in a laboratory may not reach the 'critical level' of optimum performance (that is, recall of an event). This is because they know what they are seeing is not real. Similarly, due to the experiment being artificial, they are also unlikely to experience high amounts of stress that may affect their recall, therefore being 'under-aroused' in the experiment.

Evaluation

A classic study into arousal and recall was Valentine and Mesout's (2009) London Dungeon study (see Section 6.3, *Studies*). This was undertaken with real eyewitnesses to an event, as participants did not know they would be expected to recall what they saw after visiting the museum. This study can therefore be considered a more valid study of the effect of arousal on memory recall than laboratory

Link

For more information on reconstructive memory, see Topic 2: *Cognitive psychology*.

experiments such as the Loftus et al. (1987) syringe study. She aimed to look at the weapon focus effect and found that recall of the event was greater when participants were approached by an experimenter holding a syringe than an experimenter holding a pen. The syringe created a high-arousal situation.

We know from research, however, that this is not always the case. Recall within artificial situations can be accurate, suggesting that low arousal in experimental settings may not always affect accuracy. Similarly, the Yerkes-Dodson Law does not necessarily apply in field studies of witness accuracy of real-life incidents. There are mixed findings in relation to the recall within real-life situations. Yuille and Cutshall (1986) found that the greater the reported level of arousal, the more accurate the testimony. This may be due not just to arousal levels, but those with the highest level of arousal were also those closest to the crime, and therefore would have had a better view of the crime. Alternatively, Stanny and Johnson (2000) found that within a high arousal police officer training involving a shooting, fewer details were recalled, suggesting that high arousal does not always create improved recall, as a result of the arousal level having gone beyond the point of being effective.

Flashbulb memories

'Flashbulb memories' were proposed in the 1970s to describe the belief that memory almost takes a photograph of an event that has an emotional impact on us. It was hypothesised that this type of memory was unusually clear and remained accurate over many years. The idea of a flashbulb memory has, however, been criticised, and demonstrated that while people were confident in their abilities to recall information from a significant event, their confidence did not translate into accuracy of recall (Neisser and Harsch, 1992). For example, people may be able to recall exactly what they were doing at key moments of time; the 9/11 terrorist attack in New York in 2001 or the 7/7 bombings of London in 2005, or when we learned of the death of well-known individuals such as Michael Jackson or Robin Williams. Hirst et al. (2009) investigated flashbulb memories of the 9/11 New York terrorist attack and have shown that our memories of these events will stay accurate for a period of time, but, as with other memories, the accuracy of our recall fades over time.

WIDER ISSUES AND DEBATES

The use of psychological knowledge within society

Our understanding of how we encode and later retrieve memories is helpful to wider society. Flashbulb memories can explain why individuals still recall vivid incidents such as tragic accidents for a long period of time after the event.

Similarly, it helps us to understand why recall for stressful situations remain for prolonged periods, due to the high arousal at the time. This provides an explanation for why individuals can suffer prolonged trauma, often known as post-traumatic stress disorder (PTSD) after witnessing a traumatic scene, even if they were only involved in that situation for a brief period of time.

Inconsistent outcomes of studies addressing the impact of arousal on eyewitnesses are limited by methods used to elicit arousal (for example, artificial laboratory settings) and problematic operational definitions. For example, arousal could result from anxiety or fear (as might be experienced by eyewitnesses) or simply an increased state of alertness or attention. This confusion in the use of the term 'arousal' makes comparison between studies complex.

Taking it further

What is your own memory like when experiencing high levels of stress or other emotions?

Recall an event that you witnessed or were involved in that created high emotions in you. This could be something like a happy event, seeing a scary movie, etc. How much detail can you remember about what you saw or what you did?

Now think about a typical day you have had this week, when you haven't experienced any high-level emotion. How much can you remember about what you did, who you spoke to, etc., during this day? Are you able to remember any more of this day when emotions were less than the emotional event you have described above?

The reliability of eyewitnesses has been questioned by many research studies.

Post-event information

The eyewitness is the single most common form of evidence in many criminal trials; whether a case is solved frequently depends on the thoroughness and accuracy of an eyewitness account. Unfortunately, incorrect eyewitness accounts have also been identified as the leading cause for the miscarriage of justice.

The encoding of the event seen by a witness is just as critical as the initial witnessing of the offence itself when maintaining accurate testimony. Often witnesses are interviewed over a period of time after the offence, and some time before a case may go to trial. The experiences of the witness in this time period can have an impact on what witnesses think they saw during the offence. It can result in them providing inaccurate information at crucial times as other information can confabulate the information they have already encoded. During the period between a criminal event and a trial, a witness may encounter additional information about the event from a number of sources including the media, other witnesses, lawyers or the police. Under some conditions, exposure to this post-event information may augment or degrade a witness's report. Reconstructive memories occur when we attempt to make sense of what we have seen and are influenced by our interpretation of the situation as well as our own cultural norms and expectations. We do not recall information in exactly the same form as it was encoded. Instead, there is the tendency to recall the main points or underlying meaning in a way that makes most sense to the individual. Information presented to witnesses after the event can influence a person's schema about what they think happened within the event, particularly if the event was unusual or outside their normal experience, making for less accurate testimony.

Most of what we know about the sustainability of adult eyewitness accounts comes from the work of Elizabeth Loftus. She is an American cognitive psychologist with an interest in memory. She conducted her own research in the 1970s and continues to research memory within legal contexts, including investigation of factors that can make eyewitness memory less reliable. Overall, exposure to misleading post-event information was found to decrease accuracy. In fact, for participants who received misleading post-event information, accuracy often fell below chance levels of performance (Loftus et al., 1978). This pattern of results has been referred to as the 'misinformation effect'. This is where information that is incorrect can change a person's memory of an event.

Leading questions are discussed in Section 6.3 Studies in relation to the research of Elizabeth Loftus and John Palmer. They are a critical source of post-event information and can significantly influence the accuracy of eyewitness recall.

Leading questions may come from a number of sources, including the police at interview and from legal officials within a trial setting. They may be used unintentionally while trying to gain information or may be used at court by solicitors who are attempting to confuse witnesses in order to get their client, the defendant, a verdict of 'not guilty' from the courts. The findings of Yuille and Cutshall (1986) suggest that leading questions have limited effect on accuracy within real-life eyewitness accounts. Yuille and Cutshall's (1986) research was based on a case study of a real gunshop robbery and subsequent shootout in Canada. Real witnesses to the shooting were interviewed about the incident and this was compared to police records of other testimony. The researchers found that the witnesses had detailed memories of the event and were not misled by the researchers' leading questions.

Link

For more information on Loftus and Palmer's (1974) work see Section 6.3, Studies.

Evaluation

Most research has looked at the effect of critical questions relating to key parts of an event. For example, within Loftus and Palmer's (1974) work, they asked 'About how fast were the cars going when they hit each other?' Only limited research has been carried out to look at more open-ended questioning procedures to examine the effect of misleading post-event information on adults' eyewitness accounts. Unfortunately, some of the methods used in these studies still make it difficult to draw firm conclusions about the effect of open-ended questioning procedures, such as the cognitive interview. The purpose of the cognitive interview is to avoid interrogative techniques to ensure the absence of leading questions.

In the study conducted by Zaragoza et al. (1987), for example, participants watched a slide sequence depicting a workman stealing some items from an office. Following the slides, participants read a description of the target event that contained either neutral information about one of the objects present in the slides (for example, a soft drink can) or misleading information about that object (for example, a 'Planter's Peanuts' can). Participants were given either (1) a standard recognition test or (2) a cued-recall test. In condition (1), participants were asked to choose between two alternative responses to each question (for example, 'The key to the desk drawer was next to a _____ can?') and were asked to select the type of drink from a choice of two brands. In condition (2), they were asked more open-ended questions. However, the questions were phrased in such a way that the misleading answer was not a logical response. For example, participants were asked 'The key to the desk drawer was next to a soft drink can. What brand of soft drink was it?' As participants were highly unlikely to answer 'Planter's Peanuts' in response to a question about soft drinks, this study does not tell us whether participants would have incorporated the misleading information about peanuts into their subsequent report if the question had been more general (for example, 'What items were on the desk when the workman entered the room?').

The Yuille and Cutshall (1986) study used only a small participant group. There is the potential for participant variables to affect the findings of the study, and reliability is therefore reduced. The use of field studies such as this increases the ecological validity of the study and psychological understanding of the effect of leading questions on eyewitness testimony.

Most studies of post-event information have focused on adults. A number of studies conducted with children have shown that leading questions can also influence their account of an event. Poole and Lindsay (1995) investigated the accuracy of recall of 5–7-year-olds following the presence of leading questions. They found that after a three-month delay, children were influenced by leading questions, resulting in misinformation being recalled.

The use of laboratory investigation as a measure of eyewitness testimony yields different results from those undertaken with the witnesses of real-life crimes. This suggests that caution should be applied in considering only the findings of laboratory studies in this area. Laboratory experiments arguably minimise the emotional stress placed on a participant as they are aware the crime is not real, though it can still be distressing for some to witness crime images.

Laboratory experiments for this type of research have a number of limitations. They are unlikely to create the same emotional reactions in watching a film of a crime than if the witnesses were experiencing the crime for themselves. This may also make the participants less invested in trying to remember as much information as possible, as they know it was not a real crime. Laboratory experiments have the advantage of being highly controlled settings. For eyewitness testimony research, this level of control creates an artificial environment, and the absence of extraneous

Taking it further

Elizabeth Loftus is currently conducting research into how misleading information can be used to implant false memories and reshape peoples' food preferences. This is exciting new research that you may wish to investigate further on the Internet'.

Taking it further

Using your knowledge of the theories of memory, consider why a person who witnessed a terrifying street mugging would be unable to accurately remember or identify what and who they saw.

Consider, among others, the emotional state, time taken to take statements, the speed of the offence and who they spoke to before going to trial. What other factors would also influence their accuracy?

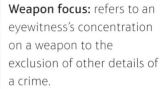

Key term

Weapon focus: refers to an eyewitness's concentration on a weapon to the exclusion of other details of a crime.

In a crime where a weapon is involved, it is not unusual for a witness to be able to describe the weapon in much more detail than the person holding it.

variables that would typically be found in a real crime setting, such as noises, the reactions of other people, etc., reduces the ecological validity of the findings from laboratory settings.

Weapon focus

One specific factor that has been proven to affect recall of an event, and therefore eyewitness accuracy, is whether there is a weapon used within the offence they witness. There are two possible explanations for the effect of a weapon on eyewitness recall. These include the influence of stress experienced within the situation and the attention paid to the weapon.

Stress

The Yerkes-Dodson Law is applicable to any crime situation, including those in which weapons are present. The high level of stress and arousal experienced by the eyewitness may have some influence on the amount of information they encode about the crime, and therefore the amount of information they are able to recall. When there is a weapon present, it creates an optimum level of arousal, which assists the eyewitness in recalling information about the weapon, though not about other details within the situation. This suggests that arousal results in the individual focusing on the weapon to the detriment of other details, so making their recall limited to the weapon itself.

Attention

A different explanation for the effect of weapon focus on the memory of an eyewitness, is that of attention. Because a weapon is unusual in many cultures, it is focused on more closely at the expense of peripheral information. Rather than a source of stress on memory, it is a focus of attention that diminishes the capacity of a witness to encode other information.

Evaluation

Loftus et al. (1987) suggest that weapon focus occurs because the presence of a weapon focuses attention away from the less dramatic visual images, such as the image of the perpetrator. They showed participants a series of slides of a customer in a restaurant. In one version, the customer was holding a gun; in the other, the same customer held a chequebook. Participants who saw the gun version tended to focus on the weapon. As a result, they were less likely to identify the customer in an identity parade than those who had seen the chequebook version.

Kerri Pickel (1998) investigated weapon focus within the context of a hairdresser's salon and used a video consisting of a scene from a hair salon. A man walks to the receptionist and she handed him money. In the different conditions, the man held a different item in his hand. These were: nothing (control situation), scissors (high threat, low unusualness), handgun (high threat, high unusualness), wallet (low threat, low unusualness) and raw chicken (low threat, high unusualness). Participants then completed a ten-minute filler exercise before completing a questionnaire asking them to recall details of what they saw, including the receptionist, the man, what he was doing in the salon and what he had in his hand. She found that the presence of either a handgun or the raw chicken resulted in the poorest recall of the man, while the wallet and scissors had less effect in comparison. This could be interpreted as both high unusualness and high threat items producing low recall. However, the handgun and scissors are both high threat items, yet scissors did not affect recall of the man. This suggests that threat alone cannot result in poor memory.

Pickel argued that it is the unusualness of an object that draws our attention, in this case, the presence of a handgun, therefore assisting our recall of it, rather than the threat associated with it. This would explain why we might recall someone dressed as a superhero walking through a shopping centre on a busy day when we talk to friends about what we have done that day. There was no threat by the person dressed up, but it is not every day you see Batman at the local shops! The weapon-focus effect will not occur for weapons consistent with the visual scene in which they appear, for example a gun at a shooting range.

In 2006, Pickel et al. published another simulation study, this time investigating whether awareness of the weapon-focus effect could diminish its effect. Participants were seated in a small classroom and informed that they were about to observe a short scene portrayed by actors. However, participants were first provided with one of two brief lectures: (a) a lecture regarding weapon focus, and how important it is to attend to perpetrator features instead of dwelling on any weapons they may carry, or (b) a lecture regarding eyewitness confidence and perceived credibility. In either case, a man interrupted the lecture by bursting into the classroom bearing a neutral object (a book) or a weapon (gun). The main finding was that participants presented with the lecture on eyewitness confidence (b) produced fewer correct details (and more incorrect details) related to the perpetrator in the weapon condition than in the neutral object condition. However, object type had no effect on those presented with the weapon focus lecture (a). Pickel concluded that with proper instruction, the weapon-focus effect could be overcome.

WIDER ISSUES AND DEBATES

The use of psychological knowledge in society

The findings of Pickel's various studies suggest that we should carefully consider the reliability of an eyewitness in court, if the crime involved a weapon. Recent studies suggest that it may be possible to overcome the effect of weapon focus, which may increase the reliability of testimony. It has particular application to police officers, who are more likely to experience such situations in their working roles. If officers can be trained in the area of weapon focus, it is possible that this will improve their recall of events when a weapon was present within a crime.

In an attempt to overcome the fact that most weapon-focus research was simulated in a laboratory, Wagstaff et al. (2003) adopted a different approach by investigating information obtained about real-life events after they had occurred. They coded police interviews taken from witnesses or victims of robberies, assaults and rapes investigated by two separate police forces in Britain. These interviews were compared against a police description of the primary suspect at the time of their arrest. They found no evidence of any effect of weapon presence on feature accuracy, therefore not supporting the weapon-focus effect.

Fawcett et al. (2013) undertook a meta-analysis to identify what it is that causes our memories to be influenced when a weapon is present, in an attempt to clarify the various findings. They concluded that weapon presence consistently demonstrated a negative effect on both feature accuracy and identification accuracy under controlled conditions as well as within real-life situations. Factors that complicate real-world research include how long the witness was exposed to the weapon, which is easily controlled within laboratory settings.

Exam tip

If you are using a number of studies to evaluate a topic, such as weapon focus, it is not always necessary to spend a long time describing in lots of detail all stages of each study, unless specifically asked for in the question. Instead, the emphasis is likely to be on showing your understanding of the studies and using that to evaluate if the studies support the topic or not. This will give you more time to demonstrate the application of your knowledge, which goes beyond simply describing what you know.

Taking it further

Look again at the studies of Pickel et al. (2006) and Loftus et al. (1987). How applicable are their findings in today's society, in a time where the presence of guns is more frequent in crime?

What influences the court process?

It is the aim of the police that as many crimes as possible are dealt with officially, to act as a deterrent for future offending. For many criminal cases, this requires a criminal trial where the decision is made as to whether the accused person is guilty or not of the crime they are charged with.

Many criminal cases are dealt with in the Crown Court. This is a court that has the power to give long prison sentences to offenders if necessary but can also give much more lenient sentences if the offence is not considered to need a prison sentence. Less serious cases may be dealt with in the Magistrates Court. Magistrates only have the power to give lighter sentences, including short prison sentences, and their powers are therefore more restricted than that of a Crown Court. For all cases dealt with by the Crown Court in England and Wales, there will be a jury selected to assist the judge in the case.

The decisions made by the jury can be influenced by a number of factors including:

- characteristics of the defendant
- pre-trial publicity
- factors that influence behaviour in the deliberation room.

Factors influencing jury decision making

Twelve adults will be asked to be jury members for one criminal case. There are strict rules they have to follow during a trial to make sure that the case is confidential. This also protects the jury members from any influences on their judgement other than what evidence is presented in the court, such as media interest if the case has been reported in the news. This is to make sure that the decisions the jury make are based solely on the facts of the case as told to them in court. The main role of jury members will be to decide, as a group, if they believe the defendant is guilty of the crime they have been charged with or not. A judge cannot decide if someone is guilty nor can they tell the jury what to decide, so the judge relies entirely on the jury. This makes the role of the jury very important.

There are a number of factors that have been shown to affect jury decision making at different times of the trial process.

Pre-trial

Publicity surrounding the offence, the defendant or other information about the case can influence the schemas the jury have about those involved. What is communicated within the media, whether via the news or social media, can create a perception of the defendant and other involved parties even before official information has been given within the court. It is difficult to change such perceptions once they have been formed.

Competence and instructions: jurors are expected to listen to often technical information, which may be far outside of their own knowledge base, and be tasked with making an informed decision about guilt as a result of the technical evidence. Forster Lee et al. (1993) found that giving instructions to jury members prior to the presentation of technical information rather than afterwards increased their ability to focus on relevant information to the trial. This suggests the instructions helped them to filter out irrelevancies and increase their ability as non-technical jury members to make sense of the evidence presented to them. Levett and Kovera (2003) have shown

Link

Pre-trial publicity is discussed in more detail later in this section.

that jurors have difficulty evaluating what scientific evidence is inaccurate, even following cross-examination by other experts, due to difficulties in understanding the meaning of the evidence.

Severance and Loftus (1982) have shown that having key terms explained to the jury, such as what is meant by 'reasonable doubt', improved understanding of legal concepts, though not all demonstrated understanding even after such explanations. Explanations appear to assist understanding for terms that the jury may have some familiarity with, but does little to improve their level of understanding for more legal, unfamiliar terms. This results in jury members potentially having limited comprehension of significant issues throughout a trial. Reifman et al. (1992) found that real jurors' comprehension of the instructions they receive at trial is not very good, and that this is also the case with mock jurors participating in jury research.

During the trial

Defendant characteristics, such as race, gender, appearance, etc., can bias the jury based on stereotypes the jury members may have towards individuals with certain characteristics.

Expert witness testimony is often used to give scientific credibility to evidence and help clarify complex issues. Experts warning the jury about the reliability of certain witness evidence does reduce the trust in such evidence, but does not necessarily discriminate between 'good' and 'bad' evidence. Research has shown that even though expert witnesses are called to warn jurors about the problems with eyewitness testimony, jurors tend to disregard these warnings and still believe eyewitness accounts. Cutler et al. (1989) demonstrated that jurors were more likely to give guilty verdicts when the expert witness used easy-to-understand language, suggesting the use of language can influence the opinion of juries.

Story models are another example of within trial influences. When faced with particularly complex information, a jury is likely to pick out key information or facts and create a story from them in order to make sense of the information given to them. Pennington and Hastie (1990) showed that if a jury is given an account of an offence in an order that was easy to understand, 78 per cent of the participants, in the role as a juror, gave guilty verdicts, compared to 31 per cent if the information was not given to them in a logical order. This suggests that legal representatives should consider how they structure their legal arguments, and that this can be used as a means of potentially influencing the outcome of the trial.

Additional consideration should be given to witness characteristics within a trial. Social psychology has identified that an authoritarian personality is most likely to be followed by others, and a confident, authoritarian witness may influence the jury. As is the case of authoritarian personalities within the jury itself, a confident witness may be persuasive to the jury. Race, accent and attractiveness of witnesses may also influence the jury, based on their schemas and stereotypes, as has been evidenced for defendants.

Post-trial

Conformity is when an individual gives up his or her personal views under group pressure. Within a jury situation, two types of conformity may occur: **normative** and **informational**. In the latter case, the individual conforms to the group norms because they do not know what to do and looks to the group for guidance. It may be that the individual does not understand the legal technicalities of the case. With normative conformity, the jury member conforms to avoid rejection by the group or to gain rewards from them, but may not in reality agree with the decision. Asch (1951) found that the most influential group size to gain conformity was 7:1. He also showed that difficult tasks and the higher status of some group members also influenced others to conform.

Link

Defendant characteristics are discussed in more detail later in this section.

Key terms

Normative conformity: the jury member conforms to avoid rejection by the group or to gain rewards from them, but may not in reality agree with the decision.

Informational conformity: the individual conforms to the group norms because they do not know what to do and looks to the group for guidance.

The understanding of the jury in the Vicky Pryce trial in February 2013 was questionable. She was accused of falsely admitting she was driving the car when her husband at the time, Chris Huhne, a Member of Parliament, was caught speeding. The jury had listened to all the information and were at the stage where they started to discuss their decisions among themselves. This is called the 'deliberation' stage and happens towards the end of a trial. They asked some basic questions that raised significant concerns to the judge about their understanding of their role and of the information given to them in court. The defendant faced a possible prison sentence if found convicted so it was important the jury fully understood their role. The judge considered that he had no choice but to dismiss the first jury, select a new one and hold a retrial in the hope that they would understand and be able to make an **informed decision**.

This is fortunately an unusual case but highlights that the jury is expected to have a sufficient level of understanding of the English language, formal discussions and an ability to evaluate the information given to them. Their abilities in this area may therefore have a significant effect on the decisions they make at trial.

Minority influence: it does not always require a large number of individuals to influence the decision of one juror. Moscovici (1976) suggests that one or a small minority of like-minded individuals may influence the majority. He found this to be the case if they are consistent, committed in their opinions and arguments, seem to be acting on principle rather than out of self-gain and incur some cost, as well as being not overly rigid and unreasonable in their opinions and arguments.

Social loafing: not every individual who serves on a jury is motivated to attend. Many people are there only because they have been summoned to participate. Such individuals may therefore be inclined to deliberate less. **Social loafing** refers to a reduction in individual effort on a collective task, in which their output is pooled with those of other group members, compared to when working alone. Knowing that the final jury decision is a collective one, an individual jury member may be inclined to review the information less than they would if it was their decision alone, thereby letting other jury members think for them and influence their decisions.

Foreperson influence: all juries will have a foreperson, who will be the individual to present the decision of the jury back to the judge. The foreperson is often perceived as leader, and the selection of the foreperson often reflects this. Leaders are more likely to influence others as they are considered best placed to make a decision. If this individual has an authoritarian personality (see Topic 1: *Social psychology*), this may further influence other jury members. Evidence for the influence of the foreperson is more limited than other post-trial factors.

This suggests that the trial process is vulnerable at many stages, as the jury members are susceptible to influence throughout the process, even before being selected as a jury member, and after all the evidence has been presented.

Characteristics of the defendant

The stereotypes we hold can influence how we see and categorise individuals, and can affect our views towards these people. Our stereotypes can be influenced by how they sound, what they look like or how they behave. This can in turn change how we would view these individuals if they were a defendant in a trial situation.

Race

Most research regarding race has focused on the relationship between white jurors and black or white defendants. One common finding has been that white jurors in mock trials demonstrate negative bias to black defendants during sentence decisions, giving them harsher sentences when compared to white defendants. A similar racial bias has been shown during verdict decisions, with more black defendants being found guilty than white defendants. Bradbury and Williams' 2013 study (see Section 6.3, *Studies*) found that that black defendants are less likely to be convicted by juries composed of a higher proportion of black jurors and are more likely to be convicted by juries composed of a higher proportion of white and Hispanic jurors.

Skolnick and Shaw (1997), however, found that while jury members of the same ethnic race as the defendant were less likely to find the defendant guilty, white jurors were more likely to find a black defendant not guilty than guilty. The same effect was not found if the jury was black and the defendant white. They summarised that a black defendant always received fewer guilty verdicts, irrespective of the race of the jury. This was speculated to be due to the white jury members being fearful of being accused as racist.

David Abwender and Kenyatta Hough undertook mock jury research in 2001. The mock trials involved black, white and Hispanic defendants. The study investigated both race and attractiveness. Black participants showed leniency to defendants of their own race, whereas Hispanics showed the opposite. White participants did not show any ethnic bias. This suggests that racial bias has a more complicated effect on jury decision making than first assumed; any such bias may not be consistent among racial groups.

Defendants are instructed when going to court to present themselves in a smart and tidy fashion, even if this is not how they would typically dress. This can help to reduce any negative stereotypes the jury may have against the defendant based on a more casual appearance and can, in turn, influence whether the jury finds the defendant guilty. Evidence for this was found in Abwender and Hough's study. Female jurors were found to be harsher to an unattractive defendant than they were to an attractive one but male jurors showed the opposite effect.

Villains in films are usually portrayed as unattractive, and are often presented as untrustworthy. The 'good guys', however, tend to be attractive, and appear more trustworthy and honest. This creates a stereotype that can be found in jury decision research, including that found by Harold Sigall and Nancy Ostrove in 1975. They asked 120 participants to make sentence recommendations for a defendant for either burglary or fraud. They were given a piece of card with a crime written on it, either fraud or burglary, and a photograph of a woman known as Barbara Helms. There were a number of conditions to the research. The participants were separated into 6 groups of 20 participants, with each group having a different experimental condition (see *Experimental conditions*).

All participants were asked to rate Barbara's attractiveness to ensure they agreed which photographs showed her as unattractive and attractive. They were then all asked to give her a prison sentence from between 1 and 15 years for the crime. They found that Barbara was sentenced to longer in prison in the fraud conditions and less time in prison for burglary in the attractive photo condition. A similar length of sentence was given for both crimes in the 'unattractive' and 'no photograph' conditions. This suggested it was the attractiveness of the photograph that influenced their decision. This could be due to an assumption that attractive people use their looks to con people out of money, whereas attractive people are not associated with burglary.

This study, while informative, would not be applicable to a real trial, as the jury only make a decision on guilt, and do not decide the length of a sentence for a defendant who has been found guilty. Only the judge has the legal power to make that decision to ensure impartiality. It does, however, provide information about the perceptions of the people towards those of different levels of attractiveness.

The negative effect of unattractiveness on decisions of guilt has been evidenced in other mock trial studies. Saladin et al. (1988) showed participants photos of eight men, and asked participants to judge how capable they thought the men would be of committing armed robbery and murder. The

Exam tip

Some studies discussed here are more than 20 years old. While they are still informative, consider their applicability to modern times as you evaluate each study. This is particularly relevant if there have been significant changes in, for example, attitudes, experiences, etc., since the studies were conducted.

Experimental conditions

1 Attractive photo of Barbara accused of burglary

2 Unattractive photo of Barbara accused of burglary

3 No photograph with the burglary case (control group)

4 Attractive photo of Barbara accused of fraud

5 Unattractive photo of Barbara accused of fraud

6 No photograph with the fraud case (control group)

Jurors can be influenced by the appearance of defendants.

findings were that the unattractive men were considered more likely to have committed either crime than the attractive men. This could be called an 'attractiveness effect'. It is most evident with serious but non-fatal crimes, such as burglary, and when females are being judged (Quigley et al. 1995). This attractiveness effect is, however, not seen if people are considered to be using their attractiveness for material gain, such as in fraud cases. It would therefore appear that the jury make some assumptions about whether the defendant has used their appearance to benefit them in crime, and if it is considered that they have are more likely to find them guilty.

Accent

John Dixon and Berenice Mahoney are British psychologists who have conducted a lot of research looking at whether the accent of the defendant can influence the decision making of the jury. They, with other colleagues, have typically focused on the Birmingham accent, likely due to the geographical area where they work. They identified that there was a probable level of prejudice occurring towards those with a strong Birmingham accent, when compared to a non-Birmingham accent. In their 1997 study, participants were just given a transcript and a tape recording to listen to with different accents. The study found that those with a strong 'Brummie' accent were considered to be more guilty, using a mock-trial research method. They found that a black defendant with a Birmingham accent was seen as more guilty than a white defendant with the same strong accent. All participants where white, non-Birmingham students. They have repeated this study a number of times, in 2002 and 2004, and in each instance, have had the same outcome. This would support a level of reliability for the findings.

Evaluation

As much of the psychological research in the area of defendant characteristics is not fully controlled for all variables, it is not always possible to establish cause and effect. Experimental research can isolate variables, but does not account for the fact that actual jury members are subject to a range of factors that can influence their decision making, unlike in a laboratory setting, hence why cause and effect cannot be established. Without a research study that controls all possible variables, we need to be cautious that we do not say for definite that the characteristics influence decision making.

There may be other factors, besides the characteristics of the defendant, that influence the jury member's decision making. This may include their own past experiences of victimisation for a similar offence, which may bias them regarding specific offences. The defendant may remind him or her of someone they know and can change their views based on this. Alternatively, the jury member may have been uncertain about the defendant's guilt and have been persuaded by the arguments of other jury members during deliberation. There are many factors internal to each individual jury member that can also influence decisions. These factors extend beyond the race, accent or other characteristics of the defendant.

Research investigating the influence of race and accent has typically been undertaken in controlled settings, such as laboratories. These do not create a realistic jury setting, and are therefore not considered ecologically valid. Real juries may react differently in real life trial settings. Conversely, laboratory settings allow for a greater control of the information presented, which helps researchers to place greater emphasis on specific variables, such as the accent of the defendant, which not be noticed within a trial setting.

Pre-trial publicity

Nowadays, the Internet, television and social media make it easy for us to acquire information or to communicate with other people, and not just people known to us. A criminal case is often documented in the media for a significant time before it goes to trial. Members of the general public, including potential jury members, may therefore form an opinion of the case and any identified suspects long before the trial.

In *Cognitive psychology* (Topic 2), you covered the development of schemas as a way of thinking that helps us to organise and interpret information and the world around us (see Schema theory). This can influence juries who are exposed to pre-trial information, as they try to make sense of the information using their own schema. During the trial, the jury member's schema can alter their perception of the evidence they are presented with in court.

Pre-trial publicity can involve two types of information: factual or emotional publicity. The former is likely to include incriminating information about the defendant or the case, such as what happened during the crime. Emotional publicity may not contain incriminating information, but is likely to present information that could arouse negative emotions. This could be information about the defendant or victim's past, for example. Emotional publicity is considered to have a longer lasting influence on jury members than factual information, which can be redressed within the trial as more information about what happened is presented to the jury.

Evaluation

There is a great deal of psychological research into the effects of pre-trial publicity on jury decision making. Many of these studies have used mock juries deliberately exposed to specific media sources and information. They may not, therefore, reflect the effects of real pre-trial publicity on real jurors. Real jurors cannot be deliberately exposed to pre-trial publicity before they serve on a jury because of the potential bias it may cause in their decision making.

Steblay et al. (1999) investigated the effect of pre-trial publicity on juror verdicts by undertaking a meta-analysis of 44 empirical tests representing 5755 subjects. They found that 'jurors' exposed to negative pre-trial publicity were significantly more likely to judge the defendant guilty compared to those exposed to less or no negative pre-trial publicity. This was more likely in the cases involving murder, sexual abuse or drugs, or when there were multiple pieces of negative information. It was also noted to be the case when there was a greater length of time between exposure to the publicity and judgment.

Ogloff and Vidmar (1994) looked at the effect of television as a form of pre-trial publicity, and whether this had a greater or lesser influence on potential jurors. They used a real child sexual abuse case in which there were extensive amounts of pre-trial publicity. They found that the potential jurors did express negative bias in the presence of negative pre-trial publicity, and that they were unaware of the biases they had. Ogloff and Vidmar concluded that television publicity alone, or television and printed articles such as newspapers, had a greater influence on potential jurors than printed media alone. This raises concerns in the current digital era of television-based news being available 24 hours a day, and the constant access to online news, so increasing the potential for biases to occur.

Kovera (2002) discusses how any type of media exposure can influence a juror's decision-making process, not just negative exposure. The study used two rape cases with varied media exposure, some of it pro-defence (positive), some pro-prosecution (negative) and the rest was neutral in that it did not address the rape. The findings were that jurors (undergraduate students) who watched a pro-defence rape trial reported that they needed more evidence in order to convict someone of rape than participants who watched a pro-prosecution rape trial.

Taking it further

There are many courtroom dramas that have looked at the decisions made by the jury. A classic one to highlight the issues of defendant characteristics, as well as how jury members are influenced by factors such as minority and majority influence, social loafing and appointment of the foreperson among others, is the 1957 film *12 Angry Men*.

While watching this film, see how many different factors influenced the jury in their decisions. Which factors were given more weight than others by the jury?

Exam tip

It is likely that you will need to apply principles of cognitive psychology, such as specific elements of memory, to analyse criminal behaviour. Therefore building on your learning from earlier topics will be more helpful throughout the year than trying to remember only the new principles discussed within criminological psychology.

Ruva and LeVasseur (2012) undertook content analyses of 30 mock-jury deliberations. It was found that pre-trial publicity exposure does influence the interpretation and discussion of trial evidence during deliberations as well as the views of potential jurors. Jurors who were exposed to negative publicity (anti-defendant) were significantly more likely than their non-exposed counterparts to discuss ambiguous trial facts in a manner that supported the prosecution's case, but rarely discussed them in a manner that supported the defence's case. This study also found that jurors exposed to pre-trial publicity were either unwilling or unable to adhere to instructions telling them not to discuss any pre-trial publicity they may have seen, and rarely corrected jury members who also mentioned it.

While there has been a lot of research undertaken about jury decision making, there are a number of issues to consider when evaluating the reliability of such studies.

A lot of research is conducted with research participants, often students, being asked to make decisions in a mock trial. This is not a representative sample of the population. Bornstein's (1999) meta-analysis of mock jury research has found that while there is little difference in the decisions of students versus non-student mock juries, any differences that are evident suggest that students tend to be more lenient than other populations. The information summarising a criminal offence is also presented in a written format rather than watching it unfold in a real trial. A real jury will be influencing the decision of a real judge so it has serious consequences for a defendant. This is not the case in mock trials and may affect how seriously the participants take the experiment. While experimental research in laboratories can isolate variables, this approach fails to account for the fact that jury members in actual trials are subject to a wider range of factors that can influence their decisions. Findings of laboratory research into jury decision making do not therefore have the realism of a real trial.

Nemeth (1977) found that there was no difference in jury decision making within mock trials for those presented in the form of a written summary or when staged live. This provides reassurances that the way in which the mock trial is conducted will not affect the outcome of the decision making. Researchers can therefore select the mock-trial approach most suited to their research aims without concern that this in itself will influence the findings. As a result, this makes the research methodology most applicable to its purpose.

In the past, real jury members have been asked to complete self-reported questionnaires after the trial has ended. There are limitations involved in self-report data but this provides a rare opportunity to obtain information about decision making in a real-life situation. This is likely to provide a more reliable account than that of mock trials. Asking real-life jurors may provide information about what they did do, whereas in a mock trial, it can only be recorded what a participant would do.

Exam tip

This section discusses different explanations about what influences jury decision making. Each explanation has supporting evidence for it, though each explanation can be significantly different from another.

A challenge within psychology is therefore deciding the value of each explanation and its contribution to the field of psychology and beyond. The value of an explanation is not necessarily how many research studies support the same outcome, although this is important. It goes beyond quantity to also consider how it influences psychology as a profession. When considering the differing explanations presented, it is therefore important to consider these areas, beyond the descriptions of each approach.

Taking it further

Different countries have very different legal processes. Research undertaken in one country may therefore not apply to other countries as the role of the jury or the influence of their decisions may vary. For example, some states in America carry the death penalty for some offences. The effect of finding someone guilty in America for a serious crime may therefore influence the jury in a different way compared with countries that do not use the death penalty. This will make comparison to different legal jurisdictions potentially inaccurate.

Studies into eyewitness testimony are conducted throughout the world. It is helpful to know in which countries studies were conducted as this may have an impact on the extent to which they will be applicable to other countries or culture, and if not, why are they not applicable. For each study you have looked at, investigate the legal process for each of the countries in which the study was undertaken. Note down any significant differences from UK legislation.

6.2 Methods

Learning outcomes

In this section, you will learn about:

- research methods used to assess eyewitness effectiveness
- sample selection
- issues of reliability, validity, objectivity and credibility in research in criminological psychology
- how to analyse data
- ethical guidelines for research.

Undertaking criminological psychology research

Many of the guiding principles for undertaking any psychological research apply when researching criminological topics. There are also additional ethical factors to consider when researching vulnerable populations – offenders or witnesses to potentially traumatic situations.

When undertaking any research, it is important that decisions about research design, sample selection and analysis are undertaken with a focus on reliability, validity, objectivity, credibility and ethics. Achieving these standards makes psychology a science.

Research methods

Laboratory experiments and field experiments can effectively be used when undertaking research in the area of criminological psychology. It is important that consideration is given to the details within the chosen methodology when designing a research study to ensure it follows ethical guidelines for psychology.

Laboratory experiments

Laboratory experiments are often used within this area of psychology, particularly in relation to eyewitness testimony. It is illegal to test real witnesses as it may bias their testimony, so participant witnesses are used in a simulated context, such as watching films in a laboratory setting.

A laboratory experiment is conducted in an artificial environment, one that is constructed by the experimenter in an unnatural setting. It involves a researcher manipulating the independent variable (IV) and measuring the dependent variable (DV). Within criminological psychology, the IV is manipulated to investigate the effect of a factor such as weapon presence or leading question types. The DV is then the testimony that is provided, or the witness recall. This may be undertaken in a laboratory experiment by watching a film.

The studies of Elizabeth Loftus and others (see Section 6.3, *Studies*) used laboratory experiments and included a number of key steps.

1 Gathering participants to take part in a study.

2 Showing them a film or photographs of an incident or a potential suspect.

3 Asking them to recall what they saw as a test of memory.

The study will introduce one or more IVs. This may involve varying the characteristics of the participants selected at step 1, for example age or gender. In step 2, participants may see different films, offences or

> **Link**
>
> For more information about laboratory experiments please see the Methods section of Topic 2: *Cognitive psychology.*

> **Link**
>
> For more information on independent variables and dependent variables, see Topic 2: *Cognitive psychology.*

suspects. At step 3, researchers may investigate the influence of post-event information by delaying the time at which the participants recall what they saw or how they recall the information.

Evaluation

As laboratory experiments use a standardised procedure, it is easier to replicate (copy) a laboratory experiment. They allow for precise control of extraneous and independent variables, and for events to be directly manipulated, which could not be achieved in a real-life witnessed event. This allows a cause-and-effect relationship to be established so that it is possible to say with greater certainty which factors, for example, influence the accuracy of an eyewitness. This would not be possible within a field experiment, where there are likely to be many variables all having a potential effect on the witness.

The artificiality of the setting may produce unnatural behaviour that does not reflect real life, that is, having low ecological validity. In Loftus' studies in the 1970s, participants watch a film clip of a car accident and are then asked questions about it. Participants are therefore expecting to see something on the clip and are more likely to be paying attention than an individual might be in the street prior to an accident occurring that they are not expecting. This means it would not be possible to generalise the findings to a real-life setting as the results from the laboratory may not reflect the findings if the research had involved a real accident. Validity is also reduced within laboratory experiments as the participants are less likely to experience stress by watching a film clip than a real accident. They will not be interviewed by the police and are unlikely to speak to others within the experiment about what they have seen, thereby minimising additional influencing variables.

Laboratory experiments often involve showing participants clips of crimes that would be unethical for them to experience in real life. Watching a film clip of a car accident is less distressing than witnessing a real one, but may still cause upset if a participant has previous experience of a similar accident themselves. In this case, they are given the right to withdraw.

Field experiments

Field experiments are similar to laboratory experiments as they both have an IV and a DV. The main difference is that a field experiment is conducted in a more natural setting. The experiment itself is, however, still artificially constructed but takes place in a setting where the phenomenon being studied would naturally occur. A researcher conducting a field experiment would attempt to realistically recreate an environment in which a particular situation is likely to occur, for example a car accident. A field experiment would follow the same three steps as a laboratory experiment, but at step 2 the participants will witness a real crime or a real suspect.

The 2009 Valentine and Mesout experiment (see Section 6.3, *Studies*) involving real visitors to the London Dungeon is an example of a field experiment. It is within its natural setting (the dungeons), but visitors would not normally be asked to complete questionnaires on their experience or asked to identify individuals whom they saw within the dungeons.

Evaluation

Field experiments are more difficult to control than laboratory experiments because many situational variables may occur in a natural setting, such as distractions from other witnesses to an event. This makes it unlikely that field experiments can be replicated exactly as the extraneous variables may affect the findings, leading to inconsistent results and low reliability. It is possible that some field experiments can create a controlled environment in which to conduct the study. For example, a field experiment testing witness recall of a bank robbery may be able to control situational variables because it is set up in a bank.

Link

For more information about field experiments please see the Methods section of Topic 2: *Cognitive psychology*.

Exam tip

Field experiments should not be confused with 'natural experiments'. These are experiments in which the IV occurs naturally and so the researcher does not have to manipulate the IV.

Behaviour displayed by participants in a field experiment is more likely to reflect real life as participants are essentially experiencing the conditions of a real witness. They are more likely to experience stress or anxiety at what they have seen and discuss it with other witnesses, and are less likely to be forewarned to recall a situation than in a laboratory experiment. This, therefore, increases the ecological validity of the study and allows the findings to be considered representative of a real situation.

As participants may be unaware they are participating in a psychological study conducted in the field, demand characteristics are minimised. This makes it more likely that the responses or reactions they give within the study are genuine and indicative of real life. This allows the findings of such studies to be relied on more than if there were concerns about response bias from participants.

Within field experiments, it is important to protect the participants as they are experiencing what they believe to be a real-life incident. As such, they are more likely to experience distress than in a laboratory experiment. A researcher will need to weigh up the nature of the incident they are intending to stage to make sure it does not create excessive distress, in order to maintain ethical principles.

Case studies

Case studies are in-depth investigations of a single person, group or event. In criminological psychology a case study usually involves conducting interviews with an individual, such as an offender. Yuille and Cutshall's (1986) weapon focus study was a case study in which they focused on witnesses to a specific crime. Case studies are particularly useful in understanding why a particular person committed an offence, from which a clinician may develop a clinical formulation to explore the factors relevant to their offending. Further clinical evaluations of case studies may determine if treatment of an offender, or group of offenders, is working.

Case studies use IVs and DVs as with other methodologies. The only difference is that at step 1 there would only be one or a small number of people participating. The information gathered at step 3 is likely to be in much more detail, typically of a qualitative nature.

Evaluation

Case studies provide information that is rich in detail. Information about an offender's response to treatment captures information from a variety of sources: asking the offender during an interview, the use of self-report questionnaires, observations by prison staff and often a review of prison documents related to the individual. A case study can therefore provide a greater insight into a real situation than can be gained by other methods, identifying motives, beliefs and decisions of the offender and not just their behaviour. The information obtained has greater reliability, as it has come from the offender themselves, providing a depth to the data that can be used to draw conclusions about the treatment effectiveness.

However, as case studies only deal with a small number of people, the findings cannot be generalised to the wider population. The reason why an offender decided to stalk an ex-partner, for example, may not be representative of the motives of all stalkers. Their beliefs and subsequent case formulation is very specific to them, and it cannot be assumed that the same applies to all who commit the same offence. Similarly, there may be specific participant variables that influence whether an offender will respond positively to an anger management programme, not just that they committed an offence while angry. This is why caution should be applied to assuming that all offenders who commit offences while angry will have the same treatment response. A full understanding of the decisions surrounding the offence is necessary in order to then consider if the treatment may also have an effect on someone with a similar formulation.

> ### Link
>
> For more information about case studies please see the Methods section of Topic 2: *Cognitive psychology*.

Link

For more information about sampling methods please see the Methods section of Topic 2: *Cognitive psychology*.

Sampling methods

Sampling methods are an important part in the research process when undertaking research in criminological psychology. Often students are selected by opportunity or randomly from a pool of research candidates for laboratory research. This poses an issue with the generalisability of the research findings to other populations as students represent a rather homogenous group of individuals who do not have the variation of possible characteristics that typical witnesses might have. In field experiments, such as that of Valentine and Mesout (2009) participants are selected by opportunity as they are available at the time of the study being conducted.

Research issues

Reliability

Reliability refers to the consistency of the research findings. A research design with many experimental controls results in high reliability. This allows for the research to be replicated.

Laboratory experiments have high reliability as the controlled nature of the design prevents other factors from affecting what is being studied. This can include controlling participant and situational variables. For example, the same film clip may be shown or a researcher can ensure only a specific age group is being researched if this is what they wanted. These high controls allow for the research to be replicated many times and provides consistency.

Field experiments are more difficult to control as there is more chance of situational variables occurring in a natural setting. This makes it difficult to replicate the exact same conditions in future research due to these extraneous variables. As a result, the findings may be inconsistent and this lowers the reliability of the findings. Similarly, in case studies, it can be very difficult to control all the participant and situational variables. It is difficult to find two identical people who have experienced the exact same situation in order to compare findings. As such, case studies also have low reliability.

Validity

Validity refers to how well a study measures what it is supposed to measure.

Doubt has been raised about the validity of the findings of laboratory experiments in relation to eyewitness testimony. They may be more or less cautious about their testimony compared to a real witness as it is known to be an experiment. Wagstaff et al. (2003) found little evidence for factors such as weapon focus, age or level of violence having any effect on witness testimony among real witnesses, despite laboratory (and field) experiments suggesting these to be influential variables.

Similarly, Yuille and Cutshall's (1986) study showed limited effect of leading questions on real witnesses to a robbery, despite this having been demonstrated within a laboratory setting. Ihlebaek et al. (2003) compared memory for a live staged robbery (field setting) and film footage of the same robbery (laboratory setting). They found those who watched the film footage recalled more details with greater accuracy than the staged robbery. The number of errors in recall was the same for both conditions. This shows that while laboratory experiments may find similar results to field experiments, they overestimate witness recall. This may be due to the level of attention to the film compared to an unexpected incident. It therefore suggests that reliance on the findings of laboratory experiments, as valid indications of the accuracy of eyewitness testimony, should be viewed with caution.

Field experiments in criminological psychology are more valid as they are less likely to suffer from these problems because essentially the participants are experiencing what a real witness would experience. The only exception is they are unlikely to be interviewed by the police. As case studies investigate real situations, the information obtained is that of a real situation. It is therefore a valid research method.

Demand characteristics can also reduce the validity of an artificial experiment such as a laboratory experiment. As people may alter their behaviour in response to the situation, this does not reflect a true-life situation and therefore lowers the validity. For example, a participant may guess that the aim of the study is to test how stress affects witness recall, so they may recall less to meet the expectations of the researcher. This may also happen in a case study, as the person being interviewed may have an understanding of the aims of the interview and provide information that would support the research. For example, an offender may guess that a researcher is looking to investigate if completion of the anger management programme has a positive effect on their ability to manage trigger situations for anger. They may therefore state that they have not experienced high levels of anger in such situations. Case studies also have the added difficulty of researcher bias as the information being gathered is qualitative data and so requires subjective analysis; in addition to this there is a high level of researcher involvement, which can potentially reduce objectivity. This can also lower the validity.

Exam tip

The terms 'validity' and 'reliability' can often be confused with each other because they are closely linked. It is important to have a clear understanding of each, as a general understanding of the terms and as part of an evaluation of known studies.

Objectivity

Researchers should remain totally value free when investigating a topic. While they might have a hypothesis about the factors that may influence the accuracy of eyewitnesses, they should try to remain totally unbiased in their investigations and simply gather facts that may prove or disprove their hypothesis. This can be achieved in laboratory and field experiments. They typically gather quantitative data that requires no interpretation by the researcher and this minimises the potential for bias.

Undertaking a case study of an offender can involve the researcher spending considerable time with the individual, and time speaking about them with others, for example, prison staff. Over time, it is possible that the researcher feels that they know the person very well, and that they have a full understanding of the reasons for their offending. The researcher may become invested in the aims of the research, for example to show that an individual has succeeded in reducing anger via treatment, and seek only evidence that supports this finding or may place greater interpretative emphasis on evidence that supports this aim.

Achieving objectivity makes the research more scientific. Quantitative data requires little interpretation and therefore is more objective. Such data is obtained in field and laboratory experiments. Case studies however, due to the depth of detail, gather qualitative data. Analysis of such data can lead to subjectivity and researcher bias.

Credibility

Psychologists want the research they undertake to be considered seriously. They aim to contribute to the field of psychological research and influence its future. In order for this to happen the research should have credibility. All three research methods can achieve credibility by striving to undertake research that is reliable, valid and objective. Research within the field of criminal psychology needs to be credible as the application of the research findings is important for the courts and police.

Data analysis

Once data has been gathered, it is subject to analysis, to determine if the data is meaningful to the research question. The analysis may look at determining relationships between variables or whether the findings from research are statistically significant. In experiments such as that undertaken by Loftus and Palmer (1974), the analysis is seeking to explore if there is a relationship between leading questions and the accuracy of recall.

Link

For more information about different methods please see the following topics:

Method	Topic location
Analysis of quantitative data: calculating measures of central tendency, frequency tables, measures of dispersion (range and deviation)	Topic 2: *Cognitive psychology*
Correlations	Topic 3: *Biological psychology*
Meta-analysis	Topic 5: *Clinical psychology*
Chi-squared	Topic 4: *Learning theories*
Spearman's rho, Mann-Whitney U and Wilcoxon and issues of statistical significance; levels of measurement and critical and observed values	Topic 2: *Cognitive psychology*
Analysis of qualitative data using thematic analysis	Topic 1: *Social psychology*
Grounded theory	Topic 5: *Clinical psychology*

Ethics

The British Psychological Society (BPS) has produced guidance for those wanting to undertake psychological research or engage in clinical practice such as psychological formulations or treatment interventions. This is known as the Code of Ethics and Conduct (BPS, 2009). It provides guidance about the general conduct of a psychologist to ensure any psychological roles they undertake fulfil a minimum standard, to protect all involved. Psychologists who practise in the field of psychology (known as practitioner psychologists, for example, 'Forensic' Psychologists and others with protected titles: 'Clinical' Psychologists, 'Health' Psychologists, etc.) also have to follow additional guidance from their legal governing body: the Health and Care Professions Council (HCPC). Practitioner psychologists who do not follow the guidelines can be 'disbarred' from the Council and are no longer allowed to practise as psychologists. Psychologists registered with the BPS can also be removed from the Register if they act in an unethical manner. The ethical guidance must therefore be taken very seriously. As many practitioner psychologists are often registered with the BPS and the HCPC, it is best practice to follow both guidelines when conducting psychological research.

Ethical guidelines

As with all research, criminological studies should follow a number of strict ethical guidelines. These include the following.

Protection of the participant

Eyewitnesses who see real-life crimes can become distressed and it would be unethical to expose someone to this for an experiment. Watching a crime in a film clip would be less distressing than seeing it in reality. However, it is possible that watching a film clip can remind them of any past similar experience that may have occurred, for example, if someone had been victim to a similar crime. Participants should be allowed to withdraw from the experiment in this case or in any other situations in which they start to feel distressed. Laboratory experiments have a greater protection for participants than field experiments or case studies, as the event is artificial. When conducting research with real situations, careful consideration is required to minimise any possible distress.

Risk management

It is important to consider any potential harm to participants when carrying out research. Risks should be identified from the outset of designing the research and protocols should be set up to manage them. Risks can range from physical harm such as discomfort or stress to psychological risks, such as affecting the participant's personal values or relationships.

Deception and consent

Deception may be used to minimise demand characteristics. This can then increase the validity of the findings. As such, a researcher may not tell participants the true aim of the study. If deception is used, there is a lack of informed consent. As the participants do not know what the study is about, they cannot be fully aware of the nature and consequences of the research.

Laboratory experiments and case studies are more likely to require consent than field experiments as the person will know they are involved in an experiment/study. Field experiments may have less need for consent if it stages an incident that someone is likely to experience in their everyday lives. This possibility is more limited in criminological psychology. Deception can still be an issue for all three methodologies. For example, in field studies, participants may not be fully aware that they are in a staged situation in which they are about to witness a specific crime. If deception and consent are issues, guidance suggests the need to debrief participants once the research is complete.

Laboratory experiments have greater protection for participants than real-life events but it is still important to debrief participants once research is complete.

Right to withdraw

This may be less of an issue in field experiments if, as with consent, they are likely to experience the situation in their everyday lives. However, laboratory experiments and case studies should always offer the right to withdraw, to comply with guidance regarding protection of participants. As with deception, participants should be debriefed if there are issues relating to their right to withdraw.

In addition to ethical guidance, the BPS has also issued documentation to support the clinical practice of psychologists, which forms guidelines to be adhered to when undertaking certain tasks such as psychological formulations or treatment interventions. These guidelines not only support the ethical principles outlined above, but specifically in relation to such tasks, they provide a framework of best practice to ensure the maintenance of high-quality psychological input.

Taking it further

The British Psychological Society has clear guidance on the ethics and professional protocols of undertaking research. Look at the BPS website for this guidance and make yourself familiar with the published guidance.

6.3 Studies
Learning outcome

In this section, you will learn about one classic study:

- Loftus and Palmer (1974) study into the effect of leading questions

and three contemporary studies, from which you will need to choose one to learn about:

- Howells et al. (2005) study into the effectiveness of offender treatment options
- Valentine and Mesout (2009) investigation into factors influencing eyewitness testimony
- Bradbury and Williams (2013) study into factors of race within jury decision making.

Reconstruction of automobile destruction: An example of the interaction between language and memory (Loftus and Palmer, 1974)

Early research into memory identified how our recollection of an event can be distorted by post-event information. Elizabeth Loftus and colleagues have expanded on these early studies of memory to look specifically into memories of crimes, and factors such as the contribution of language and leading questions to the accuracy of testimony. Her ongoing research over the past five decades has been influential both within cognitive psychology and in its application to criminal matters.

This study (1974) looked at memory in general, rather than memory under specific situations. Her work has been pivotal in influencing the practice of law enforcers.

Aim

To investigate whether leading questions would influence the estimates of the speed of a vehicle among eyewitnesses.

Procedure for experiment one

A total of 45 students were shown seven short film clips of a traffic accident. After each film clip, participants were asked to give an account of the accident they had seen and were then given a questionnaire and asked to answer specific questions about the accident. The length of the film clips ranged from 5 to 30 seconds.

All participants received the same questionnaire with the exception of one critical question that was changed. One group of nine participants were asked the critical question, 'About how fast were the cars going when they hit each other?'. The remaining four groups of nine participants were asked the same question, but the verb 'hit' was changed to 'smashed', 'collided', 'bumped' and 'contacted'. Each of the five groups were shown the film clips in a different order. Loftus and Palmer knew the actual speeds of the cars in most of the film clips.

Results for experiment one

Table 6.3 shows that those participants presented with the verb 'smashed' estimated the fastest speed of the car before the accident. The verb 'contacted' produced the slowest speed estimate. There was a difference of almost 9 miles per hour (mph) in the estimates given for these two verbs.

Hit

Smash

Figure 6.5 The language used when asking a witness to recall information can affect their memory of the event

Table 6.3 Mean speed estimates for each verb used

Verb used	Mean speed estimate (mph)
Smashed	40.5
Collided	39.3
Bumped	38.1
Hit	34.0
Contacted	31.8

Conclusion

They concluded that a change of word could significantly affect a witness's answer to a question. Loftus and Palmer believed that this might be due to two reasons:

1 The participant was uncertain of the speed being travelled and the verb used to describe the contact of the cars created a bias and influenced their decision.

2 The wording of the question causes a change in the participant's memory of the accident, so they recall the accident as being more severe than it actually was.

Procedure for experiment two

A total of 150 students watched a film showing a multiple car accident. The film lasted less than one minute, with the accident within the film lasting four seconds. They were then given a questionnaire in which they were asked to describe the accident and then answer questions about the accident.

As with experiment one, there was a critical question within the questionnaire. The participants were divided into three groups of 50. One group was asked 'About how fast were the cars going when they smashed into each other?' A second group was asked 'About how fast were the cars going when they hit each other?' The final group was not asked about the speed of the cars at all (no critical question).

A week later the participants returned to answer 10 questions about the accident, without watching the film clip again. All 150 participants were asked, among other questions, the following critical question: 'Did you see any broken glass?' The participants were asked to report 'Yes' or 'No'. In the film clip, there was no broken glass.

Table 6.4 Responses to the question 'Did you see the broken glass?'

	Verb condition		
Answer to critical question	'Smashed'	'Hit'	Control
Yes	16	7	6
No	34	43	44

Results for experiment two

In all conditions, most participants correctly identified that there was no broken glass seen in the film clip. A chi-square test was carried out to see if the results were statistically significant; they were. A significantly higher number of participants in the 'smashed' group reported seeing the glass than in the 'hit' group; 32 per cent of those in the 'smashed' condition reported seeing glass compared to 14 per cent of those in the 'hit' group; 12 per cent of those in the control group who were not asked about the approximate speed of the cars reported seeing glass.

This showed that the verb in the question influenced the participants' recall of the accident. The participants did not see any broken glass and the findings suggest that the verb used within the question changed their memory of the accident, even a week after seeing the film clip.

Conclusion

Loftus and Palmer argue that two kinds of information go into a person's memory of a complex event. The first is the information obtained from witnessing the event, and the second is the other information supplied to us after the event. As time elapses, the two sources of information may merge, making it difficult to know the source of some details. This creates one overall memory of the event; this is called the **reconstructive hypothesis**. Loftus and Palmer concluded that reconstructive memory exists. They also concluded that leading questions do influence eyewitness testimony. The wording of the questions suggests a specific response that may alter witness memory of an accident.

Key term

Reconstructive hypothesis: memory for an event when the information supplied after the event merges with the information obtained from witnessing the event.

Evaluation

Both experiments were conducted in a laboratory and therefore had a high level of control. Specifically, the questions asked (except for verb change) and the film clips used were consistent for the groups. This allows for the study to be replicated in order to determine the reliability of the findings.

The critical question was randomly included among other questions within the questionnaire. This prevented the participants from guessing the aim of the study and displaying demand characteristics, which would have resulted in flawed results. Embedding the critical question among other questions minimises the likelihood that the responses given by the participants is due to the research methodology, rather than their genuine response to the question.

The experimenters knew the actual speed the cars were travelling for most films. This allowed them to assess whether the estimates were significantly affected by the actual speed of the cars. They found that it did not affect the estimates. This allowed them to say with certainty that it was the verb used and not the actual speed that had the effect on the estimates of speed given by participants.

The use of yes/no responses within experiment two produced quantitative data, as did the estimates of speed in both experiments. This meant there was no subjective interpretation of the data in either experiment, making the findings more objective. The results are therefore less likely to be the result of researcher bias, making the results more reliable.

It may, however, be difficult to accurately distinguish the speed of the cars from watching the film clips, particularly when the participants were students so are likely to have limited experience of car speeds. Limited experience in estimating speeds may have resulted in the students being more influenced by the verb used in the question than would have been the case if a different population had been included, with more experience of driving. The findings therefore may only represent the views of this specific population, rather than it being possible to generalise the findings to the wider population.

The participants are unlikely to have been under the same emotional strain as an eyewitness of a real accident would be, as they only watched film clips in a laboratory. This makes the validity questionable as they may have responded differently as a result. It cannot therefore be said with certainty that a real eyewitness would respond in the same way as those undertaking a research study in an artificial situation.

As well as the type of question asked, many other factors could influence memory of an event, including emotions, the environment in which it occurred, etc. These are not considered in this study. As such, the study is somewhat reductionist, considering only one potential variable that may influence human memory.

WIDER ISSUES AND DEBATES

The use of psychological knowledge within society

The Devlin Committee was set up to investigate the use of eyewitness testimony in court. It found that many people have been convicted of serious crimes by eyewitness testimony alone.

As a result the police and legal professionals are guided to minimise the use of leading questions in order to ensure an accurate account is obtained. This constitutes a marked change in policing techniques within the 20th century, which are still used today.

Brief anger management programmes with offenders: Outcomes and predictors of change (Howells et al., 2005)

The work of Kevin Howells and his colleagues investigates prison and community offender populations in Australia. It focuses on real offenders engaging in real treatment and therefore offers an exciting insight into an offending population. It was conducted at a time when there had been an increase in the use of anger management interventions for offenders, following emphasis on a rehabilitative approach to managing offenders compared to a more traditional perspective of punishment. It reflects an ongoing psychological research interest in evaluating whether such interventions do indeed effect a behavioural change for the offender.

Aim

The two aims of the study were as follows.

1 To determine whether anger management is more effective than no treatment in producing change.

2 To investigate whether improvement in treatment can be predicted from pre-treatment offender characteristics, such as whether they are ready to engage in treatment.

Procedure

A total of 418 male offenders participated in the study. All had been referred to prison or community probation equivalent anger management programmes in Australia; 86 per cent of these were from prison-based anger management programmes. The offenders came from a variety of ethnic backgrounds and offence types, mainly violent. The majority (73 per cent) had not previously completed an anger management programme. Of the initial 418 participants, 285 completed the post-intervention assessment, 78 completed the two-month follow-up (93 per cent of whom attended prison-based programmes), and 21 completed the six-month follow-up assessment. A control sample was selected from the participants who were on a waiting list for the programme.

The participants attended programmes that lasted approximately 20 hours (over 10 sessions). While the programmes in the different geographical areas differed, they were very similar in content. Both programmes were based on a cognitive behavioural approach and used a treatment manual based on material developed in New Zealand and derived from Novaco's framework (1997). Programme content included structured exercises focusing on skills, such as identifying provocations, relaxation, cognitive restructuring, assertion and relapse prevention. Participants completed outcome measures (two internationally used questionnaires that asked about experiences of anger and their triggers) before and after attending the programme, with follow-up assessments at two and six months after finishing the group. Support was given to those with literacy issues and the questionnaires were verbally administered. Staff (either prison or community) also completed an observational rating scale for each participant.

Results

The offenders who completed the anger management programme showed significantly greater improvement in anger knowledge than those in the control group (mean change = 1.80 compared to 0.95 respectively). There was some improvement among those in the control group who did not complete any treatment. Although there was a relative improvement in ability to manage anger using appropriate skills among the treatment group, this was not statistically significant when compared to the control group.

WIDER ISSUES AND DEBATES

Psychology as a science

Clinical trials often do not use random allocation because it would be unethical to randomly distribute people to a trial and control group. They are often criticised, therefore, as those undertaking the trial would be likely to improve because they volunteered/were selected or are motivated to show improvement. This study takes into account these pre-treatment features.

At the two-month follow-up stage, the initial improvement was observed again, and was statistically significant. This showed that the treatment was helping to manage anger and the participants were continuing to make progress after the course finished. The same effect was not seen at the six-month stage.

The ability to predict how much change someone will make in treatment (known as **predictive validity**) was more accurate among those who had the most negative anger symptoms before attending the programme. There was a positive correlation between treatment readiness and progress made after course completion.

Conclusion

The overall impact of the anger management programmes was small and the completion of an anger questionnaire, even without treatment, may have a small benefit in itself. The improvement shown by those completing programmes is not always maintained some months after the course has finished.

Those who had the biggest difficulties in anger management made the biggest improvements when completing a programme. Motivated offenders can be predicted to make more positive change than those who are not ready to change their anger problems.

Evaluation

The data was obtained within a naturally occurring treatment programme using real offenders and consequently the findings have real-life clinical application. The study therefore has high ecological validity, making the findings more applicable to other treatment programmes of a similar content.

The study was a randomised trial, with offenders allocated to a condition (to receive treatment or be placed on a waiting list for treatment). This provides a control group to the experiment against which comparisons can be made. It also minimises any allocation bias by the researcher. This makes the findings more reliable as it is possible to identify the extent to which the treatment influenced behaviour, for example, whether the treatment programme worked.

The programmes measured used an evidence-based model and therefore are applicable to many anger management programmes undertaken with offenders, as they all follow a similar content. This makes the research generalisable to other offenders undertaking treatment of this type.

Not all variables were accounted for within the research, including individual differences in levels of understanding of the programmes that may account for the amount of change some made. Therefore it is possible that such extraneous variables may influence the outcome of the research.

As the sample size reduced so much by the six-month stage, it is difficult to say with certainty whether change is or is not maintained at this time. Further research will be required before it is possible to determine the longer-term effect of anger management programmes.

Most of the questionnaires were self-report and the offenders may not have been honest in their responses, possibly due to concerns about the impact of being honest among their peers. The staff can only rate on behaviours that they observe and they may not have seen all behaviours, so this also making their ratings limited. The findings, therefore, may have an element of response bias, which reduces the reliability of the findings.

Key term 💬

Predictive validity: the extent to which results from a test or study can predict future behaviour.

WIDER ISSUES AND DEBATES

Issues related to socially sensitive research

Undertaking research into offending behaviour can be problematic. Allocating an offender to a waiting list or placebo group within research in order to investigate if treatment works can potentially delay an offender addressing the behaviour that contributes to them committing crime. It is important that when undertaking research in this area, that the research itself does not negatively effect the offender by denying them access to treatment.

Taking it further ↗

What ethical issues might you encounter as a psychologist undertaking treatment such as anger management? What steps do you need to take to overcome these issues?

Eyewitness identification under stress in the London Dungeon (Valentine and Mesout, 2009)

Tim Valentine has undertaken research into witness identifications and factors affecting the accuracy of this. In his research with Jan Mesout in 2009, stress was the variable under investigation to see if it would have an effect on eyewitness identification. They wanted to overcome some of the limitations of laboratory research in this area by looking at eyewitness identification in a real-life scenario, in an attempt to clarify the effect of stress on witnesses. In particular, they wanted to look at situations in which the witness was not aware that their testimony would be tested.

Aim

To test the hypothesis that high arousal (high levels of stress) can reduce an eyewitness' ability to recall information and identify a perpetrator.

Procedure

Visitors to the London Dungeon were offered a reduction in the admission price to complete some questionnaires after their visit and to wear a heart rate monitor throughout their visit. A total of 56 participants completed the questionnaires; 29 were female and 27 were male.

An actor dressed up in a dark robe and wore make-up to appear very pale, with wounds or scars on their face. This actor was known as the 'scary person'. They would step out in front of the participant and prevent them from passing by blocking their way. All participants went around the dungeon in the same direction.

After they completed the tour, the purpose of the experiment was explained and informed consent was obtained. They were given the opportunity to withdraw at any stage. The participants completed a questionnaire that assessed how they felt in the dungeon (state anxiety). They were then asked to answer questions that related more to their general experience of emotions (trait anxiety). A separate questionnaire asked for free recall of a description of the 'scary person' and a cued recall asking about specific details. They were advised not to guess details if they could not remember.

Finally, participants were shown a nine-person photograph line-up. The picture of the 'scary person' was placed in a randomly selected position for each line-up. Unbiased instructions were used. Each participant was instructed that 'the person you saw in the labyrinth may or may not be in the line-up', and were guided to say if they could not identify the person. Participants then rated their confidence in their decision on a scale of 0–100 per cent confidence.

Results

Females reported feeling a higher state of anxiety in the dungeon than males (a score of 52.8 versus 45.3 respectively). The mean state anxiety score was 49.0. There was no difference in the trait anxiety between males and females.

Participants who reported lower state anxiety recalled more correct information about the scary person. Only 17 per cent of those who scored above the median on the state anxiety scale (a score of 52 or above) correctly identified the person they saw from a nine-person culprit-present photograph line-up. In contrast, 75 per cent of eyewitnesses who scored below the median correctly identified the 'culprit'. Those who reported higher state anxiety were less likely to correctly identify the scary person in the photo line-up. Males made more correct identifications than females.

Those who correctly identified the right photo showed a higher level of confidence in their identification.

Conclusion

Females show higher levels of anxiety in stressful situations. Being highly anxious reduces the accuracy of eyewitnesses in identifying perpetrators. It suggests that when considering the accuracy of eyewitnesses, experts should take into account the emotional state of the witness at the time of the event.

Evaluation

The study is a field experiment. Although it is not a typical daily experience to be scared by an actor in a ghoulish outfit, its natural setting and the subsequent findings of the study are more representative of real eyewitnesses than those conducted in a laboratory, in which participants may be able to guess the aims and respond in a way in which they think the researcher wants them to.

There were good controls among the participants as it was the same actor for each set of visitors, acting in the same manner, on the same tour. This provides a high level of replicability to the study, if conducted again in a similar setting. This allows the findings of this study to be extrapolated into other situations.

The researchers undertook an additional process of validating the questionnaires used on a set of office workers to make sure they were reliable in measuring anxiety. This provides assurances of the validity of the study, in that the researchers were obtaining information about anxiety levels rather than any other emotion when asking participants to complete the questionnaires.

The research takes into account individual differences among the participants rather than comparing a stressful situation with a control condition. For example, obtaining information about trait anxiety among the participants provided a baseline measure against which comparisons could be made to the state anxiety experienced within the dungeons.

The participants had all chosen to attend a scary place (London Dungeon). Therefore they may have a preference for scary entertainment and may be affected by scary events in a different way from those who do not like such activities. This limits the generalisability of the findings to the wider population as the reactions of the participants may be influenced by their preference for scary situations. Their reactions may not therefore be the same as those who do not choose to visit such environments.

Diversity and citizen participation: The effect of race on juror decision making (Bradbury and Williams, 2013)

Race and crime have been discussed for many years. This includes whether certain races are over-represented in crime statistics and prisons and if certain races are treated differently at various stages in the criminal justice system. The work of Mark Bradbury and Marian Williams provides an up-to-date evaluation of the work previously undertaken by Abwender and Hough (2001), which was an influential study in looking at the influence of defendant characteristics within mock trials.

Aim

To examine whether the racial make-up of a jury affects its decision making. To test the following two hypotheses:

Hypothesis (H_1): Black defendants will be more likely to be convicted by juries composed of a higher number of white jurors.

Hypothesis (H_2): Black defendants will be more likely to be convicted by juries composed of a higher number of Hispanic jurors.

Procedure

Data was collected from real trials in four American states. The cases chosen were ones in which there was a 'hung jury'; where juries could not agree on whether the defendant was guilty or not. Data included demographic characteristics of the jury, jury selection and offence type. Only trials that included black defendants were examined.

Dependent variable: Whether or not a trial resulted in a conviction.

Independent variable: The racial make-up of the jury: mostly black, mostly white and mostly Hispanic.

They included seven control variables to measure the strength of the prosecution case, to make sure that there was a sufficient case for the jury to decide on.

Control variables:

- quantity of evidence
- strength of the case
- length of the trial
- length of the jury deliberations
- presence of written instructions to the jury
- case type (violence, property or drug offences)
- lawyer type (public or private).

In order to assess whether there was a significant relationship, the researchers undertook complex statistical analysis, including a **logistic regression**. The nature of this statistical test helped them to identify which juror characteristics may influence their decision making.

> **Key term**
>
> **Logistic regression:** a statistical analysis that examines the relationship between the dependent variable and the independent variables being investigated, and calculates the probability of them being related.

Results

Bradbury and Williams' key findings were that black defendants are less likely to be convicted by juries composed mostly of black jurors. Juries comprising mostly white jurors are more likely to convict black defendants. This finding is statistically significant at the $p<.01$ level, so is highly significant. Juries comprising mostly Hispanic jurors are more likely to convict black defendants. This was significant, but only to the $p<.10$ level. It was also found that black defendants are less likely to be convicted of violent or property crimes than drug crimes.

Conclusion

Diversity within the jury pool is likely to have an impact on the outcome of their decision making. Black defendants are more likely to be convicted if the percentage of other ethnicity jurors is higher than the percentage of black jurors. The selection process of jury members can therefore bias the outcome of the trial.

Evaluation

The data represented characteristics of actual jury trials, as opposed to mock juries. This therefore provides more reliable data regarding actual jury decision making than an experiment undertaken in a laboratory. We can therefore consider the findings to be more ecologically valid than other research methodologies.

There were a number of control variables to ensure that they were truly investigating the racial composition of the jury rather than other factors. This ensures a level of validity within the research, and the findings can be confidently applied to the area of race.

The study is a content analysis, using qualitative and quantitative data. The quantitative data is less subjective as it is not open to interpretation by the researchers. Subsequently, there is less chance of researcher bias than relying entirely on qualitative data.

As it is so rare to get data from actual trials, it is difficult to be sure the findings are representative of all trials. The findings may reflect an unknown uniqueness to the trial and the jury members that may or may not be applicable to all similar trials. The general absence of real-life research makes this uncertain.

It is not possible to control for all variables in the research. Other factors that may have influenced the jury's decision may include their own personal experiences of crime and other personal biases and any pre-trial publicity that may have occurred. These may have had an unknown impact on the jury members which, due to it involving real-life trials, was not possible to control, despite attempts to control as many variables as possible.

The cases focused only on black defendants. The findings may therefore not be applicable to cases in which the defendant's race is non-black. Further research is required into other ethnic groups before it is possible to determine whether the effect found within the current research is applicable across races.

Exam tip

When evaluating theories, studies or approaches, give consideration to how each applies to wider society. For example, this may include thinking about how society has been influenced, or not, as a result of the theory etc. or if changes have been made to practice at all.

In England, juries are made up of individuals who are selected randomly.

6.4 Key questions

Learning outcomes

In this section, you will learn about:

- one key issue and its importance to society today

- concepts, theories and research used in criminological psychology to explain the key issue.

Is eyewitness testimony too unreliable to trust?

Eyewitness testimony refers to information given by a witness after seeing an event or crime occur. This is recorded in a police statement or given as verbal testimony in a court trial. Eyewitness testimony is often used to corroborate forensic evidence, although jurors may find forensic evidence more difficult to understand, particularly in complex trials, so jurors may depend more on the testimony given by a witness whom they can relate to and have confidence in. In the absence of forensic evidence, the information given by a witness can be influential, and indeed essential, to the outcome of a trial. Jurors have to decide whether or not to convict someone based on the evidence presented in court, so inaccurate eyewitness testimony may lead to the wrong person being convicted, or a guilty person getting away with the crime.

Research has been undertaken to investigate the accuracy of eyewitnesses. Some of this research suggests that eyewitnesses may be less accurate than we believe them to be. This concern was the subject of a judicial review that produced the Devlin Report (1976), which concluded that the courts should be very cautious in the sole reliance on eyewitness testimony in the absence of other corroborating evidence.

Research into reconstructive memory questions the reliability of eyewitnesses. You will remember from the cognitive approach (see Section 2.1 in Topic 2) that Bartlett's (1932) theory of reconstructive memory describes how we try to fit what we remember with what we already know and understand about the world. This can lead eyewitnesses to reconstruct their memory of an event to fit with their understanding or expectations within a situation. For example, a perpetrator's appearance or accent may trigger the eyewitnesses' schemas about the type of person who is committing the crime, influencing them to encode and then later recall the perpetrator differently from reality.

Post-event information (what the eyewitness is exposed to after the event and before the trial), can result in inaccurate memory, as new events or information can alter the memory of the event, as investigated by Elizabeth Loftus in her numerous studies on leading questions. It can then be difficult to isolate their true memory of the event without the additional influences when giving testimony at trial.

Other factors are also known to affect the reliability of eyewitness recall. These can be individual characteristics of the witness such as age, factors associated with the context of the event such as lighting or the presence of a weapon, or post-event factors such as the way a witness is questioned and the duration of time between the event and being asked to remember what happened.

Despite the concerns regarding the inaccuracy of eyewitness testimony, there is research that questions the validity of laboratory research into eyewitness testimony. Yuille and Cutshall (1986) demonstrated that when using a naturalistic case study rather than an artificial laboratory experiment, real-life eyewitnesses demonstrated great accuracy in their recall, and were not influenced by leading questions, even following a prolonged period of time between initial event and recall.

Taking it further

This section will describe an example of the key issue of whether eyewitness testimony is reliable or not. However, you can choose your own key issue and relate it to theories, concepts and research used in criminological psychology.

Thompson (1997) studied statements given by the survivors of the sunken riverboat, Marchioness, and found that, despite extreme emotional trauma, recall was very accurate after many months. This suggests that laboratory research may not reflect the conditions that are experienced by witnesses. Participants in experimental research are often onlookers, so the emotional involvement of witnessing a real event is not replicated. Participants are aware of the need to pay attention to what they have been asked to witness: a video clip or simulated event. Real-life events are often unexpected, confusing and rapid. Importantly, real-life witnesses are questioned by police and believe that their testimony is of real importance as it can affect the outcome of a police investigation or trial. This may not be the case with participants involved in laboratory research.

Steyvers and Hemmer (2012) found that in recall of naturalistic scenes, prior knowledge drawn from semantic memory could contribute to accurate recall in episodic memory tasks (see Topic 2: *Cognitive psychology*). This study seriously questions the way experimental research purporting to claim that eyewitness testimony is valid is conducted. They suggest that lots of experimental research actively constructs a situation that encourages flawed recall, such as the staging of an unusual object in a scene. This does not accurately reflect real life, where the contexts of crimes being committed are likely to be fairly normal.

Yarmey's (2004) field experiment focuses on identification of a person in the street in a later set of photographs. His findings do not support the argument for the reliability of eyewitness testimony using a more realistic methodology, as correct identification only occurred approximately 50 per cent of the time. There is, however, an argument for further research to be undertaken outside a laboratory setting so that the findings can be considered more ecologically valid.

Flashbulb memories suggest that memory of an event can be particularly clear owing to the emotional impact the event witnessed has on the individual. Hirst et al. (2009) has shown that memory recall for an emotional event remains accurate for a prolonged period of time, although it is subject to eventually fading, as are most memories. The evidence for flashbulb memory has been mixed, and there are other studies that suggest it is not a true phenomenon, and does not increase accuracy of recall (Neisser and Harsch, 1992).

There is some evidence to support the accuracy of eyewitness testimony, particularly from naturalistic research, but there is also substantial experimental evidence to suggest that we should be cautious in relying on the testimony of eyewitnesses. Psychologists have more research to conduct in order to establish which factors are an important influence on the reliability of eyewitness testimony, and perhaps how these factors interact to improve or diminish recall.

Taking it further

There are many documented cases of mistaken eyewitness identification that have led to unjust convictions. Calvin Willis was finally exonerated after serving over 20 years for a brutal rape that he did not commit, a conviction based on mistaken eyewitness testimony. You can read about this case and many more by conducting an Internet search for 'The Innocence Project'. Research some of these cases and consider why an eyewitness may have got it wrong.

Exam tip

Key issues are to be presented as a question. In your response, you need to provide a balanced account of evidence to support either side of the issue. It is important to answer the key issue identified by recording a clear conclusion based on the evidence you have presented. You may wish to consider the following structure for your key issue:

Key question: Is eyewitness testimony reliable?

Outline of the key question: What is meant by eyewitness testimony and why is the issue important for the defendant of a case and the criminal system?

Arguments for eyewitness testimony being unreliable.

Arguments for eyewitness testimony being more accurate than thought.

A conclusion.

6.5 Practical investigation

Learning outcomes

In this section, you will learn about:

- key stages of designing and conducting ethical psychological research
- how to analyse and present the findings of the research undertaken.

In this section, you will have to design and conduct a practical investigation using a questionnaire, interview or case study in an area relevant to the topics covered in criminological psychology.

Before you begin planning your practical investigation, you should review the relevant methodology sections of this book to familiarise yourself with key terms and concepts concerning questionnaires, interviews and case studies.

Conducting criminological psychology research

It is important when conducting research to follow all research guidelines as a psychologist. The planning stage of a practical investigation will ensure that the investigation follows these guidelines and is crucial to any research.

This section follows a practical from planning through to analysis and a discussion of the findings. It serves as an example only, and is **not** the only available investigation option.

This example is an investigation to see if people remember more accurately the events from video footage compared to a real-life event. You can gather qualitative or quantitative data for your practical investigation, but you must be able to convert the data you gather into quantitative data for the purpose of analysis. Here, we will gather quantitative data, but you may choose to gather qualitative data, which you then quantify using a content analysis, for example.

Aim

To investigate whether recall is more accurate when recalling a real-life event or video footage of the same event.

A huge number of laboratory and field experiments have been conducted into the accuracy of recall. Laboratory experiments into recall have often been criticised for lacking validity because the participants tend to be passive observers of staged footage, emotionally disengaged from the event and less concerned with the quality of their recall. In contrast, field experiments have provided more findings with greater ecological validity, but at the expense of adequate control. The majority of this research suggests that participants have more accurate recall under laboratory conditions compared to more naturalistic ones.

Ihlebaek et al. (2003) found that participants who viewed video footage of a staged robbery were more accurate in their recall than participants involved in the staged robbery. It might be possible that greater participation in an event to be remembered leads to subjective memories prone to distortion compared to a detached observer of an event, who recalls what actually happened rather than how they felt about it (Davies and Alonso-Quecuty, 1997).

The conclusions reached by laboratory experiments have caused some controversy over whether or not laboratory experiments over-inflate accuracy of memory. This practical investigation example will compare recall of a video footage and a live staged event. Participants' memory of the event (live or video) will be recorded using a questionnaire the next day. The questionnaire will contain closed questions (yes/no responses) concerning details of the event; the greater the number of correct answers to the questions, the more accurate the recall.

Variables

It is important to identify the variables involved in your investigation, so that your procedure and data collection methods are clear, objective and reliable. The information gathered from participants of what they remember can be gathered via interview or questionnaire techniques. If you decide to use an interview, it will need to be transcribed and quantified using a technique such as content analysis for either accuracy or amount remembered. This can be done by reading the transcript carefully and tallying the number of details or accuracy of details remembered.

In this practical investigation we are looking at how the context of the witnessed event affects the accuracy of recall. The independent variable (IV) will be the context of the event; either live or using video footage of a staged event. The dependent variable (DV) will be the accuracy of recall of the witnessed event. This will be measured by the number of correct answers given on a questionnaire.

Hypotheses

Experimental hypothesis

Participants will give more correct answers on a recall questionnaire after watching video footage of a staged event than participants watching a live staged event.

The hypothesis is directional because there is an overwhelming amount of research, which indicates the direction of difference likely to be found; that memory of video footage is more accurate than live events.

Null hypothesis

There will be no difference in the accuracy of recall of video footage or live staged event.

Planning the practical investigation

Consideration will need to be given to the nature of the staged event and the construction of your questionnaire. The staged event should be both practical and ethical, so you will need to think about what type of event you will be able to both video-record and produce as a live event with actors. It is fairly simple to ask participants to watch a video, but setting up a live event will need to be thought through carefully as participants cannot be distressed and it should be a fairly naturalistic context where all participants can see what is going on.

You will also need to consider how the questionnaire will be constructed because different questions will yield different types of data that can influence the level of analysis possible later. Remember that you can gather qualitative and quantitative data, but your analysis must be quantitative. This means that your data needs to be put into tables and graphs and subject to a statistical test.

These closed-ended questions will produce quantitative data that gives every participant a score for accuracy. The more correctly answered questions, the greater the score of recall accuracy. You can use open-ended questions that also produce quantitative data, such as 'What did the student take from the classroom?' An accurate response can achieve a score that can also be subject to quantitative analysis. If you decide to use open questions that ask for a more detailed and lengthy response from participants, such as 'Tell me what you remember from the event', it is likely that you will need to devise some form of coding system to be able to quantify whether the response is accurate or not.

Experimental design

When selecting an experimental design, you should consider the strengths and weaknesses of each design for your particular study aim. This practical investigation is testing to see if a live or video footage of an event affects recall, so an independent groups design might be more appropriate than

---

Types of interview questions

1 Did you see a teacher in the classroom? Yes/No

2 Was there a pen on the desk? Yes/No

3 Did you see a student enter the classroom? Yes/No

4 Did the student say anything? Yes/No

5 Did the student take anything from the classroom? Yes/No

a repeated measures design because participants will not have to view the staged event twice or have a different event set up. This also avoids the possibility of demand characteristics and order effects, where participants alter their behaviour because they can guess the aim of the research, become more or less accurate as a result of practise or fatigue at having to remember and recall events they have witnessed or different characteristics of two events, affecting recall. However, an independent groups design means that individual differences between the participants in each group might have an influence of the results, so this will need to be controlled. This can be done using random allocation of participants to either the live or video footage conditions, which should result in a fairly even distribution of the kinds of individual differences that could have an impact on the results.

If you choose to use a repeated measures design for your experiment, it is worth considering using counterbalancing or randomisation of conditions. You will also have to consider using different types of staged event or leaving a significant time gap between watching the video footage and witnessing the live event.

Sampling

You will need to gather a sample of participants for your study. If you decide to use a repeated measures deign, around ten participants will be enough to gather a reasonable amount of data. If you have chosen to use an independent groups design, you will need to double your sample size.

Because the aim of this practical investigation concerns anyone who is a potential witness to an event, the target population is the general population. Gathering a representative sample of the general population can be problematic and would require access to all members of the public, such as an electoral roll, from which to select participants. There are also different witness factors known to affect the accuracy of recall, such as age and experience, so producing a truly representative sample using random or stratified sampling methods is likely to be difficult. It is therefore more likely that you will use an opportunity or volunteer sampling technique to gather participants for the study. Both of these methods are convenient and relatively quick to establish a group of participants. A volunteer sample is more ethical, because they are self-selecting rather than directly approached, and the kind of personality likely to volunteer is not one that will affect the findings of this study.

For this practical investigation, 20 participants will be selected by opportunity sample from students who attend a geography club at school. Participants will be asked by the geography teacher if they would like to take part in a psychology experiment, and their names will be forwarded to the researcher so that formal consent can be gained.

Controls

When planning the experiment it is important to remember that the validity and reliability of any findings can be limited by decisions made at planning, that is, whether other factors may be influencing the outcome. You will need to consider any extraneous variables that may occur and how they may affect the results if they were to occur. To counteract some of these extraneous variables, it may be possible to control or eliminate them.

Participant variables

The participants will be tested in one of two groups; each member of the geography club that has agreed to participate will be randomly assigned to either the live or the video footage condition. The live event group will be attending the first half of the lunchtime geography club in the geography classroom and the video footage group will attend the second half of the club.

The participants will be asked if they have any visual impairment that might affect their ability, and asked to wear glasses if they normally do so.

Situational variables

Situational variables are any factor within the environment that might potentially affect the results of the study. This is particularly important if these factors affect one condition of the experiment but not the other. In any experiment it is important to control the surroundings and any potential disturbance from noise or distraction. In this investigation, a 'Do not disturb' sign will be placed on the door to prevent disruptions from other staff and students during both the first and second half of the club.

The students will be seated at a single desk facing the front of the room and will be instructed not to confer throughout the study.

The staged event will be recorded in the geography room and acted out in the same way for the live event. The actors involved will be given a script to follow and the same set of standardised instructions will be read out to participants. All participants will receive the same questionnaire the following day during a tutorial period.

Developing a procedure

The procedure should clearly outline what you are planning to do and at what stage, that is, in what order are you going to do each step. Areas to consider include:

- the standardised instructions that you will give to participants

- the timing and location of the experiment

- whether you will test individuals or groups of participants

- where and when are you going to conduct the questionnaire

- how the participants are going to be debriefed.

Once a detailed plan has been drawn up, only then is it possible to start recruiting participants and conducting the investigation.

In this investigation, the participants will be asked to attend either the first or second half of the geography club. Once in the classroom, the participants of the live condition will be seated at separate desks and read a set of standardised instructions. A student actor will then enter the room and ask the geography teacher a question about their coursework. The teacher will tell the student that they are busy and the student will respond negatively by throwing their school bag on the floor at their feet. The teacher will restart the geography club lesson and the student will pick up the wrong bag and leave the classroom. The teacher will not notice this and continue to discuss the geography topic with the club.

During the second half of the club, the video footage group will enter the classroom, sit at separate desks and receive the same instructions (but be told that they will watch a video rather than live event). They will be shown a video clip of the same sequence of events.

The participants will be asked to complete the questionnaire in a tutorial period the next day.

Ethical considerations

Consideration needs to be given to the event you ask the individual to recall. It cannot be distressing or embarrassing in any way, and does not need to contain acts of aggression or violence in order to establish whether recall is accurate.

If you choose to use a repeated measures design it may be prudent to withhold the specific aim of the study in order to prevent demand characteristics, but you should disclose as much information about the expectations of participation as possible before gaining consent. Participants should also be made fully aware of their right to withdraw from the study at any point without adverse consequence.

Review the BPS guidance on conducting research and use this as a checklist to make sure you have considered all areas of ethics. Check with your teacher that your procedure is ethical before proceeding with the investigation.

Consent form

The aim of the study is to investigate whether people recall more about video footage than witnessing live events. You will be asked to take part in a memory experiment in your geography club at lunchtime. The club members will be divided into two groups (video or live event) and required to attend the first or second half of the club. You will be informed which half of the club to attend. During the experiment you will witness an event and then you will answer a questionnaire about what you saw in tutorial the following day. The purpose of the study is to compare real life and simulated laboratory experiments to see which is a better measure of memory.

You will not be named or identified in the research and the event that you witness will not cause any distress or embarrassment. You will be asked to not discuss any of the events during the experiment with family, friends or other students and staff until after you have completed the questionnaire and spoken to the researchers involved. You can decline to take part in the experiment at any point and without consequence. The data gathered from your responses will be destroyed at the end of the year.

I can be contacted if you have any further questions and my supervising teacher will also be available throughout the experiment and afterwards.

I have understood these instructions and the implications of taking part in this experiment.

Signature of participant   Date

Signature of researcher   Date

Signature of supervising teacher   Date

Design decisions taken in this experiment

Aim: To investigate whether recall accuracy is affected by the context of the witnessed event.

Experimental design: Independent groups

Sampling method: Opportunity

Independent variable: Live staged event or video footage

Dependent variable: The total number of correct recall responses on a questionnaire.

Analysing results

The data gathered from the questionnaire must be collated and a comparison between the two experimental conditions compared. This will establish whether there is a difference in the accuracy of recall between the live and video footage staged events. Each participant will receive a score for accuracy of recall, so the data is at least ordinal level. This type of data should be presented in a histogram or bar chart of the modal scores and analysed using a Mann-Whitney U test of significance.

Quantitative analysis

Table 6.5 Raw data from the experiment

Participant	Accuracy score of recall of live event (out of 20)	Participant	Accuracy score of recall of video footage (out of 20)
1	6	11	13
2	9	12	12
3	13	13	14
4	11	14	15
5	15	15	16
6	9	16	14
7	7	17	12
8	14	18	11
9	8	19	14
10	-	20	16

Table 6.6 Results to show the mode and range of correct responses given to questions concerning a live and staged event

	Live event	Video footage
Mode of correct responses	9	14
Range of correct responses	9	5

Inferential test of significance

To determine whether the findings of the practical investigation are statistically significant, or just due to chance, you will have to run your data through an inferential test. For your practical investigation you will need to gather quantitative data and conduct a chi-squared, Mann-Whitney U or Wilcoxon non-parametric test of difference.

The investigation here produced frequencies, so is at least ordinal level and an independent groups design was used to look for a difference between the two conditions. This means that a Mann-Whitney U test will be used to establish whether there is a significant difference between the accuracy of recall of a live staged event and video footage. Any difference found using the test will indicate that the context of the witnessed event has an impact on the accuracy of recall.

$$U_a = n_a n_b + \frac{n_a(n_a + 1)}{2} - \Sigma R_a$$

$$U_b = n_a n_b + \frac{n_b(n_b + 1)}{2} - \Sigma R_b$$

(U is the smaller of U_a and U_b)

To use the Mann-Whitney U test, you will need to assign each raw score a point for each time it is beaten by a raw score in the other condition. The lowest of the sum of these points for each condition will be the U value. You will find the procedure for calculating this test in Topic 2: *Cognitive psychology*, Section 2.5.

The calculated (observed) Mann-Whitney U = 17. The critical value for a two-tailed test at $p<0.05$ is 24 with N = 9, N = 10. The calculated value of 17 must be equal to or less than the critical value at the significance level shown to be significant. The calculated value is less than the critical value, so the finding is significant.

Drawing conclusions

The conclusions you draw from the analysis should be logical, based on the findings you have presented. The conclusions can be discussed briefly to avoid repeating the findings in detail. Returning the reader back to the original hypothesis and research aims and then discussing if the results support or disprove the hypothesis is a systematic way of referring back to the original purpose of the study.

This practical investigation shows that there is a significant difference in the accuracy of recall between the live and video footage of a staged event ($p < 0.05$). This means that we can be 95 per cent confident that the results indicate that the video event was more accurately recalled than the live event, and the experimental hypothesis can be supported. This also concurs with previous psychological research in this area.

However, examining the range of the data, we can also see that participants' scores for the live event were more varied; they had a greater spread of scores. This indicates individual variability on recall compared to fairly consistent accurate recall for the video footage event. This perhaps can be explained by the mode of presentation of the event; the video footage received greater student concentration and focus compared to a live event that they may not have been expecting. It also may be that the live event could not be seen by all of the participants in the room equally compared to the video footage that was projected onto a whiteboard.

Evaluating the practical investigation

When evaluating your practical, it is necessary to consider both its strengths and weaknesses. As with the evaluation of any research study, a range of possible considerations can be made, including the validity, reliability, generalisability, application, scientific value and credibility of the research. You should also consider possible improvements that could have been made to the practical investigation if it was to be replicated in the future.

A number of general questions should be asked:

- Is the study ethical?
- Can you generalise the findings to others/different cultures/different eras?
- Is the study reliable?
- Is the study carried out in a natural or artificial environment?
- Is the task ordinary?
- Are the findings useful in real life?
- Is the research valid?
- Is there any conflicting evidence from other research?

Here are a few questions that have been explored in greater detail:

Is the study valid and reliable?

A number of issues need to be addressed in order to ensure a study is valid. One of these is how you went about operationalising memory recall. In this practical investigation, accuracy of recall was measured using a questionnaire based on the events that were staged. We know that the questions are an accurate reflection of the event, because they were based on the video footage, so can be verified.

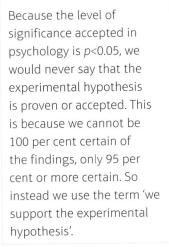

Maths tip

Because the level of significance accepted in psychology is $p<0.05$, we would never say that the experimental hypothesis is proven or accepted. This is because we cannot be 100 per cent certain of the findings, only 95 per cent or more certain. So instead we use the term 'we support the experimental hypothesis'.

However, all participants were not asked to recall the live or video recorded event, so the findings could have been affected by the time lapse between the experiment and recall task. We also know that participants may have focused more on the video footage and had a better view than participants in the live event; again this could account for the decreased accuracy of the live event.

To improve these issues, it would be necessary to ensure that all participants could view the event from the same distance and without obstruction, administer the questionnaire after the same amount of time and instruct participants in the live condition to focus as much on the event as they would if watching a whiteboard screen.

Can we generalise the findings?

Generalisability is the aim of any scientific research; it should be possible to widely apply the findings to other people in other places and times. We know that witnesses vary considerably and it is unlikely that a small sample of geography club attendees represent all potential witnesses. This means that we cannot generalise the findings to everyone and limits the usefulness of such research, particularly if it was to be used to inform police practice. It also means that the research lacks scientific credibility because it only applies to a specific group of people. However, small-scale experiments, such as this practical example, can be a useful precursor to more extensive experimental research, as it is cost effective. It can be used as a litmus test to investigate factors that affect recall before more expensive research is conducted using larger and more diverse samples.

6.6 Issues and debates (A level only)

In this section you will learn about issues and debates relevant to criminological psychology. You will have already noticed that issues and debates have been mentioned throughout this topic. This section will draw together the main themes and ideas related to the criminological approach as a whole.

Psychologists have a duty to protect individuals from distress rather than purposely expose them to it.

Ethics

Criminological psychology research can involve exposing individuals to potentially stressful situations, such as mock trials or artificial crime scenes. Some research also uses actual witnesses to real-life crimes. This may cause levels of distress for participants, whether their experiences relate to real or artificial situations.

Ethical consideration needs to be given to ensure individuals have the capacity to give consent as they may be emotional at the time, for example witnesses in a real-life crime, or they may have impairments affecting their ability to give consent. This could be the case in situations in which offenders are considered to have significant mental impairment. The use of naturalistic experiments results in the individuals providing consent after unwittingly participating in an experiment. During such occasions, the use of a debrief following the experiment is critical, but on its own cannot be used to justify such deception.

Practical issues in the design and implementation of research

Developing field experiments requires careful consideration. Efforts should be made to minimise the effect of as many external variables as possible so that the IV and DV can be more easily investigated.

Within criminological psychology, this may include consideration about the time of day that the artificial task is conducted within the field. This will minimise the likelihood that variables, such as it is getting dark, influence witness recall if the IV being explored is, for example, weapon focus.

The most significant practical issue with the design of research in criminological psychology is lack of realism. It is not legal or moral to conduct research on real life victims and witnesses, and it would be considered perversion of the course of justice to study a real jury. Therefore experiments are set up, mock juries are used and participants are exposed to tasks that lack mundane realism or simulations where participants are aware of their participation. This can result in findings lacking ecological validity and the behaviour of participants might be considered unnatural.

Reductionism

Criminological psychology aims to identify specific factors that contribute to an individual engaging in criminal behaviour, such as genetic or environmental influences. This serves to reduce the explanation of an individual's behaviour to these singular factors, rather than considering the behaviour of the individual as a whole, where it may be a number of different influences that explain antisocial behaviour. In thinking about the individual's behaviour in unitary ways, it is easy to overlook aspects of, and oversimplify, the complex nature of criminality.

Comparisons between ways of explaining behaviour using different themes

Explanations for crime come from many different perspectives, including biological psychology and cognitive psychology. Comparisons can be made directly between these two approaches, including crime being the result of the way a person thinks and their attitudes and how our biological make-up may contribute to offending behaviour. Further comparisons can be made, such as whether genetics, hormones or social factors have the greatest influence on criminal behaviour.

Psychology as a science

Criminological psychology uses various research methods, some of which are considered more scientific than others. Laboratory experiments are typically used in relation to investigations of memory for eyewitness testimony. The use of field experiments introduces the possibility for extraneous variables to affect the outcome of the experiments, and are therefore less controlled, and subsequently less scientific than similar research undertaken within the confines of a laboratory. Experiments are considered the most scientific tool used in psychology because they propose testable hypotheses and gather empirical data using objective measures.

Qualitative research methods are used within some aspects of criminological psychology. Interviews are particularly applicable when assessing effectiveness of treatment among offenders. As this methodology can be subjective, because it requires interpretation and is difficult to replicate, this approach is less scientific.

Culture

Much of the research into criminological psychology has been undertaken from a western perspective, which has particular legal systems and cultural beliefs. This can influence findings and may make it less applicable to other cultures dissimilar to that being explored. The cultural background of eyewitnesses or jury members can have a significant influence on how they interpret what they see, or the information presented to them. It is, therefore, important to understand the background culture of the individual to determine its effect on their decision making.

Gender

There is a prevalence of data regarding male offenders, as these represent the highest proportion of convicted criminals within the UK. Explanations for offending, such as elevated testosterone levels or XYY syndrome, help to explain male offending, but do not explain why females commit offences.

Similarly, structured treatment programmes have been designed with men in mind, and therefore may not reflect the needs of female offenders, thereby making them less effective for female offenders completing such treatments. Consequently, less is known about the factors influencing women and how to address these treatment needs.

Nature–nurture

Twin studies have been used within criminological psychology when looking at factors influencing an individual to engage in antisocial behaviour. The use of monozygotic and dizygotic twins within studies allows researchers to look at whether the genetic element has an effect, that is, both twins become criminals if one of them is, or if there is something within their environment that is influential. The latter would explain why one twin might not become a criminal if exposed to different factors within their environment than their twin.

The nature–nurture debate provides some information as to how to treat criminality. The nurture debate would advocate that changes to an individual's lifestyle and environmental factors can reduce their likelihood of offending, and factors such as peer influence may contribute. Alternatively, the nature debate argues that hormone levels, genes and other internal factors predispose to criminality. Addressing these is much more complex, if at all possible.

An understanding of how psychological understanding has developed over time

Many of the explanations regarding eyewitness testimony draw on an understanding of memory that was developed many years ago. Each recent study, which builds on this knowledge, helps to provide a greater application of established theories and approaches to this specific area. In particular, the understanding of the relationship between memory and eyewitness testimony has contributed to the development of the cognitive interview technique used by the police. This technique increases the accuracy of the testimony obtained, and is now commonplace when gathering such information.

Recent years have led to a resurgence of research into why individuals commit criminal acts. There has been a number of technological advances that have helped this area of criminological psychology. For example, an ability to explore the genetic make-up of an individual can identify innate factors among offenders and brain scans can help us understand the cognitive processing of a criminal brain.

The use of psychological knowledge in society

Research in the areas of eyewitness testimony and jury decision making has helped psychologists to understand the cognitive processes that witnesses and jury members go through in a criminal trial. This has aided the evaluation of the accuracy of eyewitness testimony while also influencing how witnesses are managed, to maximise memory accuracy and reduce biases, such as the use of the cognitive interview technique within police interviews. It has also influenced the structure and guidelines followed in trials to minimise the influence of external factors on jury members, such as isolating juries to prevent the influence of publicity on decision making.

Issues related to socially sensitive research

Research looking into offending behaviour can be sensitive in a number of areas, particularly in relation to the manner in which data is collected, and the application and implications this data has on societal views about offenders.

For example, in jury decision making there is substantial emphasis on the race of defendants on trial. There is a large array of research looking at the effect of race on jury decision making. Typically, the ethnic groups investigated have been black or Hispanic, with greater focus on the former. The literature base can create a bias in the perception of ethnic minorities and their true representation within criminal settings.

Similarly, using brain studies and genetic mapping to identify individuals who may be more likely to engage in offending behaviour can be considered inflammatory. With the causal effect of the presence of specific genes or brain structures not proven, it is important that assumptions are not made about such individuals, nor their future behaviour being incorrectly anticipated.

Issues of social control

Investigating offending behaviour, and the reasons why individuals commit offences influences decision making about the management and treatability of offenders. Evidence that suggests that individuals with specific biological characteristics or social experiences may have a greater tendency to commit offences has the potential to be misapplied. This is particularly the case when considering the level of risk that the individual may present to the public. It can exaggerate risk, and in turn be used as a means of controlling the freedom of the individual.

Knowledge check

Content

> In the content section you are required to explain, evaluate and apply your knowledge of crime and antisocial behaviour, offenders and their treatment, and eyewitness testimony and jury decision making.
>
> To check your evaluation skills, refer to the introduction section of this book and review 'how to evaluate a theory'. Remember that you may be asked to consider issues of validity, reliability, credibility, generalisability, objectivity and subjectivity in your evaluation of theories.

Can you explain the biological causes of antisocial and criminal behaviour, including brain injury, brain structure, hormones, genetics and personality?

Can you evaluate the role of the amygdala in aggressive behaviour?

Are you able to apply personality theories of criminality to explain the role of individual variation in the development of criminality or aggression?

Can you explain the role of neurotransmitters and hormones in the development of criminal and antisocial behaviour in some individuals?

Can you explain the social causes of antisocial and criminal behaviour, including labelling, self-fulfilling prophecy and social learning theory?

Are you able to apply the self-fulfilling prophecy as a theory to explain individual differences in the development of criminal and antisocial behaviour?

Can you evaluate social learning theory as a theory of human development to explain antisocial and criminal behaviour?

Are you confident that you can you describe the techniques used in the cognitive interview and explain how to ensure the interview process remains an ethical one?

Are you able to apply psychological formulations to explain criminal and antisocial behaviour?

Can you evaluate cognitive-behavioural treatments for offenders in terms of strengths and weaknesses?

Can you evaluate biological treatments for offenders in terms of strengths and weaknesses?

Are you able to apply your knowledge of reconstructive memory to evaluate the reliability of eyewitness testimony?

Do you understand what weapon focus is and how it can affect eyewitness recall?

Are you confident that you can describe the factors influencing jury decision making at different times of the trial process?

Methods

Can you describe and evaluate the research methods used to assess eyewitness effectiveness, including laboratory experiments and field experiments?

Are you able to explain and evaluate the use of case studies to assess eyewitness effectiveness?

Link

Some of the methods you will need to know for Criminological psychology have already been covered in earlier topics. Have a look back at the Methods section of this topic for a reminder on where to find the relevant information.

Can you describe different ways of selecting participants for research in criminological psychology, including random and stratified, volunteer and opportunity?

Can you explain what is meant by the concepts of reliability, validity, objectivity, credibility and ethics in research in criminological psychology, and understand the impact and control of these concepts within the scientific process?

For quantitative data, can you identify and calculate measures of central tendency (mean, median and mode), measures of dispersion (range and standard deviation), correlations and meta-analysis?

Are you able to analyse and draw conclusions from quantitative data, including using inferential statistical testing (chi-squared, Spearman's rho, Mann-Whitney U and Wilcoxon)?

Do you understand levels of significance and are you able to use these to interpret the results of an inferential test?

Are you able to identify levels of measurement in order to select an appropriate inferential test?

Can you compare observed and critical values on a critical values table to check whether results are significant?

Are you confident you can use thematic analysis and grounded theory to analyse and interpret qualitative data?

Do you know and understand the BPS Code of Ethics and Conduct (2009), including risk management when carrying out research in psychology?

Do you know and understand the HCPC principles for undertaking psychological formulation, and intervention?

Studies

In the studies section you are required to describe, evaluate and apply your knowledge of one classic and one contemporary study of criminological psychology.

To check your evaluation skills, refer to the introduction section of this book and review 'how to evaluate a study. Remember that you may be asked to consider issues of validity, reliability, credibility, generalisability, objectivity and subjectivity in your evaluation of studies.

Can you describe the classic study by Loftus and Palmer (1974) Reconstruction of automobile destruction: An example of the interaction between language and memory, in terms of its aim, method(s), procedures, results and conclusions?

Are you able to evaluate Loftus and Palmer's (1974) study in terms of strengths and weaknesses?

Are you able to identify and describe the aims, method, procedure, results and conclusions of a contemporary study from the following list and evaluate the study in terms of strengths and weaknesses?

- Bradbury and Williams (2013) Diversity and Citizen Participation: The Effect of Race on Juror Decision Making.

- Valentine and Mesout (2009) Eyewitness identification under stress in the London Dungeon.

- Howells et al. (2005) Brief anger management program with offenders: Outcomes and predictors of change.

Key question

Are you able to identify and describe a key question in criminological psychology that is relevant to today's society?

Can you explain this key question using concepts, theories and research that you have studied in criminological psychology?

Practical investigation

Have you designed and conducted a questionnaire, interview or case study to investigate an area of criminological psychology?

Can you justify your choice of research questions or hypotheses?

Can you justify your choice of design and sampling method, and explain the ethical considerations involved?

Can you describe and analyse (using measures of central tendency and dispersion) the quantitative data that you gathered for your study and how you presented your data?

Are you able to explain, justify and interpret the non-parametric test of difference (chi-squared, Mann-Whitney U, Wilcoxon or Spearman's rho) that you used on your data?

Are you able to collect and present an analysis of qualitative data, including thematic analysis or grounded theory?

> Remember that you may be asked to consider issues of validity, reliability, credibility, generalisability, objectivity and subjectivity in your evaluation of your practical investigation.

Can you explain the strengths and weaknesses of your study and suggest possible improvements that could have been made?

Are you able to write up the procedure, results and discussion sections of your study in a report style?

Issues and debates (A level only)

> Remember that issues and debates are synoptic. This means you may be asked to make connections by comparing issues and debates across topics in psychology or comment on issues and debates within unseen material.

Can you identify ethical issues associated with theory and research within criminological psychology?

Can you comment on the practical and methodological issues in the design and implementation of research within criminological psychology?

Can you explain how theories, research and concepts within criminological psychology might be considered reductionist?

Can you compare theories and research within criminological psychology to show different ways of explaining and understanding criminal behaviour?

Are you able to discuss whether theories, concepts, research and methodology within criminological psychology are scientific?

Can you discuss issues of culture and gender within criminological psychology, for example how they might affect jury decision making?

Are you able to discuss the nature–nurture debate in the context of criminological psychology, in terms of which parts emphasise the role of nature and nurture or the interaction between them?

Do you understand how criminological psychology has developed over time?

Do you understand what is meant by social control and how research within criminological psychology may be used to control behaviour?

Can you show how the theories, concepts and research within criminological psychology can be used in a practical way in society?

Are you able to understand what is meant by socially sensitive research and explain how research in criminological psychology might be considered to be socially sensitive?

References

Bradbury, M. D. and Williams, M. R. (2013). Diversity and citizen participation: The effect of race on juror decision making. *Administration & Society*, 45(5), pp. 563–582.

Howells, K., Day, Andrew, Williamson, P., Bubner, Susan, Jauncey, Sue, Parker, Ann and Heseltine, K. (2005). Brief anger management programs with offenders: Outcomes and predictors of change. *Journal of Forensic Psychiatry & Psychology*, 16(2), pp. 296–311.

Loftus, E.F. and Palmer, J.C. (1974). Reconstruction of automobile destruction: An example of the interaction between language and memory. *Journal of Verbal Learning and Verbal Behavior*, 13, pp. 585–589.

Valentine, T. and Mesout, J. (2009). Eyewitness identification under stress in the London Dungeon. *Applied Cognitive Psychology*, 23, pp. 151–161.

Yuille, J., and Cutshall, J. (1986). A case study of eyewitness memory of a crime. *Journal of Applied Psychology*, 71, pp. 291–301.

7

Child psychology

Child psychology is concerned with understanding the development of human behaviour from before birth, through childhood, adolescence and into adulthood. It investigates how experiences in childhood affect later adult development, so focuses mainly on how children develop. Child psychology investigates a range of developmental processes, such as the development of cognition, moral development and social behaviour. In this topic, we will consider the emotional development of children, focusing specifically on the role of attachment in early infancy, and its influence on later development. It is important to consider why children attach to a caregiver, whether these attachment types differ between children and the possible impact of disruptions to this attachment on later adult development.

In this topic, you will learn about:

- Bowlby's explanation of attachment, the effects of deprivation and privation, and whether negative effects can be reduced
- Ainsworth's research into attachment types and cross-cultural research highlighting nature–nurture issues
- research into day care
- explanations and therapies for autism, a development disorder
- factors that affect attachment, including individual differences such as child temperament
- the use of observations, questionnaires, interviews and cross-cultural research and meta-analysis when investigating development
- a classic and a contemporary study of child development
- key issues around the topic of child psychology that are of relevance to society today
- how to carry out a practical research exercise relevant to topics covered in child psychology
- wider issues and debates in child psychology (A level).

7.1 Content
Learning outcomes

In this section, you will learn about explanations and types of attachment, research and factors affecting attachment, day care and autism:

- Bowlby's work on attachment
- Ainsworth's types of attachment and the use of the Strange Situation Procedure
- research into the short-term and long-term effects of deprivation and how negative effects can be reduced
- research into privation, and whether negative effects can be reversed
- research into day care
- cross-cultural research into attachment, and issues that arise about the nature–nurture debate
- explanations and therapies for autism.

Throughout this topic, you will consider individual differences in attachment type, responses to day care, and consider the effect on a child's development of day care, deprivation, privation and autism.

Introduction to child psychology

Historically, children were viewed as little adults and it was only with the writings of Jean-Jacques Rousseau, in the 18th century, that it was considered how children think and act differently from adults. Rousseau described the four stages of development from infancy, through childhood, late childhood and adolescence as an unfolding and invariant sequence of development according to biological maturation, and which represented the recapitulation of man from primitive, to savage, to social and skilled human being.

Arnold Gesell (1880–1961) further developed the idea of **biological maturation** to explain childhood growth but also explained that a child is a product of both a biological plan and its environment. As babies grow they follow a fixed pattern of development such as learning to sit, stand and walk, that follows a biological blueprint. However, children are also born into social and cultural contexts that influence what they learn. Exposure to certain experiences from parents and carers should take account of the maturational phase of development, so a child should not be encouraged to walk until they are biologically ready to do so.

Both biological maturation and environmental influences are of key importance to child psychology today, and influence much of the research into **attachment**.

Attachment

Attachment is defined as a close, emotional bond between child and caregiver. Although there are several theories of why this attachment may occur, it is generally accepted that this attachment is necessary to promote proximity between child and caregiver in order to provide safety and security. **Deprivation** is defined as a loss of an attachment that has been formed. In this topic, we will consider both the short-term and long-term effects of deprivation, and whether day care can be considered as a form of deprivation of attachment. **Privation** is defined as an absence of attachment, that is, an attachment has never been formed. Privation occurs when a child is extremely neglected or in a situation where a caregiver is unable to bond with a child.

Key terms

Biological maturation: how development occurs naturally.

Attachment: a close, emotional, enduring bond between child and caregiver.

Deprivation: loss of an attachment.

Privation: never formed an attachment.

Attachment to the mother provides security and stability for a child.

Bowlby's work on attachment

John Bowlby (1907–1990) trained as a psychiatrist and psychoanalyst and worked for the army and later at the Tavistock Clinic in London. Importantly, he was appointed as consultant in mental health by the World Health Organization for whom he wrote many of his publications on maternal care and mental health. Beginning his work in child guidance during the 1930s, he became increasingly concerned with the disturbances presented by children who had spent time in institutional care. He observed that many children who had experienced separations from their caregiver in infancy presented with emotional problems and an inability to form close relationships with others. He hypothesised that these disturbances could be as a result of their own missed opportunity to form a close bond with their caregiver.

Bowlby's theory of attachment

Evolutionary theory

Bowlby drew on evolutionary theory to explain why children attach to their caregiver. He explained that within our ancestral environment of 'evolutionary adaptedness' we existed as hunter-gatherers, often moving to search for food and at risk of predation. In order to protect their vulnerable young, ancestral humans needed to ensure that their young maintained close proximity to an adult. Such closeness is innate and so must have evolved as a mechanism to ensure survival; therefore attachment behaviours that promote proximity developed, such as crying, grasping and smiling. Initially, babies are indiscriminate in whom they grasp and whom they cry for when left alone. However, around the age of six to nine months they begin to prefer one person in particular, maintaining close proximity to this caregiver and monitoring their whereabouts.

Stages of attachment

Bowlby described three phases or stages in the development of attachment.

Phase 1: During the first few months of life a baby will respond indiscriminately towards any adult figure. The baby will orient themselves towards an adult using eye contact/tracking, grasping and smiling to promote proximity. A baby will gaze at an adult face and smiling will become a social response after several weeks.

Phase 2: A child will use **social releasers**, such as crying and smiling, to promote proximity, but this behaviour is directly towards the primary caregiver when the child is around three to six months old.

Phase 3: At around six months the baby will show intense attachment to the primary caregiver. The child will not only maintain close proximity to the caregiver in order to establish a safe base from which to explore the world, but they also show distress at separation and joy at reunion. They treat strangers with fear and use crying as a social releaser to raise alarm about their distress. This phase continues until the child is two or three years old.

Imprinting/attachment

Bowlby drew several parallels between his own research and that conducted on animals. In particular, Bowlby used the research into imprinting by Konrad Lorenz to explain how human babies follow a similar pattern of attachment. Lorenz conducted several experiments using greylag geese immediately after hatching. He observed that the chicks would instinctively follow the closest moving object they saw and develop to follow only this object and avoid other objects. Under natural conditions, it would be the mother goose which the chicks 'imprinted' on, and Lorenz tested this by dividing hatching chicks into two groups: one group imprinted on the mother goose and the second group imprinted on Lorenz himself. This process of imprinting was more likely to occur during the

Imprinting in wild birds is crucial for their survival.

Key terms

Social releasers: an innate behaviour that helps initiate a response from a baby's mother or carer.

Imprinting: a pre-programmed behaviour that creates a bond between an animal and its offspring to maintain close proximity, for example a duck will follow its parent.

first 12–24 hours of life, but if after 32 hours, the chick had not imprinted, they were not likely to imprint at all. This led to the idea that there was a critical period for imprinting after which it became irreversible.

Bowlby used Lorenz's concept of imprinting and applied it to explain attachment in human babies. Attachment in humans is slower than in animals; but the characteristics of attachment are similar to that of imprinting. Babies increasingly and selectively use social releasers towards a primary caregiver in order to promote proximity and this occurs during the first year or so of life – so perhaps it is better described as a sensitive rather than critical period.

Safe base

Previous theories of attachment, such as learning theories and Freudian ideas, were dubbed 'cupboard love' theories because they explained attachment as occurring because of the provision of food. Learning theories described how the mother was associated with providing food which satisfied a biological need. However, Bowlby did not believe that such a complex emotional bond between child and caregiver could be explained by food alone. In particular, Bowlby drew on research by Harry Harlow that investigated attachment behaviours in rhesus monkeys.

A rhesus monkey with its cloth surrogate mother.

Harlow and Zimmermann (1959) isolated eight rhesus monkeys, with a choice of a cloth surrogate mother and a wire surrogate mother. Four of the rhesus monkeys were fed by the cloth mother and four by the wire mother. They observed that the monkeys preferred the cloth mother regardless of which provided food, and spent no more than two hours a day on the wire mother suckling for food. The monkeys' preference for the cloth mother was clear, and some monkeys were observed to lean across from the cloth mother to the wire mother in order to suckle. Harlow and Zimmermann claimed that 'contact comfort' was critical in the development of attachment, not food. This was further reinforced when the monkeys were exposed to a fear-inducing stimulus. The monkeys clung to the cloth mother when fearful, which seemed to settle the monkey to the point where it could challenge the fearful object from its safe base. Monkeys raised with the wire mother did not seek comfort from it and continued to be fearful of the stimulus.

WIDER ISSUES AND DEBATES

Nature–nurture

Bowlby's theory of attachment is an evolutionary theory that explains attachment as a biological innate process based on adaptedness formed in our environment of evolutionary adaptedness. This suggests that we do not learn to attach, but that imprinting to one caregiver is a natural part of the developmental process. Prior to Bowlby's theory of attachment, learning theories suggested that we bond with a caregiver because of the food we associate with them. Classical conditioning described a mother figure as a neutral stimulus and the milk as an unconditioned stimulus that provides pleasure as an unconditioned response. As we acquire milk from the mother figure, we learn to associate her with pleasure and she becomes a conditioned stimulus. Operant conditioning would explain that milk is a primary reinforcer that satisfies our drive for satiety. As the mother is associated with the provision of milk, she becomes a secondary reinforcer. Note how these theories contrast with one another; Bowlby's theory suggests that we attach as part of biological maturation, whereas learning theories emphasise the role of associating the mother with food as a learned response.

Monotropy

Based primarily on the research conducted by Mary Ainsworth (1967) discussed later in this section, Bowlby listed several behaviours that children tend to display towards one particular person – namely the mother figure or primary caregiver. The child will vocalise more and smile more when interacting with the mother, continue to cry when nursed by others but stop crying for the mother; the child cries only when the mother leaves the room, the child will fix their gaze on the mother, crawl and follow her, as well as many other mother-directed behaviours.

Bowlby argued that, although multiple people may care for and be attached to a child, the principal caregiver of that child was the main attachment figure and the one to which the child formed a special bond. He also argued that the principle attachment figure was most likely, but not exclusively, to be the mother. Although substitute attachment figures could adopt the same role as the mother, he argued that they would be less able to attach than the natural mother because of hormonal influences and consistency of care following birth. Bowlby named this bias of a child to attach to one person in particular 'monotropy'.

> **Key term**
>
> **Monotropy:** the bias of a child to attach to one person in particular.

Bowlby suggested that human babies instinctively grasp and grip a caregiver in order to seek an embrace. This contact comfort provides a safe base for babies.

Internal working model

Bowlby proposed that personality development into adulthood was defined by early attachment experiences that are mentally stored by the child. A child's experience of a continuous, loving and sensitive mother is formed as a mental representation, a memory or template of what relationships are like. This mental representation forms a basis for subsequent romantic relationships and attachments with their offspring. A mother who provides a safe base helps to promote competence and resilience in later life. A sensitive-responsive mother builds a positive internal working model for a child to utilise in later adulthood relationships. Different experiences in childhood can have adverse consequences for later development, including less resilience and dependency.

> **Exam tip**
>
> When revising Bowlby's theory of attachment, it can be useful to revise using key terms. Define each key term and then link them together:
>
> | | |
> |---|---|
> | Evolutionary adaptedness | Social releasers |
> | Safe base | Proximity |
> | Sensitive period | Monotropy |
> | Attachment | Internal working model |

Evaluation

The concept of monotropy has been debated as Bowlby claimed a child was more likely to attach to the mother figure and that, although the child has multiple attachments after a certain age, this mother–child relationship was qualitatively different from others. Rudolph Schaffer and Peggy Emerson (1964) conducted a longitudinal study of 60 Glaswegian babies at monthly intervals over the first 18 months of life. Observing the children within their family homes, Schaffer and Emerson found that 17 per cent of the babies had formed multiple attachments as soon as attachment behaviours were displayed, and by four months half of the babies had formed more than one attachment, and some up to five attachments. In fact, at 18 months only 13 per cent of children with a single attachment had maintained this exclusivity. On the face of it, this research seems to disprove the concept of monotropy as children were able to form multiple attachments at a very young age. However, Schaffer and Emerson found that the babies protested more intensely at separation from one particular attachment figure than others, so much so that the attachments could be arranged in hierarchical order. This seems to support the concept of the monotropic bond being qualitatively different from other attachments. Additionally, the principal attachment figure for babies in the Glasgow study was the natural mother; however this finding was largely a product of the sample used whereby the mother was typically the one who reared the child.

WIDER ISSUES AND DEBATES

Social control

Bowlby's theory of attachment remains dominant as an explanation of attachment in developmental psychology; it has made positive contributions to the development of new hospital procedures ensuring that visiting times and access rights of parents to hospitalised children were increased. It has also made a positive contribution to childcare practices to avoid bond disruption. As we will see later in this section, day care now carefully considers the nature of substitute care and child–carer ratios are set by government.

However, the legacy of Bowlby is knowledge that even temporary separation can have adverse effects on attachment, which has led to working mothers feeling guilty for having to leave their children in day care. This psychological knowledge can still be felt today, as women continue to feel anxiety about using day care and balancing their home/work environments.

Child and adult attachments

Support for the internal working model comes from correlatory research into attachment types as a child and later adult attachments. Cindy Hazan and Phillip Shaver (1987) tested whether early attachments formed a template or model for later romantic relationships by using a questionnaire known as the 'Love Quiz'. The Love Quiz consisted of questions related to recall of childhood relationships with parents and questions about individual beliefs about romantic relationships. The quiz was published in a local newspaper and responses invited. They classified the recall of 620 replies of child–parent relationships as securely attached or insecurely attached and related this to the individuals' beliefs about romantic love. Respondents classified as having secure child–parent relationships were more likely to hold beliefs that romantic relationships were trusting, enduring and accepting of partners' faults. Insecurely classified respondents tended to believe romantic relationships were either based on obsession, attraction and jealously or that they feared intimacy and did not need love.

The correlation between early and later attachments provides evidence to support Bowlby's idea that first relationships form an internal working model on which subsequent relationships are based. However, this correlatory evidence does not mean that early attachment causes later attachment style and people did change their attachment as they grew older. It is also based on recall of child–parent relationships which may not be reliable. Other researchers have also found an association between early and adult attachment types (Feeney and Noller, 1990; Keelan, Dion and Dion, 1994) and in a replication of the Love Quiz (Hazan and Shaver, 1993) a similar but more modest correlation was found.

INDIVIDUAL DIFFERENCES

An alternative explanation for the association between childhood and adulthood attachment styles suggests that the temperament of the individual, and not the internal working model per se, should be considered. Kagan's (1984) temperament hypothesis suggests that the innate individual temperament of a child can dictate whether a secure or insecure attachment is formed, which has little to do with the formation of an internal working model. A child with a difficult temperament will impact on the quality of the relationship formed with a parent, and equally this temperament can influence subsequent relationships. It is the individual temperament and not the internal working model that affects the quality of relationships.

Bowlby based much of his theoretical work on research using animals. Harlow and Zimmermann (1959) showed that rhesus monkeys attached innately to a cloth mother to secure a safe base, and Lorenz's research into greylag geese helped Bowlby formulate his idea of a sensitive period. However, we should be mindful that animal research, although supporting the concept of an evolutionary basis for attachment, may not be wholly applicable to human development.

Ainsworth's work on attachment

Mary Ainsworth worked as Bowlby's assistant for several years and developed his ideas from an explanation of attachment into the types of attachment that children form with their caregiver. Moving to Uganda, she studied 28 Ganda infants and their mothers in their homes. Observing the infant–mother interactions of 26 families, she discovered that securely attached children used their mother as a safe base from which to explore their world, while insecurely attached babies tended to cling to the mother and refuse to venture away from her with confidence. She also found that mothers who were sensitive to behavioural cues from their child were more likely to form a secure attachment, whereas mothers who were not able to understand these cues formed insecure attachments with their child. Insecure children tended to cry more frequently, even when held by their mother. Ainsworth suggested that attachment type was associated with maternal sensitivity.

In 1963, Mary Ainsworth began a second observational study in Baltimore, USA, using middle-class families recruited before the baby was born. She observed the parent–child interactions for four hours each month from the first few weeks of birth. She found additional evidence that sensitive-responsive parenting was associated with happier children who cried less. When the children were 12 months old, Ainsworth and her colleague, Barbara Wittig, invited the families to a laboratory environment to understand how the babies would respond to their safe base when in a strange environment.

The 'Strange Situation'

Ainsworth and Wittig developed a 20-minute procedure to examine infant–parent interactions when in a strange situation. The procedure involved eight episodes, which involve the mother being present or absent and the introduction of a stranger. In each episode, the behaviour of the child was carefully observed.

Eight episodes of the Strange Situation Procedure

1 Mother and child are invited to play together in a laboratory playroom by a researcher, who then leaves the room.

2 The mother sits on a chair and the child plays on the floor with toys in the room.

3 A stranger enters the room with mother and child and talks to the mother.

4 The mother leaves the room, leaving the stranger with the child.

5 Mother returns to the room and the stranger leaves.

6 The parent leaves the room and the child is alone.

7 The stranger enters the room and tries to interact/comfort the child.

8 The mother returns and the stranger leaves the room.

Attachment types

The behaviour of the children was recorded, and particular attention was paid to the following occurrences:

- separation behaviour – the behaviour of the child when separated from the mother
- stranger response – how the child responded to the presence/comfort of the stranger
- reunion behaviour – how the child behaved when the mother returned
- exploring – the extent to which the child felt safe to explore the room.

Using the different ways the children responded in the Strange Situation, they could be classified into three different attachment types.

Taking it further

Use the Internet to find video footage of the Strange Situation Procedure in action. You will find quite a few clips of securely attached children, but see if you can find an insecurely attached pattern of behaviour.

Table 7.1 Children's attachment types in response to the Strange Situation

	Insecure-avoidant (Type A)	Secure attachment (Type B)	Insecure-resistant/ambivalent (Type C)
Separation anxiety	Not upset when the mother leaves the room.	Very distressed when mother leaves the room.	Very intense distress when mother leaves the room.
Stranger fear	Stranger able to interact and comfort the child.	Avoids stranger and resists stranger comfort.	Shows signs of stranger fear.
Reunion behaviour	Did not seek closeness of mother on her return and ignored her. When picked up by mother they avert their gaze from her.	Seeks comfort from mother. Happy that she has returned and quick to soothe.	Child approaches mother on her return but pushes her away angrily.
Exploring	Able to explore the room independently but does not check mother's presence and use her as a safe base.	Able to explore the room from the safe base of the mother. This stopped when the mother left the room. After reunion comfort they were able to explore again.	Clung to mother and hardly explored at all. Cries more than other types.
Observations from home visits	Insensitive, interfering and rejecting mothering observed.	Sensitive, responsive mothering observed.	Inconsistent mothering observed; warm and responsive on occasion and rejecting on other occasions.
Approximate % of children	20	70	10

Correlating the attachments types into which the children were classified, and observations made about the parent–child interactions at home, it was suggested that sensitive, responsive parenting encouraged trust and safety for the child, which resulted in a secure attachment type. Mothers who ignored the behavioural cues of their children and were insensitive to their needs tended to be more independent (avoidant) because they were accustomed to rejection. Children exposed to inconsistent parenting strategies, both loving and rejecting, were more likely to be ambivalent towards the mother because they were uncertain whether they could rely on their mothers. This resulted in clingy children who did not trust the mother to stay close to them and who were angry at her on her return.

Exam tip

To prepare well for the exam you should be able to use your knowledge of attachment types to explain novel scenarios that you may be given. Consider the following novel scenarios and explain the behaviour of the children.

Brendan is taken to the doctor by his mother for his first injection. Brendan plays happily in the doctor's surgery waiting room, but checks that his mother is close. A nurse takes him from his mother to receive the injection from the doctor. Brendan cries at the nurse but is quickly soothed by his mother when the nurse returns him to her.

Ellie is playing nicely when her mother introduces her to a new babysitter. Her mother and father are going out for the evening. Ellie seems unconcerned and continues to play with the babysitter near her. When her mother returns the babysitter describes how Ellie played well and was easy to put to bed.

Alisha and her mum visit some relatives that they have not seen for some time. Alisha clings to her mum and does not want to play with the toys she has been given. Alisha's mum pops to the shop, leaving her with her relatives. When her mum returns, Alisha continues to cry and gives her mum an angry look.

Evaluation

The Strange Situation Procedure has been widely used and is a highly regarded standardised procedure for classifying attachment types. However, it has been criticised for lacking ecological validity as the child may behave differently in more familiar surroundings. It has also been criticised on ethical grounds as it causes distress to the child involved in the procedure. The procedure was largely based on the research by Harlow, where rhesus monkeys were exposed to threatening stimuli. In this sense it is a more natural condition for a child to experience and one a child may be accustomed to. Although the procedure does induce stress in a child, the observers are trained to recognise intense distress and stop the procedure if they feel the child will become more than momentarily upset.

Because the Strange Situation Procedure is a structured observation, the episodes are highly standardised and it is conducted in a controlled environment. The behaviour of the children can be recorded and reviewed by many observers to establish inter-rater reliability. However, it may not be a useful procedure to measure attachment types in children accustomed to separation, such as those who attend regular day care.

INDIVIDUAL DIFFERENCES

Marina Fuertes et al. (2006) conducted research on the sensitive, responsiveness of mothers and the attachment bond secured by attentive mothers. They studied 48 Portuguese babies and mothers and observed them regularly until they reached their first birthday. They assessed the baby's personality in the first few months and the mother's sensitivity to the baby's needs. When the babies were 12 months old they used the Strange Situation to categorise them into different attachment types. They found that it was not only the sensitive, responsiveness of the mother that determined the attachment type, but that the individual temperament or personality of the child had an overwhelming influence on the type of attachment that developed. This contradicts Ainsworth's maternal sensitivity hypothesis, highlighting instead the role of individual differences in the personality of the child.

Kagan's (1984) temperament hypothesis can be used to criticise Ainsworth's research into attachment, in particular the association made between sensitive, responsive mothering and attachment type. He argues instead that the child's response in the Strange Situation is a result of their temperament rather than the attachment type they have developed through interactions with their mother. Avoidant children are innately fearless and independent, rather than ignored by a parent.

WIDER ISSUES AND DEBATES

Culture

As we will discuss later in this section, the attachment type proportions found in Ainsworth's Baltimore study are not the same patterns found in different cultures. Additionally, Ainsworth's conclusion about sensitive, responsiveness and attachment may be seen as culturally biased as it only represents a westernised view of attachment. Some cultures encourage independence so it only applies to western child-rearing practices. It is also worth noting that the Strange Situation Procedure may be an inappropriate tool to use in cultures where separation from a parent is uncommon. In Japanese culture, for example, children are rarely separated from their caregiver, so the Strange Situation causes the child great distress and therefore becomes a meaningless tool for measuring attachment type.

Separation and deprivation

Bowlby's theory of attachment argues that a child should have a close bond with a mother figure during the first few years of life. Therefore, separation from the mother could have serious consequences for the emotional development of the child. He based this hypothesis on observations conducted at the child guidance clinic and those made by other researchers at the time on children in institutional care and residential nurseries.

Short-term effects of separation: protest, despair, detachment

Separation anxiety can be observed in children from around seven months old; they display a desire to be close to their mother and display distress when separated. This is quite clear in the research of Ainsworth using the Strange Situation. She observed distinct patterns of immediate emotional distress following separation and the reluctance to accept comfort from others.

The short-term effects of relatively temporary separation from the mother can also be seen in James Robertson's research. Working as an observer for Bowlby in a residential nursery and hospital setting, Robertson systematically made notes on the behaviour of the children who came to the institutions. At the time, children's distress at separation from their caregiver was rarely noted and parental visitation was very restricted. However, Robertson was able to record the distress at separation exhibited by children and this led Robertson and Bowlby (1952) to suggest three stages to the distress that children undergo.

1 Protest: The initial stage of separation can last several hours or days and the child is seen to cry profusely, throw himself around and seek for the mother figure. During this phase of protest the child will actively refuse comfort from other adults or displays exaggerated clinging to an adult.

2 Despair: Once the initial protest and screaming stops, the child no longer anticipates the return of the mother and becomes increasingly hopeless. The child will become withdrawn, apathetic and demonstrates mourning. The child self-soothes and rejects the comfort of others; often displaying rocking, thumb sucking, and cuddling inanimate objects.

3 Detachment: The child regains an interest in its environment and even accepts comfort and interaction with other adults. However, when the mother returns it is apparent that the child

does not display normal reunion behaviour. The child will reject the mother, turning away from her and not accepting her comfort. The child will seem to reject his mother as she has seemingly rejected them. Prolonged or repeated separations can lead to rather superficial interactions between the child and other adult figures.

Children who are securely attached may be wary of strangers and see their mother as a secure base.

Evaluation

The stages of distress have been observed in a series of observations conducted by Robertson. One small child named John was 17 months old when he was placed in a residential nursery for nine days while his mother was admitted to hospital to give birth to a second child. His father worked all day and he had no relatives to care for him, although his father did visit him while he was in the nursery. John displayed the three stages of distress while in the nursery: he sobbed and resisted comfort (protest), he played with toys and clung to a soft teddy bear (despair), and would not look at his mother when she returned, resisting attempts to soothe him (detachment).

Some psychologists argue that it is not the separation itself that causes such an acute distress response in a child, but the associated factors around the separation, such as the introduction to an unfamiliar environment or the length and nature of the separation or resilience of the child. However, research by Spiro (1958) reported a case of a boy brought up in an Israeli kibbutz who was left for several weeks while his parents were away travelling. In a familiar environment and with familiar people, the little boy still demonstrated the same distress documented in the case of John. This may question whether the unfamiliarity of the environment alone may account for the distress shown. In a study of matched children who were accompanied into hospital by their mother, or left in hospital alone (Fagin, 1966), it was found that only the unaccompanied children showed distress. Again, this highlighted that it is the absence of the mother figure that caused distress and not the unfamiliarity of the environment.

In extreme cases, the effects of separation can be severe, particularly if the separation is prolonged and at an early age. René Spitz (1887–1974) conducted research in children's orphanages in South America during the 1940s. In one institution, babies were separated from their mothers at three months and placed into an orphanage to await fostering. In another institution, annexed to a female prison, the babies of inmates were separated from their mothers but received regular visits so their mothers could care for them. The prison babies thrived while the orphaned children displayed **anaclitic depression** and developmental delay.

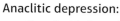

Key term

Anaclitic depression: emotional withdrawal, loss of appetite, crying.

The maternal deprivation hypothesis

Bowlby proposed the maternal deprivation hypothesis to explain the adverse consequences caused by separation between a child and caregiver during the sensitive period. The negative effects could be seen in the longer term development of the mental health of the child.

How long are long-term effects observed?

For the purpose of this book, we have described the short-term effects of separation over the course of around one week. However, Bowlby drew on additional research to describe the development of behavioural responses to separation over the course of the first year of life. Rudolph Schaffer (1958) studied 67 hospitalised children under the age of 12 months admitted for elective surgery, without apparent malnutrition or brain injury. The children were without their mother for the duration of the stay and received little attention from nurses in the form of social interaction. The children aged over 29 weeks cried and physically struggled around their cots. Those under 28 weeks did not exhibit the same protest, but maintained silence and showed bewilderment. It seemed that age played a significant role in the protest to separation, and this was marked at the 28-week stage. Bowlby claimed that the intensity of this protest response diminished around the third birthday.

Long-term effects of deprivation

The effects of maternal deprivation on the long-term development of children was largely based on research of institutionalised children conducted during the 1940s. In 1943, William Goldfarb studied the development of children raised in institutions compared to those fostered straight from their mother. The 15 children in each group were matched on maternal education and occupation, and studied from the age of around six months to three years old. At three years old the children who remained in the institution were intellectually and socially behind the fostered group, and in adolescence they maintained this development lag and showed problems with relationship formation (Goldfarb, 1947). It is clear that such research would seem to strongly suggest that early deprivation can have long-term consequences on social, emotional and intellectual development, although it could have been the very nature of the unstimulating and neglectful environment that caused these problems rather than their separation from a mother figure.

To investigate the long-term consequences of deprivation, Bowlby conducted his own research on children attending the guidance clinic where he worked. Some of the boys and girls attending the clinic had been referred by schools and parents, and some had been referred by legal services. Bowlby interviewed 44 children who had been referred because of juvenile delinquency and theft (the 44 juvenile thieves) and 44 children referred because of emotional problems (control group) but not stealing. Along with a social worker, they interviewed each child and parent and made psychiatric assessments of the children's behaviour. Bowlby classified 14 of the juvenile thieves as having an 'affectionless character', as they seemed to lack affection for others and experienced no guilt, responsibility or shame for their crimes. None of the children in the control group was classified as having an affectionless character. Of the 44 juvenile thieves, 17 had experienced prolonged periods of separation from the primary caregiver of more than six months before the age of six years, compared to only two of the control group. Of the 17 juvenile thieves who had experienced maternal deprivation, 12 of them were classified as affectionless characters. This was the most important finding as it suggested that the long-term consequences of maternal deprivation were a lack of empathy and guilt and later the development of delinquent behaviour.

WIDER ISSUES AND DEBATES

Psychology as a science
Research into the effects of institutional care are natural experiments because whether or not a child is fostered, adopted or remain in the institution is not under the control of the researchers. This means that the children cannot be randomly allocated to an experimental condition, which is a requirement of a true experiment.

Evaluation

The long-term consequences of maternal deprivation have been found to be associated with later emotional, social and cognitive difficulties. However, it cannot be firmly established that the deprivation alone led to such problems in later life. In Bowlby's study of 44 juvenile thieves, we cannot be certain of the circumstances around the separation period or the reason for such separation. It could be that the reason for the separation itself led to later problems. Correlatory research cannot firmly establish the cause of later difficulties, just that there is a relationship between them. It must also be discussed that of the 44 juvenile thieves, 27 had not suffered maternal deprivation but were still referred to the clinic for stealing. This means that other factors must also contribute to the development of these tendencies. This does not take away from the fact that many of those suffering maternal deprivation were also classified as affectionless characters, but does highlight that other factors should be considered.

Goldfarb acknowledged that factors associated with orphanages at the time, such as emotional neglect, contributed to poor development of the children who remained in care; however, he argued that it was the separation that was the most important factor. Other researchers disagree with this view. Impoverished environments lack stimulation and are associated with developmental retardation and poor language development. Therefore poor long-term outcomes could be associated with unstimulating environments rather than lack of a mother figure. Rutter (1981) extends this argument to suggest that the long-term effects of deprivation demonstrated in research involving institutionalised children may be a result of privation (lack of an attachment) rather than deprivation (loss of an attachment), as many children were for all intents and purposes emotionally neglected, which may explain negative effects in later life.

Reducing negative effects of deprivation

According to Bowlby's theory, the short-term effects of separation can only be truly **ameliorated** by reunion between the caregiver and the child. However, this is not always possible as modern society requires both parents in families to be working – meaning that children are often placed in day care.

Following on from his observations of children attending hospital and residential nursery care, James and his wife Joyce Robertson (1971) conducted a series of experimental trials that combined their roles as observers and temporary foster carers for four children whose mothers were going into hospital. It was their aim to understand the conditions under which negative effects of separation could be ameliorated.

The Robertsons decided to become temporary foster carers for four children, as shown in Table 7.2.

Table 7.2 Children fostered by James and Joyce Robertson while their mothers were in hospital (1971)

Name	Age	Days to be spent in care
Jane	1 year 5 months	10
Lucy	1 year 9 months	19
Thomas	2 years 4 months	10
Kate	2 years 5 months	27

Each child was fostered separately and the Robertsons made great efforts to get to know the habits and developmental stage of each child prior to their being separated from their parents. Based on observations both during their time with the Robertsons, and on their return to their parents, it was concluded that, although the stages of protest, despair and detachment could be seen in the children's behaviour, the intensity of distress was significantly reduced when good-quality substitute care was provided.

Key term

Ameliorate: to make a bad situation better or less harmful.

The negative effects of separation can be reduced by the provision of a substitute mother figure with concern over the child's emotional and intellectual needs. Greater contact and comfort from a substitute carer, who provides attention and stimulation, can reduce the distress experienced by a child.

The Robertsons suggested that regular contact with the parent and reminders of them, such as photographs, could help the child cope with the separation. They also suggested that placement in an unfamiliar environment would be buffered by maintaining home life routines, permitting children to bring with them familiar toys and comforters to remind them of their home and family.

These findings can be seen in practice today in our day care centres and nurseries. Government policies for childcare provision regulate the permitted child to staff ratios for childcare providers to ensure that children receive a sufficient amount of attention and stimulation from substitute carers. This has had an impact on recent developments in childcare provision that will be discussed later in this section.

Privation

Privation is defined as the complete absence of an attachment figure or when an attachment between child and caregiver is never formed. This occurs in cases where children have suffered extreme neglect or have been placed in poor-quality institutional care. Psychologists know that privation can have extremely negative effects on a child's emotional, social and cognitive development, but it is still relatively unclear whether any of these effects could be reversed or ameliorated. In this section, we will examine a number of case studies of privated (neglected) children to explore the effects of privation on a range of outcomes and also examine the effects of poor-quality institutional care.

The case of Genie (Curtiss, 1977)

In 1970, a case of extreme neglect came to light: a girl aged 13 years old who had spent most of her life locked in a room with nothing but a cot, potty chair and cotton reels to play with. Genie was seriously neglected by her parents, who claimed that she was diagnosed with mental retardation as a baby. She was confined to her cot or tied to her potty chair for most of her life, and only on special occasions allowed to play with two plastic raincoats. Her father repeatedly beat her for vocalising, and her mother, who was partially blind, claimed that she was also a victim of his abuse.

Although both of Genie's parents were charged with child abuse, her father committed suicide and her mother was never convicted. The custody of Genie was given to the Los Angeles Children's Hospital, where researchers and doctors were involved in her care and recovery. She was found with severe emotional and intellectual retardation; she was virtually mute, had an awkward gait and stooped, was seriously malnourished and often scratched and bit herself. From being tied to a potty chair, she had a ring of callus on her buttocks, she frequently urinated in her clothing; and it transpired that she could not chew as a result of being fed only baby food, she often held solid food in her mouth until it dissolved enough to swallow.

After only a few days in the hospital, Genie began to show signs of improvement; she was able to urinate independently and form attachments with members of staff. After several months, she began to play and utter words. However, her language development, particularly the use of grammar, did not improve beyond that of a toddler. Unfortunately, Genie's story was one of repeated foster carers and eventually she regressed into a world of silence and emotional disturbance.

WIDER ISSUES AND DEBATES

Ethics and socially sensitive research

Following a period of hospital care, Genie was initially fostered by one of the researchers, Jean Butler, who was working on developing her linguistic ability. However, many speculated at the time that Butler could not provide adequate care and that her care of Genie would be in direct conflict with her research ambitions. Genie was removed from Butler's care and placed in the family home of David Rigler, one of Genie's therapists and head of the research team. Genie was exposed to a number of cognitive tests, brain scans and treatments to improve her emotional and social skills. Some claimed that she was overexposed to testing and this was inappropriate for a vulnerable child. Once the project funding for Genie ran out, and further grant extensions denied, the Rigler family could no longer care for Genie and she went back to the care of her mother. Genie's mother could not cope with her so she was returned to a succession of foster care homes and was finally made a ward of the state.

There is continued speculation about whether the researchers were appropriately placed to provide both therapeutic and foster care, and whether the career ambitions of some of the researchers were placed ahead of the welfare of this child.

Taking it further

Further information about the case of Genie and Koluchová's research into the Czech twins can be found on the Internet. You can find video footage of the case of Genie, which documents her progress and the controversies surrounding her care and rehabilitation. Investigate the progress that Genie made and carefully consider the opinions of researchers in her case. Remember, even researchers can be biased in their opinions, so try to maintain an objective view.

The Czech twins (Koluchová, 1972)

Andrei and Vanya, a pair of Czechoslovakian twins, lost their mother shortly after their birth and were placed into institutional care for a year. They were subsequently cared for by an aunt before returning to their father's care at the age of 18 months. Their father had remarried and their stepmother was cruel, locking them in a small, dark room for long periods of time. Eventually discovered at the age of 6 years, the twins were malnourished and mentally retarded. Their IQ was estimated to be around 40 (the average IQ is 100), but their language development was so poor this could not be firmly established. They were taken to a children's home for rehabilitation and two years later were fostered by two sisters who provided exceptional care for the boys. At 11 years old the boys had developed normal speech, and by 14 years had attained an average IQ. At the age of 20, both boys were in relationships and had secured employment. The rehabilitative success of the boys was attributed largely to the good-quality care they received after being found.

Institutional care

Michael Rutter and Edmund Sonuga-Barke lead the English and Romanian Adoptee (ERA) Team, a longitudinal study which continues to investigate the development of Romanian orphans adopted into UK families, compared with adopted children born in the UK. A random sample of 165 Romanian orphans raised in appalling institutional conditions from the first few weeks of life were divided into those who were adopted before the age of six months or between six months and two years old. Their development after being fostered was compared to 52 adopted children who had not spent time in institutional care. Despite being developmentally delayed at the age of six months, the Romanian adoptees caught up in weight, height and head circumference and cognitive ability, to be on par with the English adoptees at the age of 11 years. Although the Romanian children adopted after six months old made progress, they still continued to experience significant problems, such as overactivity, difficulties forming attachments and social interaction, which warranted attention from psychological services. These difficulties persisted when followed up at the age of 15, particularly those stemming from attachment disorders. They concluded that the early privation experienced by the Romanian orphans seemed only to have a prolonged effect only if they were adopted after the age of six months.

Anna Freud and Sophie Dann (1951) studied and cared for six children raised in a concentration camp in Theresienstadt. Having lost their parents during the Nazi occupation, the children were raised together by prisoners at the concentration camp but this care was infrequent and the ability to form attachments was made difficult by the nature of the environment in which they were raised. These children became known as the Bulldogs Bank children. They were seen by a clinic for treatment at around the age of three years after enduring appalling conditions. Initially aggressive towards staff and having formed intense bonds with each other, the children began to form attachments with the staff at the clinic. Although one was later known to have sought psychiatric care as an adult, the remaining children seemed to have developed normal adult behaviours.

Jill Hodges and Barbara Tizard (1989) studied 65 children raised in institutional care that held a policy not to form attachments with the children and had a high staff turnover. This meant that the researchers could be reasonably certain that any long-term effects found were a result of privation and not deprivation as close relationships were actively discouraged. When the children were four years old, 24 were adopted into families, 15 were returned to their biological families and 26 remained in institutional care. The children were followed up at various ages, and parents and teachers asked to rate their behaviour. At the age of 16 years, the adopted children had formed attachments with their adoptive parents and were happy. This contrasted with those who were re-established with their biological parents who had difficulty showing affection and formed poor relationships. The story was rather different for relationships formed outside the family units as both adopted and returned children found it difficult to form friendships, were attention- and approval-seeking and indiscriminate in friendship selection. This disparity between home and school life could be explained by the nature of the relationships between the child and caregiver; the adoptive parents were desperate to adopt a child, whereas the biological parents were ambivalent towards their returning children and suffered economic hardship.

Evaluation

Case studies of privated children provide useful insights into the development of these children that could never be created under experimental conditions. Often these case studies employ a variety of methods, such as self-reports, observations, cognitive tests and EEG recordings, all of which can be triangulated to ensure valid findings. However, there are significant methodological issues associated with the information derived from such investigations. The most significant weakness is that case studies of privated children are retrospective. This means that we cannot accurately ascertain what actually happened to these children through the course of their development before being discovered. Any information about their history tends to come from accounts of family and friends or speculation as to how they were treated. This results in an uncertainty about the conditions in which they were raised and whether or not they were truly privated or were still able to form attachments and were then deprived.

This is true of both Genie and the Bulldogs Bank children. A researcher working with Genie claimed that he could not determine whether or not Genie was retarded from birth or whether her difficulties arose as a result of her treatment. A sleep spindle study recorded bursts of activity that we would normally associate with congenital retardation, but Susan Curtiss, another researcher, claimed that Genie's developmental progress after being discovered would have been uncharacteristic of someone born with developmental difficulties.

The Bulldogs Bank children received transient care from prisoners of war, and were able to attach with one another, so the extent of their privation is unclear, and perhaps their bonds with each other buffered the effects of privation.

Similarly, the Czech twins received good-quality care at a children's home following the death of their mother, and only suffered neglect after the age of 18 months. It is possible that the care they received prior to their neglect, and the fact that they had each other, ameliorated the effects of privation which could account for their recovery.

Case studies are unique one-off investigations; therefore we have a limited number to refer to and all have their own individual characteristics. This makes it difficult to generalise the findings and claim that privation would cause such effects for all children. There are significant factors identified to affect the outcome of children who have suffered privation, such as age, quality of relationships formed after being discovered and the availability of other individuals to bond with.

Studies of institutionalised children also present issues that make it difficult to establish the effects of privation on later development. Children who are adopted compared to those who remain in institutional care cannot be matched on every characteristic likely to affect their later development, in particular the reason why they were placed in institutional care or the circumstances around their adoption. Hodges and Tizard's research did not take account of the temperament of the child; it is possible that the children selected for adoption were more socially adept and emotionally stable compared to those who remained in the institution or were returned to their biological families. This may have explained why the adopted children formed better relationships with their adoptive parents.

Can negative effects of privation be reversed?

Research investigating the long-term effects of privation also helps us to understand whether these effects can be reversed and under what conditions it may be possible to overcome negative effects. Age seems a significant factor as the younger the child is rehabilitated or placed into foster care, the better the outcomes in terms of reversing negative effects. The Czech twins were discovered at the age of six, but Genie was found at the age of 13 years, which may account for the recovery of the twins but the extent to which Genie recovered was limited. This can also explain why the Romanian orphans adopted before the age of six months of age recovered from their early privation compared to those adopted into the UK after the age of six months. The length of the privation period seems to influence the extent to which early trauma can be reversed.

A further factor that may explain why some children recover from privation better than others is the nature of their isolation. The Bulldogs Bank children and the Czech twins had other attachment figures; transient adults or other children with whom bonds could be formed, Genie was held in almost complete isolation. Again this could be a factor that explains why the negative effects Genie suffered were not reversible compared to other privated children.

The quality of care following a period of privation can also ameliorate negative effects caused by early trauma. The Czech twins were cared for by two sisters who provided excellent emotional, social and intellectual support to aid their recovery, and Hodges and Tizard demonstrated that when children were adopted into loving families they fared better than those restored to biological parents. (This assumes that the biological parents may have been reluctant to have their child returned as they rated them less favourably than their children who had not been fostered.)

Day care

Day care constitutes any formal or informal arrangement to provide substitute care for a child which is not provided by the biological parent. This can be arranged in a formal setting such as nursery, with a childminder or nanny, or informally with a relative such as a grandparent. The type of day care setting can influence the social, emotional and cognitive development of the child. Grandparents are more likely to be minding one or a small number of grandchildren and also more likely to provide greater intellectual and social stimulation and emotional support compared to a childminder, who may have several children to care for. This section will focus on day care provided in the formal setting of a nursery/preschool environment.

Research into day care

Research into day care has focused on certain aspects of child development.

- Social development: refers to the ability of a child to interact with others (peers), this includes how independent, shy or aggressive they are.

- Emotional development: refers to the attachments they form and their ability to cope with situations.

- Cognitive development: refers to the intellectual growth of a child, which can be measured using IQ tests or referring to standardised assessment scores (GCSEs, etc.).

Bowlby would predict that children in day care would suffer maternal deprivation, particularly if they attend day care before the age of two and for prolonged periods away from their caregiver. However, research into the effects of day care has produced mixed findings: some suggest that day care can have positive effects, some no effects and some suggest that children suffer negative effects as a result.

The advantages of day care

Andersson (1992) conducted a longitudinal study in Sweden to track the development of 119 children until their eighth birthday. Children who attended day care at a young age, before the age of one, were rated as more socially advanced by their school teachers than those who attended day care at an older age or who were cared for at home. These children had more friends and were more outgoing because day care had offered them greater opportunity to develop social skills. These children also performed better at school at the ages of 8 and 13 years than children cared for at home or late-entry day care children. The positive effects of day care, both social and cognitive, were related to onset and time spent in day care. However, Swedish day care is particularly well funded and those children who started day care earliest were from families of higher socio-economic status and whose mother had a higher educational level. Moreover, the maternity and paternity leave in Sweden is extended in comparison with the UK, meaning that children spend a longer time with their parents before the parents are required to return to work. The positive effects of day care found in children attending day care early was mediated significantly by coming from wealthy families and also limited to this particular culture.

The Effective Provision of Preschool Education project (EPPE; Sylva et al., 2004) was a longitudinal study of day care provision (home care, nurseries, preschools and playgroups) for over 3000 children in the UK. The researchers created developmental profiles for each child, from the age of three to seven years, based on **SATs** results, preschool staff, parents and school teachers. The researchers also recorded parental qualifications, social background, and birth weight of the child, in order to examine the interactional effects of these mediating factors. They found that children benefited both socially and intellectually from preschool care, particularly if they started day care before the age of three years.

> ### Key term
>
> **SATs:** Standardised assessment tests to assess literacy and numeracy.

High-quality provision and well-qualified staff led to better social and cognitive development, and cognitive effects were still evident at the end of Key Stage 1, with children achieving higher scores in maths and literacy.

The advantages of day care seem to be largely contingent on factors such as the provision of good-quality day care, characterised by good staff to child ratios, positive interaction between staff and children, low staff turnover and staff who are highly qualified in childcare.

The EPPE study found that positive effects of day care, both social and cognitive, were related to onset and time spent in day care.

The disadvantages of day care

Other research into the effects of day care have not documented such positive effects. Jay Belsky and Michael Rovine (1988) used the findings of two longitudinal studies in America to investigate the effects of day care on attachments formed between parents and children in the first year of life. Using the data of children and their attachment types with their mothers and fathers, using the Strange Situation Procedure, they found a higher incidence of insecure-avoidant attachment types with mother (43 per cent) among children who attended more than 20 hours of day care a week during the first year of life compared with those attending fewer than 20 hours. They also found that boys whose mothers worked full time, and therefore attended day care for 35 hours per week, had more insecure attachments with their fathers. This suggests a negative effect of day care on the emotional development of children. However, Clarke-Stewart (1989) criticised the use of the Strange Situation Procedure as a measure of attachment for children in prolonged day care because they would be familiar with being left with other people and therefore would not respond in the same way as children who were unaccustomed to being left with other adults. Children who have regular experience of day care are routinely left with other adults and develop independent behaviour that may be interpreted as avoidant behaviour.

The National Institute of Child Health and Human Development (NICHD) followed 1364 families from birth to the first grade to examine the relationship between day care and development of American children from a range of socio-economic and ethnic backgrounds and family structures. They found that high-quality day care was associated with cognitive development; they also found that day care was associated with more behavioural problems, in particular aggression, compared to children cared for at home. This was particularly evident in low-quality day care provision.

INDIVIDUAL DIFFERENCES

Increasingly, researchers are examining the effects of day care on individual children, as some children are more resilient and able to cope better with separation than others. Day care may provide independent and outgoing children with social skills, but shy children may be adversely affected by a constant background of social activity.

Michael Pluess and Jay Belsky (2010) found that children rated as having difficult temperaments were affected differentially by both good- and poor-quality day care and parenting. Children rated as difficult in temperament benefited most from good-quality day care and sensitive parenting, and suffer most negative effects in poor-quality environments. It seems that good-quality care helps them regulate their emotions within a supportive and sensitive environment, but such children can become overwhelmed by poor-quality environments, leading to academic and behavioural problems and teacher–child conflicts that extend to middle childhood.

Evaluation

There are problems when investigating whether day care has advantages or disadvantages for the development of children's social, emotional and cognitive abilities. A significant issue is that children are rarely randomised to a specific type of childcare environment. A randomised controlled trial would involve children being randomly assigned to one specific type of childcare in order to distribute mediating factors such as temperament of the child, socio-economic status, etc. Clearly this is impractical in most cases and therefore researchers have to resort to conducting a complex statistical analysis of these mediating factors in order to isolate the roles and interaction effects caused against the effects of day care. This becomes a statistical challenge, as the nature of the home environment, temperament of the child, quality of the day care and other factors often interact to have differential effects on the outcomes for each child. Not every factor that could possibly mediate or interact with the effects of day care can be measured, as they are too innumerable to investigate, so significant variables may not be recorded. Day care research is correlatory and therefore any significant associations found between day care and outcomes cannot claim a causal effect.

Comparing different types of maternal and non-maternal care environments also makes research to examine their effects difficult. Every day care provider has different qualities, such as staff ratios, staff wages, resources, and so on that make them difficult to compare with other providers. This probably accounts for the lack of agreement in the findings of research into day care.

What makes good-quality day care?

Ratios and training

Clearly the quality of day care provision is associated with better cognitive and social outcomes of children. Low staff turnover to ensure consistency of care, good staff to child ratios to help form substitute attachments and staff training and qualifications, are known to be indicators of good-quality day care provision. In a review of staff ratios, training and group size, the Thomas Coram Research Unit (2002) analysed day care literature across many countries and established firm recommendations for the Department for Education and Skills that included better standards and clear guidelines for staff to child ratios and staff training. The current Early Years Foundation Stage statutory framework (2014) requires that the manager of a day care centre should hold at least a relevant level 3 qualification as a minimum and half of the staff should hold a relevant level 2 qualification.

Table 7.3 Staff:children ratios in day care in the UK and abroad (2002)

Country	Age	Staff to child ratio
UK (National standards)	0–2 years	1:3
	2–3 years	1:4
	3–5 years	1:8
	5 years	
USA (No national standards, varies state to state)	0–9 months	1:3–1:6
	10–18 months	1:4–1:9
	19–27 months	1:4–1:13
	28 months to 3 years	1:7–1:15
Spain (National standards)	0–1 year	1:8
	1–2 years	1:13
	2–3 years	1:20
	3–6 years	1:25

Taking it further

In 2013, Elizabeth Truss, Parliamentary Under-Secretary of State, proposed the relaxing of staff ratios and improvements in staff qualifications for day care providers. Conduct research into these proposals and consider the implications of such changes on the well-being of children in day care.

Key person

The Early Years Foundation Stage (EYFS) set out a statutory framework for the quality of care provided by day care provision in the UK, to include the provision of a key worker within the environment for each child. The role of this key worker was to help the child settle into the environment, provide tailored care, track progress and build relationships with parents. This substitute carer seems consistent with the work of James and Joyce Robertson to reduce the negative effects of separation.

Onset and duration of day care

Bowlby would support later and less intensive day care for children in order for secure attachment to be formed with parents before separation. This is certainly echoed in the research by Belsky and Rovine, who found that day care before the age of one for more than 20 hours a week resulted in more insecure attachment patterns. However, the EPPE project and Andersson's research suggests that early onset day care could be both socially and intellectually beneficial for children. The lack of consistent findings is probably explained by the quality of provision, so it is perhaps safer to assume that only good-quality day care is beneficial for children at an early age for full-time working parents.

Cross-cultural research into attachment types

Ainsworth's research into attachment using the Strange Situation Procedure was confined to families from Baltimore in the USA. However, the Strange Situation Procedure has become an internationally recognised tool for classifying parent–child attachment types, and therefore we can examine the outcomes across different cultures. In a meta-analysis of cross-cultural patterns of attachment, Van IJzendoorn and Kroonenberg (1988) found that attachment patterns varied considerably across cultures. You will read about this classic study later in this section, but you may find it useful to refer to this study before you read about cross-cultural issues here.

According to Ainsworth's research, parent–child attachment types are based largely on the concept of maternal sensitivity. As childrearing practices vary greatly across cultures, according to traditions and beliefs about childhood, it is important to investigate whether attachment types differ as a result. This would help us understand whether attachment is a universal or culturally specific phenomenon.

Attachment types in Germany

Klaus and Karin Grossman and colleagues conducted a longitudinal study of attachment in Germany. The Bielefeld study in northern Germany, began in 1976–77 and 49 families were recruited at hospital before the birth of their child. The sample of children – 26 boys and 23 girls – came from typical German native families with traditional divisions of labour within the family; the mother tended to be the primary caregiver and father the provider. Researchers made extensive records from observations of parent–child interactions within the family home. At two years old the children were assessed using the Strange Situation Procedure, They found that 24 out of the 49 infants studied showed Type A insecure-avoidant attachment behaviour during the Strange Situation (49 per cent) and, consistent with Ainsworth's maternal sensitivity hypothesis, that parental sensitivity was correlated with child–parent attachment types found.

However, the attachment types found were disproportionate to those found in America, perhaps due to childrearing practices in Germany. German children are taught to be more independent from an early age and accustomed to being left with other adults, which may have been interpreted as avoidant behaviour. The researchers recognised this, and later established a further longitudinal study in Regensburg (1980) using measures that were adapted to account for parent–child interactions being interpreted by traditional methods as avoidant. It is perhaps that the avoidant attachment types found were not necessarily a result of insensitive parenting, but a conscious cultural belief in the independence of children. It could also be that the sample size used by the German study was not applicable to all German families. In fact, other research conducted in Germany suggests that there are as many within-culture differences as between-culture differences. For example, the difference in attachment profiles found between Berlin and Bielefeld in Germany were as different as those found between Berlin and an Israeli kibbutz. This could be a product of subcultural differences within a culture.

Attachment types in Japan

Miyake et al. (1985) and Takahashi (1986) studied attachment types of children in Sapporo, Japan. They found an absence of Type A insecure-avoidant attachment types but a greater distribution of Type C insecure-resistant/ambivalent attachment types (>30 per cent) compared to the USA. Miyake interpreted this finding as a product of childrearing practices and the temperaments of Japanese children. Japanese children are rarely separated from the mother and attachment is characterised by close and continuous physical contact. They were also found to have fearful and irritable temperaments, making them more distressed at separation. In the Strange Situation, this distress was interpreted as resistant attachment behaviour. Specifically, Japanese children show signs of distress at episode two in the Strange Situation Procedure, which is confounded by subsequent episodes of separation and stranger activity around the child, as such they become inconsolable, a pattern misunderstood as resistant behaviour. This suggests that the Strange Situation is not a valid tool to measure attachment for Japanese children; rather than an indication of maladaptive parenting, it represents an unusual response to the procedure itself. This is further supported by the evidence that modern Japanese families often work and leave their children regularly. In these modern families, attachment distribution behaviour more similar to the USA is found.

Attachment types in Israel

Sagi et al. (1985) studied attachment types of children and their parents in a communal living environment such as an Israeli kibbutz. Children are often separated from the parents during the day; instead they are looked after in a nursery environment headed by a community member known as a metapelet. Children sleep in dormitories and are cared for collectively where childrearing is shared.

Within these communes, Sagi et al. found the highest level of Type C insecure-resistant attachment (33 per cent). They suggested that resistant behaviour was more likely because the mother was regularly absent and caregivers rotated shifts, so continuous and immediate attention could not be given by caregivers. Sagi et al. (1991) later compared kibbutz children who were raised in communal sleeping arrangements and those who slept with their biological family. They found that attachment patterns were consistent with attachment proportions found in the USA when children experienced modern kibbutz sleeping arrangements.

Explaining attachment types across cultures (nature–nurture)

Ainsworth's research into attachment types and maternal sensitivity suggest a strong association between sensitive, responsive parenting and Type B secure attachments. If we take cross-cultural research on face value, we could assume that Japanese, German and Israeli children are insecurely attached due to a lack of maternal sensitive, responsiveness. However, cross-cultural research into attachment types suggest that the beliefs and values concerning childcare practices within a culture or subculture affect the way a child responds within a strange situation.

The Strange Situation Procedure was created in America and therefore reflects the values and beliefs concerning childrearing practices of that culture; as such it may not be a useful measure of attachment across other cultures. It may simply be the case that this procedure is not appropriate to use as it is not sensitive to cultural values. This leads to a misunderstanding that different cultures produce insecure-attachment types, which is an imposed etic (the single viewpoint of a researcher). This imposed etic may lead us to assume that Japanese, German and Israeli parents are insensitive to the needs of their children relative to USA parenting, because they have been judged by the ethnocentric standards set by one culture being imposed on another. The fact is that these childrearing practices and attachment patterns are normal within their particular culture.

We can, however, establish that attachment is a behaviour that exists across many cultures and to an extent is determined by maternal sensitivity. This seems to support Bowlby's position that attachment is an innate process driven by evolutionary adaptedness. However, the type of attachment formed is largely dependent on different childrearing practices in different cultures. This affects how children respond to separation and to strangers as it is a product of nurture.

Autism

Autism is a developmental disorder that lasts for the lifetime of the individual. It affects how people interact with others and how they make sense of the world. Autism is considered a spectrum condition, meaning that each child with autism will be affected in different ways. The frequency of autism within the population is considered to be approximately one in 100 people. Boys are five times more likely than girls to have autism, although this may be because it is under-diagnosed in girls rather than it being more common in boys.

Autism is typically detected through problems in three domains of an individual's life. This is known as the triad of impairment and includes problems with communication, social interaction and imagination. As a result of the autism, individuals may have difficulty in interpreting the intentions or facial expressions of others, be somewhat rigid in their interests and misunderstand sarcasm. Speech can be limited, or if they have verbal communication, they have difficulty in understanding the two-way style of verbal conversation. It means children with autism can have difficulty in forming and developing friendships.

Symptoms of autism are typically detected in children at approximately four years old. Behaviours are likely to include a preference for routine, sensory sensitivity, such as dislike for labels in clothes, or becoming distressed by bright lights or excessive noise, etc. They may also have specific interests,

Taking it further

Search for 'autism triad' on Google to find more information about the impairments of people on the autism spectrum.

which often emerge from a young age, and which may eventually become a hobby, or an area in which they choose to work as an adult. A **learning disability** may also be present, which can range in the level of impairment.

Asperger's syndrome is a form of autism. Individuals with Asperger's syndrome are likely to be of average or above average intelligence, and their speech is less problematic.

Causes of autism

The exact cause of autism is still under investigation. It is currently considered that a combination of factors, rather than just one, can contribute to the development of autism. Some of the common explanations of autism include a genetic link, neurological factors, cognitive reasons or environmental influences. As the exact 'cause' of autism is still to be clarified, the above are considered 'risk factors', thought to increase the potential to develop autism.

Genetics

Twin studies undertaken by Bailey et al. (1995) report a 60 per cent concordance for autism in monozygotic (MZ) twins versus 0 per cent in dizygotic (DZ) twins. The higher MZ concordance suggests genetic inheritance as the predominant causative agent. When considering the broader spectrum of related cognitive or social abnormalities that included communication and social disorders, the concordance increased from 60 per cent to 92 per cent in MZ twins and from 0 per cent to 10 per cent in DZ pairs. This suggests that interactions between multiple genes cause autism but exposure to environmental modifiers may contribute to variable expression of autism-related traits. The identity and number of genes involved remain unknown.

Hallmayer et al. (2011) found a similar concordance between MZ and DZ twins when looking at pairs of female and male twins. For strict autism, concordance for male twins was 58 per cent for 40 monozygotic pairs and 21 per cent for 31 dizygotic pairs. Among female twins, the concordance was 60 per cent for 7 monozygotic pairs and 27 per cent for 10 dizygotic pairs. The lower number of female pairs reflects the smaller number of females diagnosed with autism. For autism symptoms, the concordance for male twins was 77 per cent for 45 monozygotic pairs and 31 per cent for 45 dizygotic pairs. Within the female twins, the concordance was 50 per cent for 9 monozygotic pairs and 36 per cent for 13 dizygotic pairs. A large proportion of the variance in liability can be explained by shared environmental factors in addition to moderate genetic heritability.

Despite information to suggest a genetic cause for autism, as documented by the relationship between autism and MZ twins, to date no specific 'autism genes' have been identified. The prevalence of autism in MZ twins if one has autism is not 100 per cent. This suggests that other factors besides genetics contribute to the development of autism.

Theory of mind

This cognitive skill is a person's ability to understand other people's mental states and to see the world from the perspective of the other person. When a child has theory of mind they recognise that each person they meet has their own set of beliefs, emotions, likes and dislikes that may be different from their own.

Theory of mind development begins early in life. At about five months of age, typical children can recognise different facial expressions, but understanding the meaning occurs a few months later. Once young children can reliably interpret the facial expressions of others, they begin to use this non-verbal information to guide their behaviour. Osterling and Dawson (1994) studied videotapes of first birthday parties of typical children and children who later received a diagnosis of autism. They found that the best predictor of future diagnosis was lack of attention to the face of others.

> **Key term**
>
> **Learning disability:** a reduced intellectual ability and difficulty with everyday activities that affects someone for their whole life.

Children with autism do not tend to use the gaze of others to guide their behaviour as they fail to consider the mental state of others.

It is thought that most children without autism have a full understanding of theory of mind by around the age of four. This explains why diagnosis of children comes following this age, to have allowed the child the time to develop this skill. Children with autism develop a limited understanding or no understanding at all of theory of mind. This results in them having difficulty relating to others. It can, therefore, be one of the causes of their difficulties with social interaction, and particularly in engaging in pretend play. It may also provide an explanation as to the tendency to become focused on detail, rather than seeing the bigger picture.

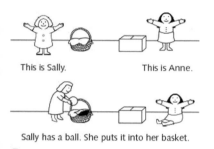

This is Sally. This is Anne.

Sally has a ball. She puts it into her basket.

Sally goes out for a walk.
Anne takes the ball out of the basket.

Anne then puts the ball in the box.

Now Sally comes back. She wants to play with the ball.

Where will Sally look for the ball?

Figure 7.1 Sally–Anne task stages in the test for Theory of Mind

> **The Sally–Anne Test for Theory of Mind (Baron-Cohen et al., 1985)**
>
> A group of autistic children, children with Down's syndrome and some with no identifiable developmental disability (the 'normal' group) took part in the experiment. They were each tested individually to assess if they had theory of mind.
>
> On a desk opposite the experimenter were two dolls, Sally and Anne. Sally had a basket in front of her, and Anne had a box. The dolls were introduced to the children (for example, 'this is Sally') and the child's ability to name them was tested (the 'Naming Question').
>
> Sally then takes a marble and hides it in her basket. She then leaves the room and 'goes for a walk'. While she is away, and therefore unknown to her, Anne takes the marble out of Sally's basket and puts it in her own box. Sally returns and the child is asked the key question 'Where will Sally look for her marble?' (The 'Belief Question'). The correct response is to point to or name Sally's basket; that is, to indicate that the child knows that Sally believes the marble to be somewhere where it is not. The incorrect response is to point to Anne's box.
>
> Two control questions are also asked: 'Where is the marble really?' ('Reality Question'), and 'Where was the marble in the beginning?' ('Memory Question'). Every child was tested twice. During the second time a new location (the experimenter's pocket) for the marble was introduced.
>
> For the children to succeed in this task they have to attribute a belief to Sally. That is, the children have to be able to appreciate that Sally has beliefs about the world that can differ from their own beliefs, and which happen in this case not to be true.
>
> The 'naming', 'reality', and 'memory' questions were answered correctly by all the children.
>
> However, whereas at least 85 per cent of the 'normal' and children with Down's syndrome gave the correct response to the belief question, only 20 per cent (4 from 20) of the autistic children did so.
>
> The autistic children who gave the wrong response on both trials pointed to where the marble really was rather than to where Sally must believe it to be. This suggests that the children with autism have an underdeveloped theory of mind.

This explanation cannot explain all difficulties experienced by those with autism. In particular, it fails to explain why a lack of theory of mind may contribute to difficulties in the verbalisation of words and in the communication they attempt with others. This skill does not rely on interpreting the intentions of others, as the reciprocal element of communication does, and therefore cannot easily be explained by the theory of mind explanation.

Research on theory of mind has typically focused on preschool children because this is when there is an apparent rapid development of mental state understanding. Less is known about theory of mind in older children, although it is acknowledged that this area continues to develop as children mature.

Theory of mind is presented as a factor contributing to the development of autism; a lack of theory of mind limits their interactions with others. However, the absence of theory of mind may be a symptom of autism, rather than a cause. It could be that due to the autism children do not develop theory of mind and the ability to understand others. The complexity of autism, and its root causes, makes this an ongoing conundrum.

Alternative explanations

In addition to those above, other explanations for autism include the following:

1 **Weak central coherence:** An imbalance of integrating information at different levels. Typically, when processing information, a child can draw information together to construct higher-level meaning, known as central coherence. For example, a child may not be able to recall a full story, but they will understand the overall gist of it. Children with autism do not have this ability. This can explain the positive attention to detail in many with autism, and their inability to recognise global meanings.

2 **Environmental factors:** The theory is that a person is born with a vulnerability to autism, but the condition develops only if that person is exposed to a specific environmental trigger. Such triggers include being born prematurely (before 35 weeks gestation) or being exposed to the medication sodium valproate during pregnancy. There is a lack of conclusive evidence to link pollution or maternal infections in pregnancy with an increased risk of autism.

3 **Neurological factors:** It has been suggested that the connections between the cerebral cortex, limbic system and the amygdala within the brain are connected in such a manner that allows for overstimulation, or 'over connection'. This can contribute to the experiences of extreme emotions or hypersensitivity often observed among children with autism.

Therapies

It is not possible to 'treat' autism, as it is a pervasive disorder, present for the lifetime of the individual. Therapies for children with autism are focused on supporting their needs and minimising the difficulties they present with. This can include enhancing social skills or supporting them to manage periods of change without becoming distressed.

Applied Behaviour Analysis (ABA)

Applied Behaviour Analysis (ABA) is a systematic way of observing someone's social communication, identifying desirable changes in that behaviour and then using the most appropriate methods to make those changes. ABA can be used to improve communication and social skills among children and adults with autism. It works by demonstrating effective ways to interact with others and rewarding the improved behaviour when it is displayed. This can be achieved by providing opportunities, both planned and naturally occurring, to acquire and practise skills in both structured and unstructured situations. Behaviours that are harmful or not indicative of positive behaviour are ignored and are not reinforced. The therapist will continually analyse the effectiveness of the approach, and make changes where necessary to improve the child's behaviour next time. This makes ABA a very reflective, evaluative and therefore dynamic therapy style.

It uses the principles of positive reinforcement (operant conditioning) to support the learning of positive behaviour, using rewards for desirable behaviour to make it more likely the child will repeat the behaviour. Therapists develop a tailored programme for each child. They customise the intervention to their skills or needs. For these reasons, an ABA programme for one child will look different from a programme for another child. This reflects the diversity of presentation among children with autism.

WIDER ISSUES

Psychology over time
Explanations for autism have changed over recent years, and this reflects updates in research findings. At one time there was thought to be a link between autism and the MMR vaccination given to children. As a result, parents were reluctant to consent to their child receiving this vaccination. The MMR vaccination has now been disproven as a cause for autism. Research is ongoing in an attempt to conclusively find a single factor contributing to its development.

Evaluation

As there are many different interventions and programmes and techniques used to help children with autism that use the principles of ABA, it makes evaluation of the effectiveness of ABA complex. Additionally, the longer-term effects of ABA interventions are required, as existing studies involve only relatively short follow-up periods, although with promising results.

There is a need for consistency and routine as part of the principles of ABA. Operant conditioning is effective when all positive behaviour is consistently rewarded. If this is not adhered to, the effectiveness of the reinforcement can be compromised.

Cognitive behavioural therapy

Cognitive behavioural therapy (CBT) can be useful for children who experience anxiety as a symptom of their autism. This technique, discussed in detail in other topics, works on the basis of exploring the child's thoughts and feelings about the source of their anxiety. It provides them with skills to manage their anxiety so that stressful situations or experiences become less distressing for them.

CBT, when undertaken with children with autism, needs to be adapted slightly from its typical structure. Children with autism are able to distinguish thoughts, feelings, and behaviours, and to work on altering their thoughts, which are all skills required within CBT. However, children with autism often have difficulty in recognising emotions and working with hypothetical or abstract thoughts. To address this, CBT for those with autism places greater emphasis on repetition and visual cues. One example might be using a picture of a thermometer to encourage a child to rate their anxiety levels, rather than using a ten-point verbal rating system. This makes the content of the session more relatable to them, thereby improving efficacy.

Sofronoff et al. (2005) found that, following a brief CBT intervention, children experienced less anxiety (based on parental self-report) and an increase in the child's ability to identify positive strategies to deal with stressful situations that would have previously been problematic for them. They also noted that if parents were involved in the treatment, this had a further positive effect on the effectiveness of the intervention.

Wood et al. (2009) found improvement in 78.5 per cent of young children with autism who undertook 16 sessions of CBT for their anxiety, compared to an improvement in only 8.7 per cent of those children in a control group, waiting to undertake treatment. The improvements made by the children were upheld when reassessed three months after completing the intervention.

Evaluation

CBT as a form of therapy has shown to have a positive impact on behaviour and psychological well-being. That it has been adapted to meet the specific requirements of children with autism is positive.

CBT requires children to talk to the therapist to explain their thoughts, or to respond to the visual cues given. Not all children with autism are verbal, or have a wide understanding of language, and this treatment is, therefore, less accessible to non-verbal children.

Biomedical interventions are an alternative therapy that can be use alongside or instead of psychological treatments. These include restrictive diets, supplements, hormone interventions and drugs. There is limited scientific evidence demonstrating the efficacy of biomedical interventions in supporting people to directly 'manage' their autism, rather than to treat other conditions. Medication can be used to support symptoms such as anxiety that is associated with autism, although does not treat the autism directly.

Taking it further

There are governmental documents that guide the application of treatment for children with autism. The National Institute for Health and Care Excellence (NICE) provides clear evidence-based guidance. Clinicians work within the guidance issued.

Look up the specific guidance relating to children with autism and note the guidance given to those working with children with autism.

7.2 Methods
Learning outcomes

In this section, you will learn about:

- the use of observations as a research method in child psychology
- the use of questionnaires and interviews as a research method in child psychology
- cross-cultural research
- the use of meta-analysis in the study of attachment
- ethical issues when researching with children
- quantitative data analysis using measures of central tendency, frequency tables and measures of dispersion
- data analysis using inferential statistics, including chi-squared, Spearman's rho, Mann-Whitney U and Wilcoxon
- the analysis of qualitative data via thematic analysis and grounded theory.

Naturalistic and structured observations

Observation as a research method does not involve the direct manipulation of the independent variable; rather the researcher simply watches the behaviour of participants. Observations fall into two broad categories – structured and naturalistic.

Naturalistic observation involves observing the behaviour of participants within their own environment. The situation has not been created by the researcher and so allows them to gain a real insight into a person's behaviour.

Ainsworth used naturalistic observations in Uganda to test out her Strange Situation hypothesis. The benefit of a naturalistic observation is that it is carried out in the person's own environment, which is familiar to them and should, therefore, make the observations more valid. Naturalistic observations can, however, have issues with reliability. They take place in the participants' natural setting which can make it harder to replicate them. Ethically, with naturalistic observations of children, it is extremely important that consent has been gained and parents are fully aware of the reasons behind the observations.

Structured observations are staged observations and are normally carried out within an environment in which the researcher has some control. Subsequent behaviour can be observed behind a one-way mirror or screen. Structured observations are set to record behaviours when it would be difficult to gain information from naturalistic observations. Ainsworth carried out structured observations during her research of the Strange Situation. Structured observations normally use a coding system by which to observe and record certain behaviours in order to gain information. Structured observations are more reliable than naturalistic observations as the coding systems used allow for replicability. Ethically, structured observations must ensure that the children being observed are not put under any undue stress.

Observations can therefore produce both quantitative and qualitative data. Tallying can produce quantitative data, for example frequencies of certain behaviour. Writing down quotes or observations is more qualitative and this is more subjective, as it relies on the gathering of information that is less easy to quantify in numbers.

Link

For more information on the use of the observational research method in psychology, please see the Methods section of Topic 4: *Learning theories*.

Exam tip

If you are asked to outline what is meant by some of the types of observation, try to illustrate with an example to show your full understanding of the concepts after you have defined them.

In child psychology a naturalistic observation will take place in the child's home, nursery, school, etc.

Key terms

Social desirability bias: the tendency for participants to respond in a manner that will be viewed favourably by others.

Interviewer effect: the age, gender and ethnicity of the interviewer can all have an effect on the answer given by a child and it is important to be mindful of this in preparing interviews.

Using questionnaires and interviews as research methods in child psychology

Self-report methods include questionnaires and interviews and at the core of both is questioning. (See Topic 1: *Social psychology* for more on questionnaires.) One problem with questionnaires is that respondents may not tell the truth or answer accurately because of **social desirability bias** – as they want to present a more positive image of themselves and this affects the overall validity of the method.

Questionnaires may not be suitable to use with young children although they can be commonly used to assess the views of parents and teachers. The CASE (Child and Adolescent Survey of Experiences) provides an example of where questionnaires can be used with children and adolescents as a measure of stressful life experiences.

Taking it further

Use an Internet search engine to find the Child and Adolescent Survey of Experiences (CASE). Compare and contrast the details of both the child and adult versions of the questionnaire in terms of the questions asked, scales and language used.

Interviews are face-to-face situations involving a series of questions. Interviews allow the opportunity for the participant and researcher to expand on questions or clarify to gather data accurately. Interviewers in child psychology need training prior to interviewing a child and, when interviewing children, the interviewer must ensure that extra care is taken. Younger children have a short attention span and so expecting the children to sit still for a lengthy interview is inappropriate. Interviewers need to adjust their language to suit a younger, more vulnerable group of people such as children, for example the language used will change according to the age of the child. To aid the interviewer, many will record the interview and later transcribe the interview to seek out common denominators of research interest.

Link

For more information on the use of questionnaires in psychology please see the Methods section of Topic 1: *Social psychology*.

The **Interviewer effect** can be especially relevant in the field of child psychology. The physical appearance of the interviewer and other characteristics, such as the gender of the interviewer, could influence the way a child responds to questions, depending on the topic.

Demand characteristics are also relevant here. In the case of interviews, these are subtle cues that the interviewer may give as to what and how they want to find out from interviewees. Participants may then alter their responses to conform to these perceived expectations and this will have a profound influence on the results obtained.

Cross-cultural research

Cross-cultural research allows psychologists to see if a behaviour is universal across countries or cultures. For example, within child psychology, researchers can examine whether attachment behaviour is universal regardless of the country. If cross-cultural research is not carried out, then the research would be relevant only to one country and, therefore, culturally biased. Takahashi (1990), for example, wanted to test whether or not the Strange Situation was a valid procedure for cultures other than America. Sixty Japanese mothers and their children were observed. The study found that 68 per cent of the children were classified as securely attached (similar to Ainsworth and Bell, 1970).

No avoidant-insecure behaviour was observed, although 32 per cent were classified as resistant. Japanese children were observed to be very distressed when left alone. The study shows that there are cross-cultural variations in how children behave when left alone. This may be a result of Japanese culture teaching that avoidant behaviour, that is, avoiding interacting with other people is impolite and this is instilled in children from a very young age. It suggested that the Strange Situation does not measure attachment behaviour effectively on a universal scale.

Researchers also need to consider whether to employ a cross-sectional or longitudinal design when undertaking research. Cross-sectional designs are used to gather information on a population at a single point in time. Researchers decide on a cross-section of the population to target and their measures are compared. For example, a researcher may be interested in examining how insecure attachments change over time and could therefore compare a group of two-year-olds assessed as insecurely attached with a group of four-year-olds with the same attachment style.

Cross-sectional studies obtain immediate results and are more cost-effective as you only need to use the researcher once. They also impose fewer demands on participants, compared to longitudinal designs, and may therefore be viewed as more ethical. However, as different participants are used, participant variables may affect the results obtained. The children might have the same attachment style but they may have experienced very different upbringings and experiences that could affect the data.

Longitudinal research on the other hand, allows you to gather data from your participants over the course of time and determine whether any changes occur. If you wanted to investigate whether attachment behaviours change over time, you might observe your sample at various time intervals to see if behaviours are consistent. Longitudinal studies avoid the **cohort effect**; the differences within social and cultural groups that change with age and time. However, longitudinal studies are more expensive and time-consuming. For this reason, they are extremely difficult to replicate. Replicating the same cross-cultural research would be extremely expensive and it is not possible to guarantee the same conditions with each study. Due to the time involved in carrying out a longitudinal study/ cross-cultural research, participants may be lost for various reasons (**attrition**), which can alter the direction or aim of the study or hold the study up while another sample is found.

Much cross-cultural research is carried out through the use of meta-analysis. A meta-analysis involves combining and reanalysing the results of a number of different individual studies investigating a specific topic through a statistical technique. This allows researchers to get a better overall feel for trends across cultures as a meta-analysis combines many smaller studies into a much bigger pool of data, making overall trends more likely to be identified. Later we will discuss Van IJzendoorn and Kroonenberg (1988) who looked at attachment types in different countries; thus attempting to make their research universal. They analysed 32 studies that had used the Strange Situation to measure attachment from eight different countries and found considerable consistency in the overall distribution of attachment types across cultures.

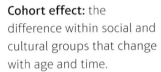

Key terms

Cohort effect: the difference within social and cultural groups that change with age and time.

Attrition: the tendency for some participants to drop out of a study for various reasons which can threaten the validity of the study.

WIDER ISSUES AND DEBATES

Practical issues in the design and implementation of research

Meta-analyses pose several problems for researchers. Firstly, all the methodological problems and biases associated with the initial studies will transfer to the meta-analysis. Therefore, only methodologically sound studies should be included. Another pitfall is the file-drawer effect. There is a bias within the scientific community to publish studies that only reveal a positive result, that is they support the original hypothesis. Studies that find no significant findings are less likely to be published but instead get filed away. This is not easy to address as it is impossible for a researcher to know how many studies have gone unreported. As a result, meta-analysis can be seen to be biased or skewed and researchers should seriously consider this issue when interpreting the outcomes of a meta-analysis. A serious flaw of meta-analysis is that it can be used to support a personal agenda. Researchers may 'cherry-pick' studies that favourably support their hypothesis and ignore those that do not, which again can present research in a biased way.

Ethical issues when researching with children

The BPS code of ethics (2009) outlines what British psychologists must adhere to when undertaking research. Guidelines are given under the headings of respect, competence, integrity and responsibility. These guidelines protect all participants but they are particularly important where children are concerned: protection from harm, informed consent, confidentiality and deception are very important ethical considerations. Parental consent must be gained before carrying out any observations or gaining any information. A child's consent is not the same as a parent's owing to their vulnerability and age. It is important for researchers to understand that, although parents have the right to withdraw their child from the study, children also have the right to withdraw. Researchers must be aware that if the child becomes too distressed, they need to stop the research to avoid any damaging long-term effects. The child's safety and emotional state must be a priority during the research. It is of the utmost importance that all details regarding the child are kept confidential and the identity of the child protected. Any information gained that may affect the child's well-being should be referred to an expert and parents allowed to follow this up after research has finished.

Any research involving children should also adhere to the UN Convention on the Rights of the Child (UNCRC). In 1989, governments across the world promised all children the same rights by adopting the UNCRC, which offers guidelines as to what countries should do to ensure children grow up as healthy as possible, can learn at school, are protected, have their views listened to, and are treated fairly. Articles governing the convention include: the best interests of the child must be a top priority, every child has the right to privacy and governments must protect children from all other forms of bad treatment. UNCRC acknowledges that children have the right to be consulted to have access to information, to freedom of speech and opinion, and to challenge decisions made on their behalf.

Under the current guidance, a fair proportion of previous research using children is now regarded as unethical. The Strange Situation experiment, for example, was criticised on ethical grounds due to the distress caused to the children on separation from their parent.

WIDER ISSUES AND DEBATES

Ethics

A key issue for researchers is balancing children's participation in research against ethical guidelines and the UNCRC. Researchers need to consider risks or costs, for example time taken, inconvenience, embarrassment, intrusion of privacy, sense of coercion and anxiety against the benefits of taking part. This could include increased confidence for the child or increased knowledge for the scientific community; or even time to talk to an attentive listener. Moreover, are there risks and costs if the research is not carried out? Researchers may therefore need to stress clearly the potential benefits of their work, and take the required steps to prevent or reduce any risks. They need to respond appropriately to children who refuse or wish to withdraw, or who show signs of distress. They may wish to consider a small-scale pilot study to address these issues before engaging in full-scale research.

Children should be given the time to ask questions whenever they want, regardless of at what point in the research it is, and should be given age-appropriate information about the procedures.

Link

This table shows you where you can find information on the other methods that are used in child psychology.

Analysis of quantitative data using measures of central tendency, frequency tables, measures of dispersion (range and standard deviation)	Topic 1: *Social psychology*
Analysis of, use of, and drawing conclusions from quantitative data using inferential statistics, including use of chi-squared	Topic 4: *Learning theories*
Spearman's rho	Topic 3: *Biological psychology*
Mann-Whitney U and Wilcoxon, and issues of statistical significance, levels of measurement, critical and observed values	Topic 2: *Cognitive psychology*
Analysis of qualitative data using thematic analysis	Topic 1: *Social psychology*
Grounded theory	Topic 5: *Clinical psychology*

7.3 Studies

Learning outcomes

In this section, you will learn about one classic study:

- Van IJzendoorn and Kroonenberg (1988) Cross-cultural Patterns of Attachment: A Meta-Analysis of the Strange Situation

and you will need to choose one contemporary study from the following:

- Cassibba et al. (2013) Attachment the Italian way
- Gagnon-Oosterwaal et al. (2012) Pre-adoption adversity and self-reported behaviour problems in 7 year-old international adoptees.
- Li et al. (2013) Timing of High-Quality Child Care and Cognitive, Language, and Preacademic Development.

Cross-cultural Patterns of Attachment: A Meta-Analysis of the Strange Situation (Van IJzendoorn and Kroonenberg, 1988)

Traditionally in psychology, culture has been viewed in terms of a distinct dichotomy between individualistic and collectivistic cultures. Individualistic cultures value independence and emphasise personal achievement regardless of group goals, resulting in a strong sense of competition between individuals, for example, in the USA. Collectivistic cultures, on the other hand, value cooperation and working towards a family or group goal. Marinus van IJzendoorn and Pieter Kroonenberg aimed to investigate cross-cultural variation in attachment types through meta-analysis, combining statistical information from a wide range of studies to identify patterns of attachment. Van IJzendoorn and Kroonenberg analysed research studies that used the Strange Situation Procedure to examine the external validity of the attachment recorded in other cultures. Ainsworth identified three attachment types: secure attachment (Type B), anxious-avoidant (Type A), anxious-resistant (Type C). Ainsworth et al. (1978) found that the attachment type ratio in America was 20 per cent Type A, 70 per cent Type B and 10 per cent Type C. They enquired whether this result might be similar in all countries; given the fact that all countries have different childrearing strategies and beliefs about childrearing.

Aim

Van IJzendoorn and Kroonenberg wanted to investigate similarities and differences in the ratio of attachment types in different countries.

Procedure

Van IJzendoorn and Kroonenberg (1988) conducted a meta-analysis of data collected from 32 separate studies carried out in eight different countries and in total represented 1990 Strange Situation classifications. All of the studies used the Strange Situation test to measure attachment type as identified by Mary Ainsworth. Van IJzendoorn and Kroonenberg looked for similarities and differences in attachment types. In selecting data, they excluded studies that included children with special educational needs in their sample, any studies with overlapping samples and any studies where the children were over 24 months.

Results

A significant finding of the meta-analysis was the prevalence of secure attachment as the most common type in all eight countries. A significant cultural difference is that in countries such as Germany (individualistic), a high proportion of anxious-avoidant attachment was found. This could be because German parents place a high value on independence and so children in the Strange Situation show less distress in the absence of the mother. In contrast, in Japan (collectivistic) a high level of resistant attachment was evident. This could be due to the high value placed on dependency within the culture. Here, children are rarely away from the mother and so obviously become very distressed by being away from the mother in the Strange Situation test.

Another highly significant finding of Van IJzendoorn and Kroonenberg was that the variation in attachment types was one-and-a half times greater within cultures than between cultures. In other words, there was a greater difference in attachment types in studies from the same culture than there were in studies from different cultures. One of the German samples was as different from another German sample as it was from a US sample.

Conclusion

Van IJzendoorn and Kroonenberg suggested that the universal consistency of attachment might be explained by the effects of the mass media, which spread ideas about parenting so that children all over the world are exposed to similar influences.

The results suggest that the significant variations in attachment cannot be accounted for by differences or applications of the coding system used: rather childrearing practices do, in fact, vary from country to country and culture to culture. Secure attachment, as the most common attachment type in all countries illustrates that there does seem to be a key factor to raising a child in all cultures and countries. This supports the notion that secure attachment is a prerequisite for healthy social and emotional development in children. However, there were significant variations of the insecure attachment type. The reasons for such could be due to economic climate of the country, poor education, environmental and cultural factors.

Evaluation

A significant issue with the use of the Strange Situation Procedure in different cultures is that it was developed by an American researcher and based on the observations of American children. This could therefore be viewed as ethnocentric bias, reflecting the norms and values that American culture places on childrearing. The test suggests that attachment is related to anxiety on separation and in doing so assumes that behaviour has the same meaning in all cultures. As we have seen, Japanese infants show high levels of distress during the test as they are very rarely parted from their mother in comparison with western infants. Ainsworth interprets this as insecure attachment and in doing so is imposing western values on a different culture.

Also, the majority of data gathered came from studies in individualistic cultures. Only one study's data was used to represent China compared to 18 from America. It is also true that many of the samples used a small or biased number of middle-class families, which cannot represent the whole culture completely. In particular, urban rather than rural families were assessed. It is likely that the studies represented distinct subcultures within the culture they attempted to represent. It is therefore an oversimplification to view one country as a single culture, as within each country there is great variation.

> **Exam tip**
>
> A meta-analysis is different from many other research methods because no primary data is collected by the researchers themselves, they simply use data that has already been gathered by other researchers and analyse it. This means that secondary data is being used. This is worth remembering because evaluation commentary, such as ethical issues involving participants, are not relevant for a meta-analysis.

Attachment the Italian way (Cassibba et al., 2013)

Rosalinda Cassibba, Giovanna Sette, Marian Bakermans-Kranenburg, and Marinus van IJzendoorn set out to research attachment types within Italy, defined as an individualistic western culture with an emphasis on family and dependence characteristic of collectivistic culture. According to Cassibba et al., this was the first meta-analysis of attachment types within Italy.

Aims

Her primary aim was to investigate if the majority of Italian children and adults are classified as having a secure attachment. She was also interested to discover whether Italian adults, the majority of whom are Catholics, would have a lower percentage of **unresolved attachments** compared to other countries, and whether children and adults from clinical samples vary in attachment type distribution compared to non-clinical samples. The research additionally investigated potential gender differences in the distribution of attachment types.

Procedure

As this was a meta-analysis, data came from studies using PsycINFO, a psychology database of academic journals, using the key word search for 'Italian', 'attachment' and 'Strange Situation Procedure'. Other research studies were obtained from Italian journals, publications and doctoral dissertations.

The selection process resulted in 627 participants within 17 studies that used the Strange Situation Procedure (SSP), and 2258 participants from 50 studies that used the Adult Attachment Interview (AAI) or similar attachment interview. Statistical tests were used to compare SSP to AAI data.

The ratios of between culture attachment types assessed using the Strange Situation Procedure were compared to American samples used in Van IJzendoorn and Kroonenberg's analysis and Adult Attachment Interview data compared to American data gathered in Bakermans-Kranenburg and Van IJzendoorn's analysis. Intercultural differences (within Italy) were assessed in terms of gender, ages and type of population.

Results

Non-clinical Italian children were classified as 33 per cent Type A, 53 per cent Type B and 14 per cent Type C. Compared to the USA sample, Italian children showed more avoidant attachment. Clinical and at-risk children showed attachment Type A of 40 per cent, Type B of 32 per cent and Type C of 28 per cent. There was a higher proportion of insecure attachment and fewer secure attachment types among Italian clinical (at risk) children than those from the USA. Additionally, there was a higher percentage of avoidant attachment type among the Italian clinical children than the USA clinical children sample. Italian children with clinical/at-risk mothers seemed to be more avoidant and less secure in their attachments.

Classification of adults using the Adult Attachment Interview

AAI has three classifications, D, F and E; these are similar to the Strange Situation classifications of attachment Types A, B and C but are classifications used for adults. In all samples of Italian mothers, the secure-autonomous (F category) was the highest with 22 per cent dismissing (Type D), 59 per cent secure-autonomous (Type F), and 19 per cent preoccupied (Type E). The combined samples of Italian non-clinical fathers showed a slight rise of dismissing fathers. Parents with children who have psychological problems were high for the E classification (preoccupied) and often less secure and more likely to have unresolved loss, although this was not characteristic of the whole sample, and

Classification types the SSP and AAI produce

SSP classifications:

Type A: Insecure-avoidant attachment

Type B: Secure attachment

Type C: Insecure-resistant attachment

AAI classifications

Type D: Dismissing

Type E: Preoccupied

Type F: Secure-autonomous

Type U: Unresolved loss

actually unresolved attachments were under-represented in the Italian adult sample. When violence was evident in the family, there was an over-representation of Type D at 52 per cent.

Testing gender, non-clinical fathers to non-clinical mothers, did not produce a significant difference.

Conclusion

The majority of non-clinical Italian infants were classified as securely attached. Similarly, the majority of non-clinical Italian adults were classified in the secure attachment category and therefore remarkably similar to those in the normative American group.

Although these cross-cultural similarities provide evidence for the universality hypothesis of attachment theory the meta-analysis also revealed cultural differences. Both non-clinical and clinical Italian infants' distribution showed an over-representation of avoidant attachments. This may be explained through differences between Italian and American childrearing practices. For example, Italian mothers tend to think that child development is largely a natural process in which adults play a very small role. American mothers, on the other hand, assume they are responsible as parents in promoting their children's development. These therefore lead to differences in how much mothers invest into parenting. Linked to this, Italian mothers display parenting styles that stimulate early independency and expect high levels of social maturity in their children. Cassibba et al. speculated that the under-representation of unresolved attachments is due to the Italians' religious faith and their capability in times of hardship.

Evaluation

This was the first meta-analysis of attachment in Italy and therefore the scientific community could benefit from the insights into the distributions of infant, adolescent, and adult attachment across Italian society. It provides a useful comparison tool for analysing samples both in Italy and elsewhere.

However, comparisons of the Strange Situation Procedure could only be made with 1992 data from America; thus questioning the contemporaneous validity of the data comparison. It does not address the father–child attachments within Italy and America. Similarly, this was also a limitation for Bowlby and his attachment theory. Cassibba et al. admit that a lack of the paternal attachment types still requires research but this seems to be a global issue rather than an Italian issue.

There is a potential for experimenter bias as Cassibba et al. were using a database and specifying search words; thus they may have dismissed studies that they felt were inappropriate. Although meta-analysis studies are normally time saving and cost-effective, there is a tendency to be subjective about the data that is analysed. There is no unanimous strategy for meta-analysis sample selection and so what may be considered appropriate research practices may not correspond to that of others; therefore generalisation of results is limited. However, they did use unpublished studies, doctoral dissertations and conference papers to avoid the 'file drawer' effect where null findings are not published.

To avoid invalid comparisons being made between the studies used in the sample undergoing meta-analysis, the researchers were careful to ensure that studies on child–parent attachments only used the 'gold standard' of the Strange Situation Procedure, and that adult attachments were only assessed using interviews that were coded for an inter-rater reliability of over 0.75, to ensure good agreement, or that used accredited adult attachment interviews endorsed by Mary Main. This control ensured accurate comparisons could be made between the samples as they employed very similar procedures and coding measures.

Taking it further

Compare and contrast the meta-analysis carried out by Cassibba et al. (2013) and Van IJzendoorn and Kroonenberg (1988).

Pre-adoption adversity and self-reported behavior problems in 7 year-old international adoptees (Gagnon-Oosterwaal et al., 2012)

Internationally adopted children typically display more behavioural problems compared to non-adopted children and are over-represented in mental health service statistics. These issues can be related to the adoptees' pre-adoption environment, but may also be linked to the functioning and specific characteristics of the adoptive families that can affect the development of behavioural problems in internationally adopted children.

Aims

Noémi Gagnon-Oosterwaal and colleagues aimed to examine the effect of pre-adoption environment and parenting stress on children's behavioural problems.

Method

The study was carried out longitudinally with a sample of 95 children (69 girls) adopted during infancy. Of these: 47 of the children were adopted from China, 28 from other East-Asian countries (Vietnam, Taiwan, Thailand, South Korea, Cambodia), 17 from Russia, 2 from Haiti, and one from Bolivia. The children had mainly been adopted from orphanages (92 per cent) and the remainder from foster care. The children's health and developmental status was evaluated soon after arrival in their adoptive country. At this stage, the children's ages ranged from 4 to 18 months. Their behavioural problems were then assessed at age 7 years using a self-report measure, the Dominic Interactive (a computerised pictorial questionnaire to assess behavioural problems in children). The Child Behaviour Checklist (CBCL) was completed by the mothers. This is also a questionnaire used to assess children's behavioural problems. Parenting stress was measured using the PSI or Parenting Stress Index, a self-report questionnaire used to assess the stress experienced by parents in relation to their parenting role. The adopted children were compared to a group of non-adopted children recruited from 15 nearby primary schools.

Results

Preliminary analyses revealed no significant differences according to the child's gender or country of origin in scores of behavioural problems, for both children's and mothers' reports. No significant correlations between scores of behavioural problems and socio-demographic variables, for example age at arrival, mother's level of education, or family income were found.

Correlations between pre-adoption adversity, maternal stress, and children's behavioural problems were examined. Significant correlations were found between three risks factors (neurological signs, small head circumference, weight/height ratio), scores of maternal stress and scores of behavioural problems. The mediational effect of maternal stress was investigated further using correlational analysis against neurological signs, head circumference, and weight/height ratio. It was clear that maternal stress has a mediating effect on these variables.

Conclusion

Neurological signs, low weight/height ratio, and small head circumference at time of adoption can be considered potential risk factors for the development of behavioural problems. The child's condition on arrival in the adoptive country was also related to higher levels of parenting (overprotectiveness and high parental control) and high level of parenting stress is related to children's behavioural problems. Moreover, maternal stress was found to be an important mediator of the relationship between pre-adoption adversity and children's later behavioural problems at school-age.

This supports other studies which have shown that high levels of parenting stress have a negative impact on subsequent parenting behaviours, with parents being less responsive, more authoritarian, and neglectful; which in turn impacts negatively on children's behaviour. Parenting stress could have a particularly profound effect on parents of internationally adopted children. According to Levy-Shiff et al. (1997), parents of such children are more overprotective, intrusive, and controlling than other adoptive parents. Such characteristics have been associated with the development of behavioural problems in childhood, especially anxiety-related problems. Alleviating maternal stress could therefore have a positive impact on the psychological health of internationally adopted children.

Evaluation

Although the children in the current sample were adopted at a young age, it is still difficult to separate the possibility that pre-adoption conditions could yield a strong and long-lasting impact on internationally adopted children. Similarly, factors related to the post-adoption environment, such as the quality of the parent–child relationship, may also explain the development of behavioural problems in international adoptees. Due to the self-report methods used it is possible that the mothers were biased in evaluating their stress level and that of their child's behaviour. According to Gagnon-Oosterwaal, other researchers also identified that as parenting stress levels increase, their own perceptions of their children's behaviour diminish in accuracy and often become more negative. The present study tried to overcome this weakness by using children's self-reports. However, it is still possible that the children's perceptions were influenced by their mother's beliefs, although correlational analysis showed no significant difference between the child's and mother's reports of behavioural issues.

A methodological problem with the study was that the control group was not large and was selected by opportunity, so there was limited ability to detect differences between the adopted and comparison groups. However, the design was longitudinal, which meant that the children could be assessed as soon as they entered the country for developmental and physical issues, and prospectively followed up during the course of the study.

Timing of High-Quality Child Care and Cognitive, Language, and Pre-academic Development (Li et al., 2013)

Improvements in the opportunities of women to access education and employment have significantly increased alongside the provision of non-maternal childcare in the USA. Concerns have therefore been raised about the effects of childcare on children's social and cognitive development. Evidence supports the view that higher-quality care during the first five years of life is linked to cognitive and academic achievement, but few studies have focused on differences in the quality of childcare in the infant–toddler period versus the preschool period and possible outcomes from combinations of quality care during these two periods. Weilin Li and colleagues (2013) set out to investigate the effects of high- versus low-quality childcare during infant–toddlerhood and preschool periods using data from the National Institute of Child Health and Human Development Study of Early Child Care (NICHD study).

Aims

Li et al. predicted that high-quality infant–toddler care would improve cognitive outcomes at the end of this period (12 months of age). However, without continuing high-quality care during the preschool period, children with high-quality infant–toddler care would not maintain higher cognitive, language, and pre-academic scores at the end of this period (54 months of age) compared to children who have received low-quality childcare during both these periods.

Secondly, high-quality care during the preschool period would improve cognitive, language, and pre-academic outcomes at 54 months of age, and that this would be mediated by both high-quality infant–toddler care and high-quality preschool care, relative to those who receive high-quality preschool care but low-quality infant–toddler care.

Both these hypotheses led to an overall prediction that high-quality childcare during both the infant–toddler and preschool periods would be associated with higher cognitive, language, and pre-academic performance at the end of the preschool period than any other childcare quality combination during the two periods.

Method

A sample of 1364 families was recruited from ten sample sites around North America in 1991 from various hospitals at the birth of a child. At the age of one month, the children and families were assessed using a variety of research methods; observations were made, questionnaires and child assessment conducted, in addition to information gathered on the family background as far as possible confounding variables.

The quality of childcare being received was assessed using the Observational Record of the Caregiving Environment (ORCE) when the children were aged 6, 15, 24, 36 and 54 months in a range of settings, including the home and nurseries. This involved a 44-minute observation over two days, and the quality of care was rated on a scale. A score of 3.0 was used to distinguish between low- and high-quality infant–toddler care and low- and high-quality care for the preschool period. Scores of more than 3.0 indicated higher-quality care where caregivers were sensitive to children's needs, provided greater cognitive stimulation and fostered greater exploration.

At the end of the infant–toddler period the Bayley Mental Developmental Index was used to assess the children's cognitive development. At the end of the preschool period the Woodcock-Johnson Cognitive and Achievement Batteries and the Preschool Language Scale (PLS) was used to measure language, memory and intelligence.

Other measures, including ethnicity, gender, birth order, child temperament, maternal attitudes on raising children, maternal age, maternal and paternal educational level, child's health, maternal separation anxiety, maternal depression, maternal employment status and family income, were taken at varying intervals.

The children were classified into four groups according to the quality of childcare at both stages:

1 Low-low: children with low-quality infant–toddler care and low-quality care during the preschool period

2 High-low: children with high-quality infant–toddler care and low-quality care during the preschool period

3 Low-high: children with low-quality infant–toddler care combined with high-quality care during the preschool period

4 High-high: children with high-quality infant–toddler care and high-quality care during the preschool period.

Statistical analysis was employed to investigate the relationship between the key variables identified.

Results

The data suggests that there was a significant positive relationship between childcare quality during the infant–toddler period and cognitive outcomes at 24 months, supporting the first hypothesis. This first hypothesis also proposed that the positive effect of high-quality infant–toddler care would decline by the end of the preschool period if children received low- as opposed to high-quality preschool childcare. The study found support for this hypothesis except where memory was the outcome. However, this hypothesis was not supported for language and reading ability.

The second hypothesis asserted that high-quality care during the preschool period is associated with improvement in cognitive and language, reading, and maths results. This was found to be true and, in addition, those who received high-quality preschool care in addition to high-quality infant–toddler care scored better than low-high comparison children on reading and maths ability at 54 months. This suggests that high-quality preschool care improves language, reading, and maths outcomes, and is additive to infant-toddler high-quality care.

The third hypothesis predicted that high-high care would produce better 54-month outcomes than any of the other combinations and the results support this hypothesis. Therefore, the high-high pattern produced the best outcomes, the low-low pattern produced the worst outcomes, and there was little observable difference between the outcomes produced by high-low- versus low-high-quality childcare. However, memory development seemed to benefit from early high-quality care in the infant–toddler period, but maths ability benefited from high-quality care in the preschool period.

Conclusions

High-quality care during the first 24 months is important for memory development, but not as beneficial for academic skill development. High-quality preschool care prepared children for scholastic achievement, and children who were also exposed to high-quality infant–toddler care benefited most. Early exposure to good-quality care that was not maintained did not benefit the children, but maintained high-quality care resulted in the greatest gains for children.

Evaluation

These detailed measures and assessments on the timings of specific cognitive outcomes provide rich information and also account for a number of confounding variables such as the home environment. Moreover, the study provides significant practical application in suggesting how policy makers should invest in childcare in the USA. This is important to prevent unequal distribution of childcare provision into either the early or preschool years, but also to encourage provision that is equally distributed throughout childhood. However, acknowledging that high-quality day care is costly, a preference to provide better care during preschool years is probably more cost-effective.

However, the data used from NICHD Study of Early Child Care is not a representative sample, which may limit generalisation. The response rate at the six-month interview was around 50 per cent and tended to be biased towards economically advantaged, white families, who do not represent the American general population. Teenage mothers and low birth weight babies were excluded altogether.

The way that quality of childcare was categorised may also be oversimplified as it did not include a wide range of quality childcare characteristics when creating the groups; they were divided into high- and low-quality care but did not distinguish between the types of care or the quantity of care received. Moreover, the current study did not look at the social benefits of quality childcare, such as attention skills and socio-emotional behaviours, including problem-solving and social skills. Research suggests that such skills are significant predictors for later achievement.

7.4 Key question
Learning outcomes

In this section, you will learn about:

- one key question of relevance to today's society
- how concepts, theories and research from child psychology can be applied here.

Is international adoption good for a child?

Daughtery-Bailey (2006) revealed that in 2001 an estimated 34 000 children from over 50 countries were adopted on an international scale, reflecting a rise of 79 per cent from previous statistics (UNICEF, 2003). However, between 2004 and 2011, international adoptions in the top 23 nations declined, from 45 299 to 23 626. The decline was linked in part to stricter international adoption laws in countries such as China and Russia. According to Selman (2009) China, Ethiopia, India, South Korea, Ukraine and Vietnam remain as major origin countries for most international adoptees. The top ten receiving countries are the USA, Spain, France, Italy, Canada, Netherlands, Sweden, Norway, Denmark and Australia. The USA is responsible for around 50 per cent of all international adoption cases. Research into this area is still, however, relatively recent and limited in scope compared with research into the adoption of children from the same country as the adoptive parents.

International adoption has sparked much political debate and controversy as to whether adoption is good or bad for a child.

A longitudinal study: ERA

The English and Romanian Adoptee (ERA) project is a longitudinal, multi-method study of the development of 165 children adopted into the UK from Romania before the age of three and a half in the early 1990s, led by Professor Michael Rutter and Professor Edmund Sonuga-Barke. Most of the children spent their early lives in institutional care where conditions ranged from poor to abysmal. The aim of the project is to examine the extent to which children could recover when extreme deprivation in early life is followed by a middle childhood within a safe family environment. The children were studied at the ages of 4, 6, 11 and 15 years and compared to a control group of adopted children from the UK who had not lived in institutions.

To date, the study has shown that these children have made huge improvements in psychological functioning following successful adoption; although a significant minority of those adopted after the age of six months will continue to experience significant problems. One-third of the Romanian children placed for adoption after the age of six months experienced problems that required the intervention of educational, psychological or psychiatric services.

Quantitative studies

A proportion of the Romanian children adopted after the age of six months demonstrated autistic-like qualities, difficulties in forming appropriate attachments and social functioning. The study has concluded that the vast majority of families made a success of the adoptions from Romania, despite many of them being considered unacceptable for domestic adoption. Research has largely focused on the adoptive parents as information from biological parents is rare, obviously because of the anonymity considerations that characterise adoption. Very little information is available, if any, regarding the biological mother. This is particularly noticeable in foreign adoptions and so the biological origins of many foreign children who have been adopted are simply unknown. Research has therefore focused on teenagers and young adults who have been adopted in addition to the experiences of teachers, doctors and other health service personnel. The majority of research projects have been carried out as interview surveys. Only a few have utilised in-depth interviews to gather qualitative data. A number of quantitative studies, for example questionnaires, have focused on foreign adoptees' living conditions, schooling and demographic information about themselves and their families.

This is advantageous as results can be generalised to the wider population. Increasingly, longitudinal studies have been used and these provide useful insight into new chapters of the children's lives. A Norwegian study by Dalen and Sætersdal (1992) examined teenagers who had been adopted from Vietnam. Several children in their sample were considered to have serious identity problems. They commonly expressed a desire to be Norwegian and to be perceived as Norwegian. Many were anxious about being associated with immigrants and refugees. However, the sample was followed up ten years later and the problems that were most important in late adolescence were no longer so important to them. They were now more interested in issues related to their partners, establishing a family, their education and careers (Sætersdal and Dalen 1999).

A disproportionally large share of adoption research is based on parents or children who have sought psychiatric or psychological help (for example Brinich, 1990, Brodzinsky, 1990). Several surveys indicate that adoptees are over-represented among such clinical populations. Moreover, in a comparison with non-adopted children, international adoptees seem to have more behavioural problems at home and in school, and many are referred to mental health services twice as often as with non-adopted children (Juffer and Van IJzendoorn, 2005). Juffer (2006) indicated that children adopted from Sri Lanka and Colombia seemed to have more behaviour problems than domestic adoptees. Moreover, children in middle childhood seemed to understand the concept of adoption and this awareness made these children especially vulnerable to stress. As a result of these stressors, it can be argued that parents and internationally adopted children should be adequately supported by adoption agencies and social services.

Scandinavian studies suggest that children who have been adopted from abroad are adopted into relatively stable families with divorce among their adoptive parents being relatively low. Botvar (1999) found that 15 per cent of the foreign adoptees between the ages of 15 to 19 years state that their parents are divorced. The equivalent figure for Norwegian-born teenagers is 25 per cent. This study also found that there are twice as many only children among foreign adoptees (14 per cent) compared with Norwegian-born children (6 per cent).

The majority, 57 per cent, state that they have adopted siblings, 10 per cent have both adopted and non-adopted siblings, while 19 per cent only have Norwegian-born siblings (Botvar, 1999; Dalen and Rygvold, 1999). This is a positive trend as these parents are more likely to have prior experience of working with children and be educated in subjects such as psychology.

Children who need additional help

Many international adoptions take place when the child is under one year old. According to Scandinavian research only around 10–15 per cent of adopted children were in bad or extremely bad physical shape. Adoptions from countries affected by war and extreme suffering will naturally have a higher percentage of children suffering from poor health. Many studies from the 1980s and 1990s suggested that the children had a very difficult time (Hallden, 1981; Cederblad, 1982; Blucher-Andersson, 1983; Berntsen and Eigeland 1987; Dalen and Sætersdal, 1992). Many children found it difficult to sleep and some children did not want to eat at all, while others overate and were completely focused on food. Most of the children showed signs of anxiety and insecurity. They became anxious every time their mother disappeared from sight and reacted with fear to strangers.

Their adoptive parents often described them as clingy. Some displayed extreme emotional reactions, for example anger or crying fits, or being inconsolable and rejecting parental contact. Grotevant and

McRoy and Jenkins (1988) coined the term 'elbow children' to describe the fact that they commonly pushed their parents away. Some problems were also linked to language and communication, but most of the children found it easy to make themselves understood with the help of gestures and simple words and phrases. Many studies found that between three and twelve months these adjustment difficulties diminished. It is important to remember that these studies were carried out a while ago and so adoption associations were still developing their professional and specialist work. In recent years, there has been much greater commitment to information, teaching and guidance of adoptive parents.

In 2013, Feast, Grant, Rushton and Simmonds published a longitudinal study on the long-term effects and outcomes for 72 girls adopted from orphanages during the 1960s via the UK Hong Kong Adoption Project. The women were mostly abandoned as infants and spent between 8 and 72 months in orphanages in Hong Kong. Although they experienced a reasonable quality of physical and medical care, they lacked consistent one-to-one care and stimulation. The study used qualitative analysis of face-to-face interviews with the women. The findings on the whole were very positive showing that 'family life that can provide nurture, care and stimulation can counteract the negative impact of a poor start in life'. The psychological outcomes for the adoptees 50 years on were found to be commensurate with matched groups of adopted and non-adopted women born in the UK. Their well-being and life satisfaction did not appear to be significantly different from comparison women; neither was there evidence of severe difficulties in adult social relationships or poor self-esteem. However, virtually all the women reported some experience of racism or prejudice in both child and adulthood, ranging from playground name calling during childhood to serious racist attacks. The authors concluded that the quality of the adoptive home is an important contributor to well-being as adults. As the orphanages in Hong Kong seem to have provided a much better level of care than, for example, those in Romania, this may explain why this group of women seem to have fared much better. It does suggest however that 'the challenges and complexities of inter-country adoption should not be underestimated'.

Support for families

A recent report entitled 'A Changing World' (2013) collated information from 1500 adoptive parents, adoption professionals in the USA and other 'receiving' countries and countries of origin, as well as interviews with senior policy makers in 19 nations. It reveals a far from positive view of international adoptions. It found that more children are remaining in orphanages for longer periods of time, thereby incurring increased developmental and psychological harm. Many countries of origin, including the largest ones such as China, are increasingly allowing the inter-country adoption of children who have special needs, who are older, and/or are in sibling groups (to be adopted together). It has meant that many adoptive families are struggling to cope with their adopted child's needs and do not know where to turn. The report strongly recommends that countries of origin should provide more complete and accurate diagnoses/records on medical and mental health issues, and receiving countries should offer more training and resources to help countries of origin improve their child welfare and adoption systems. Receiving countries should also provide preparation, services and support for adoptive families.

It can be difficult to give a definitive picture of international adoption research, since studies have been carried out in very different contexts. Moreover, adoption practice and legislation vary from country to country and the historical, social and political context also impinges on the overall picture. It is clear, however, that internationally adopted children fare better when adoptive parents are adequately supported by adoption agencies, social services and other key organisations.

7.5 Practical investigation

Learning outcomes

- to conduct a study into child psychology using an interview, questionnaire or observation

- to include a hypothesis, research method, appropriate sample and discussion

- to apply ethical considerations in the design of the study

- to analyse and present the quantitative data gathered

- to analyse research findings using a chi-squared test, Mann-Whitney U, Wilcoxon or Spearman's rho

- consider the strengths and weaknesses of the practical and suggest possible improvements.

Can day care provide positive experiences for young children?

Day care has been shown to have positive and negative experiences for children. Psychological research often establishes positive and negative effects as being concerned with social, emotional and cognitive development. In this practical investigation, we will be examining parental views about the positive experiences of young children in day care. This practical could use an observation of children's behaviour in a day care centre, an interview with parents and/or day care staff, or a questionnaire. This practical investigation has used a parental interview to gather quantitative data about their children's experiences. You may wish to use a different research method and gather qualitative data for your own practical investigation. Through interviewing parents, you will be able to examine whether parents believe that day care provides positive experiences for children and can help them to develop social and cognitive skills.

Research question/hypothesis

The aim of your study is to examine the positive experiences of using day care for parents with children under three years old. This practical will explore whether parents believe their children have more positive experiences in a nursery compared to a preschool environment. There are several key differences between nursery and preschool care that may mediate parents' responses, in particular:

- preschools operate at certain times of the day, typically alongside mainstream education, so children attending a nursery may be more likely to experience longer times in day care

- preschools often require a child to be of a certain age or developmental stage (being potty trained, for example), whereas nurseries accept children from a very young age

- although preschools may be associated with greater emphasis on academic development, nurseries are also required to provide learning opportunities in line with preschool provision

- there is a tendency for preschool staff to be more highly qualified than nursery staff.

Based on these differences, it may not be possible to predict whether children will have more positive experiences in a nursery or preschool, so a non-directional (two-tailed) hypothesis will be stated here. There will be a difference in the degree to which parents report positive experiences of their children in nursery compared to preschool. The null hypothesis will be that there will be no difference in parental reported positive experiences of day care in a nursery compared to a preschool.

Structured interview schedule example questions

1 On a scale of 1 to 5, how would you rate the experiences of your child in day care (1 being not positive and 5 being very positive)?

2 Is your child most often happy when they come home from day care?

3 Do you believe that your child has benefited intellectually/academically from being in day care?

4 Do you feel that your child has benefited socially from day care?

5 Is your child more able to play with other children as a result of being in day care?

6 Do you feel that your child has become more independent from their experience in day care?

Research method

This practical investigation uses an interview as the research method; this interview will be structured. The type of questions you pose will influence the type of data attained. Closed questions provide people with a fixed set of responses and yield quantitative data which is easier to measure and test for reliability. Qualitative data can be attained by using open questions and allowing the parents to expand on the question. It is advisable to have an interview schedule which is a series of prepared questions designed to be asked exactly as worded. This standardisation means that the same questions are asked to each interviewee in same order. However, open questions will allow flexibility in parental responses and will not be as structured as closed questions. Previous research has focused on the cognitive and social benefits of day care and questions could therefore be based around these topics by asking parents if they feel their child has benefitted socially, intellectually and emotionally from day care provision.

Interview construction

It is important that the wording of the question reflects the background of interviewees such as their age, educational background, social class, ethnicity, etc. You will also need to consider how the data will be recorded. You may wish to write notes as the interview progresses, although an obvious disadvantage of this is that you may not actually transcribe all of what is being said. Therefore, quite often interviews will be recorded and the data written up as a transcript, that is, a written description of interview questions and answers which can be analysed later. Remember that any qualitative data gathered from the interview can be turned into quantitative data for the purpose of analysis later. It will be useful to think through the way in which you are going to score the responses that you gather from parents, so that your analysis is easier.

Scoring of responses

Question 1 uses a scaled response, so a low score will indicate less positive experiences and a high score will indicate more positive experiences.

Questions 2–6 will elicit short or lengthy responses from parents. This can be quantified as either a yes/no response based on their overall answer to each question and given a score of zero for a no response and a score of 1 for a yes response. These can then be totalled up to give an overall score for positive experiences. However, you may wish to rate each response on a scale if parents provide more detail.

Example responses
Parent 1: question 1 = 3, question 2 = 1, question 3 = 0, question 4 = 1, question 5 = 1, question 6 = 1.
Total score 7

Parent 2: question 1 = 5, question 2 = 1, question 3 = 1, question 4 = 0, question 5 = 0, question 6 = 0
Total score 7

These responses are equal in total, suggesting that both parents believe their children to have reasonably positive experiences of day care. However, you may wish to break this down further and analyse the type of responses given. For example, parent 1 believes that their child benefits more academically from day care but not socially, whereas parent 2 believes their child has benefited socially but not academically from day care.

Interviewer effects can bias the results of the study and make them invalid. As the interview is a social interaction the appearance of the interviewer may influence how the interviewee responds. This includes the interviewer's age, gender, ethnicity, body language and social status. As you are interviewing parents, it may be useful to approach people who you are familiar with, because asking strangers about their children's experiences of day care may result in an uncomfortable situation. You need to be mindful that parents often feel guilty about having to place their child in day care, so you should be sensitive to this and brief them fully on the aims of your study.

Sampling

Selecting your sample is an important issue to consider as it will determine how representative of the population the findings are. A number of sampling techniques are available to researchers although not all would be suitable here. Volunteer sampling could be used to ask parents to take part in response to an advert, for instance. This method is quick and relatively easy to do and can potentially reach a wide variety of participants, depending on where you advertise. However, you should be aware that the volunteers may not be representative of the target population for a number of reasons. For example, they may be more motivated to take part or they may have a gripe that they wish to air. Nevertheless, this sampling method may allow you to gain a pool of parents who are actually are interested in the study and willing to offer their opinions.

Sometimes samples of people are difficult to access unless you have friends and family that you know. In such cases a snowball sampling technique may be more useful; gaining access to a single participant in the target population can permit access to other participants that they may know. You will also need to consider what might be a realistic target number for your sample, given that interviews are time-consuming.

For this practical investigation, an opportunity sample of family and friends who are parents of three-year-old children will be used; five parents with a child in preschool and five parents with a child in a nursery. Either the mother or father (or guardian) will take part in the interview, depending on their availability.

Ethical considerations

As we have seen earlier in the topic, adhering to ethical guidance is of the utmost importance when using children in research. You need to ensure that your study adheres to the relevant ethical guidelines that have been presented, including:

- briefing and debriefing your participants
- gaining informed consent
- allowing for the participant to withdraw at any time from the study
- competence
- avoiding deceiving your participants
- privacy and confidentiality.

Because this interview is focusing on the positive aspects and experiences of children in day care, it is potentially less problematic than asking questions about negative experiences of children in day care, as the overall assumption is reassuring for parents rather than trying to highlight the negative effects on children. However, it is still critical that the interviews are approached with sensitivity as many parents can feel guilt about leaving their child in non-maternal care. It is also critical that all the information gathered is treated with confidentiality in mind, as any identification of a particular child or indeed the day care provider could be problematic. Asking intrusive questions should be avoided as most parents will be sensitive to the needs of their child. You should also ask your teacher to check your interview schedule or questionnaire as they are a more competent judge of ethical issues.

Example brief

Thank you for agreeing to take part in an interview to investigate the experiences that you believe your child to have in their day care centre. This interview is designed to record the different positive experiences of children who attend a nursery compared to a preschool. You should try to be as honest as possible in your answers. You will be asked a series of questions and be given time to express your own opinions. The interview should last around 10 minutes and all of your answers will remain confidential and your child, you and the day care provider will be anonymised. You can choose to not answer any of the questions that are asked or decide to not take part in the interview at any point.

My research supervisor is my teacher at school, who can be contacted by phone or email on:

Again, thank you for taking part in my investigation, the findings will be written up and available at your request. Following my A-level examination, the results gathered for this investigation will be destroyed.

Data collection tools

It is important that the data gathered from your interview is recorded accurately. This could be via handwritten notes or by tape recording each interview and writing up as a transcript. Closed interview questions, for example, 'How many friends has your child made at nursery?' will yield quantitative data such as the number of friends. This can be easily counted up. If you choose to use open-ended questions, such as 'What are the social benefits of sending your child to nursery?' it will yield more qualitative data and a variety of different and personal responses as to what parents see as the social benefits. Thematic analysis typically involves the analysis of repeated themes in the data. It could be the case that parents commonly mention 'a number of friends at nursery', 'my child is more sociable', 'my child engages more with adults'. These could then be 'counted up' as instances of the social benefits of attending day care.

Data analysis

You will need to decide how to analyse your data in relation to your initial hypothesis, so you will need to decide how to measure positive experiences. For example, this could be analysed quantitatively by counting up the number of positive experiences reported by the parents or devising a scoring system for yes/no responses.

Results

As we are interested in the difference between nursery and preschool provision and positive experiences, a Mann-Whitney U test would be an appropriate test for significance in this particular instance. Results can be presented in a table and a graph to visually represent the data gathered.

Table 7.4 The total score for positive experiences (socially and academically) rated by parents of children in nursery and preschool day care

Preschool care (Total rating/10)	Nursery care (Total rating/10)	A. Rank for preschool care	B. Rank for nursery care
9	6	9	4
7	7	6.5	6.5
5	8	1.5	8
6	6	4	4
5	10	1.5	10
	Sum total of ranks	22.5	32.5

The formula for the Mann-Whitney U can be applied to the sum total of ranks as follows.

Note that R_a is the sum total of ranks for list A and R_b is the sum total of ranks for list B.

$U_a = N_a \times N_b + N_a \times (N_a + 1) / 2 - R_a$

$U_a = 5 \times 5 + 5 \times 6 / 2 - 22.5$

$U_a = 25 + 30/2 - 22.5$

$U_a = 17.5$

$U_b = N_a \times N_b + N_b \times (N_b + 1) / 2 - R_b$

$U_b = 5 \times 5 + 5 \times 6 / 2 - 32.5$

$U_b = 25 + 30/2 - 32.5$

$U_b = 7.5$

The lowest value of U_a or U_b is the U value taken. In this case the U value is 7.5. This should be compared to the table of critical values for a two-tailed test at p 0.05.

Table 7.5 Extract of a Mann-Whitney U table of critical values for a two-tailed test at p 0.05

	N_a	5	6	7
N_b	5	2	3	5
	6	–	5	6
	7	–	–	8

The calculated value must be equal to or less than the critical value in this table for significance to be shown.

The U value = 7.5, which is more than the critical value of 2 for a one-tailed test (which we will assume in this instance), therefore the results are not significant at the p 0.05 level of significance ($p>0.05$) and the null hypothesis should be accepted. This means that there is no difference in the positive experiences of children who attend nursery or preschool day care.

> **Maths tip**
>
> If $p>0.05$ it means that the probability of the results being due to chance is greater than 5 per cent, therefore the null hypothesis should be accepted as the results are not significant.
>
> If $p<0.05$ it means that the probability of the results being due to chance is less than 5 per cent, therefore the alternative hypothesis can be retained.
>
> Check the direction of the symbols that indicate probability is greater than (>) or less than (<) very carefully.

Discussion

The final section of your practical investigation is the discussion. The overall aim of this section is to interpret your findings in relation to previous research and to critically reflect on your study. This part of your practical investigation should include the following sections.

Offer an explanation of your findings

Explain what was found in relation to your hypothesis. In this particular instance, you could say that the alternative hypothesis was not supported as the difference between the positive experiences of nursery and preschool children was not significant and could be due to chance factors. It is also useful to provide a summary of your descriptive statistics; in this case no real differences between nursery and preschool children emerged from the data.

In your examination there will be tables of critical values to choose from. It is important, especially for the Mann-Whitney U test that you select the correct table to use. Carefully read the instructions at the top of the table to help with your selection. You will probably be required to use a table at the significance level of 0.05, unless otherwise instructed. So you will need to select the correct table for a one-tailed or two-tailed test based on whether your hypothesis is directional or non-directional.

Explain how your findings relate to previous research

Reflect on whether your research supports, disputes or extends the knowledge of previous research and theory. Think about whether the theory or other studies could be reconsidered as a result of your findings. Studies such as Vandell et al. (1988) found a positive correlation between children's positive interactions with adults and ratings of peer acceptance, social competence and empathy four years later. There seemed to be no difference between children attending preschool or nursery, which is perhaps predicted from the congruence in governmental policy between the different providers.

Limitations of your practical investigation

You should be critical of your research and suggest possible limitations of your current study. For instance, was your sample representative? Were there any potential biases or confounding variables that could have affected the data? If relying on parents' self-ratings of quality, for example, there may be an element of bias involved. You should suggest how such issues could be resolved and suggest improvements for any further research.

In this practical example, it is likely that parents reported their children having more positive experiences because they would not wish to appear to place their children in day care where they would have negative experiences. It is also likely that parents would be more favourable about day care choices that they have made for their own children. The motivation behind self-reported responses must be explored fully to establish whether the findings are valid or not.

The sample used can also be criticised for being based on a small number of parents recruited by opportunity sample. This sample is not only unlikely to represent the views of all parents but is likely to be biased towards those parents who are willing to discuss day care experiences of their children; these are more likely to be positive experiences as parents may not wish to participate in such an interview had their children had negative experiences of day care.

You should also consider the way in which your questions were constructed, in order to assess the validity of your findings. Questions can often be leading or generate socially desirable answers.

Strengths of your practical investigation

You should also consider the strengths of your practical investigation. Here it is useful to consider the ethical guidelines that you adhered to and the methodological considerations that made your study reliable or valid. You may also wish to consider the implications of your findings as this can also be a strength of the research.

In this practical investigation, parents were fully informed about the nature of the research aims, the procedure, and were also given the right to withdraw and have access to the report findings. Data protection was taken into account as the findings were destroyed after use. None of the questions asked in the interview violated a right to privacy and the results were anonymised to ensure confidentiality was not breached.

Although an interview was the research method used, it was a structured interview and a strict schedule was followed to ensure that all participants were asked the same questions in the same format. This standardised procedure was used to ensure the study could be repeated and improves the reliability of the research.

Identifying the strengths of your practical investigation can sometimes be difficult. It can be useful to compare your research method and procedure with alternative choices, such as a questionnaire or observation, and discuss why your design choices were better.

Suggestions for improvement

Review the weaknesses of your practical investigation to highlight possible areas for improvement. It could be argued that a larger and more diverse sample of parents with children aged three years would have produced more reliable and generalisable findings. As it is important to develop your suggestions for improvement, you need to explain exactly what you would have done to implement your ideas. For this practical, it would have been better to have accessed a range of nurseries and preschools, perhaps conducting background research on the quality of day care provided by reading their Ofsted reports. A random sample of three-year-old children could be gathered by assigning each child a number and using a random number generator to select a random sample. The parents of these children could have then been contacted for their agreement to participate.

Exam tip

Suggestions for improving your practical investigation need to be well developed. Follow this format to explain your suggestions better.

State your suggested improvement.

Explain why the improvement is needed.

Describe how you intend to implement your improvement ('how' is a process, so detail each stage of this process).

Explain the implications of your suggestion, how it will improve the practical.

7.6 Issues and debates (A level only)

In this section, you will learn about issues and debates relevant to child psychology.

You will have already noticed that issues and debates have been mentioned throughout this topic. This section will draw together the main themes and ideas related to child psychology as a whole.

Ethics

Child psychology can pose specific ethical issues that need special consideration. The capacity of children to understand what is happening and consent to research is limited, so they should always be treated as vulnerable individuals. Psychologists go to great lengths to ensure consenting participation, even from babies; they are trained to recognise non-participative behaviours and are sensitive to the needs of children. The United Nations Convention on the Rights of the Child (1989) protects the rights and welfare of children involved in psychological research, with particular emphasis on protection of human rights.

However, some research raises questions about the ethical participation of children in psychological research; one such case is the study of Genie. It is argued that the psychological knowledge gained from this study was put before the well-being and rehabilitation of the child. Although this argument still stands, it is important in that it highlights the potential problems that can occur from such research. Research into children who have suffered neglect can pose particular issues associated with confidentiality and privacy. These cases are rare, and as such, tend to be high-profile cases that attract media attention. Anonymity of these children is therefore difficult to establish and maintain.

The use of the Strange Situation Procedure also raises ethical issues, as it deliberately places children in a situation where they become distressed. Some may say that this is unacceptable, whereas others might argue that it is only momentary and the procedure is stopped if the child becomes too distressed.

Practical issues in the design and implementation of research

Different research methods can be used to investigate child development. Observational research can be subject to observer effects, where the behaviour of the child and parent may change as a result of being observed, resulting in unnatural behaviour. Similarly, the observational data may be open to observer bias, making the findings subjective. Attempts to reduce subjectivity can involve stringent controls, such as the development of specific coding that operationalises behavioural categories precisely, or the use of more than one observer/rater. Inter-rater reliability involves establishing agreement between different observers coding the same child behaviour. This agreement is often represented as a correlation coefficient, of which a coefficient of around 0.75 or above indicates good agreement.

Meta-analyses are often used where research in one area of psychology has produced a wealth of studies but perhaps demonstrate inconsistent findings. In such cases a meta-analysis is a useful tool to get an overall picture of trends and patterns found (called effect sizes). Because a meta-analysis is a study of studies, it uses secondary data in its analysis, and therefore does not collect primary data. This means that the research has been conducted by other researchers and these often vary in procedure, sample, design and data analysis. This can pose difficulties as studies that are different in methodological design are not really useful to compare to one another. Although researchers exert significant effort to ensure studies are comparable, they will never be identical, so the procedural differences themselves may account for the different outcomes under comparison.

Meta-analyses can over-rely on published and peer-reviewed studies. This research has a tendency to show positive, rather than negative/null, findings. Research studies with null findings are often not published because they do not demonstrate interesting findings, so they are filed away. This is known as the file-drawer effect. However, many meta-analyses try to use unpublished doctoral dissertations, journals and conference papers to avoid the file-drawer effect so that the effect size found is not skewed to positive findings.

Reductionism

Reductionism is not a significant debate in child psychology because much of the research takes account of the interaction of many variables on the developing child. For example, research into day care often considers the complex mediational effects of the biological disposition of a child, rearing strategies, quality of day care and family background, among other variables. Therefore, most developmental research cannot be accused of being reductionist in the methodology or explanations of behaviour. However, research into attachment types can be argued only to consider the nature of the parent–child relationship, ignoring childhood temperament as an interactional influence on how children are raised and subsequently attached to a parent.

Comparisons between ways of explaining behaviour using different themes

Explanations of attachment from learning theory used to be considered a good explanation of attachment, seeing the mother as associated with the provision of food. However, Bowlby, making use of many research studies into both animal and children's attachment, quickly demonstrated that children do not attach because of food, but instead that attachment was a complex, emotional bond with psychological and evolutionary benefits. In his theory, Bowlby draws together many themes in explaining behaviour to help understand why attachment occurs. He used the evolutionary concept of adaptedness and natural selection to describe how children use proximity-promoting behaviours that encourage proximity and a safe base, in order to survive. Bowlby also drew on cognitive themes to explain how children use their early relationships as a template for later adult attachments, and psychodynamic themes to describe how early childhood experiences affect later psychological development. Developmental theorists often take an integrative approach to understanding child development using many themes that explain behaviour.

Psychology as a science

Science demands many elements in the methodological process of scientific enquiry, such as falsifiability, reliability, empirical findings and hypothesis testing. Many of these standards are met (or researchers try to meet them) when investigating childhood development. The Strange Situation is a procedure that adopts many procedural elements consistent with being scientific: children's behaviour is coded and confirmed using inter-rater reliability, the procedure is highly standardised and controlled, and only observable behaviours are recorded.

Evolutionary theories of attachment are, however, largely speculative and therefore lack direct empirical evidence or the ability to be falsified. We cannot go back in a time machine to directly gather evidence for the evolution of attachment behaviours, directly observe the necessity of attachment to avoid predation, or any other speculative ideas put forward by the evolutionary approach. So we cannot prove or disprove (falsify) any evolutionary account of behaviour. However, it is possible to use evidence from comparative animal studies to suggest a plausible account of attachment, and we can even test hypotheses about the evolution of behaviour, therefore meeting some, but not all, standards of being truly scientific.

Culture

Different cultural practices across countries vary considerably, as different beliefs about childhood and development are evident. We have seen that childrearing practices in Germany encourage independence while in Japan they encourage dependence. Although these children are judged to be insecurely attached, this etic is one that is created by inappropriately using American western standards about maternal sensitivity. It is important to judge theories and research according to the culture in which they have been formulated and not impose the same expectations on to other people.

Nature–nurture

The universality of attachment is well recognised in cross-cultural research. All children seek a 'safe base' typically of a primary caregiver who may be the mother, father or significant other. However, the universality of the different forms of attachment type does not follow the norms found in America. The distribution of attachment types vary considerably from country to country and even within countries, suggesting cultural and subcultural differences in childrearing strategies that result in differential attachment distributions. Attachment itself may be founded largely in nature, but the qualities of attachment formed between child and parent differ according to nurture.

An understanding of how psychological knowledge has developed over time

John Bowlby's research into attachment has shaped our understanding of children's emotional, social and cognitive development today. In fact, most research exploring the nature of attachment, deprivation and separation largely stems from Bowlby's early research and publications. He helped to develop an understanding of why children may experience problems in later life based on their early childhood experiences, and today a great deal of research into day care is formulated from his writings.

Issues of social control

Many issues discussed in child psychology have the potential to be used as a form of social control. This is particularly evident in the work of John Bowlby. Bowlby's theories of attachment and maternal deprivation became public knowledge after the Second World War. During the war men were conscripted into the armed forces and female labour was necessary on farms and factories. Women embraced the liberation of employment that they had previously been denied. But after the war as the importance of mother–infant attachment was stressed, and the consequent dangers of bond disruption emphasised, many women felt pressured to give up their jobs and return to the family home. Although this was not Bowlby's direct intention, the knowledge was used to force women out of the labour market so that returning soldiers could take up positions of employment once again. Bowlby's legacy still persists today, as many women can feel pressured to extend their maternity leave or resign from employment in order to raise their children, while also worrying about the financial costs; and those parents who use day care often feel guilty about leaving their children in non-maternal care. This is a particularly salient issue in today's society, where two incomes are often essential to meet the financial commitments of a family.

The use of psychological knowledge in society

Attachment theory, and in particular the work of James and Joyce Robertson, has informed hospital practice around parental visitation rights. The Robertsons recorded the distress experienced by very young children who were separated from their parents and championed the increase in visitation times that were very restricted in hospitals during the 1940s to 1960s. Many hospitals at the time only permitted parental visits of an hour a week, and some only allowed parents to see their child behind a partition. Today, parents have almost complete access to see their child in hospital and some have parent apartments so that they can stay with their children throughout the duration of their stay.

This knowledge has extended into day care practice and current guidelines ensure that children are familiar with the day care provider, have a key worker as a substitute primary caregiver and limit the staff–child ratios to ensure that children receive enough attention and care.

Issues related to socially sensitive research

Research considered to be socially sensitive has negative implications for the participants involved in the research and for the groups that these participants represent. Research into day care, particularly research that suggests day care can have negative effects on children or which concludes that certain children are more likely to be harmed, such as those of lower socio-economic status, can have negative implications for those families and day care users. This may create guilt about using day care provision, and parents will feel responsible in case there are any negative effects on their children.

Similarly, research into attachment types based on the western proportions of secure and insecure attachment stresses the influence of maternal sensitivity in creating secure attachments, and blames rejecting or inconsistent parents for creating insecure attachments through poor bonding. It effectively blames the parents for poor attachments being formed. This is particularly salient for mothers who experience postnatal depression following the birth of their child, which can mean that the bonding process is affected – and possibly leading to poor attachment.

Research concluding that day care is damaging for children is often exacerbated by media coverage, perpetuating the idea that parents are deliberately harming their children and often not documenting the methodological problems with such research.

Knowledge check

Content

- Are you able to define attachment, deprivation and privation?

- Can you describe and evaluate Bowlby's research into attachment?

- Can you describe and identify attachment types and discuss Ainsworth's research into attachment types?

- Can you describe the short-term and long-term effects of deprivation and how negative effects might be reduced?

- Can you describe and evaluate research investigating short-term and long-term effects of deprivation?

- Are you able to describe and evaluate research into the effects of privation, and whether these effects can be reversed?

- Are you able to discuss research into the advantages and disadvantages of day care?

- Can you describe cross-cultural patterns in attachment types and explain this variation using the nature–nurture debate?

- Can you outline the characteristics of autism as a developmental disorder?

- Are you able to explain autism using one biological and one other explanation?

- Can you describe two or more therapies for helping children with autism?

Methods

- Are you able to describe how observations are designed and conducted?

- Can you explain how qualitative data collected from observations can be gathered and analysed?

- Can you explain how quantitative data collected from observations can be gathered and analysed?

- Can you describe the difference between participant and non-participant observations?

- Can you describe the difference between overt and covert observations?

- Can you explain how questionnaires can be used in child psychology to gather both qualitative and quantitative data?

- Can you explain how interviews can be used in child psychology to gather both qualitative and quantitative data?

- Do you know the difference between semi-structured, structured and unstructured interviews?

- Can you explain how a sample could be achieved for self-report methods such as questionnaires and interviews?

- Can you explain the difference between open and closed questions in interviews and questionnaires?

- Can you identify and explain issues surrounding the use of interviews and questionnaires such as social desirability bias and demand characteristics?

- Can you describe how and why cross-cultural research is conducted in child psychology? Can you explain and evaluate relevant nature–nurture issues in cross-cultural research?

- Can you evaluate the strengths and weaknesses of cross-sectional versus longitudinal designs in cross-cultural research?

- Can you describe how a meta-analysis can be conducted using cross-cultural research? Can you identify the strengths and weaknesses of such a method in drawing conclusions about the universality of attachment types?

- Are you able to identify and describe ethical issues of researching with children, including children's rights and the UNCRC (1989)?

- Can you identify the different measures of central tendency and explain how they are calculated?

- Can you construct a frequency table?

- Can you describe and evaluate the different measures of dispersion? Can you calculate the range and standard deviation?

- Can you select an appropriate inferential test?

- Can you carry out an inferential statistical test, for example chi-squared, Spearman's rho, Mann-Whitney U and Wilcoxon and draw appropriate conclusions from the data?

- Can you define what is meant by the term 'levels of measurement'? Can you identify and explain the four levels of measurement used in psychology?

- Do you understand levels of significance ($p \leq .10$ $p \leq .05$ $p \leq .01$) and are you able to use these to interpret the results of an inferential test?

- Can you compare observed and critical values on a critical values table to check whether results are significant?

- Can you explain how qualitative data can be analysed via the use of thematic analysis and grounded theory techniques?

Studies

> In the studies section, you are required to describe, evaluate and apply your knowledge of one classic and one contemporary study of child psychology.
>
> To check your evaluation skills, refer to the introduction section of this book and review 'how to evaluate a study'. Remember that you may be asked to consider issues of validity, reliability, credibility, generalisability, objectivity and subjectivity in your evaluation of studies.

- Can you describe the classic study by Van IJzendoorn and Kroonenberg (1988) Cross-cultural patterns of attachment: A Meta-Analysis of the Strange Situation in terms of its aim(s), method, procedure, results and conclusions?

- Are you able to evaluate the Van IJzendoorn and Kroonenberg (1988) study in terms of strengths and weaknesses?

- Are you able to identify and describe the aims, method, procedure, results and conclusions of a contemporary child psychology study from the following list and evaluate the study in terms of strengths and weaknesses?

  o Cassibba et al. (2013) Attachment the Italian way

  o Gagnon-Oosterwaal et al. (2012) Pre-adoption adversity and self-reported behavior problems in 7 year-old international adoptees o Li et al. (2013) Timing of High-Quality Child Care and Cognitive, Language, and Pre-academic Development.

Key question

- Are you able to identify and describe a key question in child psychology that is relevant to today's society?

- Can you explain this key question using concepts, theories and research that you have studied in child psychology?

Practical investigation

- Have you designed and conducted a questionnaire, interview or observation to investigate an area of child psychology?

- Can you explain the process of how you went about planning and designing your questionnaire, interview or observation and justifying your decision making for your choice?

- Can you write a report of your investigation including, a hypothesis, a description of the research method, the sampling process, ethical considerations, data collection tools, data analysis, results and discussion?

- Can you describe and analyse the qualitative and/or quantitative data that you gathered as a result of your investigation?

- Can you use an inferential statistical test to analyse your data such as chi-squared, Mann-Whitney U, Wilcoxon or Spearman's rho?

- Can you explain the strengths and weaknesses of your investigation into a child psychology issue and suggest possible improvements that could have been made?

Issues and debates (A level only)

> Remember that issues and debates are synoptic. This means you may be asked to make connections by comparing issues and debates across topics in psychology or comment on issues and debates within unseen material.

- Can you identify ethical issues associated with theory and research within the child psychology?

- Can you comment on the practical and methodological issues in the design and implementation of research within child psychology?

- Can you explain how theories, research and concepts within child psychology might be considered reductionist?

- Can you compare and contrast theories and research within child psychology to show different ways of explaining and understanding attachment?

- Are you able to discuss whether theories, concepts, research and methodology within child psychology are scientific?

- Are you able to discuss the concepts of culture and gender within the context of child psychology and how they may impact on observed differences?

- Are you able to discuss the nature–nurture debate in the context of child psychology, in terms of which theories emphasise the role of nature or nurture?

- Do you understand how child psychology has developed over time?

- Do you understand what is meant by social control and how research within child psychology may be used to control behaviour?

- Can you show how the theories, concepts and research within child psychology can be used in a practical way in society?

- Are you able to understand what is meant by socially sensitive research and explain how research in child psychology might be considered to be socially sensitive?

References

Cassibba, R., Sette, G., Bakermans-Kranenburg, M.J., and Van IJzendoorn, M.H. (2013). Attachment the Italian way: In search of specific patterns of infant and adult attachments in Italian typical and atypical samples, *European Psychologist*, 18(1), pp. 47–58.

Gagnon-Oosterwaal, N., et al., (2012). Pre-Adoption Adversity and Self-Reported Behavior Problems in 7 Year-Old International Adoptees, *Child Psychiatry Hum Dev*, 43, pp. 648–660.

Li, W., Farkas, G., Duncan, G. J., Burchinal, M. R., and Vandell, D. L. (2013). Timing of high-quality childcare and cognitive, language, and pre-academic development, *Developmental Psychology*, 49, (8), pp. 1440–1451.

Van IJzendoorn., M., H and Pieter M. Kroonenberg, P.M. (1988). Cross-cultural Patterns of Attachment: A Meta-Analysis of the Strange Situation, *Child Development*, 59, pp. 147–156.

Health psychology

Health psychology investigates how and why people behave in unhealthy ways and what can be done to encourage people to adopt a healthier approach. It combines different elements of psychology: the biological bases of behaviour, how our cognitions (thoughts) affect our behaviour and social influences on health-related behaviour. Health psychologists work to understand why people engage in harmful activities, such as drug taking, so that they can help by introducing strategies to reduce or prevent such activities.

In this topic, you will learn about:

- issues around drug taking

- biological and learning explanations for alcohol, heroin and nicotine addiction

- treatments for drug addiction, including an anti-drugs campaign and the psychological strategies behind it

- individual differences in drug misuse and how drug misuse may develop

- research methods used within health psychology

- research studies that examine key aspects of health psychology

- a key issue around the topic of health psychology that is of relevance to society today

- how to carry out a practical research exercise relevant to topics in health psychology

- wider issues and debates in health psychology (A level).

8.1 Content

Learning outcomes

In this section, you will learn about:

- addiction, tolerance, dependency and withdrawal in relation to drugs

- a biological and a learning explanation for alcohol, heroin and nicotine addiction

- two treatments for addiction

- how and why anti-drugs campaigns are used

- biological and social factors influencing individual differences in drug misuse

- how social influences during development can lead to drug misuse.

Drug-taking behaviour

Drugs can mean illegal substances, such as, heroin but can also refer to legal substances used by many, such as alcohol, and the nicotine found in tobacco. These drugs can become addictive, creating a feeling in the person that they need the drug. If they stop taking the drug this can result in withdrawal symptoms.

Addiction

Addiction is a condition that occurs when a person ingests a substance (for example drugs, alcohol or nicotine) that they find enjoyable, but the continued use of the drug can interfere with ordinary life responsibilities, such as work, relationships or health. Drug users will feel an increasingly overwhelming need to continue to use the drug, which can result in a person becoming overly focused on the drug use, and this is how it can cause problems in other areas of their lives. A drug user may believe that they have to have the drug and cannot function without it. Those who are addicted to a drug may find it difficult to stop the behaviour, even if they know it is causing them harm or creating difficulties.

Addiction can present itself in a physical way, where a person shows physical symptoms if they do not get the drug, resulting in physical dependency. Addiction to a drug, however, goes beyond the body's physical desire for the drug or a physical reaction; it can also cause a psychological need for the drug. In order to fully understand addiction, it is necessary to consider the cognitive, biological and social processes that contribute to the behaviour, and how these processes are influenced by using the drug. This contributes to the dependency that can occur.

It is important to remember that the effect of addiction, including withdrawal symptoms and dependency, differs depending on the drug that the person is taking.

Dependency

Psychological dependency

People typically continue to take drugs because of the psychological effects they experience when they take them. Drugs may affect their feelings, reactions and behaviours in situations. Some people may report, for example, that they feel more confident, relaxed or more able to achieve certain goals as a result of taking their specified drug. Repeated use of the drug can lead to a psychological dependence on the drug, as the person believes they cannot manage without taking it. They therefore continue to take the drug.

Physical dependency

Drugs have an effect on how the body works by changing the way neurotransmitters operate in the brain. For example, heroin increases the amount of dopamine in the reward pathways of the brain (the **nucleus accumbens** and **ventral tegmental** areas) by boosting the activation of dopaminergic synapses, causing an intensely pleasurable or euphoric experience while it lasts. People may, therefore, continue to take a drug because it has a pleasant physical side effect. Repeated use of drugs creates a physical dependency as the brain adapts to the changes imposed by the drug so that it no longer operates normally without it. Abstinence from the drug can result in unpleasant physical side effects.

Two important aspects of physical dependency are tolerance and withdrawal.

- **Tolerance:** This occurs over time as a person continues to take the drug. The body adapts to the presence of the drug and as a result needs to take greater amounts of the drug in order to get the same effect. This often occurs because the nervous system increases the number of receptor sites for the drug molecules in a process known as up-regulation.

- **Withdrawal:** This is experienced when the person stops taking the drug. These are painful or unpleasant physical symptoms that the drug user will experience as the drug leaves their body or wears off. Symptoms may include vomiting, shaking and headaches or fits. The symptoms, the severity of the withdrawal and how quickly they are experienced depend on the type of drug taken, and the frequency and quantity of the drugs being taken.

Key terms

Nucleus accumbens: an area of the midbrain associated with the brain's reward system.

Ventral tegmental area: an area of the midbrain associated with the brain's reward system and the origin of dopaminergic activity.

Exam tip

Developing a familiarity with the meaning of the terms 'tolerance', 'withdrawal' and 'dependency' (psychological and physiological), and being able to apply them when explaining substance use will help to show your knowledge of the topic. This can be achieved by creating either a glossary of terms, which can be added to when a new term is introduced, or a vocabulary book. It will also help to avoid any of the distress that can happen in an exam when you come across a term that you are less familiar with!

Why do people become addicted to drugs?

People start to take drugs for many reasons. Addiction is what influences a person to carry on using drugs. Addiction can occur due to physiological and psychological changes in the individual as a result of taking the substance. Two key explanations relate to the biological and learning approaches already covered in this book (see Topic 3: *Biological psychology* and Topic 4: *Learning theories* respectively). Theories within these approaches provide differing explanations for why people continue to misuse substances, even in the presence of any unpleasant side effects of drug use.

Biological explanation: the role of neurotransmitters

Biological explanations for addiction suggest that there are key physiological influences within our bodies that make it more likely that a person will engage in substance use and how someone deals with dependency and withdrawal. This would form the nature side of the nature–nurture debate that you have visited in previous topics.

WIDER ISSUES AND DEBATES

Nature–nurture

The nature–nurture debate suggests that an individual may engage in drug taking because of influences from the environment, for example learning to associate a drug with pleasurable feelings, or observing others taking drugs (nurture), or as a result of physiological changes that make individuals more susceptible to drug use (nature).

Drugs will create one of two reactions in the brain of the user. This is due to the effect the substance has on the availability of one or more neurotransmitters. Drugs will affect the body by either having an **agonist** role or an **antagonist** role. They can also act as reuptake inhibitors. The way in which a drug changes the anatomy or function of a cell is known as the 'mode of action'.

Agonists are drugs that mimic neurotransmitters. They fit onto receptor sites, making the post-synaptic dendrite believe that the drug is a neurotransmitter and this makes the neuron fire. Substances that act as agonists make the stimulation of one neuron by another much easier. Using stimulants can result in temporary alertness and increased levels of energy. It can also create an increased body temperature and an irregular heartbeat. Both heroin and nicotine are agonist substances.

Antagonists are drugs that bind onto receptor sites on a neuron and prevent it from firing. This then prevents the message being passed from neuron to neuron. Substances may act as a depressant and will slow the brain's activity down. As the brain activity is reduced, the transmission of messages between neurons becomes less effective. Alcohol is considered to be a **depressant**. This can result in poor concentration, sluggish behaviour, confusion and slurred speech.

Reuptake inhibitors are drugs that work by binding onto the axon terminal branches. This prevents the axon terminal from taking up the excess neurotransmitter left over in the synapse, causing an excess of that neurotransmitter. For example, cocaine is a reuptake inhibitor for the neurotransmitter dopamine. When the axon terminal cannot take up the leftover dopamine, and the dendrite from the next neuron has reached its threshold, we are left with too much dopamine, causing the stimulating effects of cocaine.

Alcohol

Alcohol is a drug that is consumed in liquid form. The type of alcohol that is in alcoholic drinks is called ethanol and it is made from plant material. Grains, fruit or vegetables are processed and allowed to ferment for differing amounts of time, which affects how much ethanol and, therefore,

Link

For more information on synaptic transmission and the effect of recreational drugs on the transmission process in the central nervous system, see Topic 3: *Biological psychology*.

Key terms

Agonist: a substance that acts like another substance and, therefore, stimulates neural action.

Antagonist: drugs which produce an antagonist effect bind to the receptor sites on neurons to prevent the substance from being absorbed in large quantities, therefore reducing the effect of the neurotransmitter.

Depressant: a drug that reduces the ability of the synapses to work effectively, so slowing down brain activity.

alcohol is in the drink. Alcohol is a substance that is legal in Britain for individuals over the age of 18 years. Many people drink alcohol.

Psychological effects

Alcohol reduces inhibitions as it targets the social control areas of the brain. Reduced effectiveness of these inhibitory mechanisms leads initially to relaxed, confident behaviour but can develop into exhibitionism and extreme behaviour at higher levels. Users may experience relaxation following a drink, which makes continued drinking more appealing. People who drink alcohol to avoid worrying about personal problems may find that the reduction in stress is positive, and they start to use alcohol as a way of coping with stress and worries. With increased use, the alcoholic becomes psychologically dependent on the alcohol, as they see it, albeit inaccurately, as a way out of their problems.

Physical effects

Initially, following a low intake of alcohol, users will feel warm and look flushed as a result of the alcohol causing blood vessels to dilate. The effect of alcohol on the **GABA** (an inhibitory neurotransmitter) becomes noticeable as reactions to situations slow down. Alcohol also affects speech, making it more difficult to form coherent words. As the frontal lobes become depressed, they will show less control over motor skills or coordination. Dehydration occurs when the alcohol inhibits the hormone controlling urination so as alcohol levels start to fall, there is increased urination.

There can be many long-term health problems as a result of alcohol misuse. Key issues include liver disease and nerve damage. The brain can also be permanently affected. Some individuals may develop Korsakoff's syndrome, a brain disorder associated with heavy alcohol use that is characterised by short-term memory loss and potential changes to their personality. Pregnant woman are advised not to drink alcohol during pregnancy, as this increases the risk of foetal abnormality.

Mode of action

Alcohol affects neurotransmission in various ways, including GABA receptors, and reduces serotonin activity. Serotonin is associated with emotions. A low level of serotonin in the brain can create feelings of depression. Alcohol is, therefore, considered a depressant as it reduces serotonin levels and can make the person feel low in mood.

Alcohol also makes GABA more effective. GABA is an inhibitory neurotransmitter that makes it difficult for messages to be transmitted from one synapse to another. The presence of alcohol further slows down the speed at which messages are passed between neurons. This includes slowing down fight or flight reflexes that are usually triggered by noradrenaline synapses. The nerve endings of these noradrenalin synapses are numbed by the alcohol so are less effective. It also makes inhibitory systems of the brain less effective, so people under the influence of alcohol are likely to take more risks than they would do when sober.

Tolerance

Short-term tolerance can develop quickly. This can lead to people feeling more sober than they actually are when their blood alcohol levels drop slightly. This often contributes to behaviours such as people believing they are safe to drive a car after drinking alcohol.

In a matter of weeks, a regular drinker will have developed a tolerance to alcohol, as a direct result of the body producing more of an enzyme that breaks down alcohol quickly. As a result, a higher level of alcohol intoxication will be required to reproduce the initial reactions to alcohol. The person is also likely to develop ways of dealing with the side effects of intoxication, such as drinking first thing in a morning to reduce the shaking symptoms of withdrawal.

> **Key term**
>
> **GABA (gamma-aminobutyric acid):** this is a very important inhibitory neurotransmitter. It makes it more difficult for messages to be transmitted across synapses, and is, therefore, known as a depressant.

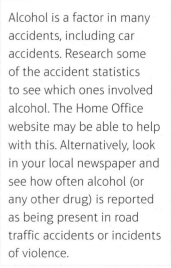

> **Taking it further**
>
> Alcohol is a factor in many accidents, including car accidents. Research some of the accident statistics to see which ones involved alcohol. The Home Office website may be able to help with this. Alternatively, look in your local newspaper and see how often alcohol (or any other drug) is reported as being present in road traffic accidents or incidents of violence.

Withdrawal

Withdrawal can be felt as early as two hours after the last drink, depending on the amount consumed. It is typically experienced 6–12 hours afterwards. Symptoms may include shaky hands, nausea, vomiting, headaches or insomnia. There may be some vivid dreaming or visual or tactile hallucinations that usually end within 48 hours.

'Alcohol withdrawal syndrome' is potentially life threatening. It can happen when people who have been drinking heavily for a long period of time suddenly stop or significantly reduce their alcohol consumption. When they stop drinking, the neurotransmitters that have been suppressed come to the fore. As they rebound, it can create hyper-excitability in the brain. People with a heavy history of alcohol use may experience delirium tremens (DTs). With DTs the brain becomes used to the effect of alcohol on GABA receptors. As alcohol levels drop, the fight-flight mechanism is overly active, and this produces hallucinations, confusion or anxiety and severe tremors. DTs can be fatal and is considered a medical emergency. Mortality rates can be up to 35 per cent unless treated, reducing to 5 per cent with early recognition and treatment.

Heroin

Heroin, or diacetylmorphine, is an opioid analgesic that is found naturally in the opium poppy. Historically, it has been used legally as a form of pain relief in the form of morphine. It is also used as an illegal recreational drug in which users aim to seek feelings of euphoria following consumption. Heroin is a highly addictive drug.

Psychological effects

Heroin rapidly produces a feeling of euphoria. The analgesic effect gives a feeling of calm and aches or pains will disappear. The intensity of the euphoria and well-being experienced by the user depends on the amount of heroin that has been taken. It is this feeling that acts as a reinforcement or motivator to use heroin again in the future.

Psychological dependency can occur as the user may become progressively less satisfied with the rest of their life, due to the contrast between reality and the feelings of euphoria. When not experiencing the immediate effects of euphoria, the addict may feel increasingly confused, anxious and restless. They may also experience paranoia. These psychological symptoms can only be alleviated by the user taking more heroin. As these negative withdrawal symptoms then disappear, it reinforces the individual to continue to use heroin.

Physical effects

The user will also feel their skin become warm, experience a dry mouth and their limbs may feel heavy. There is often a feeling of nausea or actual vomiting. As the amount of heroin builds up, they will experience nausea and vomiting on a less frequent basis, as it depresses the part of the brain associated with this action. A person's heart rate and breathing will slow down, often to life-threatening levels. This is because it changes the activity of neurochemicals in the brain stem, which is where automatic functions, including breathing and heart rate, are controlled. Mental functioning will become less clear and they will feel drowsy for a number of hours once the initial euphoria has faded. A long-term user is likely to experience lung problems because of the continual depression of the respiratory system. Depending on how the person consumes the drug, they may damage the nasal tissues (if snorted) or may get abscesses and collapsed veins if they inject heroin.

Mode of action

Heroin attaches to receptors that would typically receive input from **endorphins**. During everyday activity, a moderate amount of endorphins is naturally produced, causing the release of dopamine and facilitating the reward systems within the brain. If the body is put under stress and pain, receptors are stimulated and the level of endorphins is increased. These lock onto the receptor sites that transmit information about pain, blocking the brain's ability to register pain.

Heroin acts like a massive release of endorphin into the brain. Once heroin has been taken, it quickly hydrolyses into morphine, which binds to opioid receptors concentrated in the reward pathway (ventral tegmental area, nucleus accumbens and **cortex**) and pain pathway (**thalamus**, **brain stem** and spinal cord) of the brain. This morphine is an opiate that attaches to the opioid receptors on the post-synaptic membrane. When these opioid receptors in the brain become activated by the opiate, they inhibit the activation of GABA, a chemical known to inhibit the release of dopamine. Once GABA is inhibited, dopamine can flood the synaptic gap, which leads to sustained activation of the post-synaptic membrane. This has the same effect as having lots of natural endorphins released. In low doses of the drug, the release of dopamine activates the reward system and generates feelings of pleasure.

Exam tip

In an exam, it can be tempting to list all the information you know about a topic, for example the effects of heroin, by simply stating all the symptoms that a person may experience. It is important to read the question carefully to see if the question is asking for a list, or if the question wants you to show wider knowledge. This could include explaining why the symptoms occur, which will involve describing the mode of action of the drug at the synapse.

It can be too easy to limit the marks you can access by not filtering your knowledge and so not providing the answer that is needed. It can also waste valuable time in the exam.

Tolerance

Repeated use of heroin can create long-term chemical imbalances in the brain that are not easily reversed. The brain adapts to the high levels of dopamine caused by the drug and down-regulates its own natural production of it. This means that the baseline measure of dopamine is now lower than before, so in order to get the same 'high', the user now needs more dopamine and so more of the drug. This results in a tolerance for the drug, where the user has to increase the amount they use in order to experience the same initial euphoria. The neural changes that have occurred due to repeated exposure to heroin mean that these areas of the brain will only function normally in the presence of the drug, which creates dependency.

Withdrawal

Withdrawal may occur within a few hours of taking heroin. How quickly withdrawal symptoms are experienced directly relates to the level of use; the more a person uses, the quicker and more intense the withdrawal symptoms will be. A person may become agitated if they are unable to take any heroin when experiencing withdrawal symptoms. Withdrawal can be very painful and may include symptoms such as muscle and bone pain, insomnia, cold flashes and restlessness. Symptoms will peak 24–48 hours after the last dose of heroin, and can last up to a week. The symptoms will gradually subside as the level of drug in the body reduces.

Key terms

Endorphins: a group of hormones in the brain that bind to opioid receptors. They are involved in pain reception and emotions.

Cortex: the outer layer of the brain, consists of grey matter and involved in higher mental functioning.

Thalamus: part of the brain associated with sensory perception and consciousness.

Brain stem: a central trunk of the brain located in the very middle, and extends down to form the spinal cord.

Nicotine

Nicotine is a nitrogen-containing chemical, made from plants, mainly the tobacco plant. It can also be produced synthetically. Nicotine is included in cigarettes, which are then smoked. It can also be used as an insecticide, so is not just for human consumption.

Psychological effects

Nicotine makes the smoker feel very relaxed as soon as they inhale the drug. This makes smoking a pleasurable experience, and stimulates the reward system, making the smoker want to continue smoking. The reduction in stress experienced when smoking creates a psychological dependency. This is in part due to the fact that nicotine deprivation can be stressful in itself, and is relieved as soon as the person smokes again.

Physical effects

Nicotine is highly addictive. The effect of nicotine on the body is almost instant, as it quickly enters the brain's blood supply. Drug levels peak within 7–10 seconds of inhalation, creating a sense of relaxation. The acute effects of nicotine reduce within a few minutes, causing the need to continue repeated intake throughout the day. As the dopamine reward system is stimulated, smoking creates a positive feeling in the smoker. This happens with each inhalation of smoke, so is continually rewarding, which is why people become psychologically dependent on cigarettes. The alertness experienced by smoking quickly subsides and concentration can slow down. This creates the feeling that the person needs the nicotine in order to function, because the body has adapted to having nicotine present.

Smoking increases the levels of carbon monoxide (CO) in the blood, resulting in less oxygen being available. Less blood flows to the surface of the skin and can give the appearance of cool and clammy skin, while also making smokers look grey in the face due to the more limited blood flow. Long-term nicotine use can result in an irregular heartbeat and skin may age prematurely, making a smoker look older than they actually are. The presence of nicotine in conjunction with the additional chemicals in cigarettes contributes to lung disorders or cancers. It can also lead to insulin resistance, increasing the likelihood of diabetes.

Mode of action

Nicotine stimulates acetylcholine (ACh) synapses as nicotine molecules are the same shape as acetylcholine. Acetylcholine helps synapses to modify and change, which makes synaptic transmission easier. It also stimulates the dopamine reward system. The ACh synapses are associated with thinking and learning, with greater stimulation increasing alertness.

As Figure 8.1 shows, nicotine binds to the ACh receptors, causing the neuron to fire more frequently due to nicotine stimulation. This reaction explains why smokers often report greater feelings of alertness or quicker reaction times. Nicotine indirectly increases the neural transmission of several neurotransmitters, dopamine being one of them in the reward pathway of the brain, generating positive feelings that act as a reinforcer for continued smoking, as with other drugs such as heroin. Nicotine may also exert a sedative effect, depending on the level of the smoker's nervous system arousal and the dose of nicotine taken.

Immediately after exposure to nicotine, the sympathetic nervous system is activated and the adrenal glands release epinephrine (adrenaline) into the bloodstream. The rush of adrenalin causes a sudden release of glucose as well as an increase in blood pressure, heart rate and respiration. The glucose production raises blood sugar levels and will inhibit appetite. Nicotine also suppresses insulin output from the pancreas, causing smokers to be slightly hyperglycemic, which is when there is too much sugar in the blood. This can make smokers feel increasingly thirsty.

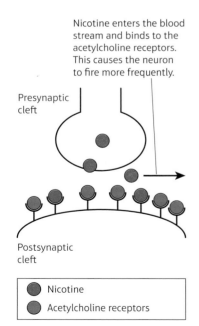

Nicotine enters the blood stream and binds to the acetylcholine receptors. This causes the neuron to fire more frequently.

Presynaptic cleft

Postsynaptic cleft

- ● Nicotine
- ● Acetylcholine receptors

Figure 8.1 Diagram to show the effect of nicotine on the synapses

WIDER ISSUES AND DEBATES

Psychology as a science

The development of technology has made a fundamental difference to our understanding of the effects of substances. It is now possible to use brain-scanning techniques to see the functioning of the brain as it occurs. This helps to further the development of health psychology as a field of science.

This understanding can help to influence the development of treatments that are more effective, as they directly address the physical symptoms experienced when withdrawing from a substance.

Tolerance

Nicotine is metabolised fairly quickly in the body, disappearing from the body in a few hours. Therefore some tolerance is lost overnight, when the smoker is not inhaling nicotine, and smokers often report that the first cigarettes of the day are the strongest as their tolerance is at its lowest. Tolerance progresses as the day develops, and later cigarettes have less effect.

The symptoms of withdrawal, rather than the effect of the drug itself create a tolerance cycle as the person smokes more frequently to avoid the negative symptoms of withdrawal. While nicotine is extremely addictive, not all smokers will feel the need to increase their intake, with some maintaining a low level of nicotine use for many years, while others quickly increase.

Withdrawal

Withdrawal symptoms may begin within a few hours after the last cigarette and include irritability, sleep disturbances, headaches, difficulties in concentrating and increased appetite. Symptoms generally peak within the first few days and may subside within a few weeks, although for some people they may persist for months or longer. Craving nicotine is considered a major obstacle to overcome when stopping smoking. Experiencing an urge to have nicotine can last for up to six months, and for some the pleasure of smoking makes it a constant battle not to reach for a cigarette.

In addition to the physiological symptoms, withdrawal can create a number of psychological difficulties. It can be difficult for some people to overcome the problem of no longer engaging in the behaviour of lighting a cigarette and smoking it, as these behaviours are associated with the pleasurable effects of smoking. Smokers often associate having a cigarette with having a good time, which makes the behaviour reinforcing and difficult to stop.

WIDER ISSUES AND DEBATES

Ethics

The biological explanations for addiction, tolerance and drug withdrawal have largely been conducted through animal research. This poses ethical questions about using adverse stimuli on animals, which can be potentially fatal and likely to cause considerable pain. It is common practise to euthanise animals after the research data has been gathered, and this should be done as speedily and appropriately for the species of animal used. A cost–benefit analysis should be conducted before such research is given ethical approval.

Evaluation

The presence of withdrawal symptoms support the biological viewpoint that the brain relies on the drug to function, as the symptoms indicate a deficit of the relevant neurotransmitter. It is possible to use brain scanning and other objective assessments such as blood tests to look at the effects of substances within the body. This provides a scientific approach to investigating the effects of substances. As the outcome of such tests can be seen, and can be replicated due to their scientific approach, the findings are considered reliable.

The biological explanation complements psychological learning theories. Classical conditioning can be observed via the experiencing of pleasure after taking a drug such as heroin. The presence of a reward system represents positive reinforcement, and the avoidance of withdrawal symptoms by continuing to take a drug is indicative of negative reinforcement. This suggests a biological foundation for learning theories to build on.

Many studies into the effects of drugs are undertaken on animals. For example, the Richardson and Roberts (1996) study to look at the reinforcing effect of opiates was carried out on rats. Rats have similar brain structures to humans but humans are influenced by social conditions, which may influence substance misuse, so the findings may not be applicable to humans. However, research using animals that highlight significant brain structures implicated in drug misuse are likely to be very appropriate in explaining human addiction.

The biological approach does not explain why someone first starts using a drug before the development of any physical addiction. Social explanations may be more appropriate at this stage, for example, peer pressure or observing others around them smoking. As a result, biological explanations cannot be considered a full explanation of addiction as they cannot account for why someone takes the drug in the first place. Therefore biological explanations are better suited to explain continuation of use, tolerance, withdrawal and physical dependency.

Peer pressure is one reason people choose to start smoking.

Exam tip

There are lots of different symptoms and neurotransmitters discussed in the biological explanation for the three substances. You will need to know these.

To help your memory, draw a table like the one below in which you can summarise all the information so it is available at a glance. You could include headings such as 'Positive effects', 'Withdrawal symptoms', etc.

You may even want to include information from later in this topic, such as 'Treatment options' for each substance.

	Mode of action	Tolerance	Withdrawal	Effects of physical and psychological dependency
Heroin				
Alcohol				
Smoking				

Learning explanations

All of the theories from the learning approach that you have studied in Topic 4: *Learning theories*, can be used to explain why someone may start to use drugs or continue to take them. It will be helpful for you to familiarise yourself with these theories so that you can confidently apply them to the topic of substance misuse.

The acquisition stage of drug use explains how an individual comes to engage in the drug-taking behaviour, for example how they come to engage in heroin use, smoking or the drinking of alcohol. This occurs through the development of an association between the drug and the positive feeling that occurs as a result of taking the substance, which may include feelings of relaxation. This is a form of classical conditioning. Social learning theory can also explain the acquisition stage. Individuals start to smoke, drink alcohol or take heroin as a result of observing those around them engaging in such behaviours and witnessing them having a positive effect from it. This acts as vicarious reinforcement.

The maintenance stage of substance use is best explained by operant conditioning. Having a positive experience from taking a substance, for example having a buzz from heroin or feeling a sense of well-being after drinking alcohol, acts as a powerful reinforcer that makes the behaviour more likely to be repeated in the future. The punishment of withdrawal symptoms should the individual stop taking the drug will also act to maintain future repetition.

Operant conditioning

Central to the learning approach is the concept of reinforcement. Positive reinforcement explains the early stages of someone continuing to take a substance after they have tried it. It explains why individuals continue to take heroin, nicotine and alcohol.

The drugs initially create positive feelings in the person. Alcohol and heroin have relaxing benefits and can induce a sense of well-being. Heroin may also remove any feelings of pain. All of these effects can be reinforcing to the individual. They make the individual want to take the drug again in order to recreate the same effect. They learn to associate the drug with the positive feelings they experience after taking the drug.

Continued smoking can be explained by operant conditioning, despite the initial reaction to nicotine often being feelings of nausea and light-headedness, which are not in themselves

WIDER ISSUES AND DEBATES

Nature–nurture
The learning explanations seek to explain specific stages of drug taking behaviour, particularly that of the acquisition and maintenance stages. It identifies drug addiction as a learned response: an individual continues to take a substance as a result of the positive consequences that occur from taking the substance and to avoid the negative symptoms of withdrawal.

This explanation highlights the nurture side of the nature–nurture debate in explaining drug use. Individuals engage in such behaviour as a result of being exposed to it from others. They then continue to participate in such behaviour as a result of the positive consequences experienced from either taking the drug or the negative consequences of withdrawing from it.

reinforcing. Smoking can reduce anxiety and increase concentration. These positive feelings are soon experienced after trying a cigarette and, therefore, quickly become reinforcing to the individual. Feelings of nausea subside, and are often only experienced during smoking the initial cigarettes.

Positive reinforcement is not always due to the consumption of the drug. Drugs, such as alcohol and nicotine, are often taken socially and reinforced by the approval of friends or peers, so continuing to drink or smoke can also be reinforced by praise from those important to us.

Operant conditioning helps to explain the maintenance of drug use. For example, the symptoms of withdrawal from heroin can be unpleasant. Heroin users, therefore, continue to use the drug to avoid the negative symptoms of withdrawal. This is an example of negative reinforcement where the drug-taking behaviour is undertaken to avoid a negative consequence (withdrawal).

Social learning theory

According to social learning theory, our observations of other people engaging in addictive behaviour can lead to the development of addiction. When we observe the behaviour and reactions of other people using drugs, we may wish to repeat what we saw, particularly if the person is considered a role model or is looked up to by the individual. It may be that the individual observes the positive experience in the other person when they use the drugs, and they therefore want to experience a similar reaction and so they use the drug.

This explanation explains smoking behaviour and alcohol use, both of which can be considered social behaviours; the drug-taking behaviour can form part of the group's culture and is, therefore, readily engaged in within social settings. For example, students leaving home and attending university make friends with other students in the first few weeks at university. This is likely to occur within a social setting such as in a bar or pub. Students see others drinking large amounts of alcohol or engaging in drinking-related activities. They may choose to copy such behaviour because it looks like the other people are having fun while drinking, and because they want to be liked by those people.

Social learning theory is particularly suited as an explanation for nicotine use, particularly as initial attempts at smoking may result in nausea and, therefore, are not initially reinforcing. For example, a person may look up to an elder sibling. If their sibling is observed smoking, the younger person may want to copy this behaviour due to their sibling being a role model.

> ### Developmental psychology
>
> Adolescence is a critical period in the development of smoking, and is, therefore, of concern to developmental psychologists. Peer modelling and pressure to initiate smoking behaviour is a key factor in the development of smoking and its continued use into adulthood. Friedman et al. (1985) used a structured interview on 157 teenagers to investigate smoking initiation. They found that peer encouragement and exposure to smoking peers were significant risk factors associated with onset and continued smoking behaviour. Urberg et al. (1990) surveyed 2334 adolescents and found that both peer influence and modelling accounted equally for smoking behaviour, but in particular that smoking was not directly affected by peer encouragement to smoke, but rather through lack of discouragement.
>
> Jackson (1997) examined initiation and experimentation stages of alcohol and tobacco use in a sample of 1272 teenagers, and found modelling of peers and perceived drug misuse in the population were strongly associated with initiation and experimental use of the drugs.
>
> As the path from initiation and experimental stages of drug misuse in teenage years through to adulthood is strong, developmental research into drug misuse has important applications in identifying at risk groups and developing health strategies and regulations to prevent drug misuse early on.

Raising the age limit to purchase nicotine and alcohol helps towards preventing teenagers being able to access these drugs, so limiting the availability within the population and, therefore, their exposure. In order for this theory to explain substance use, the person has to observe an individual undertaking the behaviour. This can occur in person, for example among friends, or can be via the media.

Many television programmes include pub scenes, for example, where everyone is shown to be having a positive and enjoyable time while drinking. This can be appealing to others who choose to copy this behaviour in order to have the same experience.

Individuals exposed to very different cultures may have different experiences of observational learning. For example, khat is an agonist drug, typically smoked and derived from a plant most commonly grown in the African continent. Growing up in an environment in which khat is an important part of decision making, a person may be more inclined to copy such behaviour than someone who does not see it as part of their cultural background.

Social learning theory is less effective as an explanation of heroin use. Individuals may experiment with heroin because they see their favourite television character doing so but are less likely to be exposed to peers engaging in such behaviour, unless they are submerged in a drug-taking subculture. However, heroin is not a drug that is particularly glamourised by the media; in fact it is often portrayed with negative consequences for the user.

Classical conditioning

Classical conditioning can be helpful to explain the development of addiction and tolerance to some drugs. The central premise of classical conditioning is based on that of a system of learned association. Behaviour is repeated as a result of developing an association between a specific behaviour, such as taking heroin and the association with the pleasurable feeling for engaging in the behaviour, such as feelings of euphoria. An association between heroin and euphoria is established quickly, explaining why it has such addictive properties. Alcohol can also be explained by a learned association between drinking and its inhibitory and sedative qualities. However, classical conditioning does not lend itself to explaining the acquisition of smoking behaviour because the first cigarette smoked is often considered to be an unpleasant experience.

An individual can also develop an association between environmental cues and the behaviour, which makes it more likely they will engage in taking the drug in specific situations. For example, a person may associate eating a meal with having a drink. The meal would, therefore, be seen as a conditioned stimulus and the individual will experience cravings for a drink with a meal. Identifying these environmental cues can help an individual in treating an addiction, as they may seek to address, and, therefore, reduce the association between the environment and drug by engaging in alternative behaviours when in such environments.

One form of learning that occurs as a result of classical conditioning is drug tolerance. Drug-taking behaviour (such as using a needle or even opening a bottle of beer) functions as a conditioned stimulus that predicts the introduction of the drug into the body. Eventually the act of drug taking triggers an anticipatory response: the secretion of drug antagonists that help eliminate the drug from the body. The ability of experienced drinkers to consume a lot of alcohol without showing much effect is a sign that the body is adapting to the drug. Classical conditioning has occurred. Alcohol consumption then triggers a strong anti-drug action that reduces the effect of the drug. As a person becomes addicted, the drug has less and less effect, and the person is considered to have developed a tolerance to the drug.

Classical conditioning explains the use of heroin as well as the consumption of alcohol. The initial aversive reaction of nicotine, however, does not create an association between a cigarette and a positive reward. As a result, nicotine use is less likely to be explained via the classical conditioning approach.

WIDER ISSUES AND DEBATES

The use of psychological knowledge in society
The principles of classical conditioning can be applied both to treat drug misuse and to explain it. Aversion therapy involves associating the drug with an unpleasant stimuli. A recent meta-analysis of the effectiveness of aversive smoking strategies (including rapid smoking) did not find significant evidence that aversion therapies worked to help individuals quit in the long-term (Hajek and Stead, 2011).

Tolerance and classical conditioning

Siegel et al. (1982) wanted to understand why some addicts died after taking a dose of the drug that they had taken many times before. He tested this by giving rats injections of heroin every other day for 30 days and gradually increasing the dose to develop a tolerance of the heroin in the rats.

The rats were placed into two experimental groups and a control group.

Group 1: These rats received their heroin injections in Room 1, which was the room that housed all the rats. They received their sugar injections in Room 2, which was a room that differed from Room 1 in two ways: no rats were housed there and a machine generated constant 'white noise'.

Group 2: These rats received their heroin injections in Room 2, and their sugar injections in Room 1.

Control group: These rats received injections of the sugar solution in both Room 1 and Room 2 on the same schedule as the other rats.

At the end of the 30 days, rats in all three groups were given a very large dose of heroin.

Almost all the rats in the control group died after being injected with the large dose of heroin because they had no tolerance for its lethal effects. Almost 64 per cent of the rats in Groups 1 and 2 who received the injection in a different room from that in which they were given their regular dose of heroin died. Almost 32 per cent of the rats given the heroin in the same room as they were usually given it died.

Siegel et al. concluded that the environmental stimuli in which drug addicts usually take the drug serve as a conditioned stimulus that produces a conditioned response that increases tolerance for the drug's effects; a conditioned response consisting of biological changes that counteracted the effects of the drug they were about to receive. They stated that when the rats received the final injection in a different room, the conditioned response didn't occur, which increased their chances of dying from the overdose.

Evaluation

Social learning theory explains why someone might start using drugs because of external influences such as peers, family or the media. This was found in the study of Ennett, Bauman and Koch (1994) where spending time with friends who either smoke or do not smoke makes it more likely individuals will also act the same way (although non-smoking friendship groups were more likely to establish anti-smoking norms). The explanation of external influences is not considered within the biological approach. Within the learning approach external influences provide an explanation for the 'nurture' side of the nature–nurture debate. This explanation, however, fails to explain why not everyone gives in to influence from peers and why some individuals engage in behaviour despite not being in a social setting where that behaviour is approved of.

Social learning theory highlights how family members may act as role models that can help to explain trends in alcohol use in families. However, families also share genes, and this may be a contributory factor. It is, therefore, not possible to clearly determine whether the influence in alcohol use is social or genetic.

Many drugs are known to create a response that is rewarding to the individual and can, therefore, positively reinforce their behaviour. Operant conditioning provides an explanation as to why individuals carry on taking drugs after a positive experience. Not every incident of drug taking, however, is positive.

Operant conditioning fails to explain why someone would continue to take drugs after a negative experience, for example after a bad hangover or after feeling ill following heroin ingestion. This explanation fails to take into account addiction, which can also explain why individuals take substances even after a negative experience.

Classical conditioning cannot explain why people start smoking, because most people report that the taste of their first cigarette was unpleasant. This should put people off but it does not, suggesting that there are additional influences other than positive reinforcement in the acquisition of an addiction to nicotine. However, it is a very good explanation for the acquisition of a heroin addiction because the first use of heroin creates feelings of pleasure.

Individual differences

There are other explanations that seek to explain why some individuals may be more likely to engage in substance-taking behaviour. These individual differences are not present in everyone, and can help to explain individual variation in drug-taking behaviour.

Personality characteristics

Sensation-seeking personality

Some individuals have a preference for engaging in risk-taking experiences. It is a personality trait and they will readily engage in sensation-seeking behaviour that creates a strong personal response. This can include undertaking extreme sports but can also contribute to drug-taking behaviour as another risky activity. Zuckerman (1979) originally identified this trait in individuals. He initially wanted to look at the reasons behind why adolescents took risks in relation to friends and sports. His study found a high correlation with this personality trait among drug users.

This personality type can help to explain why individuals begin to use drugs, as they search for new experiences, but does not necessarily explain why they continue to do so, as the experience no longer has the same risk sensations for them. The continued behaviour is likely to be due to other factors such as biological or learning explanations. As this sensation-seeking tendency is part of an individual's personality, it is not something that can easily be changed. Instead, they will be encouraged to manage their sensation-seeking feelings or channel them into other, less harmful, activities.

Personality disorder

There is a correlation between the presence of various personality disorders and drug or alcohol addiction. What is not fully clear is whether the presence of a personality disorder makes a person more vulnerable to substance use, or if the substance use contributes to the development of later personality disorders. Irrespective of the difficulties in identifying whether one contributes to the presence of the other, the presence of personality disorder and a substance use problem results in these disorders being described as co-morbid conditions. They are both present and both create difficulties for the individual.

Extraversion

Extraverted personalities are often associated with alcohol consumption and smoking, though smoking to a lesser extent. Martsh and Miller (1997) looked at extraversion as a predictor of alcohol use, and of binge drinking. They suggest regular drinkers are more extravert than light or non-drinkers, but alcoholics are more introverted than social drinkers.

> **Exam tip**
>
> When comparing explanations, it is best done in a methodical way rather than simply describing one explanation and then the other. Consider for every point you are making how the two explanations are similar or different. For example, 'The biological and learning explanations both provide explanations of addiction, however, the biological approach says... which is different from the learning approach, which argues...'

How do we treat drug addiction?

When considering how to treat addiction, it is important to consider all of the explanations for addiction previously discussed in this topic. Treatment methods will differ depending on the approach. For example, aversion therapy is suggested to treat addiction from a learning perspective.

Treatment options include:

- drug replacement programmes, such as methadone

- behavioural programmes, such as aversion therapy

- cognitive programmes, such as hypnotherapy.

Treatment for heroin

Methadone treatment programme

Drug-replacement programmes provide individuals who are taking illegal drugs, such as heroin, with an alternative drug that is controlled by a medical professional. The aim of this is to support the person, over time, to reduce the amount of drugs they use while also ensuring that they will not experience any serious side effects from taking some of the illegal drug that has been contaminated in some way. Drug-replacement programmes for heroin often include the practice of taking the replacement drug orally, in liquid form, rather than injected into the body, as this is much safer for the drug user. A frequently used drug-replacement programme is that of prescribing heroin users with a drug called methadone.

Methadone is a **synthetic opiate**. It replaces heroin at the synapse, which allows the drug user to function normally. Providing the individual with methadone as a replacement means the person avoids experiencing the withdrawal symptoms that result from not having heroin in their body. Methadone stays in the body longer than heroin would do, and only requires a once-a-day dose. Methadone reduces the effects of heroin withdrawal, but does not lead to the same 'high' associated with heroin use.

The dose given to the person is decided for each individual by a medical professional. As methadone can be harmful if too much is given at once, a doctor will start off at a low dose when the person is first prescribed methadone. Over the next few weeks, the dose may be increased so that it has a therapeutic effect. A person will need to have their use of the drugs supervised in a pharmacy until it has been decided that they can be trusted to have small amounts of methadone kept in a secure place at home.

Methadone is used as part of a maintenance programme, so ex-heroin users will often continue to take methadone for a long time. However, some people can reduce their methadone dose and eventually come off methadone for good. Once a person has been stabilised on methadone, the process of **detoxification** can start. The amount of methadone is reduced slowly. There will still be withdrawal symptoms when coming off methadone, and doing this slowly can minimise or reduce almost entirely any negative symptoms withdrawal may bring. At the end of the detoxification process, the person will not feel that they need to have methadone and, most importantly, will not consider themselves to need to take heroin in order to function.

Evaluation

This approach can take many months to achieve a full reduction and detoxification as the reduction in substance use is very gradual. It therefore requires the person to continue to engage with the programme for quite a long period of time. If an individual chooses not to carry on with the

Key terms

Synthetic opiate: a drug that mimics an opiate (heroin).

Detoxification: a treatment for addiction to drugs or alcohol intended to remove the physiological effects of the addictive substances. A person is helped to overcome the physical and psychological dependence on a substance.

treatment, it makes it likely that they will return to drugs as they will still have feelings of dependency and addiction. Similarly, because the treatment is gradual, it will only work if the person is committed to a long-term programme. It is not helpful for those who want to stop taking all drugs straightaway.

It can help to address some of the social influences of drugs, including reducing the need for a person to approach a drug dealer. This can reduce their exposure to other drugs. If a person is not spending time with other people who share drug-taking attitudes, this can have a positive effect on external influences. On this basis, drug-replacement programmes address the nurture explanations of drug use, such as those considered by social learning theory.

The treatment programme is carefully controlled and overseen by medical professionals. This is much safer, and more successful, than a person simply stopping taking heroin. As there can be unpleasant side effects when withdrawing from substances, the person is more supported by undertaking treatment in a controlled way. Hedrich et al. (2012) found that starting a methadone programme for offenders in prison and continuing the support into the community has a positive effect on success rates, with more offenders remaining drug-free when out in the community.

Methadone, and other oral medication, avoids any dangers of contracting blood-borne viruses, such as hepatitis or HIV, due to sharing needles with other drug users. It can also prevent other health complications through using needles when taking drugs, such as blood clots. This can provide an additional, short-term health benefit while reducing substance use.

While drug-replacement programmes typically relate to heroin use, they can be applied to other substances. It could be argued that the increasing use of electronic cigarettes for smokers, which reportedly contain fewer harmful chemicals, are an alternative to nicotine and, therefore, a form of drug-replacement treatment, albeit unlicensed. The treatment effectiveness of this emerging market remains to be seen.

Drug-replacement programmes do not address the reasons why the person started using heroin in the first place. This can leave people vulnerable to start using drugs again, if the reason for their initial use is not also addressed in addition to the physical addiction. Hasan et al. (2014) found that combining drug-replacement programmes with psychosocial support increases the likelihood that a person will not return to drug use. It can be argued that the psychological treatment allows the person to address the underlying motivation for their drug use.

There have been documented cases where young children have accidentally drunk methadone that was not correctly locked away in the family home. These cases show there may be risks associated with allowing a person to self-administer methadone without going to a pharmacist. Such decisions are, however, made by professionals after a full investigation about the safety of others.

Detoxification programme

A detoxification programme aims to reduce the level of heroin in the body in a controlled manner. Detoxification programmes provide supervised withdrawal from a drug of dependence so that the severity of withdrawal symptoms and serious medical complications are reduced to a minimum. It usually involves supervision in the period immediately after the person stops taking the heroin, when the typical 'rebound' symptoms of drug withdrawal are at their most severe.

During a detoxification programme, the emphasis is on the physical effects of heroin addiction. The aim is to reduce the level of heroin in the body, so that the body can return to normal functioning, without the influence of heroin on the synapses. It is a somewhat simple way of treating heroin addiction in that the individual is observed and monitored while experiencing withdrawal from heroin.

Taking it further

The giving of methadone prescriptions for the user to keep them in their home has resulted in media attention in recent years, often due to young children getting hold of the drug and drinking it themselves, or the user selling the drug to other drug users.

If you were a health practitioner, what could you do to minimise this from happening and to make sure the person was going to use it themselves?

There is likely to be a clinician to provide support to the individual within an in-patient facility, but this support is not a structured therapeutic approach during the acute withdrawal phase. Some detoxification programmes offer additional treatments such as cognitive behavioural therapy (CBT) to address the individual's beliefs and attitudes around their substance use. It is also possible that holistic treatments, such as acupuncture, are offered, which aim to reduce some of the physical discomfort experienced during a detoxification.

Heroin withdrawal is rarely life-threatening, but it has unpleasant side effects. For heroin users, detoxification is a form of palliative care for those who wish to **abstain**. It also provides a period of respite from drug use, and can act as a precursor to more specific forms of drug-free treatment for drug dependence. The unpleasant feelings of the withdrawal can act as an aversive stimulus for heroin users, which can then act as a barrier to them engaging in a detoxification in the absence of a substitute such as methadone.

Evaluation

Detoxification is a process that aims to achieve a safe and humane withdrawal from a drug of dependence. It does not address the reasons why the person started taking the drug initially, nor does it provide the individual with any strategies or support to address any future temptation to use heroin again. As a result, the potential for relapse remains high. As it only addresses the physical addiction to the drug, it can be considered an overly simplistic way of addressing heroin use.

Detoxification is often conducted in conjunction with heroin replacement programmes, such as the use of methadone. To undertake detoxification, (even in a controlled manner), in the absence of a replacement substance can be distressing and uncomfortable for the individual. This makes it less likely that an individual will want to engage in a detoxification-only programme.

The detoxification process can start as soon as an individual stops taking heroin. While it is unpleasant, after a week without taking the drug the worst of the withdrawal symptoms have passed. This therefore provides a quick way to reduce the levels of heroin in the body, whereas methadone programmes can take many weeks before an individual is no longer taking any substance.

Supervised heroin detoxification often takes place in an in-patient setting, which is more effective than if someone undertakes it as an out-patient (Mattick and Hall, 1996). This creates a resource demand where there are often waiting lists for individuals accessing such facilities due to the cost and resources required to provide such a service. As a result, an individual may have a period of time to wait before they can access a detoxification programme. During this waiting time, they remain vulnerable to continued heroin use, potential harm as a result of their use and the likelihood that they could change their mind about accessing the treatment.

Treatment for alcohol

Aversion therapy

Another approach to change substance behaviour is to directly address the behaviour itself. The behavioural approach advocates that new behaviour can be 'learned' in order to overcome addictions and, therefore, replace the addictive behaviours. Aversion therapy is one such behavioural treatment, and is based on learning theory. One of the basic principles of learning theories is that all behaviour is learned and, on that basis, undesirable behaviours can be unlearned under the right circumstances. It is based directly on the classical conditioning approach of learning theory. The goal of aversion therapy is to decrease or eliminate undesirable behaviours.

Aversion therapy is an application of the branch of learning theory called classical conditioning. Within this model of learning, an undesirable behaviour, such as smoking or drinking alcohol, is

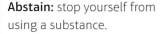

Key term

Abstain: stop yourself from using a substance.

matched with an unpleasant (aversive) stimulus. The unpleasant feelings or sensations become associated with the behaviour, and the behaviour will decrease in frequency or stop altogether. It has been applied to a number of addictions, including smoking.

Typically when someone drinks alcohol, the body metabolises the alcohol by turning it into a substance called acetaldehyde. This is a toxic compound that can cause the unpleasant symptoms associated with excess alcohol consumption such as vertigo, weakness, headache, anxiety and possibly even chest pain. Acetaldehyde is usually broken down quickly in the body and made into acetic acid, which is harmless.

Aversion therapy is most commonly applied to ensure alcoholics do not drink alcohol.

An individual undergoing aversion therapy for alcohol use is given a drug called disulfiram shortly before drinking alcohol. This drug, often in tablet form, works by interfering with the ability of the body to metabolise alcohol, that is it interferes with the mechanism that breaks down the acetaldehyde. The chemical can then build up in the body to produce unpleasant symptoms. The fear of developing these symptoms can be enough to deter the individual from drinking while on the drug. Those who do consume alcohol while on the drug will develop an aversion due to the pairing of the alcohol with the unpleasant symptoms. Individuals become classically conditioned to associate the taste, and even the smell, of alcohol with the negative symptoms. They then choose not to drink alcohol to avoid the negative symptoms.

While disulfiram has been in use for many years, there have been recent advances in similar, but more developed, medications to use within aversion therapy. Medication that works in the same way of developing aversive symptoms but also rewards abstinence with positive feelings has had encouraging results. This medication, tryptophan, is known to increase levels of the neurotransmitter serotonin, which is associated with feelings of optimism, tranquillity and general well-being. Therefore, people who take this drug will not only abstain from alcohol, but will feel more positive while doing so, which acts as a positive reinforcement for abstaining.

Evaluation

Aversion therapy differs from those types of therapies that adopt principles of operant conditioning. Therapy that uses an operant conditioning approach would present the aversive stimulus, usually called punishment, after the behaviour rather than together with it. In presenting the aversive stimulus at the same time as the unwanted behaviour, it has a greater treatment effect based on the principles of classical conditioning. Ethical concerns have, however, been raised about deliberately making people experience unpleasant symptoms, even if they do give consent to the treatment.

The person is not required to have any insight into why they engage in the behaviour, which is often the case for more cognitive treatments such as CBT. However, it could be argued that if a person does not understand their motives for drinking, this could make them vulnerable to returning to the substance again in the future.

Aversion therapy can be very effective in the short term as the unpleasant side effects are immediate, therefore creating an immediate behaviour change. However, relapse rates are high with this therapy. The individual is also still likely to have cravings as these are not addressed by taking the medication. It is usual for aversion therapy to be combined with other forms of treatment to address the motivation for the behaviour. Without other forms of treatment in addition to the aversion therapy, the person may simply replace the old undesirable behaviour with a new undesirable one.

There can be potentially serious side effects through taking toxins to support behaviour change. Side effects can include liver or nerve damage. Those with existing medical conditions may be more prone to experience these side effects. This could reduce access to this treatment for individuals with existing medical conditions that could be made worse by the side effects of the aversive medication.

This treatment can only be used for people who want to abstain completely from alcohol. It is not an appropriate treatment for those who want to reduce their drinking to within safe limits. Behavioural change is needed instead for such individuals. Learning explanations would be interested in exploring what makes them drink excessively, such as peer influence, the environment they drink in, etc.

Cognitive behavioural therapy (CBT)

CBT is a talking therapy that uses a problem-solving approach to alcohol dependence. It aims to identify unhelpful and unrealistic thoughts and beliefs that may be contributing towards an individual's alcohol dependence. These can include reasons why a person chooses to drink, which may include as a way of relaxing or to cope with problems. Once an individual has identified the thoughts and beliefs that keep them drinking, the individual is encouraged to change their thoughts to be more helpful. For example, an individual may believe that they are unable to relax without drinking. CBT may help the individual to instead believe that they have other ways they can relax, besides alcohol. They will then be encouraged to engage in the alternative behaviour to help them to relax, once they have an awareness of such alternative behaviours.

CBT is also helpful for identifying triggers that may increase the likelihood that a person will drink, such as being in a certain environment or with certain individuals, or being in a specific mindset, such as feeling upset. The therapist will then support the individual to develop strategies to manage these triggers, which are known as 'high-risk situations' to minimise the potential that the individual will feel the need to drink alcohol.

Evaluation

McCarthy (2008) found that CBT was effective in reducing binge drinking but also demonstrated an increase in the ability for individuals to refuse alcoholic drinks when in high-risk situations. This therefore indicated that the therapy was helpful in addressing the drinking behaviour itself, as well as the individual's coping abilities when in situations that would typically result in alcohol consumption.

This two-fold approach increases the likelihood that an individual will be able to manage their future alcohol consumption by providing skills that can be applied when needed as well as encouraging behaviour change.

Many evaluations for the effectiveness of CBT for alcohol use are undertaken under the umbrella of 'substance use', which also includes drug use. It is, therefore, difficult to extrapolate the effectiveness of this therapy approach solely for alcohol use.

For some people, spending time with a therapist discussing their alcohol use may be sufficient to create a change in behaviour, as the individual may feel supported by the therapist and, therefore, empowered to make a change in their behaviour. It is, therefore, possible that simply discussing their alcohol use results in behaviour change, rather than specifically the components of the therapy itself. In this sense, it is difficult to determine if the positive therapeutic relationship creates behaviour change or the skills taught within the therapy.

Treatment for smoking

Aversion therapy

Aversion therapy has been proven to be effective not only in alcohol use but also with other substances, including smoking. This treatment approach aims to pair smoking with unpleasant, aversive stimuli that remove the rewarding feeling experienced by smokers, and replace it with an unpleasant one, with a view to the individual no longer wanting to smoke. The process of aversion therapy as a treatment for smoking follows the same process as with other stimulants, such as alcohol. The only difference between aversion therapy for smoking another substance is the aversive stimuli being used.

Aversion therapy is commonly applied to smoking through the method of rapid smoking. This involves inhaling on a cigarette every few seconds for several minutes while concentrating on the unpleasant feelings that arise from smoking so quickly. The participant continues the quick-puff procedure until they begin to feel nauseated. This then serves to replace the association between the pleasurable or comforting feelings most people get from smoking with the more repulsive consequences of tobacco use.

Similarly, silver acetate products serve as a pharmacological aversive stimulus. They can be taken in the form of chewing gum, lozenges and a mouth spray. When taken with cigarettes, silver acetate produces an unpleasant metallic taste in the mouth and, therefore, has aversive qualities for smokers.

Evaluation

The effectiveness of aversive stimuli with smokers has received limited empirical evaluation to date. As a result, it is not fully known how effective this treatment is in order to achieve long-term smoking cessation. Hajek and Stead (2000) found limited evidence that rapid smoking (inhaling deeply and frequently) might reduce smoking. Existing trials show little evidence for a specific effect of silver acetate in promoting smoking cessation. The lack of effect of silver acetate may reflect poor compliance with a treatment whose rationale is to create an unpleasant stimulus, rather than the treatment method itself being ineffective.

Hypnotherapy

There are many psychological treatment programmes available that can be used to address addiction behaviour. CBT is one way in which individuals can be guided to use self-talk strategies at times of cravings to support themselves when wanting to drink alcohol or smoke a cigarette. Another approach that has been gaining credibility as a treatment, particularly for nicotine addictions, is that of hypnotherapy.

Hypnotherapy occurs when a trained therapist induces a client into a very relaxed state. This can make them more open to suggestions put to them by the therapist, thus making them more **suggestible**. The client is not put to sleep, but their focus reduces to the extent that they are no longer aware of anything other than the words of the hypnotherapist. Their level of consciousness has been altered when placed under hypnosis before the treatment commences.

In this relaxed state, ideas can be implanted into the client's unconscious that will influence the person's behaviour once they are in a more conscious state. When addressing addiction behaviours, the therapist will suggest ideas such as the person no longer wants to smoke or to imagine unpleasant outcomes if they were to smoke again. These suggestions then form part of the client's own thoughts, and are remembered when in a conscious state. When the person thinks about smoking they will then think about these thoughts, which will put them off smoking.

Evaluation

Hypnotherapy has been found to be three times more effective as a treatment in addressing nicotine addiction than nicotine replacement therapy (Hasan et al., 2014). This supports the psychological influence of nicotine addiction, whereas nicotine replacement therapy focuses on the biological sources of nicotine addiction. As such, it addresses and seeks to change the psychological components related to continued smoking behaviour. Other treatment methods tend to just focus on the physical dependency that maintains smoking behaviour.

Hypnotherapy can be more helpful than other techniques, such as drug treatments, as it supports the self-belief of the person, that they are able to make positive changes for themselves, without feeling that they need medication to help them with it. Positive treatment outcomes can often be seen after just one or two treatment sessions. This makes it a very cost-effective treatment. For treatments such as methadone reduction, treatment takes a prolonged period of time before positive outcomes can be seen.

Some people may be put off from trying hypnotherapy as they may think that they are not going to be in control of their behaviour or that they may be vulnerable during hypnosis. As a result, they may be more likely to try other treatment options.

Treatment success relies on the client being able to relax sufficiently to be hypnotised. If they cannot do this, the auto-suggestions will have no benefit on the individual. Therefore, it may not be a treatment that will be suited to everyone, although the individual will not know if it will be effective or not until they have tried it.

It is unlikely that a person will be able to access hypnotherapy on the NHS as it is not licensed by the NHS for such use and, therefore, has a personal cost implication for the client. As such, this is a treatment that is not accessible to everyone.

> **Exam tip**
>
> When evaluating a treatment programme, considering how they compare with others may be a useful part of the evaluation. For example, if there are ethical issues with this particular treatment approach, are there other treatments that are more ethical? It is best to expand on your comment to say why the other treatment may be more ethical, to show that you understand both treatments. You can do this by saying 'It is more ethical because…'

Motivation as a precursor for treatment

In order for treatment to be successful, a person using the drugs has to want to change their behaviour. A common psychological model that identifies an individual's motivation, designed specifically with drug addiction in mind, is that of the 'Stages of Change' Model (Prochaska and DiClemente, 1983). It is an influential model within psychology as a discipline, no more so than in relation to identifying treatment options for drug users.

The five stages of change are as follows.

Pre-contemplation: the person is not considering changing their drug use. They are unaware of the full negative consequences of their behaviour. As a result, they are unlikely to make efforts to change their behaviour.

Contemplation: the drug user is aware of some of the negative consequences of their drug use, but they are still thinking about whether changing their behaviour is what they want. They have not yet made a definite commitment to changing their behaviour.

Preparation: the drug user has decided to make a positive change to their behaviour, that is, to stop using drugs. They begin to plan steps towards making this change.

Action: the person tries out the plans they have made to support their decision to change their behaviour. This is likely to include attending treatment programmes and developing skills to manage any temptation they may have to use drugs.

Maintenance: the person has a set of new behaviours that supports them not using drugs. This is a long-term stage and staying in this stage will prevent the person from using drugs in the future.

If a person were to return to drug use at any point (that is, have a **relapse** or a **lapse**), they will need to make a decision about what they want to do next, and re-enter the stages of change.

The model is considered to be a cycle that a person goes through in order to manage their addiction. The model is, therefore, often referred to as the 'cycle of change'. An individual's positive, ongoing motivation to address their drug use will move through each of these stages, in the direction shown by the arrows. Motivation may also, however, go the other way, and would suggest the person is less motivated or feels less ready to make positive changes to their drug use.

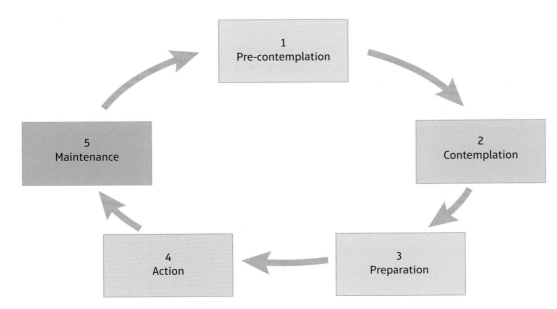

Figure 8.2 Prochaska and DiClemente's 'Stages of Change' Model

Key terms

Relapse: a person has started to use a substance again after a period of abstinence (not using the substance). A relapse is not to be confused with a 'lapse'.

Lapse: a one-off return to drug-using behaviour but which does not result in the person fully returning to such behaviour. For example, a person who is trying to stop smoking may have one cigarette, but then not have any more. This would be a lapse. People who experience both relapses and lapses will benefit from continued support with their attempt to quit.

Taking it further

There are questionnaires available on the Internet that people can fill in to look at their own motivation to make positive change in their life. Download one of these and think about something that you may want to change, such as wanting to write more neatly in exercise books or develop a more organised approach to learning, or something involving an activity, such as wanting to take up a new hobby. While thinking about this planned change, complete the questionnaire.

Are you ready to make that change yet?

Anti-drug campaigns

A psychologist will often work with other professionals, often with a medical or nursing background, to develop ways to share important health messages with the general public. These messages are known as 'campaigns', and will involve lots of advertising to encourage the general public to make positive change to their behaviour.

Previous health-related campaigns have addressed topics such as self-assessments for breast or testicular cancer or national programmes aimed at increasing the vaccination rates of children following health concerns after vaccinations. From a substance perspective, campaigns have historically included national 'stop smoking' promotions. The role of the psychologist in such campaigns is essential to ensure the strategies underpinning the campaigns are those that will have a positive outcome.

Figure 8.3 The logo for the Stoptober 'stop smoking' campaign

'Stoptober' 2014

The campaign message is simple; if you stop smoking for 28 days in the month of October, it makes it five times more likely that you will quit for good. There are still over 8 million smokers in England and smoking remains the number one cause of preventable premature death and chronic disease. It causes a staggering 80 000 deaths and costs the NHS an estimated £2.7 billion each year. The campaign title is catchy. It was designed to capitalise on a trend to give months of the year a theme in the same way as 'Movember' is associated with an increased number of men growing facial hair in November, in support of male cancer fundraising. It is focused on being positive and motivational.

The campaign was introduced in 2012 and is led by Public Health England. It is the biggest mass quit attempt in the UK. It aims to show smokers that Stoptober understands that quitting can be a difficult and intimidating proposition for many people, but with the right support and tools, they can make it through the month and beyond. Stoptober report that 250 000 people in England and Wales took part in the 2013 Stoptober challenge, and over 65 per cent made it to 28 days (160 000 people). It is estimated that 50 000 will remain smoke free after 12 months.

It looks set to be an annual event and the 2014 campaign featured comedians to supercharge the positive tone of Stoptober by adding humour to empathise with smokers and deliver the message.

The campaign crosses a number of advertising sources, including television, radio, road shows, online and social media to create a sense of scale and relevance. From 8th September 2014, Stoptober encouraged as many smokers as possible to join the challenge and prepare to quit from 1st October by signing up online for free support tools. The tools complemented the 28-day journey and were designed to offer support every day, this year peppered with humorous content to keep people engaged and smiling throughout, via a physical pack, smartphone app, text and email programs.

Stoptober launched on television with an innovative 3-minute 'sketch show' during the Emmerdale commercial break (available to download from the Internet), fronted by comedians such as Paddy McGuiness and Al Murray (The Pub Landlord) who delivered Stoptober's key messages in a humorous way.

The start of the advert includes pictures of individuals designed to represent the general public. This creates an inclusive feel to it so that all smokers who see the advert are likely to feel they are represented within those images. The pictures reflect a range of ages, ethnic backgrounds and represent both men and women. This approach helps to draw in all smokers to the campaign and is important for people to choose to participate.

The comedic tone is carefully used. It purposefully avoids mention of cancer or respiratory disease. Furthermore, the humour used is inclusive of all so as to avoid alienating a key audience. Some of the health benefits of not smoking are subtly included in the advert. Al Murray hints that taste buds will improve and his pub customers will realise how bad his beer is if they were to stop smoking. Using humour in this way avoids people seeing the campaign as pressurising and more that they have to stop because it improves their taste. Such direct health campaigns have been less effective in the past as people have reported that it can feel as if they are being lectured at. This can make people more reluctant to try to change their behaviour.

A lot of reference is made to willpower within the advert, which is needed in order for someone to succeed in stopping smoking. At this point of the advert, Al Murray speaks a lot about how willpower is a British trait, making reference to the war. This approach helps the viewer to identify with historical events that required will power and aims to instil a sense of pride in the viewer. These traits will help the person to be more resilient to the demands of quitting smoking.

While the main body of the advert aims to highlight the benefits of not smoking, there are also links to some of the negatives of continuing to smoke. This includes making a joke about the Coldplay song 'Yellow' being written for smokers, making reference to the tendency for smokers fingers to become yellowed due to the nicotine in cigarettes.

In presenting the advert as if it is a chat show, with an audience being filmed within the advert, it has a group-based approach. The viewers, while not in the actual audience are likely to feel that they are part of the wider group. In considering making change, feeling supported by others, even if not directly known to you, increases a sense of self-belief that the desired change can be achieved.

The 'sketch show' advert generated PR for the campaign and announced the arrival of a new, refreshed Stoptober. Throughout September, the comedians then delivered shorter adverts reinforcing Stoptober's key messages through television and radio to explain why smokers should act now and sign up online to start their quit attempt on 1 October. Online and social media advertising directed smokers to the sign up page and Stoptober's proven support tools.

Who is it aimed at?

The campaign is aimed at all smokers. As the legal age to buy cigarettes is 18, the campaign ultimately is directed towards adults. However, the accessibility of the language used and the use of humour is also likely to gain the attention of teenagers who have started smoking.

What psychological theories are applicable to anti-drug campaigns?

Hovland-Yale model of persuasion

This model states that there are several factors that will affect how likely a change of attitude is through persuasion. For example, how likely someone will consider stopping smoking and be open to campaigns such as Stoptober. The model states that there are three prominent factors that need to be considered in order for a campaign to be persuasive. This has led psychologists to look at the science of persuasion to discover how to change attitudes with the ultimate goal of changing behaviour.

1 The source (who is giving the message)

According to credibility theory, people are more likely to be persuaded when a source presents itself as credible, for example if the person providing the message is an expert in the field.

2 The message (what the message is saying)

The content of the message is an important factor. Two-sided messages, those which highlight both sides of the argument, have a greater influence on attitudes than one-sided messages, as long as the two-sided argument eventually gives a solid opinion. This would suggest that an effective campaign to stop smoking needs to highlight both sides of the smoking debate, and then be clearly conclusive about why the benefits of quitting outweigh reasons to smoke.

3 The audience

The characteristics of the audience strongly affect how likely someone is to be persuaded. Individuals considered to be more intelligent are more likely to be persuaded by valid arguments because they have a longer attention span and can understand the arguments better. The campaign will, therefore, need to be structured around the audience characteristics it is aiming to persuade.

Culture can also be a contributory factor in relation to how messages are received by the audience and, therefore, how persuasive the messages are. For example, Wang et al. (2000) found Americans prefer products that offered 'separateness' whereas Chinese prefer products that offered 'togetherness'. This suggests different cultures would be more influenced by messages that back up their opinions.

Elaboration likelihood model of persuasion (Petty and Cacioppo, 1986)

This model aims to look at attitude change by looking at persuasion, and factors that increase the likelihood of persuasion occurring. Under this model, persuasion depends on the level of scrutiny given to a message. The level of scrutiny falls along a continuum from close scrutiny, or 'central processing', which involves examining an argument closely, to 'peripheral processing' where short-cut cues are used to understand a message. The level of scrutiny and processing depends on motivation. People who are less motivated use peripheral cues that lead to 'less stable' attitude changes, which are less likely to lead to behaviour change. People who are well motivated undertake central processing, which is more likely to lead to sustained changes in behaviour (Crano and Prislin, 2006).

Many messages lead to both central and peripheral processing operating at once. This theory implies that information campaigns should seek to provoke central processing of their message. A campaign fronted by a celebrity may provoke interest and, through peripheral processing, lead the viewer to understand the message. However, to change habitual behaviours and bring about long-lasting change, a message has to provoke deeper thought.

Two conditions are necessary for 'effortful processing' to occur. The recipient of the message must be both motivated and able to think carefully. A person's motivation to consider messages can be influenced by a number of variables, including the perceived personal relevance of the message and whether the person enjoys thinking in general. A person's ability to think carefully can also be influenced by a number of variables, including the amount of distraction present in the persuasion context and the number of times the message is repeated. If a person is both motivated and able to think carefully about the issue and relevant information presented, it can generate an attitude that is integrated into the person's overall beliefs.

Fear arousal (Janis and Feshbach, 1953)

Fear arousal health promotions aim to inform individuals of the risks of engaging in a particular behaviour, such as smoking. Health messages based on fear arousal may include graphic images such as those that have been placed on cigarette packets in recent years, depicting the damage caused to internal organs as a result of smoking. Hammond et al. (2003) found that pictorial messages on cigarette packets were more effective in encouraging behaviour change than written warnings.

Health communications, which stimulate higher levels of fear, have been shown to increase the likelihood that individuals will accept the health recommendations being made within a health campaign. It has been shown that high-fear messages produce more attitude and behaviour change than health communications that do not highlight hazards of the behaviour, and are, therefore, seen as low-fear messages.

While high-fear messages have an impact on behaviour change, it is, however, necessary to use an appropriate fear level for the campaign, as found by Janis and Feshbach (1953). The individual must be able to identify with the message and consider it possible to happen to them. If the fear arousal is too high for the behaviour, it increases the potential for the individual to dismiss it as unlikely to happen to them and, therefore, does not contribute to behaviour change. The need to apply an appropriate fear level to the health message may contribute to the inconsistent results within the fear arousal literature as to whether high or low fear messages are most effective.

Janis and Feshbach (1953) investigated the effect of fear arousal levels within health communications on dental hygiene. Two hundred students were separated into four groups of 50 participants. Each group was allocated a fear arousal level: minimal, moderate or high arousal and a control group. Participants were exposed to different health messages as determined by their arousal level.

- The high-fear arousal group were shown pictures and descriptions of diseased mouths, including explanations about the pain of tooth decay and gum disease and awful consequences like cancer and blindness.

- The moderate-fear arousal group were shown similar pictures and descriptions to the high fear arousal group, but they were much less disturbing and dramatic.

- The minimal-fear arousal group were given a lecture about teeth and cavities, but without referring to very serious consequences and using diagrams and X-rays rather than emotive pictures.

- The control group were given a lecture of the same length as the other conditions (15 minutes), but this group was given a lecture on the structure and functioning of the human eye.

The outcome of the study was that the high-fear arousal message created the most worry in the students and was rated as more interesting. This condition also showed a high level of the individuals thinking more about the condition of their teeth than for the moderate- or minimal-fear arousal groups. However, they concluded that while the high-fear messages did generate most concern about dental health, the overall effectiveness of a health promotion campaign is likely to be reduced by the use of strong fear appeal, as it produced the least change in behaviour. The Janis and Feshbach (1953) study, therefore, showed that, after a delay between giving the message and measuring any behaviour change, a low-fear message is more persuasive than a high-fear message.

Leventhal and Watts (1966) used low, mild and strong threat messages (on lung cancer) to influence attitudes towards chest X-rays and stopping smoking. Their high-fear movie included close-ups from a lung surgery operation. The three groups were compared for the number of people who took X-rays immediately after the communications; an X-ray booth was available right outside the movie theatre. The results showed that the smokers in the audience did not take X-rays after exposure to the high-threat film, though did take X-rays after the low and moderate threat films. Reports of success in reducing smoking were collected three months later and a greater proportion of subjects exposed to the strong high-fear film claimed success in cutting back.

Taking it further

Fear campaigns have been used to promote healthy lifestyles, such as stopping smoking or taking drugs. Investigate these campaigns using the Internet, paying particular attention to the pictures and messages given in the campaign.

Evaluation

One way to evaluate an anti-drug campaign is to consider the strengths and weaknesses of the psychological theories that inform it. The Hovland-Yale model is too simplistic. The idea that processing occurs in order, through attention, comprehension, acceptance and retention is not necessarily the case. For example, once we start to think about the meaning of the message, we go back and pay some or all of it more attention, so individuals are not processing in a simple stage-by-stage manner. Furthermore, the Hovland–Yale model concentrates on external processes (the communication, the communicator, etc.) but does not take sufficient account of the underlying internal factors associated with the viewer (for example, attention, comprehension), which is accounted for in the elaboration likelihood model.

The elaboration likelihood model of persuasion does not result in quick attitudinal change. While it is likely to result in long-standing behaviour change, it develops over a prolonged period of time and, therefore, is less effective for rapid behaviour change. The model is somewhat oversimplified in considering that the two forms of processing act as separate processes, rather than on a continuum. It is likely that individuals use both forms of processing. The model is not clear as to how the two processes interact. It is also difficult to tell which type of processing people will use. This makes it difficult to predict behaviour from the model.

The elaboration likelihood model accounts for individual differences in a manner that the other models fail to do. It recognises how the same message can be processed differently by different people using different processes. It suggests that individuals with a high need for cognition use the central route, whereas individuals with low need for cognition use the peripheral route. The consideration of two routes may be considered more realistic than the one route of persuasion outlined by the Hovland-Yale model as individuals are complex in their processing.

The fear arousal approach is useful for increasing health behaviours in individuals, as it demonstrates that fear arousal may not be the most effective way of promoting healthy living. However, this approach does not consider other reasons, besides fear, as to why an individual may adopt a health behaviour. The approach suggests that graphic images on health campaigns may not be the most effective way to encourage individuals to change harmful behaviour. Despite this, cigarettes currently depict such images on their packets. This would suggest that the application of this approach, in practice, is inconsistent with the findings.

Research in this area is usually conducted using self-report techniques. These are biased on the part of the participant as they may report what they assume the researcher is looking for. As a result, the findings of research in this area may not accurately identify factors influencing attitude and behaviour change.

> **Exam tip**
>
> You will be asked to apply your knowledge of health campaigns to unseen material. Consider how you might go about explaining the following scenario, using your knowledge of why health campaigns may not be effective. John has tried several times to give up smoking after seeing a health campaign that made him consider quitting. Every time John tries to give up he fails, despite being aware of the health campaigns advertised on bill boards and the television.

> **Taking it further**
>
> There are different public organisations that have responsibility for developing and advertising health campaigns. One of these is Public Health England, though other countries usually have their own bodies for this.
>
> Spend some time researching some of these agencies to look at what their ongoing projects are. They are often influenced by what is being reported in the media or by health problems, for example alcohol campaigns came about due to an increase in antisocial behaviour by binge drinkers.

8.2 Methods
Learning outcomes

In this section, you will learn about:

- the use of animals in laboratory research to study drugs, and the ethics of animal research

- two research methods using humans to study drugs and the ethics of human research

- the use of cross-cultural research into drug misuse

- analysis of quantitative and qualitative data.

Undertaking health psychology research

Many of the principles for undertaking any psychological research apply when researching health topics. Within health research, subjects are often animals. Animal research requires consideration of a number of specific ethical issues.

When undertaking psychological research, it is important that decisions about research design, sample selection and analysis are undertaken with a focus on reliability, validity, objectivity and credibility. Achieving these standards makes psychology a science.

Use of animals in research into drug use

There is more use of animals as research subjects in health research than in other areas of psychological research. This is usually due to restrictions on using humans in research that investigates the effects of drugs on the body. Using animals in this setting is a way to ensure that the research questions can be explored, without putting humans at risk.

Historically, experiments on animals have been used to study the effect of drugs on the body and on behaviour, including the long-term consequences of drug use. They have also been used to explore effective treatments for drug use. When research aims to look at the consequences of a drug on the brain or is trying to recreate the effects of drugs on the brain, animals are used. This type of research requires surgery, including damaging or triggering parts of the brain.

Using animals allows researchers to make use of highly controlled environments such as laboratories, which may not be possible with human subjects.

Evaluation

It is possible to control the environment in which the experiment on animals takes place, much more so than for a human subject. This includes controlling the amount of exposure to the drugs. However, humans taking drugs can be a social activity, and animal research is unable to take into account the social factors that affect drug taking, tolerance and withdrawal as a human may experience them.

As animals used in research tend to have shorter lifespans than humans, it is possible to undertake research that allows scientists to look throughout the life of the animal. This allows researchers to understand the long-term effects of drug use, which may not be practical within a human research population.

There are cost reductions in using animals as, being smaller, they require less medication than humans who are typically larger in size. This may make it more financially accessible for some researchers to undertake such research.

Animals are a different species from humans. While the brains of some animals are similar to ours, for example primates, there are other fundamental differences. The drugs may, therefore, affect the behaviour and functioning of humans differently than that shown in the animal studies. As such, the findings of animal drug research may not be easily applicable to humans.

Animal research ethics

The use of animal laboratory experiments to study drugs

You will have learned about issues associated with using animals in psychological research in the Topic 4: *Learning theories*. You should remind yourself of the Animal (Scientific Procedures) Act (1986), the Animal Welfare Act (2006) and the British Psychological Society guidelines for using animals in psychological research. This legislation and regulation applies to the use of animals in the study of drugs.

Psychologists use animals to study the effects of drugs on behaviour and neurological functioning, addiction, tolerance and withdrawal. Although drug research is conducted on a variety of animals, typically laboratory-bred mice are used. This can involve administering the drug to an animal until it is addicted and looking at behaviour patterns, studying the physiological and behaviour symptoms associated with withdrawal from a drug, and investigating tolerance levels by administering high doses of a drug under certain conditions. Invariably the animal used in the procedure will be humanely destroyed afterwards. Animal research has ethical implications, but it is also important to consider the great number of advancements in our understanding of the effects of drugs on humans that have been made as a direct result of this research when looking at the benefits and costs.

Conducting drug research on humans requires a high level of ethical approval due to the potential harm it may create to the individuals. Human participants must, therefore, volunteer to take part in the research. In contrast, the guidelines for animal drug research has a lower threshold for ethical approval, as consent is not a relevant issue when researching on animals.

The drugs may cause long-lasting effects on the animals used within the research. This goes beyond the ethical guidelines that stipulate causing 'minimal' harm to animals in experiments. It is considered ethically more acceptable to cause long-term negative consequences to animals, if this is an unavoidable outcome of the study, than it is to cause the same harm to humans. Furthermore, the findings from drug research may then not be applicable to humans due to the difference in anatomical make-up, making the harm to the animals unjustifiable or unnecessary.

The strict regulations in place to undertake drug research on animals in Britain requires the researcher to consider the minimal amount of drug to which the animal will be exposed, and limits the number of animals to only what is necessary to explore the effect of the drugs on the animals. This provides the animals with a greater level of protection to ensure the experiment is conducted in an ethical, humane way.

> **Exam tip**
>
> Animal research in health psychology is focused on the psychological effect of drugs, not medical studies. When evaluating the ethics of animal research it is important to bear this distinction in mind, so as to avoid evaluating the use of animals in research in a more general way.

Human participants in drug research

While animal research provides some answers to the effect of drugs on behaviour, this does not entirely exclude the use of humans in research where ethics allow humans to be used. This reduces one of the weaknesses of conducting animal studies – whether the findings of animal research can be applied to humans. Humans are used in psychological studies looking at the effects of drugs using two specific research methodologies:

- laboratory studies

- surveys.

Laboratory studies

By now you will be familiar with laboratory studies. The controlled setting of a laboratory is helpful in minimising other variables that may affect the results, allowing researchers to have a clear understanding of the effect of drugs on the human. Such studies often look at how drugs affect the way we think or how our body works following intoxication.

Modern technology allows researchers to use brain scans within laboratories to assist with an understanding of brain function, including the effect of drugs on reaction times or how accurately someone can complete a task. Laboratory experiments provide lots of quantitative data, which can be analysed objectively using statistical techniques. The studies are also likely to include self-report data from the participants, to provide a qualitative account of experiences that cannot necessarily be captured using scanning or other techniques.

Often the studies will use existing drug users as their participants, to ensure the research is ethical. For example, Grant et al. (2000) looked at whether long-term drug use had an impact on decision making.

Evaluation

Human studies allow us to make direct comparisons to how humans react when under the influence of drugs. This is more difficult in animal studies as they are different species from humans. Therefore the results of human research apply directly to other human drug users.

Human studies can use a combination of quantitative and qualitative measures to ensure a wide range of effects are captured via self-report and scanning techniques. Using self-report data can lead to desirable responses being given, particularly as drug use is not socially acceptable behaviour. This may lead to an under-reporting of drug-taking behaviour. It may also not be generalisable to others as other people may describe their experiences differently.

Laboratories do not reflect a usual drug-taking environment for the participant, which may affect their behaviour. This may result in their drug-taking behaviour being unnatural, which can influence how they respond to the drug and their tolerance levels. This can then lead to questions about the validity of the study.

To use only existing drug users means studying a very specific group in society. Their experiences and reactions may not be applicable to non-drug users. This may make it difficult to study certain areas of drug-taking behaviour, such as how the body reacts to substances, as those who have previously used the drug may have a different reaction.

Drug research often investigates the influence of a drug on existing drug users, and the BPS ethical guidelines state that any administration of drug must be one which is normally encountered. Although this may seem to mitigate ethical issues of consent and harm, it can pose its own ethical dilemmas. If a drug user is participating in drug research in order to obtain a drug, it may be considered to lack consent, as a drug user may be compelled to participate to receive a drug that they crave. A drug user is a vulnerable individual and should be protected from harm.

Surveys

Surveys can include the collection of data in a number of formats, including interviews or use of questionnaires. They can be used to capture a one-off picture of attitudes to drugs or form part of a longitudinal study to look at influences on drug-taking behaviour over a longer period of time. A study such as Mundt et al. (2012) (see Section 8.3, *Studies*) is an example of a longitudinal study looking at alcohol use in students.

This approach can gather both qualitative and quantitative data. The surveys may gain information about attitudes to a substance or opinions about drug-related issues. This leans towards qualitative data, which is likely to require an analysis of themes within the responses in order to draw a conclusion (known as thematic analysis). Alternatively, it may capture data such as the frequency and severity of substance use (drugs or alcohol or both), which allows for quantitative data to be obtained.

Evaluation

Surveys can gather rich, in-depth data depending on the type of questions used. In-depth data leads to greater validity in the findings. Open questions will allow for individuals to provide detail to their answers without being restricted to answering 'Yes' or 'No'. This can provide more information if a person has previously used drugs, and can gain information about how much they used and why they started using drugs, for example. This produces greater ecological validity as it relates to their real experiences. As the surveys rely on self-report, the data obtained may not always be accurate. People may respond in a socially desirable way as they may not want their true attitudes or behaviour to be known. Individuals may not give an honest account of, for example, why they use drugs for fear of being viewed negatively by the researchers. Socially desirable responses can then create inaccurate results.

The use of questionnaires facilitates a large sample size. This makes the conclusions of the study more representative of the wider population, which allows researchers to have a wider understanding of drug use beyond a small sample population. Those who agree to complete the survey may not be representative of all who originally took part, or of the wider population. The survey may also result in a biased population as only those who are willing to talk about drugs will volunteer to take part, and these individuals may have different attitudes from those who decline to participate.

Human research ethics

As with all research, health studies should follow a number of strict ethical guidelines. These include:

1 Protection of the participant

Asking drug users about their own experiences, including their reasons for drug use, may be distressing for them. This may result in them recalling painful memories. If people use drugs to avoid dealing with painful memories, as can be the case for some, asking these questions may potentially increase their drug use, as they take more drugs to forget the memories brought up in the study. Alternatively, it has been argued by researchers, that some drug users find it helpful to talk about their experiences, even if it causes them distress. Even if they become distressed within the research, this does not always result in them regretting taking part. Researchers, however, have a duty to consider the level of potential emotional distress on participants.

2 Confidentiality and privacy

The duty of the researcher is to protect the participant and maintain a level of confidentiality. However, depending on the nature of the study, the participant may disclose information about illegal activities and the researcher needs to have a clear understanding of how they plan to deal with this information, and communicate such plans to the participants before the start of the study. Disclosure of illegal activities to the police may prevent the participant from disclosing information in the study, resulting in limited information being obtained. This will affect the validity of the findings. Alternatively, the researcher needs to consider their duties as a responsible citizen in terms of disclosing the information potentially to protect the participant and other individuals.

3 Consent

Drug users may not have **capacity** to make fully informed consent, due to being under the influence of substances. This may be temporary at the time of intoxication and they may be able to give full consent if asked when sober. Additionally, there is the potential for the effects of drug use to have resulted in cognitive impairments, making it difficult to obtain informed consent when sober. Their concentration, for example, may be limited when the study is being explained to them, resulting in them being unsure about what they are being asked to do. While the ability to give consent is not exclusively an issue for those under the influence of substances, it creates an additional consideration when designing research to ensure that capacity to give consent is present among the participants.

> **Key term**
>
> **Capacity:** a person's maximum ability to perform a task. This may include the extent to which a person is able to receive and retain information, due to mental ability or other factors affecting their cognitive functioning.

> **Taking it further**
>
> There are a number of interesting articles available on the Internet or in journals that discuss the sensitive nature of ethics in research, for example, Bell and Salmon (2012) 'Good Intentions and Dangerous Assumptions: Research Ethics Committees and Illicit Drug Use Research' in *Research Ethics*, 8, (4), pages 191–199. This is a particularly interesting one, but there are others. Familiarise yourself with some of the specific ethical issues relevant to research in this population. It is also helpful to consider general ethical principles and consider how they relate specifically to drug research.

Cross-cultural research

Cross-cultural research relates to studies that take place in a number of different cultural settings in order to establish patterns or differences among the differing populations. In health psychology, it is particularly useful in understanding if different attitudes and behaviours influence alcohol or drug use. One consideration when undertaking cross-cultural research in relation to drugs concerns the different measures used to determine substance use disorders and cultural attitudes towards substance use. As with mental health, there are differences in the symptoms or behaviours required for a diagnosis of substance use disorders.

Attitudes towards substances also change among cultures. For example, khat is a stimulant drug, producing effects similar to amphetamine, that has been made illegal in England and Wales and use in such countries is likely to have low levels of social acceptance. In countries such as Yemen and Somalia, however, khat is used in social contexts and dates back thousands of years. Its use is not restricted in many countries. To attempt to determine attitudes towards khat use is, therefore, likely to differ among these cultures. The findings of one culture may have limited applicability to other cultures. This may be true of other substances.

Cross-cultural research can also consider religious differences. Some religions disapprove of substance use, including the use of alcohol, for example Islam. To undertake research in a predominantly Muslim area would be likely to produce very different findings from in an area that is much more multicultural. When undertaking cross-cultural research, it is, therefore, important to consider the characteristics and attitudes of the cultures being studied prior to making attempts to generalise this to other cultures.

> **Exam tip**
>
> You will not be expected to know lots of information about substances other than those on the specification: alcohol, nicotine and heroin. However, you can use your knowledge of other substances, such as khat, to provide a depth to your arguments, in this case in relation to different cultures. The emphasis is on showing your understanding of different cultures, and not necessarily other drugs.

Link

For more information on quantitative data analysis and the use of inferential statistical tests, including Mann-Whitney U test and Wilcoxon Signed Rank test, see the Methods section of Topic 2: *Cognitive psychology*.

For information on other inferential statistical tests, including Spearman's rho, see the Methods section in Topic 3: *Biological psychology*.

For information on qualitative data analysis, including grounded theory, see the Methods section of Topic 2: *Cognitive psychology*.

For information on chi-squared see the Methods section of Topic 4: *Learning theories*.

Maths tip

Often when discussing quantitative data, you may be making reference to a number that actually represents a unit of something, such as time, cigarettes, etc. It is important when talking about a unit of measurement that you specify what the unit is. This clearly shows that you understand the study or data that you are talking about.

Nature–nurture debate

One way in which cross-cultural research can be used is to explore whether a person's substance use behaviour is determined by nature or by nurture. There are ongoing discussions as to whether it is the environment or a person's predisposed characteristics that contributes to substance use. By undertaking twin studies in which individuals have been raised apart, in different cultures, it is possible to explore further this debate.

Substance use is relatively universal in most cultures, with individuals across cultures engaging in drug-taking behaviour. The notable difference is the type of drug taken among these cultures. For example, khat has a high level of usage among African populations, compared to western cultures. This is noted even when individuals from such cultures moved to other areas. There is an increase in khat use, for example, within the United Kingdom, which reflects the increased African population. This reflects the nurture debate in which culture is influential on drug choice, even with migration.

The Rastafari movement is a form of spirituality originating from Jamaica. As part of their religious beliefs, Rastafarians advocate the use of cannabis as a demonstration of their faith and consider smoking cannabis a spiritual act. Cannabis use therefore forms a significant part of their culture and the way in which they have been nurtured and have developed their spiritual beliefs.

Kendler et al. (2012) found a relationship between genetics and drug use when investigating adoptive children. They found a two-fold increase in drug use among adopted children whose biological parents used drugs. Risk also was higher in the biological siblings of adopted children who abused drugs – both full siblings and half siblings. There was a trend towards an increased risk of drug abuse in adopted children if their adoptive parents had abused drugs, but it was not significant, suggesting some environmental influence, but to a lesser extent than genetics.

Data analysis

Quantitative data

Within health psychology research you will be required to gather information and look for statistical relationships between different variables, that is, the relationship between individual characteristics and demographics and their substance use behaviour. For example, there may be an expectation that you can determine which amount of alcohol intake is more common among young adults by looking at tables that report the frequencies of behaviours (frequency tables).

Similarly, it is necessary to have familiarity with other quantitative data collected such as range and standard deviation. Imagine you have been asked to interpret a table that shows how many alcoholic drinks a group of 30 young adults drink in an average week. It is possible that the answers will vary greatly, with some not drinking any alcohol to others drinking much more often. The range would be the difference between the highest score and the lowest score reported by the participants. In this case, the range could be from 0 units per week to 20 units per week. The standard deviation in this example would show how much the amount of alcohol reported by the participants deviates from the mean number of units drunk by the group as a whole.

Qualitative data

In health psychology, thematic analysis may involve looking at attitudes to people who drink alcohol or use drugs, or possibly analysing some of the self-reported reasons why people chose to take drugs. Qualitative data analysis goes beyond understanding how many people take drugs, or other numerical type data, but is able to more closely examine the underlying reasons why people engage in drug misuse.

8.3 Studies
Learning outcomes

In this section, you will learn about one classic study:

- Olds and Milner (1954) – a study into the effect of brain stimulation in rats on reinforcing behaviour

and three contemporary studies, from which you will need to choose one to learn about:

- Mundt et al. (2012) – a study into the effect of alcohol use among friends on personal drinking behaviours
- Dixit et al. (2012) – an investigation into individual characteristics associated with alcohol use
- Pengpid et al. (2013) – a study into the effectiveness of alcohol treatment interventions.

Positive reinforcement produced by electrical stimulation of septal area and other regions of rat brain (Olds and Milner, 1954)

The research of James Olds and Peter Milner provided some of the first key evidence for the existence of certain regions in the brain that process reward, or positive reinforcement. The study conducted was actually designed to investigate systems regulating sleep. They were stimulating different parts of the rats' brains to try to identify the brain systems that regulated their sleep. The stimulation was undertaken in a cage. As part of the experiment, they observed one of their rats returning to the location within the cage where this particular stimulation had been administered. They interpreted this as the rat finding the stimulation experience pleasurable, which is why the rat returned to the place where it had experienced the pleasure. This persuaded Olds and Milner to develop a specific research design to look at why this was happening, and where exactly in the brain the rats were being stimulated.

Aim

To explore whether electrical brain stimulation acts as a positive reinforcement in rats.

Procedure

Fifteen, male, hooded rats were used, each weighing approximately 250g at the start of the experiment. Electrodes were implanted in the brains of the rats under anaesthesia, and fastened to the skull using screws. The electrodes were inserted into different parts of the brain for each rat. Rats were given three days to recover from the implantation before being tested. The electrodes were connected to an electrical lead suspended from the ceiling of the cage. This was designed so that the electrodes had minimal interference with the health or free movement of the rats.

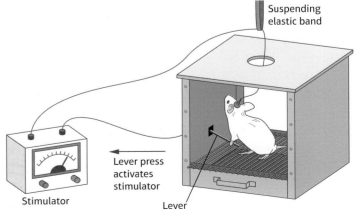

Figure 8.4 The Olds and Milner operant conditioning chamber for rats (Skinner-type box)

The rats were placed in an operant conditioning chamber (Skinner-type box). The box delivered an electric current to the rats' brains whenever they pressed the lever. For some tests, a time delay switch was used that switched off the electric current after a set amount of time if the rat continued to hold down the lever. The voltage used was just enough to observe a noticeable effect on the rats' behaviour (ranging from 0.5–5 volts). This varied between rats.

The rats were then subjected to two conditions:

1 Acquisition testing: This lasted for a total of 6–12 hours for the whole experiment. The stimulator was turned on so that an electric current would pass to the rats when they pressed the lever.

2 Extinction testing: This lasted for a total of 1–2 hours for the whole experiment. The stimulator was turned off so that no electric current would pass to the rats when they pressed the lever.

Rats were tested for between two and four days, with each day involving three hours of acquisition testing, followed by 30 minutes of extinction testing.

The amount of time the rat spent responding to the electrical stimulation in the acquisition phase was compared to the time spent not responding in the extinction phase. A behaviour was considered a 'response' if there was a clear behaviour shown at least once in 30 seconds. If there was no behavioural reaction within this time and, therefore, intervals of 30 seconds or more were noted without a behavioural reaction, this was considered to be a period of 'no response'. All the rats were killed after testing, in order to examine under a microscope which brain structures had been stimulated in the exercises.

Results

As some rats had 12 hours of acquisition and later rats had only 6 hours (as they were tested for less time), only the results in the first 6 hours for all rats were used in the analysis.

Table 8.1 shows the amount of time the rats spent responding in the acquisition and extinction phases (that is the number of 30-second intervals in which a behavioural reaction was seen) and the section of their brain being stimulated by the electrode.

The highest scores are found together in the central portion of the brain, the septal area. Rats with electrodes in this area spent more than 75 per cent of their acquisition time responding. They all spent less than 22 per cent of their extinction time responding. This shows that stimulating the septal area acts as a primary reward, making the rats press the lever more frequently when stimulated.

Those with lower percentage scores at the acquisition stage suggest that stimulation of that part of the brain is less rewarding. Areas of the brain with a 0 per cent response within the acquisition phase suggest there is a punishing effect if that part of the brain was stimulated.

Table 8.1 Response of rats in the acquisition and extinction phases

Number of rats	Location of electrode	Area of brain	Range of percentage of acquisition time spent responding	Range of percentage of extinction time spent responding
4	Septal	Fore brain	75–92%	6–21%
1	Corpus callosum	Fore brain	6%	3%
1	Hippocampus	Thalamic	11%	14%
1	Caudate	Fore brain	4%	4%
2	Cingulate	Thalamic	36–37%	9–10%
1	Medial lemniscus	Thalamic	0%	4%
1	Mammillothalamic tract	Thalamic	71%	9%
2	Medial geniculate	Mid brain	0%	21–31%
2	Tegmentum	Mid brain	2–77%	1–81%

Conclusion

Certain areas of the brain, if stimulated, have a rewarding effect on behaviour, particularly the septal area. This suggests that there is a specific 'reward centre' within the brain.

Evaluation

The study was conducted in a controlled environment in which all rats were implanted with electrodes and tested in the same way. For example, no reinforcement was used except the electrical stimulus, allowing the researchers to identify a cause and effect relationship. This provided an environment in which external variables were minimised, thereby increasing the validity of the research findings. There were, however, variations in the voltage of the stimulation given to some rats. This introduces a possible inconsistency that may affect the results. This reduces the replicability of the study as future experiments may have rats that require different voltage amounts before they respond.

In spite of being lab reared, the setting of the experiment and conditions they were exposed to are not natural for a rat, for example wires attached to their skulls and being given electric shocks. This may have influenced their behaviour, so that what was observed was a reaction to the experimental conditions, rather than their behaviour being due to reinforcement.

The study provided a unique opportunity to explore the effect of drugs on animals, despite this not being the original aim of the study. It provides some insight into why humans return to behaviour they consider to be rewarding, although rats have a different brain structure from humans. There is no guarantee that the reward centres of the brain found in rats will also be found in humans.

The number of days the rats were tested for was reduced when the experimenters realised there was little difference in the results for each day of testing. This meant that later rats were subject to less testing. This minimised the harm caused to the later rats who were tested for a shorter amount of time and, therefore, is considered to be more ethical than if they had carried on with their original research aim of testing for longer.

At no time during the experiment were the rats deprived of food or water (except when in the Skinner box) and were allowed to eat normally. As a result, the researchers protected the needs of the animals. Ethical guidelines would be supportive of this approach, and the study would not be considered to have breached any ethical guidance in relation to the storage and use of animals in research.

The researchers monitored whether the rats showed any signs of pain after the implantation of the electrode and during the testing phase. As there were no signs of this, it suggests the rats did not directly suffer. This further acts as a control to make sure the behaviour was not a result of pain. It also shows consideration of the welfare of the animals being used within the study, as does the fact that only a small number of rats were used to minimise the harm caused to the species.

The number of rats with electrodes in each area of the brain differed, with some areas of the brain only being observed in one rat. The same findings may not be found if an even number of rats were investigated for each area of the brain. It could, therefore, be argued that the sample size was insufficient to provide meaningful results or to be able to draw conclusions from the experiment. This means that animals were unnecessarily harmed for the research, particularly as the rats were destroyed following the experiment in order for Olds and Milner to look at the brain structure of the rats.

WIDER ISSUES AND DEBATES

The use of psychological knowledge in society

While the research is now over 60 years old, this study by Olds and Milner has paved the way for much investigation into the effect of deep brain stimulation to influence mood. Brain stimulation has since been used as a treatment for severe depression and to manage pain in extreme cases that are typically resistant to other medical interventions.

Exam tip

Olds and Milner (1954) is a named study in the specification. This means that you may be asked to provide quite a lot of detail about it. This could include describing or evaluating the study (or both). When you are learning studies like this, which have a lot of statistics involved, try to remember the key information. It is unlikely you will ever be asked to remember every percentage for all the variables. If you focus on remembering the results, in exam conditions you will be able to look at this data and remind yourself of the conclusions. If you cannot remember the exact figures, give an approximate figure, as it is better than not giving one at all. In addition, be sure to know how Olds and Milner collected the data and the methodology they used, as this can help in evaluating the study.

Peer selection and influence effects on adolescent alcohol use: a stochastic actor-based model (Mundt et al., 2012)

Many adolescents start drinking alcohol from a young age. There is a relationship between a young age of first drinking alcohol and alcohol dependence in adulthood. There are other risky adolescent behaviours associated with young drinking, including marijuana use, having sex with multiple partners and academic underperformance. Attempts to understand what motivates and influences an adolescent to start drinking at a young age can be informative to minimise future risks. It is possible to develop interventions for adolescents that are relevant to their needs if their needs can be greater understood.

Aim

The study aimed to answer two specific questions:

1   Do adolescents select friends with similar alcohol use?

2   Do adolescents adjust their alcohol consumption to fit with the alcohol consumption level of their friends?

The researchers believed that these questions would be answered affirmatively within their study.

Procedure

The study analysed data from an existing study. The data was originally collected from school children (13–18 years old) using a stratified sampling method to choose high schools and middle schools that were considered representative of American schools in terms of region, funding and ethnicity. A total of 2563 students were used in the study (Wave 1).

The students completed an interview and their parents also completed a survey. Researchers collected data, including expectations for the future, self-esteem and risk behaviours, such as alcohol use. One question the students were asked was who their five male and five female best friends were.

Twelve months later (Wave 2), the children completed another survey. In this survey they were asked similar questions, including the frequency of alcohol consumption over the past year: 'How often did you consume alcohol in the past year?' Categorical responses included never, 1 or 2 times, 3 to 12 times, monthly but not weekly, weekly and more than once a week. Once again, they were asked to name their five best male and five best female friends. A total of 2299 students were used in the follow up study.

Table 8.2 The changes in reported alcohol use among the individual students in the 12-month period between waves

Alcohol use	Wave 1 (n=2563) (%)	Wave 2 (n=2299) (%)
None	49.6	54.0
1–2 times	18.3	14.1
3–12 times	14.2	12.3
More than monthly, less than weekly	8.3	8.7
Weekly or more often	9.6	10.9

Results

The results were analysed looking at individual alcohol use and then in relation to their reported friendship groups.

Reported friendship groups:

- friendship selection was associated with similarity in alcohol consumption

- students were more likely to choose as friends other students of similar age, gender and ethnicity

- adolescents were more likely to nominate as friends others who drank similarly to themselves

- friend alcohol use was correlated with increased personal alcohol use.

Conclusion

One factor that influences who adolescents choose as their friends is similarities in alcohol use. This suggests that friends have little influence on alcohol use once the friendship is in place.

Peer selection plays a major role in alcohol use behaviour among adolescent friends. When working with adolescents to change their alcohol use, consideration needs to be given to their social network.

Evaluation

A large number of students were used within the sample, and were selected due to being considered representative of the wider American population of this age. This makes the findings more representative to the wider population as a wider range of people in society have been included within the research population.

The current study did not collect their own data. Instead they used secondary data, which was gathered during previous research. This can create difficulties in identifying patterns and trends. However, they were able to use the raw data from the original study, rather than having to look at data that had already been interpreted. This minimises any bias effects from the original study.

Alcohol use was self-reported within the study. There remains the possibility that the students may have answered differently from their actual alcohol use in order to provide socially desirable answers. This is particularly pertinent considering the participants were all under the legal age of consent to drink alcohol in America. Participants may have had reservations about disclosing any engagement in such behaviour as a result and, therefore, misrepresented their alcohol intake.

The study only looked at alcohol use as a factor influencing friendship selection, to the detriment of any other possible explanation. There are many other reasons why someone may choose a friend, which are not captured in this research. Other explanations may have a greater influence on friendship selection than alcohol use, leading to alternative conclusions about the effect of alcohol on friendships. Correlatory research, such as this, cannot account for other variables that are not directly being investigated.

Understanding the influences that contribute to the drinking behaviour of an adolescent is important to considering how to prevent underage drinking or excessive drinking in the future. Alcohol intervention strategies can be designed, which include encouraging the person to select friendships carefully to minimise future drinking.

Biosocial determinants of alcohol risk behaviour: An epidemiological study in urban and rural communities of Aligarh, Uttar Pradesh (Dixit et al., 2012)

Alcohol research is currently prominent throughout the world due to the large number of individuals engaging in alcohol consumption to the extent that it is harmful to their behaviour or others around them. Alcohol reduction campaigns are interested in understanding if certain populations are more vulnerable to alcohol use. With this information, they can target the campaigns to those where it is likely to have the greatest impact.

Aim

Dr Sumeet Dixit and colleagues wanted to find out the prevalence and patterns of alcohol use among populations from different demographic backgrounds. They were interested in finding out whether there was certain demographic information, such as age, socio-economic status, religion, etc. that could be associated with increased alcohol use.

WIDER ISSUES AND DEBATES

Ethics
Participants of this research were allocated randomly to either the experimental or the control condition. This raises ethical issues; if the experimental condition had worked better at reducing alcohol consumption compared to the control, the research could be criticised for deliberately exposing control participants to harm by denying them an intervention with the potential to help them.

Procedure

The study was a cross-sectional survey. It took place over one year and included 848 participants, all over the age of 15. A household survey was conducted in urban and rural health training centres. An equal number of participants came from urban health training centres and rural ones. Each household was selected randomly and a maximum of two people from each, also selected randomly, were asked to consent.

When randomly selecting which households to approach, every tenth household in a particular area was approached. A structured interview schedule was used. This asked for baseline information about the person and their family, information about any use of any form of alcohol and a final section asking about patterns of alcohol use. The researchers defined what they meant by a 'current alcohol user' (if they have used alcohol in the past month) and an 'ever user' (if they had ever used alcohol in their lifetime).

Results

The results were as follows.

- 13.4 per cent of the sample had used alcohol at some point in their life.

- Only 43 (5.07 per cent) had used alcohol in the past month, with 71 (8.37 per cent) categorised as being 'ever users'.

- 734 participants (86.6 per cent) denied ever using alcohol.

Chi-square analysis was undertaken on the data to look for characteristics that correlated with alcohol use. Some of those characteristics are included in the table.

Table 8.3 Characteristics associated with alcohol use. NB All p values were two-tailed and values of <0.05 were considered to indicate statistical significance

Factor	Alcohol use		Chi-squared test
	Yes	No	
Age group			
15–25	6	224	$\chi^2 = 14.547$, df = 1 p <0.0001
26–40	71	308	
41–60	17	119	
60+	20	83	
Marital status			
Married	91	531	$\chi^2 = 5.33$, df = 2 p >0.05
Unmarried	15	163	
Widow/divorce/alone	8	40	
Education			
Illiterate	46	345	$\chi^2 = 5.4$, df = 3 p >0.05
Up to high school	56	297	
Intermediate/diploma/graduate	12	80	
Above graduate	0	12	

Other significant findings included the following points.

- No women had any history of alcohol use.

- Hindu religion was statistically associated with greater alcohol use when compared to Islam, which may be due to restrictions placed on Muslims regarding alcohol.

- Alcohol use was seen to be significantly associated with parental alcohol use, with higher alcohol use among those whose parents also had a history of alcohol use.

- Alcohol use was seen to be more prevalent among subjects who were unemployed, skilled or unskilled labourers as compared to subjects who were professionals or well paid.

- Rural residence was significantly associated with greater alcohol use than urban areas.

- Alcohol use was significantly associated with lower socio-economic status.

Alcohol users cited peer pressure as the main reason why they started using alcohol (86.1 per cent of the alcohol users gave this as a reason). Other influences include:

- curiosity (68 per cent)

- social acceptance (25 per cent)

- unemployment (2.8 per cent)

- health benefit (2.8 per cent)

- anxiety/stress (1.4 per cent).

Conclusion

While the proportion of the sample that drank alcohol was low, there are a number of factors that correlate with increased alcohol use, most notably age, social class and gender. There is value in targeting the vulnerable populations to protect them from future alcohol use.

Evaluation

Although adolescents aged between 15 and 18 years were included within the study, consent was obtained from both the parent and the individual for this age range. This ensures that ethical guidelines relating to younger participants and consent were adhered to. All participants consented to the study after being told about the nature, purpose and procedure of the study. This allowed them to give informed consent.

The study considered a wide range of characteristics that may influence drinking behaviour. From this, researchers are more able to draw conclusions about individual characteristics that show a relationship with alcohol use than if just one variable had been investigated. This makes the data more reliable. The researchers used a large population, making for a more representative sample from which they can draw conclusions. Having more participants means that they can say with greater confidence that the finding are applicable to the culture in which the research was undertaken. This increases the reliability of the findings.

The study is based on self-report data from the participants. Those completing the data may be motivated to either over-report their alcohol use in an attempt to help the researcher, or under-report their alcohol use to avoid potential stigma or judgement. As a result, the data collected using self-report, due to its subjective nature, may be biased, providing inaccurate data on which the conclusions are then based.

The study only focuses on the demographics of individuals to understand their drinking behaviour. While it identified why people may start to drink alcohol, it fails to make any suggestions about how to address the motivators. It is important when looking at behaviour change to understand as many factors as possible that contribute to why someone starts and continues to drink alcohol, in order to target the problem behaviour most effectively. Furthermore, it is not possible to change many of a person's demographics. This may lead the individuals who fit those characteristics to believe it is inevitable that they will start to drink, leading to the self-fulfilling prophecy.

Cross-sectional studies, while they often look at many different factors, are descriptive in nature. There is no manipulation of variables and, therefore, can only be observational, studying events or phenomena that are already occurring. As a result, cross-sectional research can only suggest relationships and are not able to identify 'cause and effect' relationships. This can then be used to make recommendations for future research, but in themselves they cannot be considered causal.

WIDER ISSUES AND DEBATES

Culture

This study is an example of research undertaken in a culture that may be very different from many. Such research helps to compare if substance use behaviours in countries such as the UK are similar to that in other countries throughout the world. They can, therefore, be very important in developing a wider understanding of substance use, in this case alcohol, throughout the world.

When there are differences in research findings in different countries or cultures, it leads researchers to wonder why the findings are different. Is there something about a specific culture that makes someone more vulnerable to substance use or protects them from getting involved in substances? Understanding these questions can be essential in supporting individuals from different cultures in accessing effective treatment, even if they undertake the treatment in a different country from the one that influences their culture. This is particularly important considering the increase in multicultural societies.

Screening and brief interventions for hazardous and harmful alcohol use among hospital outpatients in South Africa: results from a randomized controlled trial (Pengpid et al., 2013)

Increasing attention has been given to the use of alcohol among the general population in the past decade. This is in part due to the increasing alcohol-related health challenges being faced by medical agencies worldwide, such as the NHS. Understanding the benefit of interventions will allow for the introduction of wide-scale treatment to minimise the negative effects, on the individual and agencies.

Hospitals have widespread access to patient populations each year and, therefore, are a valuable location for undertaking interventions to establish effective treatment. This study was undertaken in South Africa, but it reflects a lot of the challenges faced by medical professionals around the world.

Aim

Supa Pengpid and her colleagues wanted to investigate the effectiveness of brief interventions in reducing alcohol intake.

Procedure

Adult outpatients to a South African hospital were screened for alcohol problems, using an alcohol use questionnaire called the AUDIT, over a 16-month time period. All visitors were asked to complete a consent form to participate in the research while they were waiting for their appointments in various hospital departments. Those who consented completed the AUDIT. In total, 1419 people completed the audit. A second researcher scored the AUDIT.

Of the 1419 participants, 392 (27.6 per cent) were identified as having hazardous or harmful alcohol use (scored between 8 and 19 for men and 7–19 for women on the AUDIT). These individuals were randomly allocated by Researcher 2 to an experimental or a control group. Both groups included the same number of participants (196 participants). Researcher 2 administered the interventions to the two groups.

The research conditions were as follows.

- The experimental group received one 20-minute counselling session about excessive drinking, personalised feedback on their AUDIT results and a health education leaflet. The counselling included introducing them to problem-solving skills and making them realise their drinking behaviour was harmful.

- The control group was given a health education leaflet to read about responsible drinking.

The researchers excluded people who were already receiving alcohol treatment and those with mental impairment, or were pregnant. People who scored more than 19 on the AUDIT were not asked to participate as this suggested their alcohol use was more problematic. They were referred elsewhere.

Participants were offered 6- and 12-month follow-up appointments, where they were reassessed by Researcher 1, using the AUDIT. Researcher 1 did not at any point know which intervention they had been offered. A total of 282 participants (72 per cent of the sample) attended the 12-month follow-up appointment.

Participants were given money for transport to attend the two follow-up appointments. The questionnaires were administered either in English or Tswana at each stage.

Results

A Mann-Whitney U test was used for continuous data. A chi-squared test was used to examine categorical data for relationships between the two groups.

Table 8.4 The changes in AUDIT scores over time and between the two groups

Variable	Time	Control group	Experimental/ Intervention group
AUDIT total score Mean (Standard Deviation)	Baseline	11.3 (3.4)	12.7 (3.4)
	6 months	6.3 (4.6)	7.0 (4.5)
	12 months	7.3 (6.8)	7.2 (5.8)

Table 8.4 shows that, over time, there was a statistically significant reduction in AUDIT scores for both groups. This shows they had reduced the level of their alcohol use to a less harmful level. There was no difference between the two groups, so receiving interventions or a leaflet had equal effect. This shows that the interventions themselves did not have any more of an effect on drinking behaviours than being given information about responsible drinking.

Conclusion

Health education is sufficient to create behaviour change in those with hazardous and harmful drinking. The researchers also concluded that simply the process of undergoing alcohol screening, in addition to being given health information, might cause a reduction in drinking.

Evaluation

Two different researchers were used to complete the questionnaires and to administer the treatment. As a result, the researchers had limited influence on the information recorded. This reduces any potential researcher bias, which can occur when the same researcher gathers all the data and is fully aware of the aims of the study. As a result, the two-researcher approach used makes the findings more valid as the potential for bias has been minimised. Similarly, participants were randomly allocated to either the experimental or control group to minimise bias. In the same way as the researcher approach minimised researcher bias, this will minimise participant bias, once again increasing the validity of any subsequent research outcomes.

The AUDIT is a self-report questionnaire. Participants may have provided information that was not fully accurate to minimise the amount of their alcohol use, therefore giving biased information. Discussing alcohol use may carry stigma with some individuals who, therefore, under-report their drinking behaviour. Also, some participants may over-disclose and exaggerate their alcohol intake, as they may want to please the researcher, and think this is how they should respond. Under- or over-reporting of alcohol behaviour has implications for the accuracy of the data obtained.

The study had ethical approval before they started the research to ensure that all ethical guidelines were followed. This included allowing individuals the right to withdraw. Some participants used this right, and not everyone who agreed to participate at the start of the research completed the follow-up sessions. This identifies that protection was in place for participants who did not want to continue with the study, particularly considering the sensitive nature of the information being disclosed. However, the behaviour of those who did not complete the follow-up sessions may have changed the outcome of the results. It is not known if there were any similarities of alcohol use among those who did choose not to continue, which, if they had continued with the study, might have resulted in a different conclusion for the study.

The characteristics of the participants were not controlled, as it was an opportunity sample. Differences within the participants may have influenced the outcomes. Personality types can influence who participates in research studies, with some people more willing to agree to disclose personal information than others.

The research was undertaken in South Africa. There may be cultural or societal differences that make it difficult to apply the findings of the study to other countries. When interpreting the conclusions of the study, it is only reliable to do so within the context of South African cultures, rather than extrapolating it to other areas of the world.

WIDER ISSUES AND DEBATES

The use of psychological knowledge within society

The findings of this study can be used to consider which interventions to use with individuals with problematic drinking behaviour. It would suggest that there is little value in investing in brief interventions when health promotion is equally as effective. This, therefore, demonstrates potential cost savings for the NHS, allowing time and effort to be redirected into other areas of alcohol misuse.

8.4 Key questions
Learning outcomes

In this section, you will learn about:

● one key issue and its relevance to society today

● concepts, theories and research used in health psychology to explain the key issue.

Can we encourage the cessation of smoking?

A key issue of relevance to today's society relates to what a health psychologist can do to effectively promote and encourage non-smoking behaviour. In order to be able to address the smoking behaviour, it is important to consider how the person was influenced to smoke. Smoking behaviour can be the result of a number of different experiences. An individual may have family members who engage in similar behaviour, or their role models, either peers or on television, may be smokers. This can influence a person to try to smoke for themselves, as they want to be like their models. In the same manner as the individual has been persuaded to smoke due to observation or influence, smoking cessation needs to consider how to persuade the individual to stop smoking.

The elaboration likelihood model of persuasion suggests that individuals can be encouraged to stop smoking if they are initially motivated to do so and are then provided with a clear message about the behaviour change with minimal distractions. Health providers should, therefore, consider health campaigns that are concise, without lots of additional information that may appear less relevant. The Hovland-Yale model of persuasion would support this approach, by indicating that the content of the message given is significant to encourage behaviour change. It would advocate the use of a two-sided, balanced argument outlining the benefit of smoking cessation, and the implications of this. Smoking campaigns such as Stoptober are initiatives of the Department of Health and the National Health Service. These agencies have credibility and are, therefore, more likely to be influential, as health experts, than an organisation or individual who does not have such influence. Ensuring that the credibility of the source is clearly understood will maximise its influence on individuals.

Health campaigns need to consider the cognition underpinning the smoking behaviour in order to target such cognitions within the campaign. It is important that the health message is pitched to the individuals at such a level that it creates sufficient fear of the harmful effects of the behaviour to encourage behaviour change. However, to generate too high a level of fear, such as using graphic images of the harm caused by smoking, may not have the desired effect on behaviour change, as shown by Janis and Feshbach (1953).

The Hovland-Yale model assumes that simply being given a message can be persuasive, and this is not always the case. Telling someone of the dangers of smoking and that to stop smoking would be beneficial, may be insufficient to result in behavioural change. Once the individual has recognised the need to change their behaviour, the way in which they are supported to do so is just as influential in ensuring the behaviour change actually occurs. Studies by Pengpid et al. (2013) have shown that an awareness of the risks of substance use can be as effective as a brief treatment intervention. This could be achieved via a health promotion campaign such as Stoptober. Such campaigns need to appeal to the audience and try to avoid making the person feel forced to change, in order for them to be effective.

It is possible to treat nicotine addiction in a number of ways. Before treatment begins, however, it is essential that the person is ready to make the change, as this will help them to overcome any difficulties they experience when trying to stop smoking. Hypnotherapy has been shown to be effective as this gently persuades the person that they do need to stop smoking. This can be supported by medicinal treatments that reduce the physical withdrawal, such as nicotine replacement drugs. Such treatments may, however, not be available to everyone as they may be costly to the smoker. Treatment options also need to consider the physiological dependency that smoking creates, such as addressing the reduction in concentration. They will also need to manage the psychological dependency of addressing the behaviour they associate with smoking, for example after certain activities or in certain situations.

While such treatments help with the physical aspect of dependency, it is also important that a person receives ongoing support for their cravings, as these can be experienced for many months after the withdrawal symptoms have been addressed. Without an all-round (holistic) approach to smoking cessation, it is highly likely the person will smoke again due to the addictive and reinforcing powers of nicotine.

In order, therefore, to successfully support smoking cessation, consideration should be given to the reasons why the individual chooses to smoke, their cognition that maintains the smoking behaviour and that can be used to change their beliefs about smoking, and appropriate treatment options. Health campaigns, therefore, need to be carefully targeted to the specific audience in order to be meaningful to the individual. Campaigns and treatment options that do not appeal to the individual are unlikely to be effective in supporting smoking cessation.

Exam tip

Key issues may be presented in different ways in exam papers from year to year, even if the same general topic is used. If you have prepared large chunks of information for a key issue worded in a specific way, it may not fit with the question, and this could limit the number of marks you can access.

A better solution than trying to remember short essays off by heart is to learn a number of key headings that will prompt you to draw on your knowledge of the topic. This will maximise the chances of you answering the question in front of you and avoid you filling up your memory with an essay that may or may not appear on the exam paper.

Taking it further

The title 'Health Psychologist' is a protected title and is considered to be a specialist area of psychology. The role of a health psychologist involves undertaking specific skills and having specific knowledge. Understanding substance use is just one part of this role.

Look on the BPS website to explore the varied work of a health psychologist and to develop your knowledge of their interests in supporting positive behaviour change, irrespective of the behaviour. Think about how else a health psychologist can address substance use that has not been addressed in detail in this chapter.

8.5 Practical investigation
Learning outcomes

In this section, you will learn about:

- key stages of designing and conducting ethical psychological research
- how to analyse and present the findings of the research undertaken.

Conducting health psychology research

When conducting research, it is important to follow all research guidelines as a psychologist. The planning stage of a practical investigation will ensure that the investigation follows these guidelines and is crucial to any research.

Within health psychology, key investigation approaches include using:

- questionnaires
- interviews
- content analysis.

This section follows a practical content analysis from planning through to analysis and a discussion of the findings. It serves as an example only, and is not the only available investigation option.

Aim

This example investigation aims to conduct a content analysis to investigate drug references in television programmes before and after the watershed. The 'watershed' is a broadcasting deadline that prevents television programmes with adult content, including making reference to or showing drug-taking behaviour, from being shown on television before 9.00 pm.

Research question

Is there a difference in the exposure to drug references in programmes before and after the watershed?

Hypotheses

Alternative hypothesis

There will be more drug references in television programmes after the watershed than before it.

This is a directional hypothesis because legislation would predict that more drug references would be found after the watershed because that is when they are permitted to be shown.

Null hypothesis

There will be no difference in the number of drug references made before and after the watershed, and any difference found will be due to chance factors.

Planning the content analysis/practical

A key consideration in planning the investigation is what is meant by 'references to drugs'. It is important that this is operationalised so that if the study should be repeated, another person would know what you were looking for when watching the programmes and will be able to follow the same guidance. For example, you may want to consider specific words that may be spoken that relate to drug use. Are you looking at references to specific drugs, or all drugs? If all drugs, does this include alcohol? Similarly, you should outline the behaviours that you consider to be relevant to drugs.

The procedure should clearly outline what you are planning on doing and at what stage. That is, in what order are you going to do each step? Areas to consider include the following.

- Which programme are you going to watch and for how long? Are you just going to watch one episode?

- What exactly are you going to be looking for?

- How are you going to record the findings?

- How do you plan to analyse the data you collect?

It will be helpful to think about how many programmes you plan to watch – will it be just one programme, or a variety? Consider how you are going to record the data. Would a frequency chart be sufficient? In addition to the content analysis, you might want to collect qualitative data, such as specifically what was said by a television character. What is your overall plan for analysing the data?

For this example, one programme will be viewed on a specified Monday night before the watershed, and a different programme will be watched after the watershed. A frequency chart will be used to monitor how often specific references to substances are made. Focus will be on references to cigarettes and alcohol.

Once a detailed plan has been drawn up, only then is it possible to conduct the investigation.

Behavioural categories/coding

Operationalising the data to be collected is essential in ensuring clarity of the data collection. This makes the findings more reliable. In this example, it is necessary to be clear about what is considered to be a drug reference.

Specifying the behaviours to be observed is called operationalisation. The following behaviours or references from actors will be observed and noted on the frequency chart:

- smoking

- going to the pub

- buying cigarettes

- talking about wanting/needing a cigarette

- drinking alcohol at home.

Every time one of these behaviours is observed, it will be noted on the tally chart. At the end of the programme, the tallies will be added up.

Inter-rater reliability

Subjectivity will be reduced by having more than one individual watching television before and after the watershed and rating the number of drug references. The researchers can then compare their findings. When using more than one researcher, the need to operationalise the data being collected is even more important. Accuracy of coding will be increased by researchers being specific about what would be a drug reference that might be seen on television. The tallies gathered by both raters can be compared to check for agreement. The use of inter-rater reliability will ensure reliability of data.

In this content analysis, a whole episode of each soap will be watched. The tally chart will be filled in as the behaviour is observed. An example of a tally chart is shown below. Other individuals will also watch the same television programme on the same night and will be looking for the same behaviours. They will record the data on their copy of the tally chart.

Table 8.5 Example of a tally chart

	An actor smoking	An actor going to the pub	An actor buying cigarettes or talking about wanting to smoke a cigarette	An actor drinking alcohol at home
Programme 1 (before watershed)				
Programme 2 (after watershed)				

Ethical considerations

If you are undertaking the research yourself and the research involves watching a television programme, what ethical issues may occur? As this example is looking at television programmes prior to the watershed, there are no ethical issues in undertaking a content analysis of programmes. However, the raters should be old enough to be permitted to watch the programmes, particularly the one after the watershed. It is, however, possible that the research may uncover something that is considered socially sensitive. For example, that there are a large number of drug references that children are exposed to on television. If this occurs, this knowledge will be for the good of society as it can act as an agent of change.

Review the BPS guidance on conducting research and use this as a checklist to make sure you have considered all areas of ethics. Check with your teacher that your procedure is ethical before proceeding with the investigation. This is more important if you are conducting a questionnaire or interview.

Analysing results

The data gathered from the study will be collated in quantitative data. For example, the number of times a drug reference was made on television, based on the specific behaviours outlined at the planning stage of the research. Quantitative data will allow you to undertake simplistic statistical analysis, as discussed in detail in previous topics. Any qualitative data collected will need to be translated into quantitative data so it can then be analysed statistically.

In this example, you may have created a tally chart similar to the one shown in Table 8.6.

Table 8.6 Tally chart for smoking/alcohol references in Programme 1 and Programme 2

	An actor smoking	An actor going to the pub	An actor buying cigarettes or talking about wanting to smoke a cigarette	An actor drinking alcohol at home
Programme 1 (before watershed)	III	IIII	I	II
Programme 2 (after watershed)	IIII	III	II	IIII

This tally chart shows that a range of drug references were made in both television programmes both before and after the watershed.

This can be seen more clearly when references to cigarettes and alcohol are totalled and presented in a 2X2 contingency table (see Table 8.7).

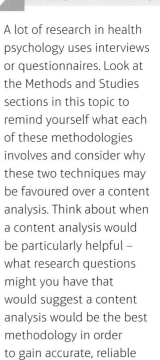

Taking it further

A lot of research in health psychology uses interviews or questionnaires. Look at the Methods and Studies sections in this topic to remind yourself what each of these methodologies involves and consider why these two techniques may be favoured over a content analysis. Think about when a content analysis would be particularly helpful – what research questions might you have that would suggest a content analysis would be the best methodology in order to gain accurate, reliable information that answers your research question?

Table 8.7 Contingency table for smoking/alcohol references in Programme 1 and Programme 2

	References to alcohol	References to nicotine	Total
Programme 1 (before watershed)	6	4	10
Programme 2 (after watershed)	7	6	13
Total	13	10	23

It is helpful to convert the tally chart into a visual record, such as a bar chart, to assist in the comparison of the data. A bar chart for the data in Figure 8.5 is shown below.

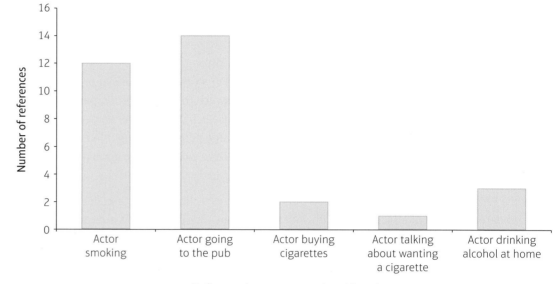

Figure 8.5 A bar graph to show the total number of drug references in a single episode of Programme 1 and Programme 2

Of the 23 references to drug use, 10 occurred before the watershed and 13 after the watershed. This may not seem a huge difference, but whether it is a significant difference or not can only really be established by conducting a chi-squared statistical test.

Chi-squared analysis

The procedure for a chi-squared analysis involves calculating the expected frequencies of the data being gathered. An expected frequency needs to be calculated for all four cells in the 2X2 contingency table, so it is useful to label each cell as a, b, c and d.

Table 8.8 Data frequencies for drug references in a single episode of each programme

Observed frequencies	References to alcohol		References to nicotine		Total
Programme 1 (before watershed)	Cell a	6	Cell b	4	10
Programme 2 (after watershed)	Cell c	7	Cell d	6	13
Total	13		10		23 (overall total)

Use the formula to calculate the expected frequencies for each cell.

1. Multiple the row total by the column total for each cell and divide this by the overall total.

    Cell a: 10 × 13 / 23 = 5.65   Cell c: 13 × 13 / 23 = 7.35

    Cell b: 10 × 10 / 23 = 4.35   Cell d: 13 × 10 / 23 = 5.65

2. For each cell subtract the expected frequencies from the observed frequencies for each cell.

    Cell a: 6 − 5.65 = 0.35   Cell c: 7 − 7.35 = −0.35

    Cell b: 4 − 4.35 = −0.35   Cell d: 6 − 5.65 = 0.35

3. Square the result for each cell calculations above.

    Cell a: $0.35^2 = 0.1225$ Cell c: $0.35^2 = 0.1225$

    Cell b: $-0.35^2 = 0.1225$ Cell d: $-0.35^2 = 0.1225$

4. Divide the sum of step 3 by the expected frequencies for each cell.

    Cell a: 0.1225 / 5.65 = 0.02   Cell c: 0.1225 / 7.35 = 0.02

    Cell b: 0.1225 / 4.35 = 0.03   Cell d: 0.1225 / 5.65 = 0.02

5. Find the sum total of all the scores calculated in step 4.

    0.02 + 0.03 + 0.02 + 0.02 = 0.09

    Chi-squared test statistic is 0.09.

This needs to be compared to a table of critical values for a chi-squared test in order to establish whether the findings are significant. Before using the critical value table, we need to calculate the degrees of freedom. This will give the figure needed to determine which row to follow in the table.

Degrees of freedom are calculated using the following formula: $df = (R–1)(C–1)$, where R refers to the total number of rows, in this case two cell rows, and C refers to the total number of columns, in this case two column cells, in the 2 × 2 contingency table.

$$df = (2–1) \times (2–1) = 1$$

Table 8.9 Critical values for a chi-squared test

Level of significance for a one tailed test			
	0.1	0.05	0.025
Level of significance for a two tailed test			
df	0.2	0.1	0.05
1	1.64	2.71	3.84
2	3.22	4.60	5.99

Calculated value of chi-square must be equal to or exceed the table (critical) value for significance at the level shown.

Drawing conclusions

The conclusions should be logical, based on the findings you have presented. The conclusions can be discussed briefly to avoid repeating the findings in detail. When discussing the conclusions, it is helpful to return to the original research question and hypothesis. You can then conclude whether the data supports or disproves the hypothesis.

This practical investigation proposed a directional hypothesis, so a one-tailed test will be used. The accepted level of significance in psychology is $p=0.05$, with $df = 1$, the critical value is 2.71. The calculated chi-square value = 0.09 must be equal to or exceed the critical value of 2.71, which it does not. Therefore the result is not significant at the significance level of 0.05. This means that there is no difference between references to drugs before and after the watershed, and the null hypothesis should be retained.

Discussion

Once the analysis has been conducted, you should present your findings in a way that is clearly understandable to the reader. The use of subheadings can help to ensure clarity within the discussion. When discussing findings, it is best to talk about all of them, including those that do not support the hypothesis. This shows a transparency of your research.

A discussion point within the current example may be: *It is noted that there were more references to drinking alcohol than there were to smoking, though there was only a small difference in the number of references made between alcohol and cigarettes. While there were a number of actors smoking on the programme, very few actually spoke about wanting a cigarette. The pub was heavily featured in the episode, with many actors going to the pub. This is where most of the alcohol observed was consumed, with very few actors drinking within their own home.*

One strength of this practical investigation was the use of inter-rater reliability. This means that the raters' scoring is compared for agreement. If there is good agreement between the tallies observed by the raters, inter-rater reliability can be established. A correlation can be conducted to establish the rate of agreement between the rates. A high positive correlation co-efficient shows good agreement. However, the process of quantifying the content of the television programmes may lose the meaningfulness of the data as it is converted into a numerical form. Additionally, only one episode for each television programme was analysed; it may be that the particular episode was dealing with a drug-related issue, which may have overinflated the depictions of such drugs being used. It would be a good suggestion for improvement to use more than one episode of each television programme to counteract this problem. We also have to consider whether the programmes analysed were representative of the content of programmes shown before and after the watershed. A suggestion for improvement would be to analyse a range of different genres of programmes both before and after the watershed to get a more generalisable sample.

8.6 Issues and debates (A level only)

Ethics

Many of the studies into the effects of substances use animals rather than humans as participants. This is due to the different ethical criteria for animal and human research subjects, with greater restrictions on human studies when there is the potential for humans to be harmed. Ethically, this is to ensure protection of the human species, but it can have implications in terms of how applicable the findings of animal studies are to human functioning. If human participants are used, the participants have to be voluntary drug users in order for the study to be ethically sound, as was the case with Blättler et al.'s (2002) study looking at heroin treatment and cocaine use.

Practical issues in the design and implementation of research

Research into drug misuse is particularly problematic when using either humans or animals in experiments. In addition to the ethical implications of administering drugs, and investigating withdrawal and tolerance effects, access to individuals who misuse drugs can be problematic, as there are access issues to vulnerable individuals. Another practical issue is whether honest information can be obtained from participants about their drug use. Drinking, smoking and drug taking are not socially desirable behaviours, so individuals are less likely to be honest about their use. The practical issue concerned with animal experimentation is the lack of generalisability of the findings to a human population.

Reductionism

Health psychology aims to explore and explain addiction from social and biological perspectives. One approach identifies how the people an individual socialises with, and their environment, can contribute to substance use. Alternatively, the role of neurotransmitters can affect how an individual reacts to substances, with explanations such as operant conditioning serving to maintain substance use. These explanations of addiction are taken from a singular perspective. This may, at times, overlook the complexity of human behaviour, where there may be more than one factor influencing substance use.

Comparisons between ways of explaining behaviour using different themes

Addiction is explained via key approaches, including biological, social and learning approaches. These differ substantially from each other in terms of how addiction occurs, as well as how addiction can be treated. Advocates from the biological approach argue that treatment for substance use should be medical, to address some of the biological influences of addiction. Alternatively, social and learning approaches advocate treatment that considers a person's environment, including their social circle, or how to provide positive reinforcement of behaviour that does not include substances. The direction taken by health campaigns is influenced by the psychological approach being attributed to substance use.

Psychology as a science

Health psychology uses a number of medical techniques to explore issues such as addiction. This includes brain scans that use highly technological processes, undertaken within strictly controlled settings. Brain scans help to establish causality, such as how substances influence the brain. It is possible to explore the influence of substances, while minimising external factors in order to enhance the biological understanding of addiction.

The use of self-reported information, such as rating scales, when exploring addiction is more subjective and, therefore, less scientific. This is dependent on the accuracy and honesty of the individual, who may report information in a less accurate manner as a means of social desirability bias, particularly due to the sensitive nature of substance use.

> In this section you will learn about issues and debates relevant to health psychology. You will have already noticed that issues and debates have been mentioned throughout this topic. This section will draw together the main themes and ideas related to the health approach as a whole.

Culture

Health psychology explores addiction and substance use across cultures. Some substances are not disapproved of within certain societies, and can in some cases form part of the identity of the culture. For example, the prevalence of khat within some African countries is accepted, whereas in the United Kingdom this substance is considered illegal. This influences societal attitudes, making comparison of substance use and addiction across cultures problematic. Similarly, substance use can play a key role within subcultures, for example young adults exploring alcohol use when first attending university.

Nature–nurture

The various explanations for addiction to substances clearly highlight the nature–nurture debate. The biological explanations seek to outline the nature argument, in that a person becomes addicted to a substance entirely as a result of the effect the drug has on neurotransmitters, and how the body does or does not function effectively as a whole. It gives no consideration to any other influences.

On the other hand, learning explanations focus entirely on the influence of people around us, including our culture and the attitudes and the behaviour of peers, as well as the reinforcement experience. Learning theories argue that we only do what we do because we have learned that it is positive to do so.

Neither argument fully considers the basis of the other, therefore failing to consider the complexity of substance use. When taken together, both the nature and the nurture explanations better explain the acquisition and maintenance of addictions.

An understanding of how psychological understanding has developed over time

With medical advances, addiction can now be understood from a number of approaches, including the biological. This has helped to influence treatment programmes to maximise effectiveness. Current treatment programmes may incorporate a number of approaches, utilising medication to address the withdrawal symptoms while simultaneously supporting the individual to address their behaviours and decisions contributing to continued substance use. This provides a holistic approach to treatment that was not previously employed.

The use of psychological knowledge in society

An understanding of psychological theories relating to substance use can be applied to the practice of professionals and organisations working with individuals using substances, or in a preventative way through health promotion campaigns.

Campaigns, such as Stoptober, adopt psychological models of persuasion to encourage an individual to consider behavioural change. A strategy such as placing health images on the back of cigarette packets is an example of how knowledge about fear arousal also has applications within society.

An appreciation of potentially vulnerable groups can allow health promotion campaigns to be targeted at these audiences, to increase the effectiveness. This can encourage more global agencies, such as the World Health Organization (WHO), to consider international strategies to address problematic behaviour.

Issues related to socially sensitive research

In order to understand addiction, it is helpful to speak to individuals who use substances. Being asked to disclose personal information such as this can be embarrassing for the individual being asked, particularly if asked directly in an interview rather than in an anonymous questionnaire. The individual may respond to questions in a way they think the researcher would want them to or may minimise their substance use due to embarrassment. This makes any information obtained potentially flawed.

Individuals may not want to be identified within the research project due to the sensitive nature of the subject matter. Anonymity and protection of the participant are, therefore, significant ethical issues to be considered.

Knowledge check

Content

Are you confident that you can describe issues around drug taking, including addiction, tolerance, physical and psychological dependency, and withdrawal?

Can you explain the biological causes of drug taking, including those associated with alcohol, heroin and nicotine addiction, in terms of physical and psychological effects, tolerance and withdrawal?

Do you understand what mode of action is and how it works in alcohol, heroin and nicotine addiction?

Can you explain the learning causes of drug taking, including those associated with alcohol, heroin and nicotine addiction?

Are you able to apply learning theories, such as operant conditioning, social learning theory and classical conditioning, to explain drug taking behaviour?

Can you evaluate two treatments each for alcohol, heroin and nicotine addiction?

Do you understand what aversion therapy is and how it can be used to treat addiction from a learning perspective?

Can you give an example of an anti-drug campaign and explain the psychological strategies behind it?

Are you able to apply personality theories to explain individual differences in drug misuse?

Can you explain how social interactions during development can lead to drug misuse?

Methods

Can you describe and evaluate the use of animal laboratory experiments to study drugs?

Do you know and understand the ethical guidelines for using animals to study drugs, including the Animals (Scientific Procedures) Act (1986), the Animal Welfare Act (2006) and the BPS Code of Ethics and Conduct (2009)?

Can you describe and evaluate the research methods used to assess the use of humans to study drugs, including laboratory studies and surveys?

Do you know and understand the ethical guidelines for using human participants to study drugs?

Are you able to explain and evaluate the use of cross-cultural research to study drug misuse?

Can you explain the use of cross-cultural research to explore the nature–nurture issues related to drug misuse?

For quantitative data, can you identify and calculate measures of central tendency (mean, median and mode), measures of dispersion (range and standard deviation) and frequency tables?

Are you able to analyse and draw conclusions from quantitative data, including using inferential statistical testing (chi-squared, Spearmans' rho, Mann-Whitney U and Wilcoxon)?

Do you understand levels of significance and are you able to use these to interpret the results of an inferential test?

Are you able to identify levels of measurement in order to select an appropriate inferential test?

Can you compare observed and critical values on a critical values table to check whether results are significant?

Are you confident you can use thematic analysis and grounded theory to analyse and interpret qualitative data?

Studies

In the studies section, you are required to describe, evaluate and apply your knowledge of one classic and one contemporary study of health psychology.

To check your evaluation skills, refer to the introduction section of this book and review 'how to evaluate a study'. Remember that you may be asked to consider issues of validity, reliability, credibility, generalisability, objectivity and subjectivity in your evaluation of studies.

Can you describe the classic study by Olds and Milner (1954) Positive reinforcement produced by electrical stimulation of septal area and other regions of rat brain, in terms of its aim, method(s), procedures, results and conclusions?

Are you able to evaluate Olds and Milner's (1954) study in terms of strengths and weaknesses?

Are you able to identify and describe the aims, method, procedure, results and conclusions of a contemporary study from the following list, and evaluate the study in terms of strengths and weaknesses?

- Mundt et al. (2012) Peer selection and influence effects on adolescent alcohol use: a stochastic actor-based model.

- Dixit et al. (2012) Biosocial determinants of alcohol risk behaviour: An epidemiological study in urban and rural communities of Aligarh, Uttar Pradesh.

- Pengpid et al. (2013) Screening and brief intervention for alcohol problems in Dr George Mukhari Hospital out-patients in Gauteng, South Africa: a single-blinded randomized controlled trial protocol.

Key question

Are you able to identify and describe a key question in health psychology that is relevant to today's society?

Can you explain this key question using concepts, theories and research that you have studied in health psychology?

Practical investigation

Have you designed and conducted a questionnaire, interview or content analysis to investigate an area of health psychology?

Can you justify your choice of research questions or hypotheses?

Can you justify your choice of design and sampling method, and explain the ethical considerations involved?

Can you describe and analyse (using measures of central tendency and dispersion) the quantitative data that you gathered for your study and how you presented your data?

Are you able to explain, justify and interpret the non-parametric test of difference (chi-squared, Mann-Whitney U, Wilcoxon or Spearman's rho) that you used on your data?

Are you able to collect and present an analysis of qualitative data, including thematic analysis or grounded theory?

> Remember that you may be asked to consider issues of validity, reliability, credibility, generalisability, objectivity and subjectivity in your evaluation of your practical investigation.

Can you explain the strengths and weaknesses of your study and suggest possible improvements that could have been made?

Are you able to write up the procedure, results and discussion sections of your study in a report style?

Issues and debates (A Level only)

> Remember that issues and debates are synoptic. This means you may be asked to make connections by comparing issues and debates across topics in psychology or comment on issues and debates within unseen material.

Can you identify ethical issues associated with theory and research within health psychology?

Can you comment on the practical and methodological issues in the design and implementation of research within health psychology?

Can you explain how theories, research and concepts within health psychology might be considered reductionist?

Can you compare theories and research within health psychology to show different ways of explaining and understanding criminal behaviour?

Are you able to discuss whether theories, concepts, research and methodology within health psychology are scientific?

Can you discuss issues of culture (and gender) within health psychology, for example when considering cross-cultural research?

Are you able to discuss the nature–nurture debate in the context of health psychology, in terms of which parts emphasise the role of nature or nurture, or the interaction between them?

Do you understand how health psychology has developed over time?

Do you understand what is meant by social control and how research within health psychology may be used to control drug use?

Can you show how the theories, concepts and research within health psychology can be used in a practical way in society?

Are you able to understand what is meant by socially sensitive research and explain how research in health psychology might be considered to be socially sensitive?

References

Dixit, S., Ansari, AM., Khan, Z., Khalique N. (2012). Biosocial determinants of alcohol risk behaviour: An epidemiological study in urban and rural communities of Aligarh, Uttar Pradesh. *National Journal of Community Medicine*, 3(3), pp. 447–451.

Mundt, M.P. et al. (2012). Peer selection and influence effects on adolescent alcohol use: a stochastic actor-based model. *BMC Pediatrics*, 12, p. 115.

Olds, J and Milner, P. (1954). Positive reinforcement produced by electrical stimulation of septal area and other regions of rat brain. *Journal of Comparative and Physiological Psychology*, 47(6), pp. 419–427.

Pengpid, S. et al. (2012). Screening and brief intervention for alcohol problems in Dr George Mukhari Hospital out-patients in Gauteng, South Africa: a single-blinded randomized controlled trial protocol. *BMC Public Health*, 12, pp. 12–127.

Preparing for your exams:
A level Paper 2

Advance planning

- You will need to revise the methodology that you have learned about in your first year as this will represent 25 per cent of this paper. The methodology will relate to your chosen application. You will also need to revise all of the statistical tests and mathematical skills. Make sure you include time for this in your revision timetable.
- There are more marks available for Clinical psychology than the application you have learned about. Your revision timetable should reflect this. Spend more time revising the clinical content than your application content.

A level Paper 2 overview

A level Paper 2	Time: 2 hours	
Section A: Clinical psychology (compulsory questions)	A mixture of short answer questions and extended response questions (8–20 marks)	54 marks
Section B: Applications in psychology (Options 1, 2 and 3)	A mixture of short answer questions and extended response questions (8–16 marks)	36 marks
	Total marks =	90 marks

The paper requires the use of a calculator. Statistical tables and formulae are provided at the beginning of the paper.

Section A

Extended response questions will require you to formulate an argument, consider strengths and weaknesses, apply your knowledge, and often come to a reasoned conclusion. It is important to understand the demands of the command words used in this paper and draw up a plan before you commit pen to paper.

You will have learned about schizophrenia and one other mental disorder, either anorexia nervosa, obsessive-compulsive disorder or unipolar depression. In the exam, your option will be referred to as 'one other disorder'.

Section B

This section contains three applications in psychology of which you will have learned about only one. You should ignore the two sections that you have not learned about. Again, you will be asked to draw on your knowledge of research methods and statistics for your chosen application.

Eight-mark questions can ask you to discuss a topic/situation or to evaluate a topic/situation; both require you to describe relevant psychology, explore the issue, consider different viewpoints and judge strengths and weaknesses to form a conclusion. However, if the question asks that you 'make reference to the context', you must instead describe relevant psychology and apply it to the context given. You do not need to evaluate.

Sample answers with comments

Section A

This is an example of a short response question that requires knowledge without application.

Question: *Describe one symptom of a disorder you have studied, other than schizophrenia.* **(2 marks)**

Student answer

One symptom of anorexia nervosa is very low body weight which is below what would be expected. They also have a fear of weight gain and believe their body is larger than it actually is.

This answer has offered more than one symptom for anorexia nervosa. It is important to read exam questions carefully, and highlight the important command words so that your answer is focused on the question demands. Here, the answer describes three separate symptoms. There is some credit given for a basic account of one of the symptoms described, but this needs further elaboration to get both available marks. The answer should have focused on, for example, low body weight and then expanded this answer to describe a BMI of 18.5 or below, or having a weight of 15 per cent less than expected based on sex, age and height.

This is an example of a set of short methodology and data response questions. Typically, you will be presented with a context to read and answer questions on, and will be required to relate your methodological knowledge and skills of data analysis and mathematics to the context.

Researchers were investigating the effectiveness of a new drug to reduce auditory hallucinations in schizophrenia patients. The new drug was cheaper than existing medication and caused fewer side effects for patients. Patient self-reports of auditory hallucinations currently taking existing medication were compared to patient self-reports taking the new drug on a one-month trial.

Table I Data from the investigation

Patients self-reported number of auditory hallucinations over a one-month period	A. Patients taking existing medication	B. Patients taking new drug	Ranks for A	Ranks for B
1	22	25	8	12.5
2	16	23	1.5	9
3	20	31	6	17
4	30	27	16	14
5	24	16	10.5	1.5
6	19	20	4	6
7	37	24	20	10.5
8	33	36	18	19
9	25	29	12.5	15
10	18	20	3	6
Sum of ranks (A and B)			99.5	110.5

This answer is complete. The sums of lists A and B have been correctly calculated in the table and the formula has been used appropriately to calculate Ua and Ub. The student has also correctly identified U being the smaller value of Ua and Ub.

The ranks for lists A and B have been calculated for you, but it is worth remembering that the ranks for lists A and B need to be been done as a whole group and divided into lists A and B after ranks have been assigned for each score.

Remember that the formula for each statistical test is at the beginning of the exam paper.

Question: *Complete the table and calculate a Mann-Whitney U test.* **(4 marks)**

$U_a = 10 \times 10 + 110/2 - 99.5 = 100 + 55 - 99.5 = 55.5$

$U_b = 10 \times 10 + 110/2 - 110.5 = 100 + 55 - 110.5 = 44.5$

$U = 44.5$

The researchers' hypothesis stated that there would be a difference in self-reported hallucinations between existing medication users and those on the trial new drug.

Question: *Using the results of the Mann-Whitney U test, explain whether the researchers should accept or reject their hypothesis.* **(3 marks)**

Student answer

The calculated value of U = 44.5, which is greater than the critical value of 23 for a two-tailed test at P 0.05 with n = 10. Therefore the hypothesis cannot be accepted and the null hypothesis should be retained which states that there is no difference between the two drugs.

This statistical statement accurately explains why the researchers should reject the hypothesis and retain the null hypothesis using the results of the Mann-Whitney U Test. It is worth learning this type of statistical statement so that your answer is explained in full, using all of the available information.

Section B

This is an example of a data response question where you are required to show your workings.

Smoking causes an increase in carbon monoxide (CO) in the bloodstream. Cessation programmes commonly monitor CO levels in exhalation tests to establish whether a nicotine replacement treatment is helping a person reduce or abstain from smoking. This is an example of data comparing two different nicotine replacement programmes.

Table 1

Patient	Nicotine patches		Nicotine gum	
	CO levels (ppm) before treatment	CO levels (ppm) after two days of treatment	CO levels (ppm) before treatment	CO levels (ppm) after two days of treatment
1	20	1	19	2
2	18	0	19	6
3	22	4	17	4
4	16	7	20	8
5	13	2	21	1
Mean	17.8	2.8	19.2	4.2

Question: *Calculate the standard deviation for CO levels (ppm) after using nicotine gum for two days. Show your workings and give your answer to two significant figures.* **(3 marks)**

Student answer

Step 1: n–mean, squared

$(2-4.2)^2 = 4.84$

$(6-4.2)^2 = 3.24$

$(4-4.2)^2 = 0.04$

$(8-4.2)^2 = 14.44$

$(1-4.2)^2 = 10.24$

Step 2: Sum of squares

Sum = 32.8

Step 3: total number of scores minus 1

$N = 5-1$

Step 4: Sum divided by n-1

$32.8/4 = 8.2$

Step 5: Square root

Standard deviation = 2.86

This response is really useful because it has used a step-by-step procedure to ensure that all workings are shown. This can be cross-checked with a statistical calculator (σ n-1), but using a calculator alone will not enable you to achieve all available marks because it will not show workings. The formula for calculating the standard deviation is at the front of the exam paper. Your workings should reflect stages of this formula. Each step gains credit. In this example, there will be credit for step one, step two and step five.

This is an example of an extended response question for Criminological psychology.

Rhys was always a naughty child, and his parents found it difficult to control his temper. As an adolescent, Rhys engaged in risk-taking behaviour and often got into trouble at school because of truancy and disobedience. He was arrested for being drunk and disorderely in a public placed and given an Antisocial Behaviour Order.

Question: *Discuss Rhys' behaviour using explanations from biological psychology. You must make reference to the context in your answer.* **(8 marks)**

Student answer

One biological explanation for Rhys' antisocial behaviour could be because he may have suffered a brain injury caused by trauma, or excessive drinking, which can lead to a deficiency of brain nutrients or contribute to a greater likelihood of trauma through falls. Because Rhys was always a difficult child, he may have suffered brain damage before or during birth or in infancy. Alternatively, he could have just been a difficult child and suffered a brain injury in adolescence because he engaged in risk taking behaviour. Williams et al (2010) found that 60 per cent of prisoners they studied had suffered some form of physical brain injury, and that this could be related to antisocial activity.

However, this research is correlatory and it cannot be established that injury caused antisocial behaviour as it is equally likely that those who engage in antisocial behaviour increase their likelihood of suffering brain injury from risk taking behaviour. Brain injury tends to also be related to other life events, such as exposure to violence as a child and substance misuse, so it is difficult to establish causation. Also Kreutzer et al (1991) found that some prisoners had suffered brain damaged post arrest, rather than pre-arrest and that it was more likely that brain injury was only related to antisocial behaviour if substance misuse was also involved. This may explain Rhys' behaviour because he also misused alcohol, so this and brain injury could be involved.

An alternative biological theory that could explain Rhys' behaviour is XYY syndrome. Rhys could have an additional Y chromosome that could explain his difficult and antisocial behaviour. Some researchers have linked XYY to aggressive behaviour. However, Theilgaard only found tentative links between XYY and aggression. In fact she found stronger associations between XYY and lower intelligence. Because Rhys was a regular truant at school and was disobedient, this may be explained because he was not intelligent and failed to succeed academically. With limited success at school, Rhys found it difficult to fit in to normal mainstream education and sought alternative routes in antisocial subculture.

A different biological explanation for Rhys' behaviour may be personality theory. Eysenck suggested that individuals have personality traits that underlie our behaviour. Combinations of certain traits are more likely to result in antisocial behaviour. Rhys could have a combination of such traits called Psychoticism, Extraversion and Neuroticism. Extraverts have an underactive Reticular Activating System that means that they require extra external stimulation, resulting in risk taking behaviour, which Rhys has shown. Rhys is also reactive to his environment as demonstrated by naughtiness and disobedience, which may be explained by his overreactive sympathetic nervous system that means he is neurotic and not emotionally stable. His psychoticism would explain why he is able to engage in antisocial behaviours and disobedience without remorse.

Although personality theory is a useful explanation for Rhys behaviour, there is little consistent research that links the PEN personality with actual delinquency, some only supporting one or two of the dimensions (Rushton & Chrisjohn, 1981). This makes it difficult to establish which dimension or relationship between the dimensions contribute to criminal behaviour.

Because Rhys is a male, testosterone may also be implicated because there is an elevated level of testosterone experienced during adolescence. High levels of testosterone have been associated with increased violence. Although Rhys has not engaged in violent behaviour, he has been challenging and difficult at school, which may precursor violent behaviour in young adulthood. As Rhys has not been violent yet, Dabbs et al (1995) would argue that testosterone is not likely to be associated with his behaviour.

Although biological explanations can account for Rhys' behaviour, they do not take account of social explanations for antisocial behaviour that could also explain why this is happening. Because Rhys has been a difficult child and known for being naughty, he could have been labelled as such by his teachers, family and friends which is a label that he could have internalised and eventually became a self-fulfilling prophesy.

This answer does well to maintain focus on the question and refer to the context of Rhys and his antisocial behaviour throughout. There is a good attempt to apply each biological explanation to Rhys directly and speculate as to why he behaves the way he does. Remember that when you are asked to 'refer to the context in your answer', this must be done throughout.

The question demands that the answer should 'discuss' biological explanations, which means that the situation should be explored fully using contrasting viewpoints. This answer does well to present relevant biological explanations, steering clear of biological explanations least likely to be associated with the context. For example, it would have been inappropriate to discuss the role of the amygdala in this instance because Rhys did not demonstrate psychotic behaviour. It may have also been a stretch to have discussed the MAO gene because it has been related to aggression, which the answer attempts to manage with limited success.

Because the question does not demand evaluation of each explanation, there is some irrelevant information presented here, such as the supporting research and additional critique. This answer would have benefitted more from selecting only descriptions of each biological explanation and applying the explanation to the context.

Psychological skills

This topic differs from the other topics you have studied, because it takes a synoptic approach. This means that, instead of providing new information, it requires you to draw on your knowledge from other areas of psychology in order to understand and explain methodological and conceptual issues. You have already learned about many psychological approaches, theories, studies, methodology and key issues. This section will guide you in applying this knowledge and these skills to other contexts. In particular, you will be asked to draw on your knowledge of research methods, classic studies and issues and debates.

Topic 9 encourages you to take a synoptic view of:

- research methods, descriptive statistics, inferential statistics, methodological and ethical (human and animal) issues

- analysis of qualitative data (thematic analysis and grounded theory)

- conventions of reporting published research, and the process of peer review

- classic studies in psychology and novel unseen research

- issues and debates in psychology across all topic areas.

Synopticity

Synopticity involves appreciating that each topic is not separate from another, taking a broader perspective and making links across topics. It is about understanding how topics relate to one another in a number of ways:

- drawing together knowledge from different topic areas to explain an issue or argument

- making links across topics through issues and debates, research methodology and ethical issues

- considering the implications and applications of research for psychology and wider society.

Throughout your studies you will have touched on the synoptic elements that are general to all of psychology, not just one particular topic or approach. Now you will have to study these synoptic elements in more depth so that you can apply them to unseen material that you could be presented with. Synoptic thinking is a skill you can learn by making sure that you have a firm understanding of issues, debates, research methodology and ethical issues in general, and that you practise applying this understanding in different contexts. The good news is that you will have already learned about these synoptic elements, so your focus now is taking a broader perspective and viewing them as general areas that can be applied to topics – rather than embedded within a topic.

Thinking critically

Exam papers 1, 2 and 3 all require critical thinking skills, but this topic emphasises this critical approach because you will be presented with unseen material to analyse and assess. The skills that you have developed throughout the course will be tested in a number of ways, focusing on methodology and data analysis, a review of studies and an understanding of synoptic issues and debates. It would be useful to refer to the introduction section of this book, where critical thinking skills for these areas were discussed, and to revise the methodology, studies and issues and debates sections throughout the topic areas. Remember, this is not new information to learn, just a new way of approaching these ideas.

History of psychology

Throughout each topic you have read about the history of each approach and how it has developed over time. It is important to understand the history of psychology because it provides a context for some of the theories and studies you have learned about, and it can be used to understand how psychological research has contributed to wider knowledge and its use in society. You will also see how synoptic themes have emerged throughout the historical development of psychology; for example, the endeavour to develop psychology as a scientific discipline, the emphasis on nature or nurture explanations and the way specific behaviours have been isolated in order to make investigating them easier (reductionism).

Social psychology

Contemporary social psychology developed from folk psychologists, a group working in Germany during the mid-19th century. They noted that the behaviour of an individual can be influenced by others around them, a central tenet of social psychology that remains important today. Experimental social psychology began in the early part of the 20th century and laboratories were opened to investigate social behaviour. The rise of social psychology as a distinct sub-discipline of psychology developed alongside specific historical events, such as economic depression and war, giving it the impetus to answer questions raised by such events. Notably, the discipline grew rapidly following the Second World War to address why individuals would be willing to harm others, blindly obey authority and discriminate against others. This led to research into obedience, conformity and prejudice.

Cognitive psychology

The modern development of cognitive psychology began during the Second World War and during the 1950s there was a cognitive revolution, largely due to the growing dissatisfaction with behaviourism, which was the dominant approach in psychology at the time. During the war there were huge developments in communication and digital computers that led psychologists to consider humans as information processors similar to the processors used in computers. As communication follows a flow of information in which humans receive, process and store information, this led to the information-processing approach. The rise of the computer led to psychologists considering the human brain as comparable to machines in the way that both problem solve and process information. Ulric Neisser (1967) published *Cognitive Psychology*, which named the approach, and today psychologists are exploring the neural basis of cognition; how cognitive systems are represented biologically in the human brain.

Learning theories

Learning theories are attributable to the behaviourist approach which was founded by John Watson. Although concepts associated with behaviourism can be found earlier, Watson published *Psychology as the Behaviourist Views it* in 1913, a paper outlining the discipline as a distinct school of thought built on scientific foundations found within the natural sciences. Edward Thorndike built on classical conditioning as an explanation for learning behaviour by proposing operant conditioning and the Law of Effect; that any behaviour followed by a negative consequence is unlikely to be repeated and any behaviour followed by a positive consequence will be likely to occur again.

B.F. Skinner further developed operant conditioning into radical behaviourism, proposing that behavioural events, like natural events, just happen without being attributed to thoughts or beliefs, or indeed any form of mental processing. Albert Bandura later bridged the gap between behaviourism and cognitive psychology, arguing that behaviour was largely acquired through observation, which required attention and memory. Behaviourism does not have the strength it once had as a separate discipline, but its roots are firmly established in behavioural therapies and the legacy of its strict scientific methodology is still dominant in modern psychology.

Biological psychology

The biological approach in psychology emerged as a discipline during the 18th and 19th centuries in many forms. Philosopher René Descartes argued that humans and animals operated like machines, except that humans had a soul (1648). Although early thinkers believed that the soul (or mind) existed separately from the body (dualism), biologists believed that the mind and body were one entity or thing (monism). This was evidenced by Pierre Paul Broca (1861) when investigating a man who could only say the word 'tan'. Following the man's death, Broca found damage to a specific part of his brain – the Broca's area (named after Broca's discovery), suggesting that mental functions were localised in specific regions of the brain. The role of heredity was advanced following Charles Darwin's publication *On The Origin of Species* (1859), suggesting that physical features could be passed on through genetic inheritance. Today biological psychology investigates how many different behaviours, such as aggression, dreaming, consciousness and memory, can be associated with the structure and function of the brain.

Evolutionary psychology

Evolutionary psychology is a sub-discipline of biological psychology that explains human behaviour today as a product of evolutionary adaptedness. Following the writings of Darwin, Jerome Barkow and colleagues (1992) promoted evolutionary psychology to explain why behaviours that may appear **maladaptive** today, such as obesity and aggression, are present because of a genome lag; these behaviours were **adaptive** in our evolutionary past and aided survival, but social conditions have developed faster than our genetic fitness. Our desire for fatty and sweet foods aided survival when food was scarce, but in modern society fatty and sweet foods are abundant and yet our desire to have them has not diminished. This genome lag may help to explain the rise in modern obesity.

Psychodynamic approach

Psychodynamic psychology is largely attributed to the work of Sigmund Freud during the late 19th and early 20th centuries. Freud's theories were established from his clinical work with patients suffering from psychological disorders that had no apparent physical cause. This led to the development of psychoanalysis as a therapy to treat psychological disorders. His work was well received by some in America and led to the establishment of the International Psychoanalytical Association. Carl Jung succeeded Freud as director of the Association, although Jung diverged from Freud, instead developing his own theories of the unconscious and moving away from psychosexual stages of development and parts of the personality. Anna Freud became an influential figure in British psychology, working with children and influencing the work of John Bowlby and Mary Ainsworth into attachment and child development.

> ### Key terms 💬
>
> **Adaptive:** in evolutionary terms adaptive refers to a behaviour that aids survival of the individual or species.
>
> **Maladaptive:** in evolutionary terms maladaptive refers to a behaviour that does not promote survival.

9.1 Methods

Throughout your course you will have learned about a variety of psychological research methods used to investigate behaviour, methodological issues and ways of analysing data that has been collected during investigations. You will have also conducted your own practical investigations using a variety of research methods, procedures and data analysis techniques. This knowledge, understanding and skills base will be further tested as you will now need to apply it to an unseen psychological investigation.

The table below shows you where you will have learned about methods in the compulsory topics 1–5, although you may also learn about them in your optional topic (6, 7 or 8). Use this table to guide your revision of Topic 9 and consider ways in which this knowledge could be drawn upon for paper 3.

Table 9.1

9.1 Methods	Where you learned about these	You will need to be able to:
Types of data: qualitative and quantitative data; primary and secondary data	Topics 1 and 2 Topic 5	Identify each type of data, when they are appropriate to use and their strengths and weaknesses.
Sampling techniques: random, stratified, volunteer and opportunity	Topic 1	Identify each sampling method, when they are appropriate to use and their strengths and weaknesses.
Experimental/research designs: independent groups, repeated measures and matched pairs	Topic 2	Identify each type of design, when they are appropriate to use, their strengths and weaknesses and how the limitations of use may be overcome.
Hypotheses: null, alternate, experimental; directional and non-directional	Topics 1 and 2	Identify alternate/experimental and null hypotheses and whether they are directional or non-directional, and write an operationalised hypothesis.
Questionnaires and interviews: open, closed (including ranked scale questions); structured, semi-structured and unstructured interviews; self-report data	Topic 1	Identify types of questionnaire/interview and question types, write different question types, understand how different types of data are generated and how they are analysed. Understand the strengths and weaknesses of self-report data, and apply this knowledge to unseen investigation examples.
Experiments: laboratory and field; independent and dependent variables	Topic 2	Identify and understand the differences between lab and field experiments, their main features and how they are conducted. Understand their strengths and weaknesses, and apply this knowledge to unseen study examples. Identify, suggest and operationalise independent and dependent variables.
Observations: tallying; event and time sampling; covert, overt, participant, non-participant; structured observations; naturalistic observations	Topic 4	Identify and understand the differences between types of observation, and their associated strengths and weaknesses. Suggest behavioural categories and understand the way tallying is done. Identify and be able to suggest appropriate sampling (time and event) as used in an observation. Apply your knowledge to unseen investigation examples.
Additional research methods and techniques: twin and adoption studies, animal experiments, case studies as used in different areas of psychology, scanning (CAT, PET, fMRI), content analysis, correlational research, longitudinal and cross-sectional and cross-cultural research and meta-analysis	Topic 3 Topic 4 Topics 2 and 5 Topic 3 Topic 4 Topic 3 Topic 5	Identify, describe the main features of and evaluate each additional research method and technique in terms of strengths and weaknesses. Use your knowledge of each method to suggest ways of devising investigations based on the research method. Understand methodological and design issues associated with each research method and technique. Apply your knowledge of each additional research method and technique to unseen investigation examples.

9.1 Methods	Where you learned about these	You will need to be able to:
Control issues: counterbalancing, order effects, experimenter effects, social desirability, demand characteristics, participant variables, situational variables, extraneous variables, confounding variables, operationalisation of variables	Topic 2	Identify and understand the control issues, recognising when they can be a potential problem for an investigation, and suggest ways of overcoming them. Identify and suggest possible variables that may apply to an unseen investigation example, and how they can be overcome/controlled. Identify and suggest how to operationalise variables in an investigation and the validity of operationalisation.
Descriptive statistics Measures of central tendency, frequency tables, graphs (bar chart, histogram, scatter diagram), normal distribution (including standard deviation), skewed distribution, sense checking data, measures of dispersion (range, standard deviation) Produce, handle, interpret data – including drawing comparisons (e.g. between means of two sets of data)	Topics 1 and 2	Identify and use appropriate descriptive statistics, draw appropriate graphs and tables, interpret data presented as descriptive statistics, calculate descriptive statistics (using formulae where appropriate). Understand what type of data is being presented as descriptive statistics and how to appropriately present different types of data. Compare different data sets to draw conclusions. Apply your knowledge of descriptive statistics to an unseen investigation example.
Inferential statistics Decision making and interpretation: levels of measurement, appropriate choice of statistical test, the criteria for and use of Mann-Whitney U, Wilcoxon, Spearman's, chi-squared (for difference) tests, directional and non-directional testing Use of critical value tables, one- and two-tailed testing Levels of significance, including knowledge of standard statistical terminology, such as p equal to or greater than (e.g. $p \leq .05$) Rejecting hypotheses Type I and Type II errors, the relationship between significance levels and p values, observed and critical values	Topics 2, 3 and 4	Identify and interpret data at different levels of measurement, and how they should be analysed and presented. Identify appropriate statistical tests and the reasons for their use. Relate directional and non-directional hypotheses to one- and two-tailed testing. Use the correct column of critical values for a one and two-tailed test at a given significance level. Use critical values tables to interpret the significance of a statistical test. Compare observed and critical values. Understand probability and the meaning of symbols related to probability in order to relay a statistical conclusion. Identify and understand Type I and Type II errors at a given significance level, and relay this in percentage form to convey the likelihood of an error being made. Apply your knowledge of inferential statistics to an unseen investigation example.
Methodological issues: validity (internal, predictive, ecological), reliability, generalisability, objectivity, subjectivity (researcher bias), credibility	Topics 2 and 4	Describe and identify different methodological issues and how they could be overcome. Use methodological issues to evaluate data. Apply your knowledge of methodological issues to an unseen example.
Analysis of qualitative data (thematic analysis and grounded theory)	Topics 1 and 5	Identify qualitative data analysis and understand how it is conducted and analysed. Evaluate qualitative data in terms of strengths and weaknesses. Apply your knowledge of qualitative data to an unseen investigation.
Conventions of published psychological research: abstract, introduction, aims and hypotheses, method, results, discussion; the process of peer review	Introduction	Identify the sections of a psychological report and understand their purposes. Select appropriate material for each section of a report. Understand the purpose and process of publishing psychological reports and the strengths and limitations of peer review.
Ethical issues in research using humans (BPS Code of Ethics and Conduct, 2009), including risk assessment when carrying out research in psychology	Topic 1	Identify, describe and explain the purpose of ethical guidelines and risk assessment in psychological research on humans. Understand how to overcome ethical issues. Apply your knowledge of ethical issues to an unseen investigation example.
Ethical issues in research using animals (Scientific Procedures Act 1986 and Home Office regulations)	Topic 4	Identify, describe and explain the purpose of guidelines and legislation associated with animal research in psychology. Apply your knowledge of ethical issues to an unseen investigation example.

9.2 Synoptic review of studies

During your course you will have learned about classic and contemporary psychological studies. This section will require you to use your knowledge of the classic studies in order to compare them or consider them in the light of synoptic themes, issues and debates.

This table shows you which classic studies you will need to know. You may also be given unseen material in the form of a study that you could be asked to comment on using the same synoptic themes as the classic studies.

Table 9.2

Classic studies	Topic
Sherif et al. (1954/1961) Intergroup conflict and cooperation: The Robbers Cave experiment	Topic 1 Social psychology
Baddeley (1966b) Working memory model: The influence of acoustic and semantic similarity on long-term memory for word sequences	Topic 2 Cognitive psychology
Raine et al. (1997) Brain abnormalities in murderers indicated by positron emission tomography	Topic 3 Biological psychology
Watson and Rayner (1920) Little Albert: Conditioned emotional reactions	Topic 4 Learning theories
Rosenhan (1973) On being sane in insane places	Topic 5 Clinical psychology
Options topics	
Loftus and Palmer (1974) Reconstruction of automobile destruction: An example of the interaction between language and memory	Topic 6 Criminological psychology
van IJzendoorn and Kroonenberg (1988) Cross-cultural patterns of attachment: A meta-analysis of the Strange Situation	Topic 7 Child psychology
Olds and Milner (1954) Positive reinforcement produced by electrical stimulation of septal areas and other regions of rat brain	Topic 8 Health psychology

Comparing the classic studies

Each classic study uses a different methodological approach to investigation and ways of analysing data. For example, Watson and Rayner used a single case experiment under controlled conditions and Rosenhan used a naturalistic observation to investigate the topic area. You could be asked to compare two classic studies in a variety of ways, drawing on your knowledge of explaining behaviour, methodology, data analysis and issues and debates.

Comparing methods

A typical way of comparing the classic studies is to consider the similarities and differences in the way they went about conducting their research. This can draw on your knowledge of their aims, variables, procedures, design issues and controls. Comparing methods will also test your critical understanding of the strengths and limitations of conducting research in this way.

Comparing data

Each study produced different types of data: primary or secondary data, qualitative and/or quantitative data. You should consider how the data was gathered and recorded by the researcher, the techniques used to analyse the data, and the strengths and weaknesses of these procedures.

Comparison of explanations

You may also be asked to consider how the classic studies have contributed to an understanding of behaviour; what theories do they relate to and how? Are they good evidence for an explanation? How do they explain behaviour in different ways?

Common study issues

You may also be asked to consider common issues of validity, reliability, credibility, generalisability, objectivity and subjectivity of classic studies. It is important to know each classic study well enough to ensure that you can cover a broad range of issues that you may be asked to consider.

The following revision table may be useful to help you get started on your review of your non-option studies. Remember that you will also have an optional topic to revise as well.

Table 9.3

Classic studies	Validity	Reliability	Credibility	Generalisability	Objectivity/ subjectivity
Sherif et al. (1954/1961)	Natural environment but the boys may have guessed that they were being studied	Three replications yielded different findings; inconsistent procedures	Low credibility as the integrity of the study was questioned and there were ethical implications	A limited number from a limited sample of competitive sporting boys	Records taken by camp researchers, often in note form and possibly reflecting their views on how the boys were behaving
Baddeley (1966b)	Tasks not an everyday use of memory	Good control over memory trials	Reputable researcher in memory; scientific procedures used	Limited to experimental conditions	Objective recordings taken of word recall
Raine et al. (1997)	PET scans are an accurate measure of brain activity	Scientific equipment is reliable	Brain-imaging equipment used, but only on a small sample with considerable ethical issues	Small sample size of selected murderers, which are not representative	Objective PET scan recordings taken
Watson and Rayner (1920)	Phobia: too many trials to condition, which questions the validity of the conditioning process as a permanent way of learning	Control over many stimuli (e.g. room and items) to ensure phobia was of rat	Ethical issues limit credibility, but regarded as evidence of classical conditioning in a human	Only one child studied, who may have been more resilient (stolid) than other children	Objective recordings taken of Albert's behaviour, film footage evidences emotional reaction
Rosenhan (1973)	High validity due to naturalistic environment	Replication study with no pseudopatients offers some evidence for reliability of findings	Credible evidence used by the anti-psychiatry movement	A range of hospitals but restricted to the USA	Pseudopatients' notes (qualitative and quantitative)

You could be asked to consider or compare classic research studies in terms of issues and debates. This requires that you draw on your knowledge of specific issues and debates and apply them to one or more classic studies. For example, you could compare classic studies in terms of their relation to the nature–nurture debate, scientific status or ethical issues. You will need to show an understanding of the issue or debate and then draw on specific details about the study that can be used to exemplify the discussion.

Once you have identified and commented on a relevant issue or debate for each classic study, remember to think critically by identifying strengths and weaknesses. For example, you may have identified flooding and systematic desensitisation as useful applications that have led from the work of Watson and Rayner's classical conditioning study. However, flooding has important ethical considerations as it is a highly distressing and therapist-directed procedure. The research of Raine et al. into the brains of murderers strongly suggests that some individuals may be born to commit murder (nature) but, as the research is retrospective, it is important to consider that the murderers could have been exposed to environmental conditions which might explain their violent behaviour (nurture). You are also required to compare the studies on these debates and issues; for example, to compare the cognitive and learning approaches in terms of the nature–nurture debate or their scientific status.

9.3 Issues and debates

Issues and debates are philosophical and methodological/ethical concepts that apply to the whole of psychology: approaches, explanations and research studies. You will have to consider issues and debates when reviewing the classic research studies, as above, and also consider issues and debates as they relate to theories and concepts you have studied throughout your course for all topics and applications. You will have read about these issues and debates in feature sections throughout this book, so it is important to revisit these sections and draw together the ideas.

This is an example of how you should go about using your knowledge of issues and debates in a synoptic way.

Ethical issues involved in research in psychology

Imagine that you have been asked to consider the following statement.

Psychological research is often held back because researchers cannot study human behaviour in a way that is meaningful without violating ethical principles relating to deception.

To what extent do you agree with this statement? You will need to carefully consider the purpose of this ethical principle: what is deception, why it is used, what the consequences are of its use on participants involved in psychological research, and whether meaningful research can be conducted if deception is not used. There is much that can be said about psychological research in relation to ethical guidelines; you will need to be selective and formulate your argument carefully so that a balanced judgement can be made.

Ethical guidelines and principles were created to ensure that meaningful research can be conducted in psychology while still protecting participants and the groups that they represent. However, some argue that ethical guidelines restrict the topics that can be investigated and the ways in which a researcher may choose to investigate them. Deception involves misleading participants about the nature of the investigation, giving participants false information, or omitting to inform participants of important information about an investigation that could result in participants choosing not to take part in the research. This relates directly to the principle of informed consent. If a participant has been deceived as to the nature of an investigation, then they do not have the capacity to give informed consent to their participation. Under such conditions the ethical guidelines state that representatives of an individual should be informed or peers and colleagues of the research should be consulted. In such cases the research may be restricted to ensure that participants are not unduly harmed by their participation. The BPS guidelines refer specifically to deception as that which should be avoided unless it threatens the integrity of the research and should be resolved by informing participants of the deception at the earliest opportunity.

Deception is often used in psychological research because participants may change their behaviour or responses if they are fully aware of the nature of an investigation. For example, Milgram deliberately lied to participants about the aims of his investigation and his procedure because if they had known that it was a study of obedience they might not have reacted in a naturalistic way. Furthermore, if participants had been aware that the learner was not receiving real shocks, they probably would have not experienced stress or responded to authority in the way that they did. In this way, Milgram used deception to protect the integrity of this experiment. It can be seen as a methodological tool to avoid suspicion by participants, prevent demand characteristics and to ensure natural behaviour.

Research into aggression poses particular issues related to the use of deception. If a researcher is examining aggression under certain situations, participant knowledge of this may result in them refraining from engaging in aggressive behaviour because it is not deemed socially desirable. This is also true of questionnaires that are designed to elicit true responses from participants; if they are aware of the objectives of a survey, they will be mindful of how their responses may look to others and possibly offer disingenuous answers.

In criminological psychology, research using deception has had important benefits for legal policy and practice. For example, mock jury studies that manipulate the attractiveness, race or accent of a defendant, without participants being aware that this variable is the one under investigation, has directly contributed to knowledge of jury bias. Similarly, research in clinical psychology involving participants being allocated to a placebo condition without their knowledge has led to an understanding of the placebo effect and actual effectiveness of treatments using the placebo as a baseline condition.

The consequences of deception may be fruitful for psychological researchers and the reliability of findings, but the impact on participants may be one of embarrassment, mistrust of psychological research or anxiety. The extent to which a participant experiences these feelings depends largely on how and why they have been deceived, and how the researcher reconciles with participants the nature of the deception following the investigation. Deception intentionally removes self-determination and autonomy away from individual participants, which violates ethical principles, and the overuse of deception can create suspicion about psychological research that could discourage participation, encourage participants to second-guess researchers and bring the subject into disrepute.

The most significant issues associated with deception are whether or not participant autonomy is affected and whether deception causes harm. To withhold or falsely misrepresent the intentions or procedure of a study mean that a participant's capacity to give informed consent is impaired. Milgram's experiment is commonly cited as research that contravenes this ethical guideline as the use of deception caused considerable harm to participants and diminished their capacity to exercise informed consent. The question is still debated as to whether the deception did actually cause harm; some argue that the harm caused was momentary and no greater than being placed in an uncomfortable situation. Some believe that the participants understood and accepted the nature of the experimental deception and believed it was necessary to achieve important psychological insights into obedience to authority. Rather than limiting the personal autonomy of an individual, knowledge of their natural reactions under such conditions could have been a self-reflection exercise for participants that might promote greater autonomy in the future; that is, knowledge that they were blindly obedient could prevent blind obedience in future situations.

The extent to which deception should be used to ensure meaningful research in psychology leads to a compelling debate. Most researchers would argue that it is a methodological and ethical 'double-edged sword' because it can ensure the reliability and validity of findings but violate ethical principles when used; but when not used, it can threaten the integrity of research but maintain the autonomy and prevent harm to participants. While much research in psychology does involve deception, it does not necessarily mean that harm is caused, as not all deception causes distress or embarrassment; indeed some participants can benefit from the psychological insight into their own behavioural patterns. However, many would argue that deception is unjustifiable and steps should be taken to inform participants that they could be subject to deception or involve third parties to gain presumptive consent.

Taking it further

Now that you have seen how ethics can be used synoptically, by drawing on relevant psychological research from across approaches and applications, you should consider how this must be achieved for all the issues and debates in Topic 9. Take a theme from each issue and debate and apply it to as many approaches, explanations and studies that are relevant to each.

A further synoptic example of how different theories in psychology can be used to explain real-life situations is explored in the 'Thinking Bigger' section. See how this is tackled here, and then practise applying your psychological knowledge to events that occur in the news or at your school.

THINKING BIGGER

What recycled sewage water reveals about human psychology

This article is about environmental psychology, an area of study which investigates how human thought and behaviour affects our relationship with the environment. Specifically, in this case, it is looking at cognition and decision making. Do we, as humans, have certain styles of thinking that are not rational and may even be detrimental and which can also impact on how we feel about aspects of our environment? Where does this thinking come from? Can it be overcome? As you go through this activity you will be drawing on your understanding of evolutionary theories, cognitive psychology and research methodology and will have the opportunity to practise applying what you have learned during the course to wider contexts.

Each year around one million people die from water-related diseases. In most cases, the causes are painfully obvious. Without access to a modern sewage system, people dump their bodily waste into the nearest river or street, which funnels their filthy excrement and urine back into the water supply. It is a catastrophic problem without a cheap solution.

Until now. A few years ago Bill Gates teamed up with an engineer named Peter Janicki to create an ingenious machine that uses the same ingredient that taints water supplies—human waste—to clean them. The "Janicki Omniprocessor", which looks something like a miniature power plant, can turn waste from 100,000 people into 86,000 litres of clean water a day while generating enough electricity to power itself. "The water tasted as good as any I've had out of a bottle," Gates wrote on his blog.

The Janicki Omniprocessor is a major technological breakthrough, but a psychological barrier remains. We know recycled water is clean, we trust the science, and it's exciting to think about how many lives it will save. And yet, that nasty "Yuk!" feeling persists. Part of our deeply rooted aversion for tainted water has clear evolutionary origins. Like many animals, we instinctually avoid food and liquid that has touched nasty substances for health reasons.

This brings me to a new survey of over 2,600 Americans conducted by disgust guru Paul Rozin and his colleagues. Participants first read a short passage explaining how recycled water is certified safe and indicated their willingness to drink it. Next, they scored how comfortable they were drinking different types of water, from commercial bottled water, to tap water, to sewage water that had been boiled, evaporated, and condensed into pure water. Finally, they rated how comfortable they felt drinking recycled water if it had spent a certain amount of time in a reservoir or aquifer before it was fed back into the water supply. The purpose of this question was to see if the contagion heuristic—"Once in contact, always in contact"—wears off over time.

Although 13 percent of the sample indicated that they would never drink recycled water, almost half said that they would,

while 38 percent remained uncertain. Disgust sensitivity, as measured by a short disgust test, correlated inversely with a willingness to drink recycled water. The more easily someone is grossed out, the less likely he or she will sip water from the Janicki Omniprocessor. The next finding revealed something important about how the human mind perceives purity. Even though sewage water that is boiled, evaporated, and condensed is purer than tap water, participants overwhelmingly preferred tap water.

The scientists also found that participants were more likely to drink recycled water the longer it remained in a reservoir or aquifer, even though feeding recycled water back into a natural system actually decreases its purity.

… And that's why I find this topic so interesting. Humans pay special attention to the history of objects – where they have been, what they have touched, and who has touched them – because we subscribe to the notion that objects have an underlying reality, an essence. Normally, this piece of mental software is helpful, but sometimes it can lead us astray. The Janicki Omniprocessor represents a major breakthrough for producing clean water and improving health in the developing world at a low cost. But before we can put it to use, we will have to overcome a bigger obstacle: ourselves.

This article has been adapted from the Research Digest of the British Psychological Society, Blogging on Brain and Behaviour, March 2015. By guest blogger Sam McNerney http://www.sammcnerney.com/. For the full article please see: **http://digest.bps.org.uk/2015/03/what-recycled-sewage-water-reveals.html**

The BPS Research Digest aims to summarise psychological research in a clear way and make it accessible to a wider audience than just academics. It also aims to put the research into a wider social context.

> **1** In what ways has the author achieved the aim of making the article clear and conveying its message to you?
>
> **2** Are there any specialist terms that impact on your understanding of the article? How could the author have addressed this?
>
> **3** How might you turn the article into a summary for a younger audience, such as primary school children, without losing its essential meaning?

Now you are going to use your knowledge of psychology from across all the topics in this course to answer the following questions.

> According to the article, 'part of our deeply rooted aversion for tainted water has clear evolutionary origins'.
>
> **1** Explain this statement using your knowledge of what evolution is and how it shaped human behaviour.
>
> **2** The studies on which this article is based were done by Rozin and colleagues using survey techniques. What would be the advantages and disadvantages of using surveys to understand how people feel about recycled water?
>
> In the article, the author refers to a correlation between disgust sensitivity and attitude to recycled water.
>
> **3** Briefly outline how you would operationalise the key variables and how you could carry out such a correlation.

Activity

1 These research findings have clear implications for the real world. Outline what these implications are, and suggest some ways that recycled water could be presented in order to make it more psychologically acceptable.

2 Imagine you have been employed by the developers of the omniprocessor as part of a marketing team. You have to give a short presentation about the current problems with water-related diseases and how the omniprocessor addresses them. You should then give some ideas about how to 'sell' the product of recycled water to those that would use it.

You might consider how you could use social media, such as Tumblr, to spread the message.

The presentation could be in the form of PowerPoint®, using appropriate images. The presentation should take no more than 10 minutes to deliver.

Links with course content

This table shows how the themes in the article link to topics that have been covered elsewhere in the book.

Content	Links
Evolutionary perspective	Topic 4: Learning theories
Methodology – surveys and correlations	Topic 2: Biological psychology
Cognitive ideas	Topic 2: Cognitive psychology
Social learning approach	Topic 4: Learning theories

References: Rozin, P., Haddad, B., Nemeroff, C. and Slovic, P. (2015). Psychological aspects of the rejection of recycled water: Contamination, purification and disgust. *Judgment and Decision Making*, 10 (1), pp. 50–63

Preparing for your exams: A level Paper 3

Advance planning

- Paper 3 draws on your knowledge and skills developed throughout the course, so you will need to take a different approach to gathering information in preparation for revision. Use the specification as a guide to find specific methodological information to begin with; tick off each method and data analysis technique as you revise.
- Paper 3 also tests your knowledge of the classic studies. You will need to know these studies in detail and be able to compare them on common themes, such as aims, procedure and findings, in addition to synoptic themes, such as ethics, science, reductionism and application.
- You will be asked to draw on your knowledge of each approach and the theories you have learned for each one. Use cue cards to help build up a resource bank of theories, making sure that you can describe, apply and evaluate each one.
- There is a significant amount of extended writing in Paper 3, so you should try to create essay plans in preparation. This is particularly the case for the issues and debates section C. Draw together information about issues and debates that you have studied through the course and create essay plans that your teacher can check.

A level Paper 3 overview

A level Paper 3	Time: 2 hours	
Section A: Research methods	A mixture of short answer questions and open response questions	24 marks
Section B: Review of studies	A mixture of short answer questions and extended response questions (up to 16 marks)	24 marks
Section C: Issues and debates	Extended response question (12–20 marks)	32 marks
	Total marks =	80 marks

This paper requires the use of a calculator. Statistical tables and formulae are provided at the beginning of the paper.

Section A

This section is focused on research methods and includes mostly short answer questions related to general methods and data analysis and application of knowledge of these skills to an unseen practical investigation example. It is important to remember that you will be required to apply your knowledge of research methods and statistics that you have learned about in your first year of study, so make sure you build this into your revision timetable.

Section B

This section contains the review of the classic studies you have learned about during the course. You will have to be able to recall all six classic studies, one from each topic you have studied, as you will be asked to compare the studies. Your revision should focus on this by taking a common or synoptic theme and making comparisons. Use your specification issues and debates section as a guide to the themes that you may be asked to compare the studies on, not forgetting that common themes such as validity, reliability, credibility, subjectivity/objectivity and generalisability may be used too.

Section B questions will be a mix of short response questions and extended response questions of up to 16 marks that require you to evaluate, assess, discuss or review 'to what extent' a statement given is considered valid. Remember that an extended response question requires balanced and formulated reasoning, often with a judgement or conclusion needed.

Section C

Section C will draw on your knowledge of issues and debates and require extended essay writing skills. You therefore need to know and focus your writing on certain skills in order to meet the demands of each question. You need to understand the command words 'evaluate', 'assess' and 'to what extent'.

- Evaluate: requires that you review and bring together knowledge in order to formulate a conclusion. You should review this knowledge in terms of strengths and weaknesses, alternative opinions or other relevant evaluative ideas. Your conclusion should be clearly stated and well founded in the context of what you have written for your argument.

- Assess: requires that you identify relevant information and consider information that may apply to the context of the question. You should formulate a judgement or conclusion.

- To what extent: this style of question will be embedded in a context, a real-life or fictional scenario, psychological knowledge or other unseen material. You should review this information and form a balanced and reasoned conclusion using your knowledge of issues and debates.

If a question asks that you 'make reference to the context in your answer' you must ensure that your response directly addresses the context provided.

Sample answers with comments

Section A

This is an example of a set of short answer questions based on an unseen practical investigation.

An investigation examining the effectiveness of systematic desensitisation as a way of treating social anxiety compared those receiving treatment to those waiting to receive treatment. All selected participants had been referred for systematic desensitisation because their doctors felt they would benefit from the treatment and showed similar levels of anxiety before they started treatment.

Participants were asked to complete a questionnaire to rate their social anxiety on the first treatment session, or those on the waiting list were asked to complete the questionnaire at home. Participants were also asked to keep a diary for the duration of the treatment/ time on the waiting list, which the researchers used in the analysis. At the end of the treatment duration, both groups were given a questionnaire to rate their end social anxiety.

As predicted, ten participants' ratings of social anxiety following the course of systematic desensitisation fell once completed. A Wilcoxon Signed Ranks test produced the observed value of 4.

Researchers compared the post-test rating for anxiety of those ten participants who received treatment to the eight participants on the waiting list. The researchers were unsure how participants would compare following treatment or no treatment, so a non-directional hypothesis was suggested. A Mann-Whitney U test produced the observed value of 8.

Question a) *Using the critical value table for Wilcoxon Signed Ranks, state whether the results are significant.* **(1 mark)**

> The results are significant because the observed value of 4 is less than the critical value of 11 at $p = 0.05$ for a one-tailed test.

a) The response correctly uses the critical values table and compares the observed and critical values appropriately.

Question b) *Using the critical value table for the Mann-Whitney U, state the best level of probability at which the results would be significant.* **(1 mark)**

> $p = < 0.01$

b) The probability level in psychology is 0.05. However, that does not mean that we always accept that level. If a finding is significant at p 0.01 it indicates a stronger result, so this is the one that should be reported.

Question c) *Explain whether the researchers could have made a Type 1 error when interpreting the significance of the post-test ratings.* **(2 marks)**

> The likelihood of making a type 1 error is less than 1%, so the researchers are not likely to have made a Type 1 error.

c) The response could have referred back to the probability level, but accurately explains why a Type 1 error was not likely.

Question d) *Write a conclusion for these results.*

There was no difference in anxiety between those who received systematic desensitisation and those who were on the waiting list before they started treatment. In addition, those who received treatment showed a significant reduction in anxiety between pre- and post-test. There was a significant difference between the groups at post-test, so it shows that the treatment worked very well.

d) There is a lot of information to identify and use in this context, so it is worth reading and highlighting important information that can be used to answer a particular question. Here, it was necessary to identify that both groups started at a similar anxiety level, the treatment group showed a reduction in anxiety at post-test and that there was a significant difference between the groups at post-test, suggesting that systematic desensitisation worked. The response does well to go through all of the findings systematically.

Question e) *Explain why the researchers chose to ask participants to keep a diary during the study.* **(3 marks)**

The researchers may have chosen to ask participants to keep a diary so that they could do a qualitative analysis on the entries. Qualitative data is useful when gathering data about how people are feeling.

e) The response is rather limited/brief and so would not achieve all available marks. A more complete response would also refer to methodological reasons for using diaries, such as to triangulate with the quantitative ratings or to understand if there were any potential stress triggers that affected particular individuals more than others.

Section B

This is an example of an open response question focused on a classic study.

Question: *Compare the methodology used in Sherif et al. (1954, 1961) and Baddeley's (1966b) studies in terms of validity, reliability and generalisability.* **(6 marks)**

Student answer

Sherif et al. conducted a field study of boys at a summer camp. Although the boys were carefully selected for the study, the environment in which they were placed was naturalistic and the sporting events and competitions would have normally occurred in such a camp. Therefore the study can be regarded as having high ecological validity, and because the tasks set for the boys were realistic, it can be regarded as having mundane realism. This is very different from Baddeley's laboratory experiment into memory. Baddeley recruited participants to learn lists of random similar and dissimilar sounding words, engage in distractor tasks and recall or recognise the words after a specified time. The conditions under which Baddeley's participants had to learn and recall the words were not as we would normally experience in real life, so this study can be argued to lack ecological validity and mundane realism.

As both studies are investigating different topics in psychology, they also differ in terms of reliability. Baddeley's study was repeated several times, and subsequently repeated by other researchers. It also had a high degree of control to establish cause and effect and increase the reliability of the findings. Sherif et al. did replicate their research over three summer camps, but although they found that prejudice emerged from all three camps, the final Robbers Cave study was different in that they attempted to reduce prejudice with superordinate goals. There was very limited control over the actions of the boys and the camp staff could not standardise any procedures in the way that could be done in a laboratory, so it has low reliability.

However, similar generalisability problems occur with both studies. Baddeley recruited a relatively small number of participants as did Sherif, and both are limited to a particular group of people; a pool of recruits from a university list, and a group of boys from one American state. This limits the generalisability of the findings of both studies to a specific group of people or culture.

This response has made a good comparison and maintained relevance to the common themes of reliability, validity and generalisability. Compare questions demand that both similarities and differences are discussed, which this response has done reasonably well, although the similarity has less elaboration.

Section C

This example is an extended response question focused on social control as an issue.

Question: *Assess how psychology could be used as a form of social control in relation to learning theories and the biological approach.* **(20 marks)**

Student answer

In the learning approach, classical, operant and social learning theories are explanations of our behaviour. One assumption of the learning approach is that all behaviour is determined by environmental forces. This assumption itself has the capacity to imply that we could control behaviour by manipulating the environment in which we live. B. F. Skinner published two books that advocate such a claim; Beyond Freedom and Dignity and Waldon Two, both discuss the deliberate manipulation of behaviour by environment control.

Classical conditioning states that we are conditioned through association and operant conditioning that we learn through reinforcement. Both of these theories have the capacity to be used as a form of social control. Watson and Rayner demonstrated this with their study of Little Albert, who they conditioned to cause an emotional response to the sight of a white rat.

Social learning theory suggests that we learn through observation of role models. In such a case, if we deliberately manipulate the type of role models that children are exposed to, it too can be seen as a form of social control.

The biological approach suggests that genes are the basis of human behaviour, and biological processes, such as neurotransmitter levels and hormones, account for our behaviour. With recent advances in medical techniques, gene manipulation is a reality, and hormone treatments and drug therapy have been used for a long time in order to control the behaviour of others. This is particularly true in clinical psychology, where a biological drug, such as Clozapine for schizophrenia, has been used to reduce dopamine in the brain and control delusions and hallucinations.

Drug treatments in particular, have been criticised by the anti-psychiatry movement as a form of social control over mental illness, and that it is only society which defines mental illness as such, drugs ensure that individuals conform to societies expectations of what is regarded as 'normal'.

Learning theories do have the potential for social control, but much of this has been put to good use. Token economy programmes, systematic desensitisation and flooding were created to help treat people with mental health issues such as phobias and anxiety, which would otherwise be debilitating and prevent them from living a normal life. Reward systems have been very productive in school to promote good, positive and cooperative behaviour in children.

However, token economy programmes in prisons has been criticised for simply forcing people to comply and denying prisoners their basic human rights, as tokens can be abused by staff and bargained between prisoners.

Observational learning has also been used to good effect. Celebrities have been used to promote healthy lifestyles which people can identify with. Classical conditioning has been used in advertising, in which products are associated with pleasurable feelings in order to promote sales, which is a direct manipulation of behaviour. In contrast, classical conditioning has also been used to help people undergoing chemotherapy to prevent them from associating sickness with important foods.

Social control exerted by the biological approach through gene manipulation and drug therapy has also been seen to have a good effect. People living with depression and other mental health issues can lead relatively normal lives on medication and it has led to the almost disappearance of institutions, in which they would otherwise be placed. Gene therapy is a real treatment for people living with physical conditions and can be used to ensure that genetic problems are not passed on to offspring. Although many object to this as selective breeding and having the potential to be misused by those who can afford to select certain attributes for their children.

Drug treatments are also criticised for being a money making scheme, costing the government and tax payers billions of pounds, when we could focus more on the individual and psychological treatments.

In conclusion, there are many ways that both learning and biological approaches have been, and have the potential to be, used as a form of social control, but many of these are used in a positive way to help people with issues and promote healthy living.

This response has done well to separate the descriptive element and judgement elements of the question. The first half of this response focuses on how each approach can be used as a form of social control and the second half attempts to weigh up the advantages and limitations of this. It is critical that you understand the command words of these extended response questions because each requires a different skill.

The conclusion made by this response is rather weak, and could be strengthened by discussing in more detail why they have reached this judgement. The response seems to have selected appropriate examples from each approach in terms of social control and presented them formulaically here. To improve this essay, it would have been good to see some psychological evidence. For example, studies that have shown the effectiveness of drug treatments and systematic desensitisation. It would have also benefitted from a greater range of ideas linked to social control, as it has tended to focus on clinical treatments. There seems a greater emphasis on positive ways in which the approaches have been used as a form of social control, leading to a slight imbalance in judgement. This could be improved by further exploring negative uses of explanations and research in each approach, for example aversion therapy for homosexuality, ECT and the lobotomy to control political dissidents, Raine's research on murderers' brains and the potential for screening for violence.

Glossary

ABC model of operant conditioning: a way of explaining how operant conditioning works showing how the consequence of a behaviour influences the replication of behaviour.

Ablate: remove or destroy the function of an organ or body tissue.

Abstain: stop yourself from using a substance.

Action potential: the electrical trigger that passes along the axon and stimulates the neuron to activate and release neurotransmitters as a result of synaptic transmission.

ADHD: a syndrome of behaviours including inability to sustain attention, impulsivity and restlessness.

Adoption study: a research method that examines the degree of similarity or difference of family members/twins that have been separated and adopted into different families.

Advanced dementia: the later stages of dementia where symptoms are more profound.

Aetiological validity: the extent to which a disorder has the same cause or causes. Aetiological validity exists when the diagnosis reflects known causes such as a family history in a disorder that is known to have a genetic cause.

Agency: when one acts as an agent for another.

Agonist: a substance that acts like another substance and therefore stimulates neural action.

Agranulocytosis: an acute condition resulting in a reduced white blood count which increases risk of infections.

Agreeableness: a measure of temper such as whether a person is willing to cooperate or compete.

Alternative hypothesis: a statement that lays out what a researcher predicts will be found. This is also known as an experimental hypothesis when the research methodology adopted is experimental.

Alzheimer's disease: a neurological degenerative disease that impairs cognitive functioning causing memory loss and impairments in thinking and language.

Amenorrhoea: lack of menstruation.

AMPA receptors: postsynaptic receptors responsible for glutamate transmission (glutamate is the most prevalent neurotransmitter in the nervous system and the main excitatory one).

Amphetamine: a drug that stimulates the central nervous system. Its effects include increased activity and energy, as well as appetite suppression and making it difficult to sleep.

Amygdala: centre in the brain responsible for emotions, emotional behaviour and motivation.

Anabolic steroids: a synthetic form of testosterone. They promote the growth of body muscle and strength in users.

Androcentric: focused on men.

Androgen: a chemical that develops or maintains male characteristics.

Angular gyrus: part of the parietal lobe associated with memory, language processing and attention.

Anoxic episode: lack of oxygen to the brain causing injury.

Antagonist: drugs that produce an antagonist effect bind to the receptor sites on neurons to prevent the substance from being absorbed in large quantities, therefore reducing the effect of the neurotransmitter.

Anterior Cingulate Cortex: surrounds the frontal part of the corpus callosum (the tissues that connect the two hemispheres of the brain) and connects to the prefrontal cortical area. It has several functions including those governing autonomic behaviours but has been implicated in such cognitive functions as reward anticipation, impulse control and empathy.

Anterograde: the loss of ability to make new memories, while memories before the injury remain relatively intact.

Anterolateral: to the front and side of.

Anti-democratic: views that oppose the fair election of government and majority rule.

Antidopaminergic: blocking the activity of dopamine.

Anti-Semitism: hostility against Jews.

Antiserotonergic: blocking the activity of serotonin.

Anti-social behaviour: acting in a way that caused or was likely to cause harassment, alarm or distress to one or more people not of the same household as the person acting in this way.

Aphasia: a disturbance in the comprehension or production of language caused by brain dysfunction or damage, such as a stroke.

Arousal theory: individuals are motivated to act in a way to maintain a certain level of physiological arousal. When arousal levels drop below our personal optimal level, we engage in stimulating behaviour to increase arousal.

Artificial neural network: computational models inspired by an animal's central nervous system (in particular the brain) which is capable of basic learning generally presented as systems of interconnected nodes or neurones which can compute values from inputs.

Ascending reticular activating system (ARAS): a system that transmits messages to the limbic system, triggering the release of hormones and neurotransmitters.

Attachment: a close, emotional, enduring bond between child and caregiver.

Attended information: information that is given attention.

Attributional bias: how we habitually locate causes for events e.g. internal cause suggests that we are responsible for what happens to us, but external would suggest that events are beyond our control.

Attrition: the tendency for some participants to drop out of a study for various reasons which can threaten the validity of the study.

Autobiographical memory: like episodic memory it is a memory for personal events.

Autonomy: acting on one's own freewill.

Avolition: a psychological state characterised by a general lack of motivation to complete usual, self-motivated activities such as work.

Axon hillock: the area that connects the cell body to the axon.

Axon terminals: the end of the axon that leads to the terminal buttons.

Axon: a long branch from the cell body that passes electrical impulses down to the end of the neuron to allow it to communicate with others.

Basal Ganglia: situated within the base of the brain, this is a group of three structures associated with the coordination of movement.

Basal model: a model that suggests the testosterone is assumed to be a persistent trait that influences behaviour.

Bilateral: both hemispheres of the brain are involved.

Biological maturation: how development occurs naturally.

Borderline personality disorder: a pattern of instability in interpersonal relationships and self-image and marked impulsivity.

Brain scan: a research method that involves examining the structure and functioning of the brain.

Brain stem: a central trunk of the brain located in the very middle, and extends down to form the spinal cord.

Brain stimulation: the use of electrodes to stimulate regions of the brain and examine resulting behavioural or cognitive changes as a result.

Broca's area: an area of the left (typically) frontal lobe associated with the production of language.

Capacity: a person's maximum ability to perform a task. This may include the extent to which a person is able to receive and retain information, due to mental ability or other factors which are effecting their cognitive functioning.

Castrated: to remove the testicles of a male animal or a man.

Catatonia: various motor disturbances characterised by abnormality of movement and behaviour.

Catharsis: the process of releasing negative energy in the mind.

Causal factors: factors that definitely make the person act in a criminal or anti-social way.

Causality: the effect of the manipulated variable on the measured variable can be reliably established as a cause and effect relationship.

Cell body: the main part of the cell where the nucleus sits. It also contains mitochondria.

Cerebral cortex: the outer layer of the brain.

Children's Yale Brown Obsessive Compulsive Scale: a self-rating scale used to measure depression in children and adolescents.

Cingulate gyrus: part of the brain which is involved in emotion formation.

Classical conditioning: a form of learning based on the association with an environmental event or stimulus with an internal response.

Clinical interview: the process of evaluating a client by gaining important personal information about them regarding their health.

Cognitive deficits: a condition caused by injury or developmental issue that affects a person's ability to learn and function.

Cognitive insufficiency: deficits and difficulties in processing information. These include problems with attention and slow processing speed.

Cognitive loading: reduced levels of a neurotransmitter cause the brain to struggle more in processing information.

Cognitive symptoms: systematic changes in the way the person processes information from the world leading to a negative view of their circumstances.

Cohort effect: the difference within social and cultural groups that change with age and time.

Comorbidity: the existence of more than one disorder in the same person at the same time.

Compulsions: repetitive behaviours or mental acts that an individual feels driven to perform in response to an obsession or according to rules that must be applied rigidly.

Concordance rate: the probability that if one twin/family member has a certain characteristic (such as schizophrenia) then the other twin/another family member will also have it.

Concurrent validity: a way of establishing validity that compares evidence from several studies testing the same thing to see if they agree.

Conditioned response (CR): a behaviour that is shown in response to a learnt stimulus.

Conditioned stimulus: (CS): a stimulus that has been associated with an unconditioned stimulus so that it now produces the same response.

Confederate: someone who helps someone else to do something.

Confidentiality: participants should not be identified as part of the study. Their names can be anonymised.

Confounding variable: a variable that affects the findings of a study directly, so much that you are no longer measuring what was intended.

Conscientiousness: a measure of dependability and self-discipline.

Consequence: an outcome of something.

Conservativism: a belief in tradition and social order with a dislike for change.

Construct validity: the extent to which the test measures what it claims to measure.

Context effects: the surrounding environment effects how an event is perceived.

Continuous reinforcement: the desired behaviour is reinforced every time it occurs.

Control group: a group of participants that does not experience the experimental situation but acts as a baseline against which to judge any change.

Control processes: conscious decisions about what to attend to from the sensory information in our environment.

Corpus callosum: a band of nerve fibres that join the two hemispheres of the brain together and allow communication between the two parts.

Correlation: a research method that examines the relationship between two co-variables.

Cortex: the outer layer of the brain, consists of grey matter and involved in higher mental functioning.

Cost benefits analysis: method for deciding whether to approve a research proposal involving balancing the suffering of the animal (costs) against the quality of the research and the medical benefit from the knowledge (benefits).

Counterbalancing: alternating the conditions of the study for each participant in a repeated measures design.

Covert observation: a form of observation where the participants do not know they are being observed. For example, you making an observation of behaviour in your student area, from simply sitting in one of the seated areas.

Critical value: a statistical cut-off point. It is a number presented on a table of critical values that determines whether the result is significant enough for the null hypothesis not to be accepted.

Cross sectional: research that looks at a group of individuals within a set period of time (as opposed to longitudinal research where the same individuals are examined over a prolonged period of time).

Cue dependent recall: recall that is prompted by a specific context or physiological or psychological state that was encoded with the original memory.

Debrief: a statement given to participants on conclusion of a study which discloses fully the nature and implications of the research.

Deception: participants should not be lied to or misguided about the nature of the study.

Deductive: using the knowledge and information you have in order to understand something.

Delusions: beliefs that are contrary to fact.

Demand characteristics: participants behaving in a way they think they should to fit what they perceive to be the aim of the experiment.

Dendrites: branches at the top end of a neuron that receive messages from other neurons.

Depressant: a drug that reduces the ability of the synapses to work effectively, so slowing down brain activity.

Depressogenic schema: dysfunctional thoughts and beliefs contributing to the symptoms of depression.

Deprivation: loss of an attachment.

Desensitisation: brought about by relaxation techniques taught before facing the phobic object.

Detoxification: a treatment for addiction to drugs or alcohol intended to remove the physiological effects of the addictive substances. A person is helped to overcome the physical and psychological dependence on a substance.

Diathesis-stress model: a theory that explains behaviour through a mixture of biological and environmental factors. A dormant genetic disposition could be triggered by an environmental life event.

Digit span: how many digits can be retained and recalled in sequential order without mistakes.

Directional hypothesis: a directional hypothesis predicts the direction of difference or relationship that the result is likely to take.

Discrimination: the practice of treating one person or group differently from another in an unfair way.

Disorganised behaviour: behaviour that is not necessarily expected in the situation they are in, or that changes rapidly and is out of context.

Disorganised thinking/speech: patients are unable to make connections between their thoughts resulting in incomprehensible language and ideas that seem loosely connected.

Dizygotic twins: siblings conceived in the same pregnancy resulting from two eggs being fertilized by two sperm. The twins share 50% of their genetic material, the same as any two siblings.

Dopamine: is a neurotransmitter. It is a chemical messenger that helps in the transmission of signals between neurons in the brain.

Double-blind procedure: neither the participant nor researcher knows the aim of the study.

Down-regulation: homeostatic mechanism where the brain produces less of something in response to an increase.

Dual task experiment: experiments that involve two tasks that either compete with for cognitive resource because they are similar tasks (two verbal or two visual tasks) or involve different cognitive resources because they are different tasks (one verbal and one visual).

Dysphoria: an intense dissatisfaction, anxiety or depression, discomfort and distress.

EAT-26 Survey: a widely used self-measure assessment of characteristics/behaviours associated with eating disorders.

Eclectic: using a broad range of sources/explanations.

Ecological validity: the extent to which the findings still explain the behaviour in different situations.

Ego: a part of the personality that attempts to satisfy the id within the restrictions of reality.

Emotional symptoms: those that deal with subjective states i.e. mood, typically in major depression the mood would be low and or negative.

Encephalitis: inflammation of the brain causing damage to the structures of the brain.

Endocrine system: the system of glands that secrete hormone messages around the body using the circulatory system.

Endocytosis: the taking in of extra-cellular materials from outside a cell by fusing with its plasma membrane.

Endogenous depression: linked to internal biological factors rather than being caused by an environmental trigger such as a stressful event.

Endorphins: a group of hormones in the brain that bind to opioid receptors. They are involved in pain reception and emotions.

Environment of evolutionary adaptation (EEA): the conditions that prevailed in the environment at the time that a species was adapting in response to. In psychology we are interested in the development of behavioural characteristics hard wired in the brain so the EEA we are interested in would be at the point when humans lived in hunter-gatherer groups.

Episodic buffer: a subcomponent of the working memory associated with interfacing with LTM and integrating information from other subcomponents.

Episodic memory: memory for events.

Ethnocentrism: belief that one's own ethnic group is superior to another.

Euphoria: an intense pleasurable feeling often referred to as a 'high'.

Evolutionary theory: a theory that explains human behaviour today as a consequence of environmental pressures placed on our ancestors in the environment of evolutionary adaptation.

Excitatory postsynaptic potential: the temporary depolarization of a neuron as a result of positively charged ions flowing into the cell which makes it more likely to fire an action potential.

External reliability: refers to the consistency of a measure.

External validity: the extent to which the findings apply to other people and situations.

Extinction: when behaviour that has previously been reinforced no longer produces reinforcement and is no longer repeated in response to the stimulus (unlearning).

Extraneous variable: a variable that may have affected the dependent variable but that was not the independent variable.

Extraversion: behaviour is outgoing, sociable and active. Individuals want excitement and may become easily bored.

Face validity: looking at each question and deciding whether they make sense in terms of the construct being measured.

Fascism: extreme intolerant views based on a right-wing political perspective.

Field experiment: a piece of research that takes place in the setting where the behaviour being studied would naturally occur.

Flooding: direct, prolonged exposure to a fearful situation or experience.

Forensic psychologist: a specialist working with offenders. They will apply psychological theory to criminal investigation, understanding psychological problems associated with criminal behaviour and the treatment of those who have committed offences.

Free recall: recall of stimulus material in any order and without memory cues.

Frontal variant frontotemporal dementia: a degenerative neurological disease that affects the frontal lobes of the brain.

GABA (gammaaminobutyricacid): this is a very important inhibitory neurotransmitter. It makes it more difficult for messages to be transmitted across synapses, and is therefore known as a depressant.

Generalisability: the ability to apply findings to other people, situations and contexts.

Genes: a unit of heredity that contains DNA carrying information from one generation to the next. Each gene influences development by triggering the production of enzymes and proteins that are involved in the production of certain cells.

Genetics: the building blocks of human life that are passed down through generations/inherited that result in certain characteristics/traits in an individual.

Glands: an organ of the body which produces a substance that the body needs, such as hormones, sweat, or saliva.

Glutamate: as a neurotransmitter, glutamate is involved in the activation of neurones, enabling neural transmission to take place.

Grandiose delusions: the individual believes they have remarkable qualities such as being famous or having special powers.

Habituation: the process by which a response to a given stimulus is seen to decrease with repetition.

Hallucinations: perceptual experiences that occur in the absence of external stimulation of the corresponding sensory organ.

Harassment: acting in an aggressive or intimidating manner to another person.

Hawthorn effect: the presence of a researcher affects performance in a task.

Hemisphere: the brain is divided into two symmetrical halves, one on the left and one on the right, known as hemispheres.

Heterogeneous: all different – in-group heterogeneity is the term given to this bias according to social identity theory.

Hierarchical: a system of social organisation that is ranked from top to bottom.

Hippocampus: a structure of the brain responsible for learning, emotion and memory.

Homeostasis: process that maintains the stability of the human body in response to changes in external conditions e.g. temperature.

Homogenous: equal or similar – out-group homogeneity is the term given to this bias according to social identity theory.

Homunculus: a noun used to describe a very small human.

Hormones: chemicals produced by glands that are used to signal between organs and tissues.

Hyperprolactinemia: abnormal blood levels of prolactin, associated with spontaneous lactation, menstruation, infertility and erectile dysfunction.

Hypoglutamatergia: reduced levels of glutamate.

Hypothalamus: area of the brain responsible for maintaining control of the body through release of hormones.

Id: a part of the personality that acts upon instinctive drives.

Implicit bias: a positive or negative mental attitude towards a person, thing, or group that a person holds at an unconscious level.

Implosion: prolonged exposure to the phobic situation or experience by imagining the feared stimuli.

Imprinting: a preprogrammed behaviour that creates a bond between an animal and its offspring to maintain close proximity, e.g. a duck will follow its parent.

In vivo: actual real life encounter (with the feared stimuli).

Incentivised: given monetary reward or other form of gift to encourage participation in the study.

Independent groups design: where only one group of participants complete one condition of the experiment and a different group complete another condition.

Individual differences: natural variation in human characteristics.

Inductive: using known facts to produce general principles.

Inferential test: a statistical test that is performed on data to establish whether or not the results found were due to chance factors or whether there was indeed a significant relationship or difference found between the data.

Informational conformity: the individual conforms to the group norms because he/she does not know what to do and looks to the group for guidance.

Informed consent: participants should be fully aware of the aims, procedure and implications of the research.

Informed decision: a decision using all the available relevant facts and information. Once the information has been gathered, the person can evaluate it to make their decision.

In-group favouritism: seeing our own group and members in a positive light and as unique.

Inhibitory postsynaptic potential: changes in the polarization of a neuron that make it less likely to fire an action potential.

Instrumental learning: the term Edward Thorndike originally gave to the form of learning where the consequence of a behaviour dictates the further repeating of it.

Interference task: a task that prevents rehearsal, such as counting backwards.

Intergroup conflict: real conflict experienced between different groups.

Internal reliability: refers to the consistency of a measure within itself.

Internal validity: the extent to which the outcome of the study is the direct result of the manipulated independent variable.

Inter-rater reliability: the degree of agreement and consistency between raters about the thing being measured.

Interval/ratio data: data where an individual score for each participant is gathered, and the score can be identified using a recognised scale with equal distances between each score, e.g. time, height.

Interviewer effect: the age, gender and ethnicity of the interviewer and style of interviewing can all have an effect on the answer given by a individual and it is important to be mindful of this in preparing interviews.

Introvert: individuals are typically reserved and reflective. An introvert is more likely to prefer solitary to social activities.

Labelling: this occurs when general and broad terms are used to describe members of a group.

Laboratory experiment: an experiment conducted in a controlled environment.

Lapse: a one-off return to drug using behaviour but which does not result in the person fully returning to such behaviour. For example, a person who is trying to stop smoking may have one cigarette, but then not have any more. This would be a lapse. People who experience both relapses and lapses will benefit from continued support with their substance use.

Lateral: towards the side of.

Law of effect: created by Edward Thorndike, suggesting that behaviour with a nice consequence following it will lead to replication of behaviour.

Behaviour with an unpleasant consequence following it will lead to it being withdrawn.

Lesion studies: investigations into the effect on behaviour of damage to specific areas of the brain.

Limbic system: a set of structures in the brain associated with drives, emotions and mood.

Lobes: specific locations in each hemisphere of the brain, frontal – is the front part, temporal is to the side and behind the ears, parietal is the top area and occipital is at the back of the brain. Brains have eight lobes, four in each hemisphere.

Logistic regression: allows for factors that are influential to be identified.

Logistic regression: a statistical analysis that examines the relationship between the dependent variable and the independent variables being investigated, and calculates the probability of them being related.

Major depression: mental health disorder characterised by low mood, behavioural changes, physical changes and negative thinking.

Maladaptive: behaviour that we commonly exhibit that is bad for us.

Mass spectrometry: analytical technique to identify the amount and types of chemicals present in a sample.

Matched pairs design: where different participants are allocated to only one experimental condition (they do not do both) but are matched on important characteristics.

Medial prefrontal cortex (mPFC): area of tissue situated within the prefrontal cortex of the brain. Medial, dorsal and lateral are signifiers of a specific part of something, medial being in the middle, dorsal at the back and lateral to the side.

Medial: situated in the middle.

Mesocortical pathways: a dopamine pathway associated with motivation and emotion.

Mesolimbic system: a dopamine pathway associated with reward and pleasure, and often linked with addictive behaviours.

Meta-analysis: a research method where a researcher examines the results of several previous studies rather than conducting new research with participants.

Methylphenidate: a psycho-stimulant drug that acts on the central nervous system. It is used medically to treat attention-deficit hyperactivity disorder (ADHD) in children and adolescents.

Mitochondria: the site of aerobic respiration, where energy is released from glucose.

Mnemonic: a system for remembering something such as an association or a pattern of letters.

Modality free: able to process different forms of information (acoustic, visual, haptic, etc.).

Modelling: a way of learning by imitating the behaviour of others.

Monozygotic twins: siblings conceived in the same pregnancy resulting from one fertilized egg 'splitting' into two separate embryos. The twins share 100% of their genetic material.

Moral strain: experiencing anxiety, usually because you are asked to do something that goes against your moral judgement.

Morality principle: the concept of understanding what is right from what is wrong.

Motivational symptoms: are to do with behaviour and the willingness to engage with the world, a persistence or determination to achieve is often missing if the person feels apathy.

MRI scan: a brain scan that produces an image of the structure of the brain, a bit like an X-ray but with more detail.

Multi-wave: where there are several different measurements being used in the study.

Mundane realism: the extent to which the test used in an experiment represents a realistic activity.

Mutation: a change in the genetic structure of an animal or plant that makes it different from others of the same kind.

Myelin sheath: the fatty deposit that provides electrical insulation for an axon and allows electrical nerve impulses to be passed along.

Narcissistic: a personality type that results in the person focusing on themselves, and have a need to be admired by others. It can lead to the exploitation of others.

Natural selection: the gradual process by which heritable traits become more or less common in an environment.

Naturalistic experiment: a type of experiment which occurs in a natural setting (and where the independent variable is not being manipulated by the experimenter).

Negative out-group bias: seeing members of a different group as all the same and in a negative light.

Negative schema: habitual ways of thinking that are self-critical and damaging.

Negative symptoms: symptoms that mean the person has 'lost' an element of normal functioning.

Neonatal: relating to babies that have just been born.

Nervous system: the system of nerves that send signals as messages about the brain and body.

Neuroimaging: images produced about the structure or function of the brain using scanners such as an MRI or CAT.

Neuron: a cell within the nervous system.

Neuroticism: emotional instability associated with anxiety, fear, depression and envy.

Neurotransmitters: chemicals that pass messages from one neuron to another.

Neutral stimulus (NS): an environmental stimulus that does not of itself (without association) produce a response.

Nodes of Ranvier: gaps between adjacent myelin sheaths.

Nominal data: where data forms discrete categories, e.g. hair colour can only be nominal data because it can only be described in its categories of blond(e), brown, red or black.

Non-directional hypothesis: a non-directional hypothesis predicts that a difference or relationship will be found, but not the direction that the difference or relationship will take.

Non-participant observation: a form of observation where the researcher observes behaviour of others but does not form part of the group they study.

Noradrenalin: (also known as norepinephrine) is a catecholamine hormone and neurotransmitter with multiple roles including maintaining concentration.

Normative conformity: the jury member conforms to avoid rejection by the group or to gain rewards from them, but may not in reality agree with the decision.

Nucleus accumbens: an area of the midbrain associated with the brain's reward system.

Nucleus: houses the genetic material for that particular neuron.

Null hypothesis: predicts no difference/relationship will be found or that any difference/relationship is due to chance factors.

Observed value: the value given by a statistical test, such as rho for Spearman's. It is compared with the relevant critical value to see if a null hypothesis should be retained or not.

Obsessions: recurrent and persistent thoughts, urges or images that are experienced as intrusive or unwanted.

Openness to experience: whether a person is open to new experiences, adventure and ideas – general curiosity for novelty.

Operant conditioning: learning based on the consequence for the operator of the action performed, actions that are reinforced are repeated and learned.

Operational definitions: what the variables are and how you will measure them.

Operationalisation: defining the variables specifically so that they are directly tested.

Order effects: the problem with presentation order of stimulus material. Participants may become practised at the test so improve performance or they may become tired so that performance deteriorates.

Ordinal data: a level of measurement where numbers are rankings rather than scores in themselves, e.g. a rank order for attractiveness on a scale of 1 to 5.

Overt Aggression Scale-Modified for Outpatients: a rating scale which is used to identify the level of aggression presented by an individual within the past week. The scale is completed by people who know the individual well.

Overt observation: a form of observation where those being observed are aware of the presence of an observer. For example an inspector coming into classroom to observe teacher/ pupils.

Oxytocin: a hormone released by the posterior pituitary gland which has been shown to increase trust between people.

Paranoid: a personality type which results in a distrust of others and suspiciousness. A paranoid person takes criticism very personally and can bear grudges.

Paraphernalia: apparatus or equipment used for a particular activity.

Partial reinforcement: the desired response is only reinforced some of the time.

Participant observation: a form of observation where the researcher takes an active role in the situation being observed.

Participant variables: natural variation in human characteristics.

Peptide: chain of biological molecules containing 50 or fewer amino acids.

Periaqueductal grey matter (PAG): an area of grey matter located within the midbrain. It plays a role in the modulation of pain and in defensive behaviour.

Persecutory delusions: the individual reports believing that others are 'out to get them' and trying to harm them in some way.

Personal identity: our own unique qualities, personality, self-esteem.

Phencyclidine: (aka PCP; Angel dust) is a drug originally created as an anaesthetic because it induces 'numbness', but is no longer used for this purpose because of its other effects. These include hallucinations loss of touch with reality, and changes in mood, often making the user feel as if they are 'not in control' of their actions.

Phonological similarity effect: similar sounding words and letters are acoustically confused in short-term memory, making them more difficult to recall.

Phonology: speech sounds.

Phrenology: the practice of mapping the bumps on a person's skull and using these to deduce aspects of their character.

Physical dependency: a state where chronic and prolonged drug abuse results in a physical need for a drug in order to function, categorised through tolerance for the drug and withdrawal symptoms when the drug is absent.

Pituitary gland: the small organ at the base of the brain which produces hormones that control the growth and development of the body.

Placebo: an inactive substance often used as a control in a study to see the effect of a drug.

Plasticity: changes in neural pathways and synapses which are due to environment or behaviour.

Population validity: the extent to which the findings can be applied to other people.

Positive reinforcement: a rewarding outcome for behaviour.

Posterior cingulate cortex: the posterior cingulate cortex lies behind the anterior cingulate cortex and has been linked with human awareness. It connects to multiple neural networks and is known to play a role in pain perception and episodic memory.

Postsynaptic neuron: the neuron where a chemical message travels to.

Predictive validity: the extent to which results from a test or a study can predict future behaviour.

Pre-frontal cortex: the front area of the brain situated just behind the forehead.

Pre-frontal Lesions: damage (either accidental or deliberate) to the brain that causes areas to die.

Prejudice: dislike or unfair behaviour based on false or misguided opinion.

Presynaptic neuron: the neuron where a chemical message starts from.

Prevalence rate: the number of people in a given population that have the disorder at any one time.

Privacy: participants should not be asked personal questions that they may find intrusive, and the researcher must not obtain personal data that a participant would not voluntarily disclose.

Privation: never formed an attachment.

Progressive muscle relaxation: in each session the therapist focuses the client on tensing and relaxing one particular muscle group to create awareness of tension and relaxation.

Pro-social behaviour: behaviour that takes account of the welfare of others and avoids harming others deliberately.

Prospective design: a study that begins at the starting point of a change and tracks development over time, looking forward rather than looking back (retrospective).

Protein: main component of the physical metabolic pathways of cells made up of chains of peptides.

Psychological formulation: a way of making sense of a person's difficulties, by looking at their relationships, biological and social circumstances, life events, and how they have interpreted the events that have happened to them.

Psychopath: a person with a serious mental illness that effects how they think and interact with others, resulting in abnormal or violent social behaviour.

Psychoticism: individuals lack empathy, are aggressive, impersonal and cold.

Qualitative data: descriptive data

Quantitative data: numerical data.

Random allocation: participants are allocated to a condition of the study at random (names drawn from a hat).

Randomisation: randomising the conditions of the study for each participant in a repeated measures design.

Randomly allocated: randomly dividing the participants into each condition by, for example, picking their name out of a hat.

Reality principle: the rules of what is socially acceptable. The ego uses these principles to control the demands of the id.

Receptor sites: areas on the post synaptic neuron that allow neurotransmitters to lock onto the membrane.

Receptors: sites on the dendrites that are designed to bond to and absorb a specific type of neurotransmitter molecule.

Recidivism: a tendency to relapse into a previous mode of behaviour such as criminal behaviour.

Reciprocal inhibition: two contrasting emotions cannot co-exist – you cannot be relaxed and scared at the same time.

Reciprocal model: something cannot happen in one part of the relationship without it affecting the other.

Reconstructive hypothesis: memory for an event when the information supplied after the event merges with the information obtained from witnessing the event.

Reconstructive memory: the idea that we alter information we have stored when we recall it, based on prior expectations/knowledge.

Referential delusions: the individual holds a belief that certain behaviours or language from others is being directed at them personally.

Refractory OCD: obsessive compulsive disorder that is difficult to treat.

Rehearsal: consciously rehearsing and repeating items.

Relapse: a person has started to use a substance again after a period of abstinence (not using the substance). A relapse is not to be confused with a 'lapse'.

Repeated measures design: where all participants complete all conditions of the experiment.

Repeated reproduction: a participant recalls information at increasing time intervals (e.g. after 10 minutes, a week and a month).

Resting membrane potential: the difference in electrical potential (meaning how 'ready' the neuron is for action) on each side of the cell membrane while the cell is at rest.

Retrograde: the loss of ability to recall events prior to the injury.

Reuptake: the process by which unused neurotransmitter molecules are absorbed back into the presynaptic neuron and then destroyed by enzymes.

Right to withdraw: participants should be offered the opportunity to leave the study at any point without consequence. This means that they can withdraw their data after the study if they choose (up to a negotiated point in time).

Role models: significant individuals in a person's life. You are more likely to imitate role models such as parents, teachers or idols (e.g. celebrities).

Schema: core information and beliefs about how we think about the world.

Self-efficacy: a person knowing their own ability to do something and being confident with it.

Self-fulfilling prophecy: a stereotype that leads someone to act in a manner consistent with the stereotype.

Semantic dementia: a degenerative neurological disorder resulting in loss of semantic memory.

Semantic memory: memory for facts.

Serial position effect: recall of information at the beginning and end of a list is higher than the middle of the list.

Serotonin: a chemical created by the body that works as a neurotransmitter. It is responsible for managing moods.

Sexual selection: a form of natural selection, individuals that are successful in attracting a mate out-reproduce others in the population.

Single-blind procedure: to control for demand characteristics, participants may be unaware that they are part of an experiment, or may have been deceived as to the true nature of the study.

Skewed distribution: when the values in a data set do not conform to a normal distribution (many scores around the mean and fewer at the extreme ends).

Social desirability bias: the tendency for participants to respond in a manner that will be viewed favourably by others.

Social identity: the attributes of the group to which we belong.

Social influence: when an individual's behaviour, attitudes and emotions are affected by those of another.

Social loafing: a reduction in individual effort on a collective task, in which their output is pooled with those of other group members, compared to when working alone.

Social phobia: a fear of interacting with others.

Social releasers: an innate behaviour that helps initiate a response from a baby's mother or carer.

Socialisation: the process by which we learn the rules and norm of society through socialising agents such as teachers and parents.

Sociometric data: quantitative data gathered about personal/social relationships.

Sociotrophy: a personality trait characterised by dependence on relationships with other people and an excessive need to please others.

Somatic symptoms: changes to physiological patterns such as sleep or appetite.

Spatial: relates to where something occurred.

Specific Language Impairment: individuals whose language skills are much lower than other cognitive skills such as IQ and non-verbal abilities.

Split-half method: splitting the questions into two halves and comparing the findings from both halves during analysis to ensure reliability.

Stability: an individual is emotionally calm, unreactive and unworried.

Statistical significance: the probability that the data is a result of an actual relationship existing between the variables rather than a coincidence.

Stereotype: an overgeneralised belief about someone or something typically based on limited information.

Stimulant medication: drugs prescribed to treat ADHD that change neurotransmitter levels and increase focus.

Stimulation: artificial activation of brain areas often through use of electrodes giving off small electrical charges.

Successive approximations: rewarding behaviour for acting in a way that gets closer and closer to the desired behaviour.

Suggestibility: this is a personal quality where the individual is inclined to accept and act on the suggestions of other people. They may be aware that they are following the suggestions of others or it may occur unconsciously.

Superordinate goals: goals that can only be achieved by cooperation of all group members together.

Supramarginal gyrus: an area of the parietal lobe of the brain associated with the perception of language.

Synaptic gap: the tiny space between the dendrite of one neuron and the terminal button of another where chemical messages can be passed.

Synthetic opiate: a drug that mimics an opiate (heroin).

Systematic: gradually facing up to the phobic object via a hierarchy of exposure (from least fearful to most fearful).

Tachistoscope: a device used to present visual information in a controlled way, typically to test sensory memory.

Tardive dyskinesia: involuntary muscle spasms that commonly occur around the mouth and can affect speech.

Temperance: abstinence from drinking alcohol.

Temporal lobe: an area of the brain, called a lobe, situated below the ear.

Temporal: relates to when something occurred.

Terminal buttons/terminal boutons: the very end of a neuron where the nerve impulse becomes a chemical message that can be passed to the dendrite of another neuron.

Testosterone: principal male sex hormone and an anabolic steroid.

Test-retest method: the same people are given the same questionnaire to complete again on a different occasion.

Thalamus: part of the brain associated with sensory perception and consciousness.

The dopamine system: pathway in the brain which operates on the neurotransmitter dopamine, the release of which leads to feelings of reward.

Thematic analysis: recording themes, patterns or trends within data.

Thematic Apperception Test: where individuals are shown abstract images (inkblots) to interpret in an attempt to uncover motivations and attitudes towards a particular subject.

Tic disorder: uncontrolled spasms of muscles or vocal emissions.

Token economy: a treatment method which provides secondary reinforcement for a desirable behaviour that can be saved up or exchanged for a primary reinforcer.

Tourette's: a disorder characterised by unwanted and uncontrollable noises and movements (tics).

Trepanning: surgical intervention in which a hole is drilled into the skull to treat problems related to the surface of the brain.

Triangulate: to take multiple pieces of information and draw them together to make an overall conclusion.

Trigram: a set of three digits or letters.

Twin study: a research method that examines the degree of similarity or difference between twins on a particular characteristic.

Type 1/Type I error: when the null hypothesis is rejected and the alternative hypothesis supported when the effect was not real.

Type 2/Type II error: when the alternative hypothesis is rejected and the null retained when there was actually a real effect.

Unconditioned response (UCR): a response that occurs naturally without any form of learning (a reflex action).

Unconditioned stimulus (UCS): any stimulus producing a natural, unlearnt response.

Unconscious mind: a psychodynamic concept of a part of the human mind that is not in our conscious awareness but that influences our thoughts and behaviour.

Unilateral lobectomy: the surgical removal of parts of the brain from one hemisphere.

Up-regulation: homeostatic mechanism where the brain produces more of something in response to a depletion.

Unresolved attachment: a type of attachment that is indicative of unresolved loss, typically from trauma or abuse.

Ventral tegmental: an area of the midbrain associated with the brain's reward system and the origin of dopaminergic activity.

Vesicles: tiny sacs that contain molecules of neurotransmitter chemicals.

Vicarious reinforcement: learning through the consequence of another person's behaviour.

Virtual reality exposure therapy: a method of therapy using virtual reality technologies to treat phobias and anxiety disorders.

Visual array: an arrangement of digits or letters.

Weapon focus: refers to an eyewitness's concentration on a weapon to the exclusion of other details of a crime.

Whole and partial report technique: participants are asked to recall the whole array or part of the array, such as a line.

Index

Note: **Bold** page numbers indicate key term definitions.